Obasanjo, Nigeria and the World

Obasanjo, Nigeria and the World

JOHN ILIFFE
Fellow of St John's College, Cambridge

JC JAMES CURREY

James Currey
www.jamescurrey.com
is an imprint of Boydell & Brewer Ltd
PO Box 9, Woodbridge, Suffolk IP12 3DF, UK

and of

Boydell & Brewer Inc.
668 Mount Hope Ave, Rochester, NY 14620, USA
www.boydellandbrewer.com

The publisher has no responsibility for the continued existence or accuracy of URLs for
external or third-party internet websites referred to in this book, and does not guarantee
that any content on such websites is, or will remain, accurate or appropriate.

1 2 3 4 5 14 13 12 11

British Library Cataloguing in Publication Data
Iliffe, John.
   Obasanjo, Nigeria and the world.
   1. Obasanjo, Olusegun. 2. Presidents – Nigeria – Biography.
   3. Nigeria – Politics and government – 1960–
   I. Title
   966.9'05'092-dc22

ISBN 978–1–84701–027–8 (James Currey cloth)

Papers used by Boydell & Brewer are natural, recyclable products
made from wood grown in sustainable forests.

Printed and bound in Great Britain by
CPI Antony Rowe, Chippenham and Eastbourne

Contents

Preface

Adekeye Adebajo, Adewale Adebanwi, David Easterbrook, Marilyn Glanfield, Simon Stevens, Megan Vaughan, and Ruth Watson have helped me in preparing this book. I am grateful to the staff of the National Archives, Kew; University Library, African Studies Centre Library, and St John's College Library, Cambridge; Library of the School of Oriental and African Studies, London; Commonwealth Secretariat, London; Library of Congress; Herskovits Memorial Africana Library, Northwestern University; and Bayero University Library, Kano. The book draws heavily on Nigeria's lively political press. I am especially indebted to the work of Reuben Abati, Olusegun Adeniyi, Dare Babarinsa, Ray Ekpu, and Stanley Macebuh, both for political analysis and for the pleasure of reading good journalism.

In this book I have tried to understand General Obasanjo, which I believe to be the chief task of a biographer. Although I spent a period in Nigeria during his tenure as military head of state, I have not approached him in writing the book. My African travelling days are over and he is a busy man who has never been slow to tell his own story in print. I hope, however, that it will be clear to him and others that I write with respect.

John Iliffe
May 2010

Abbreviations

ABU	Ahmadu Bello University, Zaria
AC	Action Congress
AD	Alliance for Democracy
AG	Action Group
AIDS	acquired immune deficiency syndrome
ANC	African National Congress (of South Africa)
ANPP	All Nigeria People's Party
APGA	All Progressive Grand Alliance
APP	All People's Party
BBC	British Broadcasting Corporation
CAB	Cabinet (records in TNA)
CRO	Commonwealth Relations Office (records in TNA)
DO	Dominions Office (records in TNA)
DTA	Democratic Turnhalle Alliance
ECOMOG	ECOWAS Monitoring Group
ECOWAS	Economic Community of West African States
EPG	Eminent Persons Group
FCO	Foreign and Commonwealth Office (records in TNA)
FESTAC	Festival of Arts and Culture
FNLA	Frente Nacional de Libertação de Angola
GDP	Gross Domestic Product
GNPP	Great Nigerian People's Party
HIV	human immunodeficiency virus
IDA	International Development Agency
IMF	International Monetary Fund
INEC	Independent National Electoral Commission
LNG	liquefied natural gas
MDC	Movement for Democratic Change
MPLA	Movimento Popular de Libertação de Angola
MW	megawatt
N	naira
NADECO	National Democratic Coalition
NCNC	National Council of Nigeria and the Cameroons
NEEDS	National Economic Empowerment and Development Strategy

NEPA	Nigerian Electrical Power Authority
NEPAD	New Partnership for African Development
NGO	non-governmental organisation
NIPP	National Integrated Power Project
NITEL	Nigerian Telecommunications Corporation
NLC	Nigerian Labour Congress
NNOC	Nigerian National Oil Corporation
NNPC	Nigerian National Petroleum Corporation
NPC	Northern People's Congress
NPN	National Party of Nigeria
NPP	Nigerian People's Party
NRC	National Republican Convention
NUON	National Unity Organisation of Nigeria
OAU	Organisation of African Unity
OFN	Operation Feed the Nation
OPEC	Organisation of Petroleum Exporting Countries
PDP	People's Democratic Party
PFN	Patriotic Front of Nigeria
PREM	Prime Minister's Office (records in TNA)
PRP	People's Redemption Party
RH	Rhodes House, Oxford
RUF	Revolutionary United Front (of Sierra Leone)
SAP	structural adjustment programme
SDP	Social Democratic Party
SWAPO	South-West African People's Organisation
TNA	The National Archives, Kew, London
TRC	Truth and Reconciliation Commission
UAC	United Africa Company
UN	United Nations
UNAIDS	United Nations AIDS Organisation
UNAMSIL	United Nations Mission in Sierra Leone
UNECA	United Nations Economic Commission for Africa
UNITA	União Nacional para a Independência Total de Angola
UPE	universal primary education
UPN	Unity Party of Nigeria
ZANU	Zimbabwe African National Union
ZAPU	Zimbabwe African People's Union

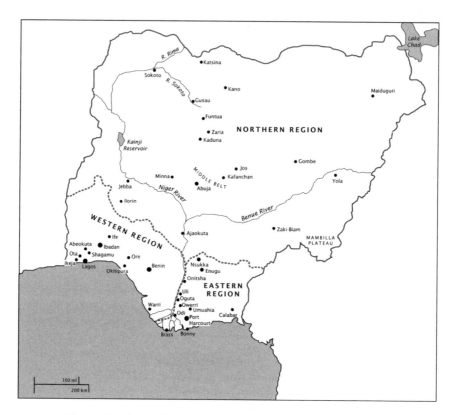

Map 1. The three regions (in 1960) and places mentioned

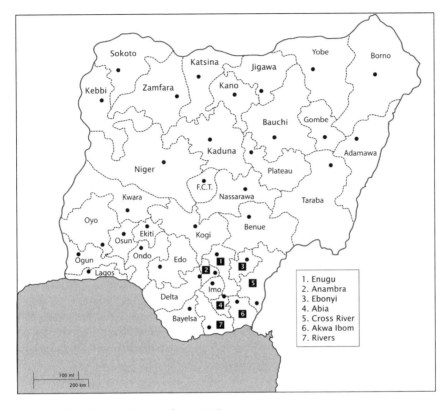

Map 2. The 36 states (from 1996)

1
A Man of Controversy

When Olusegun Obasanjo left office as President of Nigeria in May 2007, at the age of seventy, he suffered a torrent of abuse. The country's leading constitutional lawyer described the departing regime as 'a bad dream, a nightmare for the Nigerian people and a disaster for the Rule of Law, democracy and good governance'.[1] The playwright and Nobel laureate Wole Soyinka dubbed the retiring president a Master of Hypocrisy.[2] A formerly close colleague called him 'the most toxic leader that Nigeria has produced'.[3] A political enemy recommended 'that Obasanjo should go back to jail. I think he belongs there and should die there.'[4] The president's first wife published a memoir of their marriage alleging violence and neglect.[5] His second son accused him publicly of adultery with the son's wife.[6]

If this were the truth about Obasanjo, he would surely find a biographer. Yet the truth was more complicated and interesting. He had led a life of extraordinary activity and achievement. Born in an obscure Yoruba village in south-western Nigeria, too poor to go to university, he rose by ability, hard work, and sheer luck to lead the most populous black country on earth. As a soldier, he secured the victory in a civil war. Appointed military head of state at the age of 39, he returned Nigeria to democratic rule and retired to his farm, emerging to contribute to the destruction of apartheid, to contest election as Secretary-General of the United Nations, to challenge a military dictator, and to spend three years in prison, where a religious experience transformed his life. Head of a large polygynous family and author or editor of a dozen books, he also travelled and befriended leading men in every continent. In his sixties, as elected president for eight years, he dominated one of the most ungovernable countries in the world and was a principal architect of the African Union.

To unravel the contradiction between Obasanjo's life of achievement and the obloquy that surrounded his retirement is one purpose of this book. The contradiction reveals much about the first half-century of Nigerian and African independence. It also reveals much about the contradictions in Obasanjo himself. Perhaps four themes run through his contentious life.

First, despite the diversity of his experience, Obasanjo remained rooted in his Yoruba culture, one of Africa's richest and most embracing. In speech and manner, tastes and dress, he remained a Yoruba farmer and a Yoruba chief. His notions of proper gender and generational relationships remained those of his village origins. The sense of honour that he cultivated as a youth and the sense of destiny that he felt

as an elder both appear to have drawn deeply on Yoruba beliefs. His determination
to succeed through personal enterprise grew out of a fiercely competitive culture, as
did his political ruthlessness and his thirst for education and enlightenment, which
opened his mind to many intellectual currents of his time. For with his Yoruba
inheritance Obasanjo blended ideas and innovations from the larger world: from
his restless travels, his training as a military engineer, his taste for books and intellectual debate, his long experience of public life, and his deepening commitment to
Christianity. The resulting synthesis was not perfect, so that conflict between Yoruba
instincts and derived ideas contributed to the complexity and unpredictability that
many acquaintances remarked in his character. Nevertheless, this personal synthesis
forms the core of his biography, as it must of any twentieth-century African.

Ironically, given his commitment to Yoruba culture, the second theme of
Obasanjo's life was his distinctively Nigerian patriotism. Too young to have taken
a significant part in the nationalist movement, he came to maturity at the moment
of Nigerian independence and was marked for ever by its optimism and dedication. For Obasanjo, Nigeria was a given. 'We have no choice', he insisted, 'but to
make this country work and that is the responsibility of all Nigerians.'[7] There was
no choice because there was no way of unscrambling Nigeria without intolerable
violence and chaos. 'Assuming that the larger ethnic groups can go it alone, can
the smaller ethnic groups do so?' he asked. 'If not what will be their fate? Many
Bosnias will be created in many parts of Nigeria if the country breaks up. This is
too frightening a possibility to contemplate.'[8] This commitment to Nigeria set
Obasanjo at odds with many Nigerians – especially the Yoruba elite from whom his
birth and limited education distanced him – who saw their country as a colonial
agglomeration of the ethnic groups to which their first loyalties lay. Soyinka, for
example, speaking from a Yoruba perspective, denounced the 'demagogic' and
'ridiculous' notion 'which says there's an entity called Nigeria and that entity is
sacrosanct.'[9] Instead he quoted Obafemi Awolowo, the dominant figure in twentieth-century Yoruba politics: 'I've always insisted to myself that my first duty is to
the Yoruba nation. We are a nation, you know. And I put that nation first, then the
one called Nigeria.'[10] By contrast, Obasanjo's long-term goal, as he declared in 2001,
was 'the nullification of all forms of identification except Nigerian citizenship'.[11] In
the shorter term, he strove to make Nigeria work, both economically and politically,
an immensely difficult task when state-building must take place democratically in
a context of popular loyalties to component ethnic groups. Politics in Nigeria, as
elsewhere in Africa, is often dismissed as being purely about personal advantage, but
that is untrue; it is chiefly about political structures, as in most new countries, the
early history of the United States being a good example. At times, especially early in
his civilian presidency, Obasanjo seemed to be fighting the battle for Nigerian unity
almost on his own. As he said at the age of 67, with full justification, 'I have always
put Nigeria above everything else in my life.'[12] It is as the outstanding member of the
second generation of independent African leaders who dedicated themselves to the
consolidation of their postcolonial states that Obasanjo merits his place in history.

This dedication to 'the Nigerian project' made Obasanjo willing to accept the
responsibilities, constraints, and compromises of power from which elite sceptics like
Soyinka shrank. As the journalist Reuben Abati wrote, 'Obasanjo is effectively a man
of power. He radiates·it. He looks it.'[13] In the Yoruba manner, he flaunted it. Power,
his use of it, and its effects upon him form the third theme of his life. Endowed with
great authority as a military commander in his early thirties, he became exceptionally

2

sensitive to the location of power, whether in international affairs or the streets of Nigerian cities. His decisions were invariably based on political calculations, rather than the legal and constitutional principles that concerned his elite critics. A man of great physical and intellectual energy, he exercised power with skill and ruthlessness, sometimes unscrupulously but seldom cruelly. To study his career is to gain some sense of the immense demands that the government of a large African state places on those who undertake it. His critics believed that power corrupted him, that an 'inordinate desire for absolute, unfettered power'[14] became the driving principle of his administration, especially during his second term as president, when he flouted democratic procedures and attempted, as they believed, to entrench himself permanently in office. This issue is essential to an assessment of the man and will dominate the penultimate chapter of this book. Power, age, self-righteousness, lack of scruple, the relentless hostility of his critics, and an obsessive sense of responsibility did indeed warp his judgment, but behind the actions at the end of his career, it will be argued, any thirst for personal power was subordinate to his anxiety to retain sufficient command of the political process to ensure a successful transfer of authority to his successor. Paradoxically, Obasanjo was corrupted chiefly by the strength of his own patriotism.

Moreover, Obasanjo's behaviour at the end of his career must be understood in the light of the rapid changes taking place in the global and national context within which he worked, a pace of change accentuated by his unique experience of exercising national leadership on two occasions separated by a full twenty years.[15] On the international scene, the liberation of southern Africa, which dominated his first tenure of power in the late 1970s, gave way to the consequences of the end of the Cold War and the marginalisation of Africa that led him to share in the creation of the African Union twenty years later. At the national level, he had to come to terms with the enormous changes in Nigerian society taking place around him, especially the growth of the country's population during his adult lifetime from something over 30 million in 1952–3 (the census figure) to 140 million in 2006,[16] which posed immense problems for the governments he headed. He had, also, to adapt his thinking to changing strategies of Third World development, moving in the course of his career across the entire spectrum from faith in state investment in heavy industry, the orthodoxy of the 1970s, to overt commitment to the private enterprise and market liberalism that dominated the 1990s, although he never lost his real enthusiasm for the most modern, large-scale projects. Similarly, it was the failure of the civilian regime to which he had transferred power in 1979 that dominated his political strategy when he became civilian president in 1999, shaping especially his determination to control the choice of his successor. In this respect, however, Obasanjo failed to adapt to the changing expectations of Nigeria's increasingly educated and sophisticated population, for whom democratic procedures were becoming a priority alongside the unity and development to which the aging Obasanjo was dedicated. This failure to adapt explained much of the bitterness surrounding his retirement.

Many sources needed for a definitive biography of Obasanjo are not yet available to a historian and may not become available for many years to come. This provisional account may nevertheless be justified by his importance to the modern history of Nigeria and by Nigeria's importance to the world.

NOTES

1. Ben Nwabueze, *How President Obasanjo subverted the rule of law and democracy* (Ibadan, 2007), p. xxiii.
2. Wole Soyinka, 'Between nation space and nationhood', *Guardian*, 5 March 2009.
3. Danjuma in *Guardian*, 17 February 2008.
4. Abubakar Rimi in *Newswatch*, 14 April 2008.
5. Oluremi Obasanjo, *Bitter-sweet: my life with Obasanjo* (Lagos, 2008).
6. *This Day*, 16 January 2008; below, p. 305.
7. Broadcast quoted in *Guardian*, 28 October 2001.
8. Olusegun Obasanjo, 'A dangerous diversion', *African Concord*, 14 February 1994.
9. Wole Soyinka, 'The shape of things to come', *Index on Censorship*, 22, 8 (1993), 33.
10. Quoted in Wole Soyinka, *You must set forth at dawn: a memoir* (London, 2007), pp. 129–30.
11. Broadcast quoted in *Guardian*, 28 October 2001.
12. Olusegun Obasanjo, *Standing tall* (Lagos, 2005), p. 11.
13. *Guardian*, 24 November 2004.
14. Nwabueze, *How Obasanjo subverted law*, p. 90.
15. The closest parallel is perhaps with General de Gaulle, whose two periods of power were separated by twelve years (1946–58).
16. James S. Coleman, *Nigeria: background to nationalism* (Berkeley, 1960), p. 15; *Newswatch*, 15 March 2009.

Part I

Making a Career
(1937–70)

2
Yoruba Boy

Matthew Olusegun Aremu Obasanjo was born at Ibogun-Olaogun, a village in south-western Nigeria about half-way between Lagos and Abeokuta. His passport later showed his date of birth as 5 March 1937, but there was no written record and the date was estimated from other family events. He was the first of his parents' nine children and the only one to survive childhood except a younger sister.[1] There are several interpretations of the baby's names, all suggesting his parents' joy and hope. By one account, Olusegun meant 'God conquers', Aremu was a praise name with royal connotations, and Obasanjo – his father's first name – signified 'the king rewards'. He abandoned Matthew at secondary school as an act of cultural nationalism.[2]

Linguistic evidence suggests that ancestors of Obasanjo's Yoruba people had lived in this broad region of West Africa for several thousand years. By about A.D. 1000 they were forming kingdoms with capital towns.[3] Obasanjo's ancestors came from one of the oldest, Owu, which was defeated and destroyed by its rivals during the 1820s in a war initiating an Age of Confusion that engulfed Yorubaland for the remainder of the nineteenth century.[4] During the 1830s many Owu refugees settled at Abeokuta, a new town built by the similarly uprooted Egba branch of the Yoruba. Occupying a distinct southern quarter of the town, Owu people gained a reputation for industry, pride, truculence, and military valour.[5]

Ancestral kingdoms and their capital cities largely determined Yoruba identities. Especially during the Age of Confusion, when much of a kingdom's population might seek security within the city wall, life in the capital and participation in its competitive and colourful public arena were the essence of civilisation. Social honour, long sought through the display of authority, esteem, courage, wealth, decency, moderation, and generosity, was now gained especially by military prowess.[6] Abeokuta, like other nineteenth-century Yoruba cities, was dominated by warchiefs and swarmed with military slaves and 'warboys'. Watching one warchief enter his city in triumph, a young man declared, 'If I enjoy such a glory for only one day and I die the next, I shall be content.'[7]

Most townsmen were agriculturalists with fields and temporary houses in surrounding farm settlements. Obasanjo's Owu ancestors carved out a chain of settlements south-west of Abeokuta along the trade route through Ota to the coast at Lagos. His birthplace, Ibogun, was a late and relatively distant village founded in the early 1920s by settlers who included his father, remembered as a hard-working

7

farmer and proud bicycle owner.[8] Until he was eleven years old, the young Obasanjo helped his father in the fields. Doubtless he experienced the severe upbringing traditional among the Yoruba, who demanded extreme deference to seniority[9] – a principle on which Obasanjo would insist throughout his life. Ibogun was small and remote, but it enjoyed a community life. Obasanjo's village church was Baptist, a branch of the Southern Baptist mission from the United States that had reached Abeokuta in 1850. Yet, as he recalled, 'I grew up in a village where Muslims and Christians lived together. As a kid, I partook in the Rammadan fast with my Muslim cousins and relations; we celebrated all Muslim festivals together, in addition, we prayed in mosques during the fasting and on Fridays and we all went to the church on Sundays and during the Christian festivals.' His sister, through her marriage, was to become a Muslim.[10]

Ibogun's remoteness was to shape Obasanjo's entire career. The village was a farm settlement of Abeokuta, but Obasanjo probably did not visit the town until he was at least nine years old.[11] He had no part in the intellectual vitality that Western education had brought to Abeokuta, where Anglican missionaries had established their main base in Yorubaland in 1846. Once supported and protected by British rule, from 1893, a Christian elite took control of the town from its former warchiefs and made it a centre of enlightenment for Yorubaland and Nigeria as a whole. Among Obasanjo's contemporaries growing up there in the 1940s, for example, were Wole Soyinka and his Ransome-Kuti cousins – Olikoye (future Minister of Health), Femi (civil rights activist), and Fela (musician) – all four the sons of headmasters, all socialised in the complex households characteristic of Yoruba towns, all enjoying the vivid childhoods that Soyinka would describe so brilliantly.[12] To this urban elite, Obasanjo was a farm boy. He lacked even an elite patron, an invaluable aid to advancement in Yoruba society. He was, quite literally, on his own and would remain so for the rest of his life.

Yet that had advantages. Obasanjo lacked the family and community ties that bound most Yoruba (and other Nigerians) to champion localities and ethnic groups. As a man from the rural periphery, he could, if he chose, belong solely to Nigeria. His upbringing gave him a lasting preference for rural life and a rapport with village people. He learned to work hard, to get his hands dirty, and to live simply. 'Very early in life,' he later wrote, 'I had to know that in terms of experience, poverty has greater purchasing power than wealth.'[13] His social attitudes, especially towards women and youth, remained essentially rural. 'It takes a village to raise a child,' he observed in old age.[14] As a child, his ambitions were limited and practical. He said later that he had wanted to become either a motor mechanic, like one of his cousins, or a barman. His father, however, wanted the boy to have an education. 'If you want me to', Obasanjo acquiesced, knowing little about it. He was already nine years old and another two years elapsed before a place could be found at the village school in Ibogun.[15] To start so late was not unique at that time – his contemporary Frederick Fasehun entered primary school at twelve and secondary school at twenty[16] – but it marked him out. Together with his evident intelligence, it may have helped him to jump classes and make rapid progress. In 1951, after only three years, he gained a place at the Baptist Day School in the Owu quarter of Abeokuta.[17]

It was an exciting moment to enter the town. In 1951, seeking to bring the western, eastern, and northern regions of Nigeria together, the British government created a federal structure in which each region enjoyed much self-government. Yoruba Christian professionals and businessmen launched the Action Group to

control their Western Region. Its leader, Obafemi Awolowo, was a brilliant political organiser and administrator determined to unite the Yoruba, preserve their
identity within Nigeria, and ensure that their advantages in education and wealth
made them its leaders. Funded by high world prices for the local cocoa crop, the
Action Group operated the most efficient administration in tropical Africa, with an
ambitious programme of economic development, institutional modernisation, and,
above all, education.[18]

Obasanjo was a beneficiary, for in 1952, aged fifteen, he transferred to the Baptist
Boys' High School in Abeokuta, partly financed by state grants. Founded in 1923 for
'youths of above average and average ability and little means, including those with
no means at all', it was known as the Penny School to Canon Oludotun Ransome-
Kuti, the headmaster of the Abeokuta Grammar School that the town's Anglican
elite attended.[19] Yet the Baptist School, with stern discipline and compulsory
daily worship, had a high reputation and produced many distinguished Nigerians.
Obasanjo, somewhat older than the average, stood out in several ways. His father
had failed as a farmer and had abandoned his family, leaving his wife to support her
children as best she could by trading.[20] Obasanjo was now poor in a culture that
despised poverty. His future wife, Oluremi, then a younger schoolgirl, remembered
their first encounter: 'I looked him over.... He wore no shoes, not even the cheap
tennis shoes sold for 7 shilling and 6 pence students wore then. He introduced
himself and started to talk to me about beginning a friendship. I didn't take him
seriously.'[21] The school allowed Obasanjo to earn part of his fees by cutting grass,
washing plates, and cleaning the premises during holidays. He worked on cocoa
and kola farms, fished, collected firewood, and gathered baskets of sand to sell to
building contractors.[22] A somewhat clumsy youth, never athletic, he made no mark
at games but was an enthusiastic boy scout. A teacher remembered him as jealous of
his status, 'very self-assertive, a stickler for procedure and would not brook cheating'.
He added that Obasanjo was 'a very brilliant student', a judgement echoed by other
accounts and confirmed in 1956 by success in the school certificate examination.[23]

Although he remembered Awolowo lecturing to the school on 'The sky is the
limit', there is no evidence that Obasanjo took any part in Nigerian national politics either as a schoolboy or for several years thereafter. Of the 30 million Nigerians
counted in the census of 1952–3, some 5 million were Yoruba, who predominated
among the 6 million people of the Western Region. In the Eastern Region, the
7.7 million included 5.5 million listed as Igbo, a linguistic group divided, like the
Yoruba, into many smaller units. Over half Nigeria's population (16.1 million) lived
in the vast and less developed Northern Region, where the 8.6 million Hausa-
Fulani people had been amalgamated in the early nineteenth century into a single
Islamic caliphate, subdivided into numerous emirates. Thus the three major
ethnic groups – Yoruba, Igbo, and Hausa-Fulani – each dominated a region and
together composed 63 % of the total population. The remaining 'minority' peoples,
particularly numerous in the southern part of the Northern Region (known as the
Middle Belt), were divided into many (some said about 250) linguistic and ethnic
groups.[24] Just as British constitutional engineering stimulated the Yoruba to form
the Action Group (AG), so the Igbo-dominated National Council of Nigeria and the
Cameroons (NCNC), led by Nnamdi Azikiwe, controlled the Eastern Region, while
the Northern People's Congresss (NPC) represented the caliphate and was led by a
member of its ruling family, the Sardauna of Sokoto. To win support, these leaders
had to satisfy voters whose concerns were overwhelmingly parochial. Nationalism in

Nigeria during the 1950s was less about ousting the British than about competing to succeed them and devising a mutually acceptable constitution for the successor state, a competition fought out at elections that grew increasingly frenetic, corrupt, and expensive. The final federal election in 1959 was a victory for the NPC, whose larger regional constituency gave it 134 of the 312 seats in the federal assembly, against 89 for the NCNC and only 73 for the AG. Awolowo was not only denied the victory he expected, but his attempt to challenge the 'feudal' NPC's control of the North bred a bitterness on both sides that left him in opposition to the NPC/NCNC coalition formed to govern the new state, a coalition headed by the NPC's federal leader, Abubakar Tafawa Balewa, as Prime Minister. Not only did this party rivalry endanger stability, but so did the constitutional structure, which left most internal functions to the three regions but enabled the North, with over half the population, to dominate the federal centre.[25] On Independence Day (1 October 1960) the Prime Minister himself confessed privately that 'he was apprehensive of the high hopes built in the world for Nigeria.'[26]

For younger Nigerians, however, the new world was full of hope and opportunity. Obasanjo was one of them. In 1956, already nineteen years old, he refused to delay his school certificate examination until the school chose to enter him. Instead he borrowed a guinea (£1.1s., or £1.05) from a local bookseller, entered privately, and passed all the papers. The school refused him a testimonial, so he left for the bustling city of Ibadan, eventually finding a teaching job, giving him time to study for the entrance examination to the University College there, the apex of Nigeria's educational system. Although successful, he could not afford the fees and did not know how to obtain a scholarship. Instead, hoping now to become a civil engineer and seeking access to training without the expense of a university, he answered in 1958 an advertisement by the Nigerian army for applicants with a background in science to be trained as officer cadets.[27] He was 21 years old and it was the most important decision of his life.

NOTES

1. Onukaba Adinoyi Ojo, *In the eyes of time: a biography of Olusegun Obasanjo* (New York, 1997), pp. 31–5. My account of Obasanjo's early life relies heavily on this book, which uses extensive interviews but ends in 1976.
2. Dapo Olaosebikan, *Olusegun Obasanjo: father of new Nigeria* (Lagos, 2002), pp. 3–5; Adinoyi Ojo, *In the eyes of time*, p. 33.
3. Christopher Ehret and Merrick Posnansky (eds), *The archaeological and linguistic reconstruction of African history* (Berkeley, 1982), p. 242; Bassey W. Andah, 'Early urban societies and settlement of the Guinea and savannah regions of West Africa', *West African Journal of Archaeology*, 25, 1 (1995), 139–40.
4. Akin Mabogunje and J.D. Omer-Cooper, *Owu in Yoruba history* (Ibadan, 1971), pp. 30, 51–6; J.D.Y. Peel, *Religious encounter and the making of the Yoruba* (Bloomington, 2000), Ch.3.
5. Saburi O. Biobaku, *The Egba and their neighbours 1842–1872* (Oxford, 1957), pp. 13–18, 24, 54, and map 3; Mabogunje and Omer-Cooper, *Owu*, pp. 44, 94–6.
6. John Iliffe, *Honour in African history* (Cambridge, 2005), Ch.5.
7. Samuel Johnson, *The history of the Yorubas* (London, 1921), p. 395.
8. Mabogunje and Omer-Cooper, *Owu*, p. 100; Adinoyi Ojo, *In the eyes of time*, pp. 31–5.

9. N.A. Fadipe, *The sociology of the Yoruba* (reprinted, Ibadan, 1970), pp. 108–9, 129.

10. Olusegun Obasanjo, *Not my will* (Ibadan, 1990), p. 62.

11. Adinoyi Ojo, *In the eyes of time*, p. 36.

12. Wole Soyinka, *Ake: the years of childhood* (London, 1981).

13. Olusegun Obasanjo, *This animal called man* (Abeokuta [c.1998]), p. 270.

14. Olusegun Obasanjo, 'Obama's election and the needed change', *Guardian*, 6 November 2008.

15. Adinoyi Ojo, *In the eyes of time*, pp. 34–7; *Nigerian Tribune*, 29 October 2006.

16. Frederick Isiotan Fasehun, *Frederick Fasehun: the son of Oodua* (Lagos, 2002), pp. 25, 38.

17. Adinoyi Ojo, *In the eyes of time*, pp. 36, 43.

18. Richard L. Sklar, *Nigerian political parties: power in an emergent African nation* (Princeton, 1963), Chs. 6 and 7.

19. Adinoyi Ojo, *In the eyes of time*, p. 50.

20. Ibid., pp. 43–5.

21. Obasanjo, *Bitter-sweet*, p. 14.

22. Adinoyi Ojo, *In the eyes of time*, pp. 43–5, 50–3; *This Day*, 5 and 29 May 1999.

23. *Sunday Concord*, 24 June 1984; *African Guardian*, 5 June 1986, p. 22.

24. Coleman, *Nigeria*, p. 15.

25. The best account is still Coleman, *Nigeria*, part 4.

26. Alan Lennox-Boyd in A.H.M. Kirk-Greene (ed.), *The transfer of power: the colonial administrator in the age of decolonisation* (Oxford, 1979), p. 63.

27. Adinoyi Ojo, *In the eyes of time*, pp. 56–63; Obasanjo, *Bitter-sweet*, pp. 15–17.

3
Nigerian Soldier

Military service suited many aspects of Obasanjo's personality: his sense of discipline and duty, his compulsive activism, his ambition, perhaps his need for a surrogate family and for a cause, which he was to find in the Nigerian nation. When he retired after twenty years' service, he told his assembled colleagues that 'for the total development of man within his environment physically and intellectually, there is no better ground than military training and full military career.'[1]

Not all of this can have been clear to him in March 1958 when he enlisted and was sent to the Regular Officers' Training School at Teshie in Ghana. His main concern then was to find a job that would pay him to acquire further training. Owu people were proud of their military past, but unlike many officer cadets, Obasanjo had neither family connections to the army, fascination with military display, nor athletic prowess. What he shared with many was relatively lowly social origin and a readiness to defy his parents, whom he did not even inform.[2] 'A message just came to us at Abeokuta that we should come and pick his property because he had gone to Angola [Ghana] to join the army', his sister recalled. 'When he came back and was asked why he did not inform our parents before going, he said he was sure that our parents would not have allowed him if he had told them.'[3] Opposition by family and friends to an educated young man joining the army was common. 'I was appalled', Obasanjo's girl-friend Oluremi remembered. 'Images of drunken soldiers, drinking *burukutu* and patronising prostitutes in Sobo area of Abeokuta flooded to my mind.'[4] Not only had the army been an occupying force, but its men were often brutal and illiterate, poorly paid – much less than policemen – and subject to harsh discipline. 'He who joins the army plunges himself into trouble', ran a Yoruba song.[5] Few of Nigeria's 7,500 soldiers were Yoruba and most of those were in technical branches, while the bulk of foot-soldiers came from northern 'minorities'.[6] Obasanjo joined this colonial army at exactly the moment when the Nigerian Government took control of it. Only 32 of its 280 officers were then Nigerians, the highest in rank being a major.[7] Obasanjo was one of the young men recruited to transform the institution.

The first six months of basic training at Teshie were 'pure unadulterated Hell', according to Benjamin Adekunle, Obasanjo's fellow-cadet.[8] Doubtless the unathletic Obasanjo suffered equally, but Emmanuel Erskine, who shared a room with him, remembered him as 'an extremely hard working, assiduous cadet who was among the few Nigerian cadets selected at the end of the course in September 1958 for further training at Mons, Aldershot, U.K'.[9] Whereas Ghana's recent independence seems to have made little impact on Obasanjo, Mons left a more lasting impression, for he found it class-ridden and racist, giving him a disdain for Britain's fading power that was to colour his later policy. Moreover, his mother died while he was in England, followed a year later by his father. And although Obasanjo gained his commission and a certificate in engineering, he failed, unlike Adekunle, to win selection for further training at the more prestigious Royal Military Academy at Sandhurst.[10] It was his first failure.

Back in Nigeria in 1959, Obasanjo was posted to Kaduna as an infantry subaltern with the Fifth Battalion, generally considered Nigeria's best. There he lived for the first time in the savanna lands and Muslim culture of Northern Nigeria and entered happily into regimental soldiering. Nearly thirty years later he idealised this period:

> The army itself was happy, young Nigerians were for the first time, being given the opportunity to command units and even battalions. The officer ranks were still dominated by British officers and the few Nigerian officers knew that in the fullness of time, they would inherit commanding positions within their chosen careers. There was camaraderie within the officers corps and a sense of brotherhood was building up. One's ethnic background was never a subject of discussion, and the tendency of those days was to see one's colleagues as officers and gentlemen. This was the legacy bequeathed to the Nigerian Army by the British, and it was felt that it was a legacy worth keeping and defending.[11]

Obasanjo's Owu origin and detachment from the Yoruba elite may have predisposed him towards a specifically Nigerian nationalism, but it was probably during this time as a young officer at the cusp of national independence that commitment to Nigeria became the guiding passion of his life. As he was to say frequently later, 'I am a Nigerian who happens to be a Yoruba man. I am not a Yoruba man who happens to be a Nigerian.'[12] Other young officers shared his conviction. 'Only in the army do you get true Nigerianism', claimed his friend Chukwuma Nzeogwu.[13]

The young officers gained, too, a notion of military honour that blended with indigenous notions and distinguished the military from civilians, even those enjoying greater education, wealth, or political power. 'I was trained in the classic military mould as an officer and a gentleman,' Obasanjo later recalled.[14] That phrase, a sociologist observed during the 1960s, was 'one of the most frequently heard expressions in the Nigerian Army':

> The notion that officers are gentlemen ... is a device of collective military honour, being in this respect not unlike the practice of duelling in the German officer corps. It affirms the professional identity of the individual officer and the corporate identity of the officer corps as a differentiated status group with its own system of values. There is no clearly defined status of gentleman outside the army.[15]

For Obasanjo, this notion became a vital distinction between soldiers and politicians, a moral justification for military power that must not be sullied. And along with these principles of patriotism and honour the young officers imbibed a third: the transcendent importance and duty of leadership, which Obasanjo liked to summarise by the military dictum that 'there are no bad soldiers but bad officers'.[16] Exaggeration of the importance of leadership was a trait he shared with many Nigerians.

13

These ideals were soon tested in the anarchic conditions of the newly independent Congo. Having failed to prepare its colony for independence, the Belgian government undertook a precipitate decolonisation in June 1960. The frail successor regime of Patrice Lumumba almost immediately faced a mutiny by the 25,000-strong Congolese National Army, accompanied by administrative collapse, Belgian military intervention to protect its citizens, and secession by the mineral-rich Katanga province. When Lumumba sought international aid, the United Nations intervened to prevent the Cold War extending into the Congo. Its peacekeepers concentrated not on supporting Lumumba but on restoring order, especially by curbing the mutinous troops. Shortly after Nigeria gained independence in October 1960, Obasanjo's Fifth Battalion joined the peacekeepers, under the command of Colonel Ironsi. They were posted to the eastern Kivu province, with their headquarters at Bukavu.[17]

It was a difficult mission. The Nigerians found themselves defending the civilian population, including Belgian settlers, against mutinous Congolese soldiers. Obasanjo's company initially patrolled the countryside from a base at Kasongo, where 'our military operations ... consisted in confidence building, removal of suspicion and dispelling rumours which came in many and varied forms.... We moved from one tense situation to another.'[18] When they rejoined the main force at Bukavu in January 1961, the political situation had deteriorated further, for Lumumba, escaping from captivity and heading for his power base at Kisangani, had been recaptured and murdered.[19] His followers set up a rival government in Kisangani and sought to extend its control across the region of Nigerian operations. On 2 February, after an incident at a road block, the Fifth Battalion had a major engagement with troops from Kisangani, killing 49 Congolese for the death of one Nigerian.[20] Three weeks later, Obasanjo, sent to evacuate Catholic missionaries from a station near Bukavu, was waylaid by Congolese troops and bundled into the boot of a car. His captors sought permission to kill him but were ordered to release him. His Company arrested the soldiers responsible, roughed them up, and secured their dismissal. It was probably the most dangerous moment of his life.[21]

Obasanjo left the Congo with the Fifth Battalion in May 1961 and did not return, although other Nigerian troops served there for another three years. 'As young officers, the Congo operation had tremendous implications and made deep impressions on our lives and military careers', Obasanjo recalled:

> We were able to compare at that early stage in our military careers the effects of colonization by two colonial powers.... There were only shades of difference in the methods employed.
>
> By and large, both Britain and Belgium were only interested in exploitation of the colonies for the development of their home countries ...
>
> Our Congo experience, however heightened our Pan-African fervour. We realised that Africa divided by outsiders and within itself, would remain perpetually exploited, suppressed and backward.[22]

Perhaps the experience also reinforced the young officers' distaste for politicians, whose squabbles had brought the Congo to such chaos,[23] and it left a profound fear of anarchy – especially the anarchy of undisciplined private soldiers – which many officers saw as a warning to their own country. 'When I remember the situation I

14

saw in Congo 47 years ago ... and the situation the Republic of Congo faces now,' Obasanjo said on Nigerian Independence Day in 2007, 'we must thank God.'[24]

There was a brighter side. 'Dag's Dash', as the Congolese service allowance was known,[25] enabled Obasanjo to buy his first car. He liked to recall that his superiors immediately demanded proof that the money had not been gained corruptly; when satisfied, they replaced it by a car loan that enabled him to invest the £700 in his first parcels of urban land.[26] His returning battalion marched proudly through the streets of Lagos, but the press paid it little attention, for 'progressives' who regarded Lumumba as the legitimate leader of the Congo denounced the use of Nigerian troops to kill Congolese and defend European settlers.[27] The controversy added to the hostility between Awolowo's Action Group and Abubakar's conservative coalition government. Awolowo was increasingly frustrated. Powerless in opposition in the federal assembly, his attempt to reassert his authority in Yorubaland led to conflict that Abubakar exploited to declare a state of emergency there, arrest Action Group leaders, and impose federal control. Subsequent enquiries revealed extensive misappropriation of public funds and amateurish preparations for armed insurrection, possibly in association with elements in the army. Awolowo was sentenced to ten years imprisonment (later reduced to seven).[28]

Although Obasanjo later wrote that at independence, 'No Nigerian army officer, in his wildest dreams, would have imagined the army playing any part in political governance',[29] this displayed his own political naivety at the time. Several young officers were alert to the possibility – Emeka Ojukwu, commissioned in 1957, later said that he joined the army because he thought Nigeria 'headed for an upheaval and that the army was the place to be when the time came'[30] – as also were some politicians, including Abubakar and Awolowo. The Action Group's preparations were the most serious to date, but until 1964, while up to half the army was engaged in the Congo, it had little opportunity for conspiracy.[31]

Beneath the surface of detribalised harmony, the army in which Obasanjo served in the mid 1960s was a snake-pit. Its priority was rapid Africanisation of the officer corps. Between 1960 and 1966, the number of Nigerian officers increased from 50 to 517, while expatriates fell from 237 to nil.[32] This drew into the army the ethnic rivalries that permeated Nigerian life. In 1960 about two-thirds of Nigerian officers were Igbo, owing to their high levels of education and relative scarcity of employment opportunities. A year later, the Minister of Defence, a tough northern politician, imposed quotas on new appointments, with 50% to come from the North and 25% each from the East and West. Much pressure was put on northern schoolboys to 'show that they were not women' by enlisting. By 1966, 41% of officers were Igbo, 33% from the North, and 27% from the West (mostly from the newly-excised Mid-West region rather than Yorubaland).[33] This policy embittered many eastern officers. 'Anybody in trousers could become an army officer, so long as he was a Northerner', one later complained.[34] Yet in 1966 most northerners were still junior officers while easterners filled the middle ranks as majors and lieutenant-colonels.[35]

To these tensions were added rivalries between officers trained at Sandhurst, Mons, or elsewhere; disputes over seniority between those with or without university degrees; and especially the divisions of age and culture between senior officers who had risen through the ranks, such as Ironsi, and the younger, better-educated, junior officers recruited as cadets. Obasanjo's friend Nzeogwu scarcely concealed his contempt for Ironsi, who 'joined the army as a tally-clerk and was a clerk most of the time'. Ironsi, in turn, told Obasanjo, 'You are a good officer but I don't like you because you don't drink. You will always be too sober.'[36] Ironsi's appointment in 1965 as the first Nigerian Commander in Chief was due chiefly to his seniority and his eastern origin, at a time when his Yoruba rivals were politically unacceptable to the ruling coalition.[37]

Obasanjo took little part in these cross-cutting rivalries. Although sharing the widespread dissatisfaction with developments in the army, he was no partisan and, as one of the few Yoruba middle-ranking officers, he stood outside the main rivalry between northerners and easterners. Quiet, thoughtful, reliable, a lifelong teetotaller, and already portly in his later twenties, he was a threat to nobody and progressed steadily through the ranks, reaching major in 1965.[38] Most important, on returning from the Congo he transferred to the small Army Engineering Corps and, after a long period in hospital with a stomach ulcer, began a series of training courses in his new profession, spending the year 1962–3 in Britain at the Royal College of Military Engineering, where he won distinction as 'the best Commonwealth student ever'.[39] He also married.

Oluremi Akinlawon was the daughter of a station master. Obasanjo first noticed her when they sang together in the Owu Baptist church choir. Despite initial rejection, he pursued her with characteristic persistence from 1956, when he was nineteen and she was fourteen. In 1958, when Obasanjo joined the army, Oluremi told her mother that he was her fiancé. Mother was not keen: Obasanjo was poor, soldiers were disreputable, and Oluremi had other suitors. But Obasanjo wrote persistently from Ghana, Britain, and the Congo, returning each time with presents. Mother was persuaded by his helpfulness, father by Obasanjo's blunt declaration that he had even more grounds to encourage Oluremi's education because he wanted an educated wife to bring up his family. When he left for England in 1962 he was in a position to buy her a ticket to follow him and to find her a room and a training course in London, vetoing her wish to train as a nurse because he thought them wayward. They were married at Camberwell Green Registry Office in June 1963, five days after her twenty-first birthday, without informing their families.[40]

He was an assiduous but domineering husband. 'I was in my early teens when we met, just about to begin my secondary education', Oluremi recalled:

> He was in the last lap of his and for seven years we courted before marriage. I was a school leaver of barely six months when we married. He is the only man I have known all my life. I had not the luxury of mixing or experimenting like some other women before I married.
>
> He manipulated me at his will, knowing my experience in the world was limited to him. He raised me, so to speak; gave me the books I should read; dictated the course I studied; sent me to England, paid my fees at school there; hired a flat for me, paid my way back. In short, he took control of my life and moulded me.[41]

Yet this was only part of the truth. Oluremi was an educated Yoruba woman from a culture in which women enjoyed an unusual degree of economic independence and married couples often lived apart. She showed her independence when he completed his engineering course in 1963 and asked her to return to Nigeria with him. 'I felt devastated,' she wrote. 'I hadn't achieved my purpose in coming to the U.K. and my husband was already asking me to put an end to my dreams ... I told him I couldn't go back home without something to show for it.' Obasanjo acquiesced. He was expecting to return to Britain for another course, but this fell through. Instead, Oluremi spent most of the next three years alone in London, visited sporadically by Obasanjo's friends but often lonely and unhappy.[42]

Back in Nigeria in 1963, Obasanjo took command of the Field Engineering Squadron at Kaduna until 1965, when he was sent abroad again, this time to India, visiting Oluremi in London on the way there and back. He studied at the Defence Services Staff College, Wellington, and the School of Engineering, Poona, where again he earned excellent reports. None of these courses gave him the professional engineering qualification he coveted, but India made a considerable impact on him. While appalled to see people dying of starvation in the streets of Calcutta, he was impressed by the ethos of hard work, austerity, and piety, which led to reading in the field of comparative religion and enlarged the open-mindedness acquired during his childhood.[43]

His absence in Britain and India meant that Obasanjo escaped much of the escalating tension within the army and Nigeria as a whole between 1963 and 1965.[44] With the Action Group fragmented, the dominant northern party had little need to humour its NCNC coalition partner. During 1962–4, the two quarrelled over inflated census figures that showed a sufficient northern majority of population to guarantee the NPC control of the federal legislature, provided it monopolised its region. This it did so effectively in the December 1964 election that the NCNC boycotted the polls and began to plan secession, creating a constitutional crisis that brought the military more directly into politics. While the army command supported Prime Minister Abubakar in a power struggle with President Azikiwe, eastern and radical officers contemplated intervention on Azikiwe's behalf. Many soldiers already resented orders to suppress protest by the Tiv people of the Middle Belt against NPC domination. They were further alienated when the rigging of regional elections in Yorubaland in October 1965 provoked popular violence that the army was again ordered to repress. The Premier of the Eastern Region asked the British Government at this time whether he could expect its support in the event of civil war.[45] With recent models of military intervention in neighbouring Benin and Togo, discussion of coups was so prevalent late in 1965 that some officers avoided parties lest they be suspected of subversion.[46] 'There was a kind of paranoia everywhere', an acute observer remembered. 'Everybody was feeling somebody was going to kill them. This was when the army came and hit.'[47] It was exactly the moment when Obasanjo returned from India.

NOTES

1. [Olusegun Obasanjo,] *A march of progress: collected speeches of His Excellency General Olusegun Obasanjo* (ed. L.E. Scott-Emuakpor, Lagos, n.d.), p. 478.
2. Adinoyi-Ojo, *In the eyes of time*, pp. 63–6; Robin Luckham, *The Nigerian military: a sociological analysis of authority and revolt 1960–67* (Cambridge, 1971), pp. 111–14.
3. *This Day*, 17 May 1999.
4. Obasanjo, *Bitter-sweet*, p. 18.
5. Rasheed Olaniyi, *Diaspora is not like home: a social and economic history of Yoruba in Kano, 1912–1999* (Munich, 2008), p. 57.
6. N.J. Miners, *The Nigerian army 1956–1966* (London, 1971), pp. 2, 22–32.

17

Making a Career (1937–70)

7. Ibid., pp. 45, 49.
8. Abiodun A. Adekunle (ed.), *The Nigeria Biafra war letters: a soldier's story: volume 1* (Atlanta, 2004), p. 38.
9. Emmanuel A. Erskine, 'My heartiest congratulations', in Hans d'Orville (ed.), *Leadership for Africa: in honour of Olusegun Obasanjo on the occasion of his 60th birthday* (New York, 1995), p. 85.
10. Adinoyi Ojo, *In the eyes of time*, pp. 66–71; Adekunle, *War letters*, pp. 40–2.
11. Olusegun Obasanjo, *Nzeogwu: an intimate portrait of Major Chukwuma Kaduna Nzeogwu* (Ibadan, 1987), p. 44.
12. *This Day*, 12 September 2000.
13. *New Nigerian*, 18 January 1966, quoted in John Olukayode Fayemi, 'Threats, military expenditure and national security: analysis of trends in Nigeria's defence planning, 1970–1990', Ph.D. thesis, King's College, London, 1994, p. 127.
14. *Tell*, 6 July 1998, p. 32.
15. Luckham, *Nigerian military*, pp. 160, 127–8. A classic statement is Patrick A. Anwunah, *The Nigeria-Biafra War (1967–1970): my memoirs* (Ibadan, 2007), p. 21.
16. *Tell*, 26 April 1993, p. 19.
17. See Festus Ugboaja Ohaegbulam, *Nigeria and the UN mission in the Democratic Republic of the Congo: a case study of the formative stages of Nigeria's foreign policy* (Tampa, 1982), Chs. 2–5.
18. Obasanjo, *Nzeogwu*, p. 55.
19. Ludo de Witte, *L'assassinat de Lumumba* (Paris, 2000), p. 236.
20. *RNA* [Royal Nigerian Army] *Magazine*, 2, 3 (May 1962), 78–9.
21. Obasanjo, *Nzeogwu*, pp. 63–7; G. Norton, diary, 22–3 February 1961, Norton papers, RH.
22. Obasanjo, *Nzeogwu*, pp 67–8. Adejunle, by contrast, thought that 'Nigerians were incomparably better off' than Congolese: Adekunle, *War letters*, p. 45.
23. B.J. Dudley, *Instability and political order: politics and crisis in Nigeria* (Ibadan, 1973), p. 98.
24. *Guardian*, 2 October 2007.
25. After Dag Hammarskjöld, the UN Secretary-General.
26. Obasanjo, *This animal*, pp. 193–4.
27. *Nigerian Tribune*, 19 January and 15 February 1961.
28. See Richard L. Sklar, 'Nigerian politics: the ordeal of Chief Awolowo, 1960–65', in Gwendolen M. Carter (ed.), *Politics in Africa: seven cases* (New York, 1966), Ch. 4.
29. Obasanjo, *Nzeogwu*, p. 43.
30. Quoted in John J. Stremlau, *The international politics of the Nigerian Civil War 1967–1970* (Princeton, 1977), p. 42.
31. Miners, *Nigerian army*, pp. 130, 71.
32. Luckham, *Nigerian military*, p. 163.
33. Miners, *Nigerian army*, pp. 115–19; Luckham, *Nigerian military*, p. 244.
34. Ben Gbulie, *Nigeria's five majors: coup d'état of 15th January 1966: first inside account* (Onitsha, 1981), p. 11.
35. Dudley, *Instability*, p. 91.
36. Dennis D. Ejindu, 'Major Nzeogwu speaks', *Africa and the World*, 3, 31 (May 1967), 16; Obasanjo, *Nzeogwu*, p. 60.
37. Luckham, *Nigerian military*, p. 243.
38. Luckham's meticulous *Nigerian military* mentions Obasanjo only once, in a list of promotions.
39. Adinoyi Ojo, *In the eyes of time*, pp. 79–82.
40. Obasanjo, *Bitter-sweet*, pp. 14–26; Adinoyi Ojo, *In the eyes of time*, pp. 54–63, 82.
41. Obasanjo, *Bitter-sweet*, p. 64.
42. Ibid., p. 26.

43. Adinoyi Ojo, *In tne eyes of time*, pp. 82–6; Olusegun Obasanjo, *Africa embattled: selected essays on contemporary African development* (Ibadan, 1988), p. 21; Obasanjo, *Not my will*, p. 63.
44. See John P. Mackintosh, *Nigerian government and politics* (London, 1966), Chs. 12 and 13.
45. Treadwell, 'Record of meeting at Premier's Lodge', 18 October 1965, DO 195/283/239.
46. *Newswatch*, 10 April 1989, p. 42.
47. M.D. Yusufu in Yusufu Bala Usman and George Awale Kwanashie (ed.), *Inside Nigerian history 1950–1970: events, issues and sources* (Ibadan, 1995), p. 73.

4
Coups and Civil War

When Major Obasanjo landed at Kano airport on 13 January 1966, nobody met him. Surprised, he continued to the Engineers' base at Kaduna. Again nobody met him. He telephoned his closest friend, Major Chukwuma Nzeogwu, who promptly arrived to take him home, then left for his office, explaining that they were conducting night training exercises: 'Operation Leopard'. The acting commander of the engineers had left a note telling Obasanjo that he could not take over until 15 January. Obasanjo decided to catch up on his unit's files. The night of 14–15 January was disturbed by explosions and gunfire, but when he woke, everything was silent. Puzzled, he made for army headquarters. Nzeogwu was there, with a bandaged neck wound and his arm in a sling. He had just assassinated the Premier of Northern Nigeria.[1]

The coup d'état had been planned since August 1965, first by young officers in southern Nigeria clustered around Major Emmanuel Ifeajuna, then drawing in Nzeogwu and others in the North. Accounts differ, but there were probably five core conspirators: four Igbo and one Yoruba, including several of the best educated, best trained, and most politically conscious middle-ranking officers in the army. They planned to sweep away the political and military leadership by simulta-neous strikes in Lagos, Kaduna, and perhaps other regional capitals. 'Our enemies', Nzeogwu proclaimed, 'are the political profiteers, swindlers, the men in the high and low places that seek bribes and demand ten per cent, those that seek to keep the country divided permanently so that they can remain in office as ministers or VIPs of waste, the tribalists, the nepotists.'[2] Whether these targets were to be killed or merely arrested remained unclear, as was the regime to replace them.[3]

When Obasanjo saw him early on 15 January, Nzeogwu was triumphant that he had 'gunned down the bloody tyrant'.[4] Kaduna, the northern military headquarters, was in his hands. News of events elsewhere came in slowly, by telephone, and it was bad. In Ibadan, Captain Nwobosi had killed the unpopular Western Premier, Akintola, but failed to control the city or its garrison. In Kano, the battalion commander, Lt Col Ojukwu, refused to be involved.[5] In Lagos, the results were disastrous. Ifeajuna and his men had shot several senior officers and abducted (and later killed) the Federal Prime Minister, but they had not won over the infantry battalion at nearby Ikeja or prevented the Commander-in-Chief, Ironsi, from using it to control the capital. Next day the rump of the civilian government transferred power to Ironsi.[6]

Nzeogwu told Obasanjo that it had been too late to involve him in the conspiracy, had he wished it, and too dangerous to give him information, had he not. Obasanjo had been lucky: although he shared the conspirators' discontents, neither then nor later was he coup-making material. Instead, for the next 48 hours he gave Nzeogwu personal support, preparing his food for fear of attempted revenge. Isolated and exposed, Nzeogwu consolidated his hold on Kaduna and contemplated an advance southwards towards Lagos. Obasanjo and others warned against civil war. A meeting of officers decided to open negotiations with Ironsi by sending an emissary to Lagos.[7] When the officer selected refused the task, Obasanjo, by his own account, offered to replace him. According to one report, the meeting specified five terms on which they would recognise Ironsi's authority: safe conduct, freedom from legal action, no reinstatement of the former regime, compensation to the families of those killed, and release of conspirators already arrested.[8]

When Obasanjo reached Lagos, Ironsi and Nzeogwu had already spoken by telephone, Nzeogwu offering his loyalty under conditions and Ironsi accepting the loyalty without referring to the conditions.[9] When Obasanjo met him,

> Ironsi … made one point. He said, 'Nzeogwu talked about safe conduct for him and his colleagues, when I spoke to him. What exactly does he mean? Does he want medals for what they have done?' I explained that I could only understand it to mean pardon or amnesty for them. General Ironsi then remarked that it would be the responsibility of the Supreme Military Council when it was constituted, to decide. I bade the general good-bye and left.[10]

Later that day, Nzeogwu announced that Ironsi had accepted the five conditions for submission.[11] Although some in Kaduna suspected that Obasanjo might have misled them,[12] it seems more likely that Nzeogwu, accepting that submission was better than civil war, tried to claim more than had been conceded.[13] He flew to the capital, asserting that Ironsi had 'virtually accepted' his terms.[14] He was immediately detained, as gradually were the other leaders.

Although almost all conspirators were Igbo and those they killed were not, they claimed to have acted in the national interest. All major political parties and newspapers welcomed the new order. Even the Sultan of Sokoto, whose people had most reason for anger, urged acceptance of the *fait accompli*.[15] Nzeogwu, however, wrote to Obasanjo from prison complaining that 'my colleagues in the South made such a nonsense of this affair with result that people are accusing us of being one sided.'[16] In a larger sense, too, the coup had been sectional, expressing the centralising, meritocratic vision of Nigeria championed by educated young southerners, especially Igbo. Ironsi's actions reinforced this. 'All Nigerians want an end to Regionalism', he proclaimed, quite falsely.[17] His most influential advisers were mainly Igbo centralisers. When he promoted 21 officers to be lieutenant-colonels in April 1966, the ethnic composition of the officer corps ensured that 18 were Igbo, who now commanded 10 of the army's 13 combat units.[18] The coup leaders were neither prosecuted nor released.

The Unification Decree of 24 May 1966 brought the crisis to a head. It stated that 'Nigeria shall … cease to be a Federation…. All officers in the service of the Republic in a civil capacity shall be officers in a single service.'[19] Fearful northerners launched peaceful demonstrations that degenerated into violent attacks on the Igbo who had long lived on the fringes of northern cities. Some demonstrators shouted

'*A raba*' (separate us). A careful estimate was that some 600 people were killed. Northern emirs may have warned Ironsi that the North might secede unless the expected new constitution provided a federal structure.[20]

The army, too, was in turmoil. Enlisted men at Ikeja declared:

> They wanted a leader and he must come out now to lead them, so that they could hit back…. Apparently the Igbo soldiers or the Southern soldiers, in the barracks, were talking in disparaging terms toward those wives of Northern soldiers, when they go to take water from the pump. The Southern wives would push away Northern wives, saying, 'Get out, let us take it first, after all, we are now in charge.' And the women were pestering their husbands and asking 'When are you going to hit back to redeem our image?'[21]

The Fourth Battalion in Ibadan, whose commander had been murdered during the January coup, refused obedience to his Igbo successor, who had to be replaced. When Ironsi visited Kaduna, where Obasanjo was stationed, officers attending a party for him had to be searched for weapons.[22] Rumours of planned coups abounded, many centring on an impetuous officer from Kano, Lt Col Murtala Muhammed, who 'later on admitted that they had to do it as they couldn't allow sergeant-majors to take over'.[23]

In the event, violence began almost accidentally during the night of 28–9 July at Abeokuta, where the commanding officer assembled his (largely Igbo) officers to warn them against a coup, leading suspicious northern troops to attack them. Fearing that 'otherwise our boys in Abeokuta will be surrounded', troops in Ibadan seized and murdered Ironsi.[24] Over 200 Igbo officers and men were killed, most extensively at Ikeja. What Obasanjo later called 'the lack of planning and the revengeful intention of the second coup' bred three days of chaos until the troops at Ikeja obliged Lt Col Gowon, the senior surviving northern officer, to assume command.[25] By then northern soldiers were preparing to return to their region in readiness for secession from Nigeria, but Gowon – strongly advised by senior civil servants and American and British diplomats – persuaded them to suspend this until the idea lapsed. Gowon's authority was recognised by other senior officers except Lt Col Ojukwu, the Military Governor of the Eastern Region.[26]

When this July coup began, Lt Col Obasanjo was visiting Maiduguri, in the extreme north-east. Returning hastily to Kaduna – where Oluremi had joined him from Britain a few days earlier - he found great danger. Northern troops of the Third Battalion were arresting its southern personnel, torturing and killing many of the Igbo, but eventually releasing the Yoruba. Obasanjo sought to calm his engineers, who included many southern troops and a Regimental Sergeant-Major who at one point drunkenly asked permission to go out and kill Igbo. Believing that Obasanjo's life was in danger, the Military Governor of the North, Hassan Katsina, arranged for him and the pregnant Oluremi to be flown back to Maiduguri for ten days until Kaduna became calmer. Sending Oluremi to Lagos, Obasanjo then returned to Kaduna and remained there until January 1967 as the most senior Yoruba officer in the North, from which several others had fled.[27] 'Meetings of officers and civilians of Northern origin were regularly called at Lugard Hall' in Kaduna, he remembered, 'while senior officers like myself who were of non-Northern origin were excluded.'[28]

Meanwhile Gowon and his military governors were seeking to restore order. They released Awolowo and other imprisoned leaders and separated northern from eastern troops by returning both as far as possible to their regions. On 12 September regional representatives met to discuss future constitutional arrangements, but the negotiations were aborted by renewed violence against Igbo in northern cities, made especially brutal by the participation of mutinous soldiers. At least 10,000 Igbo – some accounts said up to 100,000 – were killed. Perhaps a million fled back to the East, often arriving in a condition that spread fear and hatred throughout the region.[29] Eastern delegates refused to return to the constitutional talks. Ojukwu, in the East, had once been a fervent unitarist but now saw the loosest confederation as the only current alternative to outright regional separation. He probably kept both options open for the next six months while he armed his regional forces and sought to win Yoruba support against the North.[30]

In Kaduna, Obasanjo was dangerously exposed, both physically and politically. The decision after the July coup to return soldiers to their own regions wherever possible had resulted in all northerners leaving the East and all easterners leaving the North and West, while approximately 3,000 northern troops remained in the West and Lagos. The federal government claimed that the approximately 700 western troops could not replace these northerners or guarantee the government's security in the capital. In addition, however, the northern troops guaranteed northern dominance of the federal government and constrained the West's freedom of action.[31] Most westerners saw them as an occupying army. Awolowo, released from prison and almost immediately elected 'Leader of the Yoruba' by a meeting of chiefs and opinion leaders, demanded that the northern troops be removed.[32] So did Ojukwu, who gave their presence in Lagos as his reason for refusing to attend federal meetings.

That Obasanjo remained in the North with fewer than 150 western soldiers weakened the Yoruba leaders' case. From August 1966 they tried to induce these troops to desert their posts and return to the West. In September intelligence sources reported that the four Yoruba officers in the North were to be killed. When they met Hassan Katsina to warn him of their fears, Obasanjo, the senior officer, refused to be their spokesman.[33] In the event, the officers held to their posts, not only because the journey to Yorubaland and their reception by northern soldiers there would have been dangerous, but as a matter of duty. 'We stood firmly with all our men, and we commanded them as officers of the Nigerian Army', Obasanjo recalled. 'Not one of the senior officers deserted his post, in spite of intimidation by soldiers and civilians alike and open danger to his life.'[34] 'He told me he would not leave Kaduna until he was officially reassigned', Oluremi recalled.[35] A fellow-officer pointed out that this decision, backed by Gowon and Hassan Katsina, helped to prevent the complete regionalisation of the army and possibly of the country.[36] Obasanjo maintained his stand until he was posted to Lagos in January 1967 to become Chief Army Engineer. While he and Awolowo both sought to preserve Nigeria's integrity, they differed - not for the last time - on the best way to do it, with Obasanjo insisting on the need for accommodation with northern power-holders.

For eight months after the September massacres, Gowon and Ojukwu negotiated at long range, Gowon seeking a federation that would ensure the survival of Nigeria, Ojukwu a confederation that would ensure the survival of the Igbo, and each under pressure from extremists demanding war or secession. For Gowon, a major anxiety was to preserve the unity of the federal side, especially against the possibility that the West might assert neutrality between North and East or even join the East in a southern alliance, as many Yoruba intellectuals preferred. On 1 May 1967, at Awolowo's initiative, a meeting of western leaders of thought approved four 'imperatives': the East must be kept within Nigeria by a looser constitutional settlement; force must not be used for this purpose; the northern 'army of occupation' must be removed from the West; and 'if by any act of omission or commission Eastern Nigeria is allowed to secede, Western Nigeria shall follow suit' – a resolution that Ojukwu chose to regard as an undertaking to secede if the East did so, but equally a warning that any such attempt must be frustrated.[37] At this meeting, Awolowo was flanked by the senior Yoruba officers in the Western Region. Obasanjo was not mentioned, but after the meeting he joined a delegation of Yoruba officers who complained to Gowon of abuses by northern soldiers and demanded their removal from both the West and Lagos.[38] 'It is a measure of how far morale had sunk', a northern officer remarked, 'that such officers as Obasanjo ... who went on to fight valiantly for Nigeria and distinguish themselves in the process, would even consider entertaining such thoughts.'[39] Obasanjo did not mention this in his war memoirs, while Gowon later said that the officers 'came back individually to dissociate themselves from that point of view'.[40] Alternatively, it may be that western disaffection and the imminent risk of violence between westerners and the northern troops had come to take precedence over the longer-term danger of regionalising the army. That was presumably Gowon's assessment, for he agreed to remove northern troops from the West, although he could persuade northern commanders to withdraw them no further than Ilorin and Jebba, just across the regional border. At Awolowo's prompting, he also rescinded an economic blockade of the East, provided Ojukwu reciprocated.[41]

It was too late, for Ojukwu had decided to act, probably believing that he had sufficiently divided the West from the North. On 27 May, the Eastern Region Consultative Assembly welcomed his invitation to authorise him to declare the region's independence as Biafra. Four hours later Gowon responded decisively. He assumed full powers, declared a state of emergency – thereby halting the removal of northern troops – and announced the division of Nigeria into twelve states, a critical step that he had long desired. In the short term, this robbed Biafra of the main oil-bearing regions, threatened potential western secessionists with loss of the newly created Lagos State, satisfied Awolowo's desire to see the North broken up, and gained the support of minorities throughout the country, especially in the army. In the long term, it superseded the rivalry between three over-mighty regions, 'the fundamental problem that has plagued this country since the early 50s', as Gowon described it. Ojukwu replied on 30 May 1967 by proclaiming Biafran independence. Gowon ordered mobilisation.[42]

Fighting began on 6 July when the federal First Division crossed Biafra's northern frontier to take Nsukka on 14 July and Enugu on 4 October. The long delay between these two victories witnessed to the relative weakness of federal forces (about 9,000–10,000 men), their shortage of trained officers (some 184), their lack of mechanical equipment apart from lorries and a few armoured cars, and the difficulty of supplying troops over hundreds of kilometres of gravel roads in heavy rain. It witnessed to resistance by the Biafran forces, perhaps half as numerous at this stage and even worse equipped, but defending prepared positions across the main roads that the attackers generally followed. And it witnessed also to the federal strategy of committing Biafra in the north and surrounding it to the east while conducting amphibious landings in the south to occupy the oil-producing states with their non-Igbo populations, beginning with the capture of Bonny on 26 July. The federal expectation was that a surrounded and isolated Biafra would negotiate, without incurring the mutual slaughter likely to result from invasion of the Igbo heartland.[43]

Obasanjo was far from these events but quickly felt their impact. While remaining Chief Army Engineer, he was posted on 3 July to Ibadan as commander of 2 Area (the Western State), following 'gentle pressure' by Yoruba officers on Gowon, who was impressed by Obasanjo and did not trust his predecessor. Obasanjo's command consisted of the Third Battalion at Ibadan and an Eleventh Battalion still in formation. The northern majority of the Third Battalion were still on venomous terms with Yoruba civilians and the minority of Yoruba soldiers, who feared to sleep in barracks and trained separately, each group in its own language. Obasanjo, always a disciplinarian, ordered that all soldiers must sleep in barracks, all communication must be in English, and molestation of civilians must cease – an order he was prepared to enforce by flogging. Only two weeks after he assumed command, however, the Third Battalion was transferred to the Nsukka front, leaving the Western State defended only by the 700 recent recruits of the Eleventh Battalion.[44]

Ojukwu seized the opportunity. His main hope of preventing encirclement lay to the west, across the Niger, where the small Mid-Western State had a population that was nearly 20 per cent Igbo and a garrison with a large Igbo majority. Still further to the west lay Lagos and the Western State, lightly defended, widely opposed to the war, and with groups known to share Biafra's hostility to the North. At 3 a.m. on 9 August, Ojukwu launched a motley column of over 100 vehicles and between 1,000 and 3,000 men across the newly built Niger bridge, whose garrison made no attempt to stop them. By nightfall they controlled the Mid-West, aided by a mutiny among its garrison. The column apparently had orders to instal a Mid-Western Igbo officer as military administrator and move on to capture Lagos and Ibadan with the aid of Yoruba sympathisers, thereby reinforcing Biafra's independence.[45]

News of the invasion reached Obasanjo on 9 August. He immediately sought to block the roads leading from the Mid-West into Lagos and the Western State with troops from the Eleventh Battalion.[46] At the same time his loyalty was tested. The commander of the Biafran invasion was Victor Banjo, a Yoruba of radical nationalist and pan-Africanist views who had been detained by Ironsi, released by Ojukwu, and had ostensibly thrown in his lot with Biafra. Banjo had many contacts with Yoruba leaders, including Awolowo, the playwright Wole Soyinka, and Obasanjo, who had visited him in detention. On arrival in the Mid-West, Banjo informed a diplomat 'that he does not ... agree with Ojukwu on the separate existence of Biafra. He is convinced that a united Nigeria is essential.'[47] His immediate goal was to free the West and Mid-West from northern domination without replacing it with Biafran control. In this he sought Obasanjo's collaboration. His intermediary was Soyinka, a leading figure in the 'third force' of Yoruba intellectuals who deplored the war and Yoruba participation in it. Visiting Biafra three days before Banjo's invasion, Soyinka had agreed to pass on to Obasanjo – of whom he heard for the first time – that 'Victor wanted an unimpeded passage to Lagos, that he wished to avoid a battle in Western Nigeria.'[48] Following Banjo's invasion, Soyinka passed on his message in suitably conspiratorial style while driving around Ibadan at night in Obasanjo's Volkswagen. 'His expression remained inscrutable', Soyinka recalled, 'but his voice sounded relaxed, even self-confident.... Nothing whatsoever to indicate which way he felt about the war, no sense of his awareness of the critical position in which he found himself.'[49] After listening impassively to Banjo's proposal, so Soyinka claimed, Obasanjo replied:

Well, tell him I have taken an oath of loyalty to Lagos. There are other routes to Lagos – by water through Ukitipupa for instance. If he makes it to Lagos and takes over, well, my oath of loyalty is to Lagos, and I'll stand by that. But to let him pass through my Western Command, that would be betraying my oath of loyalty. Whoever is in power in Lagos – that's the person to whom I owe my allegiance.[50]

Obasanjo had already informed Gowon of the meeting. Soyinka spent the next two years in detention.

While Banjo's sympathisers were preparing to join 'the liberation army' once it reached Ibadan,[51] his invasion had in reality swung Yoruba leaders decisively to the federal side. Awolowo, now Vice-Chairman of the Federal Executive Council and Minister of Finance, declared that 'all Yoruba people, particularly those in the Western and Lagos States which now face the threats of invasion by the rebels from the East and the mid-West, must ... spare no efforts in giving every conceivable support to the Federal troops in defence of their homeland, and of the Fatherland.'[52]

Obasanjo's priority was to use his scanty forces - some taken straight from the recruiting depot to the front - to delay the Biafran column while Gowon in Lagos put together an effective resistance. His men briefly defended a position at Ofugu on the Western State's border before falling back to Otu and then to Ore, a junction from which roads fanned out into the Western State and Lagos. There Nigerian resistance and the demolition of the bridge over the Oluwo River to the west held up the Biafran column. By 22 August, federal reinforcements were arriving, first units of the elite Federal Guard from Lagos and then the nucleus of a new Second Division under Murtala Muhammed that recaptured Ore and forced the Biafrans back through the Mid-West and across the Niger.[53] This was Obasanjo's first experience of warfare. 'The thriving road junction and market village of Ore was a ghost village after the guns had stopped', he remembered. 'Corpses lay on the roadside and houses were reduced to ashes.' Yet it was also, he added, 'the turning point of the civil war', a view that Ojukwu came to share.[54]

While Murtala's Second Division operated in the Mid-West, Obasanjo acted as its rear commander, based in Ibadan and organising its supplies. Diplomats described him drawing pistols with the irascible Murtala during a dispute over transport.[55] Obasanjo also doubled as Chief Engineer, visiting all divisions and their attached engineering units. In Ibadan he made extensive contacts with the Yoruba elite, teaching a course on military science at the University of Ibadan. As garrison commander he cultivated the image of a straightforward soldier striving to avoid the corruption and internecine politics that flourished as the old rivalries between Awolowo's Action Group and northern Yoruba factions became embroiled with popular dissatisfactions. These ranged over northern dominance of the military regime, its failure to end the war, the austerity measures widely blamed on Awolowo, and the wartime profiteering particularly charged against the local military governor. According to diplomatic reports, in August or September 1968 Gowon had to ask Obasanjo if there was any truth in rumours that he was to lead a coup d'état, the first that Obasanjo said that he had heard of it.[56] Some months later Gowon permitted him to resign quietly from the Western State Executive Council because 'he did not wish to share responsibility for many things that were going on in the Western State'.[57]

The most serious crisis there was agrarian unrest led by the Agbekoya (Farmers Reject Suffering) Association, beginning in November 1968 and aimed against low cocoa prices, high wartime taxation, corrupt and unpopular local government, and 'an underlying awareness of inherent conflict between farmer-members and the state's ruling elite'.[58] Obasanjo was away from Ibadan on 26 November when about 2,000 armed villagers attacked the Ibadan City Hall and were driven off by his soldiers, leaving some ten villagers dead.[59] He ordered a court of inquiry. A month later the troops were involved again in a mass round-up of protesters near Abeokuta. 'Obasanjo indicated he [was] sick and tired [of] having his men do police work and getting killed while undertaking routine duties', a diplomat reported, '... he indicated his lack of confidence in police by forcefully expelling breath between pursed lips.'[60] A few days later he called a meeting of 'the people of Ibadan' and 'invited them to air their grievances which, according to him, were very numerous and mostly petty.... At least two speakers complained about the prolongation of the war ... Colonel Obasanjo seemed to think this meeting ... had lowered the temperature', the diplomat reported, adding, 'Altogether I found Obasanjo in a pretty relaxed frame of mind despite his current problems.'[61] In the event, the disturbances were still continuing when he left Ibadan in May 1969 and did not end until Awolowo intervened later in the year.

The war had reached stalemate. Gowon, with humanity and foresight, insisted that his 'police action' must cause minimum casualties and minimum bitterness when the Igbo were reintegrated into Nigeria. As Obasanjo later put it, 'It was fighting to unite, not to destroy, to do what a war is not supposed to do.'[62] While keen to occupy Biafra's peripheries, Gowon restrained his divisional commanders from penetrating the Igbo heartland. The Second Division, after capturing Onitsha on the eastern bank of the Niger, was unable to break out further and fraternised extensively with the opposing forces.[63] The First Division moved slowly southwards. The chief activity during 1968 was therefore in the South, where the Third Marine Commando Division – so named from its initial amphibious landings at Bonny and Calabar – quickly occupied the non-Igbo coastal states, taking Port Harcourt on 19 April 1968. Recruited from unemployed school leavers, especially from Yoruba towns and the southern minority regions it conquered, and given six weeks' training, the division's uncertain discipline rested perilously on the drive and ruthlessness of its Yoruba commander, the 'Black Scorpion' Colonel Benjamin Adekunle. By mid 1968, however, Adekunle too was stalled, demanding authority to move forward on 'a non-stop march to Igboland'.[64]

One consequence of Gowon's 'slow squeeze' was escalating starvation and misery within what remained of Biafra, where the Red Cross estimated in late June 1968 that 3,000 people were dying each day.[65] On 31 July, however, the French government transformed the situation by defending the Biafran people's right to 'dispose of themselves', thereby exploiting humanitarian feeling within France while hoping to weaken Nigeria within West Africa. The federal commanders decided that they must advance without delay into the Igbo heartland. Adekunle took Aba on 4 September, Owerri on 16 September, and drove recklessly towards the Biafran capital at Umuahia. But at the same time the French began to airlift arms into the enclave on a scale that maintained resistance throughout 1969. On 26 April 1969 the Biafrans re-took Owerri, an event that Adekunle neglected to report. Exhausted and convinced that he was being victimised by northern officers, he had lost the confidence of headquarters and many of his troops.[66]

This was the first of the three great opportunities of Obasanjo's life. Replacing Adekunle, a popular hero, was a grave political risk, so grave that it was concealed by replacing all three divisional commanders simultaneously. Adekunle was the only Yoruba among them and his division had a large Yoruba contingent. His successor had to be a senior Yoruba officer.[67] Obasanjo was one of the few candidates, despite the fact that he was an engineer rather than a combat officer and that his experience of commanding troops in action was confined to a fortnight's skirmishing around Ore. He learned of his new appointment on 11 May 1969, receiving the news 'without emotion and without expression.'[68] He and Adekunle loathed each other and the transfer of command was 'carried out in an atmosphere of bitterness'.[69] After a brief discussion at Lagos airport and a deliberately low-key press interview, Obasanjo took up his command at Port Harcourt on 16 May 1969. He was 32 years old and commanded between 35,000 and 40,000 men.[70]

In his account of the war, published in 1980, Obasanjo summarised his contribution in a passage befitting a nineteenth-century Yoruba hero:

> The recapture of Owerri by the rebels was quickly followed by a southward thrust to Port Harcourt. The Federal toe-hold on Aba was slipping. The morale of Federal soldiers was at its lowest ebb. The despondency and general lack of will to fight was glaringly manifest in the large number of cases of self-inflicted wounds among Federal soldiers. Officers were apathetic, if not downright disloyal …
>
> Within a space of six months I turned a situation of low morale, desertion and distrust within my division and within the Army into one of high morale, confidence, co-operation and success for my division and for the Army.[71]

Much of this was true. In May 1969 tactical advantage lay with the Biafrans, who were advancing towards Port Harcourt and occupying the countryside between and behind federal positions on the main roads, creating a long, winding, indefensible federal line whose forward units had to fall back. Ojukwu declared at this time that Biafra could if necessary fight for another decade. Gowon thought the war might last another year. Even in December 1969, observers predicted several more years of fighting.[72]

Obasanjo spent his initial six weeks of command repelling a Biafran attack on Aba, which commanded the road to Port Harcourt. He succeeded, but it exhausted his reserves and ammunition, compelling a long delay while he rebuilt them. In the meantime he straightened his defensive line, thereby releasing troops for aggressive action, toured every part of the front – being wounded in the process – and sought to transform Adekunle's idiosyncratic organisation into an orthodox military formation. Morale was certainly low in many units. In his first month of command, over half the division's casualties were suspected to be self-inflicted. On his orders, a dozen offenders were court-martialled and shot.[73] But Obasanjo also cared for his men. 'When he came', a subordinate recalled, 'he established a … system whereby the normal rule of the game was applied – soldiers were paid their salaries, all supplies of food which by right were supposed to be given to us.'[74] He also established a rest and recuperation camp. Looting was banned and travelling complaints officers appointed to improve relations with civilians. 'Adekunle instilled such fear even into his officers; he couldn't give you orders and you dare refuse', an officer remembered. '… While Obasanjo would come and say, "Old boy, we want you to do that, okay? – Good luck."'[75] But his courage was widely recognised – his second-in-command said simply, 'As a soldier, he is a brave man'[76] – and he displayed the remarkable capacity for work that was later to carry him to power. Sixteen hours a day were said to be his minimum during the campaign.[77] He was a meticulous planner and, although headquarters halved his demands for reinforcements, he built up the reserves of men and stocks of equipment and ammunition that would at last make possible the overwhelming and sustained attack that had hitherto eluded federal commanders.

Moreover, Obasanjo was lucky. He was lucky to build on the hard fighting of Adekunle's division and the other federal forces. He 'was lucky', as a fellow-officer put it, 'because by then everybody was getting tired of the war, both the enemy and the Federal troops. That type of heavy resistance … wasn't there again because everybody was weak and there were very strong rumours that the enemy in so, so place have surrendered.'[78] Evidence from within Biafra bears this out: by late 1969, hunger and suffering had driven its people 'to the limit of human endurance', according to the Governor of the Aba Province, where the Biafran front was to collapse:

> Demoralized, disenchanted and distraught all at once, a large majority of our people, soldiers and civilians alike, had become altogether despondent about their future. Many of our soldiers, having discarded their personal weapons and shed their tattered uniforms, had taken to the bushes as deserters and stragglers. A handful of others, taking the line of least resistance, had ultimately defected to the enemy side …
>
> Under the circumstances, they shared a common bond in one expectation only: their individual survival, no matter what.[79]

In a third sense, also, Obasanjo was lucky. His orders – summarised in the 'Handing and taking over notes' that he signed with Adekunle on 15 May – were first to straighten his defensive line and then, having built up his supplies, to advance northwards through Owerri and Oguta towards the key Uli airstrip through which Biafra was supplied, linking up with First Division, which would previously have captured Umuahia.[80] By November, however, probes had identified gaps in the Biafran defences and Obasanjo was convinced that it would be better to advance on a broad front towards Umuahia, link up with First Division, and cut Biafra in half before turning west against Uli. On 4 December, he visited First Division to urge concerted action on these lines. Its second-in-command, Obasanjo's future colleague, Theophilus Danjuma, was enthusiastic, but the divisional commander insisted that he could not move before 15 January.[81] Obasanjo decided to act on his own and assembled his troops. 'Obasanjo himself was there, right among his men, and officers, giving orders and encouragement', wrote the novelist Ken Saro-Wiwa.[82] Operation Finishing Touch began on 22 December. Biafran resistance crumbled. Without pausing to consolidate, Obasanjo's troops reached Umuahia on Christmas Day, taking 2,000 prisoners. After breaking initial resistance in Biafra's surviving eastern rump, he concentrated all his forces against the west. Operation Tail Wind, launched on 7 January, captured the Uli airstrip on 12 January, three days before First Division had prepared to move. Ojukwu had flown out two nights earlier, leaving his army commander, Philip Effiong, to broadcast Biafra's surrender.[83]

Obasanjo and Effiong met on 13 January:

> A very healthy-looking, rather corpulent Colonel Obasanjo emerged from a gleaming staff car, a number of plain-clothes men dancing attendance upon him, a broad smile of ostensible goodwill glued to his somewhat boyish face. Immediately he advanced towards us, his gait and carriage clearly symptomatic of the authority he had been fated to wield.

After greetings, Obasanjo distributed the beer he had thoughtfully brought with him and the two groups 'sat reminiscing about the good old times' until he indicated that they should talk business. He said that he would deal only with former officers of the Nigerian Army, not with militia leaders who had emerged during the war. He then criticised Effiong's broadcast reference to a 'peaceful settlement on the basis of OAU resolutions'. 'What settlement?' he asked, 'And what armistice were you talking about, Philip?' Obasanjo insisted that Biafran troops must surrender their weapons at assembly areas. Effiong must select leaders to fly to Lagos for a formal surrender ceremony at which they must renounce secession and accept Nigeria's twelve-state structure. Next day Obasanjo spoke on former Radio Biafra, urging the region's people to return to their homes, guaranteeing their safety, and announcing that the Nigerian Police had taken over the maintenance of order from the troops, who were confined to barracks.[84] In Lagos, on 15 January, he had a preliminary meeting with Gowon, who asked what form the peace talks should take. Obasanjo replied that they had already taken place in the field and only formal surrender remained. 'The ceremony started with my being called forward, and a short citation highlighting my qualities and exploits as an Army officer and a field commander was read', he recalled. 'After this I formally reported the accomplishment of my mission to the Commander-in-Chief and I presented Philip Effiong, the officer administering the government of the Republic of "Biafra" and his colleagues to the Head of State.' Gowon said, 'Welcome back, Philip.'[85]

In the East there was work to do. Many Biafrans, Western statesmen, and a sensation-hungry foreign press expected a holocaust of genocide and starvation. Obasanjo had ordered his men to return to barracks and hand over security to the police. 'He pulled his troops back into their camps ...', a well-informed journalist wrote in a report published on 18 January. 'Nigerian police are now operating throughout the area.'[86] During the next few days, however, Obasanjo's announcement proved premature. The Third Division, thinly officered, poorly disciplined, and extended over a front of nearly 200 kilometers, had advanced so fast and so far that many units were scarcely in contact with headquarters, had no camps to return to, and, being far ahead of supply lines, could only live on the country. For about a fortnight after the surrender, Igbo civilians in the Third Division's area of operations suffered extensive rape and looting. A British military observer reported on 24 January:

> The main factor that is affecting all aspects of behaviour, relief and rehabilitation ... is the breakdown of law and order and the confused and undisciplined state of federal troops. This will only be corrected when the troops are withdrawn into garrisons and this is being done as quickly as possible. Until it is achieved and order is restored, food stores are liable to be raided, doctors and nurses will not return to hospitals for fear of molestation and the existing fear of federal troops will not be allayed. I do not believe that the authorities in Lagos are aware of the full extent of the undisciplined conduct of federal troops but senior officers on the spot are doing their best to implement the decision to withdraw troops to garrison areas.[87]

Obasanjo was acutely aware of the situation. He punished offenders brutally, enforcing the standing order that rapists should be shot and personally flogging looters. He resented the blatant sensationalism of press reports and Gowon's order to hand over part of the territory his men had taken to the better disciplined First Division.[88] This did improve the situation, however, and by the end of January discipline was returning. Most important of all, despite isolated killings, the surrender was not followed by any sign of genocide, as an international observer team confirmed.[89] 'During the civil war', Obasanjo later declared,

> we were accused of barbarism and genocide and yet after the war, the ease of the reconciliation, the absence of any rancour or reprisals, not only belie the accusations of genocide, but also did not receive the praise it justly deserves from the Press – as the only case in human history where the bitterness of a civil war has been eradicated with such magnanimity – a fact which all black men ought to know and be proud of.[90]

Nor was there mass starvation, for villagers returned quite quickly to their homes, cassava was widely available in the fields, and the planting season was just beginning. To encourage this was Obasanjo's priority, as he told the observer team on returning from the surrender ceremony. Next day he asked a group of over a thousand surrendered Biafran soldiers, 'Have you taken your food? YES SIR! they said, in such a way that you will think a goal was scored in a nearby football stadium. The time was 4 p.m. The colonel has taken no food since morning.'[91]

Estimates of deaths as a result of the civil war and the attendant famine range from 50,000 to 2,000,000, with a middling figure perhaps the best guess.[92] The conflict left the Igbo people desperately impoverished. Despite Gowon's magnanimity – there were no war medals, no monuments – they also retained a sense of collective suffering and marginalisation.[93] The immediate responsibility for displaying magnanimity and implementing reintegration fell on Obasanjo. He treated defeated Biafrans with consideration and expected them to reciprocate. 'Just as it will be wrong for us to go about with an air of superiority,' he told one group, 'it is equally wrong for you to parade yourselves with an air of achievement. This won't help anybody.' At which, according to the report, 'the officers cheered him lustily.'[94] He denounced opposition in the new Rivers State to the return of its previously dominant Igbo business community, observing that 'he did not fight the war to reduce the Igbo to serfs in Nigeria.'[95] His 'admirable show of humility and understanding' won wide respect at this time. 'If he was ambitious,' wrote Saro-Wiwa, 'it was a closely guarded secret.'[96] His experience as an engineer was also valuable. By May 1970 the water supply was restored to all major towns in former Biafra. Congratulated on this by Aba residents, he replied, 'We are here for the maintenance of law and order and the protection of lives and property. We are not here to steal or molest anyone or be a nuisance to the people.'[97]

Obasanjo's civil war experience was probably the most important of his life. He was proud of his role. 'I fought it as cleanly as anyone has ever fought a civil war,' he later claimed. 'I knew I was fighting to unite and not to divide.'[98] He was proud, too, of the support and loyalty of his troops, which confirmed his belief that ethnic differences among ordinary Nigerians were superficial.[99] Oluremi believed that wartime experience made him more confident but also more impatient, intolerant, and ruthless. He 'confessed to being utterly disappointed by the human frailties he saw on the battlefield.'[100] Above all, he learned to hate war. On the 31st anniversary of Biafra's surrender he declared that 'the greatest horror in this world is to witness and participate in military combat.'[101]

Nevertheless, to the victor the spoils. Early in June 1970 Obasanjo made a triumphal return to Abeokuta. 'People lined the highway with drums, cymbals and other musical instruments', Oluremi remembered, 'singing my husband's praise. Guilds of hunters, ancient warriors and other such local traditional fighters staged their art, with the crowd complementing.' Seated in a limousine, the couple drove with the Alake of Abeokuta to his palace for the reception. There the military governor praised the young colonel's victory, describing him as 'A soft-spoken, humble man, brave and brilliant.' It was the kind of triumph for which Yoruba warriors had wagered their lives.[102]

NOTES

1. Obasanjo, *Nzeogwu*, pp. 84–90; Adinoyi Ojo, *In the eyes of time*, pp. 86–9.
2. A.H.M. Kirk-Greene (ed.), *Crisis and conflict in Nigeria: a documentary sourcebook 1966–1969* (2 vols, London, 1971), vol. 1, pp. 125–6.
3. Among the many accounts, see ibid., pp. 115–24; Luckham, *Nigerian military*, Ch.1; Gbulie, *Nigeria's five majors*, Chs. 1 and 2.
4. Gbulie, *Nigeria's five majors*, p. 82.
5. Ibid., pp. 89–96; Victor Ladijo Akintola, *Akintola: the man and the legend* (Enugu, 1982), p. 112; *Tell*, 18 September 2000, pp. 31–2.
6. H.M. Njoku, *A tragedy without heroes: the Nigeria-Biafra War* (Enugu, 1987), pp. 12–33; *Newswatch*, 5 May 1997, pp. 11–16.
7. Alexander A. Madiebo, *The Nigerian revolution and the Biafran war* (Enugu, 1980), pp. 22–5.
8. Gbulie, *Nigeria's five majors*, p. 99; Obasanjo, *Nzeogwu*, p. 93.
9. Obasanjo, *Nzeogwu*, p. 95; 'Kaduna summary', 14–17 January 1966, DO 195/286/94A; Cumming-Bruce to CRO, 17 January 1966, DO 195/294/46.
10. Obasanjo, *Nzeogwu*, p. 95.
11. *West Africa*, 29 January 1966, p. 127; Chuks Iloegbunam, *Ironside: the biography of General Aguiyi-Ironsi, Nigeria's first military head of state* (London, 1999), p. 118.
12. Gbulie, *Nigeria's five majors*, pp. 103–4.
13. Ejindu, 'Major Nzeogwu speaks', p. 15.
14. Reuters cable, 19 January 1966, DO 195/294/57A.
15. *West Africa*, 5 February 1966, p. 158.
16. Nzeogwu to Obasanjo, 4 February 1966, in Obasanjo, *Nzeogwu*, p. 150.
17. Kirk-Greene, *Crisis and conflict*, vol. 1, p. 154.
18. Ibid., vol. 2, p. 285; Luckham, *Nigerian military*, pp. 56–8.
19. Kirk-Greene, *Crisis and conflict*, vol. 1, pp. 167–73.
20. Douglas A. Anthony, *Poison and medicine: ethnicity, power, and violence in a Nigerian city, 1966 to 1986* (Portsmouth NH, 2002), Ch. 2; Laird to Hawley, 16 June 1966, DO 195/286/114B; Hawley to Greenhill, 4 June 1966, DO 195/297/860; Alhaji M. Yakubu, 'Emirs and soldiers: aristocratic response to the *coups d'état* of 1966 and their immediate aftermath', in A.M. Yakubu, I.M. Jumare, and A.G. Saeed (ed.), *Northern Nigeria: a century of transformation, 1903–2003* (Kaduna, 2005), pp. 251–3.
21. Yusufu in Usman and Kwanashie, *Inside Nigerian history*, p. 74.
22. 'Situation report, Nigeria: 17th March, 1966', DO 195/296/47; T.Y. Danjuma in *Newswatch*, 2 November 1992, p. 14; Obasanjo, *Bitter-sweet*, p. 39.
23. Yusufu in Usman and Kwanashie, *Inside Nigerian history*, p. 75.
24. P.J. Okoli in *Guardian*, 23 January 2007; A. Shelleng in H.B. Momoh (ed.), *The Nigerian Civil War, 1967–1970: history and reminiscences* (Ibadan, 2000), p. 817.
25. Olusegun Obasanjo, *My command: an account of the Nigerian Civil War, 1967–1970* (reprinted, London, 1981), p. 7.

26. Among many accounts, see Luckham, *Nigerian military*, Ch.2; Kirk-Greene, *Crisis and conflict*, vol. 1, pp. 54–79, 196–8; J. Isawa Elaigwu, *Gowon: the biography of a soldier-statesman* (Ibadan, 1986), pp. 64–9; Cumming-Bruce, note, 1 August 1966, DO 195/303/75.
27. Liman Ciroma in *Weekly Trust*, 18 September 1998; Obasanjo in ibid., 8 January 1999; Obasanjo, *Bitter-sweet*, pp. 39–44; Adinoyi Ojo, *In the eyes of time*, pp. 103–7.
28. Obasanjo, *My command*, p. 9.
29. Anthony, *Poison*, Ch. 3.
30. Cumming-Bruce to James, 1 October 1966, PREM 13/1041; Luckham, *Nigerian military*, pp. 328–31, 336–8; Dudley, *Instability*, pp. 187–8.
31. Larmour to Norris, 25 November 1966, DO 195/304/50; 'Points made by Lt. Col. Ojukwu during a conversation at his residence on 16 October 1966', DO 195/299/329B.
32. Luckham, *Nigerian military*, pp. 332–4; Obafemi Awolowo, *Awo on the Nigerian Civil War* (Ikeja, 1981), pp. 10–11, 24.
33. Obasanjo, *My command*, pp. 8–9; James J. Oluleye, *Architecturing a destiny: an autobiography* (Ibadan, 2001), pp. 91–2.
34. Obasanjo, *My command*, p. 9.
35. Obasanjo, *Bitter-sweet*, p. 44.
36. James J. Oluleye, *Military leadership in Nigeria 1966–1979* (Ibadan, 1985), pp. 45–9.
37. Awolowo, *Awo on the Nigerian Civil War*, p. 15; Luckham, *Nigerian military*, p. 332.
38. Luckham, *Nigerian military*, p. 320; Adinoyi Ojo, *In the eyes of time*, p. 113.
39. Joseph Nanven Garba, *'Revolution' in Nigeria: another view* (London, 1982), p. 90.
40. Elaigwu, *Gowon*, p. 111 n. 82.
41. Kirk-Greene, *Crisis and conflict*, vol. 1, pp. 426–7.
42. Ibid., pp. 428–53.
43. Obasanjo, *My command*, pp. 15–20; Oluleye, *Military leadership*, pp. 51–3; Cabinet: Joint Intelligence Committee, 'Special assessment: Nigeria', 31 May 1967, FCO 38/201/58.
44. Obasanjo, *My command*, pp. 27–9.
45. John de St Jorre, *The Nigerian Civil War* (London, 1972), Ch.6; Dudley, *Instability*, p. 212; Njoku, *Tragedy*, p. 219. St Jorre (p. 153) says about 1,000 men; Frederick Forsyth, *The Biafra story* (Harmondsworth, 1969), p. 116, says 3,000.
46. Obasanjo, *My command*, pp. 30–1.
47. Hunt to CRO, 9 August 1967, FCO 38/284/73. For Banjo's thinking, see F. Adetowun Ogunsheye, *A break in the silence: a historical note on Lt-Colonel Victor Adebukunola Banjo* (Ibadan, 2001), esp. pp. 42, 50–5.
48. Soyinka, *You must set forth*, p. 156.
49. Ibid., p. 154.
50. Ibid., p. 160. Obasanjo's account is in *My command*, p. 31.
51. Edwin Madunagu, *Understanding Nigeria and the new imperialism: essays 2000–2006* (Calabar, 2006), p. 372.
52. Awolowo, *Awo on the Nigerian Civil War*, p. 80.
53. Obasanjo, *My command*, pp. 31–43; G. Ejiga in Momoh, *Nigerian Civil War*, pp. 475–84; Garba, *'Revolution'*, pp. 105–6.
54. Obasanjo, *My command*, pp. 168, 34; Stremlau, *International politics*, pp. 77–8.
55. Strong to State Department, 7 January 1969, FCO 65/163/10.
56. Smallwood to Anderson, 12 September 1968, FCO 38/288/537.
57. Strong to State Department, 5 March 1969, FCO 65/176/59A.
58. Christopher Beer, *The politics of peasant groups in Western Nigeria* (Ibadan, 1976), p. 162.
59. *Daily Times*, 27 November 1968.
60. Strong to State Department, 31 December 1968, FCO 65/175/22A.
61. Smallwood to Anderson, 2 January 1969, FCO 65/175/23A.
62. *This Day*, 11 September 2002.

63. C.E. Arachie, *The bye-gone: horrors of a crude war: Biafra experience* (Lagos, 1991), pp. 80–2.
64. Adekunle to Gowon, July 1968, in Adekunle, *War letters*, p. 177.
65. Joseph E. Thompson, *American policy and African famine: the Nigeria-Biafra War, 1966–1970* (Westport, 1990), p. 59.
66. Daniel Bach, 'Le Général de Gaulle et la guerre civile au Nigeria', *Canadian Journal of African Studies*, 14 (1980), 261–5; Hunt to CRO, 16 August 1968, FCO 38/288/504; Obasanjo, *My command*, pp. 52–5; Oluleye, *Military leadership*, pp. 129–36; Adekunle to Gowon, July 1968, in Adekunle, *War letters*, pp. 174–5.
67. Oluleye, *Military leadership*, p. 135.
68. Obasanjo, *My command*, p. 63.
69. G.A. Innih in Momoh, *Nigerian Civil War*, p. 617; Obasanjo, *Bitter-sweet*, pp. 52, 54.
70. Obasanjo, *My command*, pp. 61–5; Adekunle, *War letters*, p. 13; *Daily Times*, 17 May 1969.
71. Obasanjo, *My command*, pp. xii-xiii.
72. Ibid., p. 62; *West Africa*, 7 June 1969, p. 633; Scott to McEntee, 4 July 1969, FCO 65/359/217; *Times* (London), 4 December 1969; *Sunday Times* (London), 21 December 1969.
73. Obasanjo, *My command*, Chs. 7 and 8.
74. M. Abdu in Momoh, *Nigerian Civil War*, p. 208.
75. E.A. Etuk in ibid., p. 525.
76. Quoted in Ademiluyi, *From prisoner to president*, p. 277.
77. *Daily Times*, 2 February 1970.
78. M. Abdu in Momoh, *Nigerian Civil War*, p. 208.
79. Ben Gbulie, *The fall of Biafra* (Enugu, 1989), pp. 55, 108–9.
80. Adekunle, *War letters*, pp. 205–8; Obasanjo, *My command*, pp. 68–9, 102.
81. Obasanjo, *My command*, pp. 102–4; Danjuma in *Guardian*, 17 February 2008.
82. Ken Saro-Wiwa, *On a darkling plain; an account of the Nigerian Civil War* (Port Harcourt, 1989), p. 222.
83. Obasanjo, *My command*, pp. 107–20; 'Visit by Mr. A.B. Ingledow to the Third Marine Commando Division area (3–6 January, 1970)', FCO 65/738/1.
84. Gbulie, *Fall of Biafra*, pp. 249–53; Obasanjo, *My command*, pp. 124–7, 130–1.
85. Obasanjo, *My command*, p. 135; *Jeune Afrique*, 15 October 1975, p. 17.
86. J. de St Jorre in *Observer*, 18 January 1970.
87. Cairns in Glass to FCO, 24 January 1970, FCO 65/784/12. See also Axel Harneit-Sievers, Jones O. Ahazuem, and Sydney Emezue, *A social history of the Nigerian Civil War: perspectives from below* (Enugu, 1997), Chs. 4 and 5.
88. *Times* (London), 22 and 24 January 1970; *Sunday Telegraph*, 25 January 1970; *Financial Times*, 26 January 1970; *Africa Confidential*, 17 April 1970, p. 4; *Africa Research Bulletin*, January 1970, p. 1652.
89. *Africa Research Bulletin*, February 1970, p. 1675; *Financial Times*, 3 February 1970.
90. *Daily Times*, 7 November 1977.
91. *Times* (London), 17 January 1970; *Daily Times*, 18 January 1970.
92. David Hunt, *On the spot: an ambassador remembers* (London, 1975), p. 190; Cervenka, *Nigerian War*, p. 168; St Jorre, *Nigerian Civil War*, p. 412.
93. Harneit-Sievers et al., *Social history*, Chs. 5 and 6.
94. *Daily Times*, 16 February 1970.
95. Adinoyi Ojo, *In the eyes of time*, p. 154.
96. Bernard Odogwu, *No place to hide (crises and conflicts inside Biafra)* (Enugu, 1985), p. 181; Saro-Wiwa, *On a darkling plain*, p. 216.
97. *West African Pilot*, 1 June 1970.
98. *This Day*, 12 September 2000.
99. Obasanjo, *March of progress*, pp. 478–9.

100. Adinoyi Ojo, In the eyes of time, pp. 157–8.
101. Ad'Obe Obe (ed.), A new dawn: a collection of speeches of President Olusegun Obasanjo (volumes 2 and 3, Ibadan, 2001 and 2004), vol. 2, p. 230.
102. Obasanjo, Bitter-sweet, pp. 57–8; Daily Times, 8 June 1970.

Part II

Military Rule
(1970–9)

5
Chance and Power

In 1970 Obasanjo returned to peacetime soldiering as Brigadier commanding the Corps of Engineers in Lagos. Professionally, the next five years were perhaps the quietest of his life. Privately, they were a time of turmoil. And in 1975 everything would change.

He was becoming a property-owner and a businessman In the early 1960s he had invested 'Dag's Dash' in parcels of land at Ibadan, Kaduna, and Lagos. In 1970 he bought a former Lebanese company in Ibadan and secured an agent to run it. By 1974, with a salary approaching $15,000 a year, he had two houses in Lagos, one in Ibadan, another (built at a cost of about ($60,000) in Abeokuta, and planned 'to build a few houses that are commercially viable', for 'After paying the mortgage on them, they would provide regular income before and during retirement', which, for a soldier, was likely to come early.[1] In seeking security through urban property, Obasanjo was obeying a powerful Yoruba tradition and demonstrating, as a man born and brought up 'in farm', that he had achieved respectability. Yet he was still an outsider, unashamed of his village origins. Somewhat awkward, earnest, moody, but humorous and sensitive, he was alternately withdrawn and outgoing. Notoriously careful with money, he lived modestly, not seeking popularity through the generosity of a Yoruba 'big man'.[2]

His family life was more turbulent. His marriage to Oluremi under English law had been in the monogamous, companionate style common among young, educated Yoruba and perhaps especially desired by educated women like Oluremi. Yet in the mid twentieth century a large proportion of married Yoruba men were polygynous.[3] In this tradition, the accumulation of wives and children was a natural component of a successful man's life, while a woman found fulfilment chiefly in her children and her ability to raise and educate them, for many women ran their own businesses (especially as traders) and did not always reside with their husbands. 'Childbearing, not companionship, is the main perceived function of marriage', an anthropologist observed.[4] When Obasanjo left Oluremi in London to complete her training in institutional management, one element of this older tradition entered their relationship. When they came together again in Kaduna in 1966, childbearing became central. At the birth of their first daughter, Iyabo, in 1967, Obasanjo – despite his assumption that the child would be a boy – 'started singing and dancing to the amusement of the nurses and paramedics'.[5] Oluremi later recalled how solicitous her husband was when they lived in Ibadan early in 1969. By then she was already pregnant with their third child.[6]

Nevertheless, Oluremi already suspected Obasanjo's unfaithfulness. 'The first time Obasanjo beat me', she claimed, was when she questioned him about 'a gorgeously dressed woman' who visited their home in Ibadan.[7] She believed, however, that it was the confidence and ruthlessness he gained as a wartime commander that damaged their marriage and attracted other women to him. One was a reporter, Gold Oruh, who formed a relationship with him in Port Harcourt and later bore him two children.[8] Many others followed. 'He took full advantage of his stature', his first biographer alleged:

> Casual affairs that led to babies. In all, there would be nearly two dozens of them from half as many women. He later married some of them…. In a society where male promiscuity or adultery is so often overlooked, Obasanjo tried to justify his actions by appealing to the age-old traditional African practice of polygyny. But that did not make it right. For in all honesty, Obasanjo had a major weakness for women – many of whom he did not treat well (lack of love and companionship, inadequate and irregular financial support, separate homes, long absences, and the typical old-style macho aloofness of his generation of men in Nigeria).[9]

Oluremi, by her own account, lived at intervals away from her husband but refused to be considered merely one among a polygynist's wives, insisting that she was his only legal wife, challenging his other relationships, quarrelling and sometimes fighting with the other women, offending his notions of male supremacy, suffering his violence, complaining of his neglect of their children, and contesting the custody of them that he claimed as a Yoruba father. In April 1975, when Obasanjo refused to support a further baby she was carrying, she complained to Yoruba leaders and his fellow officers, leading him to threaten resignation from the army if they interfered in his private life.[10] By then the marriage was virtually ended. In 1974, while attending a course in London, Obasanjo had again met Stella Abebe, a daughter of the first African chairman of the United Africa Company. They married under Yoruba custom in 1976, shortly after the dissolution of his British marriage to Oluremi, although, for the sake of the children, that too was eventually replaced by a customary relationship and she was to bear him a sixth child in 1982.[11]

On the wider national scene, Nigeria in the early 1970s was a place of great optimism. It had survived the war with little long-term external debt or economic damage. Gross National Product had increased by 19 per cent during the war despite the temporary loss of the Eastern Region.[12] Moreover, the war had alerted Nigerians for the first time to the potential wealth of their oil reserves. Located in the Niger Delta and first exported in 1958, oil provided 93% of Nigeria's export earnings and 82% of federal government revenue in 1974. Between 1970 and 1974 the average price of Bonny light crude (the standard Nigerian product) rose from $2.25 to $14.69 per barrel, thanks to concerted action by the Organisation of Petroleum Exporting Countries (OPEC), which Nigeria joined in 1971.[13] Determined to convert the foreign-dominated oil industry into the leading sector of national development, the government declared all the country's oil and gas reserves to be federal property, formed a Nigerian National Oil Corporation (NNOC), and in 1974–5 acquired a controlling 55% share in the foreign producing companies.[14] Between 1970 and 1975 real Gross Domestic Product (GDP) grew at about 8%

per year and manufacturing employment roughly doubled.[15] These were 'the years of champagne and lace', when 'Yoruba society was the place to be' and southern Nigeria enjoyed remarkable cultural florescence.[16] Yet little of this prosperity reached the countryside, where national food production per head fell by an estimated 21% during these five years.[17]

In so far as anyone presided over these developments, it was not General Gowon, the head of state until 1975, nor the officers of the Supreme Military Council, but a small group of senior civil servants who had gained influence during the war and now headed key ministries and parastatals.[18] The most influential of these 'Super Permsecs' were western-educated economists dedicated to economic nationalism and a mixed economy in which 'a programme of public expenditure' provided 'the hard core of a development programme'.[19] Their strategy built on the growth of federal power due to the abolition of the old regions, a new revenue allocation system heavily favouring the federal government, a sevenfold increase in federal revenue between 1970 and 1975, a tripling of the federal civil service between 1970 and 1979, and federal control of income tax, produce marketing, education and the oil industry.[20] Their ambitions found expression in the Third National Development Plan (1975–80), which proposed to spend ten times as much as the previous plan, to achieve an average GDP growth rate of over 9% per cent a year, and to raise average income to the levels of developed countries within twenty years.[21] 'Nigeria is rich', the Governor of the Central Bank declared, 'the problem is how to spend the money.'[22]

The political future was more difficult to plan. Obasanjo declared 'that the Army should form the bedrock of the political stability and effectiveness of any future Nigerian Government.' A month later, by contrast, Awolowo asserted a civilian politician's demand for the immediate formation of a constituent assembly.[23] Gowon temporised by announcing in October 1970 that the army would transfer power to civilians in 1976. 'Six years in the life of a nation is nothing', he declared. He did not detail a political timetable but stated that in the interim his regime would reorganise the army, implement the 1970–4 development plan, appoint a new revenue allocation commission, hold a census, eradicate corruption, prepare a constitution, foster 'genuinely national' parties, and, after an interval, consider the creation of additional states.[24]

Gowon failed to implement this programme. A Demobilisation Committee (including Obasanjo, Murtala, and Danjuma) recommended that the 250,000-strong wartime army should be reduced to 100,000-150,000 by the end of the 1970s, with an ultimate goal of 50,000, but wartime recruits had been promised peacetime rehabilitation and employment, which was seldom available. By 1975 natural wastage had reduce the numbers only to about 200,000 and the defence budget to some 46% of federal recurrent expenditure.[25] Obasanjo, as an engineer, urged 'that the military should contribute in real physical terms to the development of the state', but infantrymen resisted becoming unskilled labourers.[26] The army was also riddled with corruption, whose eradication demanded more than Gowon's good intentions. Probably incorrupt himself – when deposed, he was said to possess only £2,000 – he was incapable of checking the corruption of others, especially of his twelve military governors, ten of whom were later dismissed for it.[27] Obasanjo, too, was widely suspected of corruption at this time, with ample opportunity in the Engineering Corps, but although he may quite legally have acquired large holdings of shares sold to the Nigerian public at this time, there was no hard evidence that he was corrupt and he was cleared of involvement in the most notorious scandal of the period, the ordering of 20 million tons of cement at inflated prices.[28]

Gowon failed to implement other aspects of his programme. The 1973 census did not convince the South that – most improbably – it had little more than half the population of the North.[29] Nothing was done to create new states. The economy ran into 34% inflation in 1975, fuelled by a 74% increase in the money supply, partly to fund the Udoji pay award of December 1974, which raised the government minimum wage by 130% and provoked over 200 trade disputes.[30] Yet Gowon's crucial failure was the lack of progress towards the civilian rule that he had promised for 1976. With no preparations made, he announced in October 1974 that 'it will be utterly irresponsible to leave the nation in the lurch by a precipitate withdrawal which will certainly throw the nation back into confusion.' Although he insisted that 'we have not abandoned the idea of return to civilian rule' and announced that a panel would begin to draft a new constitution, the ban on party politics remained and he gave no date for civilian rule.[31]

Although this decision had much initial support,[32] hostility to Gowon had long existed in the army. It generally centred on Murtala Muhammed, who had resented Gowon's emergence as head of state during the July 1966 coup, opposed his gradualist wartime strategy, and sought unsuccessfully to recruit Obasanjo into a bid for collective leadership at the end of the war, thereafter nursing his contempt.[33] Middle-ranking combat officers resented the power and corruption of military governors. Gowon's announcement in October 1974 extended this disaffection by appearing to entrench the existing leadership and dishonour the army. Obasanjo, for one, regarded the announcement as a disaster and recalled that some officers came to be ashamed to be seen in uniform.[34] He was in Britain at the time, taking a coveted course at the Royal College of Defence Studies designed to prepare senior officers for future responsibilities 'by imparting knowledge and stimulating thought about international and regional issues, particularly those related to defence and security'. The course included writing a thesis, in which Obasanjo discussed Britain's overseas aid policies with a scepticism that apparently caused some British anxiety.[35] When he returned to Nigeria, Gowon appointed him in January 1975 to be Commissioner for Works and Housing. He spent seven months in the post, attracting little public attention, concentrating on building military barracks, touring construction sites, dismissing unsatisfactory contractors, and suffering his first exposure to the intractable problems of landownership, planning, and construction in Lagos. He caused one minor but characteristic sensation by ignoring protocol and ordering armed troops to surround a building next to the Cabinet Office occupied by the United States Agency for International Development, which had been slow to comply with the government's request to vacate.[36] His mind, however, was partly on the future. In 1973 he had registered a business, Temperance Enterprises Limited, in readiness for possible retirement from the army should civilian rule be established.[37]

This scheme evaporated late on the evening of 28 July 1975, when the Director of Military Intelligence, Colonel Abdullahi Mohammed, told Obasanjo that a coup d'état against Gowon would take place that night. Obasanjo had learned of a plot a week or two earlier and had told Gowon, who already knew of it and replied that everything was under control, much to Obasanjo's relief. On 27 July Obasanjo had visited Enugu, where the Brigade Commander invited him to join the conspiracy, saying, 'If you senior ones don't act, the junior ones will.' When Abdullahi Mohammed now warned him that action was imminent, Obasanjo asked whether it could be stopped. Abdullahi said not. When Obasanjo urged it should be bloodless, Abdullahi replied, 'Our plans are generally along that line.'[38]

The two chief conspirators were Lt Cols Joseph Garba and Shehu Musa Yar'Adua. Garba, a Middle Belt officer related to Gowon and known in the army as 'Gowon's boy', was the Commander of the Brigade of Guards, many of whom came from Gowon's region. Tall, handsome, vain, and ambitious, he had come to think Gowon 'bloody ineffective' and preferred to mount a coup rather than be a prime target for someone else's.[39] Yar'Adua was a young, ambitious, and ruthless staff officer, 'the hero of the Onitsha campaign' during the civil war and a partisan of his former commander, Murtala Muhammed, who was widely seen by younger officers as the natural replacement for Gowon.[40] With some difficulty, Garba and Yar'Adua persuaded Murtala to become their candidate. They also won the acquiescence of the influential Brigadier Danjuma but did not approach Obasanjo, who commanded no combat troops and was known to oppose coups.[41]

Gowon's intelligence officers warned him of the plan. When Garba denied it, Gowon told him to shed no blood. The conspirators' troops occupied the airport, radio station, and telecommunications headquarters. There was no resistance. Gowon heard the news in Kampala during a meeting of the Organisation of African Unity (OAU). He pledged loyalty to the new regime, quoted 'All the world's a stage,' and left to play squash.[42]

Obasanjo spent 29 July at home, glued to the radio and newspapers, until the conspirators took him to a stormy meeting with Murtala, Danjuma, Garba, Yar'Adua, and Abdullahi Mohammed. The conspirators said that rather than take power themselves, they wanted to hand it over to the three brigadiers. *Realpolitik* – meaning northern predominance within the army – demanded that Murtala be invited to become head of state, at which Obasanjo, who was marginally his senior, said that he was willing to serve as second-in-command provided that he had substantial responsibilities. The conspirators agreed, wanting the three brigadiers to share power rather than instal the personal rule of 'another Gowon'. They also wanted the Supreme Military Council to have a veto over the triumvirate's decisions. Murtala exploded: 'To hell with all of you! I have said I don't want to be anybody's Head of State. But if you're inviting me to be one, I'm not going to allow you [to] tie my hands behind my back. I must have executive authority and run the country as I see best.' After twenty minutes of argument, Garba asked Murtala to leave the room and, as the conspirators had previously agreed, suggested that Obasanjo become head of state and that it be announced that Murtala had refused. 'I was neither stupid nor over ambitious enough to accept such an offer on such conditions', Obasanjo recalled. In effect, he could be the Yoruba representative in a triumvirate together with a northerner and Danjuma (a Middle Belt man), but the army was not ready to accept a Yoruba commander. According to Obasanjo he then walked out and helped to persuade Murtala to accept the top position. Other accounts say that it was first offered to Danjuma, who also turned it down in favour of becoming Army Chief of Staff, before Abdullahi Mohammed intervened to tell Murtala that if he continued to refuse, they would announce the terms on which he had refused the post. 'This is blackmail!' Murtala protested, but eventually he accepted. The conspirators then announced that they wished not to participate in the new administration, which Obasanjo immediately vetoed, realising that it would be a recipe for a second coup.[43]

The three leaders – with Obasanjo as Chief of Staff, Supreme Headquarters – now discussed their immediate steps. They decided to remove all military governors and officers above the rank of Brigadier. After some days of juggling offices, Garba became Commissioner for External Affairs and Yar'Adua Commissioner for Transport (to handle a current crisis in the ports). Obasanjo later claimed that he undertook to prepare proposals for the political transition at which Gowon had balked. The 1973 census results were cancelled. Panels would consider the creation of new states and the location of a new capital.[44]

Not for the last time, Obasanjo had gained power without seeking it. Initially he was largely a silent figure at Murtala's side. The two men were friends and Obasanjo was content to demonstrate the administration's intention 'to adopt a low profile which we believe is in keeping with a military rule'.[45] Nearly twenty years in the army had also taught Obasanjo a deference to northern notions of propriety that most southern leaders neglected at their peril. Behind this public image, however, was 'a patient, shrewd man whose carthorse appearance conceals a fox-like intelligence.'[46] Insiders soon realised that Obasanjo was both the work-horse and the brains of the regime. 'We met very frequently, usually in the evening after close of work', Danjuma remembered,

> and at every meeting, Obasanjo would have a pad in hand with a pen. As we were talking, he would take down the minutes of the conclusions of the meetings and, unfailingly, the following morning when I got to the Ministry of Defence and sat at my desk, I would find on top of my in-tray the minutes of the previous day's meeting already written out, noting who's to do what on each item ... I thought Murtala was very lucky to have a staff officer who was that efficient.[47]

So hard did Obasanjo work that at one point he collapsed in his office and revived only when rushed to hospital.[48]

Whereas Gowon had instinctively avoided difficulties, Murtala and Obasanjo tackled them head on. They gradually reduced the 'cement armada' of some 450 ships waiting outside Lagos harbour. They implemented austerity measures to check inflation. They established a Corrupt Practices Investigation Bureau. They replaced all military governors by new officers who no longer sat on the Supreme Military Council but reported to Obasanjo as Chief of Staff.[49] Less wisely, they also retired the Super Permsecs, whose power under Gowon had angered senior officers but whose removal left Nigeria without skilled economic management.[50] This was only part of a wider purge of the civil service, known as 'Operation Deadwood', in which some 11,000 officials – over 80% of them from the lower ranks – were dismissed in eight weeks, ostensibly on grounds of inefficiency or disloyalty, without opportunity to defend themselves or appeal. Often, as Obasanjo admitted, the process degenerated into 'callousness and sadism ... gross indiscipline and selfishness'.[51] In a country where weakness of execution was the chief obstacle to development, the purge, as one insider admitted, was the government's most serious mistake.[52]

Much of the regime's radicalism probably came from the younger members of the Supreme Military Council who had made the coup and insisted on maintaining its momentum, especially with regard to restoring civilian rule. Murtala himself seems to have been in no haste to introduce this and Danjuma, too, was cautious, although Obasanjo was almost certainly more eager.[53] During September 1975, according to a statement attributed to Danjuma, the Council had an 'exceedingly free and frank' debate on the issue, in which, 'though they all reached agreement in the end, there was a clear division along age/rank lines over the timing of the return to civilian rule – and it was the view of the younger and junior (and more numerous) group which prevailed.'[54] The argument advanced, he explained,

> was that the army had no moral right to hang on to power. They should carry out their promise to restore civilian rule and then present themselves for election if they wished. Another consideration was that they wished to arrest the incipient signs of demoralisation in the army which prolonged involvement in politics was already producing.[55]

The programme that Murtala announced on 1 October 1975 appears to have drawn on a plan originally prepared for Gowon by his officials.[56] The first steps were to establish new states and appoint a committee to draft a new constitution for the approval of a partly-elected constituent assembly by October 1978, when party politics would resume prior to the election of a civilian government by 1 October 1979.[57] Selection of the 49 members of the Constitution Drafting Committee was left largely to Obasanjo, who drew on his wide range of acquaintances to appoint a relatively conservative (and exclusively male) body that nevertheless contained many of Nigeria's best legal, academic, and political minds, chaired by its most distinguished lawyer, Rotimi Williams.[58] Murtala charged them to pay special attention to federalism, an executive presidency, a free and fair electoral system, and, if a party system was unavoidable, then an arrangement of parties national in scope that would 'discourage institutionalized opposition to the Government in power and, instead, develop consensus politics'.[59]

This emphasis on consensual politics was a guiding principle throughout Obasanjo's career. In a pioneering television interview at this time, he claimed that most Nigerian languages had no word to describe loyal opposition:

> The word for opposition is the same as the word for enemy. And what do you do with your enemy? Of course you crush him. And if you have to crush your enemy, you don't spare anything. The opposition, too, sees itself being nothing but on the war-path and taking the position of being at war against the government. I think these are some of the ills of the past constitution which we should try to remove.[60]

The military regime 'made consultation and discussion essential ingredients of military government,' Obasanjo recalled.[61] Rather than relying on civil servants and former politicians, as Gowon had done, it turned to advisory commissions and other groups of professionals. Obasanjo had long cultivated academic contacts, especially at the University of Ibadan. An instinctively cautious man of practical mind who believed that 'Things had to mutate their normal, slow way',[62] he nevertheless eagerly sought fresh ideas from the 'eggheads and political activists' – as Oluremi described them – who thronged their home and from the bright young technocrats he assembled in the Cabinet Office Political Department, the government's think-tank. In these early months, Obasanjo, as the regime's 'closet radical',[64] even cultivated relations with student activists. 'Many of us, the then young socialist forces in Nigeria had believed that the Ethiopian scenario [i.e. a military-led socialist revolution] was going to be enacted in Nigeria', one remembered.[65]

In November 1975 the regime's radical nationalism and openness to innovation came together to transform Nigeria's external relations. During the 1960s, Nigeria had pursued a low-profile, pro-Western foreign policy with little sympathy for African liberation movements.[66] External interference during the civil war, especially by France, had sharpened national sensitivities and led Gowon into an active personal diplomacy that culminated in 1975 in the formation of the Economic Community of West African States (ECOWAS), designed to expand Nigeria's regional influence and loosen francophone ties to France. Gowon's regime had also displayed a generalised hostility towards apartheid in South Africa and the white settler regime that had unilaterally declared independence in Rhodesia (Zimbabwe) in 1965.[67] Murtala and Obasanjo, however, shared a strongly emotional commitment to the liberation of southern Africa, Obasanjo claiming that 'right from my days as a young military officer, I have always felt that I would have achieved a life ambition the day I fight for liberation in southern Africa.'[68] On taking power in July 1975, Murtala told the new Commissioner for External Affairs, Garba, 'that he wanted a very activist foreign policy' and ordered the formulation of appropriate guidelines.[69]

The opportunity for vigorous action arose from a crisis in Angola, where the Portuguese revolution of 1974 had led to a decision to withdraw the colonial army and grant independence on 11 November 1975. This threatened to leave a power vacuum, for Angola's armed liberation struggle had been fought by three largely regional organisations: Frente Nacional de Libertação de Angola (FNLA) in the north, Movimento Popular de Libertação de Angola (MPLA) in the centre, and União Nacional para a Independência Total de Angola (UNITA) in the south. By the Alvor Agreement of January 1975, the three movements undertook to form a transitional coalition and participate in elections, but this collapsed in fighting in which the Marxist MPLA gained control of the capital, Luanda, during July 1975, and expelled its FNLA rivals. Zaire (the Democratic Republic of Congo) sent troops to support the FNLA. The American Central Intelligence Agency began to supply and train the FNLA and UNITA. Soviet arms and Cuban advisers reinforced the MPLA. South African troops moved into southern Angola to defend hydraulic installations there, aid UNITA, and, on 14 October 1975, launch an armed column northwards towards Luanda. To resist this, the first of some 36,000 Cuban combat troops arrived in Angola on 8 November.[70]

Until November 1975, Murtala's government followed the OAU policy of supporting the Alvor Agreement, pressing for a government of national unity, and denouncing foreign intervention. As late as 8 November, Garba 'strongly deplored the USSR's "flagrant interference" in Angola.' On 20 November, the OAU Chairman urged African states not to recognise any Angolan party until a united front was formed.[71] Five days later, however, Nigeria recognised the MPLA regime and began lobbying other governments to follow suit, causing consternation not only within the OAU but in the Ministry of External Affairs in Lagos.[72]

The decision appears to have been made on 23 November by the inner circle of Murtala, Obasanjo, Danjuma, and the Inspector-General of Police, M.D. Yusufu. Like other observers outside Angola, they had only slowly realised that the South African army had launched a full-scale advance on Luanda in collusion with UNITA, FNLA, and probably the United States.[73] Garba was summoned to meet the leaders. 'Murtala turned to me,' he recalled, 'explaining, in a voice full of contempt for South Africa's move, that we would recognize the MPLA with immediate effect.' When Garba said the OAU's stance dictated delay,

They unanimously refused, and I suddenly sensed that the dramatic effect of our recognition was as important to them as recognition itself. Murtala, though usually sensitive to diplomatic nuances, was intransigent, shouting, 'We must recognize the MPLA *now*. The

Americans must be behind this, and any further delay will just give them an advantage. We want surprise!'[74]

Garba was sure that South African involvement was the reason for the decision and that the policy was chiefly developed by Obasanjo through the Cabinet Office. Others, including the American State Department and the British Foreign Office, agreed that Obasanjo 'had a major influence' in the decision.[75] Yusufu probably also played a large part, for as the head of Special Branch he had been responsible for contacts with liberation movements and was the channel through whom an MPLA representative was introduced to Obasanjo and Danjuma. The trio then convinced Murtala, whose eagerness to confront South Africa no doubt crystallised the decision.[76] Yet while South African involvement gave recognition of the MPLA its urgency and emotional force, there were other reasons for the decision. One, as Garba sensed, was the desire to make a dramatic impact in international affairs consonant with Nigeria's size and claim to African leadership. As one senior officer put it, 'We were fully in the arena of Super Power confrontation on the issue of Angola.'[77] It was an opportunity, also, to deepen Nigeria's sense of nationhood. Moreover, there were good practical reasons for the decision. All communist countries had already recognised the MPLA regime, which was in danger of becoming their prisoner. The MPLA controlled the capital – always a key consideration – and neither of the other parties had as strong a claim to recognition. The OAU's alternative, a government of national unity, was increasingly unrealistic. The real alternative to recognising the MPLA was probably intensified violence and deeper superpower involvement of the kind that Obasanjo and other Nigerian soldiers had witnessed in the Congo.[78] In the event, it would take the MPLA another 26 years to impose its power throughout Angola, but that was not forseeable in 1975.

Although South African intervention may not have been the only reason for recognising the MPLA regime, it was the argument that Nigeria employed most effectively in persuading other African countries to do so, a role in which the American Secretary of State, Henry Kissinger, thought Nigeria's example was of crucial importance.[79] Kissinger himself facilitated Nigeria's task with a patronising letter from President Ford urging OAU members to equate Cubans with South Africans, an intervention that Murtala denounced at the OAU summit on 11 January 1976.[80] Following intensive lobbying, in which Obasanjo visited Sierra Leone, Mali, and Burkina, the OAU was evenly divided at that meeting on whether to admit the MPLA regime, until Ethiopia added its voice in favour. Six weeks later, 41 of the 46 OAU members had recognised the MPLA government. The South Africans, checked by Cuban forces, withdrew to Angola's southern border. The United States Congress, fearing another Vietnam, banned further covert intervention.[81] The Cubans remained in Angola, transforming power relations in southern Africa and precipitating its liberation, which now became for the first time the central focus of Nigerian foreign policy and one of Obasanjo's chief preoccupations. In February 1976 he led a Nigerian delegation to MPLA anniversary celebrations in Luanda. 'This is a symbolic date', he told the crowd, 'marking the beginning of the final struggle against colonialism, imperialism and racism in Africa.' Doubtless recalling his own experience of civil war, he urged 'that in your hour of victory, you will show magnanimity' and remember that 'all Angolans, whether now within the MPLA or outside it, have to be welded together for the great task of reconstruction'.[82]

While the Angolan crisis dominated external affairs, the government's plans for internal reform were maturing. Late in 1975 a committee in the Cabinet Office began the elaborate collection of information that eventually produced a homogeneous local government system. Following a report by the Irikefe Commission, on 3 January 1976 Murtala announced the addition of seven new states to the existing twelve; one of the seven, Ogun, was to have its headquarters at Abeokuta, thanks to Obasanjo's insistence that his home town had been the provincial headquarters in colonial days. The government also accepted a commission's recommendation that the national capital should move over a period of ten to fifteen years from cramped and overcrowded Lagos to Abuja, at the heart of the country.[83] Army reform was proceeding, including a decision in January 1976 to retire or dismiss 244 officers judged inadequate. At the same time, the junta's leaders promoted themselves. In January 1976 Murtala became a full General, Obasanjo and Danjuma Lieutenant-Generals, Danjuma being promoted over several officers senior to him on the grounds that at the highest levels, rank should accord with responsibility.[84]

Students at the University of Ibadan denounced these promotions as 'contradictory to the proclaimed low profile of the military regime'.[85] Other resentments were more violent. At approximately 8.00 a.m. on 13 February 1976, Murtala Muhammed was shot by dissident officers, who ambushed his unmarked car in a Lagos traffic jam.[86] Half an hour later, a conspirator detailed to assassinate Obasanjo shot and wounded another officer by mistake. Obasanjo had been delayed before leaving his home. Informed of Murtala's death and experienced in the behaviour of coup plotters, he changed into civilian clothes and was driven to a friend's house where he could telephone Yusufu, the police chief, who said he and Danjuma were taking control and Obasanjo should stay where he was. Meanwhile, the coup leader, Colonel B.S. Dimka, the head of the army's physical training corps, announced on Lagos Radio that young revolutionaries had taken power. He also sought to contact Gowon in London through the British High Commission, but was refused. Danjuma telephoned military commanders around the country to ensure their loyalty and summoned troops from the camp at Ikeja, outside Lagos. Dimka fled and was arrested three weeks later close to the eastern frontier.

In the mid afternoon of 13 February, the radio ceased to broadcast martial music and the crisis was over. Alerted by Yusufu, Obasanjo left his hide-out around 5.00 p.m., visited his family, and then, much shaken by his friend Murtala's death, chaired a meeting of senior officers that surveyed the day's events, decided immediate security steps, and fixed a session of the Supreme Military Council for the next morning. 'At the end of the meeting, Obasanjo asked M.D. Yusufu and I to stay', Danjuma recalled. Obasanjo told them that

> what had happened had destroyed his faith in the loyalty of the Nigerian Army. That he had decided that after the funeral, he would retire, leave the Army and go home. But before that he would name me as the successor to Murtala. I told him that, that amounted to desertion and that he could not run away.

Yusufu told them to sleep on it. Instead, he and Danjuma lobbied their colleagues to insist on Obasanjo's acceptance.[87]

The minutes of the Supreme Military Council meeting next morning[88] show that Obasanjo repeated his determination that 'for personal and political reasons, he was not available for the job.' Danjuma said he must accept: 'It could not be otherwise in the tragic circumstances.' Another officer agreed that 'a contrary choice could not be satisfactorily explained to the nation.' That went to the heart of the matter. If Obasanjo, the natural successor, did not take over, the officers feared 'the adverse repercussions appointing a third Northerner in succession could breed among the Yoruba populace'.[89] Moreover, the attempted coup had been the work chiefly of Middle Belt officers – Dimka was an Angas, from the same small ethnic group as Gowon – so that Murtala, a far northerner, could not be replaced by a Middle Belt officer like Danjuma, the obvious alternative to Obasanjo, without threatening to split the army.[90] Memories of the ethnic bloodletting of 1966 were surely strong here. One officer, the Chief of Air Staff, dissented, claiming that the army had faith in Danjuma and that it was widely felt that since Gowon's overthrow the Yoruba 'were getting everything', but Danjuma overruled this. Obasanjo still held out, pointing to 'grumblings and suspicion' and saying that he 'thought it would be better for him to get out of the way,' presumably fearing hostile northern reaction to his appointment.[91] By now, however, the members were impatient. When a general suggested they find Dimka and give him the job, Obasanjo at last accepted, but only for six months, a qualification that was swiftly rejected. To achieve an ethnic and religious balance, Danjuma, fearing 'that if we were not careful, we would end up with a religious conflict on our hands', suggested that Obasanjo's former post as Chief of Staff, Supreme Headquarters, should go to the 32-year-old Colonel Shehu Yar'Adua, a member of the northern aristocracy. 'Senior officers were bound to grumble', someone observed, but the proposal was accepted. From Obasanjo's view-point it was ideal, for Yar'Adua was not only a northern Muslim and a leader of the radical younger officers in the Council, but he was too young and unacceptable to northern conservatives to seek the highest office for himself.

That these calculations were of critical importance to Obasanjo's elevation became clear the same afternoon when Murtala's body was flown home to Kano for the prompt burial required by Islamic custom. Obasanjo entered the plane to pay his last respects, but he did not accompany the body or attend the funeral. As Danjuma had implied, Murtala's assassination had aroused dangerous emotions in the North, where an influential Muslim teacher, Abubakar Gumi, had described the assassination as a Christian coup.[92] Since the civil war, the Yoruba had largely replaced the Igbo as objects of rivalry and suspicion in northern cities, so that rumours quickly spread that Yoruba had induced Middle Belt Christians to carry out the coup. As during other crises in independent Nigeria, northerners and southerners were rumoured to be returning to their homes.[93] A curfew was imposed on Kano on the night of Murtala's funeral and the emir, describing Obasanjo as Murtala's 'closest confidant', 'warned that anybody who tried to instigate one group of people against the other was doing so to achieve their selfish motives or to prepare the ground for the men of disrepute to go on the rampage and to loot.'[94] While the northern press abstained from publishing photographs of the funeral, Obasanjo urged Yoruba-controlled newspapers not to publicise himself.[95] These measures prevented violence. A week later, Yar'Adua carried the Supreme Military Council's condolences to the emir. Obasanjo followed only three months later, leaving Lagos for the first time as head of state and promising that the government would finance the splendid mosque that was built over Murtala's tomb, only the most overt expression of the cult of martyrdom deliberately constructed around a man who had been killed at the height of his reputation.[96]

On the evening of Murtala's funeral, Obasanjo broadcast a tribute to his predecessor, who 'gave this country a unique sense of direction and purpose'. With a probably sincere diffidence that nevertheless induced gentle mockery among cynical Nigerians, he declared that 'I have been called upon, against my personal wish and desire, to serve as the new Head of State. But I have accepted this honour in the interest of the nation and in the memory of the late Head of State', whose views he had shared and whose policies he vowed to continue.[97]

Retribution was already under way. Two days after the assassination, the press published a government statement describing Dimka's request to the British High Commissioner to contact Gowon, without mentioning that the request was refused. A further statement three days later claimed 'ample evidence' from conspirators that Gowon – distantly related to Dimka by marriage – had known of the plan, which the general immediately denied 'on his honour as an officer and a Christian'.[98] Thereafter the campaign against Gowon was pursued with a fury and disregard for the truth that revealed a thoroughly frightened and vindictive regime. University students at Ibadan had taken to the streets within six hours of Murtala's death to blame it on the Central Intelligence Agency, while the British High Commissioner was withdrawn two weeks later at Nigerian request.[99] Other reasons for the coup attempt soon became clear. Dimka's broadcast had complained that Murtala's regime was supporting 'commies', presumably a reference to Angolan policy. Middle-ranking officers involved feared compulsory retirement. Senior officers resented the junta's self-promotion. This suspicion focused on General Iliya Bisalla, the Commissioner for Defence, who had protested when Danjuma, his Second-in-Command during the civil war, was promoted over his head. He had opposed and apparently attempted to subvert the Angolan strategy, had been close to Gowon both personally and ethnically, and had behaved at least suspiciously during the coup.[100]

These suspicions came to a head when Dimka was arrested and interrogated. His incoherent confession[101] – allegedly 'edited, Nixon-style, to implicate General Gowon'[102] – depicted Dimka as merely the intermediary between Bisalla (the chief organiser), Gowon (whom Dimka visited in London), and a group of disgruntled majors. Dimka 'sang like a canary', as Obasanjo put it.[103] While Gowon denied any knowledge of the coup, the government loudly demanded that the British should return him to face trial, knowing that this was impossible. Instead he was dismissed from the army and barred from Nigeria until 1981.[104] Bisalla, too, protested his innocence, but he and Dimka were among the 39 executed, most of them before a crowd that 'surged forward in their thousands chanting "Shoot! Shoot!! Shoot!!!"'[105] There was opposition to such extensive killing within the army, the Supreme Military Council, and especially the Middle Belt, where it was believed that some entirely innocent men had died. Obasanjo's critics accused him of particular severity.[106] Certainly the broadcast in which he announced Dimka's execution sought to display the new leader at his sternest:

> Our purpose is to instil a new sense of public morality among all classes of Nigerians. Let me, therefore, here and now give notice that we shall not tolerate indiscipline. We shall not condone corruption. We shall not allow inefficiency or improper conduct on the part of any public officer.... We shall not allow selfish elements or those who appear bent on breaching the solidarity between the Government and the people of this our great country to unleash industrial, student, economic and other forms of unrest.[107]

One journalist described the executions as 'Obasanjo's finest hour', which had 'endeared' him 'to many Nigerians ... who had thought the new head of state would be a "walk over".'[108] His initial hold on power had indeed appeared uncertain. His behaviour during the coup had been prudent but scarcely heroic. His reluctance to accept leadership was genuine, for he lacked his predecessor's following within an army that was again riddled with suspicion, including predictions of a revenge coup like that of July 1966. Obasanjo was reported in April to have told his friends that he doubted whether he would survive the year.[109] One symptom of his uncertainty was that portraits of Murtala remained in place in administrative offices for a year after his death. Keener than ever to return to barracks, the Supreme Military Council discussed fruitlessly whether it could accelerate the transition to civilian rule.[110] In the meantime, there was a new concern with security. The country's borders were closed and a night-time curfew operated in Lagos for nearly a month after the coup. The Brigade of Guards was largely disbanded and replaced in Lagos by troops judged loyal to the new leaders.[111] Unlike Murtala, Obasanjo moved into Dodan Barracks and scarcely left them during his first three months in office. All members of the Supreme Military Council were given military escorts. Yusufu's proffered resignation was refused, but Special Branch was incorporated into a new National Security Organisation, an incipient secret police.[112]

It was normal in African history for a new ruler's tenure to begin with nervous insecurity, grow into imperious maturity, and end in faltering decline. Six months after Murtala's death, there were still observers who believed that Obasanjo's tenure remained insecure.[113] Others, however, noticed that he was behaving with greater confidence and that his strengths were becoming more apparent: his modesty and austerity, his energy and capacity for work, his ability to secure consensus within the Supreme Military Council, his transparent patriotism, his intelligence, his willingness to learn.[114] And he had one overriding advantage: his luck had held. He was a military head of state who had never made the slightest bid for power.

NOTES

1. Obasanjo, *Nzeogwu*, pp. 73–4; Obasanjo, *Bitter-sweet*, p. 53; Obasanjo, *Not my will*, p. 204.
2. Ademiluyi, *From prisoner to president*, p. 99; Adinoyi Ojo, *In the eyes of time*, p. xiv.
3. Peter C. Lloyd, *Power and independence: urban Africans' perceptions of social inequality* (London, 1974), p. 103.
4. Peter C. Lloyd, 'Divorce among the Yoruba', *American Anthropologist*, 70 (1968), 78.
5. Obasanjo, *Bitter-sweet*, p. 45. See also Olusegun Obasanjo, *Sermons from prison* (Ota, 2000), p. 73.
6. Obasanjo, *Bitter-sweet*, p. 51.
7. Ibid., p. 67.
8. Ibid., p. 56; Adinoyi Ojo, *In the eyes of time*, pp. 157–8, 185.
9. Adinoyi Ojo, *In the eyes of time*, p. 161.
10. Obasanjo, *Bitter-sweet*, pp. 60–81; Adinoyi Ojo, *In the eyes of time*, p. 199.
11. Adinoyi Ojo, *In the eyes of time*, pp. 162, 165–7, 199–201; Obasanjo, *Not my will*, p. 203; *Guardian*, 17 and 23 October 1984.
12. Stremlau, *International politics*, p. 384.
13. Douglas Rimmer, 'Elements of the political economy', in Keith Panter-Brick (ed.), *Soldiers and oil; the political transformation of Nigeria* (London, 1978), pp. 150, 152.
14. Sarah Ahmed Khan, *Nigeria: the political economy of oil* (Oxford, 1994), pp. 16–18.

15. Akin Iwayemi, 'The military and the economy', in Oyeleye Oyediran (ed.), *Nigerian government and politics under military rule, 1966–79* (London, 1979), p. 49; Festus Iyayi, 'The impact of business companies and corporations', in Yusufu Bala Usman (ed.), *Nigeria since independence: the first twenty-five years: volume I: the society* (Ibadan, 1989), p. 20.
16. Toyin Falola and Akanmu Adebayo, *Culture, politics and money among the Yoruba* (New Brunswick, 2000), p. 304.
17. Folabi K. Olagbaju, 'Seasons of cooperation: a study of peasant politics in south-western Nigeria (1960–1989)', Ph.D. thesis, George Washington University, 1999, p. 324.
18. See Ladipo Adamolekun, *Politics and administration in Nigeria* (Ibadan, 1986), Ch.5.
19. A. Akene Ayida, 'Development objectives', in A.A. Ayida and H.M.A. Onitiri (ed.), *Reconstruction and development in Nigeria: proceedings of a national conference* (Ibadan, 1971), p. 9.
20. Adamolekun, *Politics and administration*, pp. 106–7, 113; John F.E. Ohiortenuan, 'The state and economic development in Nigeria under military rule, 1966–79', in Takena N. Tamuno and J.A. Atanda (ed.), *Nigeria since independence: the first twenty-five years: volume IV: government and public policy* (Ibadan, 1989), p. 143.
21. Nigeria, *Third national development plan 1975–80* (2 vols, Lagos [1975]), vol. 1, pp. 30–1, 48.
22. Quoted in S. Ogoh Alubo, 'Doctoring as business: a study of entrepreneurial medicine in Nigeria', *Savanna*, 11, 2 (December, 1990), 62.
23. *Daily Telegraph*, 9 March 1970; 'Address delivered by Chief Obafemi Awolowo, Chancellor, University of Ife', 11 April 1970, FCO 65/740/8.
24. *West Africa*, 10 October 1970, pp. 1177–9, and 24 October 1970, p. 1265.
25. Lindsay Barrett, *Danjuma: the making of a general* (Enugu, 1979), p. 72; Shehu Othman, 'Nigeria: power for profit – class, corporatism, and factionalism in the army', in Donal B. Cruise O'Brien, John Dunn, and Richard Rathbone (ed.), *Contemporary West African states* (Cambridge, 1989), p. 129; Billy J. Dudley, *An introduction to Nigerian government and politics* (London, 1982), p. 84.
26. Ian Campbell, 'Army reorganisation and military withdrawal', in Panter-Brick, *Soldiers and oil*, pp . 61–2.
27. Penfold to FCO, 11 August 1975, FCO 65/1668/148; *Daily Times*, 4 February 1976.
28. Le Quesne, 'Nigeria: annual review for 1975', FCO 65/1779/1; *African Guardian*, 16 April 1990, p. 25; *Punch*, 2 August 1991; Nigeria, *Report of the Tribunal of Inquiry into the Importation of Cement* (Lagos, 1976), p. 27.
29. *West Africa*, 15 July 1974, p. 875.
30. Obasanjo, *March of progress*, p. 393; *West Africa*, 22 November 1976, p. 1742; Tom Forrest, *Politics and economic development in Nigeria* (2nd edn, Boulder, 1995), p. 54.
31. 'Fourteenth independence anniversary broadcast by H.E. General Yakubu Gowon', 1 October 1974, FCO 65/1531/104.
32. Elaigwu, *Gowon*, pp. 224, 238 n.20.
33. Profile of Murtala Mohammed (1975) in FCO 65/1667/3; Obasanjo, *Not my will*, p. 7; Adinoyi Ojo, *In the eyes of time*, pp. 175–7.
34. Amy to Crompton, 26 February 1974, FCO 65/1529/26; Obasanjo, *Not my will*, pp. 3–4.
35. Adinoyi Ojo, *In the eyes of time*, pp. 163, 167–8; S. Macebuh in *Daily Times*, 1 October 1979.
36. Adinoyi Ojo, *In the eyes of time*, pp. 170–2; *Daily Times*, 9 July 1975; *New Nigerian*, 23 July 1975.
37. Adinoyi Ojo, *In the eyes of time*, p. 21.
38. Obasanjo, *Not my will*, pp. 7–8; Adinoyi Ojo, *In the eyes of time*, p. 180.
39. Elaigwu, *Gowon*, pp. 225–30; *Newswatch*, 1 September 1986, p. 20.

40. Jacqueline W. Farris and Mohammed Bomoi (ed.), *Shehu Musa Yar'Adua: a life of service* (Abuja, 2004), pp. 88–92; M. Chris Alli, *The Federal Republic of Nigerian Army: the siege of a nation* (Ikeja, 2001), p. 76.
41. Joe Garba, *Diplomatic soldiering: Nigerian foreign policy, 1975–1979* (Ibadan, 1987), pp. xiii–xiv; Obasanjo, *Not my will*, pp. 9–10; Barrett, *Danjuma*, pp. 77–9.
42. Elaigwu, *Gowon*, Ch.13; *West Africa*, 4 August 1975, p. 913.
43. This account is based on Obasanjo, *Not my will*, pp. 11–14 (quotation on p. 13); Garba, *Diplomatic soldiering*, pp. xiii–xv (quotation on p. xiv); Barrett, *Danjuma*, pp. 79–81; Danjuma in *Guardian*, 17 February 2008.
44. Obasanjo, *Not my will*, pp. 14–16; Garba, *Diplomatic soldiering*, pp. xv–xvii; *Daily Times*, 30 July 1975.
45. Obasanjo, *March of progress*, p. 2.
46. Crompton to Roberts, 3 November 1975, FCO 65/1669/63.
47. Danjuma in *Guardian*, 17 February 2008.
48. *Nigerian Tribune*, 28 February 2003.
49. Obasanjo, *Not my will*, p. 5; *Daily Times*, 1 August 1975, 4 December 1975, 5 April 1976.
50. Ahmed Joda, 'Foreword', in Femi Kayode and Dafe Otobo (ed.), *Allison Akene Ayida: Nigeria's quintessential public servant* (Lagos, 2004), pp. ix–x; Peter M. Lewis, *Growing apart: oil, politics, and economic change in Indonesia and Nigeria* (Ann Arbor, 2007), pp. 148–9.
51. *Daily Times*, 13 September 1977.
52. Patrick Dele Cole, 'An assessment of contributions', in Peter P. Ekeh, Patrick Dele Cole, and Gabriel O. Olusanya (ed.), *Nigeria since independence: the first twenty-five years: volume V: politics and constitutions* (Ibadan, 1989), p. 278.
53. Kayode and Otobo, *Ayida*, p. 100; Bola Ige in *Daily Times*, 10 August 1975.
54. Le Quesne to Callaghan, 5 January 1976, FCO 65/1778/2.
55. Le Quesne to FCO, 26 September 1975, FCO 65/1669/34.
56. Le Quesne to Heath (citing Graham-Douglas), 3 October 1975, FCO 65/1668/164; Farris and Bomoi, *Shehu Musa Yar'Adua*, p. 113.
57. *Daily Times*, 2 October 1975.
58. Obasanjo, *Not my will*, p. 20; *New Nigerian*, 6 October 1975.
59. *Daily Times*, 19 October 1975.
60. *Daily Times*, 27 October 1975.
61. Obasanjo, *March of progress*, p. 478.
62. Saro-Wiwa, *On a darkling plain*, p. 221.
63. Obasanjo, *Bitter-sweet*, p. 83.
64. Ademiluyi, *From prisoner to president*, p. 23.
65. Ebenezer Babatope, *Not his will: the Awolowo Obasanjo wager* (Benin City, 1990), p. 85.
66. Okwudiba Nnoli, 'Nigerian policy towards southern Africa', *Nigerian Journal of International Affairs*, 2 (1976), 14–34.
67. Daniel C. Bach, 'The politics of West African economic co-operation: C.E.A.O. and E.C.O.W.A.S.', *Journal of Modern African Studies*, 21 (1983), 605–25.
68. Obasanjo, interviewed in *Africa* (London), June 1976, p. 14.
69. Garba, *Diplomatic soldiering*, p. 9; Alaba Ogunsanwo, *The Nigerian military and foreign policy 1975–1979: processes, principles, performance, and contradictions*, Research Monograph no. 45, Center of International Studies, Princeton University, June 1980, p. 2.
70. See John Marcum, *The Angolan revolution* (2 vols, Cambridge MA, 1969–78), vol. 2, Chs 5 and 6; Piero Gleijeses, *Conflicting missions: Havana, Washington, and Africa, 1959–1976* (Chapel Hill, 2002), Chs. 11–15 (chronology on pp. 298, 305).
71. BBC monitoring report on Lagos Radio, 8 November 1975, FCO 65/1670/57; *New Nigerian*, 21 November 1975.

72. Abiodun Olufemi Sotumbi, *Nigeria's recognition of the MPLA government of Angola: a case-study in decision-making and implementation*, Nigerian Institute of International Affairs Monograph Series no. 9 (Lagos, 1981), pp. 2, 9–10; Hennessy to FCO, 1 December 1975, FCO 65/1598/21.
73. Gleijeses, *Conflicting missions*, pp. 321–3, 327.
74. Garba, *Diplomatic soldiering*, p. 22.
75. Ibid., pp. 21, 23; State Department to Secretary's Delegation, 17 February 1976, in United States: Department of State, 'Foreign relations, 1969–1976: volume E-6: documents on Africa, 1973–1976', no. 210 (http://www.state.gov/r/pa/ho/frus/nixon/e6); 'Leading personalities in Nigeria, 1977', s.v. Obasanjo, FCO 65/1902/30.
76. Obasanjo, *Not my will*, pp. 123–4.
77. Oluleye, *Military leadership*, p. 177.
78. Johnson to Lewis, 2 December 1975, FCO 65/1670/67.
79. Minutes of National Security Council meeting, Washington, 11 May 1976, in United States: Department of State, 'Foreign relations, 1969–1976: volume E-6: documents on Africa, 1973–1976', no. 44 (http://www.state.gov/r/pa/ho/frus/nixon/e6).
80. Obasanjo, *Not my will*, pp. 245–50.
81. Garba, *Diplomatic soldiering*, pp. 26–8; John Stockwell, *In search of enemies: a CIA story* (London, 1978), pp. 231–4.
82. Obasanjo, *March of progress*, pp. 28–9.
83. *Daily Times*, 4 and 6 February 1976; Adinoyi Ojo, *In the eyes of time*, p. 196.
84. *Daily Times*, 9 and 18 January 1976.
85. *Daily Times*, 10 January 1976.
86. There is a detailed account in Adinoyi Ojo, *In the eyes of time*, pp. 4–25. See also Obasanjo, *Not my will*, pp. 27–9, and Danjuma's account in *Newswatch*, 2 November 1992, pp. 20–1.
87. Danjuma in *Guardian*, 17 February 2008; Mathias Okoi-Uyouyo, *M.D. Yusufu: beyond the cop* (Calabar, 2005), p. 65.
88. In Farris and Bomoi, *Shehu Musa Yar'Adua*, pp. 122–3. See also Obasanjo, *Not my will*, pp. 30–2; Danjuma in *Guardian*, 17 February 2008.
89. Oluleye, *Architecturing a destiny*, p. 136.
90. Bola Ige, *People, politics and politicians of Nigeria (1940–1979)* (Ibadan, 1995), p. 392.
91. See Liman Ciroma in *Weekly Trust*, 18 September 1998.
92. *Newswatch*, 2 November 1992, p. 14.
93. Wilson to British High Commission, Lagos, 16 February 1976, FCO 65/1780/32; Obasanjo, *Not my will*, p. 36.
94. *New Nigerian*, 16 and 17 February 1976.
95. Williams, note, 12 April 1976, FCO 65/1782/8.
96. *New Nigerian*, 3 May 1976; *Daily Times*, 27 June 1978.
97. Obasanjo, *Not my will*, p. 33; Ademiluyi, *From prisoner to president*, pp. 25–6.
98. *Sunday Times* (Lagos), 15 February 1976; BBC monitoring report on Radio Lagos, 18 February 1976, FCO 65/1780/32; *Daily Times*, 20 February 1976.
99. Le Quesne to FCO, 13 February 1976, FCO 65/1780/10; 'Record of conversation between the Minister of State for Foreign and Commonwealth Affairs and the Nigerian High Commissioner', 1 March 1976, FCO 65/1781/94.
100. *Daily Times*, 19 February 1996; Obasanjo, *Not my will*, pp. 35–6, 42; Barrett, *Danjuma*, pp. 84–6.
101. Text in *New Nigerian*, 13 March 1976. There is a lucid summary in *West Africa*, 22 March 1976, p. 392.
102. Allison A. Ayida, *Reflections on Nigerian development* (Lagos, 1987), p. 53.
103. Obasanjo, *Not my will*, p. 39.
104. Elaigwu, *Gowon*, pp. 257–68; *Daily Times*, 16 May 1976
105. *Daily Times*, 12 March 1976.

106. Elaigwu, *Gowon*, pp. 272–3; Kayode and Otobo, *Ayida*, p. 115. But see also *Newswatch*, 16 April 1990, p. 10.
107. [Olusegun Obasanjo,] *Call to duty: a collection of speeches* ([Lagos] n.d.), p. 65.
108. *Daily Times*, 29 July 1976.
109. *Times*, 22 July 1976; Wilson to British High Commission, Lagos, 14 April 1976, FCO 65/1782/7.
110. Campbell in Panter-Brick, *Soldiers and oil*, p. 88; Williams to FCO, 30 March 1976, FCO 65/1782/5.
111. *New Nigerian*, 9 March 1976; West African Department, 'Reporting from Kaduna', 23 April 1976, FCO 65/1782/10.
112. Oluleye, *Military leadership*, pp. 191–3; Obasanjo, *Not my will*, pp. 41, 46–7.
113. Williams to FCO, 18 August 1976, FCO 65/1793/133.
114. Sam Uba, 'Reluctant leader with will for discipline', *Times*, 22 July 1976.

6

State-directed Development

Once Obasanjo was installed as military head of state during the first months of 1976, three issues dominated his attention until he transferred power to a civilian successor in October 1979: economic and social development, foreign affairs, and the creation of democratic institutions. Murtala's regime had laid down the main lines of policy in several fields. These Obasanjo followed 'religiously', as his chief official adviser remembered.[1] Yet it would be wrong to think that Obasanjo's regime 'was like a tired anchor leg of a relay race'.[2] In Nigerian circumstances, implementing policies was more difficult than formulating them.

In carrying out the programme, Obasanjo, as he insisted, was only executive chairman of the Supreme Military Council, where he encouraged debate and consensus. During his first year of office, especially, he continued to cultivate a low profile of modesty and austerity that won him much popular sympathy.[3] He could not defy the Council's powerful complement of northern officers, especially the army chief, Danjuma. He relied heavily on his young Chief of Staff, Yar'Adua. For ideas, Obasanjo looked beyond the cowed civil service to the Cabinet Office think-tank and to his wide circle of professional and academic acquaintances, holding an informal seminar on a current issue each Saturday morning. 'Anyone who had any moving idea was free to speak out and be challenged', a participant remembered. 'Originality was his greatest fetish.'[4] Above all, Obasanjo sought to master his job as he had mastered everything to which he had set his mind. 'He worked long hours,' his chief adviser recalled, 'he ensured that he brought himself up to date in all the fields that he had to tackle. He got things done.'[5]

The economy was the most difficult task. Murtala's regime had broadly adopted the strategy of the Third Development Plan, with its emphasis on rapid, investment-driven development financed by oil revenue, with the state taking the leading role in infrastructure and heavy industry, while light industry and agriculture were left chiefly to private enterprise. This had been the standard model for capitalist development in the Third World since the Second World War and it was adopted especially by the newly rich oil producers of the 1970s like Venezuela, Algeria, and Iran. As Obasanjo later wrote, 'Our industrialization policy was orthodox, and the thrust was heavy industry as the base for medium and light industries.'[6] Neither he nor his colleagues were in any position to challenge this orthodoxy. Although he resented being described as an economic illiterate,[7] Obasanjo had no economic schooling and no cadre of skilled economic advisers. Throughout his career his thinking on economic issues – although not always his economic instincts – followed the changing orthodoxies of the time. For ideological disputes between capitalism and socialism he had nothing but contempt.[8]

Early in 1976, once security was restored, the government's most urgent problem was the overheating of the economy, indicated by a 34% inflation rate and a 25% decline in external reserves during 1975. Emphasising this in his first budget speech on 31 March 1976, Obasanjo warned that, with a population of 72 million, Nigeria was not a rich country but only one of rich potential.[9] In what a newspaper called 'a remarkable show of seriousness', he proposed to balance the budget by reducing government spending by one-sixth, curtailing prestige projects while expanding expenditure on education, health, housing, and agriculture. Two months later the government launched several emergency measures, including rent and price controls, land reform and a wage freeze.[10]

The regime also confronted underlying issues. Especially difficult, in view of the military grievances expressed in Dimka's coup, was to reduce the cost of the swollen army, but by January 1978 Danjuma could declare that 'the backbone of opposition to demobilisation has been broken.'[11] Numbers are uncertain, but by 1979 army personnel may have fallen to about 160,000, although savings were partly balanced by equipment purchases – including 64 main battle tanks – designed to create a more modern and mobile force.[12] A more profound problem was the crisis in agriculture. 'In the last few years,' Obasanjo explained in May 1976,

> the country has witnessed an alarming decline in agricultural production. Government has had to import increasing quantities of a variety of food items from abroad. Prices of food stuffs have galloped. To make matters worse, young men and women have been drifting from rural areas into the cities in unprecedented numbers, leaving behind them old men and women who cannot be expected to meet the growing needs of the country for food.[13]

Nigeria's Central Bank reckoned that agricultural production fell by 27% between 1970 and 1979. Some later economists have reported comparable (if smaller) declines, although others believe that output kept pace with population growth.[14] Four things, at least, are clear. First, the figures are thoroughly unreliable. Second, food imports rose between 1971 and 1980 from about $130 million (N88 million) to $2,830 million (N1.560 million), the bulk being wheat consumed chiefly but not exclusively by townspeople. In 1976 Nigeria produced some 7,000 tons of wheat and imported 773,000 tons.[15] Third, agricultural exports fell dramatically. Between 1970–1 and 1976–7 the cocoa crop, long the staple of the Western Region's economy, fell from a record 308,000 tonnes to 165,000 tonnes, while groundnut exports from the North dwindled from 291,000 tonnes to nothing, a fate paralleled by the East's palm oil exports.[16] Fourth, the reasons for these changes were more complicated than Obasanjo realised. Labour did flow from agriculture into the towns in response to the oil boom. Aging cocoa trees, plant diseases, drought, and increased domestic consumption all reduced cash-crop exports. Yet both exports and food imports were also affected by an increase of 87% in the value of the Nigerian naira as against foreign currencies between 1970 and 1981, which made imports cheap but reduced the naira returns from cash crops sold on world markets for foreign currencies.[17] This was an example of the notorious Dutch Disease, in which oil exports, by raising the value of the currency, damaged other sectors of the economy.

Like most Nigerians of the time, Obasanjo did not understand Dutch Disease and believed for the next twenty years that an appreciating naira was an indication of national prosperity and that devaluation was 'a sordid act of economic sabotage'.[18] His rural upbringing suggested rather that the country's apparent inability to feed itself was a moral failure. His response, Operation Feed the Nation (OFN), was inaugurated on 21 May 1976 , when the head of state, in Yoruba farmer's dress, was extensively photographed hoeing his small farm at Dodan Barracks.[19] Schools, universities, military units, and individuals were to be mobilised to produce food for their own consumption and the market. Some 27,000 students were paid N7.7 million to spend their vacations working on farms and helping to distribute the heavily subsidised fertiliser used as an incentive to increased production. Between 1975 and 1980 Nigeria's annual fertiliser consumption rose from 80,000 to over one million tons.[20] Obasanjo believed that small-scale farming must be revitalised by reducing its drudgery through mechanisation and improved tools and seeds, increasing its profitability by better marketing arrangements, and fostering a 'large-scale programme of co-operativization'.[21] He later insisted that OFN was 'an exemplary success' that brought significant progress towards self-sufficiency. Others thought it succeeded only as a publicity measure. Yar'Adua's office, which administered the scheme, concluded that 'Obasanjo Fools the Nation', as cynics described it, achieved little.[22]

OFN sought to improve peasant farming. Other policies aimed rather to transform it. The most spectacular were three massive irrigation schemes in the arid North – the Kano River Project, Bakalori Scheme (in the Sokoto-Rima basin), and South Chad Irrigation Project – which were incorporated into the 1975–80 development plan and were passionately advocated by northern leaders. Between 1974–5 and 1976–7 federal funds allocated for irrigation rose from N4 million ($6.5 million) to N190 million ($297 million); by 1983 they had risen to N897 million ($493 million).[23] The schemes rested on shoddy preparatory studies and their economic viability was doubtful from the first, so that the World Bank refused to fund them.[24] These fears were fully borne out. A report in 1981 found that Nigerian schemes had cost N2,470 per irrigated hectare, as against N500 in Côte d'Ivoire; at Bakalori the cost had been N7,540 per irrigated hectare.[25] The intention was to produce irrigated wheat, rice, sugar, and other crops to replace imported food. In reality, at Bakalori, the best known scheme, the local economy did benefit but the profit went largely to contractors and to richer farmers who used most of the irrigated land to grow indigenous crops (including rice), after a blockade by poorer peasants evicted without compensation had led the police to shoot a number estimated variously from nineteen to over a hundred.[26] At the South Chad Project, the falling level of the lake meant that by 1985 the irrigation intake was over 70 kilometres from the nearest water.[27] Obasanjo inherited these schemes and implemented them, but he did not extend them or treat them as models.

A third strand of agricultural policy appealed more strongly to Obasanjo's peasant background and entrepreneurial energy. In 1972 the World Bank agreed to finance pilot Agricultural Development Projects in the northern areas of Funtua, Gusau, and Gombe, providing local infrastructure and subsidised inputs for progressive smallholder farming in a capitalist manner. Views of their success varied, although all agreed that the chief beneficiaries were the larger farmers who secured most of the inputs. The World Bank was especially enthusiastic and promoted the strategy as a general model for sub-Saharan Africa.[28] Obasanjo visited and admired the Gombe Project in 1977 and later explained that the success of the Funtua Project led to a decision in 1980 to launch similar schemes in all states and make them, rather than large scale irrigation, the core of rural development policy. This was the chief positive outcome of an agricultural programme that, despite his enthusiasm, absorbed only about 2.5% of government expenditure between 1975 and 1980, less than in earlier or later periods.[29]

Agriculture was still the core of Nigeria's economy, but economic fluctuations followed the oil market. When Obasanjo came to power early in 1976, the great oil boom of 1973 was slowing into three years of relative recession. The official price of Nigerian light crude continued to rise slightly, from $12.72 per barrel in October 1975 to $14.33 in January 1978, but output declined from 2,325,458 barrels per day in October 1974 to only 1,557,128 in May 1975, before recovering to slightly over 2,000,000 during 1976 and most of 1977.[30] Between 1974–5 and 1975–6 the government's oil revenue fell from $8.1 billion to $6.7 billion, causing Obasanjo to make his one-sixth reduction in budgeted expenditure.[31]

These fluctuations resulted from Nigeria's place in the international oil market. OPEC's massive price increase in 1973–4 had led to a recession in the industrial countries, had reduced demand, and had stimulated the development of new fields that might previously have been uneconomic, notably in Alaska, Mexico, and the North Sea. In response, OPEC maintained its price levels by reducing production quotas. This partly explained Nigeria's reduced output, but its oil industry also suffered special difficulties. The Niger Delta's oil came from many relatively small wells in an exceptionally difficult, marshy environment and was consequently expensive to produce, especially compared with Middle Eastern fields. It was light, high quality oil and had enjoyed a premium price, but the new oil from the North Sea was of similar quality and closer to the Western European markets that Nigeria had hitherto largely supplied. By maintaining its price premium in accordance with OPEC policy, Nigeria found itself in 1975–6 trying to sell the most expensive oil in the market in competition with non-OPEC members.[32] Moreover, a reduced production quota was more damaging to a populous country like Nigeria, which spent all its oil revenue, than to OPEC's sparsely populated member states, which invested much of their revenue abroad. In addition, the contracts between the Nigerian government and the oil-producing companies gave the latter relatively stable revenues, whereas the government profited largely from windfall gains but bore the brunt of recessions.[33] These difficulties prevented Obasanjo's government from making the oil industry a more dynamic leading sector in the economy. Late in 1977 it was even obliged to break OPEC's rules and cut oil prices unilaterally in order to compete more effectively.[34]

The major changes in the oil industry had taken place during Gowon's regime. Obasanjo made only cautious progress towards bringing the industry further under national control, given that the need for the international companies' expertise made full nationalisation impossible. His chief initiative was to amalgamate the Ministry of Petroleum Resources and the Nigerian National Oil Corporation into a Nigerian National Petroleum Corporation (NNPC) that both regulated the industry and operated as a commercial marketing (and potentially producing) company. In 1979 the NNPC increased its share of the equity in all oil operations from 55% to 60%.[35] Obasanjo's chief disappointment was the failure to construct Nigeria's first Liquefied Natural Gas (LNG) plant. The Niger Delta had vast gas reserves, greater than its oil resources. During 1973 natural gas worth an estimated $793 million was produced along with oil and merely flared, with damaging environmental effects.

Obasanjo encouraged a characteristically ambitious plan for a liquefaction plant at Bonny costing over $4.5 billion, 60% financed by the NNPC, with an elaborate network of collecting pipelines. When he left office in 1979 the plan was almost complete, but cost increases, financial stringency, and market contraction forced his successor to abandon it.[36]

In the short term, the partial recovery of oil production during 1976 alleviated the crisis that Obasanjo's government had faced on taking office. His second budget speech on 31 March 1977 could claim that real GDP had grown by 10% during 1976–7, as against only 2.8% in 1975–6, while annual inflation had fallen from 35% to about 20%. An adverse balance of payments led him to 'discourage vulgar ostentation' by banning the two imports that had given their names to the years of champagne and lace, thereby precipitating a scramble for the country's surviving stocks. Generally, however, the budget set out an ambitious programme of capital expenditure on infrastructure and industry. 'The nation', he proclaimed, 'is entering a period of rapid industrialization.'[37]

Although Nigeria gained an evil reputation for wasting its oil wealth on conspicuous consumption, in reality the military regimes of the 1970s maintained high levels of investment: 22.7% of GDP over the decade as a whole, compared with 21.8% in Indonesia, an oil producer that achieved greater long term economic success. Between 1973 and 1978 the proportion of Nigerian federal expenditure that was capital expenditure rose from 24% to 52%.[38] Of total investment between 1975–6 and 1978–9, however, 64% was in building and construction, where unit costs were exceptionally high. The military regime's dangerous legacies were over-investment and inefficient investment, especially in large-scale projects that were ill-conceived, uncompleted, or beyond the country's capacity to manage and maintain.[39]

The most conspicuous illustration of these problems was the integrated steel mill at Ajaokuta, designed to enable Nigeria to advance from light, import-substitution manufacturing into heavy industry. Gowon negotiated the project with the Soviet Union in 1970, rejecting advice from the World Bank and his own civil servants that it was unviable. Five years later the two parties agreed on a site at Ajaokuta, located symbolically at the centre of the country but in economic terms absurdly distant from the coast. In 1977 Obasanjo expected the complex – 'basic to our industrial take-off' – to begin production in 1980, but it was only very shortly before he left office in 1979 that construction began. It involved building not only a steel mill but a new port, roads and railway lines capable of carrying 100-tonne loads, a power station, and a town for the workers. The smelting process – already outdated by international standards – required suitable coking coal, which was not found in Nigeria. All the elements of the project had to be constructed concurrently, for otherwise those left unused would deteriorate, as indeed happened. Abandonment, however, would mean waste and defeat. 'It has to be viewed from the strategic point and from the amount of money already sunk', Obasanjo would reflect in 1990. Ajaokuta would haunt him to the last days of his career.[40]

According to Central Bank figures, manufacturing output grew at a remarkable 23% per year between 1975 and 1979, although capacity utilisation fell from 77% to 67%, suggesting inefficient investment.[41] Most manufacturing was light processing industry, such as the more than 3,500 bakeries and innumerable enterprises producing construction materials that existed in 1980. About 60% of industrial inputs were imported, most blatantly by the motor assembly plants that were a growth point of the period.[42] The most vigorous innovation was probably in the textile factories of northern cities and the small-scale engineering and other enterprises of the south-east, neither of which received much encouragement from Lagos.[43] Governmental attention focused rather on heavier industrial plants: steel rolling mills, a fertiliser project, pulp and paper factories, and a petrochemical scheme that did not come to fruition. An ambitious plan to expand the telephone network failed largely because of poor choice of technology.[44] The government was more successful in developing road transport, adding two new petrol refineries to the pioneer enterprise at Port Harcourt, creating a petrol distribution network of 21 depots and 3,000 kilometres of pipeline, and trebling the modern road mileage.[45]

Obasanjo's government also attempted to keep pace with the rapidly growing demand for electricity resulting from industrial development and urbanisation. The country's main source, the Kainji hydroelectric scheme on the River Niger, had been built in the 1960s when water levels were high. A sequence of droughts during the 1970s roughly halved its output. To meet intense public dissatisfaction, average annual budgetary allocations to electricity were raised from $44 million in 1974–5 to $271 million in 1976–9 in order to build two new hydroelectric projects and a thermal plant.[46]

In accordance with the 1975–80 development plan, government followed a dual economic strategy. While the state invested in infrastructure, irrigation, and heavy industry, its approach in other fields was characterised as 'nurture capitalism', employing state resources to foster indigenous private enterprise.[47] The centrepiece was the indigenisation programme initiated in 1972 and expanded in 1977. The initial decree had classified private enterprises into three groups, chiefly according to technical complexity and capital requirements, reserving for Nigerians the whole of the least demanding group and a minimum 40% share in the middling group. The 1977 decree raised the minimum Nigerian share to 60% in the middling group (and all banks) and 40% in the most demanding. It also sought to prevent evasion and to widen the distribution of shares among Nigerians. Indigenisation certainly expanded Nigerian capitalism, although it also absorbed Nigerian resources that might have pioneered new enterprises and it became a major deterrent to future foreign investment.[48]

'It is impossible to convey to anyone who did not work closely with General Obasanjo, Yar'Adua, Danjuma and M.D. Yusuf the almost fanatical allegiance these men had to the concept of Nigerianness', a member of the Cabinet Office think-tank later recalled.[49] Even Obasanjo's left-wing academic critics recognised the urgency of his economic nationalism, although they denounced the 'sterile capitalism' it fostered, in which the Nigerian business man 'is largely a middleman between the overseas capitalist and the Nigerian consumer'.[50] By contrast, later economists, influenced by the neo-liberalism of the 1980s and 1990s, criticised Obasanjo's strategy from a different angle. They compared Nigeria's experience with that of Indonesia, an oil-producing state with a comparable population and average wealth in the early 1970s. Guided by a skilled cadre of economic managers such as Nigeria no longer possessed, Indonesia saw the oil boom of the 1970s as potentially dangerous, refrained from spending all its revenue, ensured that investment did not exceed the economy's absorptive capacity, and saved a proportion of revenue to carry it through the succeeding slump without suffering extreme discontinuity or paralysing debt. Indonesia also deliberately devalued its currency, thereby encouraging agricultural exports – in which it invested heavily – and discouraging manufactured imports to the advantage of domestic industries.[51] The contrast highlights key weaknesses in

Obasanjo's strategy of state-directed development, but it ignores some of the distinctive reasons for them. Unlike Indonesia, Nigeria became an oil producer only shortly before the boom of 1973–4, so that it had little experience of regulating the industry, little infrastructure through which oil revenues could be efficiently invested, and little capacity to manage the enterprises created. Oil also came to dominate Nigeria's government revenue to a greater degree than in any other populous oil state, because its domestic taxation system and administration were unusually weak, the country was still recovering from civil war, it was located in a region of political weakness, it suffered from clientelism and corruption, and its political leadership was fragmented by ethnic and other divisions.[52]

A further consequence of Nigeria's state-directed development was a rapid growth in the size and cost of the public sector. Between 1973 and 1981 public employment roughly tripled, from 0.5 to 1.5 million. In 1980 there were an estimated 850 parastatal enterprises.[53] This centralising thrust of military nationalism characterised other spheres of government activity. Obasanjo's regime 'unified anything and everything unifiable', a military dissident complained. By 1979 the supposedly federal states generated less than 3% of their revenue, depending on federal grants for the remainder.[54] Perhaps the most striking act of centralisation was an ambitious reconstruction of local government, decreed in 1976, which replaced great previous diversity by 301 local government areas of roughly equal population size, each electing a council with a paid chairman and subordinate staff, receiving revenue direct from the central government, and exercising concurrent responsibility together with state governments for primary education, basic health care, and local services. Devised largely by Yar'Adua and the Cabinet Office staff, the scheme was designed to make local authorities both effective agents of development and locally accountable training grounds for democracy. In the event, the scheme worked poorly. The funds allocated to local authorities became irresistible targets for corruption, patronage, and rivalries that multiplied local government areas to 774 by 1996. Local services often collapsed. State governments, charged to organise regular local government elections, replaced them with favoured 'caretakers'. By early 1980 only two of the nineteen states had fully elected local councils.[55]

Greater, but still qualified success attended another initiative of centrally directed development: the provision of universal primary education (UPE). In 1970, the proportion of primary school-age children at school ranged from some 95% in Lagos State to 7% in the north-west. To rectify this imbalance and its implicit threat to national unity was a major reason for the programme.[56] Long advocated by Awolowo, it was taken up by Gowon in 1974 and implemented with great conviction by Obasanjo in September 1976. Perhaps recalling his own childhood, he promised 'equal education opportunities for all children of school age, irrespective of circumstances of their birth', as 'a right and not a privilege'. Initial preparations included the training of 163,000 new teachers.[57] Between 1975–6 and 1979–80, free but voluntary primary school enrolment doubled from 6 million to 12.5 million, far outrunning the expected numbers. The central government bore the entire initial cost, raising its education budget from 3% to 11% of its total expenditure between 1973–4 and 1976–7.[58] Inevitably there were shortages of teachers, classrooms, materials, and especially finance; by 1977, several states were considering reintroducing fees. Yet the scheme went far to rectify regional imbalances, raising the share of the North in primary school enrolment from 19% to 47%.[59] It facilitated citizenship training, including daily singing of the national anthem and reciting of a national pledge. It also reduced the agricultural labour force, encouraged urban migration, and bred the alert but disillusioned citizens who made late twentieth-century Nigeria so difficult to govern. The scheme itself foundered in 1984 for lack of money, but was resurrected when Obasanjo regained power in 1999.[60] A parallel scheme for countrywide primary health care, proposed in the 1975–80 development plan, established 403 basic health units but was checked by expense and the hostility of health professionals.[61]

Many experts of this period shared Obasanjo's view that 'primary education has relatively greater *social* benefits than secondary and higher levels.'[62] Given his training as an engineer, his practical cast of mind, and his distaste for theoretical debate, it is understandable that his regime first introduced free education at post-primary level only in technical subjects, in 1977–8, extending free tuition to secondary schooling as a whole in 1979–80.[63] At the university level, government policy was especially contentious. In the later 1950s, university education had been confined to a few hundred students at the University of Ibadan, which, so Obasanjo complained, 'emphasized the concept of ivory-towerism from its inception'.[64] By 1975, however, Nigeria had thirteen universities with 32,286 students, a number increased by 1980 to 77,791. This expansion coincided with growing discontent and radicalisation among both staff and students.[65] Partly in response, the Udoji Commission of 1974 incorporated university teachers into the civil service and Gowon's government increased state control of universities.[66] Obasanjo set high value on university education but was contemptuous of Nigerian universities, while his own youthful deprivation and the patriarchalism of his generational attitudes made him intolerant of protest by those who 'forget their station in life'.[67] Antagonism culminated in 1978 when the government sought to economise by abandoning its system of student loans and trebling university food and accommodation charges, which provoked student demonstrations at all major universities and fatal shootings at Zaria and at Lagos, where the security forces lost control of parts of the city for two days.[68] Suspicion linked the protest to an embryonic military conspiracy uncovered in February 1978,[69] which may partly explain the government's fierce response, closing several universities, proscribing the National Union of Nigerian Students, and banning political activity on campuses.[70] Nigeria's universities, Obasanjo reflected, 'had come to epitomize most of the ills of the society, if not all of them…. In the interest of the future of Nigeria the universities have to be saved from themselves.'[71] The animosity survived throughout his career.

For Obasanjo, riotous students were symptoms of the indiscipline that hampered Nigeria's development and of a neglect of indigenous cultural values that was especially important to his thinking at this point in his career, perhaps owing in part to his role as Grand Patron of the Festival of Black and African Arts and Culture (FESTAC) held in Lagos in January 1977.[72] 'The major cause of most of the ills of the society … is … discarding the good part of our traditional society', he declared in September 1977:

> What, for example, is wrong with our traditional society which respects age, experience and authority; or the norm that everybody is his brother's keeper which makes ethical standard universal; or the practice of stigmatising and ostracising evildoers and the indolent; or the extolling of virtues and values not necessarily based on materialism but on the service to the community and the encouragement of excellence? These are ideals which have remained with us over the ages and which we must never allow the new wave of individualism, egotism, materialism and so-called sophistication to sweep away.[73]

Appeals to the past, however, were of little assistance in coping with the immense social problems that faced the regime. Obasanjo later admitted that in the 1970s he had not even noticed the most profound of these: a nearly 3% annual growth rate that was doubling the nation's population in little more than 25 years, owing to reduced mortality while fertility remained high. Nigeria had no population policy. Only a tiny minority of (mainly educated) women yet used artificial contraception. Although much land remained unused in the Middle Belt and the North, some 90% of farms in the South-East and 60% in the South-West were already smaller than one hectare.[74] An even more immediate consequence of population growth was rapid urbanisation, further encouraged by the civil war and the concentration of oil money and educational opportunities in the towns. Between 1965 and 1980 the proportion of Nigeria's population classified as urban rose from 17% to 27%, with an average increase in the urban population of 5.7% per year, or twice the general population growth rate.[75] The increase was most spectacular in Lagos, which in 1975 produced 70% of Nigeria's industrial output. Figures vary, but between 1963 and 1977 its population may have grown from about 1,100,000 to 3,500,000.[76]

Of some 10 million urban people of working age in the late 1970s, little more than one-quarter earned wages within the modern sector, fewer than 400,000 of them in formal manufacturing.[77] The remaining economically active townspeople engaged in the informal sector, which embraced everything from backyard manufacturing and the army of market women to the frequently unpaid apprentices, who were estimated in the early 1960s at two million.[78] Some older towns like Ibadan and Zaria also housed many farmers. This occupational pattern made it difficult to estimate levels of unemployment, but surveys in the 1970s recorded national urban unemployment rates of 4%-6%, with a majority aged less than 25.[79]

Rapid urbanisation presented Obasanjo's government with acute problems of social welfare, remuneration, and public order. The most obvious was the urban housing shortage, estimated in 1979 at one million units. Average density in Lagos in the early 1970s was at least 3.5 persons per room, commonly about ten feet square.[80] The scale of urban poverty was a question of definition, but several estimates in the late 1970s suggested that between 25% and 33% of townspeople lived below national poverty lines, with perhaps higher proportions in the countryside.[81] Obasanjo's government did almost nothing for the poor except provide free primary schooling.

Mass urbanisation also placed immense demands on services. No Nigerian city possessed a central sewerage system. In Ibadan, fewer than 10% of households had piped water.[82] Water and electricity were more widely available in Lagos, but oil wealth exacerbated its appalling traffic problems and extended its longstanding patterns of armed robbery from the poorer quarters into the commercial and elite residential areas, creating a moral panic to which the authorities responded with public executions. The entire country had only about 80,000 policemen, or little more than one for every thousand people.[83]

The military regime's first attempt to tackle social problems focused on housing. Obasanjo's budget of April 1976 undertook to build 200,000 new housing units by 1980, as the development plan specified. In fact the government built only 28,500, although it also constructed accommodation for over 70,000 military personnel, arguing that this would reduce friction and free housing for civilian occupation.[84] The government also tried to control rents, an especially acute problem in Lagos, where most land and housing were owned by landlords who commonly rented rooms at 30–40% of a tenant's income.[85] That rent control failed can scarcely have surprised Obasanjo, for whom it was probably chiefly a populist gesture,[86] but it focused his attention on the immensely complicated ownership of land in southern towns. Adopting the radical minority report of a land use panel, the Land Use Decree of March 1978 in effect extended to southern Nigeria the system of land tenure that the British had imposed in the North, giving the state proprietary rights in all land and leaving individuals with only usufructuary rights to land they actually used. Previous owners of undeveloped land were entitled to certificates of occupancy for up to half a hectare in towns, 500 hectares for farming, and 5,000 hectares for grazing. Aspiring landowners could obtain similar areas by application to the authorities – state governors in urban areas and local governments in the countryside – who could charge rents and revoke grants almost at will.[87]

Obasanjo claimed that this remarkably authoritarian decree 'was meant to discourage land hoarding and land speculation'. It won immediate applause from the left as 'a solid foundation for an egalitarian social and economic order in Nigeria. We should all be proud of this great soldier; this illustrous [sic] son of Nigeria.'[88] On the right, by contrast, it was denounced by chiefs, whose control of unused land was a major source of power and income, and by the Yoruba elite, with whom Obasanjo was so often in conflict. They condemned the measure as 'an unjustifiable attack on landowning families … the most explosive legislation ever enacted in this country'.[89]

Although Obasanjo considered the Land Use Decree one of his regime's main achievements and deliberately entrenched it in the 1979 constitution,[90] it remained a subject of controversy for the next thirty years. Its practical impact was less than many had expected, partly because it was badly drafted and almost unworkable in the South, where much land was held by families rather than individuals. Illegal private sales of unused land continued, more expensively. Land speculation in Lagos greatly increased, while the opportunities for corruption in issuing certificates of occupancy were enormous. The chief effect – and, some thought, the chief intention – was to make access to unused land more easily available to aspiring capitalists such as military officers, civil servants, and businessmen. As one critic observed, 'There is some irony in the prospect of agrarian capitalism being founded upon the abolition of private property in land.'[91]

A further area of government intervention concerned wages and industrial relations. The best available data suggest that although better-off urban families prospered during the oil boom, overall living standards fell by about 10% between 1974–5 and 1978–9, with an increase in rural wages outweighed by a decline in urban earnings due mainly to the erosion of the massive Udoji increases of 1974 by subsequent inflation.[92] One estimate suggests that between 1973–4 and 1982 the share of labour income in total income fell by perhaps one-third, despite the increase in the labour force.[93] Such increased inequality was characteristic of economies experiencing oil booms. The surprising point is that it did not provoke industrial unrest. One reason probably was that the rural background of most Nigerian industrial workers and the great social mobility of recent decades encouraged workers to hope that a period of stable wage-labour would enable them to move into self-employment. Another reason was the fragmentation of the multi-ethnic labour force in many small enterprises and economic centres: in 1975, Nigeria's 881,198 trade unionists were divided among 1,170 distinct unions. Since independence, these workers had come together in widespread strikes only on the three occasions – in 1964, 1971, and 1975 – when official commissions had recommended across-the-board pay increases and workers had struck to enforce them. Obasanjo's government made no such award.[94]

Yet the most important restraint on industrial action during Obasanjo's regime was state repression. Legislation in 1976 defined almost all major industries as essential services, banned strikes in them, laid down dispute settlement procedures, and authorised the detention of troublesome union leaders.[95] Having encouraged the four existing trade union federations to unite into a single organisation, the government then refused to recognise it on the grounds that its leadership was undemocratic and corrupt. Instead, the authorities amalgamated existing organisations into 42 industrial unions and a single federation, the Nigerian Labour Congress, inaugurated in February 1978. 'I encouraged the Union leadership to be openly and occasionally antagonistic to maintain credibility with their followers,' Obasanjo patronisingly recalled.[96] When they issued an ultimatum to the government to end the wage freeze and restore trade union rights, however, he forced them to withdraw it under threat of disbandment.[97]

By 1978 Obasanjo had moved far from the unwilling successor of February 1976. As Reuben Abati later remarked, 'Running Nigeria is such a complex assignment that can bring forth hitherto uncharted depths of a man's character.'[98] In February 1977 Awolowo's newspaper wrote of Obasanjo's 'brilliant performance' during 'his first major outing' at FESTAC. In the same month he directed that Murtala's portrait need no longer accompany his own on office walls.[99] In March he removed several senior officers from the Federal Executive Council. By October, diplomats were reporting his growing confidence, his domination of council meetings, and his successful forays into international diplomacy. A year later they were describing him as 'increasingly domineering'.[100] In the meantime, evidence of extensive corruption within the regime had come to light, implicating Yar'Adua in seeking payment for awarding contracts for new ships, two senior public figures in receiving commissions from suppliers to FESTAC, two Commissioners for Industries in demanding kickbacks from the establishment of a motor assembly plant, several individuals close to the government in illegal foreign exchange transactions, and the regime as a whole in lavish award of contracts during its last weeks in office.[101] By his own account, Obasanjo had sold all his shareholdings when he became head of state. Diplomats reported him to be notoriously corrupt, but, if so, he was remarkably discreet about it, for no hard evidence has appeared and his critics' flimsy accusations were easily refuted.[102] In other respects, too, discontent mounted, peaking in April 1978 when student riots coincided with the first serious difficulty in the political transition programme.[103] 'Like in the final days of Gowon,' a periodical commented,

> there is now widespread disaffection and disillusionment evident in the recent student unrest, the grumblings of the middle class, the hardships suffered by the masses, the soaring consumer prices (in this case aggravated by a wage freeze and disincentives to national productivity) and the intimidation and self-censorship of the mass media …
>
> All these are worsened by the emphasis on discipline and sacrifice which has gone further into regimenting the lives of individuals, whilst the nation continues to bear the brunt of a heavy and grandiose military budget.[104]

Behind this discontent lay renewed economic instability. With some exaggeration, a new Commissioner for Finance who took office in March 1977 recalled that 'the country was on the brink of economic collapse' as expenditure outran revenue.[105] Austerity measures averted the immediate crisis, but it returned in January 1978 when oil prices fell for the first time since the great increases of the early 1970s. The decline was checked, but only at the cost of lower output that reduced the government's annual oil revenue by 15%.[106] This and a severely deflationary budget in April 1978 reduced GDP by about 7% during that year, open default being avoided only by delaying payments. Obasanjo's last budget in March 1979, which banned foreign exchange allocations for schooling abroad and abolished car loans to civil servants, came in retrospect to be seen as the end of the post-independence boom and the beginning of middle class decline.[107]

In the event, rather than Obasanjo bequeathing an economic crisis to his civilian successors in October 1979, the oil market came to his rescue when the Iranian Revolution of 1978–9 drove up the price of Nigerian light crude from less than $15 per barrel at the beginning of 1979 to $40 in early 1981, a price not equalled in real terms for another 27 years.[108] In another sense, however, Obasanjo did bequeath a new problem. The oil boom of the 1970s had left the world awash with funds seeking profitable investment outlets. During 1977, he recalled, 'international bankers were descending upon my government in droves. They pressed the case that our economic strength was such that we were grossly underborrowed, especially for a nation with such a visionary development program.'[109] Although he was averse to borrowing, the alternative was to interrupt the development programme. With IMF and World Bank approval, the government decided in July 1977 to seek a 'jumbo' loan of $1 billion – an exceptionally large sum for a new borrower – from a syndicate of banks. The agreement was signed in January 1978. Although the government declared that the loan was 'not intended for balance of payments purposes,' it was in fact used to meet a deficit on imported plant and machinery.[110]

This was not Nigeria's first foreign borrowing – the World Bank had lent independent Nigeria nearly as much, including the money for the Kainji Dam – but the jumbo loan was the first large sum on commercial terms from private creditors. It aroused immediate radical criticism. 'The network of subservience to western capitalism which it further entrenches is going to lead us to further debts, further loans, ad-infinitum,' the Marxist historian Bala Usman protested.[111] The government was not swayed. In July 1978 it announced its intention to raise a second $1 billion loan on slightly worse terms, again to pay for imported equipment.[112] This proved more difficult, because the oil market and Nigerian finances had meanwhile deteriorated and the negotiations became confused with other deals in which Nigeria and the bankers were interested. Only $750 million was subscribed. Thereafter international bankers were wary of Nigerian jumbos, but they continued to support loans for specific federal projects to the extent of $3,233 million by the end of Obasanjo's tenure, plus $258 million for state projects. The security for all these loans was future oil revenue. In all, Nigeria borrowed $4,983 million from financial markets during the last two years of Obasanjo's regime.[113]

Some later critics were to see the balance of payments problems of 1977–9 and the attendant jumbo loans as the beginning of Nigeria's subsequent economic disaster.[114] Yet the revival of the oil market relieved the payments crisis and the level of Nigeria's external debt in 1980 – 14% of GDP – was relatively low, comparing favourably, for example, with Indonesia's 27%.[115] The major increase of foreign debt came after Obasanjo left office: by 1983 it amounted to $16,890 million.[116] Later in his career he would claim to have set Nigeria on a growth path and handed over 'a healthy economy with robust reserve[s] in which the naira exchanged for two dollars [actually $1.67].'[117] 'On the basis of the foundation which we have laid,' he declared on leaving office, '… I see Nigeria among the leading ten countries in the world by the year 2000.'[118] Later critics, by contrast, saw rather a catalogue of weaknesses: an overvalued currency; a stagnant agriculture; an over expanded public sector; restraints on investment rather than consumption; pervasive inefficiency and corruption; inflation; and a mass of expensive, ill-planned, and often uncompleted projects.[119]

Perhaps the truth lay between these extremes. Between 1973 and 1979, by one calculation, real per capita GDP had grown at an average of 0.6% per cent per year.[120] This was a poor result when compared with Nigeria's ambitions and opportunities, but not a total disaster where population was growing so fast. Obasanjo did not succeed in launching Nigeria into sustained growth. Nor was he responsible for the catastrophe that befell the economy after he left office. But he did not cushion his successors against the deteriorating global economic environment that they would face.

NOTES

1. Liman Ciroma in *Weekly Trust*, 18 September 1998.
2. Quoted in Okion Ojigbo, *Nigeria returns to civilian rule* (Lagos, 1980), p. 74.
3. Obasanjo, interviewed in *Africa* (London), June 1976, p. 11; *Newbreed*, end December 1977, p. 32.
4. Stanley Macebuh in *Daily Times*, 1 October 1979.
5. Liman Ciroma in *Weekly Trust*, 18 September 1998.
6. Obasanjo, *Not my will*, p. 82.
7. Soyinka, *You must set forth*, p. 276.
8. Obasanjo, *March of progress*, p. 185.
9. *Daily Times*, 1 April 1976.
10. *New Nigerian*, 3 April 1976; *Nigerian Tribune*, 1 April 1976; *Daily Times*, 30 June 1976.
11. Facey to Mackilligin, 10 January 1978, FCO 65/2070/1.
12. Othman in O'Brien et al., *Contemporary West African states*, p. 129; Fayemi, 'Threats', pp. 167 n.42, 214.
13. Obasanjo, *Call to duty*, pp. 67–8.
14. Central Bank of Nigeria, *The changing structure of the Nigerian economy and implications for development* (Lagos, 2000), p. 53; David Bevan, Paul Collier, and Jan Willem Gunning, *Nigeria and Indonesia* (Oxford, 1999), p. 186; Forrest, *Politics*, pp. 136–7, 184.
15. *West Africa*, 6 December 1982, p. 3147; Tom Forrest, 'Agricultural policies in Nigeria 1900–78', in Judith Heyer, Pepe Roberts, and Gavin Williams (ed.), *Rural development in tropical Africa* (London, 1981), p. 241.
16. *West Africa*, 15 May 1978, pp. 929–31.
17. Bevan et al., *Nigeria and Indonesia*, p. 186; *New Nigerian*, 18 March 1978; Forrest, *Politics*, p. 136.
18. 'Femi Ademiluyi, *From prisoner to president: the political metamorphosis of Olusegun Obasanjo* (Osogbo, 2006), p. 43.
19. *New Nigerian*, 22 May 1976.
20. Abiodun O. Falusi, 'Agricultural development: Operation Feed the Nation', in Oyeleye Oyediran (ed.), *Survey of Nigerian affairs 1976–1977* (Lagos, 1981), pp. 61–4; *West Africa*, 11 October 1982, p. 2642.
21. Obasanjo, *March of progress*, p. 258; Obasanjo, *Call to duty*, pp. 67–9.
22. Obasanjo, *Not my will*, p. 80; Shehu Shagari, *Beckoned to serve: an autobiography* (Ibadan, 2001), p. 189; Farris and Bomoi, *Shehu Musa Yar'Adua*, pp. 130–1.

23. Francis Idachuba, 'Policy options for African agriculture', in Jean Drèze and Amartya Sen (ed.), *The political economy of hunger* (3 vols, Oxford, 1990–1), vol. 3, p. 201.

24. Gunilla Andrae and Björn Beckman, *The wheat trap: bread and underdevelopment in Nigeria* (London, 1985), Ch.6; Gavin Williams, 'The World Bank in rural Nigeria: revisited', *Review of African Political Economy*, 43 (1988), 63.

25. Z.A. Bonat, 'Agriculture', in M.O. Kayode and Y.B. Usman (ed.), *Nigeria since independence: the first twenty-five years: volume II: the economy* (Ibadan, 1989), p. 78. Andrae and Beckman, *Wheat trap*, p. 118, reckoned the cost of Bakalori at N20,000 per hectare.

26. Muhammed Muhammed Gwandu, 'The politics of rural development in the area of the Sokoto-Rima River Basin Development Authority', Ph.D. thesis, University of Leeds, 1987, pp. ii, 186–7, 276, 296–307, 325–52.

27. A. Kolawole, 'Environmental change and the South Chad Irrigation Project (Nigeria)', *Journal of Arid Environments*, 13 (1987), 169.

28. Hans-Otto Sano, *The political economy of food in Nigeria 1960–1982: a discussion on peasants, state, and world economy*, Scandinavian Institute of African Studies Research Report no. 65 (Uppsala, 1983), pp. 37–58; World Bank, *Accelerated development in sub-Saharan Africa: an agenda for action* (Washington DC, 1981), p. 53.

29. *New Nigerian*, 18 November 1987; Obasanjo, *Not my will*, p. 79; Bevan et al., *Nigeria and Indonesia*, p. 171.

30. Elizabeth Kirk Stewart, 'Banks, governments, and risk: medium-term, syndicated international capital market loans to Nigeria, 1977–1983', Ph.D. thesis, London School of Economics, 1985, p. 114; *Petroleum Economist*, March 1975 p. 109, January 1976 p. 13, July 1976 p. 262, July 1977 p. 277, March 1978 p. 105.

31. *West Africa*, 20 April 1976, p. 586; *Daily Times*, 2 April 1976.

32. L.H. Schätzl, *Petroleum in Nigeria* (Ibadan, 1969), pp. 33, 38; *Petroleum Economist*, January 1976, p. 13.

33. Nicholas Shaxson, 'New approaches to volatility: dealing with the "resource curse" in sub-Saharan Africa', *International Affairs*, 81 (2005), 313.

34. *Petroleum Economist*, November 1977, p. 454.

35. P.C. Asiodu, *Nigeria and the oil question* (Lagos, 1979), pp. 12–13, 39–40; Obasanjo, *Not my will*, pp. 82–3; Khan, *Nigeria*, p. 72.

36. *Petroleum Economist*, July 1974 p. 273, January 1978 pp. 27–8, March 1978 p. 107; Obasanjo, *Not my will*, pp. 83–4.

37. Obasanjo, *March of progress*, pp. 127–33.

38. Lewis, *Growing apart*, p. 190; Bevan et al., *Nigeria and Indonesia*, p. 58.

39. Bevan et al., *Nigeria and Indonesia*, pp. 114–16; Xavier Sala-i-Martin and Arovind Subramanian, 'Addressing the natural resource curse: an illustration from Nigeria', IMF Working Paper WP/03/139 (2003), pp. 13–17, http://www.imf.org/external/pubs/ft/wp/2003/wp03139.pdf (accessed 5 October 2008).

40. Forrest, *Politics*, p. 151; Olujimi Jolaoso, *In the shadows: recollections of a pioneer diplomat* (Lagos, 1991), p. 130; *Daily Times*, 1 April 1977; Obasanjo, *Not my will*, p. 87; below, pp. 207, 271, 275, 305.

41. Central Bank, *Changing structure*, pp. 68–9.

42. *West Africa*, 1 December 1980, p. 2415; Paul Collins, 'The state, foreign enterprise and local equity participation: the West African experience', African Studies Association of the United Kingdom conference paper, September 1980, p. 14; *Daily Times*, 2 October 1979.

43. Forrest, *Politics*, p. 139; Tom Forrest, *The advance of African capital: the growth of Nigerian private enterprise* (London, 1994), passim.

44. Obasanjo, *March of progress*, pp. 387–8; Obasanjo, *Not my will*, pp. 92–5.

45. Terisa Turner, 'Two refineries: a comparative study of technology transfer to the Nigerian refining industry', *World Development*, 5 (1977), 242–6; Obasanjo, *Not my will*, p. 85; *African Guardian*, 5 June 1986, p. 19.

46. Ayodeji Olukoju, '"Never expect power always": electricity consumers' response to monopoly, corruption and inefficient services in Nigeria', *African Affairs*, 103 (2004), 64; *Daily Times*, 21 December 1977, 3 January 1978, 2 October 1979.
47. Sayre P. Schatz, *Nigerian capitalism* (Berkeley, 1977), p. ix.
48. Thomas J. Biersteker, *Multinationals, the state, and control of the Nigerian economy* (Princeton, 1987), pp. 86, 191–3; Obasanjo, *March of progress*, p. 391.
49. Cole in Ekeh et al., *Nigeria*, p. 290.
50. Claude Ake in *Daily Times*, 15 December 1978.
51. Lewis, *Growing apart*, Ch.4; Bevan et al., *Nigeria and Indonesia*, passim.
52. Terry Lynn Karl, *The paradox of plenty: oil booms and petrol-states* (Berkeley, 1997), pp. 198–207.
53. Sala-i-Martin and Subramanian, 'Addressing', pp. 16, 39; Bevan et al., *Nigeria and Indonesia*, p. 65; Soares, *Oil and politics*, p. 67.
54. Alli, *Federal Republic*, p. 253; Bevan et al., *Nigeria and Indonesia*, p. 61.
55. A.D. Yahaya, 'Local government reform: the military initiative', in Ekeh et al., *Nigeria*, Ch.13; Rotimi T. Suberu, *Federalism and ethnic conflict in Nigeria* (Washington DC, 2001), p. 108; Dudley, *Introduction*, p. 112.
56. Obasanjo, *March of progress*, p. 167.
57. *Daily Times*, 7 September 1976.
58. Patrick Avwenagbiku, *Olusegun Obasanjo and his footprints* (Abuja, 2000), p. 38; Olagbaju, 'Seasons', p. 329.
59. Forrest, *Politics*, p. 148.
60. Bade Onimode, 'The performance of the economy', in Kayode and Usman, *Nigeria*, p. 284; below, p. 210.
61. Onukaba Adinoyi-Ojo, 'Lest we forget: the Obasanjo years in government', in Hans d'Orville (ed.), *Beyond freedom: letters to Olusegun Obasanjo* (New York, 1996), p. 672; Obasanjo, *Not my will*, p. 82; Obasanjo, *Africa embattled*, p. 77.
62. Obasanjo, *Africa embattled*, p. 76.
63. Obasanjo, *March of progress*, p. 84; *Nigerian Tribune,* 1 April 1979.
64. Obasanjo, *March of progress*, p. 64.
65. *Daily Times*, 29 September 1989; *New Nationalist*, April 1976.
66. *Nigerian Tribune*, 14 December 1978; Elaigwu, *Gowon*, p. 161 .
67. *Nigerian Tribune*, 1 May 1978.
68. *Nigerian Tribune*, 7 and 20 April 1978; *Daily Times*, 27 April 1978; Williams to Owen, 5 January 1979, FCO 65/2215/2.
69. *Nigerian Tribune*, 29 April 1978; British High Commission, Lagos, to FCO, 31 March 1978, FCO 65/2070/35; Wilson to Hodge, 2 May 1978, FCO 65/2070/37; *African Concord*, 26 June 1986, p. 19.
70. *Nigerian Tribune*, 1 May 1978; Claude S. Phillips, 'Nigeria's new political institutions, 1975–9', *Journal of Modern African Studies*, 18 (1980), 17–18.
71. Obasanjo, *Not my will*, p. 89.
72. Below, p. 74.
73. Obasanjo, *March of progress*, pp. 190, 186.
74. *Daily Times*, 28 November 1992; Lewis, *Growing apart*, p. 183; J.C. and P. Caldwell, 'Cause and sequence in the reduction of postnatal abstinence in Ibadan City, Nigeria', and I.O. Orubuloye, 'Child-spacing among rural Yoruba women: Ekiti and Ibadan divisions in Nigeria', in Hilary J. Page and Ron Lesthaeghe (ed.), *Child-spacing in tropical Africa: traditions and change* (London, 1981), pp. 187, 228; 'Dupe Olatunbosun, *Nigeria's neglected rural majority* (Ibadan, 1975), p. 11.
75. World Bank, *World development report* (New York), 1990 p. 238, and 2000–1 p. 277.
76. Sandra T. Barnes, *Patrons and power: creating a political community in metropolitan Lagos* (Manchester, 1986), pp. 3, 11; Akin Ogunpola and Oladeji Ojo, 'Housing as an indi-

cator of urban poverty – the case of metropolitan Lagos', in Nigerian Economic Society, *Poverty in Nigeria* (Ibadan, 1976), p. 112.

77. International Labour Office, *First things first: meeting the basic needs of the people of Nigeria* (Addis Ababa, 1981), p. 217; Francis Teal, 'The objectives of development policy in Nigeria and the growth of the economy since 1950', conference paper, School of Oriental and African Studies, London, 1983, p. 18.

78. Archibald Callaway, 'Nigeria's indigenous education: the apprentice system', *Odu,* 1, 1 (July 1964), 62.

79. Bevan et al., *Nigeria and Indonesia,* p. 127; Margaret Peil, *Lagos: the city is the people* (London, 1991), p. 92.

80. International Labour Office, *First things first,* p. 13; Ogunpola and Ojo in Nigerian Economic Society, *Poverty in Nigeria,* p. 115.

81. International Labour Office, *First things first,* pp. 9, 13, 232; Lewis, *Growing apart,* p. 198.

82. Anthony Kirk-Greene and Douglas Rimmer, *Nigeria since 1970: a political and economic outline* (London, 1981), p. 117; A.L. Mabogunje, 'The problems of a metropolis', in P.C. Lloyd, A.L. Mabogunje, and B. Awe (ed.), *The city of Ibadan* (Cambridge, 1967), p. 265.

83. Laurent Fourchard, 'A new name for an old practice: vigilantes in south-western Nigeria', *Africa,* 78 (2008), 18–19; *West Africa,* 19 January 1981, p. 136.

84. *Daily Times,* 2 April 1976; Femi Olokesusi, Boye Agunbiade, J.E. Ogbuozobe, and Demola Adeagbo, 'Housing perspective of poverty in Nigeria', in D. Olusanya Ajakaiye and Ade S. Olomola (ed.), *Poverty in Nigeria: a multi-dimensional perspective* (Ibadan, 2003), p. 293; Abiodun Olufemi Sotunmbi, 'Nigeria's policy towards southern Africa – 1966–1979', Ph.D. thesis, University of Keele, 1989, p. 58.

85. Barnes, *Patrons and power,* pp. 67–8.

86. *Newbreed,* end January 1977, pp. 22–3.

87. *Daily Times,* 30 March 1978; Wilson to Hodge, 2 May 1978, FCO 65/2070/37; Ohiortenuan in Tamuno and Atanda, *Nigeria,* pp. 152–3.

88. Obasanjo, *Not my will,* p. 109; Lam Adesina in *Nigerian Tribune,* 5 April 1978.

89. *Daily Times,* 31 March 1978; *Nigerian Tribune,* 3 April 1978.

90. *Daily Times,* 21 September 1989; below, p. 91.

91. Paul Francis, '"For the use and common benefit of all Nigerians": consequences of the 1978 land nationalization', *Africa,* 54, 3 (1984), 5–28 (quotation on p. 24); George Taiwo Irele, 'Land and agricultural policy in Nigeria under military governments, 1966–1985', Ph.D. thesis, University of Cambridge, 1990, Ch.3; Peil, *Lagos,* pp. 142–5, 170; Peter Koehn, 'State land allocation and class formation in Nigeria', *Journal of Modern African Studies,* 21 (1983), 461–81.

92. International Labour Office, *First things first,* pp. 224, 227; Bevan et al., *Nigeria and Indonesia,* pp. 54, 102; D. Olu Ajakaiye and V.A. Adeyeye, *The nature of poverty in Nigeria* (Ibadan, 2001), p. 38.

93. Iyayi in Usman, *Nigeria,* p. 37.

94. Peter Waterman, 'Consciousness, organisation and action amongst Lagos portworkers', *Review of African Political Economy,* 13 (May 1978), 50–1; Iyayi in Usman, *Nigeria,* p. 31; Robin Cohen, *Labour and politics in Nigeria 1945–71* (London, 1974), pp. 186–96.

95. Julius O. Ihonvbere, *Labour, state and capital in Nigeria's oil industry* (Lewiston, 1998), p. 81.

96. *Daily Times.* 16 and 26 February 1977, 3 March 1977; *Africa* (London), August 1979, p. 58; Obasanjo, *Not my will,* pp. 76–7.

97. Boldt to Dunlop, 19 June 1979, FCO 65/2211/122.

98. *Guardian,* 27 July 2007.

99. *Nigerian Tribune,* 15 February 1977; Hodge to Roberts, 16 February 1977, FCO 65/1903/14.

100. Falle to Owen, 18 October 1977, FCO 65/1904/71; Johnson to Falle, 19 October 1977, FCO 65/1904/73; Brown to Carrington, 24 October 1979, FCO 65/2213/276.
101. Falle to FCO, 28 April 1977, FCO 65/1930/2; *Daily Times*, 17 November 1977; Heath to Mansfield, 20 October 1977, FCO 65/1930/34; Kennedy to Johnson, 30 October 1979, FCO 65/2214/281.
102. Obasanjo, *Not my will*, pp. 216–25.
103. See below, p. 90.
104. Chris Okolie, 'The drift begins', *Newbreed*, mid May 1978, p. 3.
105. Oluleye, *Architecturing a destiny*, p. 139.
106. *Daily Times*, 11 January 1978; Stewart, 'Banks', p. 114; *Petroleum Economist*, June 1979, p. 224.
107. Lewis, *Growing apart*, p. 149; *Daily Times*, 2 April 1979; Brown to Owen, 26 April 1979, FCO 65/2224/63; *Newswatch*, 3 October 1988, pp. 38–9.
108. Stewart, 'Banks', p. 114.
109. Olusegun Obasanjo, *Africa in perspective: myths and realities* (New York, 1987), p. 22.
110. Obasanjo, *Africa embattled*, p. 31; Stewart, 'Banks', pp. 158–60; *Newbreed*, end May 1978, p. 19; Oluleye, *Architecturing a destiny*, p. 137.
111. Yusufu Bala Usman, *For the liberation of Nigeria: essays and lectures 1969–1978* (London, 1979), p. 195.
112. Padraic Fallon, 'The extraordinary Nigerian jumbo', *Euromoney*, November 1978, pp. 10–23.
113. Stewart, 'Banks', p. 154.
114. E.g. Olu Falae, *The way forward for Nigeria: the economy and polity* (Akure, 2004), pp. 29–33.
115. Lewis, *Growing apart*, p. 192.
116. *West Africa*, 3 December 1984, p. 2461.
117. *Newswatch*, 16 November 1998, p. 20.
118. Obasanjo, *March of progress*, p. 487.
119. Lewis, *Growing apart*, pp. 149–50.
120. Bevan et al., *Nigeria and Indonesia*, p. 185.

7
African Liberation

The seven months of Murtala Muhammed's leadership had set clearer lines of foreign policy than economic strategy. Nigeria's security was little threatened by its weak neighbours, among whom it sought to assert a leadership consequent on its size and oil wealth. The main external challenges came from two other directions. One was the revival of the Cold War between the two superpowers during the mid 1970s, now fought less in Europe or South-East Asia than in Afghanistan and tropical Africa. Between 1970–3 and 1977–8, the average annual value of arms imported into sub-Saharan Africa, at constant prices, rose from $370 million to $2,500 million, the chief recipients being Angola and Ethiopia.[1] Angola was the link with the other major challenge of the period, for the presence there of a Cuban army numbering at its peak some 36,000 men accelerated the destruction of white power in southern Africa and the final liberation of the continent from colonial rule.

Obasanjo was eager to contribute to that liberation and to give his country a leading position in the African continent. To that extent he continued the two main lines of policy that he had helped to formulate during Murtala's regime. In both fields he gained only modest success. Further major advances in southern Africa came only after he left office, although some came as the result of policies he had supported. Nigerian leadership, similarly, proved difficult to assert where every African state jealously guarded its still novel independence, although Nigeria's influence within the continent certainly increased during Obasanjo's tenure. His grasp of foreign affairs was surer than his command of economics and he moved with remarkable ease into the world of international statesmen, who valued his good sense and intelligence. His chief innovation in foreign policy was to loosen Nigeria's remaining ties with Britain, which had been so important to Gowon, and to align Nigeria more closely with the United States, a step that contrasted with Murtala's attitude but was dictated by Nigeria's interests and the realities of world power. It demonstrated the open-minded pragmatism that generally informed his statesmanship.

The immediate reason for tension with Britain was suspicion of British collusion in Murtala's assassination and resentment of the British government's refusal to return Gowon to Nigeria for trial. During 1976 Nigeria seriously considered breaking diplomatic relations.[2] Obasanjo refused to visit Britain, discouraged his officials from doing so, and obtained the Supreme Military Council's authority to withdraw Nigeria from the Commonwealth if necessary.[3] He may have used this tension to foster Nigerian nationalism, but probably his chief aim was to mobilise Nigerian public opinion against Britain's southern African policies.[4] Deliberate polarisation of this kind – a common feature of Yoruba political behaviour, perfected by Awolowo – was a tactic Obasanjo used several times during his career.

The changing relationship also had economic roots, for the development of North Sea oil made Britain a competitor rather than a customer for Nigerian oil, while the rapid increase in Nigeria's imports made it Britain's largest market outside the United States and Europe.[5] As Nigeria's balance of trade with Britain deteriorated, its ties grew more distant, although Obasanjo was on reasonable terms with Prime Minister Callaghan and the two countries collaborated at intervals over southern African affairs.

Another staple of Gowon's foreign policy to which Obasanjo gave lower priority was ECOWAS. Although he declared it in 1978 to be 'the last bastion of hope for the economic development of our sub-region',[6] his earlier treatment of the organisation had been cavalier. To win francophone support for ECOWAS, Gowon had agreed that its headquarters should be in Lomé, but Obasanjo insisted that if Nigeria was to provide 30% of the budget, the headquarters must be in Lagos. When President Eyadema of Togo demanded compensation, an angry Obasanjo replied that 'Nigeria would not give him a kobo [cent].' An office finally opened in Lagos in 1977, but the organisation achieved nothing during Obasanjo's tenure, chiefly owing to the extreme suspicion shown by its francophone members, who saw it as a potential means of Nigerian domination, and the offence that Nigeria's young leaders caused by insisting on their country's 'historical responsibility' to make Nigeria 'a national focus, the point of reference for all black peoples in the world'.[7]

Resentment of these pretensions nearly wrecked the climax of Obasanjo's first year in office, the Second World Black and African Festival of Arts and Culture (FESTAC) held in Lagos in February 1977. Originating in the *négritude* cultural movement most powerful in Senegal, the plan for the festival was adopted by Gowon, postponed by Murtala, and finally implemented by Obasanjo as a display of Nigerian cultural leadership. President Senghor of Senegal threatened at one point to boycott it when North African delegates were invited to the associated symposium. Mired in corruption and costing Nigeria at least the official figure of N141 million ($217 million), it was denounced for extravagance and for seeking, in Awolowo's words, 'to revive a primitive culture'.[8] Obasanjo, as Grand Patron, may equally have approached the festival with misgiving, but his contributions impressed the delegates and he was himself impressed by the demonstration of 'an underlying common core which symbolises the political awareness and unity of African and Black peoples the world over'.[9] At the finale, as Soyinka patronisingly put it, 'his childlike appreciation was quite touching, revealing an unexpected aspect of the soldier.'[10] This was probably the period in Obasanjo's life at which cultural authenticity was most important to him.

Yet he had harder purposes. During Murtala's tenure, Obasanjo had already shown his commitment to the liberation of southern Africa from white control, seeing it, like many Nigerians, as a struggle for noble ideals less prevalent in their own nationalist movement.[11] Obasanjo made it the centrepiece of his foreign policy. Nigerian armed intervention, although considered, was not logistically feasible. Instead the regime made financial grants to liberation movements, enabled them to open offices in Lagos, and offered sanctuary and education to refugees.[12] 'You've given us hope', Obasanjo told a group of young South African activists from the Soweto Revolt of 1976. 'Young people with stones facing an army – imagine what you would be able to do if you had better weapons and training.... So we *are* going to support you. But whatever you do, do not get trapped in exile like the others. Go home and fight.'[13] In the event he was often disappointed by the refugees' disunity and reluctance to go home and fight, but Nigeria claimed to have invested well over a billion dollars in the liberation struggle.[14] Yet Obasanjo did not romanticise war, having experienced and hated it. He was willing to cooperate with any initiative likely to facilitate liberation, even if it earned him political unpopularity. As a diplomat remarked, 'The pursuit of Nigerian aspirations is less brash than it was under Muhammed's regime. But it is no less determined.'[15]

The dominant fact of the international situation facing Obasanjo in February 1976 was the Cuban army's presence in Angola and its implications for the Cold War and the liberation of southern Africa, especially Zimbabwe (Rhodesia) where conflict was most acute. In 1965 its white regime had declared Rhodesia independent. By 1976 two externally based black guerilla movements had penetrated into the border regions: the Zimbabwe African National Union (ZANU), based among the majority Shona people and led by Robert Mugabe, and the Zimbabwe African People's Union (ZAPU), based among the minority Ndebele of the south-west and led by Joshua Nkomo. An unarmed political movement, the African National Council, operated within Zimbabwe.[16] That the Cuban presence might transform this situation was widely recognised, not least by the American Secretary of State, Henry Kissinger, who feared that if the guerillas could not defeat the white Rhodesian forces, they might seek Cuban aid, which 'would put us in the position of either acquiescing to another Cuban move in that area and thus destroying governments on our side or resisting in the name of white supremacy, and the latter would be impossible'.[17] The white Rhodesians might even provoke Cuban intervention in the hope of attracting Western protection. Alternatively, if white Rhodesia collapsed, the rival guerilla movements might fight one another and call in foreign aid, as in Angola.[18] In April 1976, when the Central Intelligence Agency predicted that Cuban troops would be involved in Zimbabwe before the end of the year, Kissinger abandoned his previous indifference and visited southern Africa, proposing a plan for majority rule in Zimbabwe within two years, with very substantial safeguards for the white population. The plan was to be pressed on the white regime by the South African government in return for a reduction of Western pressure on its own policies, especially in Namibia, while the African frontline states would press the proposals on the guerilla forces, undertake to keep the Cubans out, and neutralise potential African opponents of the scheme, among whom Kissinger counted Nigeria.[19]

Kissinger's estimate was correct. When the guerilla leaders rejected his proposed safeguards for Europeans and his plan for whites to retain control during the crucial transition period,[20] Osabanjo's government endorsed the rejection, refused to receive a visit from Kissinger, declared that talks with Smith were futile, and insisted that armed struggle was the only solution.[21] While supporting uncompromising positions, however, experience of Angola made the Nigerians anxious to foster unity within the Zimbabwean nationalist movement. In February 1977 they persuaded the OAU Liberation Committee to reject the frontline presidents' advice to recognise only the guerilla movements, instead leaving it open to internal political organisations such as the African National Council to join the newly-formed Patriotic Front.[22]

Nigerian policy on Zimbabwe became more flexible during 1977 in response to the election at the end of 1976 of a more liberal American president, Jimmy Carter, whose victory was greeted by Nigeria's Federal Executive Council with a round of applause.[23] Carter relied heavily on black votes, had experienced the collapse of segregation in the American South, and was a born-again Christian anxious to moralise foreign policy.[24] Zimbabwe and the rest of southern Africa were immediate priorities. As the new Secretary of State, Cyrus Vance, explained, 'Like the previous administration after its conversion, we recognised that identifying the United States with the cause of majority rule was the best way to prevent Soviet and Cuban exploitation of the racial conflicts of southern Africa', but in addition the new regime *believed* in majority rule.[25] Obasanjo was convinced of its good intentions by Carter's special ambassador, Andrew Young, an Afro-American civil rights campaigner who established a close personal friendship with the Nigerian leader and, as the British Foreign Secretary wrote, 'was able to enthuse Third World countries in a way I never could'.[26] When Young visited Lagos in February 1977, Obasanjo said he wanted to see a negotiated settlement in Zimbabwe leading to a multi-racial society, but doubted if it would be possible while Smith remained in power. Young warned that the United States would not assist military action against Rhodesia or press the British to adopt economic sanctions against South Africa, but he did not share the prevailing fear of Cuban intervention – believing that African nationalists would reject foreign domination of any kind – and he believed that a combination of guerilla action and diplomatic pressure could force Smith's regime to relinquish power without full-scale war. He sought Obasanjo's aid to bring the Zimbabwean nationalist groups together at a conference whose demands could then be presented for discussion with Smith and the South Africans. It was now 'a question of kick up arse', as he put it, to which Obasanjo replied that he knew how to deliver that.[27]

Obasanjo later wrote that 'The trio of President Jimmy Carter, Cyrus Vance and Andy Young was the best thing that had ever happened in the history of U.S. policy towards Africa.'[28] He immediately redirected Nigerian policy towards cooperation with them, illustrating his acute sensitivity to power. 'It was thrilling', said the American ambassador, 'to see a strong, powerful leader with control of his country changing the whole relationship between it and the United States.'[29] Short of war, only the United States could put real pressure on the white rulers of southern Africa. Moreover, the reorientation of Nigerian policy coincided exactly with the country's economic interests as its oil exports shifted away from Europe towards the United States, which bought over half of Nigeria's oil exports in January 1977, at a time when Carter's chief domestic priority was energy supply and Obasanjo was eager to secure an American market for Nigeria's projected output of liquefied natural gas.[30] Officially sponsored anti-American protests disappeared from Lagos early in 1977 and left-wing critics were ignored.

The election of the Carter administration also encouraged a new British Foreign secretary, David Owen, to collaborate with Young in drawing up Anglo-American proposals by which a British Resident Commissioner, with Commonwealth or United Nations troops, would take control of Zimbabwe for six months to conduct a democratic election under a constitution providing for majority rule with safeguards for the white population.[31] Although the Patriotic Front immediately rejected this initiative, the fact that it had the American administration's backing made Obasanjo more receptive when he learned of the plan, in April 1977. He later explained that, although sceptical, 'he had eventually gone along with them for two reasons: firstly, because he believed that there were sufficient forces in Rhodesia to edge Smith out and, secondly, because he believed that the United States and the United Kingdom could put sufficient pressure on South Africa to make the South

Africans pressure Smith.'[32] In July 1977 Obasanjo told an OAU meeting that the Nigerian government hoped that the Anglo-American initiative would succeed.[33] His moderation may have been reinforced by a Nigerian mission that visited Zambia and Mozambique in July and August 1977, was disappointed by the slow progress of the guerilla campaign, and reported that it would not be likely to capture Harare within the next five years.[34]

At the end of August, Owen and Young visited Lagos to seek Nigerian agreement to supply troops for the Commonwealth force – which was granted – and to secure Obasanjo's support before attempting to persuade the frontline presidents and the South Africans to press the combatants towards agreement. Obasanjo asked searching questions about the proposed transition and cannot have been fully satisfied by the uncertain answers. In conclusion, however,

> *General Obasanjo* said that despite all the critical factors involved, he thought the plan had a good chance of success. He was not worried about the Front Line Presidents nor about the liberation forces, for whom African leaders could accept partial responsibility.... It was not easy to get Robert Mugabe to give up leadership of the Patriotic Front to Joshua Nkomo but he had been told point blank that he had no choice.[35]

Six days later Owen and Young published their plan[36] and presented it to Smith, while Obasanjo made an 'unofficial' visit to Tanzania, Zambia, Mozambique, and the Democratic Republic of the Congo, urged acceptance of the plan as a basis for negotiation, and believed that he received pledges of support from Presidents Nyerere, Machel, and Mobutu, although President Kaunda of Zambia had reservations.[37] Obasanjo insisted, however, that everything depended on securing the agreement of the Patriotic Front, which regarded the proposals only as a basis for negotiation.[38]

Obasanjo now reaped the reward for his boldness in cooperating with the Carter administration. Hitherto hesitant to travel outside Nigeria, in October 1977 he paid a six-day official visit to the United States that aroused only limited interest in Washington but gave him a new level of international exposure and experience.[39] Addressing Congressmen, he repaid his hosts by stressing 'how much we believe in the good intentions and sincerity of the present United States Administration and their current efforts aimed at averting racial war on our continent'.[40] In a characteristically blunt speech at the White House banquet in his honour, he insisted that armed struggle in southern Africa 'is justifiable and bound to succeed', urging the United States at least to stop investing in South Africa and supplying it with arms.[41] At Howard University he called on black Americans to give the same support to Africa as American Jews gave to Israel.[42] His address to the United Nations General Assembly returned to the Anglo-American proposals, which, despite 'various defects and weaknesses ... may well deserve to be given a chance', provided they led to 'the unequivocal surrender of power by the minority to the majority of the population'.[43] Two weeks later, Nigeria won – on the sixth vote – a long-coveted seat on the Security Council, relying on superpower and Commonwealth support to defeat the OAU's candidate, Niger, in a much resented contest that Obasanjo insisted upon fighting because he believed that the southern African issues preoccupying the Council demanded the greater weight that Nigeria could exert.[44]

When told of this vote, Obasanjo 'was screaming with joy over the telephone'.[45] It was the first concrete advantage to accrue from the new direction he had given to

Nigerian policy and was some reply to the increasingly fierce criticism it incurred. 'Enough of globe-trotting', the *New Nigerian* had greeted his return from America, reminding him of what had happened to Gowon when he became addicted to state visits.[46] More profoundly, Bala Usman denounced a policy that supported Anglo-American proposals 'to instal a puppet regime' designed to frustrate the liberation movements: 'If some Nigerians are so close to Andrew Young, then they have the simple alternative of joining Andrew Young in the U.S.; they have more room for house niggers in the White House.'[47] This was telling criticism and Obasanjo is said to have attempted at this time to secure Usman's dismissal from his university post.[48]

David Owen had known when he published the Anglo-American proposals that they had no chance of acceptance, because the war in Zimbabwe had not yet deadlocked sufficiently for the combatants to prefer negotiation. In the meantime his priorities were to prevent foreign military intervention and to fend off pressure for economic sanctions against South Africa. Within a fortnight of receiving the proposals, both Smith's regime and the South African government had judged the plan unacceptable, while waiting for the guerillas to reject it.[49] Obasanjo soon reached the same conclusion. In discussion with the proposed British Resident Commissioner early in November, Obasanjo said he was happy that nobody had yet rejected the plan:

> In essence, however, he believed that there were only two options now open to us. Either the United States and the United Kingdom should take steps to get rid of Smith, whereupon the frontline presidents (and Nigeria) would get the Patriotic Front to negotiate with us [i.e. Britain] and Smith's successors. Or, we should pause for a time, and allow the Patriotic Front to soften up the regime until it became more reasonable.[50]

'There is increasingly activist, articulate and virulent criticism of Obasanjo's policies, of which Obasanjo himself is very conscious,' the British High Commissioner reported two days later.[51]

In late November 1977, Smith put the matter beyond doubt by announcing that he would negotiate an internal Rhodesian settlement with moderate African leaders, which meant chiefly Bishop Abel Muzorewa of the African National Council. An agreement signed on 3 March 1978 formed Smith, Muzorewa, and two other African internal leaders into an Executive Council and promised an election after one year for those Africans who rejected violence. The Patriotic Front rejected the settlement two days later and the Nigerian government immediately dismissed it as a 'sell-out'. Owen, by contrast, alienated Nigerian leaders by welcoming Smith's ostensible willingness to share power with Africans.[52] As President Carter prepared to pay a return visit to Lagos in April 1978, his National Security Adviser told him that 'Obasanjo ... looks increasingly to us as his distrust of the United Kingdom grows and his personal prestige is engaged in the American connection.'[53] The meeting between the two leaders was described by the British High Commissioner as 'this superb American achievement.'[54] On Zimbabwe, they issued a joint communiqué rejecting the internal settlement but reaffirming the Anglo-American proposals. Privately, the Americans agreed with the foreign ministers of the frontline states, who had been invited to Lagos, on a new attempt to press the two sides in Zimbabwe to negotiate.[55] These talks achieved little, however and Obasanjo distanced himself further from the Anglo-American proposals. In a powerful speech at the OAU summit meeting in July 1978, he declared that the proposals 'appear to have been largely overtaken by events', that 'the Internal Settlement settled nothing', that 'it is only the Patriotic Front which had been fighting the armed struggle', and that it must be supported until a final transfer of power could be negotiated.[56]

During 1978, as the guerilla forces infiltrated deeper into the Zimbabwean countryside, fighting intensified, and the costs of war to the government escalated, most frontline African presidents, their Nigerian supporters, and the American negotiators concentrated on ensuring that those who controlled the guerillas – which meant chiefly Mugabe of ZANU – would be fully represented in any predominantly African government, because otherwise the war against white control would become a civil war among Africans on Angolan lines. The white regime, the internal African leaders, British negotiators, and perhaps President Kaunda of Zambia, on the other hand, would have preferred to exclude the potentially predominant Mugabe, possibly by splitting the Patriotic Front and bringing the more moderate Nkomo into the internal settlement. Smith attempted the latter tactic in June 1978 by suggesting a secret meeting with Nkomo in Lusaka. The British and Americans agreed in the hope that it might lead towards a negotiated settlement. Garba had become close to Nkomo and attended to protect him against accusations of betrayal. Obasanjo appears to have been unhappy with this plan but allowed it to go ahead, sending Garba with a letter to Nkomo warning him to do nothing without Mugabe's agreement. Nkomo took the advice and told Smith at the meeting in August 1978 that he must involved Mugabe in the discussions, but the internal Zimbabwean leaders – fearing to be supplanted by Nkomo – leaked news of the meeting, Mugabe's colleagues and frontline supporters were furious, and Garba was embarrassed.[57] Obasanjo refused to apologise. He tried unsuccessfully to persuade Mugabe to join the talks or accept Nkomo's leadership in a unified Patriotic Front, whose divisions exasperated Nigerians. For a time Obasanjo encouraged a British proposal for an all-party conference that found no support in southern Africa. But at the end of 1978, like all those involved, he could only watch the fighting continue and say that eventually there would have to be talks, external troops, and some neutral authority to restore order.[58] In January 1979, Yar'Adua told Owen 'that enthusiasm for detailed involvement in Rhodesia was waning' as Nigeria's transition to civilian rule absorbed the regime's attention.[59]

Yet Obasanjo's intense commitment to southern African liberation immediately faced a new challenge. In May 1979 the British Conservative Party under Margaret Thatcher won election on a programme undertaking to lift sanctions, restore Rhodesia to legality, and seek the country's international recognition if a settlement could be found acceptable to its people as a whole. Many in the party believed that this condition had been met a month earlier when Muzorewa had won an internal election, in which the Patriotic Front had not participated, held under a constitution that left effective power in white hands.[60] Thatcher, a fellow virtuoso of political power, evoked none of the confidence in Obasanjo that Carter and Young had enjoyed. Fearing that she might shortly recognise Muzorewa's regime, he launched a diplomatic offensive and threatened Britain's economic interests in Nigeria by seizing a tanker believed to be shipping Nigerian oil to South Africa, barring British firms from competing for Nigerian contracts, and nationalising British Petroleum's Nigerian operations, announcing this last decision one day before a Commonwealth Conference in Lusaka in August 1979 that the Nigerians feared might be a prelude to recognition. Obasanjo instructed his representative at the conference to announce

Nigeria's withdrawal from the Commonwealth if treatment of the Rhodesian issue was unsatisfactory.[61]

This was a miscalculation. Although the British government was determined to end the Rhodesian war, abandon sanctions, and grant independence, it was anxious to do so with maximum international support, undertaking at the conference to institute a genuinely democratic constitution, comparable to those granted when decolonising other African states, and to conduct new elections before independence. The latter concession satisfied Nyerere, Kaunda, and other Commonwealth leaders.[62] Although Obasanjo claimed that his threat to British interests had forced a dramatic reversal of policy,[63] in reality British policy had been decided well before the conference and in full awareness of the threat to British interests in Nigeria, including the likelihood that British Petroleum might be nationalised, although the timing of Obasanjo's announcement infuriated the British Foreign Secretary because it cheapened his motives and diminished his political standing.[64]

With characteristically ruthless brinkmanship, Obasanjo authorised Nigeria's continued membership of the Commonwealth only two hours before the conference ended. He remained sceptical of the Lusaka Agreement and the subsequent Lancaster House negotiations, insisting on maintaining the measures against British firms until he left office two months later.[65] The chief effect of his intervention was to exclude Nigeria from any significant role in Rhodesia's independence process, Nigerian troops being barred from the Commonwealth force that monitored the ceasefire arrangements.[66] Nigeria did give financial aid to the Patriotic Front parties that won the final election and Obasanjo rightly reflected that the independence settlement drew heavily on the Anglo-American proposals to which he had committed himself.[67] Yet it was with breathtaking arrogance that he claimed in 1987 that 'Zimbabwe would not have achieved independence at the time it did if not for Nigeria's contribution. That, of course, is not saying that others outside and inside Zimbabwe did not make some significant contribution.'[68]

While the Cuban presence in Angola gave urgency to international concern with Zimbabwe, it also sparked an initial flurry of activity in Namibia that eventually faded into stalemate. Namibia had been administered by South Africa since the First World War. The main liberation movement there, the South-West African People's Organisation (SWAPO), had launched guerilla insurgency in 1965 and had been recognised by the United Nations as sole representative of the Namibian people in 1973, but it made little headway until Portuguese control of neighbouring Angola collapsed in 1975. In January 1976, a United Nations resolution called for supervised elections and South African withdrawal. Three months later, SWAPO's leader, Sam Nujoma, visited Lagos, where Obasanjo permitted him to open an office and made a grant of $500,000.[69] In September the South African government accepted a target date for Namibian independence at the end of 1978, but it also fostered a coalition of minority ethnic groups, the Democratic Turnhalle Alliance (DTA), as an opposition to SWAPO. Believing that South African withdrawal from Namibia was necessary before the Cubans would agree to leave Angola, the Carter administration established a Contact Group of five Western nations to facilitate negotiations between SWAPO and the South Africans, an initiative towards which the OAU and the Nigerians were initially cautiously hopeful. When the DTA published its own independence plan in March 1977, the Contact Group warned that it would not receive international recognition.[70] Obasanjo pressed SWAPO to negotiate, seeking, in mid 1977, to convince Nujoma that, despite his UN recognition, his forces could not simply take control of Namibia. SWAPO, however, rejected any decolonisation scheme that left South Africa in control when the decisive election took place.[71] When Carter visited Lagos in April 1978, he explained the Contact Group's plan for free elections and independence under UN supervision. Obasanjo welcomed it and offered to persuade the Soviet government not to veto it, as he did, although he insisted on including in the communiqué the Nigerian view that SWAPO were the 'authentic leaders of the people'.[72] Yet both Nujoma and the new South African President, P.W. Botha, proved inflexible, so that the negotiations bogged down until the South Africans organised their own elections for a constituent assembly in December 1978, which the DTA won. Addressing the OAU in July 1979, Obasanjo restated his insistence that without SWAPO there could be no settlement, but there had been no progress when he left office three months later.[73]

That was equally true of South Africa itself. Nigeria had firmly opposed apartheid since Abubakar Tafawa Balewa had been instrumental in pressing South Africa to leave the Commonwealth in 1961. Since 1973 Nigeria had chaired the UN's Special Committee on Apartheid. In 1974, it backed a proposal to expel South Africa from the world body, which Western countries vetoed.[74] Obasanjo felt strongly on this subject and appreciated both its significance and its complexity. 'Africa must be saved the holocaust of a racial war', he declared in 1978, while insisting on the need to 'remain open for peaceful change'.[75] His first intervention after taking office was a boycott of the Olympic Games in 1976 because one participant, New Zealand, had sporting ties with South Africa. His discussions with Young and Owen, who both made clear their governments' refusal to impose economic sanctions on South Africa, may have provoked more active Nigerian intervention, as did pressure from radical Nigerian opinion.[76] In March 1977 Garba warned of action against Western firms with South African interests. In July, Obasanjo urged the OAU to 'exert all its weight on the more influential Western powers to bring about a drastic change by vigorously pursuing the sanctions passed by the UN. It is my belief', he added, 'that if these nations respected and implemented the sanctions, the South African Apartheid regime would have been brought round to changing its evil system.'[77]

Once launched on this course, Obasanjo pursued it with characteristic vigour, especially against Britain, whose trade with Nigeria was almost as large as that with South Africa, breeding deep anxiety to avoid choosing between them.[78] In August 1977, Obasanjo opened a United Nations Conference for Action against Apartheid at Lagos with one of his most effective speeches. 'It is in the economic aspects that apartheid is most criminal and most dangerous', he argued. 'It is in that aspect too that it is most vulnerable.' Nigeria, he announced, was listing governments and enterprises economically active in South Africa. 'Such enterprises must decide now to choose between us and our enemies and all that goes with their choice... Foreign contractors who are known to have links or connections with South Africa are already barred from taking part in any tenders of any kind or nature for any transactions or construction works in Nigeria.'[79] In reality, instructions to bar such contractors seem to have gone out after the speech, during September, and purely on Obasanjo's authority, without consideration by the Supreme Military Council. They aroused much opposition among bureaucrats, northern members of the Council, and Nigerian businessmen.[80]

In practice it appears that, apart from British Petroleum, the only British firm to be penalised was Barclays Bank (Nigeria) – already majority owned by the government – from which the regime withdrew all its accounts in March 1978 and imposed further sanctions to punish a statement by the parent bank's chairman that 'Our policy ... is to stay in South Africa and use all the influence we have to try to bring about a happier and fairer society', which Obasanjo was thought to have taken as deliberate defiance and to have exploited in order to serve as warning.[81] The action threw Barclays (Nigeria) into financial difficulty and led at least one firm with large interests in South Africa to liquidate smaller interests in Nigeria, but no other British company appears to have been penalised for its South African connections.[82] Carter was advised in April 1978 that 'the Nigerians seem not to be pressing this anymore,' while Chancellor Schmidt of Germany bluntly announced in Lagos in June that his country would not stop trading with South Africa, without provoking retaliation. A month earlier, Obasanjo's top civil servant told a leading British businessman 'that the Nigerians wished to avoid any overt reference to this matter for as long as possible.' [83] Not only had Obasanjo's initiative clearly run ahead of official opinion, but the deterioration of the economy during 1978 made action increasingly difficult. The records show, however, that Obasanjo's threat caused great anxiety to the British government at that time.[84]

A more important victory, which followed closely on Obasanjo's speech to the United Nations denouncing the arming of South Africa by Western governments, was a mandatory arms embargo imposed by the Security Council in November 1977, although the Western powers vetoed a simultaneous proposal for mandatory economic sanctions.[85] As yet, however, these manoeuvres had no significant impact within South Africa, where Obasanjo's period in office saw growing repression: the crushing of the Soweto uprising in 1976, the outlawing of the Black Consciousness movement, and the murder of Steve Biko, all culminating in November 1977 in the National Party's most sweeping electoral victory.[86]

In July 1979, three months before Obasanjo's regime left office, Danjuma confessed that there was 'precious little to show by way of successes' in foreign policy since the recognition of the MPLA in Murtala's time.[87] This was true not only of southern Africa but of Obasanjo's well-intentioned but ambitious attempts to mediate in disputes elsewhere in the continent. He had one success in 1977 in persuading the rulers of Benin and Togo to settle a border dispute and reopen their frontier.[88] With his other neighbour, Cameroun, he suffered a more significant defeat, for in August 1977 he failed to persuade President Ahidjo to reopen an agreement made by Gowon ceding to Cameroun the disputed Bakassi Peninsula on their southern border, an area newly important for the claims it allowed to offshore oil.[89] In more distant parts of the continent there was also little success. An attempt in 1976–7 to mediate between the quarrelling governments of East Africa, on the grounds that the collapse of the East African Community might react badly on ECOWAS, was both resented and unsuccessful.[90] In equatorial Africa, similarly, Obasanjo failed to heal the breach between Angola and the Democratic Republic of the Congo that had resulted from the Angolan War. He also sought to mediate in the Ogaden dispute between Ethiopia and Somalia during 1977–8, in this case as chairman of an OAU mediation committee, but again without success.[91]

The most complicated and enduring of these efforts concerned Chad, whose proximity to Nigeria made its tangled conflicts particularly threatening, especially because they involved troops from France and Libya, the two countries whose interference in West African affairs most alarmed Nigerians. In 1975 Chad's civilian government, based among the southern agricultural peoples, was overthrown by a military junta that was then challenged by rebel groups based in the arid north, in a complicated civil war involving both French and Libyan forces. In March 1979, acting on behalf of the OAU, Obasanjo hosted a conference in Kano at which several Chadian factions agreed to a ceasefire, the formation of a government of national unity, and the stationing of an 850-strong Nigerian peacekeeping force at Ndjamena. This, Obasanjo declared, was how African states should solve their own problems. Once back in Chad, however, the factions quarrelled, foreign intervention continued, Nigeria refused to recognise the government of national unity actually formed, and that government demanded the withdrawal of the Nigerian troops. Nigeria replied by cutting off Chad's oil supply, which, along with other pressures, forced the leaders to attend a new conference at Lagos in August 1979. This created another transitional government that soon collapsed amidst renewed fighting, obliging Nigeria to withdraw its forces before they became hopelessly bogged down. 'The Chadian conflict', wrote a critical French scholar, 'put into relief the gap between Nigerian pretensions to regional influence and the country's economic, financial, and military capacity.'[92]

This generally unsuccessful experience of mediation made Obasanjo increasingly dissatisfied with the OAU's arrangements for handling African conflicts. At his first OAU summit in July 1977, he suggested the establishment of a standing committee to adjudicate and mediate in conflicts between member states.[93] A year later, in a speech at the Khartoum summit that one journalist thought 'moved the West African country to the centre of the continental stage', Obasanjo warned against interference from both sides of the Cold War. Of a recent French and Belgian intervention to protect their citizens in the Congo, he complained that 'Paratroop drops in the twentieth century are no more acceptable to us than gunboats of the last century were to our ancestors.' 'To the Soviets and their friends,' he added, 'I should like to say that having been invited to Africa in order to assist in the liberation struggle and the consolidation of national independence, they should not overstay their welcome. Africa is not about to throw off one colonial yoke for another.' Yet he recognised that

> we cannot be asking powers to leave us alone while in most cases it is our own actions which provide them with an excuse to interfere in our affairs. We must begin to depart from the diplomatic habit of closing our eyes to what should be depracated [sic] simply because it is happening in an African country or because it is being committed by an African leader.[94]

This criticism offended his fellow heads of state, but he followed it up at the next summit meeting by urging that the OAU should be given continental powers similar to those of the United Nations, should be equipped with a 'truly Pan African Force', and should extend its concern to economic union – a proposal that resulted in the Lagos Economic Summit of 1980 and the largely ineffective Lagos Plan of Action for Africa's economic development.[95] This willingness to intervene across national borders also informed Obasanjo's diplomatic actions during his last year in power, when he headed an OAU mission to resolve the conflict in the Western Sahara between Morocco, Mauritania, and the Polisario guerillas, cut off sales of Nigerian oil to Ghana to check the execution of political opponents by Jerry Rawlings' newly installed junta, and condemned Tanzania's unilateral invasion of Uganda to depose General Amin as 'a dangerous precedent in African inter-state relations, the consequence [sic] of which are unimaginable'.[96]

During Obasanjo's final year in power, Nigeria's international situation worsened. The Carter administration's radical thrust weakened as first Young and then Vance resigned and as it became likely that Carter would lose the forthcoming election to the conservative Ronald Reagan. 'While it lasted, it was sweet,' Obasanjo wrote of his friend Carter's government, 'but it did not last long enough.'[97] Progress in Zimbabwe hung fire until the Lancaster House Conference. Progress elsewhere in southern Africa halted throughout the eight years of Reagan's presidency. Nigerian diplomacy weakened after the flamboyant but vigorous Garba returned to military service in 1978. The international economy, too, turned against Africa as the wind-fall profits of the mid-1970s oil boom were succeeded by the increased transport costs, foreign debts, and international recession that were to make the 1980s a period of continental decline. The difference was seen in the two Lomé Conventions negotiated between African states (under Nigerian leadership) and the European Community, the first in 1975 being a bargain between negotiating partners, whereas that of 1978–9 was closer to an aid package negotiated, on the Nigerian side, with much less enthusiasm and success.[98]

'Nigerians seemed to be able to walk tall and talk with pride and self-confidence any where in the world during the period of our administration', Obasanjo later boasted.[99] It was true, and more true than it was to be during the next twenty years. But it was somewhat less true in 1979 than in 1975. The fiercely nationalistic assertion of the Angolan crisis and the oil boom had given way to a calmer recognition of the complexity of Nigeria's place in the world. What had not given way was Obasanjo's personal determination to change both Nigeria's place and the world.

NOTES

1. Christopher Clapham, *Africa and the international system: the politics of state survival* (Cambridge, 1996), pp. 7, 153–4.
2. Garba, *Diplomatic soldiering*, p. 170.
3. Ibid., p. 172; *Newswatch*, 12 January 1987, p. 15.
4. Clapham, *Africa*, p. 54; Sotunmbi, 'Nigeria's policy, p. 204.
5. Stewart, 'Banks', p. 241.
6. Obasanjo, *March of progress*, p. 278.
7. Garba, *Diplomatic soldiering*, pp. 38–9; Bach, 'Politics', pp. 613–17; BBC monitoring report of Radio Lagos, 18 March 1976, FCO 65/1791/13; *Daily Times*, 7 November 1977.
8. Soyinka, *You must set forth*, p. 230; Andrew Apter, *The pan-African nation: oil and the spectacle of culture in Nigeria* (Chicago, 2005), pp. 90–1, 202; *New Nigerian*, 9 December 1975.
9. Obasanjo, *March of progress*, p. 108.
10. Soyinka, *You must set forth*, p. 230.
11. Reuben Abati in *Guardian*, 21 December 2007.
12. Sotunmbi, 'Nigeria's policy', pp. 63, 240, 249; A. Bolaji Akinyemi, 'Mohammed/ Obasanjo foreign policy', in Oyediran, *Nigerian government*, p. 158.
13. Mark Gevisser, *Thabo Mbeki: the dream deferred* (Johannesburg, 2007), p. 377.
14. Akinjide Osuntokun, 'Gulliver and the Lilliputians: Nigeria and its neighbours', in Adekeye Adebajo and Abdul Raufu Mustapha (ed.), *Gulliver's troubles: Nigeria's foreign policy after the Cold War* (Scottsville, 2008), p. 142.

15. Johnson to Roberts, 23 March 1977, FCO 65/1915/22.
16. See Terence Ranger, 'Zimbabwe and the long search for independence', in David Birmingham and Phyllis M. Martin (ed.), *History of Central Africa* (3 vols, London, 1983–98), vol. 3, Ch.8.
17. Minutes of National Security Council meeting, Washington, 11 May 1976, in United States: Department of State, 'Foreign relations, 1969–1976: volume E-6: documents on Africa, 1973–1976', no. 44, http://www.state.gov/r/pa/ho/frus/nixon/e6 (accessed 29 July 2007).
18. 'Extract from record of meeting between the Secretary of State (Mr A. Crosland) and Dr Kissinger at Waddington on 24 April, 1975', FCO 45/1876/16; Henry Kissinger, *Years of renewal* (London, 1999), p. 990.
19. Kissinger, *Years of renewal*, pp. 918–21, 939–41; 'Southern Africa: Secretary of State Henry A. Kissinger's Lusaka speech', 27 April 1976, Commonwealth Secretariat records 2007/168.
20. Kissinger, *Years of renewal*, Ch.32; Ian Douglas Smith, *The great betrayal* (London, 1997), pp. 199–211; Cyrus Vance, *Hard choices: critical years in America's foreign policy* (New York, 1983), p. 259.
21. Garba, *Diplomatic soldiering*, p. 150; 'Official statement issued by the Federal Military Government of Nigeria on the 28th of April, 1976', Commonwealth Secretariat records 2007/168.
22. Miles to FCO, 4 February 1977, FCO 65/1914/17; Johnson to Roberts, 9 February 1977, FCO 65/1914/21.
23. Garba, *Diplomatic soldiering*, p. 151.
24. 'Carter on Africa', *Newbreed*, September 1976, pp. 12–13; Nancy Mitchell, 'Tropes of the Cold War: Jimmy Carter and Rhodesia', *Cold War History*, 7 (2007), 265. I am grateful to Simon Stevens for discussion of Carter's policy.
25. Vance, *Hard choices*, p. 257.
26. David Owen, *Time to declare* (revised edition, Harmondsworth, 1992), p. 284.
27. Falle to FCO, 14 February 1977, FCO 65/1911/5. See also Jolaoso, *In the shadows*, pp. 144–5.
28. Obasanjo, *Not my will*, p. 138.
29. Olayiwola Abegunrin, *Nigerian foreign policy under military rule, 1966–1999* (Westport, 2003), p. 71.
30. *Petroleum Economist*, January 1977, p. 20; Mitchell, 'Tropes', p. 265; Brzezinski to Carter, 1 June 1977, United States National Archives, declassified documents reference system, document CK3100466188 (electronic resource).
31. Owen, *Time to declare*, pp. 271–83, 309; Mitchell, 'Tropes', pp. 267–8.
32. Cartledge to Walden, 25 September 1978, FCO 65/2085/24.
33. Obasanjo, *March of progress*, p. 153.
34. Olajide Aluko, *Essays on Nigerian foreign policy* (London, 1981), p. 252.
35. 'Record of a meeting between the Foreign and Commonwealth Secretary accompanied by Ambassador Andrew Young and General Obasanjo', 26 August 1977, FCO 65/1914/54. See also Olayiwola Abegunrin, *Nigeria and the struggle for the liberation of Zimbabwe: a study of foreign policy of an emerging nation* (Stockholm, 1992), p. 136.
36. Great Britain, *Rhodesia: proposals for a settlement* (London, 1977).
37. Garba, *Diplomatic soldiering*, p. 59; Stratton to FCO, 8 September 1977, FCO 65/1914/52; *Newbreed*, mid August 1977, p. 25.
38. Falle to FCO, 20 September 1977, FCO 65/1914/59; Cabinet conclusion (77) 29th of 15 September 1977, CAB 128/62.
39. See the account in Jolaoso, *In the shadows*, pp. 149–51.
40. Obasanjo, *March of progress*, p. 216.
41. Ibid., pp. 205–6.
42. *Daily Times*, 19 October 1977.

43. Obasanjo, *March of progress*, p. 220.
44. Garba, *Diplomatic soldiering*, pp. 179–87.
45. Ibid., p. 187.
46. *New Nigerian*, 17 and 21 October 1977.
47. Usman in ibid., 15 October 1977; Usman, *For the liberation*, p. 73.
48. Gevisser, *Thabo Mbeki*, p. 386.
49. Owen, *Time to declare*, pp. 312, 315–16; Sue Onslow, 'South Africa and the Owen/Vance Plan of 1977', *South African Historical Journal*, 51 (2004), 157.
50. Falle to FCO, 9 November 1977, FCO 65/1914/61.
51. Falle to FCO, 11 November 1977, FCO 65/1914/64.
52. Ranger in Birmingham and Martin, *History*, vol. 3, pp. 217–18; *Nigerian Tribune*, 6 March 1978; *Daily Times*, 7 March 1978; Richard to FCO, 10 March 1978, FCO 65/2081/6.
53. Brzezinski to Carter, n.d., United States National Archives, declassified documents reference system, document CK3100137202 (electronic resource).
54. Falle to Owen, 7 April 1978, FCO 65/2083/3; 'Interview with Donald B. Easum', 17 January 1990, http://memory.loc.gov/cgi-bin/query/r?ammem/mfdip:@field (DoclD+mfdip2004es01) (accessed 15 February 2009).
55. Cartledge, 'Brigadier Garba's call on the Prime Minister, 28 April 1978', PREM 16/2195.
56. Obasanjo, *March of progress*, p. 319.
57. Garba, *Diplomatic soldiering*, pp. 78–91; Vance, *Hard choices*, pp. 291–2; Smith, *Great betrayal*, pp. 262–4.
58. Lewen to FCO, 2 October 1978, FCO 36/2207/64; Abegunrin, *Nigeria and the struggle*, p. 164; Cartledge to Walden, 25 September 1978, FCO 65/2085/24; Falle to FCO, 13 December 1978, FCO 65/2081/59.
59. Owen to British High Commission, Lagos, 15 January 1979, FCO 36/2508/4.
60. Robin Renwick, *Unconventional diplomacy in southern Africa* (Basingstoke, 1997), pp. 14–15; Cabinet conclusion (79) 2nd of 17 May 1979, CAB 128/66.
61. Obasanjo to Mobutu, 15 June 1979, in Donald to FCO, 23 June 1979, FCO 65/2219/181; Sotunmbi, 'Nigeria's policy', pp. 230–2; Olajide Aluko, 'The nationalization of the assets of British Petroleum', in Gabriel O. Olusanya and R.A. Akindele (ed.), *The structure and processes of foreign policy making and implementation in Nigeria, 1960–1990* (Lagos, 1990), Ch. 20; Brown to Carrington, 24 October 1979, FCO 65/2213/276.
62. 'Extract from Lusaka Commonwealth Heads of Government Meeting communique, 5 April 1979', FCO 65/2212/191; Cabinet conclusion (79) 13th of 10 August 1979, CAB 128/66.
63. Obasanjo, *Not my will*, p. 145.
64. Cabinet Defence and Overseas Policy Committee minutes (OD [79] 5th) of 23 July 1979, CAB 148/183.
65. Barltrop to Johnson, 19 September 1979, FCO 36/2509/131; Brown to FCO, 30 August 1979, FCO 65/2221/381; Kennedy to Johnson, 17 October 1979, FCO 65/2222/437.
66. Carrington to British High Commission, Lagos, 9 November 1979, FCO 36/2509/169.
67. Obasanjo, *Not my will*, p. 131.
68. *Daily Times*, 30 November 1987.
69. Peter H. Katjavivi, *A history of resistance in Namibia* (London, 1988), pp. 59–93; Vance, *Hard choices*, pp. 272–3; Sotunmbi, 'Nigeria's policy', p. 213.
70. Katjavivi, *History*, Chs. 15–17; Vance, *Hard choices*, pp. 273–7; Kenoye Kelvin Eke, *Nigeria's foreign policy under two military governments, 1966–1979: an analysis of the Gowan [sic] and Muhammed/Obasanjo regimes* (Lewiston, 1990), pp. 53–4.
71. 'Record of a meeting between the British High Commissioner to Nigeria, Sir Sam Falle, and the Commissioner for External Affairs of the Federal Republic of Nigeria, Brigadier J.N. Garba', 11 July 1977, FCO 65/1919/11; Vance, *Hard choices*, pp. 281–2.
72. Easum, interview, 17 January 1990 (above, n. 54).

73. Katjavivi, *History*, p. 123; Sotunmbi, 'Nigerian policy', pp. 214–15; Obasanjo, *March of progress*, p. 456.
74. Ronald Hyam, *Britain's declining empire: the road to decolonisation, 1918–1968* (Cambridge, 2006), pp.322–3; Eke, *Nigeria's foreign policy*, pp. 63–4.
75. Obasanjo, *March of progress*, pp. 373, 335.
76. *Nigerian Tribune*, 17 July 1976; Falle to FCO, 14 February 1977, FCO 65/1911/5; 'Record of a discussion between the Foreign and Commonwealth Secretary and Nigerian Commissioner for External Relations', 17 April 1977, FCO 65/1906/22; Garba, *Diplomatic soldiering*, pp. 97–9.
77. *Observer* (London), 27 March 1977; Obasanjo, *March of progress*, p. 150.
78. Rhodes to Potter, 22 April 1977, FCO 65/1915/W.51; Vance, *Hard choices*, p. 261.
79. *Daily Times*, 26 August 1977.
80. Heath to Mansfield, 7 October 1977, FCO 65/1913/17; Holding to Mansfield, 13 October 1977, FCO 65/1916/36; British High Commission, Lagos, to FCO, n.d., FCO 65/1913/ 70.
81. Johnson to Mansfield, minute, 30 March 1978, FCO 65/2078/50; 'Extract from Chairman's report to Barclay's Bank Ltd', 31 December 1977, FCO 65/2077/1.
82. Holliman to Permanent Secretary (Finance), 6 July 1978, FCO 65/2079/137; Williams, 'Nigerian attitudes towards firms with South African trading links', 11 September 1978, FCO 65/2079/173.
83. Brzezinski to Carter, n.d., United States National Archives, declassified documents reference system, document CK3100137202 (electronic resource); *Africa Research Bulletin*, June 1978, p. 4902; Johnson to Mansfield, minute, 19 May 1978, FCO 65/2079/98.
84. See Cabinet conclusion (78) 24th of 29 June 1978, CAB 128/64.
85. *Daily Times*, 14 October 1977; Cabinet conclusion (77) 35th of 10 November 1977, CAB 128/62.
86. Aluko, *Essays*, p. 256.
87. *Daily Times*, 3 July 1979.
88. Adekeye Adebajo, *Building peace in West Africa: Liberia, Sierra Leone, and Guinea-Bissau* (Boulder, 2002), p. 30.
89. Obasanjo, *Not my will*, p. 127; below, pp. 222, 284–5.
90. Garba, *Diplomatic soldiering*, pp. 113–20.
91. Ibid., pp. 122–38.
92. Daniel Bach, 'Le Nigeria et le Tchad: échec d'une politique de stabilisation du conflit', *Politique Africaine*, 16 (December 1984), 125–8 (quotation on p. 128); *Nigerian Tribune*, 19 March 1979; Obasanjo, *Not my will*, p. 129.
93. Obasanjo, *March of progress*, p. 155.
94. *Africa Research Bulletin*, July 1978, pp. 4912, 4915; Obasanjo, *Not my will*, pp. 254–5.
95. Sotunmbi, 'Nigeria's policy', p. 309 n. 48; Obasanjo, *March of progress*, p. 459; Garba, *Diplomatic soldiering*, p. 207.
96. *Nigerian Tribune*, 1 May 1979; *Africa* (London), August 1979; Obasanjo, *March of progress*, p. 457.
97. Obasanjo, *Not my will*, p. 138.
98. Clapham, *Africa*, pp. 100–1.
99. Obasanjo, *Not my will*, p. 240.

8
Return to Civilian Rule

Nigerians remembered Obasanjo's tenure as military head of state chiefly for the fidelity with which his regime restored power to a civilian government on 1 October 1979. It was the basis for the high reputation that he bore for the next twenty years. In managing this transition, Obasanjo followed closely the political programme that Murtala had announced in October 1975,[1] but he did not merely execute decisions already taken. The creation of new political institutions – the most novel that any West African state devised[2] – raised major questions of principle and judgment, especially the question that was to trouble Obasanjo throughout his career: how much democracy was compatible with the unity of Nigeria?

The first stage in the transition process had taken place in October 1975 with the appointment of the 49-man Constitution Drafting Committee, which reported in September 1976. Their chairman explained, 'What we have designed is to counter the difficulties of the past', especially the weaknesses that had destroyed the First Republic and precipitated civil war.[3] This explained their chief innovation, recommended to them by Murtala: an executive presidency on the American model rather than a British parliamentary system. The committee explained that the coexistence of a purely ceremonial president with an executive prime minister had been 'meaningless in the light of African political experience and history' and 'difficult to maintain in practice', as the conflict between Azikiwe and Abubakar in 1964 had shown. Moreover, 'The single executive has the merit of unity, energy and despatch' needed in a country eager for national integration and economic development, especially because an executive president, unlike a prime minister, would have a personal electoral mandate.[4]

The drafting committee recognised that an executive president 'could easily become a dictator', as was so obvious elsewhere in Africa. One critic described its proposal as 'a one-way ticket to fascism'.[5] The committee thought that the best check on this was to require that the president should have widespread support when taking office, by providing that he must win both the largest number of votes and at least one-quarter of the votes in at least two-thirds of the states. Presidential power would also be limited by a federal structure in which the three levels of government – federal, state, and local – would have independently elected institutions and separately allocated funds. The federal government would have exclusive control of the military and police and power of overriding legislation in most fields, but the federal executive was to include at least one member from each state and institutions at all levels must similarly embody the country's 'federal character', an original device by which balanced ethnic and community representation became a central feature of the political system.[6] Observers later complained that this fostered mediocrity and made each Nigerian 'a stranger in 35 out of 36 states ... and in 773 of the 774 Local Government Areas'.[7]

The third way to prevent the president from becoming a dictator was the familiar American device of separating his powers from those of the legislature and judiciary. The federal legislature, the National Assembly, would consist of a Senate, with equal representation from each state, and a House of Representatives, elected in proportion to population. This arrangement, together with the existence of 19 states, largely evaded the divisive census issue that had disrupted the First Republic. The Assembly's approval was needed for all legislation and appropriation of federal funds. It could override a presidential veto on legislation by a two-thirds majority and could impeach and remove a president for grave cause. After much discussion and as part of its concern to restrain the executive, the drafting committee recommended that the president's appointed ministers should not be members of the National Assembly, thereby reproducing the potential for conflict between legislature and executive that the committee themselves recognised to be the main weakness of the American constitution. This was an ironic decision, given that the military government had urged the committee to exclude 'institutionalised opposition', but even Obasanjo, who held that view strongly, does not appear to have objected.[8]

The drafting committee believed that conflict between executive and legislature would be mediated by party organisation, as it had come to be in the United States. They wrote, 'We feel that in practice the President or a [State] Governor would normally have some form of understanding with a party or group of parties in the legislature which will ensure that its major bills are passed. Prudence and common sense require such a course.' This proved an optimistic assumption, but it illustrated the committee's virtually unthinking acceptance of a competitive party system, as most Nigerians desired, despite the military government's hostility towards it.[9] The electoral law concentrated rather on the character of parties, requiring them to be open to all Nigerians, embody federal character in their institutions, and have branch offices in at least two-thirds of states.

Publication of the draft constitution in October 1976 was followed by a full year of public discussion. Most dispute focused on 'the executive president: an invitation to tyranny', the lack of specific protection of freedom of the press, and the proposal for a federal court of appeal for civil cases under Islamic law.[10] Radicals complained that the draft 'explicitly seeks to entrench and legitimate the existing social and economic system built to produce parasitic affluence for a few based on poverty, injustice and indignity for most of the people', in the words of Bala Usman, who, with a fellow member of the committee, produced an alternative draft that received no serious consideration.[11]

The Constituent Assembly to discuss the draft met in October 1977 with 230 members, 90% of them elected by representatives of the new local government councils, with strong representation of lawyers, academics, businessmen, and former politicians.[12] Inaugurating the Assembly, Obasanjo urged its members to bear in mind not only 'the views of those who write in the press or talk on the radio and television', but those who 'labour under very primitive conditions of eking out a livelihood'. He also reminded them that 'The African genius is a child of moderation not given to unnecessary and excessive intellectual inflexibility…. It prefers to arrive at consensus through compromise and conciliation.'[13]

Obasanjo may have foreseen how the debates might develop. Four issues divided the Assembly most deeply. One was the executive presidency, which was eventually approved by a large majority.[14] The second was a proposal, eventually accepted, to extend a ban on candidacy for office to anyone found guilty of a serious offence since 1960, allegedly a device to exclude Awolowo.[15] A third conflict arose over the creation of additional states, until the Supreme Military Council dissolved the Assembly with the issue still unsettled.[16]

This dissolution also ended the fourth and most contentious dispute, over the proposed Federal Sharia Court of Appeal. During the First Republic, such an appeal court had existed in the Northern Region to hear civil cases between Muslims appealed from lower Islamic courts. When the Northern Region was abolished in 1967 and replaced by smaller states, each state received its own appeal court administering Islamic civil law, but the regional court was abolished. Further appeals lay only to the Supreme Court of the Federation, whose judges were not necessarily Muslims or learned in Islamic law.[17] At the insistence of its Muslim members, the Constitution Drafting Committee rejected the statement in the First Republic constitution that Nigeria was a secular state, specifying instead that 'The Government of the Federation or of a State shall not adopt any religion as State religion.' The Committee then proposed a Federal Sharia Court of Appeal to hear civil cases, which was widely welcomed by Muslims, although purists demanded that the court should also hear criminal appeals.[18]

The proposal alarmed some Christians, especially in Middle Belt states, where ambitious Christian politicians presented the proposal as a new threat of Muslim domination by Hausa-Fulani from the northern emirates. Their protests gave Muslim politicians an emotional issue on which to bid for for leadership.[19] Within a week of the Constituent Assembly's inauguration, opponents of the new court had walked out. A month later a leading opponent was shouted down, the session was adjourned, and Muslim members declared it an issue for which they would die.[20] After six months of controversy, the Assembly appointed a committee of leading members to formulate a compromise. Its chairman reported that it agreed that appeals from state Sharia courts should go not to a distinct Sharia Court of Appeal but to the existing Federal Appeal Court, where they would be heard by three of its judges who were versed in Islamic law. At the full Assembly, however, some Muslim members of the committee denied that there had been agreement and other Muslims complained that they were given no time to consider the report. Some 93 Muslim members withdrew. The rump of the meeting then adopted the committee's reported 'compromise'.[21] Protest marches took place in northern cities, threatening the political transition at exactly the moment when student riots and the balance of payments crisis brought the regime to its nadir.[22]

After nine days of tension, Obasanjo summoned all members of the Assembly, met them in the company of the entire Supreme Military Council, and made what one delegate described as a 'point-blank address'.[23] 'You cannot afford to disappoint the nation', he told them:

> You also have to remember that your actions and utterances in this Assembly have direct effect on our people all over the country for good or for ill in our most arduous task of national integration and national unity. The experience of the last civil war and, perhaps

more, the heartaches and tragic incidents that preceded that holocaust ... [are], I think, a sufficient reminder... In the event of a breakdown of law and order and chaos and disorder ensuing it will be the common people who will suffer most. Those of you who understand the real motive behind your actions, attitudes and utterances will fly into safety and use the common man as cannon fodder and as if they were expendable items, for self and selfish interest...I appeal to all of you to continue your deliberations on the Draft Constitution in the atmosphere of harmony and concord.[24]

It was one of his best speeches and was supported by appeals for peace and unity from the Sultan of Sokoto and other northern leaders. When the Assembly met again five days later, the Muslim members resumed their seats and their leader, Shehu Shagari, seconded a motion of thanks to Obasanjo for the wisdom with which he had handled the crisis.[25] In reality, the conflict continued, and members were awaiting an opportunity to reopen it when the chairman abruptly adjourned the Assembly as soon as the draft constitution had been read for a third time, telling Obasanjo that things would otherwise have got out of hand. The head of state assured angry members that he would not regard their work as finished until their report was submitted to him. It was submitted on 30 August 1978 and they never met again.[26]

When Murtala had inaugurated the Constitution Drafting Committee, he had stated that the Constituent Assembly would consider and accept the Draft Constitution, but when Obasanjo opened the Assembly two years later he declared that it would make recommendations to the military government, which would then issue a decree.[27] Despite protests, Obasanjo's view prevailed, although the Supreme Military Council sought to minimise its amendments. Obasanjo wished to limit the number of political parties and the tenure of office holders, but the final text announced by the Council on 21 September 1978 contained only seventeen changes, including a relaxation of the clause that might have excluded Awolowo from contesting the presidency and the entrenchment of some of the Council's major legislation, notably the Land Use Decree. At the same time, Obasanjo removed the ban on party politics and handed over the conduct of the election campaign to a Federal Electoral Commission, almost exactly a year before the military planned to leave office. 'Fears and lack of faith have led to whisperings and unaltruistic campaigns in some quarters for the military to reconsider their political programme', he added, but he rejected these because to leave military honour untarnished was a duty second only to bequeathing 'a united, stable and economically strong country'.[28]

In reality, party politics had never entirely ceased. Awolowo and his followers had organised a shadow party, the Committee of Friends, as soon as the Action Group was banned in 1966. It emerged as the Unity Party of Nigeria (UPN) one day after Obasanjo's announcement, with a ready-made manifesto promising immediate free education at all levels, free health care, integrated rural development, and full employment. Its first national congress, ten days later, unsurprisingly chose Awolowo, aged 70, as its presidential candidate. By February 1979 he could claim to have travelled 20,000 kilometres by road, visited every state, and held 401 rallies. He predicted that he would win 15 of the 19 states. Perhaps he even believed it. In reality, he united the Yoruba as never before, but could not find a single suitable northerner as a vice-presidential running mate.[29]

The Nigerian People's Party (NPP) also announced itself on the day after the ban was lifted. Its founder, financier, and aspiring presidential candidate was Waziri

Ibrahim, a First Republic minister. With support in his own Borno State and periph-
eral northern areas, he had allied with anti-Sharia politicians from the Middle Belt
and the South-East. That proved his undoing, because when a party congress met
in November 1978 and Waziri Ibrahim insisted on becoming both party chairman
and presidential candidate, most of the allies broke away and chose the 74-year-old
First Republic President, Nnamdi Azikiwe, as their presidential candidate. Their
party, which retained the NPP name, relied heavily on Azikiwe's unique standing
among the Igbo. Waziri Ibrahim renamed his faction the Great Nigerian People's
Party (GNPP).[30]

The National Party of Nigeria (NPN) took slightly longer to organise but also
had deep historical roots. Its core consisted of northern politicians from the First
Republic, such as Shehu Shagari, and younger northerners – often known as the
Kaduna Mafia – who had come to prominence as bureaucrats or businessmen
during military rule. The Sharia dispute consolidated this northern grouping,
which then allied with individual leaders from other regions while retaining an
overall northern predominance. In December the party chose the ostensibly reluctant Shagari as its presidential candidate, but he did not dominate it in Awolowo's
manner. Instead the NPN remained 'a loose amalgam of baronies', sharing its
leadership offices among the regions by a 'zoning' procedure that was to become
general in Nigerian politics, selecting an Igbo architect, Alex Ekwueme, as its vice-
presidential candidate, and finding its support equally within the northern states
and among minority groups elsewhere.[31] In the process the party alienated the most
prominent northern radical, Aminu Kano, who broke away to form the People's
Redemption Party (PRP), whose support was confined to his own Kano State and
neigbouring Kaduna.[32]

Parties hoping to contest the elections in July 1979 had three months in which to
establish branches and recruit leaders in at least two-thirds of the states in order to
secure registration. This was widely criticised as preventing the formation of genuinely new political organisations, ensuring that the parties and leaders of the First
Republic would re-establish themselves, and favouring the best-financed political
groups. Yet the new parties did not simply recreate those of the First Republic The
need to win support in two-thirds of the states forced them to seek a new breadth
of coverage, although with varying success: the PRP and UPN remained largely
regional, but the NPN was to win only half its votes in its northern stronghold,
which splintered along its new state boundaries. Similarly, although the presidential
candidates were old-breed politicians, most other candidates and organisers were
younger people, including the vice-presidential candidates and most of those elected
as state governors. One sample of elected legislators found that over three-quarters
were in their thirties or forties and about half were businessmen. The position of
the 47-year-old Ekwueme, who had taken the Biafran side during the civil war, was
especially striking.[33]

One consequence of the need to appeal to the widest possible audience was
to reinforce the temptation to promise everything to everyone. Awolowo's vow to
institute free education at all levels immediately became a target for attack by his
rivals. Shagari, whose trademark was moderation, mocked such extravagance but
promised to build five million housing units in four years, distribute free fertiliser,
and supply every rural constituency with piped water, electricity, a health centre,
primary schools, markets, motor parks, forest reserves, banks, and post offices.[34]
Voters expected such promises, but they aroused Obasanjo's well-honed contempt

for politicians. 'There are two types of politicians in Nigeria', he told an interviewer. 'There are those who don't know what they are talking about and they are talking out of ignorance and those should be pitied. There are those who know what they are talking about who are deliberately misleading, misinforming and being mischievous.'[35]

When the elections for state, legislative, and presidential offices took place in July and August 1979, turnout was low – between 30 and 40% of genuinely registered voters – and the voting, despite rigging on all sides, was unusually peaceful and orderly for a Nigerian election.[36] Except in the presidential contest, not a single candidate stood outside his state of origin. Yoruba voted solidly for UPN; Igbo predominantly supported NPP; PRP and GNPP won their respective strongholds in Kano and Borno; and the NPN won almost everything else, coming first or second in 90 of the 95 senatorial seats but winning only 36 of them.[37] In the presidential contest, Shagari won over 25% of the votes in 12 states and 5,688,857 votes overall; Awolowo won 25% of the votes in only 6 states, but because turnout was highest in Yorubaland, he gained a total of 4,916,651 votes. An attempt to form a coalition against Shagari failed.[38]

The presidential result created a dilemma, because the winning candidate was required to have the highest number of votes and to have won at least 25% of the votes in at least two-thirds of the 19 states, otherwise the election passed to an electoral college of federal and state legislators. Shagari won 25% of the votes in only 12 states and 20% in a thirteenth. The general presumption had been that two-thirds of 19 meant 13 states.[39] The NPN now argued that it meant twelve and two-thirds, so that one-sixth of the votes in the thirteenth state was enough. When the Electoral Commission put the question to the Supreme Military Council, it refused to interfere and told the Commission to make the decision, which could then if necessary be challenged in court. On 16 August, the Electoral Commission declared Shagari elected. Four days later Obasanjo met the party leaders, told them 'in a highly diplomatic manner' that he had no power over the Electoral Commission, and urged them to follow constitutional procedures.[40] Awolowo took the issue to the Supreme Court, which upheld the Electoral Commission's decision by 6 votes to one, the Chief Justice adding that even if they had interpreted the requirement as 13 states they would still have confirmed Shagari's election as having substantially met the requirements, as the law stipulated.[41] The Supreme Military Council then amended the future constitution to specify 13 states as the minimum and to replace the electoral college, which was generally expected to be spectacularly corrupt, by a run-off election if the first vote was inconclusive. At Shagari's request, the Council also delayed the opening of the National Assembly until he had secured a working majority through agreement with the NPP.[42]

This controversy had two important consequences. One was to weaken Shagari's position when he took office in October 1979. The other was to create lasting antagonism towards Obasanjo on the part of Awolowo and most Yoruba political opinion. Obasanjo was an outsider to Yoruba politics and proclaimed his primary loyalty to Nigeria, but he was nevertheless a distinguished soldier and a Yoruba head of state. Awolowo had frequently expressed his admiration – 'highly talented, shy, fearless, swift in action and deep'[43] – and his newspaper, the *Nigerian Tribune*, had supported Obasanjo's regime with more warmth than was normal for Nigeria's independent press.[44] Now attitudes changed overnight. Awolowo believed – however questionably – that by being denied recourse to the electoral college he had been cheated of his lifelong ambition to lead Nigeria. He blamed Obasanjo for it. He and his supporters accused Obasanjo and his colleagues of favouring a northern candidate and voting for Shagari (as Obasanjo did, although he voted for other parties in the legislative elections).[45] Further, they were accused of rigging the ballot paper and the voting in the North; prejudicing the electorate against Awolowo by saying the best man would not necessarily win; pressing the Electoral Commission to recognise Shagari; refusing to overrule the Commission's decision or to amend the constitution before the Supreme Court hearing; appointing a new Chief Justice favoured by Shagari; and facilitating an alliance between the NPN and NPP in order to entrench Shagari in power.[46] The last point was true,[47] but Obasanjo refuted most other accusations, insisting that the military had left the Electoral Commission to run the election and had removed the clause in the draft constitution that might have debarred Awolowo. 'Throughout the period of our administration as a government', he wrote, 'we had no plan to instal any party or any individual to succeed us. And if we had had such a plan, you know that we are courageous enough and determined enough to have said so openly and acted so publicly.'[48]

As the dispute grew more heated, Obasanjo took the precaution of strengthening his bodyguard.[49] He was also pursued by wild allegations of corruption, none of them substantiated.[50] On the other side, he was being pressed to remain in office by eminent figures ranging from Presidents Kaunda of Zambia, Houphouet-Boigny of Côte d'Ivoire, and Eyadema of Togo, to senior officers, chiefs, and civil servants.[51] He would later claim that he had transferred power when he could easily have retained it, but that was not his view closer to the event, for especially during his last 18 months, from the crisis of April 1978, the military regime had become an increasingly unpopular, lame-duck government.[52] In 1986 Obasanjo would declare 'that he could not have stayed a day longer than planned ... and there was no way he could have told Nigerians that 1979 was no longer feasible.'[53] President Nyerere of Tanzania commented that he had never seen anyone work so hard to give up power.[54]

Obasanjo was already preparing his exit. In April 1979 he promoted himself to full General, denying the same distinction to Danjuma, who never forgave him.[55] The head of state addressed religious leaders, public servants, and media personnel on their duties to the new republic. He completed a farewell tour, following an earlier inspection of each of the nineteen states. In Sokoto, the Sultan presented him with a sword. Taking leave of his military colleagues, he assured them that 'we have kept our pledge like men of honour.' Toasting Shagari, he claimed 'a clear, straight-forward feeling of joy in accomplishment'.[56]

It rained throughout Shagari's inauguration on 1 October 1979. The four defeated presidential candidates were absent. Obasanjo presented the president with a copy of the constitution, saluted him, toured the stadium with him, and then, refusing official transport, drove himself home. He prayed, changed into civilian clothes, and set off with Yar'Adua by car for Abeokuta with two helicopters over-head, unsure whether his reception into Yorubaland would be hostile or friendly. His fears were groundless. He was met on the outskirts of Abeokuta with gun salutes and dances. The Olowu and the Egba chiefs accompanied him to the cenotaph to honour Egba warriors. Then, on a white horse, a symbol of great distinction, he rode ahead of the crowds to the palace, where the Alake danced to welcome him. At the reception following a thanksgiving service in the cathedral, Obasanjo said, 'I believe our country and Africa have been enriched by what modest service I have been privileged to render for our fatherland, Africa and the world at large. I went, I served, I accomplished, I returned. Thanks be to God.'[57]

It was the second of the homecomings that punctuated his life.

NOTES

1. Above, p. 45.
2. A.H.M. Kirk-Greene, quoted in *Newswatch*, 29 January 1996, p. 8.
3. *West Africa*, 27 September 1976, p. 1426.
4. Nigeria, *Report of the Constitution Drafting Committee: volume I* (Lagos, 1976), pp. xxix–xxx.
5. Ibid., p.xxx; Ibrahim Tahir, quoted in *West Africa*, 28 February 1977, p. 437.
6. Nigeria, *Report of the Constitution Drafting Committee*, vol. 1, pp. viii–ix, xxxi; Suberu, *Federalism*, Ch.5.
7. Axel Harneit-Sievers, *Constructions of belonging: Igbo communities and the Nigerian state in the twentieth century* (Rochester NY, 2006), p. 141.
8. Nigeria, *Report of the Constitution Drafting Committee*, vol. 1, pp. xx–xxvi, xxxii; *Daily Times*, 2 October 1975.
9. Nigeria, *Report of the Constitution Drafting Committee*, vol. 1, p. xxii; Margaret Peil, *Nigerian politics: the people's view* (London, 1976), p. 110; *Daily Times*, 2 October 1975.
10. *Daily Times*, 28 November 1976.
11. Usman, *For the liberation*, p. 129; text in *Nigerian Tribune*, 9 March 1977 et seq.
12. *Daily Times*, 7 October 1977; *West Africa*, 12 September 1977, pp. 1855–9.
13. *Nigerian Tribune*, 7 October 1977; *Daily Times*, 7 October 1977.
14. *West Africa*, 23 January 1978, p. 135. The Assembly's recommendations were printed in *New Nigerian*, 15–16 June 1978.
15. *New Nigerian*, 25 May and 20 June 1978.
16. James S. Read, 'The new constitution of Nigeria, 1979: "the Washington model"?' *Journal of African Law*, 23 (1979), 163–4; Sir Udo Udoma, *History and the law of the constitution of Nigeria* (Lagos, 1994), pp. 317–18; *Nigerian Tribune*, 8 June 1978.
17. Philip Ostien, 'An opportunity missed by Nigeria's Christians: the 1976–78 Sharia debate revisited', in Benjamin F. Soares (ed.), *Muslim-Christian encounters in Africa* (Leiden, 2006), pp. 223–34.
18. Toyin Falola, *Violence in Nigeria: the crisis of religious politics and secular ideologies* (Rochester NY, 1998), pp. 75–7; Nigeria, *Report of the Constitution Drafting Committee*, vol. 1, p. xxxiv; *Daily Times*, 28 May and 6 August 1977.
19. E. Alex Gboyega, 'The making of the Nigerian constitution', in Oyediran, *Nigerian government*, p. 253.
20. *Nigerian Tribune*, 8 November and 6 December 1977.
21. *New Nigerian*, 7, 14, 18, and 19 April 1978; Udoma, *History*, pp. 314–16.
22. *West Africa*, 24 April 1978, pp. 776–9; Hodge to Mackilligin, 21 April 1978, FCO 65/2070/15; Obasanjo, *Not my will*, p. 63; above, pp. 63, 66–7.
23. Chuba Okadigbo, *Power and leadership in Nigeria* (Enugu, 1987), p. 55.
24. *Daily Times*, 20 April 1978.
25. *Punch*, 25 April 1978; *Nigerian Tribune*, 25 April 1978.
26. *Daily Times*, 8 and 29 June 1978, 30 August 1978; Obasanjo, *Not my will*, p. 179.
27. *Daily Times*, 2 October 1975; *Nigerian Tribune*, 7 October 1977.
28. Obasanjo, *Not my will*, p. 64; *Daily Times*, 22 September 1978.
29. Oyeleye Oyediran, 'Political parties: formation and candidate selection', in Oyeleye Oyediran (ed.), *The Nigerian 1979 elections* (Lagos, 1981), pp. 46–7; *Daily Times*, 26 and 28 September 1978, 1 December 1978, 30 January and 23 February 1979.

30. Oyediran in Oyediran, *Elections*, p. 54; *West Africa*, 26 April 1976 p. 586, 28 November 1977 pp. 2399 and 2425, 4 December 1978 p. 2397.

31. Oyediran in Oyediran, *Elections*, pp. 57–65; *Punch*, 2–3 October 1978; Bevan et al., *Nigeria and Indonesia*, p. 89; Shagari, *Beckoned*, pp. 210–13.

32. G. Nicolas, 'Contradictions d'un parti révolutionnaire: le PRP nigérien', *Politique Africaine*, 8 (December 1982), 74–102.

33. Eghosa E. Osaghae, *Crippled giant: Nigeria since independence* (London, 1998), pp. 118–30; Patrick F. Ollawa, 'The 1979 elections', in Ekeh et al., *Nigeria*, p. 145; *Daily Times*, 12 December 1978; A.Y. Aliyu, 'The nature and composition of the legislature: some selected states', in Abubakar Yaya Aliyu (ed.), *Return to civilian rule* (Zaria, 1982), pp. 309–11.

34. *Nigerian Tribune*, 15 March and 4 July 1979; *Daily Times*, 6 January 1979.

35. Quoted in *Nigerian Tribune*, 7 February 1979.

36. Oyeleye Oyediran and Oladele Arowolo, 'In defence of the Nigerian electorate', in Oyediran, *Elections*, pp. 124–33; Haroun Adamu and Alaba Ogunsanwo, *Nigeria: the making of the presidential system: 1979 general elections* (Kano, c.1983), pp. 140–55, 198–200, 255–6.

37. Dudley, *Introduction*, p. 223; *West Africa*, 23 July 1979 p. 1302 and 6 August 1979 p. 1406.

38. *West Africa*, 20 August 1979, pp. 1491, 1520; Adamu and Ogunsanwo, *Nigeria*, p. 238.

39. Oyeleye Oyediran, 'Presidential election result controversy', in Oyediran, *Elections*, p. 142.

40. Obasanjo, *Not my will*, pp. 191–2; *Newswatch*, 20 May 1985, p. 17; *Nigerian Tribune*, 21 August 1979; *Sunday Concord*, 11 May 1980.

41. Judgment in Read, 'New constitution', pp. 175–82. For a fuller account, see Dudley, *Introduction*, pp. 169–78.

42. Obasanjo, *Not my will*, p. 192; Shagari, *Beckoned*, p. 233.

43. Quoted in Avwenagbiku, *Olusegun Obasanjo*, p. 324.

44. See the editorial in *Nigerian Tribune*, 25 September 1978.

45. Obasanjo, *Not my will*, p. 171.

46. *Daily Sketch*, 12, 13, 17, and 22 December 1979; Babatope, *Not his will*, passim.

47. Shagari, *Beckoned*, p. 233.

48. *Nigerian Tribune*, 14 December 1979.

49. *National Concord*, 1 August 1980.

50. Obasanjo, *Not my will*, pp. 216–25.

51. Adinoyi Ojo in d'Orville, *Beyond freedom*, p. 670; Ademiluyi, *From prisoner to president*, p. 11; Ebenezer Babatope, *Murtala Muhammed, a leader betrayed (a study in Buhari's tyranny)* (Enugu, 1986), p. 29; Kennedy to Brown, 21 November 1979, FCO 65/2214/302.

52. Obe, *New dawn*, vol.3, p.269; *Daily Times*, 9 January 1978; Williams to Heath, 9 January 1978, FCO 65/2070/7; Young, 'Visit to the North: 12–21 May [1978]', FCO 65/2070/64; *Newbreed*, mid May 1978, pp. 3–4.

53. *African Guardian*, 5 June 1986, p. 17.

54. *Newswatch*, 12 January 1987, p. 13.

55. *Daily Times*, 12 April 1979; *Guardian*, 24 February 2008.

56. Obasanjo, *March of progress*, pp. 479, 483.

57. Obasanjo, *Not my will*, pp. 203–12; *Daily Sketch*, 4 October 1979; *Daily Times*, 3 October 1979.

Part III

Private Citizen
(1979–99)

9
The Farmer

On 8 October 1979, a week after leaving military office at the age of 42, Obasanjo began a new career as a farmer by visiting his land and arranging for it to be cleared for cultivation.[1] 'It was the job for which I was born', he said. He considered farming a fitting occupation for a senior officer, as it had been for a Yoruba military chief.[2] Moreover, he wanted to set an example:

> Our commitment to an agricultural and food production enterprise stems from our belief that Nigeria must be self-reliant in agriculture and food production as a nation.... Our success will encourage others to follow the same path. While not underplaying the tedium, difficulties and hazards of agricultural pursuit, we hope to glorify it, giving it a new look and a new image as a respectable, interesting, exciting, and absorbing occupation.[3]

At the farm gate he placed a notice:

> Temperance Enterprises Limited
> This farm is in part a demonstration of the Operation Feed the Nation. You too can be a farmer, have an exciting occupation and join in feeding yourself and the nation.[4]

Beside the notice stood a cement statue of a Yoruba farmer shouldering a hoe. The statue was bathed each morning.[5]

Obasanjo's selection of land at Ota had deep roots in the Yoruba past. Close to his birthplace, Ota was some 60kms south of Abeokuta and 40 kms north of Lagos. Originally settled by the Awori group of Yoruba who also founded Lagos, Ota was subordinated in 1842 and subsequently colonised by the Egba people (including Obasanjo's Owu group) who had recently established Abeokuta. By 1933, Egba outnumbered Awori in rural Ota by 6,072 to 2,622. Half a century later, when Obasanjo arrived, Ota was experiencing a further transformation as light industries expanded out of Lagos, provoking a host of land disputes.[6]

That the arrival of an exceptionally powerful Owu chief in pursuit of extensive farmland should have caused apprehension in Ota is not surprising. Six days after Obasanjo arranged for land there to be cleared, a correspondent in the hostile *Nigerian Tribune* reported that he had needed police protection to take possession. The newspaper claimed that in 1975 he had bought 230 hectares of land in Ota from a local family for N200 ($322) per hectare. It quoted the family head as saying, 'We sold the land to General Obasanjo at that price because of his position. We feared that he could confiscate our land if we refused to sell'. The family claimed to have heard no more from Obasanjo until a few days before he came to take possession.[7] During the next few weeks, three other local families claimed to own part of the contested land. One petitioned the State House of Assembly that Obasanjo had used the police to scare them away, bulldozers to destroy their crops, and '20 stalwarts, hooligans and thugs who were harassing the family daily'. The Chief of Ota complained that the transaction should not have taken place without his knowledge, the State Land Allocation Committee refused to give Obasanjo a certificate of occupancy, and the State Government (controlled by his UPN critics) was rumoured to be planning to acquire the land for industrial purposes because Obasanjo had infringed his own Land Use Decree.[8]

Asked his views on the matter, Obasanjo 'gave a garbled reply in the vernacular'.[9] He had marched into the kind of Yoruba land dispute that his decree had been designed to prevent but had in practice often exacerbated. How he extricated himself and gained ownership is unclear, although it must have been expensive. A decade later, it was said that 'he had to wade through a barrier of litigations (and threats of it) to finally hold onto his farm.'[10] At least he achieved that. Another area of land he held at Ibadan in 1979 was revoked by the UPN State Governor, although restored four years later. Some 2,500 hectares that Obasanjo secured in 1985 in Niger State – conveniently close to the new capital at Abuja – was also revoked 'as a result of persistent opposition from the community'.[11] Yet he developed farms elsewhere in Yorubaland and acquired pasture and cattle on the remote but potentially rich Mambilla Plateau, where he had served as a young engineer. By 1987 he employed over 400 workers at eight locations.[12]

Obasanjo was one of several senior officers to take up modern farming at this time. Often in their forties, they retired on generous terms, including free medical attention, free schooling for their children, and certain tax advantages, while those who had held high office received free drivers, personal servants, batmen, cook-stewards, gardeners, and an ADC. From 1981, a four-star general such as Obasanjo was quoted as receiving an annual salary (not pension) of N16,260 (then worth $26,650) for life.[13] An incentive to enter farming was the relative ease with which entrepreneurs could borrow capital. Under the Agricultural Credit Guarantee Scheme introduced by Obasanjo's government, banks were protected against losses on agricultural loans to limited companies at rates well below normal bank lending rates and the rate of inflation, so that the real rate of interest paid by the borrowers was negative.[14] According to press reports, it was with the scheme's support that Obasanjo personally raised a bank loan of $1,500,000 to launch Temperance Enterprises Limited, later renamed Obasanjo Farms Limited.[15] He devoted particular attention to poultry farming, which the banks favoured for its anticipated low risks and quick returns.[16]

Unlike some former colleagues, Obasanjo was no briefcase farmer. Shortly after arranging to clear his land, he undertook a personalised six-week course at an agricultural training centre.[17] Moreover, Ota was to be not only an enterprise but a home, after years of life in barracks. Its 'handsome burnt-brick farm house',[18] with ceiling boards of local wood, had two living rooms, two dining rooms, a study, four bedrooms, a squash court (Obasanjo's favoured exercise), bar, roof garden, fish pond, and large grounds. At a cost, it was said, of N320,000 (perhaps somewhat over $500,000), 'Every part of the house was designed to suit his taste.'[19] Obasanjo employed an Indian general manager but also handled paperwork from a farm office with a ceiling fan, a somewhat rickety desk, and a stiff-backed chair.

100

Although suffering from diabetes and high blood pressure, he was mostly on the move. 'Everyday, except when he travels,' it was reported, 'he is at the farm, dressed in shorts and shirts, sandals or slippers and sometimes with a cap, roaring like a tractor from one end of the farm to another, talking to aides, barking out orders, cracking jokes with staff and visitors.'[20] By 1987,

> The farm enterprises include crop, vegetables and seed production, cassava processing, livestock feed production, poultry hatchery, broiler, meat and egg production, piggery, rabbitry, fresh water fish culture, mushroom cultivation and cattle raising. The gari and cassava flour produced in the farm is sold in markets in Nigeria and also exported to Saudi Arabia, Europe, the United States and some West African countries.[21]

In the mid 1980s, the poultry section hatched 140,000 chicks every week.

In 1991 the Ota enterprise employed over 600 workers[22] but it is not clear whether these were all farm workers or whether they included the ancillary staff, for Ota was much more than a farm. It was, for one thing, a retreat and fortress for a man with much to fear from intruders. A notice at the farm gate warned: 'Dogs and armed guards are kept on this farm against robbers, mischief makers, intruders, pressmen and women.'[23] After a police inspector who ventured to check the General's car had been flogged by security staff and locked in the guardroom, he was reduced to posting a court summons on the farm gate after repeated failure to serve it on the proprietor.[24] Yet Ota was nevertheless a meeting place, ideally situated within reach of Lagos international airport and Ibadan University, where Obasanjo could base his discussions of national and global problems and his schemes to train African leaders to solve them. In addition to meeting rooms, there was a canteen, a bar, a disco-theque, a shop, and, in time, a 50-room hotel. For some years, Nigeria's national football team used it as a training camp, preferring its facilities to the Games Village in Lagos. When the austere President Nyerere visited Obasanjo in 1986, he was astonished that anyone could have accumulated the capital invested at Ota.[25]

Ota was a home, but perhaps more for a man than a family. Obasanjo's polygynous lifestyle was as private as it was complicated and no proper account of it can be given here. His first wife, Oluremi, had largely been excluded from his public life as head of state, in accordance with a decision taken when Murtala gained power in 1975 that it was inappropriate in a military regime for the leaders' wives to have the high-profile role that Gowon's wife had enjoyed.[26] Obasanjo's marriage with Oluremi was in any case already breaking down. Of his departure from office in 1979, she later wrote:

> When we went for thanksgiving at Owu Baptist Church, Abeokuta, I was also in the same car. At the church I sat with him on the front pew. During the reception I was in control of events and sat his mistresses and other guests as their importance demanded. I made Stella take one of the middle seats…. After the ceremony I told my husband that I had risen to the top with him by the grace of God. Now I was giving him a free rein to misbehave with his mistresses as I would not stay with him at Abeokuta.[27]

Stronger-minded than he had probably expected when he married her, she returned to Lagos and devoted herself to her children and business activities. Obasanjo visited her and provided her with a separate apartment at the Ota farmhouse, but she refused to share the house with his other wives. Their eldest child, Iyabo, remained close to her father, although later observing that '[he] has a penchant for not giving his children prominence in his life'.[28] His other children shared this grievance, for although Obasanjo enjoyed the company of children and rejoiced at their educational success, they complained that he 'was not there for his children through their bid for western education'. Instead he insisted that they must struggle like other children, with much assistance from their mothers, rather than be privileged because their father had been head of state.[29] At the same time, like many prosperous Yoruba, he sponsored poor children making their way through his own former school at Abeokuta. Several of his own children achieved academic success, but their experience and the treatment of their mothers left some resentful.[30]

With Oluremi estranged, Stella, whom Obasanjo had married in 1976, described herself eight years later as 'a full-time housewife' and appears to have performed that role at Ota throughout the 1980s. She also accompanied him occasionally on public occasions, as on a visit to Japan in 1986. They eventually had three children.[31] But Obasanjo had other wives at this time, often with independent lives in the Yoruba manner, including the television producer Gold Oruh and a glamorous Lagos businesswoman named Lynda (née Soares) who was murdered by car thieves in 1987. His relations with his growing personal staff were similarly patriarchal. A man of immense appetite in all fields of life, Obasanjo, as a journalist wrote, ruled Ota 'like an emperor'.[32]

Once his farm was in working order, Obasanjo emerged as a spokesman for modern farming and a critic of Shagari's government, whose actions threatened not only commercial agriculture but the success of the transition to civilian rule on which Obasanjo's reputation chiefly rested. He had invested his young manhood in this transition and sacrificed his military career for it. To watch the regime fail, and to be unable to prevent it, was 'personally agonizing for me'.[33] The agony probably came not only came from frustration but from a sense of guilt that shaped the remainder of his life, especially when he became civilian president.[34]

Although Obasanjo had voted for Shagari, he thought him unfit to be president. 'Shagari did not court power and he wanted to be nothing more than a senator', Obasanjo later wrote. '… He was pushed into power by those who wanted to make use of him and he was unfortunately too weak and somewhat ill prepared for the trappings of political power to check the abuses of his power by those who made use of him.'[35] Shagari bitterly resented the accusation. First elected to the Federal Assembly 27 years earlier when Obasanjo was still a schoolboy, the president was an experienced politician and administrator 'proud to have been "pushed" by millions of Nigerian voters … while General Obasanjo was pushed by only a handful of military officers … even though he was definitely ill-prepared for "the trappings of political power".' Rather, Shagari insisted, 'Running a democratic government is quite a different problem from running a military dictatorship. General Obasanjo would appear to have failed to appreciate this simple fact.'[36] A strong-minded, scrupulously honest, and deeply religious man, Shagari had played a leading role in the Constituent Assembly and saw it as his duty to establish a democratic regime in strict accordance with the new constitution. He sought to do so with the modesty expected of a pious ruler in Northern Nigeria but alien to the more ostentatious Yoruba political tradition.

Obasanjo refused to recognise the difficulty of Shagari's task. Perhaps defensively, the General insisted that there was little if anything wrong with the constitution. Rather, 'the fault has lain less in the systems than in their operators.'[37] Yet Shagari's inheritance was parlous. With the votes of only some 14% of properly registered electors, he headed a heterogeneous coalition of local party notables controlling little more than one-third of state governorships and National Assembly seats. A loose alliance with Azikiwe's NPP gave him an unreliable majority in the Assembly, but his attempt to draw other parties into a national government met the 'savage opposition' of Awolowo, who refused to regard the 'glorified Grade Two Teacher' as president and did everything possible to damage his regime.[38] The Senate took nearly three months to approve Shagari's executive appointments. Members of the National Assembly delayed his first budget somewhat longer in a dispute over their salaries and expenses, fixing the latter at N88,000 (nearly $150,000) each. They also buried Shagari's bill to establish a Code of Conduct Bureau, thereby adding to the regime's notorious corruption.[39] Shagari blamed the Assembly for the Second Republic's failure, describing it as 'some kind of Frankenstein which tended to destroy what it could not create.'[40] The constitutional division of powers so destructive at the federal level extended into the relationship between the federal government and the twelve states governed by opposition parties, which 'seemed to think of themselves as separate kingdoms,' obstructing the president's programmes and even his visits.[41] The elaborate federal structure was also extremely costly, employing, among others, an estimated 515 permanent secretaries.[42]

Yet Shagari knew that his greatest danger lay elsewhere. As he said in 1979, 'In this country, in the end there are only two parties, the civilians and the military.'[43] Two days after taking office, he appointed a man from his own Sokoto State to head the National Security Organisation. Perhaps unwisely, he reduced military expenditure and expanded the police, increasing their armaments budget from N30,000 in 1979 to over N36 million in 1982.[44] As early as March 1980, military officers complained to Obasanjo about the new government's behaviour. He told them to be patient. A month later, Shagari summarily retired six senior officers, including the former coup leader, Joseph Garba, aged 37. These developments may have moved Obasanjo to comment in a lecture that the military had tried to build bridges between different sections of society and it would be tragic if they were destroyed by hostility and abuse.[45] Ibrahim Babangida, who had sat on the Supreme Military Council and now commanded the mechanised brigade, later recalled that 'the whole thing crumbled by about the beginning of 1981…. Both the economy and the polity.'[46]

For Obasanjo, in 1981, the economy was the focus of concern. In September 1981, it appears, he warned Shagari that he intended to raise the issue at the Council of State, but Shagari asked him to refrain because opposition governors would make it a political issue.[47] There was little communication between the two men. Shagari later wrote that he understood that Obasanjo 'had expected me to be constantly consulting him on all matters of government since he had an obsession of being a super-administrator, super-diplomat and of course a military genius'. Shagari declined to do so because he had greater governmental experience, Obasanjo knew nothing about democracy, the General was unwilling to visit State House, and the President presumably thought it inappropriate to journey to Ota.[48]

The economy was indeed entering crisis, precipitated, as usual, by fluctuating oil prices. The official price of a barrel of Nigerian light crude reached a peak of $40.02 in January 1981, largely owing to the Iranian Revolution. Artificially maintained by OPEC, this bred reduced consumption and eventually a global recession, which left Nigeria unable to sell its oil at OPEC prices against competition from non-OPEC producers.[49] Between 1979 and 1983, Nigeria's average oil exports fell from

2,229,400 to 951,500 barrels per day, a figure maintained only by breaking ranks with OPEC, slashing prices, and initiating a global price collapse.[50] Consequently, between 1980 and 1983, government revenue declined from $27.4 billion to $11 billion. Foreign exchange reserves fell between mid 1980 and April 1982 from $10 billion to $1 billion.[51] Whereas the grandiose development plan for 1980–5 had projected that real GDP would grow by 8.3% per year, real per capita GDP actually fell between 1979 and 1984 by 5.9% per year. Yet imports in 1983 still exceeded those in 1979. The budget deficit was 16% of revenue in 1980 and 72% in 1983.[52]

The balance was met chiefly by borrowing. Estimates of Nigeria's external debt vary, but Shagari stated that it increased during his tenure from $6.8 billion to $18 billion.[53] He responded in March 1982 with an Economic Stabilisation Act designed to impose austerity, but the IMF denied Nigeria a loan to cover balance of payments deficits because the government refused to remove petrol subsidies, liberalise trade, or devalue the naira – devaluation being opposed by Obasanjo and many others on nationalistic grounds.[54]

While economic discontent was universal, the military were especially angered by Shagari's ineffective interventions in the continuing civil war in neighbouring Chad. In 1983, when the President failed to retaliate against Chadian forces violating the Nigerian border, the local commander, Maj.Gen. Buhari, launched a hot pursuit operation into Chad on his own responsibility.[55] The incident lost Shagari any surviving military support. Intelligence sources reported half a dozen coup plots against him during the first nine months of 1983. Senior officers especially feared action by lower ranks that might lead to the bloodletting recently seen in Ghana. In May 1983 they invited Obasanjo to take power again, but he refused to violate the constitution he had proclaimed. On his advice, they deferred their action, planned for July, until after the election due in August, 'otherwise the entire Nigerian populace will accuse the military of subverting the wishes of the people', as Babangida recalled. Shagari knew that the soldiers were waiting for the politicians to fail.[56]

The election gave the military their chance. The opposition parties failed to coalesce against the NPN, which won 60 of the 96 seats in the Senate, 305 of the 449 in the House of Representatives, 12 of the 19 state governorships (one later reversed), and 47% of the presidential vote for Shagari, against 31% for Awolowo. The NPN made genuine inroads into former opposition strongholds and proved itself the only party with a national following, but the poll was accompanied by massive rigging on all sides.[57]

Obasanjo avoided Shagari's re-inauguration. He had been harvesting his fish-pond, he told a rare visiting journalist six weeks later. Speaking in anger, he said that the previous four years had been 'the worst in the life of the Nigerian Republic'. The politicians had made the presidential system unaffordable by voting themselves inflated salaries. Shagari's new government had an 'assembly-hall cabinet' with 36 ministers for only 18 ministries. His regime had spent money mindlessly, wasting the reserves the military had left, importing food that could be produced locally, and lavishing money on the new capital at Abuja that Obasanjo had not seen and did not wish to see. Shagari's government, he claimed, had ignored the 'mountain of studies' that Obasanjo had left for it, yet had not 'started any major project of its own'.[58]

Six weeks later, while Shagari was trying to arrange a meeting with Obasanjo, the generals overthrew him on 31 December 1983, partly to preempt a coup by lower ranks. There was little violence and much public relief. Shagari evaded arrest but surrendered when he learned that Buhari, whom he respected, was the new leader. By the end of January, the regime had detained 453 people, including most leading politicians, many of whom received long prison sentences for corruption.[59] Buhari, former Commissioner for Petroleum Resources under Obasanjo, described his regime as 'an offshoot of the last military administration', whose structure it inherited, although its leadership was overwhelmingly northern. 'We have dutifully intervened to save this nation from imminent collapse', Buhari declared in his first broadcast. 'We shall remain here and salvage it together'. Asked how long that would take, he replied, 'I don't know'.[60]

Obasanjo told journalists that although he regretted the failure of the political system he had installed, he nevertheless supported the new regime enthusiastically. After the failure of both British and American democratic structures, he had

> come to the conclusion, painfully though, that democracy as it is understood by the West is not what we can toy with here. It is something we cannot afford.... We'll probably have to accept that the military will be a major factor to reckon with in the political life of the country. This is a country which needs to be governed. I believe that we have to look at our society and devise for ourselves a system that has everybody chipping in to participate in one form or another. A system that gives us direction, that gives us decisive and purposeful leadership and galvanises us together as a nation. I don't believe that the ritual of voting every four years really does that.[61]

This was the nadir in Obasanjo's fluctuating faith in democracy. For the next two years of Buhari's regime he continued to admire aspects of its policy, notably its War Against Indiscipline and its austerity measures that halved imports, restored a balanced budget, paid interest on foreign debts, and defended the value of the naira.[62] Gradually, however, he distanced himself, denying the government's claim to be an offshoot of his own and defying the ban on politics in August 1985 in a speech cautiously critical of the regime's predominantly northern character.[63]

Popular dissatisfaction with the government's authoritarianism and apparent lack of a plan to restore civilian rule was much stronger. On 27 August 1985, three weeks after Obasanjo's mild criticisms, a bloodless military coup replaced Buhari by the more flexible Army Chief of Staff, Babangida, with support more among Middle Belt officers than those from the far north. 'We had to act so that hope may be restored', Babangida declared. Disturbed by such disloyalty among senior officers, Obasanjo refused to comment beyond saying of Babangida, 'He is a nice man.'[64] There would be much opportunity to reconsider that during the next eight years.

NOTES

1. Obasanjo, *Not my will*, p. 214.
2. *Daily Times*, 2 February 1979; Obasanjo, *Not my will*, p. 205; Karin Barber, *I could speak until tomorrow: oriki, women, and the past in a Yoruba town* (Edinburgh, 1991), pp. 207–8.
3. Quoted in *Newswatch*, 12 January 1987, p. 13.
4. *National Concord*, 21 November 1983.
5. *African Guardian*, 5 June 1986, p. 23.
6. Biobaku, *Egba*, p. 27; Mabogunje and Omer-Cooper, *Owu*, p. 100; *Daily Times*, 22 March 1986.

7. *Nigerian Tribune*, 14 and 22 October 1979.
8. Ibid., 22 October, 25 November, and 3 December 1979.
9. Ibid., 7 December 1979.
10. *Newswatch*, 14 August 1989, p. 15.
11. *National Concord*, 20 January 1984; *New Nigerian*, 31 January and 23 March 1987.
12. Obasanjo, *Not my will*, pp. 214–15; *Newswatch*, 12 January 1987, p. 13.
13. J. 'Bayo Adekanye, *The retired military as emergent power factor in Nigeria* (Ibadan, 1999), pp. 21–2.
14. Irele, 'Land and agricultural policy', pp. 153–4; Obasanjo, *Not my will*, p. 78.
15. *African Guardian*, 5 June 1986, p. 18; *Daily Times*, 3 October 1990; *New Nigerian*, 17 August 1998.
16. Irele, 'Land and agricultural policy' pp. 155–9; Ayodele Aderinwale, 'The essence of Obasanjo', in d'Orville, *Leadership*, p. 142.
17. Obasanjo, *Not my will*, p. 215.
18. *Tell*, 11 November 1991, p. 12. For a description, see *African Guardian*, 5 June 1986, pp. 11–18.
19. *Newswatch*, 12 January 1987, p.16.
20. Ibid., p. 14.
21. Ibid., p. 13.
22. Joan Holmes, 'A great son of Africa', in d'Orville, *Leadership*, p. 121.
23. *Daily Times*, 25 April 1980.
24. *Newbreed*, 1 July 1991, p. 50; *Daily Times*, 20 January and 3 March 1989.
25. Avwenagbiku, *Olusegun Obasanjo*, p. 60; *Daily Times*, 31 May 1989 and 15 August 1990; *Punch*, 24 May 1991.
26. *Punch*, 22 October 1984.
27. Obasanjo, *Bitter-sweet*, p. 93.
28. *This Day*, 14 September 2008.
29. Jonathan Adio Obafemi Olopade, 'The man Obasanjo – a discrete negotiator and mediator', in d'Orville, *Leadership*, p. 138; *Nigerian Tribune*, 10 February 2003; *Newswatch*, 4 February 2008, p. 19.
30. Tunji Oseni, *Media all the way* (Lagos, 2005), p. 540; Obasanjo, *Bitter-sweet*, p. 120; *Newswatch*, 4 February 2008, pp. 14–19.
31. *Guardian*, 17 October 1984; *African Guardian*, 5 June 1986, p. 19; Avwenagbiku, *Olusegun Obasanjo*, p. 236.
32. *African Guardian*, 5 June 1986, p. 19; *Newswatch*, 2 March 1987, p. 12; Aderinwale in d'Orville, *Leadership*, pp. 142–3; *Newswatch*, 14 August 1980, p. 16.
33. Obasanjo, *Not my will*, p. 227.
34. See *African Guardian*, 5 June 1986, p. 21; below, p. 287.
35. Obasanjo, *Not my will*, p. 173.
36. Shagari, *Beckoned*, pp. 453–4.
37. Obasanjo, *Africa in perspective*, p. 10.
38. Shagari, *Beckoned*, p. 243; *Weekly Trust*, 21 August 1998; *West Africa*, 5 May 1980 p. 774 and 16 March 1981 pp. 537–8.
39. *Africa Confidential*, 30 January 1980, p. 1; *West Africa*, 9 June 1980, p. 1039; *Newswatch*, 16 May 1994, p. 14.
40. *National Concord*, 22 January 1993.
41. Shagari, *Beckoned*, p. 437.
42. Daniel C. Bach, 'Managing a plural society: the boomerang effects of Nigerian federalism', *Journal of Commonwealth and Comparative Politics*, 27 (1989), 225.
43. *West Africa*, 30 January 1984, p. 195.
44. *West Africa*, 12 August 1985, p. 1637; Oyeleye Oyediran, 'The 1983 elections', in Ekeh et al., *Nigeria*, p. 179.

45. Obasanjo, *Not my will*, p. 227; *West Africa*, 16 June 1980, p. 1087; Adekanye, *Retired military*, p. 11; *National Concord*, 2 May 1980.
46. *Newswatch*, 10 July 2000, p. 16; *West Africa*, 30 January 1984, p. 243.
47. Obasanjo, *Not my will*, p. 228; *National Concord*, 26 September 1981.
48. Shagari, *Beckoned*, pp. 453–4.
49. Stewart, 'Banks', p. 114; Khan, *Nigeria*, pp. 1, 29.
50. Akin Iwayemi, 'Le Nigeria dans le système petrolier international', in Daniel C. Bach, Johny Egg, and Jean Philippe (ed.), *Le Nigeria: un pouvoir en puissance* (Paris, 1988), p. 20; *West Africa*, 14 February 1983, p. 695.
51. Soares de Oliveira, *Oil and politics*, p. 84; Stewart, 'Banks', p. 96.
52. Bevan et al., *Nigeria and Indonesia*, p. 185; *West Africa*, 30 September 1985, p. 2023.
53. Shagari, *Beckoned*, p. 399.
54. Toyin Falola and Julius Ihonvbere, *The rise and fall of Nigeria's Second Republic: 1979–84* (London, 1985), pp. 149–50; Ademiluyi, *From prisoner to president*, pp. 42–3.
55. Shagari, *Beckoned*, pp. 353–5; Buhari in *News*, 5 July 1993, p. 23.
56. *Africa Confidential*, 4 January 1984, p. 1; *West Africa*, 30 January 1984, p. 195; Obasanjo, *Not my will*, p. 227; *Newswatch*, 10 July 2000, p. 15; Shagari, *Beckoned*, p. 443.
57. Daniel Bach (ed.), *Le Nigeria contemporain* (Paris, 1986), p. 115; Osaghae, *Crippled giant*, pp. 146–8; Christopher Hart, 'The Nigerian elections of 1983', *Africa*, 63 (1993), 397–418.
58. *National Concord*, 21 November 1983.
59. Ibid., 17 April 1984; Shagari, *Beckoned*, p. 462; *West Africa*, 30 January 1984, p. 242.
60. *West Africa*, 9 January 1984 pp. 55–7, 16 January 1984 p. 101, 27 February 1984 p. 427.
61. Ibid., 30 January 1984, pp. 197–8.
62. Obasanjo, *Africa embattled*, p. 62; Osaghae, *Crippled giant*, p. 184.
63. *Newswatch*, 12 August 1985, pp. 20–1.
64. Osaghae, *Crippled giant*, pp. 189–90; Alli, *Federal Republic*, p. 216; *West Africa*, 2 September 1985, p. 1791; Ademiluyi, *From prisoner to president*, p. 45.

10

The Author

During his first eleven years after leaving office, Obasanjo published four books covering his military career and looking forward to Nigeria's future. They were his most important publications. All were valuable contributions to the history of the period, but they were also controversial works related to contemporary politics.

Obasanjo's account of the civil war, *My Command*, was written in 1980 when he was a Distinguished Fellow at the University of Ibadan, perhaps a convenient base while preliminary work took place at Ota. After recounting the war's origins and his role during its first two years, the book dealt chiefly with his command of the Third Marine Commando Division during the final months of conflict. His pious hope that the war was sufficiently distant to prevent the opening of old wounds proved vain, but his wish that this first war memoir should stimulate others was abundantly fulfilled.[1]

My Command first alerted the Nigerian public to Obasanjo's role in ending the civil war.[2] This had received little publicity at the time. The Third Marine Commando Division was linked in the public mind with its first commander, Benjamin Adekunle. Gowon had occupied the centre stage at the end of the war. Obasanjo had conducted his final campaign in a news blackout and had then disappeared back into routine soldiering. The first extensive account of the war from the Biafran side, also published in 1980 by Alexander Madiebo, Biafra's Army Commander, did not mention Obasanjo.[3] The claims asserted in *My Command* were therefore all the more provocative.

This was certainly part of Obasanjo's purpose, for he loved to shock and had reason to feel that his contribution had been overlooked. Yet he clearly also had the contemporary situation in view. He was writing in the wake of Shagari's contested election, amidst personal abuse from the Yoruba press. He later claimed that there had been an attempt to assassinate him during his time at Ibadan.[4] *My Command*, therefore, carried a strong contemporary message. It blamed the origins of the civil war on narrow ethnic politics of the kind the UPN was pursuing. The regionalised constitution of 1951, which Awolowo's followers saw as having instituted 'true federalism', had rather been 'a turn for the worse'. 'All along, from 1954 onwards, the direction was consistently away from a strong centre towards a formidable strengthening, almost insulation, of the regional base of each major political party.' In the late 1950s, 'The leaders rode on the crest of this cancerous tribalism and the ignorance of the people to power, at the expense of national unity and the nation. Instead

108

of regionalism ensuring and preserving national unity, it became its bane.'[5] The military coup of January 1966 had possessed noble aims but its divisive execution had 'hastened Nigeria's collapse', as had Ironsi's insensitivity to northern thinking.[6] On the eve of the war, the lead in self-aggrandising ethnic separatism had passed to Ojukwu. 'If he could not achieve his long-cherished ambition of ruling an independent Nigeria,' Obasanjo wrote, 'he could break it up and rule an independent and sovereign "Biafra".'[7] By contrast, the Igbo hero in Obasanjo's story was Ukpabi Asika, the Ibadan lecturer whom Obasanjo claimed to have recruited as civilian administrator of the Igbo areas occupied by federal troops, a man regarded by most Igbo as a collaborator and condemned after the war for corruption, but held up by Obasanjo for 'his total commitment and loyalty to national cause'.[8] On the federal side, the hero was not Gowon but Obasanjo himself, who had held together western and northern troops in Ibadan in 1967 and led them to victory two years later.[9]

The attack on *My Command* began at the launching ceremony in November 1980, when Obasanjo's sharp-tongued friend, Bola Ige, Governor of the Oyo State containing Ibadan, used his keynote speech to denounce Obasanjo's 'massive rigging' of the 1979 election and then to condemn his book's egotism and its depreciation of other military commanders, especially Murtala Muhammed, whom Obasanjo had eulogised after his death. Ige conceded, however, that the book was the best existing account of the war.[10] Obasanjo's criticism of Murtala aroused particular condemnation, not only as disloyal to his former chief but as near blasphemy against a martyr. Obasanjo had described Murtala's bloody and unsuccessful attempt to capture Onitsha by direct assault across the Niger as 'a grave and calculated risk which could be called bravado', while Murtala's subsequent abandonment of his division and repeated disobedience towards federal headquarters were denounced as indiscipline.[11] 'That was long before [Obasanjo] became General Muhammed's Friday', a journalist sneered, while another revived the gossip that Obasanjo might have had wind of Dimka's coup.[12]

It was now open season for generals. Adeyinka Adebayo, Military Governor of the West before the war and a senior Yoruba political figure, urged Obasanjo to withdraw the book to avoid dividing the army and destabilising the country. 'I do not think this is the time anybody should claim credit for anything', he wrote. 'The war was not fought by one man. It was fought collectively.' He also noted that Obasanjo had omitted 'the historic battle of Ore which he led and lost' during Banjo's invasion of the Mid-West, an account of those events at odds with Obasanjo's version.[13] Ibrahim Haruna, who had been among those removed from office in 1977 and was accused in the book of failing to make his Second Division an effective unit, wrote a long and penetrating review condemning the author for 'a disservice to this nation' in pursuit of 'instant glory' and 'public acclaim as a scholar/historian'. He accused Obasanjo of endangering the army by urging the removal of northern troops from the Western State before the war, of professional incompetence as an engineer, of leading 'the onslaught against universities and intellectual freedom,' of attempting to destroy the nation by destroying its heroes, and of publishing 'a danger to peace'.[14]

The fiercest controversy focused predictably on Obasanjo's replacement of Adekunle in command of the Third Marine Commando Division in May 1969. Obasanjo's claim to have converted the division's 'low morale, desertion and distrust … into high morale, confidence, co-operation and success' especially aroused Adekunle's ire.[15] He declared the book 'an intellectual fraud', 'full of bundles of 'balderdash', written to gain money and a false reputation. In reality, he claimed, the bulk of the war had been fought and won before Obasanjo took over to reap where others had toiled.[16]

Equally angry was Obasanjo's most persistent and articulate critic, Wole Soyinka, who saw him as personifying military rule, blamed his 'betrayal' of their meeting during Banjo's invasion for his own wartime incarceration, and resented the implication in Obasanjo's account that Soyinka had tried to persuade and bribe him to allow Banjo's force to enter Yorubaland.[17] 'The stories told by Obasanjo that I came to persuade him is bullshit', Soyinka declared in 1991; '… in a way I saved his life by agreeing to meet him during the Victor Banjo crossing, because his subordinates were ready to arrange an accident for him.'[18]

The author himself was all innocence. A cartoon showed the book as a huge bomb accompanied by a grinning Obasanjo, with halo.[19] 'I have written my own account about my command, not theirs', he told his military critics. 'Anyone who disagrees with any portion of the book, is free to write his.'[20] As indeed they did: one virtue of *My Command* was to provoke a series of war memoirs, one of which Obasanjo was himself to sue for libel.[21]

There were other virtues. 'General Obasanjo has done not only what an army officer had never done, but also what our "academics" would find difficult to accomplish. He has produced a first class book on the civil war', a correspondent wrote from Benin.[22] Obasanjo's friend, the novelist Ken Saro-Wiwa, described it as masterly, although he suspected that the author had enjoyed editorial assistance.[23] It was indeed a remarkable book, providing a brief, generally lucid, simply written, fast-moving reconstruction of a complicated bush war, a reconstruction that remained after thirty years the best account yet written. The message of Nigerian unity was powerfully conveyed, but so also was the horror of war. The most memorable section is Obasanjo's account of his tour of frontline positions when he took command of Third Marine Commando. It contains vivid character sketches of individual soldiers, their reactions to war, Obasanjo's concern for their welfare, and his capacity to establish relationships with them:

> The battalion commander was a field commissioned officer nicknamed A.P.P. (African Patch Patch). A.P.P. is an interesting character. He is a dark, well-built, tall man. He is a bully who maintains iron discipline over his men. His nickname came about because of his belief that an African is naturally inefficient and will never do a thorough job. But, ironically, A.P.P. believed in his own ability to do a good job. There was a story that once when his brigade commander became a casualty, A.P.P. went with his escorts to take over command of the brigade without any authority to do so. He also had an abiding faith in rifle-launched rockets, and walked around and slept with one. He was handicapped by poor education. All the education he had he obtained in the Army. He also seemed to know his limitations, at least educationally. He had a brilliant young officer as his adjutant whom he made write down all his points for discussion with me. He pushed his adjutant forward and said, 'Talk now.' I cut in and asked A.P.P. to present his points himself. I told him I would be able to understand him. He put his points across in admirably understandable 'pidgin English'. To his surprise, I replied to him in equally good 'pidgin English'. He entertained us to cold soft drinks, fried meat and kola nuts and appealed to me not to go forward of his battalion front line as I would easily be shot at by the rebels who were within earshot. I ignored his appeal and warning and visited his men in their trenches. The trenches were not as good as those of 106 Battalion location or those of the next. And I was not shot at. I told him so.[24]

This sensitivity to character – especially the characters of soldiers – was also the chief feature of Obasanjo's second book, *Nzeogwu*, published early in 1987 as a memoir of his friend and comrade in the Congo, who had led the coup d'état of January 1966 in Kaduna and died early in the civil war fighting on the Biafran side.[25] Obasanjo focused on the contradictions in that career:

> I have not set out to praise Chukwuma [Nzeogwu] nor make him a villain … I feel I owe it to Chukwuma and to Nigerian posterity, to record what I knew about this idealistic and thoroughly patriotic Nigerian who in his approach to our political problems, has been described as exhibiting more enthusiasm and naivety than wisdom and prudence.… He played for high stakes and gambled with his own future and eventually his life. He was a man full of life, and he obviously wanted to live a full life; but he saw no contradiction in denying others theirs, when according to him they stood in the way of national progress.[26]

Obasanjo described Nzeogwu's patriotism in terms that could equally have described his own:

> Chukwuma had a dream of a great Nigeria that is a force to reckon with in the world.… He had a dream of an ordered and orderly nation, through a disciplined society. He also dreamt of a country where national interest overrides self, sectional or tribal interest. He wanted a country where a person's ability, output, merit and productivity would determine his social and economic progress, rather than political and ethnic considerations.[27]

All this Obasanjo admired, as he also admired Nzeogwu's qualities of leadership: that he 'stood out, and allowed nobody else to take the blame. He bore the responsibility and consequences of leadership.'[28] Yet Nzeogwu had other qualities that Obasanjo could not admire: his rebelliousness, recklessness, and resort to violence.

To explain these contradictions of character, Obasanjo looked to Nzeogwu's turbulent upbringing and youth, so different in many ways from his own.[29] One reviewer commented that the book made its subject sound like a juvenile delinquent, a man 'allowed to grow wayward', whom even the army could not discipline until he 'murdered the most powerful premier of the time and caused the untimely death of the most efficient cream of our officer corps.'[30] Admirers of Nzeogwu thought that Obasanjo had depreciated their hero. Some questioned the reality of the friendship Obasanjo claimed.[31]

Obasanjo replied that he was seeking only to understand the man. Yet, as in *My Command*, he surely also had a political objective. 'I would not mind if this book is sensationalised or even scandalised,' he was reported to have said at the launching, which took place on 15 January 1987, the anniversary of Nzeogwu's coup and the Sardauna's death, a choice that angered many northerners.[32] Members of the Gamji Club at Ahmadu Bello University, an organisation dedicated to the Sardauna's memory, burned copies at a ceremony attended by 6,000 students and workers, demanding that the university withdraw Obasanjo's honorary degree and condemning the book's 'hypocritical and grossly naive analysis' of the coup.[33] Letters to the press urged the author to withdraw his publication for the sake of his reputation for non-partisanship or demanded that the government ban it 'to avert the threat it posed to the existence of Nigeria as a united country'. More subtly, a northern reviewer suggested that Obasanjo was seeking popularity among the Igbo in order to foster southern unity in time for the return of civilian politics.[34]

More probably, *Nzeogwu*, although primarily a memoir of an intimate friend, was at least coloured by the dissatisfaction with northern military dominance that Obasanjo had hinted at in August 1985[35] and that other southern officers had echoed more recently. Adekunle had complained that 'The Officers corps has been bastardised.' David Ejoor, a former Chief of Staff, had protested that 'Southern officers have been gradually eliminated by posting and retirement from competing for the highest position available.'[36] Now Obasanjo wrote in his introduction:

> Attempts to re-examine the lives of those who have made contributions to this country may not only provide a better insight, but offer possible solutions to our many difficulties, which centre on the search for possible ways of co-existence in a country torn by ethnic differences, not to talk of greed and selfishness and the new apparent danger of religion.[37]

It was again a cautious hint, but one reviewer, describing the book as 'an act of courage by General Obasanjo', claimed that its chief lesson was that Nigeria should free itself from military rule.[38] Certainly it was enough for the Chief of General Staff to order retired officers to 'refrain from making indiscreet and unguarded statements.'[39]

Obasanjo's accumulated skill in combining recent history with covert political comment peaked three years later in *Not My Will*, whose cleverly ambiguous title covered an account of the Murtala/Obasanjo regime of 1975–9. He now expected, indeed courted, controversy and was not disappointed, for it was banned from sale by a court injunction.[40] At one level, this was unreasonable, for most of the book was a careful, lucid, admirably composed but pedestrian account of Obasanjo's administration, showing none of the literary skill of *My Command*. As a reviewer commented, 'By writing the book at all, Obasanjo has done an incalculable service to Nigeria, whose citizens, for once, have been let into some of the processes that ended in decisions that affected them for good or for ill.'[41] Obasanjo claimed credit for his smooth management of the political transition: 'I have voluntarily left the stage while the ovation was high for others to play their part.'[42] He was proud of the national revitalisation achieved by the regime, its contribution to liberation in southern Africa, its Universal Primary Education programme, its reform of local government, its attempts to modernise agriculture, and its extensive investment in industry and infrastructure. He showed no doubt that state investment in industry and modern farming had been the correct strategy.[43] Nor did he recognise the dangers of an overvalued currency or the need to cushion the economy against fluctuations in the oil market. Some claims were exaggerated, for example the extent of military demobilisation.[44] Failures, such as the unsuccessful programme to expand telecommunications, were blamed on others.[45] Nevertheless, *Not My Will*, like *My Command*, was a historical source of lasting value.

Like *My Command*, too, it was also a battleground, an opportunity to strike back at critics, including almost all the generals who had objected to his earlier book.[46] In addition, he indulged his distaste for politicians by criticising all five presidential candidates of 1979, especially Awolowo, whose acolytes had continued to pursue Obasanjo even after their leader's death in 1987. 'I had nothing but sympathy for Chief Awolowo who seemed incapable of achieving his life long ambition to be his country's chief executive', Obasanjo now wrote, adding, 'What he had been struggling in vain to achieve … until he died had come my way, unsolicited.' Awolowo's 'tribal chauvinism', he wrote, 'was surely not a catalyst for easy attainment of national political leadership.' Even as Yoruba leader, Awolowo had been 'blinded by his ambition.... The Yorubas whom he claimed to be working for while assiduously working for himself, would continue to be the dregs of Nigerian politics and eat the crumbs from the national political table, unless and until their attitude encompasses Nigeria.'[47] This hatchet job infuriated the acolytes. Awolowo's widow denounced it as 'a tissue of lies told only to prove how much its author hated her husband'.[48] Ebenezer Babatope published an immediate denunciation:

> Obasanjo's displeasure at being born poor has grown to such a pitiable condition that he has developed a kind of pathological rejection of all persons who clearly are his intellectual and political superiors. It is a kind of dangerous complex problem that has led him, in all he has done and written, to develop a style of running such persons down. The man certainly deserves the pity and sympathy of all rational minds.[49]

In addition to scoring blows on former adversaries, the publication of Obasanjo's book in February 1990 had a deeper contemporary purpose. It described, he claimed, 'a single-minded pursuit of the programme to hand over the reigns [sic] of administration of the country to elected civilian administrators. It was clear to us that such an exercise could not be carried out without some form of party political activities.'[50] This was a reference to Nigeria's political situation as it had developed since Babangida's coup d'état in August 1985. Whereas the previous Buhari regime had been corrective, the astute and ambitious Babangida sought to reshape Nigeria's economy and political system. He released the Second Republic politicians gaoled by Buhari but banned them from political activity in order to create opportunities for 'newbreeds' to emerge - a step that Obasanjo thought an unwise waste of experience and 'an illusion at which old politicians take a good laugh'.[51] In January 1986 Babangida announced that he would restore civilian rule on 1 October 1990. The Political Forum appointed to draw up a programme recommended a two-party political system in order to avoid both the multi-party confusion of the Second Republic and the one-party pattern that had bred authoritarianism elsewhere in Africa. To permit a more gradual transition than Obasanjo had conducted, the date for handover was postponed to 1992.[52] In the interim, a Constituent Assembly of 567 members spent ten months suggesting amendments to the 1979 constitution, most of which the military rejected. Party organisation was permitted from May 1989 on the understanding that the two most effective parties would be registered to contest election, but in October Babangida rejected all thirteen parties seeking registration and announced that he would establish two new parties, 'one a little to the left and the other a little to the right of centre'.[53]

This was the political background to *Not My Will*. Never enthusiastic towards Babangida's seizure of power, Obasanjo was angered on an especially sensitive issue when Babangida justified deferring his handover to civilians by saying that 'we need to learn a lesson from an abrupt handover of power to civilian politicians' in 1979, implying that Obasanjo's misjudgment had been responsible for Shagari's failure.[54] Obasanjo replied to this 'explanation or maybe an apology for the new 1992 disengagement date' by pointing out that Babangida had been a member of the Supreme Military Council that had approved the transition timetable of 1979. In a passage hinting at his suspicions of Babangida's intentions, he added that the integrity of the military 'should not be sacrificed on the altar of "responsibility".... As officers and gentlemen in the military our words used to be our bond.... What is expected of us, as gentlemen after such accomplishment, is to walk away with dignity and not to run away or stay put.' Babangida's spokesman commented that Obasanjo had a duty to weigh his words.[55]

Obasanjo was also pondering Babangida's proposed two-party system in relation to his own evolving thought about democracy. In the immediate disillusionment following Buhari's overthrow of the Second Republic, Obasanjo had felt that 'democracy as it is understood by the West ... is something we cannot afford.'[56] Eighteen months later, he commented that any future party system must be tailored to Nigeria's needs and foster constructive criticism rather than mere opposition.[57] This was a view widely held in Nigeria during the mid 1980s. In 1986, for example, northern traditional rulers recommended that Nigeria should become a one-party state, as did many submissions to the Political Bureau at that time. [58] One-party states were unpopular and outdated elsewhere in Africa, but in March 1987, lecturing in the United States, Obasanjo said he saw nothing wrong with such a political system, provided it ensured general participation, human rights, and freedom of expression. (He did not mention freedom of association.) What was anathema to him was 'institutionalized opposition, a concept ... profoundly incongruent with most African political culture and practice'. Nor did he think that election was necessarily the only way of choosing leaders. 'Perhaps we should instead enlist the age-old practice of sounding out local opinion, and selecting representatives within communities, with urban centers being divided into wards and quarters.'[59]

Obasanjo's reaction to Babangida's proposed two-party system was published in February 1989 as *Constitution for National Integration and Development*. During the five years since Buhari's coup, Obasanjo had lost much of his faith in military government and regained some of his sympathy for democracy, perhaps in step with the international climate of opinion that in 1989 led to the fall of the Berlin Wall and the beginnings of a democratisation movement in tropical Africa.[60] In his new book, he recognised that 'The yearning for democracy i.e. popular participation in the governmental processes with guarantees of fundamental human rights and freedom of expression within the law remain [sic] a basic desire of all peoples.' He still maintained, however, that the failure of imported Western models meant that Nigerians must create new structures, seeking precedents especially in their pre-colonial political systems, which had been consensual rather than conflictual. This would meet the most blatant feature of Nigeria's recent democratic experiments – 'that people do not want to be in opposition' – and it would counter the tendency, already appearing in preparations for Babangida's two-party system, for the new groupings, like the old, to rest on 'ethnic and linguistic affinity into which ethno-religious sentiment is creeping'.[61] 'Two parties', he warned at this time, 'will split the Nigerian society right down through the weakest seams', by which he clearly meant the division between Muslim North and Christian South,[62] a danger that led other observers to describe Babangida's two-party scheme as 'like blowing a kiss to a sex maniac'.[63] 'As a democrat, I will prefer that the number of parties be allowed to evolve rather than be legislated', Obasanjo insisted, yet if the choice was between two parties and one, he would prefer a one-party state, as a temporary device and with provision to prevent power being concentrated in one person, which had been the weakness of one-party states elsewhere.[64]

His scheme proposed that the single party would formulate policy and engage in political education and mobilisation, while the government, headed by a president, would be distinct from party leaders and would execute policy. His most original

114

suggestion was a non-partisan Council of State, composed of the president, former presidents and chief justices, and representative traditional rulers, to control the census, electoral commission, code of conduct bureau, and judicial service commission.[65] This last suggestion attracted some interest, but otherwise Obasanjo's 'bankrupt prescription'[66] found little sympathy among Nigeria's political elite, whose hostility to a one-party state was reinforced by the resumption of competitive politics during 1989. The book's most important consequence was to leave the misleading impression that Obasanjo was an enthusiast for a one-party state.

When *Not My Will* appeared a year later in February 1990, it did not debate the desirable number of parties, although it did insist that electoral choice was an essential element of democracy.[67] Remarkably, for a man who in 1984 had feared that democracy was impossible in Nigeria, the book began with an affirmation of restored faith in it:

> Democracy may not necessarily ensure rapid economic development or affluence but it is, at least, the best form of government so far devised that ensures reasonable participation by [the] majority of people in the means and issues that concern their governance. Democracy is the option which the governed prefer …
>
> In the Nigerian situation, democracy is the only integrative glue that can bind different sub-national groups together into a nation with common destinies, equal status and common identity on a permanent basis.[68]

By a circuitous route and despite his contempt for politicians, Obasanjo had become convinced that democracy in Nigeria was indispensable. He did not waver from that for the rest of his career. The problem, however, was how to define it and reconcile it with national unity.

Alongside their political dispute, Obasanjo and Babangida were at odds over economic issues. Babangida had inherited an immensely difficult economic situation in which real per capita GDP had fallen by nearly 6% per year during the previous five years.[69] He was convinced that Nigeria must meet this crisis by adopting a structural adjustment programme (SAP) of the kind that the International Monetary Fund generally imposed on needy countries during the 1980s, with the aim of reducing inefficient and costly state economic interventions and allowing market forces to operate more freely.[70] Recognising the unpopularity of such a policy, Babangida skilfully initiated a public debate on the issue, found that 65% of participants opposed an SAP formulated by the IMF, announced that 'democratic patriotism' required Nigeria to formulate its own, and instituted one acceptable to the IMF.

Babangida's SAP cut petrol subsidies by 80%, introduced a two-tier foreign exchange system that effectively devalued the naira, reduced government spending, designated 96 federal enterprises for privatisation, deregulated the banking system, and negotiated an agreement with foreign creditors limiting Nigeria's debt service payments to 30% of its exports. It was Africa's most comprehensive SAP and initially had positive economic effects, especially in expanding agricultural production by 5% per year between 1985 and 1989, raising manufacturing output by 14% per year between 1986 and 1990, and increasing GDP by 5.3% per year during the same period. Yet Babangida failed to control budget deficits, money supply, and inflation, which rose by 20% per year between 1986 and 1990, resulting in much suffering for the urban poor, a major erosion of living standards for the middle class, and the deterioration of public services, which together outweighed SAP's positive stimulus to economic growth in the eyes of most Nigerians. Nor did the programme check the accumulation of foreign debt, which rose between 1983 and 1990 from about $18 billion to $33 billion.[71]

Obasanjo's initial response to structural adjustment was to urge cooperation with the government at a time of economic emergency, but he was intuitively opposed to devaluation of the currency – not appreciating that it was essential to expanding non-oil exports – and by 1987, when the first popular protests against SAP took place, he was losing patience with the entire policy and its Western backers.[72] During November, he announced that

> It appears to me that we now have a structural adjustment programme which seems to drastically reduce the living standards of all classes of productive workers except speculators and commission agents ...
>
> If we are substantially dictated to, let us tell those who preach trade liberalisation and other harmful measures to us, and which they do not practise on the ruins of their own economy and at great hardship to their own people, that they are leading us along the path of great economic decline, social dislocation and turbulence and political consequences that we can ill-afford ...
>
> Adjustment ... must have human face, human heart and milk of kindness and must not ignore what I call human survival and dignity, issues of employment, food, shelter, education and health.[73]

The speech received a standing ovation, but the government press condemned it as 'a blow below the belt for an administration that found the courage to take unpalatable but sound economic decisions that General Obasanjo's own administration had not had the courage to take'.[74]

'Adjustment with a human face' was a phrase borrowed from the United Nations Children's Fund.[75] It was the theme of a conference organised in Abuja in June 1987 by the United Nations Economic Commission for Africa (UNECA), which was directed by Obasanjo's former colleague, the economist Adebayo Adedeji.[76] As usual, Obasanjo was absorbing the economic ideas of the moment, and he became increasingly convinced of them during the next two years. In June 1989 he set out the view, recently endorsed at a UNECA conference, that devaluation could only damage African economies unless it was accompanied by positive government action to stimulate production in order to take advantage of foreign markets.[77] In September he publicly disputed Babangida's claim that there was no viable alternative to adjustment:

> 'Any programme that almost wipes out our past gains overnight and mortgages the future of Nigeria in education, health, manufacturing, agriculture and in post [sic] of debt repayment ... cannot have my support ...'
>
> General Obasanjo said adjustment without growth amounted to stagnation at best, stressing that the World Bank and IMF 'authors of SAP want us (Nigeria) to pay our debt and not necessarily to grow, transform and develop.'[78]

Three years later he pointed out that international opinion was moving in the same direction:

> I am unrepentant on my stand on SAP. It is heartening to note, though, that the architects of the programme in Washington DC have acknowledged some defects in it. That is enough to convince us that we cannot build a solid edifice with the SAP architectural

plan. Short-term adjustment measures and medium- and long-term development and transformation should be complementary. Should we pursue industrialisation and development of certain projects at all cost? I have always wondered in recent times whether or not due to delay caused by frequent political changes and ineptitude in our management and handling, we have not missed the boat in two or three of the basic infrastructures like modernization of the railway and strategic industries including iron and steel.[79]

This was the point in Obasanjo's thinking at which *Not My Will* appeared, with its justification of the state-directed development strategy that he had pursued during the late 1970s. He had complained early in Babangida's regime that 'If I had remained in office, in 10 years, I would have made Nigeria a world power. I had a programme and a vision. But we were committed to handing over power. See the mess that followed.'[80] By the early 1990s, Obasanjo was no longer content to agonise at Ota. The farmer had already become an international statesman and was about to become a politician.

NOTES

1. Obasanjo, *My command*, p. x.
2. Ademiluyi, *From prisoner to president*, p. 38.
3. Madiebo, *Nigerian revolution*.
4. Obasanjo, *Not my will*, pp. 224–5.
5. Obasanjo, *My command*, pp. 2–3.
6. Ibid., p. 6.
7. Ibid., p. 10.
8. Ibid., p. 21.
9. Ibid., pp. 27–8, xii–xiii.
10. *Sunday Concord*, 9 November 1980; *National Concord*, 21 November 1980.
11. Obasanjo, *My command*, pp. 42, 57–8.
12. *National Concord*, 24 and 21 November 1980.
13. Ibid., 14 November 1980; *New Nigerian*, 15 November 1980; Obasanjo, *My command*, pp. 30–4.
14. *New Nigerian*, 22 November and 11 December 1980.
15. Obasanjo, *My command*, pp. xii-xiii.
16. *African Guardian*, 5 June 1986, p. 22; *National Concord*, 10 November 1980; *African Concord*, 30 September 1988, p. 13; Adekunle, *War letters*, pp. 20–1.
17. Soyinka, *You must set forth*, pp. 155–9.
18. *African Concord*, 14 October 1991, pp. 42–3.
19. *National Concord*, 5 November 1980.
20. Avwenagbiku, *Olusegun Obasanjo*, p. 65.
21. Adewale Ademoyega, *Why we struck: the story of the first Nigerian coup* (Ibadan, 1981), pp. 96–7; *National Concord*, 9 February 1983.
22. *New Nigerian*, 3 December 1980.
23. Saro-Wiwa, *On a darkling plain*, p. 214; Ken Saro-Wiwa, *Similia: essays on anomic Nigeria* (Port Harcourt, 1991), p. 75.
24. Obasanjo, *My command*, pp. 75–6.
25. Above, pp. 20–1.
26. Obasanjo, *Nzeogwu*, pp. 4, 145.
27. Ibid., pp. 143, 145.
28. Ibid., p. 81.

29. Ibid., Chs 1–5.
30. *New Nigerian*, 7 March 1987; *Daily Times*, 5 February 1987.
31. *African Concord*, 12 March 1990, p. 33; *New Nigerian*, 31 January 1987.
32. Ademiluyi, *From prisoner to president*, p. 52; *Newswatch*, 23 February 1987, p. 27.
33. *New Nigerian*, 8 March 1987.
34. *New Nigerian*, 15 February 1987; *Daily Times*, 9 February 1987; *New Nigerian*, 15 March 1987.
35. *Daily Times*, 7–8 August 1985; *Newswatch*, 12 August 1985, pp. 20–1.
36. *Newswatch*, 23 February 1987, p. 27.
37. Obasanjo, *Nzeogwu*, p. 4.
38. *New Nigerian*, 28 February 1987.
39. *Newswatch*, 23 February 1987, p. 27.
40. Obasanjo, *Not my will*, p. v.
41. *Newswatch*, 16 April 1990, p. 15.
42. Obasanjo, *Not my will*, p. 182.
43. Ibid., pp. 77–89.
44. Ibid., pp. 91–2.
45. Ibid., pp. 92–3.
46. Ibid., pp. 26–7, 157–9.
47. Ibid., pp. 181–2, 173.
48. *Newswatch*, 5 March 1990, p. 25.
49. Ibid., 16 April 1990, p. 9. Babatope later recounted the controversy in *Not his will*.
50. Obasanjo, *Not my will*, introduction.
51. Ibid., pp. 52–3.
52. *West Africa*, 3 August 1987, pp. 1482 et seq.; *Africa Confidential*, 8 July 1987, p. 8.
53. Osaghae, *Crippled giant*, pp. 207–23.
54. *Daily Times*, 3 July 1987.
55. Ibid., 30 November and 2 December 1987.
56. *West Africa*, 30 January 1984, pp. 197–8; above, p. 105.
57. *Daily Times*, 7 August 1985.
58. *West Africa*, 3 November 1986, p. 2313, and 3 August 1987, pp. 1482 et seq.
59. Obasanjo, *Africa in perspective*, pp. 8, 13, 15.
60. See below, p. 130.
61. Olusegun Obasanjo, *Constitution for national integration and development* (Lagos, 1989), pp. iii–v.
62. Obasanjo to Nwankwo, 26 April 1989, in Arthur Nwankwo, *Before I die: Olusegun Obasanjo/Arthur Nwankwo correspondence on the one-party state* (Enugu, 1989), p. 84.
63. Raufu Mustapha and Shehu Othman in *West Africa*, 28 September 1987, p. 1908.
64. Obasanjo in Nwankwo, *Before I die*, p. 86; Obasanjo, *Constitution*, pp. 3–4.
65. Obasanjo, *Constitution*, pp. 78–99.
66. *Daily Times*, 17 March 1989.
67. Obasanjo, *Not my will*, p. 1.
68. Ibid., pp. 1–2.
69. Bevan et al., *Nigeria and Indonesia*, p. 185.
70. For the economic thinking, see Tony Killick, *A reaction too far: economic theory and the role of the state in developing countries* (London, 1989), Ch.2.
71. Thomas Biersteker and Peter M. Lewis, 'The rise and fall of structural adjustment in Nigeria', in Larry Diamond, Anthony Kirk-Greene, and Oyeleye Oyediran (ed.), *Transition without end: Nigerian politics and civil society under Babangida* (Boulder, 1997), Ch.13; Gary Moser, Scott Rogers, and Reinold van Til, *Nigeria: experience with structural adjustment*, IMF Occasional Paper 148 (Washington DC, 1997); Shagari, *Beckoned*, p. 399.
72. *Daily Times*, 7 August and 30 October 1985; Avwenagbiku, *Olusegun Obasanjo*, p. 146.

73. *Daily Times*, 30 November 1987.
74. Ibid., 4 December 1987.
75. See G.A. Cornia, R. Jolly, and F. Stewart (ed.), *Adjustment with a human face* (Oxford, 1987).
76. Adebayo Adedeji, Owodunni Teriba, and Patrick Bugembe (ed.), *The challenge of African economic recovery and development* (London, 1991), pp. 780–90.
77. Olusegun Obasanjo, 'SAP: path of sanity', in *Newswatch*, 12 June 1989, p. 48; United Nations Economic Commission for Africa, *African alternative framework to structural adjustment programmes for socio-economic recovery and transformation* ([Addis Ababa, 1989?]), pp. ii, 47.
78. *Daily Times*, 12 September 1989.
79. Ibid., 18 March 1992.
80. *African Guardian*, 5 June 1986, p. 15.

11

The Statesman

'I do not believe that one must occupy the government house to make useful contributions to one's society', Obasanjo wrote in 1990. 'And out of public office, one becomes unconstrained in creating a larger constituency for oneself, even a constituency as large as the world itself.'[1] This he had indeed achieved during the previous decade. He had become a world statesman, called upon to mediate in international disputes and advise on global problems, considered for the most demanding of international posts. This in turn had compelled a deeper involvement in Nigerian public life. 'How else can I be credible in condemning injustice, racism, violation of human rights and lack of democracy in South Africa or in any foreign country for that matter, if I condone similar tendencies or practices in my own country or region?' he demanded.[2] Moreover, his international activities provided the education that he had been denied in youth and had lacked when he hesitantly accepted office. 'I believe that learning is a continuous life-long process', he said.[3] Nor was it enough merely to learn; it was necessary also to teach. His most continuous activity during these years was to organise the Africa Leadership Forum, based at his Ota farm, to provide potential African leaders with the preparation he had lacked. This chapter is about Obasanjo's globalisation.

His first and perhaps most formative international involvement after leaving office was membership, in 1981–2, of a commission chaired by the former Swedish Premier, Olaf Palme, which studied issues of disarmament and international security.[4] Other members included Cyrus Vance and David Owen, who may well have recommended Obasanjo for membership. The Palme Commission grew out of the Helsinki Conference of 1975, at which the Western Powers had accepted existing European frontiers (and hence Soviet domination of Eastern Europe) in return for Soviet acceptance of cooperation in trade, science, technology, and humanitarian and cultural matters.[5] During the next fifteen years these apparently innocuous arrangements helped to undermine Soviet communism and end the Cold War and the division of Europe. This 'Helsinki process' showed Obasanjo how continental cooperation could coexist with, undermine, and eventually supersede the immutability of national borders enshrined, for example, in the OAU's charter. It was, in fact, one origin of the African Union formed in 2001. The Palme Commission itself was chiefly concerned with the prevention of nuclear war in Europe, but it also proposed the creation, through the United Nations Security Council and regional organisations, of preventative peacekeeping structures for Third World conflicts, financed by the entire international community. Whether Obasanjo helped to suggest this is not known, but during the Commission's discussions ECOWAS adopted an analogous Protocol on Mutual Assistance in Defence Matters, while Obasanjo devoted much effort during the next twenty years to organising for Africa the regional conference on security and cooperation that the Palme Commission recommended.[6] Obasanjo was never content to allow a major initiative to remain on paper.

Membership of the Palme Commission led during the 1980s to membership of similar panels on security and disarmament issues convened by the United Nations, the World Health Organisation, and the Inter-Action Council of Former Heads of Government, an informal body that Obasanjo joined in 1983 and used as a dignified launching-pad for international initiatives.[7] The issue that brought him to greater global prominence, however, was South Africa.

In October 1985, attempts by Third World Commonwealth members to press the British Prime Minister, Margaret Thatcher, to implement economic sanctions against South Africa came to a crisis at a conference at Nassau in the Bahamas. To avert an open split, the meeting decided that an Eminent Persons Group (EPG) should try to initiate dialogue between the South African government and its opponents with a view to establishing a non-racial and representative government. If, within six months, the South African regime proved unwilling to move in this direction, further sanctions would be imposed.[8] Despite fears that this was only a delaying tactic, the Nigerian government decided to seek representation in the group. The Nigerian Deputy Secretary-General of the Commonwealth, Emeka Anyaoku, urged Presidents Kaunda of Zambia and Mugabe of Zimbabwe to propose Obasanjo as the joint chairman, along with the former Australian Prime Minister, Malcolm Fraser.[9] Obasanjo hesitated. As he later explained to Thatcher,

> I came to the EPG mission with reluctance. It was difficult enough for me, as an African and especially a Nigerian to contemplate exchanging pleasantries with those responsible for the institutionalised oppression of so many of my brothers and sisters. My repugnance was exacerbated by the widely-held perception that the EPG was a substitute for action won by you at Nassau for the benefit of P.W. Botha [the South African president]. However, I persuaded myself that, whatever the odds, the prize was so great that I should overcome my personal feelings.[10]

In his dealings with southern Africa, Obasanjo had always held that armed liberation and negotiation must work in parallel.

The South African government also hesitated. Faced by Cuban troops and hostile African states to the north (where the African National Congress [ANC] leadership was in exile in Lusaka) and by a revolt in the townships that had begun in 1984, the regime was divided between those favouring uncompromising defence of white supremacy, led by President Botha and the military, and those, represented especially by Foreign Minister 'Pik' Botha, willing to contemplate negotiation with the ANC and the release of its imprisoned leader, Nelson Mandela.[11] Under pressure from Thatcher and President Reagan of the United States to demonstrate cooperation, the government decided in December 1985 to accept the EPG mission, provided it 'confines itself to promoting peaceful dialogue, and, moreover, can be seen to be unbiased in this respect'.[12]

On 16 February 1986, Obasanjo, Fraser, and Dame Nita Barrow (from Barbados) came together in Cape Town as the EPG's advance party to explore opinions and the possibilities for negotiation. The key question was whether they could meet Mandela in his Pollsmoor prison near Cape Town, for that would test the government's willingness to enter dialogue and open the way to negotiations with the suspicious ANC leadership in exile. After hesitation, Obasanjo alone was granted a secret visit. Four years later, he remembered that 'A sort of chill went through me' as he entered the prison.[13] They met alone in the commandant's office. Mandela entered 'gaily, straight and stately', looking fit and well groomed. 'His commanding presence and physique were engaging.' He saw the EPG as a welcome opportunity to open negotiations with the government.[14] Presuming the conversation to be monitored, Mandela first expressed pleasure at the group's political balance. Asked his general view of the South African situation, he said the government would not move without pressure, which must be both internal and external. For the presumed white listeners, Obasanjo asked if the ANC was communist. Mandela replied that it was diverse, with communist members, but was not a communist party, adding, 'with the innocence and naiveté of a child', that its president, Oliver Tambo, was a Christian. Obasanjo then asked what Mandela expected from negotiations. Mandela said that he must consult his colleagues and could not negotiate as a prisoner, but that if discussions were free, peaceful, and without preconditions, he believed they could produce a negotiated government, perhaps by stages. However, 'A freedom fighter could not give up fighting until he could be assured of redress of his cause for taking up arms.' The terms for release hitherto offered to him had been unacceptable. White fears of his release were unfounded: 'While he would not compromise on principles, he has also passed the stage of reckless or irresponsible behaviour or act'. Violence must be stopped and whites must be seen as South African citizens. Obasanjo recalled,

> For me, that first contact was an encounter never to be forgotten. I saw in Nelson Mandela a South African indeed an African and a world leader of no mean order. He towered physically and metaphorically above all the leaders we met inside South Africa.
>
> His intellect, perception and vision did not appear to have been dimmed by years of isolation and solitude, if anything, they seemed to have been focused and sharpened. In thought and perception, he was freer than his gaolers who were encapsulated and imprisoned in thought, vision and perception!!!

Two days later, Obasanjo left South Africa to brief the leaders of the frontline states and meet the ANC executive in Lusaka. There Thabo Mbeki had persuaded the reluctant leaders that they must at least appear to cooperate with the EPG. The leaders said they had regretted the group's appointment, seeing it as relieving pressure on the South African regime, but were keen to know what it hoped to achieve and how the government responded. They saw Mandela's release as a necessary precondition for negotiations.[15]

At the beginning of March 1986 the group's four additional members – Lord Barber (Britain), John Malecela (Tanzania), Edward Scott (Canada), and Swaran Singh (India) – joined their three colleagues on a full-scale visit to South Africa. They made no public statements but consulted the widest range of opinion in order to draft a possible 'negotiating concept' to put to the government and ANC as a basis for dialogue.[16]

Thatcher had welcomed Obasanjo's appointment because '[he] would see for himself what the reality of life in South Africa was.'[17] Certainly he was struck by

South Africa's wealth and modernity. 'Such a beautiful and economically strong country in Africa must be preserved for all South Africans, all Africans, and all citizens of the world', he concluded.[18] But, like other members of the group, he found that 'whatever I had heard, read or been told about apartheid, the effect of it on the ground is much worse than I could ever have imagined.'[19] 'As a contrivance of social engineering', the group reported, apartheid 'is awesome in its cruelty.'[20] 'I have seen extremes of poverty and of oppression in many parts of the world', Obasanjo later told Thatcher, 'but South Africa unashamedly moulds both elements into a system which enables the white minority to enjoy a "Dallas" lifestyle at the expense of the great majority forced to endure conditions as degrading as anything I have seen anywhere.' As for the whites, he told a London press conference, 'God probably left human kindness out of their hearts when he created them.'[21]

The group's visit coincided with the peak of the township revolt, in which at least 757 people were killed and 7,996 detained during an eight-month period. 'We encountered or heard of violence and its manifestations nearly everywhere we went', the group reported.[22] Obasanjo's experience of violence enabled him to enter this environment with unusual self-assurance. The group's legal adviser remembered him

> standing in the pulpit of a crowded church in Graff-Reinet [sic], where boys danced in the sanctuary with wooden AK-47s and the General preached a sermon on liberation theology of which any Latin American Jesuit would have been proud. So, too, would any Southern Baptist of the Martin Luther King school of oratory.
> 'We have come to see apartheid!' His eyes squinted and a low growl rose from the congregation. 'We have come to smell apartheid!' He screwed his nose up theatrically and the growl grew louder. 'We have come to touch apartheid!' His pointed finger leapt as though electrocuted as the growl became a shout. 'And we have come to taste apartheid.' His face was contorted and gagged, as if by a mouthful of salt and the audience erupted in a full-throated roar. This, too, from a speaker taken completely by surprise when the parish priest offered him the pulpit.

Later that day the group met an emotional audience in a township occupied by armed troops and reeking of tear gas. Obasanjo turned to Archbishop Scott: 'No liberation theology here, Ted. The slightest provocation and they'll try to take the casspirs [troop-carriers] apart.' After a prayer, he quietly persuaded the crowd to go home, leading each party himself past the troops. The lawyer described it as 'perhaps the most courageous and principled act I have ever witnessed … an ability to empathise with any one and everyone.'[23]

Obasanjo was the key figure in the Eminent Persons Group, especially in Afrikaner eyes. General Magnus Malan, the Defence Minister who met the group on its first visit, clearly thought that Obasanjo was its sole chairman.[24] Pik Botha 'saw in the EPG a real chance of achieving a breakthrough' and claimed to have established 'a strong personal bond of friendship' with the Nigerian, whom he regarded as a realist:[25]

> General Obasanjo stood out as the dynamic kernel of the EPG, its heart and its brain. There was a quiet authority about him. He spoke in a conciliatory tone, avoiding petulance. He reacted to tension with composure. He was mild without being weak, relaxed but by no means lacking in concentration. He was self-possessed, unruffled, striving to soothe heated discussions and able by his presence and manner to do so. He discreetly explored every possible avenue of reconciliation in attempting to bring opposing views together.

> I will remember General Obasanjo's role as that of a leader, a statesman, a man who could talk to you as someone who had gone through the vortex of more than one storm. He had experienced at first hand the futility of using violence as a means of resolving problems. He could speak with legitimacy and credibility and carry it with an inner force of persuasion.[26]

In this assessment, both obsequious and patronising, was a desire to co-opt Obasanjo as an African with 'a deep understanding of the position of the Afrikaner'.[27] It was attempted more crudely, after the EPG's mission had failed, by the Minister for Constitutional Development and Planning, J.C. Heunis, who assured Obasanjo that 'If we as Africans were permitted to address the issues of South Africa in this way, the whole continent is sure to be a far better place than it is today.' Obasanjo replied brutally that the regime's behaviour ruled out any possibility of 'a common African heritage as guidance in my relationship with you'.[28]

After ten days in South Africa, the full EPG met Mandela at Pollsmoor prison on 12 March. They too were impressed by his appearance, the respect he commanded even among his gaolers, and his apparent lack of bitterness. He insisted that he could not speak for the ANC, but he wanted his party to open discussions with the government. He regretted violence but could not renounce it, a position they thought reasonable. Nevertheless, he thought that the ANC might suspend violence if the security forces withdrew from the townships. He insisted that he was a nationalist and not a communist. The group concluded that his release would reduce violence.[29] Later that day, however, they met P.W. Botha, whom Obasanjo later described as the most intolerant man he had ever met. Botha lectured them for forty minutes on South Africa's power and restraint, declared his refusal to negotiate with men of violence and communists like Mandela, and accused Obasanjo of having fought a war of genocide and imposed press censorship. As the group left, one of Botha's aides whispered, 'Now you know what we have to contend with.'[30]

Nevertheless, next day the Group formally presented its 'possible negotiating concept' to the South African government and left for London to await a considered response. 'This negotiating concept of General Obasanjo', as Pik Botha described it,[31] was based largely on terms outlined at the Commonwealth Conference at Nassau. It proposed that the government should withdraw troops from the townships, end emergency measures, release Mandela and other political prisoners, legalise the nationalist parties, and permit normal political activity. In return, the ANC and other political groups should suspend violence and enter negotiations.[32] After six weeks of consideration and urging from Thatcher and Reagan to accept the terms, Pik Botha sent the group a cautious reply, outlining recent measures to reduce conflict, stating that 'a suspension of violence' was essential to further liberalisation, and encouraging the group to return to South Africa for further discussions.[33] They decided to do so.

When negotiations resumed on 13 May 1986, the group sensed that the government's position was hardening. In a speech on 15 May, P.W. Botha denounced external interference and demanded renunciation rather than suspension of violence. Next day, however, when the group again visited Mandela, he quickly accepted the negotiating concept on his own behalf as a starting point. On 17 May, they presented the concept to the ANC leaders in Lusaka, who promised a response in about ten days.[34]

In reality, the balance had already swung against them. The division within the white regime between hardliners and moderates had been widening for several years as pressure on South Africa mounted. It was especially bitter between the military and Pik Botha's Foreign Ministry, which was suspected of leaking military information to the enemy.[35] P.W. Botha kept the two groups apart, but as a former Defence Minister he was a committed hardliner. At some point in the middle of May 1986 he resolved to act. A month earlier the military had sought permission to attack ANC installations in Botswana, Zambia, and Zimbabwe. Botha had agreed, but the raids had been suspended because warning was thought to have reached the ANC, perhaps through the Foreign Ministry. In the middle of May the generals asked again. Without consulting anyone – so he later claimed – Botha agreed. Early on 19 May 1986, South African planes bombed ANC facilities near Lusaka while airborne commandos carried out raids near Gaborone and Harare.[36]

Obasanjo and his colleagues heard the news as they were preparing to meet the government's Constitutional Committee. They decided to attend the meeting, lest the South Africans accuse them of breaking off the talks. Both sides at the meeting knew what had happened; neither mentioned it. Instead, they restated with particular clarity the distinction between suspending and renouncing violence that divided them. Then the group left for London.[37]

Although Pik Botha wrote to invite them back, the group replied that they saw no merit in further negotiations and concentrated on writing their report, which appeared on 12 June 1986. They concluded that there was an overwhelming desire among South Africans for a non-violent negotiated settlement and that the basis for one existed, but that the government was not yet willing to contemplate this and had not made the significant progress required by the Nassau Conference. Rather, the regime was attempting to entrench a more sophisticated form of white domination. The group therefore recommended 'further measures' – avoiding the word 'sanctions' in order to secure the British representative's signature – claiming that these were 'the last opportunity to avert what could be the worst bloodbath since the Second World War'.[38] On the day of publication, P.W. Botha reimposed a state of emergency.

Two months later a committee of Commonwealth heads of government accepted the report, with Britain dissenting, during a meeting at which Thatcher is alleged to have cited the repeal of the Mixed Marriages Act as an instance of South African liberalisation, at which Obasanjo asked whether she believed that '25 million blacks are queueing up to marry or have sex with five million whites.'[39] The other governments agreed to a range of sanctions that Obasanjo thought worse than useless because their ineffectiveness would discredit the tactic.[40] Exasperated by Thatcher's 'lack of vision', Obasanjo wrote her an open letter stating that 'those who seek to minimise sanctions and their effects will have the blood of thousands if not millions of innocents on their hands and on their conscience. My heart will be heavy but my hands will be clean, will yours?'[41]

Even without the raids on ANC facilities, the EPG's negotiating concept had little chance of success, for the majority of ANC leaders in Lusaka were unwilling to suspend violence and thereby discredit themselves in their followers' eyes while the townships were in flames.[42] Yet in another sense the group's mission was successful, for its failure provided the necessary justification for sanctions, which in African eyes had been its main purpose.[43] Only six days after the publication of the report, the United States House of Representatives passed an Anti-Apartheid Bill imposing total trade and investment sanctions on South Africa, later overriding a presidential veto. A month later Barclays Bank withdrew from South Africa, following the example of several leading American companies.[44] Thatcher might profess to doubt the efficacy of sanctions, but the South African government and Oliver Tambo of the ANC did not.[45] Tambo later described the EPG's visit as 'the watershed' in the breakthrough to a negotiated end to apartheid – an exaggerated word, perhaps, but one that Obasanjo himself claimed when he published *Not my will* in 1990, as the South African racial order at last began to crumble.[46]

Obasanjo followed that process to the end. Preserving hope of 'a dim chance of bringing about settlement by negotiation', he and Fraser contemplated a new EPG visit to South Africa in March 1987.[47] Then in 1989 the agreed withdrawal of Cuban troops from Angola and the collapse of Soviet communism created an opportunity for a new South African President, F.W. de Klerk, and the Western Powers to seek resolution of South Africa's conflicts. Their objectives differed, but both involved legalising the ANC and releasing Mandela. One of his first journeys outside South Africa was to Obasanjo 's farm. 'General Obasanjo made the EPG a very important group that has ever visited that country', he told Nigerians, 'and after their visit to that country South Africa has never been the same.'[48] Two months later, Obasanjo led a Nigerian government delegation to South Africa for talks with de Klerk, Mandela, and other politicians, urging the outside world to support 'a process of jumping the psychological hurdle of negotiation' and speaking already of Pretoria and Abuja as 'a kind of axis on which the continent would spin'.[49] On a further visit in September 1991, Obasanjo appears to have been instrumental in persuading the discontented Chief Buthelezi of KwaZulu to participate in negotiations. Three years later, while technically assisting the electoral commission at South Africa's first democratic election, he helped to persuade Buthelezi to contest the poll, before attending Mandela's inauguration as South Africa's first black president.[50]

During these negotiations in South Africa, Obasanjo was also being considered for the wider role of United Nations Secretary-General. The incumbent, Javier Perez de Cuellar, had undergone heart surgery and might not stand for a second term. If not, some felt that an African should succeed him. By one account, Obasanjo was first suggested by Andrew Young. Certainly two of Obasanjo's other acquaintances from the 1970s, Helmut Schmidt and James Callaghan, urged him to allow himself to be considered. In July 1986, following his prominent role in South Africa, the London *Times* reported that Obasanjo was 'the name most often mentioned'. In the event, Perez de Cuellar decided to continue and the issue was dropped.[51]

Nevertheless, the EPG had brought Obasanjo to prominence as an international conciliator, although much of his work during the next five years took place in private. Obscurity surrounds his role in Angola early in 1988, during the later stages of the crucial Battle of Cuito Cuanavale, in which MPLA and Cuban troops fought South African and UNITA forces to a standstill that each side claimed as a victory. This outcome, together with the waning of the Cold War, enabled the Cubans to leave the region with honour, despite their vow to remain until apartheid was destroyed. That in turn allowed the South Africans to withdraw from Namibia, which became independent in 1990 after an election won by the SWAPO liberation movement. The Cuban withdrawal was agreed in December 1988.[52] Obasanjo visited Angola twice early in 1988 and was himself visited by an Angolan delegation. There are indications that he helped to persuade President Castro of Cuba that Cuito Cuanavale gave him the opportunity to withdraw his troops, whose

126

departure was now as important to the liberation of southern Africa as their arrival had been.[53]

At the same period, Commonwealth leaders commissioned Obasanjo to head a committee investigating the security needs of frontline states threatened by South African incursions, Mozambique being the most vulnerable. Their report was confidential, but it urged Western nations to provide non-lethal military equipment such as vehicles, medical supplies, uniforms, tents, and communications.[54] Most of Obasanjo's mediation during the 1980s concerned these last stages of southern African liberation, but he also became involved in the Sudanese civil war between north and south that had begun in 1955. After attending a meeting that suggested a secular and pluralistic substitute for Sudan's specifically Islamic constitution, he visited the Sudan three times between 1987 and 1989, along with the former Sudanese Foreign Minister, Francis Deng, to encourage northern and southern leaders to negotiate on that basis, but without success.[55]

During the mid 1980s, in the face of political disorder and economic decline in Nigeria and elsewhere in the continent, Obasanjo grew increasingly despondent. 'Where are we going? We are not heading anywhere', he complained to a companion in 1986 while admiring Japan's rapid modernisation.[56] Yet along with pessimism of the mind went optimism of the will. Ad'Obe Obe, an experienced Nigerian journalist who became Obasanjo's speech-writer, remembered that when they first met in the late 1980s, Obasanjo talked him out of the prevailing African cynicism of the time.[57] It was in that defiant mood that Obasanjo first sketched his ideas for the Africa Leadership Forum in June 1987.

Obasanjo's military experience had accustomed him to the repeated career development courses provided for officers. His first attempt to extend this to civilian personnel was the Nigerian Institute of Policy and Strategic Studies at Kuru, near Jos, which he opened shortly before leaving office in 1979. It offered a one-year retreat for mid-career officers, officials, and executives.[58] Moreover, his experience of taking power without adequate preparation sharpened his perception that the first generation of independent African leaders had failed to achieve political stability and economic development partly because they were ill-prepared and ill-supported. Instead, they 'merely blundered and fumbled in the dark from day to day'. Their greatest weakness, he wrote in 1987, embracing himself in the criticism, 'was their lack of adequate experience and exposure in economic matters…. We opted for projects, rather than programs', especially grandiose urban projects.[59]

This was the thinking behind the plan for the Africa Leadership Forum that he discussed with his academic and political friends, especially the veteran civil servant and diplomat Simeon Adebo, who had trained international civil servants for the United Nations and became the first head of the Forum's Nigerian section. The next step was to seek the support of incumbent African heads of state. Funds came from the Japanese government, the United Nations Development Programme, the Carnegie and Rockefeller Foundations, and Nigerian companies and individuals.[60]

The Forum sponsored three main forms of leadership training. The earliest was a series of Farm House Dialogues held at Ota roughly every two months to discuss issues of Nigerian public policy. Obasanjo tried to ensure that half of those present were under forty. The first meeting, in May 1988, discussed leadership for development, concentrating on middle-level leadership. The 23rd meeting, in July 1993, discussed the military in society. Over time, as Nigerian conditions worsened, the debates became increasingly self-lacerating, but the published volume of conclusions is one of the best available surveys of African development problems at that time. Some discussions had an identifiable influence on policy, notably the abolition of the Ministry of Local Government (as tending to suffocate local initiative), the creation of a National Commission for Women, and a national policy of nine years of compulsory education.[61] The longterm impact on individual participants is impossible to assess.

The Forum's second and more ambitious activity was a series of quarterly international meetings, beginning at Ota in October 1988 with a discussion of the challenge of leadership, at which participants included Julius Nyerere and Helmut Schmidt. Of the five subsequent meetings, two were held at Ota and the others in Brussels, Washington, and Paris. Most discussed the implications for Africa of major global developments. Apart from the personal networking that would become important when Obasanjo needed international political support, no concrete outcome from these meetings is visible.[62]

The third activity, publication, is easier to trace. The most ambitious project was a glossy quarterly magazine, *Africa Forum*, launched in London in 1991 at a price of $75 per year, with offices in Abeokuta, London, and New York, a 15,000 print-run, and plans for a French edition. Edited by Ad'Obe Obe (formerly editor of *West Africa*), it aimed 'to extol things that work and to unfold things that do not work' for the benefit of 'those that matter'.[63] It contained several excellent articles, but its price and limited advertising presumably explained its rapid demise, apparently in 1993. More practical and enduring was a series of modest books published by the Forum in Nigeria, including the papers of its conferences, texts on issues like democracy, and several of Obasanjo's writings.[64]

The Africa Leadership Forum survived through the 1990s, although with waning vitality after 1993 as Nigeria's international image was tarnished and Obasanjo was eventually imprisoned. Whatever its influence on emerging leaders, it had an important impact on Obasanjo himself, not only expanding his international reputation but exposing him to current thinking on many issues. One was rapid population growth, which he had neglected during the 1970s.[65] Like most African governments, Nigeria first recognised the problem publicly in 1984 at the Second International Population Conference in Mexico. Babangida espoused population control when he took power a year later.[66] Obasanjo's first statement on the point dated from the same year and marked a striking change of attitude for a man who had fathered numerous children and held conservative views on family matters. 'If the adults of yesterday and today have helped in creating population explosion because of security and strong cultural preference for large families', he told the Agricultural Society of Nigeria, 'we must encourage and assist the children of today to go for small size families in their own economic and national socio-economic interest.'[67] Africa's population explosion, he explained five years later, constituted not only 'the most serious threat to economic… progress' but 'a danger to the survival of the majority of the African people arising from the destruction of Africa's physical environment'.[68] He and other Nigerians had been especially alarmed by World Bank projections that, at the current growth rate of about 3% per year, Nigeria's population would more than quintuple by 2035 to 529 million. In 1988 the second Farm House Dialogue discussed the issue, noting that 'one remarkable change about the population debate in Nigeria is that it can now be conducted calmly and objectively.'[69] Two years later, the Africa Leadership Forum devoted its meeting to 'Population, environment and climatic changes: their impact on development'. Robert McNamara of the World

Bank gave the keynote speech and Obasanjo made his most important statement on the subject, blaming the population explosion on the combination of African cultural tradition and modern science. To reduce the speed of growth, he suggested improved legal rights for women, social security measures for peasants, minimum marriage ages of 18 for women and 20 for men, male contraception, and incentives for families to limit their children to three per mother.[70]

Another concern to crystallise at Forum meetings was the importance of managerial skills, whose inadequacy had been a major obstacle to economic growth during the late 1970s. 'We seem to be short of a body of men and women, the type that … created the modern industrial South Korea and Taiwan', Obasanjo complained in 1988. 'Managerial development is perhaps the single, most important challenge facing Nigeria at the present time', a Farm House Dialogue concluded.[71] This was one of several changes taking place in Obasanjo's economic thinking. By the 1990s, while still championing active government, he aligned himself publicly with the prevailing orthodoxy that 'African countries [should] promote a strategy of private-sector led growth with government mainly concerned with providing the hospitable environment and unsuffocating regulatory framework.' Such 'economic democratisation', as he described it, 'would be different from the situation where the state controlled the commanding heights of the economy and actively participated in the ownership and management of economic enterprises. As our experience in Africa has shown, in most cases, these state enterprises were not only poorly run, they also gave rise to and exacerbated corruption in our economies.'[72] He also turned his back on the indigenisation policy of the 1970s, even urging that the constitution should prohibit the confiscation of foreign investments.[73]

Behind this change of stance lay his chief economic preoccupation of the 1990s, foreign debt, which he described as 'probably the gravest problem yet to face Africa since the onset of independence', bringing a new colonialism that 'cannot be agitated away'. According to World Bank figures, sub-Saharan Africa's external debt rose between 1980 and 1995 from $84 billion to $226 billion, Nigeria's from $9 billion to $35 billion.[75] Obasanjo's concern was probably sharpened in 1989 by membership, alongside several distinguished economic administrators, of Helmut Schmidt's Independent Group on Financial Flows to Developing Countries, whose recommendations included international initiatives to reduce Third World debt.[76] Yet he was probably moved more deeply by a sense of personal guilt at having started Nigeria along this road by the jumbo loans of 1977–8, however much he stressed that his successors had 'succumbed more readily to the bankers' siren song'.[77] He cited the bankers' role as grounds for claiming that creditors should assist in solving the problem by rescheduling, reducing, or forgiving debt, suggesting in 1993 that forgiveness should be granted in return for self-imposed conditionalities by the debtor nations, such as 'political reform, economic discipline, social equity, commitment to the rule of law, limitation of military expenditure, environmental development, etc.'[78]

Obasanjo was convinced that Africa's economic recovery could be achieved only by closer integration of its numerous and often unviable states. He saw a revitalised ECOWAS as a potential regional confederation and suggested five others in Africa: Maghreb, Nile, Southern, Eastern, and Central. From them might emerge a continental parliament and an OAU that operated as an economic organisation.[79] These concerns were sharpened by the consequences he expected from the ending of the Cold War, whose significance he was quick to see. In 1987, two years before the

Berlin Wall fell, he suggested that arms reduction and Soviet *perestroika* might 'lead to consensus in seeking solutions to existing conflicts in parts of Africa', as they did in Namibia and South Africa.[80] Shortly afterwards, however, he realised that the consequence for Africa might also be marginalisation. 'The signal from the international community is that Africa is now on its own', the Africa Leadership Forum's first conference concluded in 1988. 'The rest of the world is no longer particularly interested in Africa.' Aid might cease, a continent already in decline risked 'imminent economic collapse', political systems might disintegrate, and Africa's influence in world affairs might disappear. 'An international train to greater security, stability and prosperity is leaving the station', Obasanjo said in 1990. 'Africa is not on that train.'[81]

It was to meet this crisis that Obasanjo revived the Palme Commission's proposal for regional conferences on security and cooperation similar to the Helsinki Conference. Sponsored jointly by the Africa Leadership Forum, the OAU, and UNECA, such a Conference on Security, Stability, Development, and Cooperation in Africa met at Kampala in May 1991 under Nyerere's chairmanship, with some 300 invited delegates, including several heads of state. The underlying idea was that the four issues for discussion were so integrally related that problems in one field could be solved only if all four were tackled. That would require the restructuring of the OAU, giving it peacekeeping and conflict-resolution capabilities and reorientating it towards the economic integration essential to development. That, in turn, meant challenging the principle of non-intervention in the affairs of member states. The conference produced an elaborate Kampala Document setting out the norms of a new continental order for President Museveni of Uganda to present to OAU heads of state at their meeting in Abuja in June 1991.[82] There, however, it faced opposition chiefly from older members, because, as Obasanjo declared, 'it threatened the status quo and especially the power positions of a few governments whose domestic hold on unscrupulous power rendered them vulnerable and insecure'. The initiative faded until Obasanjo himself revived it in 1999.[83]

While Obasanjo feared that the end of the Cold War might marginalise Africa, he also celebrated its liberating effects, especially its contribution to the sequence of democratisation movements that began in Benin in January 1989 and spread across much of tropical Africa, sweeping away many one-party states.[84] The euphoria reinforced his personal reconversion to democracy. In November 1991 he welcomed attendants at an Africa Leadership Forum meeting

> to the fascinating epoch of Africa's rediscovery of itself. Some have chosen to call it Africa's democratic revolution. But whatever one may call it, one thing is clear, a rising tide of change in Africa is now irresistible.... Today, the issue is no longer whether all African countries – and I mean the entire African continent, will achieve a democratic form of government within the next two years or so. The uncertainty is whether most African leaders will allow such changes to be achieved peacefully or rather democratically. Those sufficiently wise, to recognize the inevitable, may have a rare chance of managing the change. But those who, even at this eleventh hour, continue to believe that they can stop this tidal wave of Africa's historical movement, may be obliterated by this mighty force and end up in the dust-bin of history.[85]

At this moment of mingled anxiety and optimism, the post of United Nations Secretary General fell vacant. Not until July 1991 did Perez de Cuellar renounce a further extension of his tenure, but public discussion of possible candidates began late in 1990, with a widespread feeling in Africa and elsewhere that it was Africa's turn. Obasanjo was among several possible candidates mentioned, along with two other Nigerians: Joseph Garba, former military Commissioner for External Affairs and President of the UN General Assembly, and Ibrahim Gambari, Nigeria's Permanent Representative at the UN. In April 1991 the Foreign Minister in Nigeria's military government announced that he was seeking support from heads of state for Nigeria's candidate.[86] He did not name the candidate, but Obasanjo's enemies were quick to mobilise against him. Wole Soyinka demanded the exclusion of all military candidates as products of 'unfair competition instituted by military muscle', apparently visualising the appointment as an honour akin to a Nobel Prize rather than a search for the best equipped candidate.[87] The estranged Oluremi took the opportunity to denounce her husband, 'not out of malice', she later insisted, but 'to save Africa and the black man of ridicule. Obasanjo's competence was not the issue but Stella's style. He had her around him as his showpiece.'[88] Activists added allegations of corruption, brutality, antidemocratic tendencies, and human rights abuses that obliged the General to take action for libel.[89] There is no evidence that this campaign affected the voting in the Security Council. More important was a decision by the OAU heads of state not to support any single candidate, partly because the single candidate they had proposed in 1981 had been vetoed and partly because they could not agree on a candidate, Obasanjo facing the invariable suspicion of Nigerian domination. Other African candidates with OAU support included Bernard Chidzero, Zimbabwe's Minister of Finance and a former UN official, and Boutros Boutros-Ghali, Egypt's Deputy Prime Minister for Foreign Affairs, with wide diplomatic experience, fluency in Arabic, French, and English, and support within the Group of Seven industrial powers. Once Perez de Cuellar announced his intention to retire, Obasanjo toured world capitals seeking support. He also took private French lessons, for it was widely believed that the French would veto any candidate ignorant of their language.[90]

In three straw polls in the Security Council during October and November, Boutros and Chidzero ran neck and neck, with Obasanjo a vote or two behind them. In the final vote on 21 November 1991, the United States chose Boutros, Chidzero lost backing from other major powers, and Boutros won by 11 votes to 7 for Chidzero and 6 for Obasanjo.[91] The General had insisted that 'it is not a matter of life and death', although he had lobbied hard and was eager to focus the United Nations on southern African issues and aid to poor countries.[92] He would surely have found the diplomatic constraints on the Secretary General intolerably frustrating.

It was instead as a freelance mediator that Obasanjo was chiefly involved in international affairs during the early 1990s. The main issues now were not the liberation of southern Africa but conflicts among Africans arising from the end of the Cold War, economic decline, and the collapse of authoritarian regimes. After the optimism that democratisation had engendered, he recalled, 'we were taken aback by the eruption of violent conflicts in many countries – Somalia, Rwanda, Liberia, and Burundi, to mention only the African ones – and by the continuance of wars in Angola and Sudan.'[93] On these long-standing wars there was no progress, although Obasanjo took part in negotiations over the Sudan in 1992 and 1995 and was an observer at the abortive Angolan election of 1992. There was more success, however, in Mozambique, where the withdrawal of South African support from the Renamo guerilla movement had made it possible to negotiate peace and hold multi-party elections in 1994. Obasanjo was again an observer. A companion remembered him mingling with the voters and telling Afonso Dhlakama, the Renamo leader, that although he had lost the election he had won a victory for democracy.[94]

The most ambiguous of these interventions was in Burundi, which Obasanjo visited twice, in 1994 and 1995, to assist the United Nations representative. Here the long-standing hostility between the Hutu majority and the Tutsi military had escalated in 1993 when the Hutu party won a free election but Tutsi troops murdered the new Prime Minister. A civilian government was restored, but amid violence on both sides, exacerbated by the genocide that began in neighbouring Rwanda in April 1994. Obasanjo's role was to calm both sides:

> As a former soldier, a former head of state of Nigeria, a promoter of democracy, and a member of the international civil society, I had important cards and a role to play.... To assess the situation, I visited many villages and camps within the country. Both the military establishment and the civilian political elite were keen and pleased to come and meet me in the UN premises. Hence, I was able to discuss the situation with them, advise them, and, when necessary, admonish them. In Africa, seniority gives one a number of rights that one should use when necessary.... I was pleased to hear that my two visits contributed to...efforts to prevent Burundi from following the genocidal course of its sister state, Rwanda. I was also made to understand that my visit had played a part in the establishment of a power-sharing government in September 1994. Maybe I was being given more credit than I deserved.[95]

Burundi was spared a genocide of Rwandan proportions, but violence escalated to terrible levels during 1995–6 and it would be another decade before peace was established.[96]

In 1995 Obasanjo was 58 years old. As a peacemaker, a counsellor, and an initiator he was constantly active. He had a global range of interests and said that he was busier than when he had been head of state.[97] Yet he was at the same time deeply involved in the gravest crisis to face Nigeria since the civil war.

NOTES

1. Obasanjo, *Not my will*, p. 65.
2. *Nigerian Tribune*, 3 October 1993.
3. *This Day*, 16 August 2000.
4. Independent Commission on Disarmament and Security Issues, *Common security: a programme for disarmament* (London, 1982).
5. P.M.H. Bell, *The world since 1945: an international history* (London, 2001), pp. 310–13, 380.
6. See below, pp. 130, 220.
7. For a slightly inaccurate list of Obasanjo's international activities, see d' Orville, *Beyond freedom*, pp. 683–5.
8. Emeka Anyaoku, *The inside story of the modern Commonwealth* (London, 2004), pp. 88–9; Commonwealth Group of Eminent Persons, *Mission to South Africa: the Commonwealth Report* (Harmondsworth, 1986), pp. 13–14, 142–5.
9. Anyaoku, *Inside story*, pp. 89–93.

10. *Daily Times*, 11 August 1986.
11. Dan O'Meara, *Forty lost years: the apartheid state and the politics of the National Party 1948–1994* (Randburg, 1996), parts 2 and 3.
12. Commonwealth Group, *Mission*, p. 148; Anyaoku, *Inside story*, p. 103.
13. This account is based on Olusegun Obasanjo, 'Face to face with Mandela', *Daily Times*, 12 February 1990.
14. Nelson Mandela, *Long walk to freedom* (London, 1994), p. 516.
15. Gevisser, *Thabo Mbeki*, p. 534; Commonwealth Group, *Mission*, pp. 85–7.
16. Commonwealth Group, *Mission*, pp. 103–4.
17. Margaret Thatcher, *The Downing Street years* (London, 1993), p. 519.
18. Obasanjo, *Africa in perspective*, p. 36.
19. *African Concord*, 26 June 1986, p. 28.
20. Commonwealth Group, *Mission*, p. 23.
21. *Daily Times*, 11 August 1986; *Newswatch*, 30 June 1986, p. 28.
22. *Africa Research Bulletin (Political)*, 15 April 1986, pp. 8014–15; Commonwealth Group, *Mission*, p. 61.
23. Jeremy Pope, 'Images of a Nigerian in apartheid South Africa', in d'Orville, *Leadership*, pp. 72–3.
24. Magnus Malan, *My life with the SA Defence Force* (Pretoria, 2006), p. 321.
25. South Africa: Truth and Reconciliation Commission, 'Proceedings' (typescript), vol. 171, pp. 9–10 (Cambridge University Library).
26. Roelof F. Botha, 'His South Africa connection', in d'Orville, *Leadership*, p. 69.
27. South Africa: TRC, 'Proceedings', vol. 171, p. 10.
28. *Newswatch*, 30 June 1986, p. 26.
29. Commonwealth Group, *Mission*, pp. 68–74; Mandela, *Long walk*, p. 517.
30. *Daily Times*, 23 March 1989; *African Concord*, 21 June 1986.
31. South Africa: TRC, 'Proceedings', vol. 171, p. 13.
32. Commonwealth Group, *Mission*, pp. 103–4.
33. Ibid., pp. 106–7.
34. Ibid., pp. 110–17.
35. South Africa: TRC, 'Proceedings', vol. 204, pp. 241–3, 281–4; Hilton Hamann, *Days of the generals* (Cape Town, 2001), p. 41.
36. South Africa: TRC, 'Proceedings', vol. 204, pp. 241–3, 281–4; Malan, *My life*, pp. 323–5; Anthony Sampson, *Mandela* (London, 1999), p. 351.
37. Commonwealth Group, *Mission*, pp. 117–20; *African Concord*, 19 August 1986, p. 7.
38. Commonwealth Group, *Mission*, pp. 140–1; Anthony Barber, *Taking the tide: a memoir* (Norwich, 1996), pp. 171–2.
39. *Times*, 17 October 1989.
40. *Newswatch*, 18 August 1986, p. 25.
41. *Daily Times*, 11 August 1986.
42. Gevisser, *Thabo Mbeki*, p. 534.
43. Stephen Chan, 'British and Commonwealth actors in the 1980s', in Stephen Chan and Vivienne Jabri (ed.), *Mediation in southern Africa* (London, 1993), p. 36.
44. Chester A. Crocker, *High noon in southern Africa* (New York, 1992), p. 306; *African Concord*, 4 December 1986, p.34.
45. Onslow, 'South Africa', p. 155; Allister Sparks, *Tomorrow is another country* (reprinted, Johannesburg, 2003), pp. 49–50.
46. Pope in d'Orville, *Leadership*, p. 72; Obasanjo, *Not my will*, p. 139.
47. Obasanjo, *Africa embattled*, p. 98; Cohen to Carlucci, 9 March 1987, United States National Archives, declassified documents reference system, document CK3100479957 (electronic resource).
48. *Daily Times*, 16 May 1990.

49. Ibid., 30 July 1990; Olatunji Dare, 'Pretoria-Abuja-Cairo axis', *Africa Forum*, 1, 2 (1991), 50.
50. Robert von Lucius, '"Archaic Rock" – mediator for a better South Africa', in d'Orville, *Leadership*, p. 82; Sampson, *Mandela*, p. 487.
51. *African Guardian*, 5 June 1986, p. 23; *Daily Times*, 19 April 1986; *Times*, 26 July 1986.
52. Edward George, *The Cuban intervention in Angola, 1965–1991: from Che Guevara to Cuito Cuanavale* (London, 2005), pp. 196, 234–5, 247–8, 277.
53. *Daily Times*, 11 and 14 January and 18 and 25 February 1988; Pope in d'Orville, *Leadership*, p. 79; Marion Gräfin Dönhoff, 'Hope for a better future', in d'Orville, *Beyond freedom*, p. 61.
54. *Daily Times*, 23 April and 4 August 1988.
55. Francis M. Deng, *Partners for peace: an initiative on Sudan with General Olusegun Obasanjo* (Abeokuta, 1998), passim.
56. *African Guardian*, 5 June 1986, p. 16.
57. Ad'Obe Obe, 'A committed optimist', in d'Orville, *Leadership*, p. 87.
58. Obasanjo, *Not my will*, p. 170.
59. [Olusegun Obasanjo,] *Hope for Africa: selected speeches of Olusegun Obasanjo* (Abeokuta, 1993), p. 3; Obasanjo, *Africa in perspective*, pp. 29–30.
60. Ayodele Aderinwale, 'For leadership's sake: the story of the Africa Leadership Forum', *Africa Forum*, 1, 1 (1991), 45–6; *Punch*, 14 July 1991; Olusegun Obasanjo and Hans d'Orville (ed.), *Challenges of leadership in African development* (New York, 1990), p. vii.
61. Obasanjo, *This animal*, p. 184; Tony Momoh, *Experiment with disintegration* (Lagos, n.d.), p. 78; Olusegun Obasanjo and Akin Mabogunje (ed.), *Elements of development* (Abeokuta, 1991), preface.
62. *New York Times*, 30 October 1988; Aderinwale, 'For leadership's sake', pp. 46–7.
63. Olusegun Obasanjo, 'Leadership for development', *Africa Forum*, 1, 1 (1991), 2; *Tell*, 12 August 1991, p. 52.
64. Olusegun Obasanjo and Akin Mabogunje (ed.), *Elements of democracy* (Abeokuta, 1992).
65. *Daily Times*, 28 November 1992.
66. Robert Cassen et al., *Population and development: old debates, new conclusions* (New Brunswick, 1994), p. 3; *African Concord*, 17 April 1986, p. 8.
67. *Daily Times*, 8 August 1985.
68. Obasanjo, *Hope*, p. 92.
69. Olusegun Obasanjo and Hans d'Orville (ed.), *The challenges of agricultural production and food security in Africa* (Washington DC, 1992), p. 6; Obasanjo and Mabogunje, *Elements of development*, p. 19.
70. Obasanjo, *Hope*, Ch.7.
71. *Daily Times*, 19 November 1988; Obasanjo and Mabogunje, *Elements of development*, pp. 85–6.
72. Obasanjo, *Hope*, pp. 145, 9.
73. Obasanjo, *Constitution*, p. 131.
74. Olusegun Obasanjo, 'Africa in today's world', in Ibrahim B. Babangida and Olusegun Obasanjo, *Africa in today's world and the challenges of leadership* (Ota [1988?]), p. 14.
75. World Bank, *World development report*, 1997, p. 247.
76. Independent Group on Financial Flows to Developing Countries, *Facing one world* (n.p., 1989).
77. Obasanjo, *Africa in perspective*, p. 22.
78. Obasanjo, *Hope*, p. 11.
79. Obasanjo, *Africa in perspective*, pp. 16–17; Obasanjo, *Africa embattled*, pp. 20–1.
80. Obasanjo, *Hope*, p. 24.
81. Obasanjo and d'Orville, *Challenges of leadership*, p. 18; *Punch*, 22 June 1991; Olusegun Obasanjo and Felix G.N. Mosha (ed.), *Africa: rise to challenge* (Abeokuta, 1993), p. 342.
82. An edited version of the document was published in *Africa Forum*, 1, 3 (1991), 59–64.

For the meeting, see Olusegun Obasanjo, 'Rendezvous with history', ibid., 1, 3 (1991), 2–3; Obasanjo and Mosha, *Africa: rise to challenge.*

83. Thomas Kwasi Tieku, 'Explaining the clash and accommodation of interests of major actors in the creation of the African Union', *African Affairs*, 103 (2004), 258; below, p. 220.

84. See Michael Bratton and Nicolas van de Walle, *Democratic experiments in Africa* (Cambridge, 1997).

85. Olusegun Obasanjo, 'Opening remarks', in Ayodele Aderinwale and Felix G.N. Mosha (ed.), *Democracy and governance in Africa: conclusions and papers presented at a conference of the Africa Leadership Forum, 29 November – 1 December 1991, Ota, Nigeria* (n.p., n.d.), p. 17. See also above, p. 115.

86. *Times*, 3 January 1991; *African Concord*, 18 March 1991, p. 173, and 6 May 1991, p. 34; *Punch*, 11 April 1991.

87. *Punch*, 13 May 1991.

88. Obasanjo, *Bitter-sweet*, p. 105.

89. *Newbreed*, 1 July 1991, pp. 45–50; *African Guardian*, 21 October 1991, p. 3.

90. *Tell*, 29 July 1991, 21 October 1991, and 11 November 1991.

91. *Punch*, 23 November 1991; Boutros Boutros-Ghali, *Unvanquished: a U.S.-U.N, saga* (London, 1999), pp. 7–12.

92. *Tell*, 11 November 1991.

93. Olusegun Obasanjo, 'Preface', in Ahmedou Ould-Abdallah, *Burundi on the brink 1993– 95: a UN envoy reflects on preventive diplomacy* (Washington DC, 2000), p. xvi.

94. D'Orville, *Beyond freedom*, pp. 94, 389–91, 684; Deng, *Partners*, pp. 146–8.

95. Obasanjo in Ould-Abdallah, *Burundi*, p. xvii.

96. Filip Reyntjens, 'Burundi: a peaceful transition after a decade of war', *African Affairs*, 105 (2006), 117–35.

97. *Tell*, 10 June 1991, p. 19.

12
The Politician

By 1992, Obasanjo's hostility to Babangida's political deviousness and structural reform programme had become a determination to oblige the president and the military as a whole to withdraw from power with as much dignity as could be preserved, so that Nigeria could share in the democratisation taking place throughout the continent.[1] In this, Obasanjo failed, a failure that brought shame to the army, misery to Nigerians, and imprisonment to himself.

The charming, clever, and enigmatic Babangida fascinated Nigerians. Nearly twenty years after leaving office he had still not explained the manner of his departure. Many believed that he had clung to power for as long as possible, perhaps hoping to convert himself into a civilian president. Some thought that he had manoeuvred himself into a situation from which he was glad to escape alive. The truth may have been more complicated, involving two central actors rather than one. When he took power, Babangida envisaged himself as 'the architect of a modern Nigeria'. Not only did he call himself president, but he reportedly commissioned a paper on Nasser's model of government.[2] Yet he had made the lack of progress towards democracy a reason for ousting Buhari and he knew that he might suffer the same fate if he did not institute a transition. Once that programme began, however, it became increasingly difficult to stop, except by violent means, while at the same time it both revealed Nigeria's politicians at their most irresponsibly competitive and strengthened elements in the army opposed to restoring civilian rule in any form. When Babangida finally realised in 1993 that public patience was exhausted and power must be transferred, he found that a section of the army refused to let him transfer it. All he could do, for his own safety, was to leave behind an appointed puppet government, which the military would oust after a few months, presenting Obasanjo and other partisans of civilian democracy with a more ruthless enemy.

Babangida's project was defeated by its excessive complexity, but it was also undermined from two other directions. One was his declining control of military force. Initially the most powerful ruler independent Nigeria had seen, as head of state he inevitably lost the direct command over troops necessary either to mount or to resist a coup d'état. That power passed to subordinate commanders, especially during an attempt to overthrow the regime in April 1990 by discontented minority elements within the army. The attempt nearly took Babangida's life and was suppressed, after bloody fighting, by Lt Gen. Sani Abacha, who regarded himself as the president's natural successor.[3] Thereafter, Abacha, as Defence Minister, was the dominant figure within the army. Seeing his succession blocked by any transition to civilian rule, he appears to have decided to convert the transition into an opportunity to supplant Babangida as military ruler, a course he followed with skill and ruthlessness. Ironically, Obasanjo, seeing Babangida as the major obstacle to democratisation, may unwittingly have facilitated Abacha's rise to power.[4]

The second process undermining Babangida's regime between 1990 and 1993 was a renewed economic crisis. His structural adjustment programme had brought some recovery during the later 1980s, reinforced in 1990 by a high oil price due to the Gulf War over Kuwait, but thereafter the annual growth rate of GDP fell from 8.2% in 1990 to only 2.6% in 1993, below the rate of population growth.[5] Government spending remained high, however, so that during 1992 money supply increased by 66% to cover the budget shortfall, annual inflation rose to at least the official figure of 45%, the value of the naira fell by 55%, and the IMF withdrew the endorsement on which debt rescheduling depended. Popular protest climaxed in major 'SAP riots' in May 1992 during which at least twenty protesters were killed.[6] This public anger and disorder formed the background to the subsequent political crisis.

The immediate political priority in 1990 was to consolidate the two parties into which Babangida insisted on channelling Nigerian politics. The party 'a little to the right', the National Republican Convention (NRC), had at its core a regrouping of Shagari's northern-based NPN, supplemented by a number of wealthy southern businessmen. The rival Social Democratic Party (SDP), leaning 'a little to the left', was an uneasy fusion of the Yoruba-based AG-UPN, inherited from Awolowo, and a new grouping, the Patriotic Front of Nigeria (PFN), largely created by Shehu Musa Yar'Adua, Obasanjo's former deputy, who recruited local political entrepreneurs throughout the country in order to create a party strong enough to exclude the military from power.[7]

The first major contest between the two parties took place in December 1991, when the NRC won 16 state governorships, the SDP 14, but the SDP gained a majority of seats in state legislatures. Broadly speaking, the NRC won the core North and the East, the SDP won the West and the Delta, and many minority areas split between them.[8] The conduct of the election alarmed Obasanjo. Although adamant that the military must leave, he was

> extremely worried by the type of leadership that our idea of grass-root politics and the open ballot system [i.e. queuing behind a candidate's photograph] is throwing up. People change places on the queue on the basis of the monetary inducement which each candidate is ready to offer before the electoral officer starts his body count …
>
> Candidates are being sold to the public irrespective of their credentials. Obvious rogues, liars, con men fill up our list of presidential aspirants. Candidates with better track records are unable to show up either because they cannot muster the money necessary to purchase the presidency or because they are disenchanted with the system …
>
> But equally disquieting is the fact that those outside Africa who now clamour for so-called democracy as the panacea of all our problems will declare us a failure again as soon as this experiment fails and that will be another stigma against Nigeria, Africa and the black race.[9]

Obasanjo's fears were borne out in August 1992 when the two parties held their first primary elections to choose presidential candidates. The first sequence of elections was so blatantly rigged that Babangida ordered it to be held again, in three successive groups of ten states.[10] In this second sequence, the first two rounds of voting, covering twenty states, produced a clear pattern. The NRC had two northern front-runners, Adamu Ciroma, a former governor of the Central Bank, and Umaru Shinkafi, a former security chief married into the Sokoto royal family, but neither had any chance of winning one-third of votes in two-thirds of states, a qualification required for presidential candidacy. In the SDP contest, however, Yar'Adua, also a northern aristocrat, trounced his rivals with a campaign that he had been planning for five years with the help of two politicians who were later to manage Obasanjo's political campaigns: Atiku Abubakar, a wealthy young northern businessman, and Tony Anenih, a retired police commissioner from the Benin region. Yar'Adua won the SDP ticket in all those states where there was no favourite son. Other SDP aspirants then abandoned the third round of the contest, leaving Yar'Adua with at least one-third of the votes in 23 of 30 states.[11]

Babangida now faced a potential presidential contest between, on the one side, an SDP candidate whom he personally distrusted and who was a northerner accused by other party leaders of large-scale corruption, and, on the other, an NRC candidate who would also be a northerner but had not met the minimum criteria for selection and must be chosen by a run-off election.[12] At a turbulent meeting on 15–16 October 1992, the military government suspended the primary process, dissolved the two party executives, and instructed the National Electoral Commission to propose a trouble-free presidential selection process. It also decided to defer once more the transition to civilian rule, a decision that divided the military leaders and, by one account, led Abacha to make his first, unsuccessful moves to oust Babangida on the grounds that the country had lost confidence in his programme.[13]

Early in November 1992, Babangida planned a meeting of the Council of State to endorse the government's decisions. Alerted to this, and with his patience exhausted, Obasanjo drafted a speech for the meeting and sent an advance copy to Babangida. 'The primary elections for the presidency, it now seems in retrospect, were designed to fail', he claimed:

> ... In the name of political engineering, the country has been converted to a political laboratory for trying out all kinds of silly experiments and gimmicks. Principle has been abandoned for expediency. All kinds of booby-traps were instituted into the transitional process. The result is the crisis we now face ...
>
> Prolongation of military rule cannot be the answer under the present circumstances. The honour and integrity of the armed forces in whose name you have governed this country these past seven years, are at great risk. The handing over of power to an elected civilian government on January 2, 1993, must proceed apace. There lies the honour of the military which must not be destroyed ...
>
> Nigeria needs peace and stability. It is too fragile to face another commotion. In God's good name, drag it not into one. This is the time for you to have some honourable exit.

What should be done, Obasanjo suggested, was for each party to hold a convention to select a candidate so that the election could take place.[14] When Babangida received this draft, he cancelled the meeting and Obasanjo released the speech to the press. A day after its publication, Babangida announced that all 23 candidates at the recent primary were disqualified, each party would select a new presidential candidate through a series of conventions, the election would take place on 12 June 1993, and civilian rule would follow on 27 August.[15] A furious Yar'Adua accused him of having a 'hidden agenda'. Obasanjo shared his former deputy's anger. 'I don't believe that Babangida will go in August 1993', he declared, 'I believe he is playing games and I believe Nigerians who know what is good for the country and democracy must realise that they must now have to struggle to get what is good for the country'. The Governor of Babangida's Niger State suggested that Obasanjo might have to be arrested.[16]

To demonstrate the military's intention to withdraw, Babangida appointed a largely civilian Transitional Council to conduct the election, with a prominent businessman, Ernest Shonekan, as chairman, although ultimate power remained with a military council. Through a sequence of conventions from ward to national level, culminating in March 1993, the SDP chose as its presidential candidate an immensely wealthy Yoruba businessman, Moshood Abiola, who had grown up in poverty alongside Obasanjo in Abeokuta, attended the same Baptist school, cultivated an extravagantly populist style, and long nursed presidential ambitions. The NRC, with its best candidates barred from consideration, chose a wealthy but colourless Muslim businessman from Kano, Bashir Tofa.[17]

Obasanjo watched these events in the despondent conviction that Babangida had no intention of transferring power. In a rare interview on 9 April 1993, he denounced the regime's lack of integrity and revealed his increasingly obsessive hostility to Babangida:

> We now have an administration in deficit. Deficit budgeting, deficit financing, deficit trading but more importantly, we have an administration that is deficit in credibility.... It's deficit in honesty, deficit in honour, deficit in truth. The only thing it has in surplus, is saying something and doing something else.... All these have increased cynicism and skepticism about government and governance in Nigeria.... It has now got to a stage that when government says good morning, people will look out four times to ascertain the time of the day....
>
> I have not shifted from what I have held firmly to and that is that the transition programme is a charade. We have had a caricature of democracy. We have had President Babangida manouvering [sic], manipulating, playing the game his own way and until he decides that he has scored a goal or he has over-dribbled himself, I don't believe that we will know where we are....
>
> There's no leader that has been credited with so great a capacity for mischief, for evil as Babangida.[18]

The government seized 70,000 copies of this interview and issued a sedition decree threatening the death penalty for spoken or written words that might disrupt the country's 'general fabric'. Babangida told a meeting of officers that Obasanjo seemed to believe that he alone could conduct a political transition, just as, with 'the height of immodesty', he claimed single-handedly to have won the civil war.[19]

By now Obasanjo was moving from criticism to political action. Following Awolowo's death in 1987, the General had made several gestures towards reconciliation with Awolowo's widow – the guardian of her husband's political legacy – and other Yoruba leaders, but he stood aside from the inward-looking organisations seeking to reunify the Yoruba in preparation for competitive politics, the most important of these being Afenifere, with whose leader Obasanjo had fruitless discussions in 1991 over the selection of an agreed Yoruba presidential candidate.[20] Obasanjo was happier to operate at the national level. In March 1989, on the eve of the resumption of party politics, he had brought together at Ota a spectrum of leaders ranging from Danjuma, Adamu Ciroma, and Yar'Adua to radicals like

Balarabe Musa and Samuel Ikoku. They had agreed on two main objectives: 'to unite members of the political class and give succour to the masses of the people so as to avoid any social upheaval akin to a Rawlings-like coup that may wipe out the entire past leadership in Nigeria'. The meeting had appointed working committees, but the initiative seems to have been submerged by the active political competition of the next three years.[21] Late in 1992, however, the cancellation of the presidential primaries and postponement of civilian rule revived Obasanjo's activism. In coopera- tion with the veteran politician Anthony Enahoro, he planned an Association for Democracy and Good Governance in Nigeria 'to rescue the nation from its present drift and set it firmly on a course of real democracy and economic revival'.[22]

A wide range of leaders, including all 23 disqualified presidential aspirants, were invited to the Association's foundation meeting at Ota on 25 May 1993. Thirty-one attended, under strict security in view of the regime's current paranoia. A journalist described those present 'as the cream of the Nigerian elite gathered … to set the agenda for the still putative Third Republic'.[23] Many were senior figures on the right of the political spectrum, including military notables like Danjuma and Buhari, but there was a scattering of more populist leaders, such as Michael Ajasin, the leader of Afenifere, and Abubakar Rimi, the radical former Governor of Kano. Obasanjo opened this 'unholy conclave', as a government newspaper described it,[24] by stressing that they were pro-Nigerian rather than anti-government. As a civil war veteran, he lamented that people were again talking of breaking up Nigeria, stressing that expe- rience in Yugoslavia and the Soviet Union demonstrated how disastrous that would be. The association, he insisted, must look beyond Babangida to the need to stabilise the civilian regime that should follow. The meeting agreed, but resolved that its first goal was to enthrone democracy and prevent further tampering with the transition process. The association would stand for unity, democracy, genuine federalism, and accountability. Membership would be open to all Nigerians, with branches at all levels. Obasanjo was to head an interim committee to draft its constitution.[25]

Whether the presidential election would take place as planned three weeks later was uncertain until the last minute. Babangida had apparently given his blessing to both candidates, who were his personal friends. When Abiola told Obasanjo of this, the General was sceptical but undertook to smooth Abiola's relations with groups within Nigeria and political leaders abroad, although he had a low opinion of Abiola's integrity.[26] Meanwhile military opposition to the transition was hardening. In May 1993 Abacha warned the colonel of a key reconnaissance battalion that his troops might be needed to remove Babangida in order to complete the transi- tion to civilian rule, although when the colonel discussed this with fellow officers, he concluded that Abacha was in fact plotting to supplant the president. A week before the election, Abacha called a meeting of officers and urged them to press for suspension of the poll.[27] Concern seems to have been strengthened by intelligence reports predicting that the amenable Tofa would lose to Abiola, whom some senior officers thought unacceptable as Commander-in-Chief. Apparently with Babangida's acquiescence, those of his close advisers who opposed the transition turned to the the courts to halt it, using the Association for a Better Nigeria, an organisation controlled by a wealthy maverick named Francis Nzeribe who was disgruntled at having failed to win the SDP nomination. On its application, the High Court ordered the suspension of the election on 10 June, in a judgment allegedly written by Babangida's attorney-general.[28] This order had no legal force, however, and at a meeting of the ruling National Defence and Security Council next day, the chairman of the electoral commission persuaded Babangida that it was too late to halt the voting.[29]

Some 37% of registered voters cast ballots on 12 June 1993, with very low figures in the North – only 13% in Tofa's home state, Kano – probably influenced by the lack of a strong northern candidate and uncertainty over whether voting was to take place. Babangida is said to have described it as the best election in Nigeria's history. Certainly it was unusually orderly, but it was definitely not free and fair - as was often subsequently claimed – because so many of the strongest candidates had been excluded. Abiola, an exuberant and generous campaigner, won a clear victory, with 58% of the votes, 19 of the 30 states, and an unprecedentedly wide range of support across regional and religious boundaries.[30]

When journalists found Obasanjo sitting outside his farmhouse on the morning after the poll, he was delighted by the first results they gave him. 'He was particularly concerned about any incident that could have marred the election and provided Babangida a ready excuse to once more, postpone the end of his dictatorship.' Commenting, 'We seem to be winning', he phoned the Ogun State Governor:

> When the conversation ended, Obasanjo, his cellular phone in one hand and the note-books and pencil in the other, suddenly sprang up, jitterbugging all over the place.... He stopped to catch his breath just as suddenly as he had started dancing, and said triumphantly: 'Boys, we have made it; we have won. Now I want to see how Ibrahim Babangida will not leave on August 27.'[31]

It was premature. On 15 June, with all the results reported, half of them announced, and Abiola far ahead, Nzeribe and his military and legal backers persuaded a High Court judge to halt the declaration of further results until the legality of the election had been decided.[32] Next day the much divided National Defence and Security Council delegated the issue to a committee, headed by Abacha, under whose pressure the electoral commission agreed to suspend further announcements of results while petitioning the Appeal Court to overrule the High Court judgement. The Appeal Court fixed the hearing for 25 June.[33] Tofa, who had drafted a letter conceding defeat, was allegedly summoned to the capital and told to start complaining, as the NRC immediately did, protesting violation of electoral laws.[34] Obasanjo, by his own account, sought without success to persuade the leader of the Nigerian Labour Congress to call his members into the streets, advised Abiola to go to court while appointing committees to draft policy statements, and then left on delayed visits to South Africa and New York.[35]

While Nigerians waited to hear the outcome of the election, a dangerous power struggle took place within the military leadership. The details are obscure and contested, but three factions seem to have been involved: those who wished to accept Abiola's election; those around Babangida (the 'Abuja group') who wished him or one of their own number to remain in power; and those (the 'Lagos group') who sought to use the crisis to replace Babangida by Abacha, whose Defence Ministry was in Lagos.[36] The Abuja and Lagos groups agreed in refusing to accept Abiola as their Commander-in-Chief. Brigadier David Mark (of the Abuja group) was said to have vowed to shoot Abiola if that happened, while Abacha snorted, 'Abiola to retire me? God forbid!'[37] After two days of confusion, when Babangida told a visiting officer, 'I don't know what is going on', the President moved to his home at Minna with members of the Abuja group, who convinced him that the election could not stand. Returning to Abuja on 21 June, Babangida said that his own life and Abiola's had been threatened.[38] With the Appeal Court due to consider the legality of the election on 25 June and likely to uphold it, the National Defence and Security Council met on the night of 22–3 June and decided, by a majority, to annul the election, cancel the transition process and bar further legal proceedings. The decision provoked almost immediate sanctions from the United States, United Kingdom, and European Community.[39] On 26 June, Babangida spoke on television, claiming that the electoral process had been corrupt and divisive, that both candidates had business relationships with the state that led to conflicts of interest, and that it was essential to protect the integrity of the courts. He promised a further election in time for him to leave office by 27 August as planned. Three days later he told state governors that Abiola 'could not have commanded the support and loyalty of the armed forces'. Much later, in 2009, he said he had been convinced that an Abiola government would have been overthrown by a military coup within six months.[40]

Obasanjo was in New York when he heard of the annulment. He immediately blamed Babangida, telling the Voice of America that he had always known that the president did not want to quit. It was a view he maintained to the end of his career. He also warned Abiola by telephone not to announce the election results and declare himself president-elect, advice that Abiola ignored.[41] 'I spoke to the State Department and the National Security Council in Washington DC and the Whitehall in London before I left New York on June 24', Obasanjo recalled, 'and I stopped over briefly in Paris to speak to the Ministry of Foreign Affairs.' Once back in Nigeria, he telephoned Babangida just before his broadcast on 26 June, urging him to reconsider the annulment:

> I came away with the impression that Babangida would not yield on the cancellation of the election in spite of the danger for the nation. I had opportunity to meet and discuss with about half a dozen senior military officers on the same day. It became clear to me that Babangida acted almost alone in canceling the election but he had been able to cultivate the support of a substantial number of senior military officers. There was a story of element of threat to Babangida's life which made him to cancel the election. But I saw perpetuation in office as the main reason. I shared my observations and conclusions with Chief Abiola.[42]

While continuing to demand the recognition of Abiola's victory, Obasanjo recognised the strength of military opposition to it and encouraged the alternative of holding a second election before Babangida was due to leave on 27 August, if both parties agreed.[43]

The parties did not agree. When Babangida, in his television broadcast, suggested a second election, most NRC leaders quickly accepted it, hoping to reverse the June 12 verdict,[44] but the SDP rejected the proposal outright on 5 July. Some of its leaders insisted on defending Abiola's 'sacred mandate', encouraged by popular protests in the south-west that began with demonstrations by Ibadan University students on 27 June and climaxed in popular riots in Lagos early in July during which over a hundred people were said to have died. Other SDP leaders, especially Yar'Adua and his supporters, shared Obasanjo's view that there was no realistic hope of fighting the military and had long resented Abiola's candidacy, but nevertheless opposed a new election lest it extend Babangida's tenure and provoke a partial boycott that would lead their divided party to defeat.[45] Thus political factionalism and the artificiality of Babangida's two parties prevented unified civilian response. Instead, ignoring Abiola, Yar'Adua's majority in the SDP executive agreed with the NRC on 7 July to pursue Babangida's alternative suggestion and jointly constitute an Interim National Government. Babangida had said that this could consist entirely of civilians, take over from him on 27 August, and organise fresh elections.[46] Babangida 'jumped for joy' on hearing this, although the military leaders objected to the parties' proposal until a compromise was reached on 31 July.[47] On 3 August Abiola left for Europe and the United States, apparently on advice from Abacha, who warned him that his life was in danger and undertook to safeguard his interests.[48]

Obasanjo insisted that an Interim National Government was not his idea, but his realism quickly convinced him that the end of military rule – his first priority throughout the crisis – could not be achieved by popular pressure or an agreed second election, so he turned to the idea as the only available alternative. By 7 July both he and Yar'Adua had discussed it with Babangida. Their initial plan was for a broad-based government to which the SDP, NRC, and military would each nominate one-third of members. Obasanjo may have hoped to accommodate Abiola in this, but Abiola rejected the idea and his departure on 3 August lost him Obasanjo's little remaining support.[49] A proposal that Babangida might himself head the interim government was rejected by senior officers. Another suggestion was that Obasanjo should do so, but he is said to have refused a brief tenure that would not allow him to implement a lasting transition. He made this clear to the Association for Democracy and Good Governance in Nigeria at a meeting on 9 August that rejected his recommendation to accept an interim government and instead reaffirmed its commitment to the June 12 result, a split that would soon destroy the organisation.[50]

Following extensive discussions with the parties, Babangida announced on 17 August that the government had accepted an all-civilian interim government to replace him on 27 August. To head it the military chose Shonekan, the leader of the Transitional Council, who, like Abiola, came from Abeokuta and who had strong support from Western diplomats. 'If an interim government will get Babangida out of the way, I will support it', Obasanjo declared.[51]

Abacha agreed. An interim government, as a fellow officer explained, was 'the weakest spot he could attack to get to power without initially alienating the people'.[52] Ten days before the new government was to take office, Abacha, as Minister of Defence, convened a meeting of senior officers, to which Babangida was not invited, and there established his followers' predominance over the Abuja group who had surrounded Babangida.[53] Allegedly hinting at a possible coup d'état, his followers then insisted that Abacha remain in office as the sole military member of the new regime. Shonekan objected but was told that Abacha's presence was essential to a smooth transition and was a guarantee against a coup by junior officers. Obasanjo was never taken in by Abacha and was furious at this breach of Babangida's promise. Yar'Adua, eager for an election that he expected to win, regarded Abacha as the price that must be paid for an interim government to arrange one. Abacha, in turn, assured a left-leaning officer that he intervened to ensure that power was transferred to Abiola. 'I just didn't understand', the officer recalled.[54]

Shonekan was sworn in as head of state on 26 August 1993, although not as Commander-in-Chief because officers refused to accept his authority in military matters. He was specifically to hold office for six months in order to conduct a new presidential election, which he fixed for 19 February 1994. Obasanjo expressed the views of many Nigerians when he said on 27 August that the interim government, although not ideal, 'was the most realistic and practical means and instrument to save Nigeria from unimaginable danger'. As one of Shonekan's advisers put it, 'Nigerians don't want another civil war, that has to be the bottom line.'[55] Returning to his political vision of the late 1980s, Obasanjo hoped that the months before the election could see 'a dialogue drawing in all the active and progressive elements that have worked to see the end of military dictatorship', with 'a limited goal of producing a national government that will ... set a genuine democratic process on track while at the same time tackling vigorously the economic and social problems of the country'.[56]

In reality the interim government never had a chance. It was trapped between Abacha's ambition, the demands of Abiola and his largely Yoruba loyalists for implementation of his June 12 victory, and the disastrous state of the economy.[57] Within a month of the new government's installation, but without consulting Shonekan, Abacha – still letting it be thought that he favoured Abiola's presidency – had consolidated his control of the army by retiring or marginalising the Abuja group of officers on the grounds that, as supporters of Babangida, they were a danger to the interim government. Meanwhile the SDP governors in the south-west refused to recognise or cooperate with Shonekan's regime and political leaders of the region insisted they would boycott any future election, although the party executive favoured one.[58] The hapless Shonekan declared on 29 September that he saw no point in an enquiry into the annulment of the June election, announced next day that he would appoint one, was promptly told that the NRC regarded the issue as closed, and stated a week later that the enquiry could not reverse the military government's decision.[59]

Shonekan had more immediate problems. With annual inflation probably over 80% and police, army, and civil service salaries paid only irregularly, he was anxious to withdraw Nigeria's peacekeeping troops from their expensive operation in Liberia, earning further military hostility, and to reduce the subsidy on petrol prices that cost the state N41 billion (about $1 billion) a year and obstructed negotiations with the IMF.[60] Babangida had tried to do this a few days before leaving office, so that Shonekan faced an immediate stay-at-home strike in Lagos and the south-west that also demanded Abiola's installation. Shonekan withdrew the price increase, but on 8 November, in desperation, he suddenly raised the price again from N0.70 to N5 per litre. Strikes and riots began almost immediately. By 16 November they were spreading beyond the south-west to other parts of the country. A week earlier the Lagos High Court had formally declared the interim government to be illegal. A further declaration invalidating the annulment of the election was expected on 18 November.[61]

Abacha seized his moment. He was under pressure from the army to take power and end the growing disorder. He feared that Shonekan might be overwhelmed by the popular movement.[62] At the same time, several democratic leaders in the south-west were urging Abacha to intervene because they expected him to instal Abiola, as did Abiola himself, who had returned to Nigeria on 24 September and had been led by Abacha and his Yoruba deputy, Oladipo Diya, to believe that the military would make him president.[63]

On 17 November 1993, Abacha and Diya told Shonekan to resign. The coup was widely popular, open opposition coming only from the powerless Senate and some student groups.[64] Obasanjo was more enigmatic. Shortly after the court declared the interim government illegal, Abacha had asked Obasanjo's advice on what should be done. Obasanjo had suggested an appeal. When Abacha had pressed him further, Obasanjo had 'sensed the sort of the direction he wanted to go, then I said "look, let me tell you if Nigeria can tolerate … military government … the international community cannot. I believe Nigeria is now pissed off, is fed up rather, with military government." So I left.' Shortly afterwards, hearing clearer news of Abacha's plan, Obasanjo had telephoned him to urge him to stay his hand and instead give full military support to Shonekan.[65] At midnight after taking power, Abacha invited Obasanjo to a meeting next day. Obasanjo deliberately arrived late. There are several later accounts of what took place. According to one, Obasanjo asked, 'Sani, what are you doing here? You better pack your things and get out of here fast. Stop disgracing the military.' When Abacha asked for his support, Obasanjo demanded to know the regime's agenda and intended length of stay. Abacha said that would depend on the constitutional conference he planned. Obasanjo refused support until a departure date was announced, suggesting that it should be no more than eighteen months.[66] Later that day he told the BBC that the coup had been 'unfortunate but necessary'. A week later, at a book launch in Lagos, Obasanjo said the regime should admit that Shonekan's 'resignation' had been 'procured at gunpoint' and should return to barracks and tackle its own corruption. 'Until the military can put itself on a moral and ethical high ground', he added, 'it will not be able to infuse new life and pull the nation together and move it forwards.'[67]

Abacha moved swiftly and skilfully to establish his regime. By reducing the new petrol price to N3.25 per litre he persuaded the Nigerian Labour Congress back to work. He abolished all existing parties and democratic institutions, but Diya promised a brief regime that would restore democracy by means of a constitutional conference. It was a sop to demands by southern politicians for a sovereign national conference to restructure Nigeria on the lines of conferences held in many African states at this time.[68] 'I will beat Obasanjo', Abacha told the American ambassador, 'I will even quickly return the government back than Obasanjo.'[69] He succeeded in attracting civilian politicians of all complexions into his Federal Executive Council, including Abiola's running-mate, Babagana Kingibe; the former NRC chairman, Tom Ikimi; the northern presidential front-runner, Adamu Ciroma; the civil rights lawyer, Olu Onagoruwa; and disciples of Awolowo like Lateef Jakande. Sixteen of the 33 members of Nigeria's first 'truly national government' were vocal advocates of Abiola's installation.[70] Although some were doubtless eager for office and wealth, many expected Abacha to fulfil his promise to transfer power to Abiola, while others saw office as a patriotic duty at a time of crisis and an opportunity to give Nigeria a new start. 'We were convinced that there was a major crisis,' remembered Iyorchia Ayu, who had led the Senate's support for Abiola and now became Minister of Education:

> … The reactions were dangerous as people were attacking others from different parts of the country and it was as if we were re-enacting the 1966 crisis which ultimately precipitated the civil war. It was our collective conviction that no country survives two civil wars and we should do everything to stop the crisis from degenerating to a war situation. We went in to save the country from collapse or disaster.[71]

Obasanjo did not share this view. He refused to suggest any names for Abacha's council.[72] On 2 February 1994, six weeks after Abacha's seizure of power, Obasanjo addressed a conference on the state of the nation at Kaduna in one of his bravest and most thoughtful speeches.[73] He was alarmed at renewed talk of Nigerian disintegration, which, he warned, would mean that 'many Bosnias will be created in many parts of Nigeria.' 'I have had to fight a war to keep Nigeria together, I cannot and will not fight another war to tear Nigeria apart.' Maintaining his earlier analysis of the recent crisis, he laid the blame firmly on Babangida, 'a great master of intrigue, mismanagement, deceit, settlement, cover-up and self-promotion at the expense of almost everybody else and everything else':

> General Babangida is the main architect of the state in which the nation finds itself today, and … General Abacha was his eminent disciple, faithful supporter, and beneficiary …
>
> General Sani Abacha reminds one of a man, who with other do-gooders proposed a meal for a blind man. As soon as the others turned their back, this seemingly good Samaritan … went back to snatch the pot of soup from the blind man for himself.
>
> Again, most of us Nigerians, as spectators, applauded. Under all sorts of excuses, there was no shortage of partakers in the meal. And they were not troubled by the moral implications.

Why, he asked, should a government expect confidence or understanding when it refused to state a programme or date of departure? An insider had warned him, he said, that Abacha's 'brief period' might last from one to ten years, a prediction reinforced two months later when the recently retired Brig. David Mark – unquestionably an insider – warned in an interview that Abacha was planning to stay five years.[74] Obasanjo asserted that

> The greatest danger lies in the failure of the military to break the vicious cycle of succeeding itself. Unless Nigerians stand up against this trend, it may continue indefinitely…. Since independence, Nigeria has not been able to unite behind one non-military leader, I believe we can unite behind one political issue. It is democracy.

Obasanjo then turned to analyse the major problems that the restoration of democracy must solve. He had no time for Abacha's planned constitutional conference, which eventually met in June 1994 and meandered on for a year, producing a little-changed constitution that was not published until 1999.[75] Obasanjo believed that it was 'a dangerous diversion' designed 'to satisfy the agitators', unlikely to affect Abacha's thinking and capable of widening national divisions. But at this time he saw more virtue in a national conference on larger issues, provided all conclusions were subject to a referendum, in line with his long-standing belief that ethnic conflict was the work of the elite:

> I still believe that a major issue to be settled at the conference should be the issue of our living together – the corporate existence of Nigeria. We must settle this matter once and for all and do away with constant threats to our corporate existence. After we have agreed to live together, we can settle the issue of how we will live together. I am convinced that when we are confronted with the reality of a break-up, our leaders will prefer living together on the basis of mutual respect and mutual benefit to breaking up. If our leaders cannot appreciate the need and the necessity, our people can and they will give the final verdict.

A central question was how to satisfy minority demands, such as those expressed most strongly at this time by the Ogoni people of the Niger Delta, whose territory was the location of Nigeria's pioneer oil industry, causing acute environmental pollution but doing little to relieve local poverty. Obasanjo reflected,

> There are many Ogonis, our dispensation must allow for the right of minorities including the enjoyment of part of the God-given resources in their area and there must be a delicate balance between the rights and interests of the minorities and the rights and common interests of all Nigerians. We must listen to them.

At the same time, however, he was alarmed by the atomisation of Nigeria through the creation of unviable new states, whose number Abacha was to swell to 36. Obasanjo suggested that states should be replaced by a smaller number of larger zones as the component units of the federation, with local government areas below them, an idea widely sponsored at this time and partly adopted by the constitutional conference. One advantage of the change might be to counteract the 'settler-stranger syndrome', the reverse side of Nigeria's cherished 'federal principle' by which full citizenship rights in a state or even a local government area – rights to free schooling or public employment, for example – were confined to 'indigenes' of the area, a divisive pattern that Obasanjo opposed throughout his career. These problems and others, he claimed, could be solved only by the immediate creation of a civilian national government. 'Nigeria has the responsibility to the whole of the Black race to put her house in order and show that the race is not doomed.'

While Obasanjo was urging unity, civilian opposition to Abacha's regime was in fact polarising around the figure of Abiola, once it became clear that Abacha had no intention of making way for him but sought instead to channel civilian politics into the constitutional conference. In February 1994, Abiola called on his largely Yoruba supporters to boycott the conference and defend his claim to the presidency, a call taken up in May by the founders of the National Democratic Coalition (NADECO), whose core consisted of the recently proscribed Yoruba ethnic organisation, Afenifere, reinforced by democratic groups from elsewhere in the south. As the anniversary of the June 12 election approached, NADECO called on Abacha to step down and allow Abiola to form a national government and convene a sovereign national conference.[76] On June 11, Abiola evaded the police, declared himself president at a tin-roofed sports centre on Lagos Island, and went into hiding. He then emerged to address a rally of 5,000 people, drove in a motorcade through the length of the city, and was arrested on June 23 on a charge of treason.[77]

Abiola's unacceptability to military commanders and northern political leaders had lost him all credibility in Obasanjo's eyes. In a comment that won him much Yoruba hostility, Obasanjo told an audience of Nigerians in Harare, 'I will not support Abiola taking power. I know him very well, much more than all of you. He was my classmate but I don't think he is the messiah Nigeria is looking for.'[78] He nevertheless advised Abacha not to arrest Abiola and on 18 July led a galaxy of traditional rulers to a meeting with Abacha designed to initiate a dialogue between the military ruler and his prisoner. The meeting was a disaster. Obasanjo asked for Abiola's release and a statement of Abacha's programme. Abacha said Abiola could be freed if he renounced his claim to the presidency. The chiefs insisted that Abiola be brought before them and then pressed the unprepared prisoner to apologise to Abacha for claiming to be president-elect and to abandon his mandate in return for freedom:

... facing Abacha, an angry Abiola was reported to have called him a 'usurper', and that the head of the junta had no right to be seated where he was because it was rightly and legitimately his (Abiola's). He was said to have sworn that nothing would stop him from claiming that mandate, and that the worst they could do was either to jail or kill him. There was pin-drop silence in the chamber.[79]

By now Obasanjo was hopelessly at odds with Yoruba opinion. On 16 July rioting spread through the region:

When the protesters got to Obasanjo's home at the Onikolobo area of the town [Abeokuta], they descended on the windows and smashed all louvres. After that, they made to set the building ablaze but for the entreaties by tenants. Not much damage was done to his second house at Itoko where two armed soldiers on guard threatened to shoot. His four-storey office building on Quarry Road Junction was however not so fortunate. The interiors were seriously vandalised. The mob actually made to set the house ablaze but for the arrival of armed mobile policemen. Even then, two cars and a jeep belonging to Obasanjo Holdings Limited were effectively burnt ... Obasanjo himself reportedly put the cost of the damage to his property at some N3 million [over $30,000], But he said he was taking it all as a sacrifice he would not mind making towards peace and unity in Nigeria.[80]

Obasanjo was shaken by what he saw as unfair reward for his selfless service and as punishment for his refusal to be a tribal leader. 'We do not need fighting in the streets, burning of properties, petrol bombing, paralysing national strikes, and a shutdown of the economy', he protested. 'We need the speediest return to civilian administration under an agreed leadership imbued with the spirit of compromise and capable of creating an inspiring national programme round which all the people can gather.'[81] His new attempt to achieve this appears to have begun in May 1994, when he and Yar'Adua created the National Unity Promoters.[82] An attempt to expand this into a National Unity Organisation of Nigeria (NUON) at a meeting in Ota early in June was obstructed by security agents, who cordoned off the farm and arrested those seeking to enter, but the organisation nevertheless came into being and apparently gained the backing of influential figures in the Northern Elders Forum who saw Obasanjo as the most plausible leader of a government of national unity at a time of incipient disorder.[83] By November 1994 Obasanjo claimed that NUON had interim officers and members in all states, but could not legally propound a programme. When party politics resumed, the organisation would sponsor a presidential candidate, although it would not be him. Many thought it would be Yar'Adua, who was at this time organising his own party and taking a leading role in the constitutional conference.[84]

In December 1994, Obasanjo organised the first of two meetings between Yoruba and Igbo politicians, but they did not attract either the Afenifere leaders who championed Abiola or representatives of the counterpart Igbo ethnic organisation, Ohanaeze Ndigbo, who told him to reconcile first with Afenifere.[85] Such an approach to Afenifere in February 1995 brought only recrimination. Obasanjo made a passionate speech about national unity, at which his Yoruba audience asked how there could be unity without justice. Reminding him of his earlier dismissal of 'Yoruba sectional politics', they refused to listen to him unless he clarified his attitude towards Abiola. Obasanjo lost his temper and the meeting ended in acrimony.[86]

Instead, Obasanjo turned back to the North, where his approaches to emirs and political leaders met a response whose warmth was said to have alarmed the military regime.[87] He had been warned in January 1995 that Abacha was threatening to deal with him and Yar'Adua.[88] Nevertheless, before leaving for the United Nations World Summit on Social Development in Copenhagen at the beginning of March, Obasanjo arranged to visit the North for talks a few days after his return.[89] In Copenhagen he apparently spoke of military rule as an obstacle to development and urged the conference to exclude military rulers.[90] While there, he learned that Yar'Adua had been detained in connection with a suspected coup plot. American diplomats and Nigerian friends warned Obasanjo that he would also be arrested if he returned to Nigeria. Knowing himself innocent, he decided that arrest was better than becoming a fugitive. At Lagos airport on 12 March his passport was confiscated. Next day, plain-clothed policemen collected him from Ota, saying his help was needed. 'If you think I am a fool, I am not', he replied, taking a towel and toilet bag.[91]

NOTES

1. See above, pp. 113–15, 130.
2. *Newswatch*, 10 July 2000, p. 9; *Africa Confidential*, 27 September 1991, p. 3.
3. Osaghae, *Crippled giant*, pp. 246–8; Omo Omoruyi, *The tale of June 12: the betrayal of the democratic rights of Nigerians (1993)* (London, 1999), pp. 200–11.
4. As suggested in Omoruyi, *Tale*, p. 275.
5. Osaghae, *Crippled giant*, p. 281.
6. Biersteker and Lewis in Diamond et al., *Transition*, pp. 321–2; Forrest, *Politics*, p. 247; Osaghae, *Crippled giant*, p. 206.
7. Babafemi A. Badejo, 'Party formation and party conflict', in Diamond et al., *Transition*, ch. 7; Farris and Bomoi, *Shehu Musa Yar'Adua*, pp. 182–95.
8. Dan Agbese and Etim Amin, 'The state elections of 1991', in Diamond et al., *Transition*.
9. Obasanjo, *Hope*, p. 86.
10. *West Africa*, 17 August 1992, p. 1386; *Daily Times*, 4–7 August 1992.
11. *Daily Times*, 14–29 September 1992.
12. Omoruyi, *Tale*, pp. 59–64.
13. *Daily Times*, 17 October 1992; Alli, *Federal Republic*, pp. 267–84; *Tell*, 14 December 1998, pp. 32–4.
14. *Guardian*, 16 November 1992.
15. *Guardian*, 18 November 1992.
16. *Daily Times*, 12 December 1992; *West Africa*, 25 January 1993, p. 97; *Guardian*, 23 November 1992.
17. *West Africa*, 11 January 1993, p. 8; Osaghae, *Crippled giant*, p. 238; *Sunday Times* (Lagos), 23 August 1992.
18. *Tell*, 26 April 1993, pp. 13–22.
19. *Africa Research Bulletin (Political)*, May 1993, p. 11003; Omoruyi, *Tale*, p. 79.
20. *African Concord*, 1 May 1989, p. 9, and 12 March 1990, p. 33; Michael Adekunle Ajasin, *Ajasin: memoirs and memories* (Lagos, 2003), pp. 476–8.
21. *African Concord*, 1 May 1989, p. 11.
22. *Tell*, 26 April 1993, p. 12.
23. *Tell*, 7 June 1993, p. 12.
24. *New Nigerian*, 10 June 1993.
25. *Tell*, 7 June 1993, pp. 11–15; *African Guardian*, 7 June 1993, pp. 20–7; *African Concord*, 7 June 1993, pp. 15–19; Francis C. Enemuo and Abubakar Momoh, 'Civic associations',

in Oyelede Oyediran and Adigun A.B. Agbaje (ed.), *Nigeria: politics of transition and governance 1986–1996* (Dakar, 1999), pp. 92–3.

26. Ademiluyi, *From prisoner to president*, pp. 62–3; *New Nigerian*, 19 August 1998; Obasanjo in *Nigerian Tribune*, 31 October 1993.
27. Abubakar Umar in *Tell*, 18 August 1998, pp. 16–18.
28. *Tell*, 26 June 1995, pp. 13–14; Abimbola Davis in *African Guardian*, 26 July 1993; *African Concord*, 24 January 1994, pp. 33–7; Olawale Oshun, *Clapping with one hand: June 12 and the crisis of a state nation* (London, 1999), p. 72; *Daily Times*, 11 June 1993.
29. H.N. Nwosu, *Laying the foundation for Nigeria's democracy: my account of June 12, 1993 presidential election and its annulment* (Lagos, 2008), pp. 285–91; *Tell*, 26 June 1995, p. 15.
30. Nwosu, *Laying the foundation*, pp. 292–8; Omoruyi, *Tale*, p. xiii.
31. *Tell*, 26 July 1994, p. 11.
32. *Daily Times*, 16 June 1993.
33. Nwosu, *Laying the foundation*, pp. 299–304.
34. *Tell*, 26 June 1995, p. 16; *Daily Times*, 16 June 1993.
35. *Nigerian Tribune*, 31 October 1993.
36. See Omoruyi, *Tale*, pp. 15–21; Abubakar Umar in *Tell*, 18 August 1998, pp. 16–23; Ebenezer Babatope, *The Abacha regime and the June 12 crisis: a struggle for democracy* (Lagos, 1995), pp. 1–3; Tunji Olurin in *This Day*, 30 September 2004.
37. Omoruyi, *Tale*, pp. 166, 185.
38. *Tell*, 26 June 1995, pp. 19–20, and 18 August 1998, p. 19; Omoruyi, *Tale*, pp. 26, 97, 161–70.
39. Omoruyi, *Tale*, pp. 176–8; *West Africa*, 28 June 1993, pp. 1078–81; Rotimi T. Suberu, 'Crisis and collapse: June-November 1993', in Diamond et al., *Transition*, p. 284.
40. *Daily Times*, 28 June and 3 July 1993; *This Day*, 5 February 2009.
41. *Tell*, 26 September 1994, pp. 11–12; *Guardian*, 4 June 2007; Farris and Bomoi, *Shehu Musa Yar'Adua*, pp. 223–4.
42. *Nigerian Tribune*, 31 October 1993; *Newswatch*, 26 July 1993, p. 42.
43. *Times*, 14 July 1993; *Newswatch*, 19 July 1993, p. 11, and 26 July 1993, pp. 42–3.
44. Oshun, *Clapping*, Ch.1.
45. *Daily Times*, 28 June – 7 July 1993; *Newswatch*, 19 July 1993, pp. 10–12, and 26 July 1993, p. 44; *African Guardian*, 12 July 1993, p. 25; Farris and Bomoi, *Shehu Musa Yar'Adua*, pp. 225–9.
46. *Daily Times*, 7–8 July 1993; *Newswatch*, 19 July 1993, pp. 12–14, and 26 July 1993, p. 44; *African Guardian*, 19 July 1993, p. 22; Farris and Bomoi, *Shehu Musa Yar'Adua*, pp. 228–30.
47. Omoruyi, *Tale*, pp. 273–4; *Newswatch*, 26 July 1993, pp. 11–13; *West Africa*, 9 August 1993, p. 1403.
48. Farris and Bomoi, *Shehu Musa Yar'Adua*, pp. 230–1
49. *New Nigerian*, 19 August 1998; Farris and Bomoi, *Shehu Musa Yar'Adua*, p. 228; Oshun *Clapping*, p. 62; *Daily Times*, 12 July 1993.
50. *African Guardian*, 23 August 1993, pp. 12, 16–17; Farris and Bomoi, *Shehu Musa Yar'Adua*, p. 230.
51. *Newswatch*, 30 August 1993, p. 2; Omoruyi, *Tale*, pp. 247, 277.
52. Adetunji Olurin in *Tell*, 14 December 1998, p. 33. See also *Tell*, 26 September 1994, p. 12.
53. Omoruyi, *Tale*, p. 15.
54. *Newswatch*, 6 September 1993, p. 13, and 20 September 1993, pp. 14–15; *Tell*, 18 August 1998, pp. 21–2; Farris and Bomoi, *Shehu Musa Yar'Adua*, p. 230.
55. Alli, *Federal Republic*, p. 220; *Daily Times*, 28 August and 11 September 1993; *West Africa*, 8 November 1993, p. 2017.
56. *Nigerian Tribune*, 3 October 1993.

57. See Suberu in Diamond et al., *Transition*, pp. 290–6.
58. *Newswatch*, 27 September 1993, pp. 14–15; *Daily Times*, 8 September and 14–15 October 1993.
59. *Daily Times*, 30 September and 1, 2, and 9 October 1993.
60. Biersteker and Lewis in Diamond et al., *Transition*, p. 326; Adekeye Adebajo, *Liberia's civil war: Nigeria, ECOMOG, and regional security in West Africa* (Boulder, 2002), p. 133; *West Africa*, 29 November 1993, p. 2156; *Daily Times*, 9 November 1993.
61. *Daily Times*, 3 September and 9–17 November 1993; Suberu in Diamond et al., *Transition*, p. 296.
62. Alli, *Federal Republic*, pp. 294–329; *Newswatch*, 11 April 1994, pp. 11–12; Omoruyi, *Tale*, p. 30.
63. Osaghae, *Crippled giant*, pp. 275–6.
64. *Newswatch*, 10 January 1994, p. 13; *Africa Confidential*, 3 December 1993, pp. 4–5.
65. *Newswatch*, 25 January 1999, p. 12; *Tell*, 20 May 1996.
66. *Newswatch*, 13 December 1993 p. 12, 21 September 1998 p. 14, 25 January 1999 pp. 12–13.
67. *Daily Times*, 20 November 1993; *Newswatch*, 27 March 1995, p. 12, and 6 December 1993, p. 14.
68. *Daily Times*, 19, 22, and 24 November 1993; *Newswatch*, 30 March 1994, p. 17.
69. *This Day*, 22 October 2000.
70. *Daily Times*, 26 November 1993; Osaghae, *Crippled giant*, p. 276 n. 2.
71. *Newswatch*, 3 January 2000, p. 43.
72. Obasanjo, *This animal*, p. 225.
73. *Daily Times*, 4–7 February 1994; extracts in *Newswatch*, 14 February 1994, pp. 30–2.
74. *Newswatch*, 11 April 1994, pp. 10–18.
75. Osaghae, *Crippled giant*, pp. 287–90.
76. *West Africa*, 14 February 1994, p. 250; Oshun, *Clapping*, pp. 175, 178.
77. *Newswatch*, 27 June 1994, pp. 9–11, and 4 July 1994, pp. 9–11.
78. *Daily Times*, 4 June 1994.
79. *Tell*, 1 August 1994, p. 9.
80. Ibid., p. 16.
81. *Newswatch*, 29 August 1994, p. 18.
82. *Newswatch*, 30 May 1994, p. 12.
83. *Newswatch*, 20 June 1994, p. 14; Farris and Bomoi, *Shehu Musa Yar'Adua*, p. 253; *Tell*, 18 July 1994, p. 14, and 1 August 1994, pp. 10–12.
84. *Daily Times*, 30 October 1994; *Newswatch*, 14 November 1994, p. 10.
85. *Daily Times*, 27 December 1994; *Tell*, 12 June 1995, p. 16.
86. Oshun, *Clapping*, pp. 248–9; *Newswatch*, 13 March 1995, pp. 18–19.
87. *Tell*, 3 April 1995, p. 14.
88. *Guardian*, 6 July 1998.
89. *Tell*, 12 June 1995, p. 16.
90. Orji Agbonnaya Orji, *Inside Aso Rock* (Ibadan, 2003), pp. 188–9.
91. *Newswatch*, 25 January 1999, pp. 13–14.

13
The Prisoner

Abacha's headquarters at Aso Rock in the new capital at Abuja seethed with intrigue, suspicion, and rumour. The head of state himself was rarely seen, seldom attended meetings, frequently neglected official business, and did not attempt to tour the country. A man of few words and no intellectual pretensions, he hated reading but was a good listener, an astute schemer, and a ruthless executor, greedy for wealth, obsessed by security, and uninhibited in resort to violence. His sinister Chief Security Officer, Major Hamza al-Mustapha, controlled an Israeli- and Korean-trained Strike Force with its own detention camps, interrogation centres, and assassination unit.[1] The obsession with security was not merely paranoid. Major-General Chris Alli, Chief of Army Staff in the first months of the regime, recalled that both the Director of Military Intelligence (Army) and Abacha's deputy, Lt Gen. Diya, had suggested a coup to him before he was retired in August 1994 on suspicion of planning one.[2]

The alleged coup plot used to ensnare Obasanjo surfaced late in 1994 and centred on Brig.Gen. Lawan Gwadabe, who had commanded Babangida's elite armoured troops but had been rusticated by Abacha to distant Yola, a most unlikely place from which to launch a coup. Gwadabe was arrested late in February 1995 with other officers and civilians. Yar'Adua was picked up on 9 March.[3] According to an account that Obasanjo transmitted from prison, presumably based on allegations during his interrogation, the regime had ordered security operatives in Abeokuta to report any information incriminating him, at which a zealous agent had claimed that Yar'Adua was planning a coup with Obasanjo's support. 'I was arrested on that basis in March,' he explained, 'and so was Shehu and six former SDP ... members from Abeokuta.'[4] Yar'Adua had publicly criticised Abacha's seizure of power, refused to join his government, and led demands at the constitutional conference in December 1994 for Abacha to restore civilian rule in January 1996. 'I will get him, including that Obasanjo,' Abacha had told Alli.[5]

When Obasanjo was arrested at Ota on 13 March 1995 he was 'rudely thrust into an empty room at the police officers mess, Ikeja', near Lagos, and then shuffled around detention centres for a week, without being interrogated.[6] He had left instructions to inform the Oni of Ife (the senior Yoruba chief) and the American ambassador. When chiefs from the Abeokuta area visited Abacha on 15 March, by one account, he told them that investigation had shown Obasanjo to be the central figure in the failed coup attempt.[7] Six days later, Obasanjo's friend, ex-President

152

Jimmy Carter, spent two hours with Abacha, allegedly carrying a blunt instruction from the American government to release the General. Abacha agreed to return him to house arrest at Ota. Obasanjo spent the next two months there, guarded by fourteen armed policemen and denied access to media, the telephone, and visitors. The regime announced that he was suspected of involvement in the coup.[8] The unlikelihood of this in a man who notoriously avoided coups – as he said, it was 'a thing I could not even do when I was in uniform' – led to a chorus of international protest.[9] Abacha told former Prime Minister Callaghan that he hoped to release Obasanjo after questioning. He told Commonwealth Secretary-General Anyaoku that the General would be tried for conspiracy, then bluntly rang off. Nelson Mandela sent a deputation. Ambassadors were turned away from the Ota complex.[10]

The regime now manufactured the evidence for a trial. Under torture, Colonel Bello-Fadile, a military lawyer who had spoken unwisely about possible military interventions, was forced to sign a statement that he had visited Ota and informed Obasanjo of the plans for a coup. This made Obasanjo guilty of the capital offence of concealment of treason, under his own decree issued at the time of Dimka's coup.[11] Equipped with this material, on 30 May the authorities took Obasanjo from his farm to the State Security Service Interrogation Centre at Ikoyi, in Lagos, where questioning began. The Special Military Investigation Panel first asked his views on the 12 June crisis and its resolution. Then the interrogators said a witness claimed to have visited Ota and told him of a coup. Obasanjo demanded to see him. Bello-Fadile was brought in, chained. Obasanjo asked the date and location of the meeting, then denied that he had ever received visitors in the manner described. The subsequent events are confused, but it appears that the Investigation Panel, having checked and confirmed Obasanjo's statement, recommended that he had no case to answer.[12] Abacha, however, insisted on a trial before a military court, which took place on 19 June 1995. Obasanjo was refused his own counsel and was allocated a military lawyer whom he met only a few minutes before the trial. The judges dismissed his objection to a trial by a court headed by an officer junior to himself. A video clip seen later on television showed Obasanjo 'staring in disbelief' as Bello-Fadile gave his evidence. To counter it, Obasanjo produced the register of visitors admitted to the farm to show that Bello-Fadile's name was missing. He also demonstrated that they could not have been there simultaneously during the period when Bello-Fadile said they had met, only for the court to extend the period in question. At a later trial, Bello-Fadile reportedly claimed that his confession had been made under duress, but the court rejected such claims unless they were supported by visible wounds.[13]

In a note smuggled from prison, Obasanjo described the trial as 'all naked frame-up, satanic deceit, grievous oppression and fraudulent elimination of other voices'. Nevertheless, on 14 July the government announced that he had been sentenced to 25 years' imprisonment for concealment of treason, while Yar'Adua and fourteen others were sentenced to death. The sentences divided the military leadership and provoked protest from within and outside Nigeria, the most effective reportedly being three telephone calls from President Clinton warning Abacha that Nigerian oil would be embargoed if executions took place. On 1 October, Abacha commuted all death sentences to imprisonment and reduced Obasanjo's sentence to 15 years.[14]

Obasanjo would spend three years in four Nigerian prisons. For the first four months he was held at the Ikoyi Centre, initially in solitary confinement, chained, in a small, windowless, insect-infested room with a bucket latrine in the centre, sleeping on the floor.[15] His only special treatment was to receive diabetic food. Later, it appears, his conditions were somewhat relaxed, according to an account pieced together by a journalist from interviews with fellow-prisoners:

> He sat on the bare bed, reading his Bible, and praying that 'God establish my innocence.' He did not wallow in self-pity. Instead, he immediately assumed the role of elder, holding out hope to the men, sending out messages of encouragement through his window assuring them that God was 'in control' of the situation and the battle being waged outside. The repressive climate did not seem to blunt his characteristic folksy disposition. He walked around the cell on bare feet, grabbed groundnuts from people's hands as he passed their cells, and even tried to share the miserable food sent to inmates.[16]

Once his sentence was confirmed, Obasanjo was moved to the main Lagos prison, Kirikiri, whose maximum security section, in 1993, had an average of 2,596 inmates in accommodation designed for 956. Chris Anyanwu, a journalist convicted in connection with the supposed coup plot, remembered that the smell of Kirikiri immediately made her sick.[17] Obasanjo was apparently accommodated in the prison hospital. Suffering from diabetes and hypertension, he had lost much weight and had several visits from prison doctors. Yar'Adua was also in the hospital. Obasanjo later wrote of his 'great undisguised delight and happiness' at their brief opportunity to share reminiscences and thank God for sparing their lives. He congratulated his former chief of staff on the strength he had shown in the face of his initial death sentence. It was their last meeting.[18]

One other incident at Kirikiri had immense significance for Obasanjo. By one account, Bello-Fadile, who was also incarcerated there, accepted Gwadabe's suggestion that he should apologise to Obasanjo for giving false evidence against him under duress. Obasanjo asked for the apology in writing, it was 'passed from prison cell to prison cell', and Obasanjo smuggled it out for publication. 'As my Commander-in-chief,' Bello-Fadile wrote, 'accept me like the Biblical prodigal son.' 'I forgave him and I told him so', Obasanjo recalled, 'and I believe that if he genuinely asks God for forgiveness, God will forgive him as well. God has proved my innocence and established it in a dramatic way.'[19]

For Obasanjo, this proof of his innocence not only cleared his reputation – 'I felt violated', he declared[20] – but it was quite literally the answer to a prayer. 'My prayer during the dark, bleak and confused early days of the so-called conviction for coup-plotting by the Kangaroo tribunal was that God should prove and establish my innocence', he remembered. 'My first prayer was for God to prove and establish my innocence for the world to know. It was a fervent prayer.' And God had answered it, rapidly and completely. When, later in his confinement, Obasanjo came to write a book on prayer, Bello-Fadile's letter was his key illustration of its efficacy.[21] It initiated his spiritual transformation during imprisonment.

After a few weeks at Kirikiri, Obasanjo, still in poor health, was flown with other 'conspirators' to spend several months at Jos prison on Nigeria's central plateau. During the flight, a companion recalled,

> I looked at Obasanjo, who opened the Bible on his lap. Where did he get the inner strength to read? This was a former Head of State, innocent of the crime of treason, but now being treated as a common criminal. The only concession to his former status was that he was not in chains like the rest of us.[22]

Anyanwu, who also travelled with them, remembered that 'His good spirit despite the indignity helped to deflate the tension around. All eyes were on him. How was he taking it? It was reassuring to see that he held up well, finding the strength to discuss other things.'[23]

Jos was typical of Nigeria's notoriously dreadful prisons. Anthony Rilwan spent thirty months there in the early 1990s before being acquitted:

> I could not believe it the first time I went there. That was in 1991. The cell was jam-packed, people everywhere. There was even no space to move; that is, like to go from one end or corner to another. And when you step on somebody they might fight you or the marshal [the cell headman] can flog you. But you cannot move without stepping on people.[24]

Each inmate's 'post' in a cell was normally about 12–24 inches square. In the prison system as a whole, the number of inmates was about twice the official capacity. More than half were awaiting trial, often, like Rilwan, for several years. The daily feeding allowance per prisoner, fixed in 1992 at N10 (less than U.S. 50 cents), had remained unchanged while the naira had lost about 75% of its value.[25] According to a fellow-prisoner at Jos, Obasanjo had been unaware of prison conditions and secured the release of some who had long awaited trial.[26] He later described Nigerian prisons as some of the worst on earth and his own experience as awful: 'I would not wish it on my worst enemy.'[27]

As usual in Nigeria, however, money and influence could lessen these horrors. Many prisoners supplemented the prison ration with food brought by family and friends, without which, according to Rilwan, most at Jos would have died. Many prisons had 'back cells' occupied by small groups or even individual prisoners who could bribe the warders for the privilege.[28] Obasanjo is said to have found it difficult to bribe his warders, but his numerous visitors had fewer inhibitions. Danjuma came and gave him money. Maj.Gen. Abubakar Abdulsalami, the Army Chief of Staff, also visited and secured him a private room with a linoleum floor, sparse furniture, a refrigerator, and even an air-conditioner.[29] At first, his reading was confined to the Bible and the Koran, but this was also relaxed with time, although many of the books allowed were religious and some he read several times. Writing materials, when eventually permitted, were especially welcome.[30] Probably even more impor-tant to his survival was the austerity of his normal lifestyle. 'Over the years,' he wrote at the end of his ordeal, 'I have been taught what I call four lessons of *less* and four lessons of *more* – eat less, sleep less, speak less and frequent people less; work more, learn more, physically exercise more and spiritually exercise more.'[31] At Jos, he practised physical exercises and spent an hour each day jogging. He fasted once a week. His health improved. He regretted the lack of intellectual companionship but maintained a correspondence.[32]

Correspondence gave Obasanjo some knowledge of the continuing international pressure for his release. In December 1995 the OAU Secretary-General gave Abacha a message to that effect from Mandela, who had become a virulent critic of what he called 'an illegitimate, barbaric, arrogant military dictatorship'. Two years later the Pope added his voice while visiting Nigeria.[33] Indian and German foundations awarded Obasanjo international prizes. The House of Lords and the Bundestag debated his release. The Africa Leadership Forum produced two volumes of essays and letters in his honour by his remarkable range of friends and acquaintances. One of these volumes at least reached his prison cell.[34]

Obasanjo's most regular contact with the outside world was his wife Stella, who is said to have insisted on accompanying him when he was first arrested and was later allowed to visit him once a month, bringing news, reporting on his condition, and on one occasion receiving an international prize on his behalf. Despite malicious gossip, her role at this time seems to have given her a larger, more companionate place in his life, as became clear after his release.[35] Oluremi also visited him at Jos, although she was barred when his visitors were limited to two, while their son Gbenga visited him until a quarrel with Stella soured the relationship.[36] Their father's incarceration created many difficulties for his children, several of whom were at university and had to change their plans or be supported by friends.[37] Branches of his extended family contested control of his business interests and 'openly fought each other over the formula by which his estate should be shared,' until the Alake and Olowu intervened to silence the quarrels.[38] Thieves robbed his Abeokuta home and injured Stella, while the Ota farm, so he complained, 'went into ruins'.[39] The Africa Leadership Forum was obliged to abandon its headquarters there and take refuge in Accra.[40]

Obasanjo remained at Jos until early 1996, when he was moved to a more remote jail at Yola, allegedly because Abacha considered that his conditions and status at Jos were too privileged. The authorities at Yola had no warning, so that for the first month he shared a common cell with many other prisoners.[41] Thereafter, following pressure from high-ranking friends, he was again given a private room with amenities similar to those he had previously enjoyed. Local notables provided his meals, but now there were few visitors apart from Stella, a perennial shortage of water, and reported periods of ill-health that confined him at one point to the prison hospital.[42] After one visit Stella knelt before the Interior Minister, Babagana Kingibe, to plead for some relief for her husband, but Kingibe said he could do little because there was 'a serious quarrel between the two generals'.[43] One of Obasanjo's former drivers who saw him early in 1997 described him as 'gaunt, unkempt and emaciated': 'He now looks like an 85-year-old farmer who has lived the last 25 years in a bad state.'[44] At first he was barred from writing and his reading was again confined to the Bible, but these restrictions were gradually relaxed and he was also permitted to cultivate a 'two-room size' garden with a hoe and watering can. He recalled, 'I worked on it twice a day with another prisoner assisting me to water the crops and vegetables, tend them, weed, apply manure or fertilizer, apply insecticide, apprehend prisoners and warders with itching fingers and prune out crops.'[45]

For a frenetically energetic man like Obasanjo, imprisonment must have been almost unbearably frustrating. Yet he came to see it as one of his most positive experiences:

> For me, God made the prison next to heaven because he used the hardship, deprivation and the tribulation to draw me closer to Him in faith, obedience, worship, prayers and fasting, study of the Word of God and in praises and thanksgiving.
>
> For me, it was a thrilling experience with God in charge and in control. He granted me His peace and joy out of His love and grace. He gave me satisfaction and contentment and kept my spirit high, my conscience free and clear and my hands clean ...
>
> The suffering for me is the forced period of relative inactivity which I again interpret as God's way of slowing me down to hear His message and His words.[46]

That a prolonged period of enforced confinement should lead to such a deepening of faith was not unusual, either in Nigeria or elsewhere. 'Prison experience sobers the body, the mind and the soul', Mandela had told Obasanjo at Pollsmoor in 1986, providing a model that the younger man clearly sought to imitate.[47] Alex Ekwueme, Shagari's vice-president, who suffered thirty months of unjustified confinement between 1983 and 1986, later described them as 'a religious retreat' in which his political colleagues of all religious persuasions displayed 'intense religious fervour'. His colleague Ishaya Audu, the former Foreign Minister, had cause to 'reflect on how best to spend the rest of my life' and decided to become a priest. Adamu Ciroma, also incarcerated at that time, deepened his Islamic faith, as did Shehu Musa Yar'Adua when imprisoned by Abacha.[48] At a secular level, Frederick Fasehun emerged from Abacha's prison with his Yoruba ethnic nationalism raised to passionate intensity, while Wole Soyinka, imprisoned during the civil war, remarked: 'Whatever it was I believed in before I was locked up, I came out a fanatic in those things.'[49] Perhaps that was the key point: all these experiences deepened an existing faith. Obasanjo was born again in prison, but he was not converted there. As he pointed out, 'I was born a Baptist and brought up a Baptist, and I nearly went to seminary. It's not a road-to-Damascus-conversion sort of thing.' His religious background had survived into his military career – 'a situation that requires faith,' as he wrote – and he had retained his ties to the Baptist Church. But 'religion had never really been an emotive issue' for him until his imprisonment.[50] He had scarcely mentioned his faith while military head of state. The language and imagery of the Bible had not dominated his mind. By the time he left prison, they did.

This religious experience began at Ikoyi with extensive time to read the Bible and pray for justification from false accusation. The answer to that prayer in Bello-Fadile's confession at Kirikiri was a decisive moment. At Jos, Obasanjo participated in daily Christian fellowship and Sunday prayer meetings among the prisoners.[51] His role expanded at Yola, where his arrival coincided with a ban on visiting preachers after inmates had escaped in cassocks smuggled in by impostors. On 11 February 1996 Obasanjo was invited to preach at a Christian fellowship meeting there. He spoke on the story of Jonah. It was the first of 28 weekly sermons that he preached before visiting ministers were again admitted. He wrote them out at the time and published them when he was released.[52] Preaching not only strengthened his faith and gave him intense satisfaction; it also transformed his style of public speaking. He preached for the rest of his career.

Obasanjo's best sermons were those in which he expounded an Old Testament story or a New Testament parable and applied it to the lives of prisoners. That Jonah had failed to pray during the storm but had been released when he prayed inside the whale demonstrated that prayer must be the response to adversity, that God answered prayer, that affliction had an educational purpose, and that everyone had a second chance to go straight and live a more religious life.[53] Obasanjo introduced this first address by identifying himself with his fellow prisoners:

> My limited experience so far in Nigerian prisons has confirmed to me that, at least, half of those who are in prison should not have been there if the society had been more sane, more wholesome, more just, more fair, more equitable, more God-fearing and less corrupt. If that were the case, on the other hand, some of the millions outside the prison walls ought to have been within the prison walls.[54]

His second sermon made the same point by posing Job's question why the righteous suffered, with a reference to his own experience.[55] Yet by the eighteenth sermon, on the rich man told to sell his possessions and give to the poor, the tone had changed. 'With very few exceptions,' Obasanjo told his congregation, 'most inmates in this institution are here on good grounds.'[56] Five weeks later, discussing the parable of the prodigal son, he denounced young criminals 'sucked or absorbed into notorious gangs' who 'become arrogant, puffed up and unreachable'. 'Once parental care and guide, discipline and self-control with God's guidance and spiritual discipline are lost in a youth, all is lost', he declared, returning to his deeply entrenched patriarchal views.[57] Perhaps he had gained closer experience of hardened young criminals. He tried to reform some of them and followed up their progress after leaving prison.[58]

Sermons from Prison was one of four books that Obasanjo wrote (or largely wrote) in prison and subsequently published, along with *Guides to Effective Prayer*, *Women of Virtue*, and *This Animal Called Man*. Taken together, their dominant feature was the impact on his mind of repeated Bible reading.

This Animal Called Man, for example, began with a fiercely creationist account of human origins, in contrast to 'the most debasing, devaluing and dehumanising suppositions on the origin of man' to be found in Darwinism.[59] *Women of Virtue*, similarly, took all its examples from biblical characters,[60] as did *Guides to Effective Prayer*, with the one exception of the prominence given to Bello-Fadile's confession. The scripturalism of these books was absolutely literal. Obasanjo held that the Flood lasted 371 days and that unbelievers were condemned to an 'everlasting lake of burning sulphur'.[61] He treated stories like Jonah's as accounts of actual events, not as allegories, and described Eve as 'a good housewife, a good companion, a confidant, a pillar of support for her husband and a good house-keeper', adding, 'The lot of pioneers is always an unenviable one, and Eve was not an exception.'[62] His treatment of a second major theme, 'the mystery and the miraculous power of prayer',[63] was more subtle, combining an insistence on Christ's promise that prayer would be answered with the caveat that it might be answered 'not always in the manner or time one may hope or expect'.[64]

Another powerful strand in the books was providentialism, which emerged from the Bible, from Obasanjo's Baptist training, and from the manner in which chance had often shaped his life. 'I have been on the mission of God all through my life', he declared shortly after his release, 'because most of the things I have done, they have come to me almost involuntarily.'[65] His arrest, survival, and eventual release all fitted into this notion of an overarching destiny. 'Only God who has given us life and the purpose for our existence can tell us what the purpose is,' he wrote in *This Animal Called Man*. 'If we miss that destiny and purpose then our life is an abysmal failure no matter what position, power, possession, popularity or pleasure we might have attained, acquired or enjoyed.'[66] This notion blended with his belief in the importance of leadership: 'When God rules the heart of the leader, God rules the people. The leader becomes like Moses.'[67] This combination, in turn, reinforced his already well developed self-righteousness. It would give him the strength to pursue his convictions despite the relentless criticism and abuse that surrounded a Nigerian leader. It made him ruthless and justified for him the moral compromises inherent in exercising power. It also made him breathtakingly arrogant:

> Criticism never distresses me, rather it delights me for three main reasons. If and when it is not frivolous and is not born out of envy, malice and pull-him-down syndrome, it makes me reflect to satisfy my conscience and God. It makes me appreciate and acknowledge with gratitude the love and grace of God. It makes me learn more about man and his

depravity in a fallen and perverted world. Invariably, criticism serves as a confirmation of the rightness of my cause, my course and my action and as an inspiration to soldier on.[68]

This messianism, as his critics called it, made the born-again Obasanjo strikingly different from the uncertain, self-doubting, and perhaps more attractive Obasanjo of 1976. As Reuben Abati put it, Obasanjo had lost his humility.

The providentialism that became so central to Obasanjo's thought while in prison probably drew not only on the Bible but on indigenous Yoruba beliefs. The need to identify the meaning and direction of his life – 'I believe in my own fate'[69] – closely paralleled the Yoruba notion of individual destiny that was determined for each person at his creation, was to be discovered through divination by the *ifa* oracle, and must then be pursued as the only way to happiness.[70] When Obasanjo read the Book of Esther and was convinced by it that God could release him from prison, he was using the Bible much as Yoruba had long used the oral texts identified and recited to them by *ifa* diviners.[71]

Yet much more of the worldview that Obasanjo framed while in prison was distinctive to the born-again Christian. Whereas earlier in his career he had often referred to traditional culture as a guide to current morality,[72] these references became less common after his release from prison and the only mention of Yoruba culture in his four prison books is a brief allusion to myths of human origin.[73] Instead, like many born-again Christians in West Africa at this time, he turned his back on the pagan past. 'Our old way of life before we believe in Jesus Christ is completely in the *sad past*', he wrote. 'We should put it behind us like old clothes to be thrown away.'[74] Nevertheless, the new world of contemporary Nigeria was equally to be condemned in the sweeping terms that born-again Christians shared with fundamentalist Muslims. 'Honesty is disregarded, indolence is extolled, probity is derided, and waste and ostentation are paraded' he bewailed.[75] Although convinced of the active existence of the Devil, he rejected the idea current in much West African Christianity that sin was the Devil's work, insisting rather on human responsibility and the internalisation of guilt.[76] He also rejected the crude form of 'prosperity gospel' taught by some Pentecostal churches. Virtue certainly had its reward. 'You receive from God in multiples of what you give as God loves a cheerful giver (II Corin. 9:7)', he assured the prisoners at Yola. 'If you give out with a shovel, you will receive with a front-end loader bucket.'[77] The reward, however, would be in the afterlife. 'A righteous life does not guarantee health, wealth and earthly pleasures', he warned. 'The reason for being good is not entirely for this world.'[78]

Obasanjo's born-again Christianity was strikingly orthodox, faithful to mainline Baptist teaching, and free from syncretism, except that the polygyny he practised – he admitted that 'monogamy was God's original intent for marriage'[79] – had long been a matter of controversy among Yoruba Baptists.[80] He was an extremely well-instructed layman in a society where religion – both Christian and Muslim – was rapidly being democratised.[81] Born-again Christianity appealed to him as a moralist, a moderniser, and a man with an overpowering sense of vocation. Its stridency, while offending some Muslims and educated sceptics, was to be a political asset in a country where 96% of people declared themselves to be religious and where, it was claimed, no-one could aspire to political office without overt religious affiliation.[82]

It was during the last period of his imprisonment, at Yola, that Obasanjo heard of the death of his friend Yar'Adua in December 1997. In a final letter to Obasanjo in November – revealingly addressed 'Dear Sir' – Yar'Adua had reported that he was keeping fairly fit 'playing some sort of tennis'. 'My present worries and prayers are that the present junta do not so devastate the country that it becomes impossible to rehabilitate,' he had written.[83] A month later he collapsed and died on the way to hospital. Doctors had diagnosed liver failure and hepatitis. The death certificate recorded cancer of the liver, but many Nigerians believed that he had been poisoned by a forced injection.[84] Obasanjo wrote in his notebook, 'When and how will it end.'[85]

Obasanjo, too, feared poisoning. 'Attempts were made to inject me with a deadly virus', he later claimed. 'I managed to refuse to have my blood taken when I was told the authorities wanted to give me a physical examination and take the blood for tests. My doctor, who had connections with the local hospital, was able to make his own arrangements for the tests.'[86] A military doctor later confirmed that orders had been given to poison Obasanjo and also for an extraordinary plan to kill him during a commando raid on Yola prison, designed to look like the work of 'Chadian brigands'. There is no clear evidence that either plan was attempted.[87]

Another death ended the story. On 8 June 1998, Sani Abacha died suddenly – probably of a heart attack, although poison was again suspected – after arranging a scenario by which he could transform himself into a civilian president, although without having announced a final decision to do so. As his successor, military commanders immediately elected the apolitical Lt Gen. Abdulsalami Abubakar, who was eager to restore civilian rule.[88] A warder at Yola informed an incredulous Obasanjo the same afternoon. He responded by writing a generously sympathetic letter to Abacha's widow. Abdulsalami ordered his release a week later and sent a plane to bring him home.[89]

It was a different homecoming from those of the past. He went first to Ota, where the farm had been hastily smartened up. There he held a prayer meeting with the workers before being driven to Abeokuta.[90] Civic leaders, family, and friends had planned a grand reception, but were forced to abandon it, 'not because they could not afford a white horse,' as it was explained, but because Obasanjo was officially confined to Ota and they feared to complicate the hoped-for release of their other imprisoned townsman, Abiola. Consequently, 'they resolved that instead of organising a flamboyant welcome, the people of the city should hold prayer sessions for the released General.'[91] Perhaps they did not realise how appropriate this would be. Gaunt and frail, 'his facial traditional marks … jutting out of his cheeks,' Obasanjo was nevertheless jubilant as he was welcomed to his home by family, friends, and the Egba chiefs who came in state to greet him.[92] The main ceremony, however, took place on 20 June at Owu Baptist Church, where, in an address punctuated by biblical references, cries of 'praise God!' and dancing led by Obasanjo himself, he told the congregation of his ordeal and rebirth:

> This day is a day of thanksgiving, not a day of celebration, it is a day of joy, not a day of merrymaking, it is a day of sober reflection, not a day of anger, bitterness or animosity. It is a day of praise and prayer to God …
>
> Much water has passed under the bridge over the past months and years. For some, not much has changed, but for me something significant has changed.[93]

NOTES

1. *Newswatch*, 25 September 1995, pp. 10–15, and 31 August 1998, pp. 9–16.
2. Alli, *Federal Republic*, pp. 294, 357, 361.
3. *Newswatch*, 13 March 1995, pp. 13–18; *Tell*, 15 May 1995, pp. 10–12; Farris and Bomoi, *Yar'Adua*, p. 260.
4. *Tell*, 20 May 1996, p. 11.
5. Farris and Bomoi, *Yar'Adua*, pp. 242, 247–8, 258–9; Alli, *Federal Republic*, p. 332.
6. *Tell*, 27 March 1995, p. 11, and 10 April 1995, p. 17.
7. *Newswatch*, 27 March 2000, p. 13; Ademiluyi, *From prisoner to president*, pp. 84–5.
8. *Newswatch*, 3 April 1995, pp. 10–12; *Tell*, 3 April 1995, p. 13.
9. [Olusegun Obasanjo,] *Selected speeches of President Olusegun Obasanjo: volume II* (Abuja, n.d.), p. 244.
10. Lord Callaghan, 'Military trials in Nigeria', in d'Orville, *Leadership*, p. 14; Anyaoku, *Inside story*, p. 178; Ademiluyi, *From prisoner to president*, p. 85; *Tell*, 10 April 1995, p. 17.
11. *Tell*, 3 July 1995, p. 12, and 23 October 1995, pp. 10–16.
12. *Newswatch*, 25 January 1999; *Africa Confidential*, 23 June 1995, p. 8.
13. Olusegun Obasanjo, 'The country of anything goes', *New York Review of Books*, 24 September 1998, pp. 55–7; Farris and Bomoi, *Yar'Adua*, p. 268; *Tell*, 23 October 1995, pp. 12–13; *Newswatch*, 6 July 1998, p. 20; Nigeria: Human Rights Violations Investigation Commission (Oputa Panel), 'Report', 7 vols (2002), vol. 4, Ch. 2, pp. 18 and 24, http://www.nigerianmuse.com/nigeriawatch/oputa/OputaVolumeFour.pdf (accessed 27 August 2007).
14. *Tell*, 20 May 1996; *Africa Research Bulletin (Political)*, July 1995, pp. 11903–4, and August 1995, p. 11956; Ademiluyi, *From prisoner to president*, pp. 91–2; *Newswatch*, 16 October 1995, p. 20, and 23 October 1995, p. 10.
15. *Newswatch*, 25 January 1999, p. 16, and 25 December 2000, pp. 24–6.
16. Chris Anyanwu, *The days of terror – a journalist's eye-witness account of Nigeria in the hands of its worst tyrant* (Ibadan, 2002), p. 104.
17. Osaze Lanre Ehonwa, *Behind the wall: a report on prison conditions in Nigeria and the Nigerian prison system* (2nd edn, Lagos, 1996), p. 17; Anyanwu, *Days of terror*, p. 80.
18. *Tell*, 30 October 1995, p. 17; Farris and Bomoi, *Yar'Adua*, pp. 275–6.
19. Obasanjo, 'Country of anything goes'; *Newswatch*, 6 July 1998, p. 20; *Tell*, 23 September 1996, p. 12. Although Bello-Fadile confirmed this account before the Oputa Panel (above, note 13), he denied it on other occasions: *This Day*, 14 July 1999; *Punch*, 10 November 2007.
20. *Tell*, 20 May 1996, p. 9.
21. *Newswatch*, 6 July 1998, p. 19; Olusegun Obasanjo, *Guides to effective prayer* (Abeokuta, n.d.), p. 7.
22. Kunle Ajibade, *Jailed for life: a reporter's prison notes* (Ibadan, 2003), p. 114.
23. Anyanwu, *Days of terror* , p. 142.
24. Ehonwa, *Behind the wall*, p. 24.
25. Ibid., pp. 2, 14–16, 24.
26. Karl Maier, *This house has fallen: Nigeria in crisis* (London, 2000), p. 169.
27. *New Nigerian*, 7 August 1998.
28. Ehonwa, *Behind the wall*, pp. 25, 45, 91.
29. *Tell*, 20 May 1996, p. 14, and 30 May 2006; *Guardian*, 24 February 2008; Ademiluyi, *From prisoner to president*, pp. 93–4.
30. *New Nigerian*, 17 August 1998; Obasanjo, *This animal*, pp. 117, 269; d'Orville, *Beyond freedom*, pp. 13–14; Ademiluyi, *From prisoner to president*, p. 94.
31. Obasanjo, *This animal*, p. 270.

32. Obasanjo, 'The country of anything goes'; Obasanjo, *This animal*, p. 269; *New Nigerian*, 17 August 1998.
33. *Times*, 7 December 1995; *Africa Today*, January 1996, p. 5; *This Day*, 25 February 2005.
34. D'Orville, *Beyond freedom*, pp. 13–14, 32.
35. Anyanwu, *Days of terror*, p. lxv; *Tell*, 23 September 1996, pp. 10–11; *Newswatch*, 4 February 2008, p. 14; *Insider Weekly*, 23 July 2001, pp. 20–1; below, p. 173.
36. Obasanjo, *Bitter-sweet*, pp. 109–11; *Newswatch*, 4 February 2008, p. 15.
37. *New Nigerian*, 17 August 1998; Ademiluyi, *From prisoner to president*, p. 145; *This Day*, 14 September 2008.
38. *Sunday Concord*, 30 May 1999; *Nigerian Tribune*, 19–22 June 1998; Obasanjo, *Bitter-sweet*, pp. 112–13.
39. Avwenagbiku, *Olusegun Obasanjo*, p. 218; *New Nigerian*, 17 August 1998.
40. African Leadership Forum, *Objectives and structure and review of activities until August 1997* (Accra, 1997), p. 36.
41. *Tell*, 20 May 1996, p. 14; Avwenagbiku, *Olusegun Obasanjo* , p. 216.
42. *Tell*, 20 May 1996 pp. 9–11, 23 September 1996 p. 11, and 29 December 1997; *Nigerian Tribune*, 20 June 1998.
43. *Tell*, 30 September 1996.
44. *Tell*, 10 March 1997, p. 12.
45. Obasanjo, *This animal*, p. 374.
46. *Newswatch*, 6 July 1998, pp. 17–20.
47. *Daily Times*, 12 February 1990.
48. Alex I. Ekwueme, *From State House to Kirikiri* (Enugu, 2002), pp. 179–80; *Daily Times*, 5 May 1988; *Weekly Trust*, 18 September 1998; Farris and Bomoi, *Yar'Adua*, p. 285.
49. Fasehun, *Frederick Fasehun*, pp. 257, 263; *Daily Times*, 13 October 1969.
50. *This Day*, 24 May 1999; Obasanjo, *My command*, p. 170; *Daily Times*, 30 July 1988; Obasanjo, *Not my will*, p. 63.
51. *New Nigerian*, 17 August 1998.
52. Obasanjo, *Sermons*, pp. x–xi.
53. Ibid., pp. 3–12.
54. Ibid., p. 3.
55. Ibid., pp. 15, 20.
56. Ibid., p. 189.
57. Ibid., pp. 249–52.
58. Obasanjo, *This animal*, pp. 324–35.
59. Ibid., p. 15 .
60. Olusegun Obasanjo, *Women of virtue: stories of outstanding women in the Bible* (Abeokuta, n.d.).
61. Obasanjo, *This animal*, pp. 66, 176.
62. Obasanjo, *Women*, pp. 6, 9.
63. Obasanjo, *This animal*, p. 383.
64. Obasanjo, *Guides*, p. 16.
65. *Newswatch*, 25 January 1999, p. 19.
66. Obasanjo, *This animal*, p. 55.
67. Ibid., pp. 76–7.
68. Ibid., p. 228.
69. *Newswatch*, 25 January 1999, p. 17.
70. William Bascom, *Ifa divination: communication between gods and men in West Africa* (Bloomington, 1969), esp. pp. 115–17.
71. *Guardian*, 6 December 2004.
72. Above, p. 63.
73. Obasanjo, *This animal*, p. 2.
74. Ibid., p. 311.

75. Ibid., p. 191.
76. Ibid., pp. 96–8.
77. Obasanjo, *Sermons*, p. 135.
78. Obasanjo, *This animal*, p. 115.
79. Obasanjo, *Women*, p. 49.
80. Travis Collins, *The Baptist mission of Nigeria 1850–1993: a history of the Southern Baptist Convention missionary work in Nigeria* (Ibadan, 1993), pp. 67–8.
81. Rosalind I.J. Hackett, 'Women as leaders and participants in the spiritual churches', in R.I.J. Hackett (ed.), *New religious movements in Nigeria* (Lewiston, 1987), p. 208.
82. *Punch*, 23 December 2007; Toyin Falola, quoted in Matthew Hassan Kukah, *Religion, politics and power in Northern Nigeria* (Ibadan, 1993), p. 228.
83. Obasanjo, *This animal*, p. 385.
84. Farris and Bomoi, *Yar'Adua*, pp. 1–2, 283, 293–4, 300; *Source*, 15 February 1999, pp. 10–11, and 25 October 1999, pp. 10–12; *Tell*, 10 May 1999, p. 28.
85. Obasanjo, *This animal*, p. 220.
86. Obasanjo, 'The country of anything goes'.
87. *Tell*, 10 May 1999, p. 27, and 28 August 2000, pp. 12–17; Ademiluyi, *From prisoner to president*, p. 101.
88. *Newswatch*, 22 June 1998, pp. 5–12; *West Africa*, 6 July 1998, p. 528.
89. *New Nigerian*, 17 August 1998; *Nigerian Tribune,* 15–16 June 1998.
90. *Nigerian Tribune*, 18 June 1998.
91. Ibid., 21 June 1998.
92. Olawale Oshun, *The open grave: NADECO and the struggle for democracy in Nigeria* (London, 2002), p. 210; *New Nigerian*, 18 June 1998.
93. *Newswatch*, 6 July 1998, p. 17.

14
The Candidate

Leaders in Abeokuta were right to think that the great problem in June 1998 was the future of Abiola. He had been in prison since 1994, with deteriorating health, refusing to gain release by renouncing his claim to be the elected president. His supporters in NADECO and the south-west insisted that he must head any civilian government, although that remained anathema to many in the army and the North.

General Abdulsalami sought help from Africa's two leading diplomats, Kofi Annan, Secretary-General of the United Nations, and Emeka Anyaoku, Secretary-General of the Commonwealth. They visited Abiola in detention early in July. Anyaoku insisted afterwards that he had not pressed Abiola to abandon his mandate, but warned him it could have no legal or international credibility five years after his election.[1] Annan appears to have offered release in return for abandoning the mandate, reporting that Abiola replied, 'I cannot be naive enough to make assumptions that I am going to come out and be president', which was denied by Abiola's supporters but seemed to offer Abdulsalami grounds to release him.[2] Abiola's own notes claimed that he had bluntly refused a deal: 'If IBB[abangida] and Abacha could not obtain my surrender after over 4 years, it is naive for anyone to suggest that one month old newcomer, using international diplomats can do it.'[3] Abdulsalami claimed that he had nevertheless intended to release Abiola on 9 July, but two days before that the prisoner died after drinking a cup of tea in the presence of two American diplomats. International pathologists blamed 'rapid deterioration in a diseased heart', but the death was so extraordinarily opportune for Abiola's opponents that his supporters inevitably suspected poisoning and rioted in south-western cities.[4]

Abiola's death freed the military government to prepare a transition to civilian rule. Abacha had planned a presidential election on 1 August 1998, at which he was expected to be the only candidate of all five contesting parties. Only the most successful party wanted to preserve this schedule, while the bulk of political opinion demanded a fresh start. Abdulsalami was anxious to leave power and feared a violent coup d'état by lower ranks. On 20 July, therefore, he dissolved existing elected parties and institutions and announced a sequence of elections culminating in the inauguration of a civilian president on 29 May 1999.[5]

Although there had been suggestions that Obasanjo might head a transitional regime to conduct these elections, he denied this publicly. 'What I need now,' he said, 'is a bit of rest and a little bit of knowing what was on during the time I was in prison.'[6] His finances were parlous – he was said to have had only N20,000 ($200) and substantial debts when released – until military and political associates apparently assisted him.[7] During July 1998 he visited South Africa before travelling to Britain and the United States for rest and medical treatment. Interviewed in New York during August, he said he had been visiting Jimmy Carter and others to thank them for support during his imprisonment. Probed for his political thoughts, '[he] affirmed that a true leader would emerge from this crop of politicians … "Only a great fool will say he is the only one that can be in a particular institution."'[8]

The comment suggested that the possibility of political office was already in his mind. Exactly how this happened is uncertain, but at least four powerful men were working in this direction before Obasanjo left for America. One was General Aliyu Gusau, a veteran security operative and close subordinate of Obasanjo who took part in discussions of possible candidates with other northern military and political leaders. When these threw up Obasanjo's name, Gusau suggested it to Abdulsalami, who told him to raise it with Ibrahim Babangida. Gusau also contacted Atiku Abubakar, the politician who had taken effective control of the dead Shehu Musa Yar'Adua's party, now the People's Democratic Movement (PDM), and was keen to put it at the service of Yar'Adua's former superior. When Babangida visited Ota on 27 June, it was he, according to Atiku's later account, who first suggested to Obasanjo that he should seek the presidency, although reports at the time said only that they discussed how Obasanjo could contribute to the transition to civilian rule.[9]

Abdulsalami's broadcast on 20 July stimulated the customary rush to form political parties.[10] Over a hundred emerged by the end of August. Most were in the South or the Middle Belt and most were purely ethnic associations, for there was widespread feeling, after years of centralised rule by northern soldiers, that the new president should be a southerner and that localities must enjoy greater power, either by dividing the country into largely autonomous zones – six were commonly identified – or through a sovereign national conference, perhaps representing ethnic groups, to create a new basis for the state. 'Nigeria is marching ahead to the 1950s', a journalist observed.[11] The Electoral Commission, however, ruled that, to secure registration, parties must pay N100,000 (about $1,000) and win 10% (later reduced to 5%) of the votes in 24 of the 36 states at local government elections in December 1998. This provoked a scramble for alliances. In the event, only 26 parties sought registration, nine gained it, and three survived the local elections to enter the state and national polls.[12]

The most successful of the three was the People's Democratic Party (PDP). This originated with groups of political leaders – G18 and G34, as they became known – who had bravely written public letters to Abacha in February and May 1998 urging him to obey the constitution and his own undertakings by withdrawing from the presidential contest.[13] When political organisation resumed in June 1998, most G34 leaders combined their local networks into the PDP under the initial leadership of Alex Ekwueme, Shagari's former vice-president, who had signed the G34 letter. Their model was the African National Congress of South Africa and their aim was to create a mass party large enough to deter future military coups. Beyond that, the party had no definable programme. Stretching across almost the entire political spectrum, with an umbrella as its symbol, it was said to embrace over 280 organisations, including important elements from Yar'Adua's PDM and Shagari's NPN. In January 1999, its members were also said to include 46 retired generals, a significant group both politically and financially. It was committed to 'power shift', i.e. to choose its first presidential candidate from the South. Its broad geographic support won it some 62% of the local government councils contested in December 1998.[14]

Another 25% of councils were won by the All People's Party (APP), a coalition of politicians who had often been closer to Abacha's regime – enemies called it the Abacha People's Party – with a northern bias. Its strongest presidential candidate would have been the NRC veteran, Umaru Shinkafi, but after much dispute the party decided that the national interest demanded 'power shift' to the South, which forced it into alliance with the third party, the Alliance for Democracy (AD), a Yoruba organisation in the tradition of the AG and UPN. Yoruba leaders, dominated by the aging men of Awolowo's circle who controlled the Afenifere ethnic association, had seen the annulment of Abiola's election as yet another ethnic grievance. They had led NADECO's militant opposition to Abacha and mourned what they believed to be Abiola's murder. At a Pan-Yoruba Conference in August 1998, their elderly leader, Abraham Adesanya, had demanded a southern president and an immediate sovereign national conference to divide Nigeria into six or more zones, each with its own army and police, in order 'to review the future of the Nigerian federation,' while Bola Ige, Awolowo's leading disciple, declared that the aim was to unite the Yoruba against their common foe: northern domination.[15] Ige had helped to found the PDP, but had withdrawn when it admitted former Abacha supporters and decided to select its presidential candidate from the south rather than specifically the southwest. Ige and the Afenifere leaders had then helped to establish the APP, only to withdraw again for the same reasons and found their separate party, which swept Yorubaland in the local government elections but won nothing elsewhere. In Afenifere's habitually authoritarian style, a caucus of 23 leaders passed over Ige as the party's presidential candidate and chose Olu Falae, who had been Babangida's Finance Minister, a strong contender for the SDP presidential nomination in 1992, and another inmate of Abacha's gaols.[16]

When Obasanjo returned from the United States late in August 1998, Atiku and the PDM organisation – now an important PDP faction, with activists throughout the country – were already working hard to persuade men of influence that, as Atiku stated during September, Obasanjo was the country's best presidential material. A southern president, so Atiku told fellow northerners, was 'crucial to the unity and stability of the country'; his hearers will have added that the southern president must not be a southern partisan, a test that Obasanjo had passed in 1979. A president with military experience, Atiku added, 'would provide a gradual transformation of leadership from the military to civilian government'.[17] That, at least, was how he put it to the wealthy retired officers like Danjuma who were to become financiers of Obasanjo's campaign. Danjuma esteemed Obasanjo far above any other potential candidate.[18] So did Babangida, another large financial contributor, who spoke from experience:

> We said for a country like this, we needed a man who has the experience, we needed somebody ... with nerves because the country is such that it vibrates. If you don't have somebody who keeps his cool, somebody who has nerves and somebody who could take [a] decision and say get the hell out of here things will not move. And if you look across, he stands out as the most qualified person to hold this post for the sake of this country, that was why we put our support there.[19]

For many other Nigerians, Obasanjo's military background was the major reason to oppose him, lest he should prove incapable of democratic behaviour and instead 'herald another cycle of military rule, this time by soldiers in mufti'.[20] To these, however, Atiku and his colleagues could reply that Obasanjo's military rank and reputation would rather give him the authority to keep the soldiers in their barracks and restore their professionalism. As an observer put it, he was 'touted as one of the few Nigerians who could run a "coup-proof" and "secession-proof" government'.[21] The risk of Nigeria fragmenting was real at this time and was alarming especially to the North, now heavily dependent on oil revenues, and also, ironically, to the oil-producing states of the delta region, ethnically fragmented and conscious of their dangerous attraction to more powerful neighbours.[22] That Obasanjo was a patriot and a unitarist was indisputable. Even Balarabe Musa, former Governor of Kaduna State and the most consistently radical of Nigerian politicians, believed that 'of all the aspirants, he is the only one that can unite this country and carry us with credibility before the international community.'[23] The latter point added strongly to the case. Nigeria needed international sympathy, especially debt relief, if it was to restore its economy. Obasanjo was the only Nigerian with the international reputation to win that sympathy. Not only was he widely believed to be the candidate favoured by Western governments, but some looked further ahead and saw him 'as the only Nigerian leader with international clout to take over the leadership of Africa from Mandela when he retires next year'.[24]

The case was powerful. The problem was to convince the potential candidate. Obasanjo had never concealed – indeed, had delighted to display – his distaste for politics. When leaving office in 1979, so he claimed, he had vowed never to run guns, manage a brothel, or join a political party.[25] Now, friends, rivals, and enemies crowded to warn him that he lacked the temperament, especially the patience, for politics and that if he succumbed to the temptation he would ruin his historical reputation. His family opposed a presidential bid: 'They are going to kill you this time.'[26] During September he gave out conflicting messages, alternately denying interest, 'though without vigour', and implying that he might be persuaded by an overwhelming popular demand. As throughout his life, he knew that reluctance was more effective than eagerness.[27] Both Mandela and Jimmy Carter were said to have urged him forward. He appears to have been especially anxious for support in Yorubaland, touring the region late in August, meeting with its more nationally minded politicians, but making no headway with Afenifere, whose leaders regarded him as a 'Sokoto Yoruba' who had sold out to the North.[28] A key moment came on 3 October when a former schoolfellow, Sunday Afolabi, led a group of PDM members from the south-west to Ota and handed Obasanjo a PDP membership application form. 'Today', he responded, 'take it that I have not reacted', adding, in a favourite metaphor, 'If you are caught in an ambush, you don't move back…. You engage the gear and forward you zoom.' He joined the PDP on 28 October, declaring, 'It has no ethnic and religious leanings unlike most of the other parties.' A week later he told a gathering of some 2,000 at Ota: 'I have decided to offer to serve our country again. I therefore intend to seek nomination of our party, the PDP.'[29]

In his speech to this gathering, Obasanjo emphasised what was probably his strongest motive: the desire to salvage what he saw as the achievement of his young manhood:

On the first of October 1979, when our administration handed over power to a democratically-elected government, I, together with all those who served in the government, left behind the following: a nation with a purpose; a workable constitution; a military institution with great honours and high professional ethics; a healthy economy with robust reserve in which the naira exchanged for two dollars; the conviction that a government can honour its commitments; an independent and courageous judiciary; a nation that commanded and could compel international respect; a nation in which every citizen had a hope and chance of self-fulfillment and a democratic federal structure.

These had been lost, he complained, through leadership insensitivity, executive arrogance, and institutional lawlessness. He wished to seek a popular mandate from Nigerians in order to restore that legacy, but under a democratic dispensation.[30]

This desire to restore his legacy became the core of Obasanjo's routine campaign speech and a driving motive of his presidency. 'If Nigeria had remained as it was in 1979,' he told an audience in Enugu, 'I wouldn't have aspired to come back.'[31] Not only did the theme emphasise his experience and proven achievement, while fending off accusations of greed for a second taste of power, but the vision of a born-again Nigeria blended with his conviction of a providential calling. 'On my release from prison,' he later declared, 'I went into a pact with my Lord to do his bidding at all times. I saw my survival and freedom as a message from God to do what needs to be done in Nigeria. I could not disregard the call of God to duty.'[32] Like Jonah, he was offered a second chance. While sceptics viewed the messianic element in Obasanjo's campaign at first with irony and then with alarm, it helped the candidate himself to overcome his distaste for political competition:

> He stated that it was his belief that the current transition process was divinely ordained to succeed and usher in an era of good governance. General Obasanjo said he was confident that God has at last answered the prayer of Nigerians and is ready to forgive them of their transgressions to pave way for an era of greatness and plenty.[33]

This ringing declaration of faith was made in the unlikely setting of a fund-raising dinner that netted N356 million (about $3.5 million). Of this, N120 million was donated by Nigeria's most successful young industrialist, Aliko Dangote, a sugar and cement tycoon from Kano; N80 million by 'friends of Abubakar Atiku'; N30 million by Sir Emeka Offor, a sparsely-educated oil trader with a papal knighthood; and N20 million by the newly elected and urbane young Governor of Cross River, Donald Duke. They were a representative cross-section, both north and south, of the new business class that backed Obasanjo with their money and enjoyed in return his enthusiastic support for their entrepreneurial ambitions. Before they contributed, however, earlier donations – in addition to Atiku's – had come especially from military men. Danjuma, with a wide range of business interests, later claimed to have raised $7 million, slightly more than half of it from his own pocket. Improbably large contributions were attributed to Babangida. Atiku also introduced to Obasanjo his longstanding business associate, Otunba Fasawe, who was to become the General's fund-raiser and business manager.[34] Among the first things Obasanjo had to learn about democratic politics was its expense and the need to be accommodating in meeting it. He learned quickly. At a PDP finance meeting on 12 November he made the grandiose gesture of donating to the cash-strapped party the N130 million that he said he had collected for the pursuit of its presidential nomination, while his chief rival, Ekwueme, could offer only N20 million. These were not exceptional sums when compared with those disbursed by millionaires like Abiola or employed in subsequent elections, but Obasanjo's gesture altered both his own image and the terms of the contest, for it declared his intention to defeat political rivals at their own game. In reality, he appears to have held back another N90 million for his own campaign, while the bulk of his 'donation' never passed through party channels, much being distributed by his agents to the party's branches in the 774 local government areas, where, as an opposition sceptic pointed out, the N100,000 each received would only hire the vehicles for two meetings. Obasanjo himself refused to handle money.[35] Throughout his campaign for the nomination and the presidency, he was vastly better financed than his opponents, but not on a scale to buy election. That turned on other issues.

The local government elections of December 1998 were followed by voting for state assemblies and governors in January 1999 and for the Senate and House of Representatives in February. The PDP won all these elections convincingly, with 20 of the 35 state governorships contested and secure majorities in both houses of the National Assembly.[36] For Obasanjo, however, the results were less auspicious. The AD won everything in (and only in) Obasanjo's Yoruba homeland, even his own electoral ward, meaning that he could not meet the PDP's minimum requirement that a presidential aspirant must deliver his own constituency. This was reinforced by solid support for the PDP in the south-east, the base of Obasanjo's chief rival, Ekwueme, which might be lost to the party if he was not chosen as its candidate. Furthermore, as the sequence of elections proceeded, the APP became increasingly effective in the north, winning all its nine governorships there with Muslim candidates in a region to which Obasanjo, the born-again Christian, must look for much of his support. And everywhere voting relentlessly followed ethnic lines. It became clear that the presidential contest would counterpose the two different notions of nationality that dominated Obasanjo's career and Nigeria's politics: the ethno-linguistic nationalisms represented by the AD and by support for favourite sons in the south-east and north, against the exclusively Nigerian nationalism that Obasanjo represented.[37] The irony was not only that his public style, in speech and dress, was distinctively that of a Yoruba farmer, but that it was precisely his ethnic identity that made him attractive to the PDP.

Obasanjo met this challenge in two ways. First, he stressed that whether he could win a particular Yoruba ward or state was irrelevant. 'I did not contest the local government election', he insisted. 'What I am contesting is a national and not a section election.'[38] Second, as befitted the victor of the civil war, he mounted a better planned and more energetic campaign than any of his rivals for the PDP nomination. The nucleus of a campaign organisation was set up in Abuja even before Obasanjo announced his intention to contest. It was then expanded into a network of state branches, with Atiku as overall chairman and Aliyu Gusau as director-general. Later, when the campaign ran into difficulties, Atiku also brought in Tony Anenih, the former policeman who had been Yar'Adua's campaign director in 1992 and became known as the man with the portable telephone, a formidable political fixer.[39] The campaign spent heavily on newspaper advertising of a rather amateurish kind, although its radio advertising was said to be better.[40] Its chief strategy, however, was that perfected by Yar'Adua in the early 1990s: recruiting a countrywide network of activists, for which the PDM machine provided a basis, supplemented by relentless touring in which the candidate interspersed public speeches – Obasanjo was fluent in Hausa and Pidgin as well as Yoruba and English – with personal approaches to men who truly controlled local votes. It was here that his immense energy, his popular touch, his knowledge of the entire country gathered as soldier and head of state, and his acute sensitivity to the location of real power made Obasanjo a formidable campaigner. 'Watching the General throughout the primaries and the subsequent elections proper,' a member of his team recalled, 'he had become some kind of tireless super human at 62. On regular day he would go to bed at 3.00 a.m. and it was not unusual for you to be woken up by 6.30 a.m. by a call from one of his aides informing you that the General wanted to see you.' His Director of Publicity said that Obasanjo won because 'he reached out to every corner of this country.'[41]

The strategy was not effective in Yorubaland. Youths of the ethnic Oodua People's Congress and students at Obafemi Awolowo University in Ife – who once held Obasanjo hostage and humiliated him for two hours – had vowed to make campaigning impossible there, while few men of influence were willing to risk ostracism by Afenifere and its political party, except Pentecostal ministers who threw their support behind a born-again candidate in all parts of the country.[42] When Obasanjo moved eastwards across the Niger into the delta area, however, the campaign gathered momentum. In Bayelsa State, Obasanjo drove into the one-street capital at Yenagoa with *okada* (motor-cycle taxi) outriders doing tricks on their bikes, to be greeted by cultural dancers. He told the crowd that he had last been there in 1969–70, when God had saved their country from disintegration. Pointing to the poverty of the only state capital still lacking electricity, he promised, 'Within the first few years of my tenure, I will make sure that Yenagoa compares favourably, in terms of infrastructure with any other state capital in the country.' 'This young state cannot afford to be in opposition', he warned. Yenagoa, so it was reported, declared for Obasanjo.[43] His next stop was in Port Harcourt, for a warm welcome from the astute new Governor of Rivers State, Peter Odili, who thanked Obasanjo 'for ensuring his victory at the last gubernatorial election', and was to remain his close ally. Then on to Akwa Ibom, where Clement Isong, leader of the Ibibio people, assured him of the state's support.[44] Obasanjo was replaying the civil war: taking the south-eastern minorities away from a potential Igbo rival. But he did not stop there. With a large entourage and considerable ceremony, he visited Ekwueme's home to commiserate on an uncle's death. More practically, the campaign opened an Obasanjo-for-President office in Imo State, encouraged the candidacy of Jim Nwobodo, Ekwueme's long-standing rival for influence in Anambra State, and established relations with the new governors of Enugu and Ebonyi.[45]

This courting of the state governors, often relatively young men who had gained office after fierce competition, was a key element – perhaps *the* key element – in Obasanjo's political strategy for the next eight years. As sole executive, a forceful governor like Odili controlled large finance, immense local patronage, and potentially a state's entire political system. The post was the most contested in the federation after the presidency itself. Obasanjo quickly grasped that an executive alliance between president and governors could protect them all against legislators and party managers. The architect of the strategy may have been Atiku, for when Ekwueme attracted the support of older northern politicians who had often worked with him in the NPN, Atiku – himself the elected Governor of Adamawa – invited the generally younger northern governors to his house in Kaduna and, as he later said, 'poisoned' their minds against Ekwueme. In January 1999, six PDP northern governors declared for Obasanjo, probably his most important step towards winning decisive northern support. While campaigning strenuously there, Obasanjo remained careful to seek the personal support of emirs, imams, and opinion leaders of all kinds, but the days when native authorities could deliver their subjects' votes had died with the Sardauna. Now it was governors who delivered votes.[46]

'Obasanjo's entry into the presidential race enlivened the whole process', a journalist wrote. 'No sooner did he declare his ambition than he became the central issue around whom all controversies revolved. It quickly became apparent to everyone that Obasanjo was the man to beat.'[47] In particular, Obasanjo's noisy campaign overshadowed that of Alex Ekwueme. As Shagari's vice-president, Ekwueme was Nigeria's most distinguished civilian politician, an architect by training, a generous philanthropist, and a man of high integrity who had shown courageous leadership during Abacha's regime, becoming the PDP's first chairman and natural presidential candidate. But Ekwueme was distrusted. He was distrusted by many northern leaders because during the constitutional conference in 1994–5, he had led southern demands for a looser Nigerian federation, with a presidency rotating among six geopolitical zones, each with a vice-president, and a large share of oil revenue remaining with the producing states. 'Ekwueme hates northerners,' it was alleged, no doubt unfairly.[48] He was distrusted by younger PDP leaders who thought he was too wedded to the old men of the NPN. He was distrusted by the military, not only because it was feared that he might seek revenge for his deposition and imprisonment during the 1983 coup, but because he denounced political intervention by retired officers: his campaign posters described him as '100 per cent civilian'. Some even feared that Ekwueme's election might lead the military to abort the transition as in 1993.[49] Moreover, Ekwueme was a gentleman who plainly disliked electioneering and, as a journalist wrote, 'never seemed to want power badly enough'.[50] His poorly organised campaign, less well funded than Obasanjo's, was controlled by supporters from his own Igbo area to a degree that reawakened old fears of Igbo domination – a disadvantage that Obasanjo was spared by his lack of Yoruba support.[51] An experienced northern campaigner observed that Ekwueme was a Rolls Royce chauffeur and Obasanjo a truck driver – and Nigeria was a truck.[52]

Three main issues faced the aspirants to the PDP nomination. Ekwueme's most effective line of attack concentrated on Obasanjo's military background, instincts, and supporters, relentlessly pursued in press advertisements. 'To read some of the broadsides, you could think that Obasanjo is still wearing his fatigues and epaulettes', an observer commented. This had genuine popular resonance: delegates at a primary election in Plateau State chanted, 'We don't want soldiers.'[53] Obasanjo replied, wryly, 'I am learning very fast to be democratic…. I have become a reformed man who has forgotten that he was once giving orders and commands.' But he also stressed the danger of emphasising a military-civilian divide and he gave equal prominence to Ekwueme's background in the notoriously corrupt NPN regime.[54] Militarism was also a campaign issue because since 1990 Nigerian troops had been engaged in widely unpopular 'peacekeeping' operations in Liberia and Sierra Leone. They had left Liberia, but the 10,000 men in Sierra Leone were costing Nigeria $1 million a day and were engaged in heavy fighting, with some hundreds killed during January 1999 alone. Obasanjo blamed this on Abacha's adventurism and joined other candidates in promising withdrawal 'as soon as possible … without danger to the existence of Sierra Leone'.[55]

The second issue facing the aspirants was the future structure of the state. Obasanjo and Ekwueme both advocated 'true federalism' rather than the centralisation of military rule. Obasanjo insisted that this was possible under the existing constitution, but, as he had suggested before his imprisonment, he was willing to accept a restructured federation of six geopolitical zones – a scheme pioneered by Ekwueme – if public opinion demanded it. He insisted, however, that such a change must pass through the National Assembly and the prescribed procedures for constitutional amendment. Consequently, he continued to oppose the fashionable idea of a sovereign national conference, which he had previously wished to subordinate to a referendum but now to the elected National Assembly. Like some other experienced leaders, he believed that a sovereign conference would be less likely to reconstruct the federation than to destroy it.[56]

The third main electoral issue was how to rebuild Nigeria's economy. Obasanjo's campaign was strong on promises, including a master plan for the Niger Delta, an aggressive anti-corruption agency, living wages, and the restoration of the Universal Primary Education scheme he had launched in 1976 but watched his successors abandon. On economic strategy, however, he was vague, perhaps deliberately, describing himself as a 'market-oriented social democrat' with an agricultural priority.[57] 'Vote Obasanjo for President ... and you are guaranteed prosperity, development, social justice, transparency, accountability', an advertisement proclaimed. Another, reproducing Mandela's letter to him in gaol, reminded readers of his international stature: 'Nelson Mandela and Olusegun Obasanjo have a lot in common. Both are the most famous African ex-prisoners of our generation. Both are crusaders for DEMOCRACY, FREEDOM AND HUMAN RIGHTS. Both are super statesmen and world leaders.'[58]

The convention to choose the PDP's presidential candidate was to meet on 14 February 1999 at Jos. Four days before the meeting, the aspirants were summoned before a group of northern party leaders and asked to sign a prepared document allegedly undertaking, if elected, to appoint northerners to certain security positions and ministries (finance, defence, petroleum, agriculture, and water resources), not to dismiss northern military officers arbitrarily, to continue development programmes targeted at the region, not to hound the Abacha family, and to be satisfied with only one four-year presidential term in the first instance. Several aspirants signed without demur. According to a well-informed account,

> Ekwueme requested and was granted the permission to sign the document as amended by him after some negotiations.
>
> When this document was, however, given to Obasanjo to sign, he was said to have expressed surprise that a few people at the meeting who he counted as personal friends and with whom he had worked before would want to tie his hands.
>
> 'I cannot and will not sign this paper. You people can keep the presidency,' Obasanjo was said to have declared. 'If I sign a paper here, I get to the East and they give me another to sign and I go to the West and I am made to sign a document, what kind of president are we producing?'
>
> After Obasanjo had expressed his displeasure uninterrupted, he turned the paper over and wrote with his handwriting: 'I have met with a caucus of Northern leaders who have intimated me of the concerns and demands of their people which I intend to take serious consideration of when I became president.' Then he signed.

Although some present reportedly pressed Obasanjo to withdraw his candidacy, other northerners urged him to persevere.[59]

Before the convention met, Ekwueme's supporters had demanded Obasanjo's disqualification for not winning his ward and local government area, but the party chairman, Solomon Lar, had bent the rules to prevent it. Ekwueme's men had succeeded, however, in ensuring that representation at the convention included all PDP state assembly members, local council chairmen, and their deputies, which meant that because the party had fared badly in the south-west, there would be few Yoruba votes for Obasanjo to collect. In the event, of the 2,472 zonal delegates expected to attend, only 217 were from the south-west, against 627 from the north-west. There were more delegates from Kano State alone than from the six Yoruba states taken together. In all, 1,462 northern and 1,010 southern delegates were expected.[60] A week before the meeting, a newspaper estimated 1,092 votes for Obasanjo, 1,013 for Ekwueme, and the rest uncertain.[61] Obasanjo arrived in Jos by chartered train, together with the south-western delegates. With Atiku and Anenih, he established headquarters in the house that Yar'Adua had used as his base in 1993. Ekwueme came in a motorcade of 250 vehicles. Both were attended by numerous dance and masquerade groups. Ekwueme was thought to have brought off a coup by booking all the hotel rooms in the town for his delegates, forcing Obasanjo to locate his supporters far away in Bauchi or Kaduna, but this allegedly backfired because it gave Obasanjo's men the chance to work on their accessible opponents.

Obasanjo's agents had reportedly rewarded all state delegations with 'logistics and support fund' before they left home. Ekwueme was said to give N20,000–30,000 ($200–300) per delegate. Crowds cost N500 ($5) per head per day. Estimates of the money changing hands at the convention ran into hundreds of millions of naira. Yet, as posters said, 'Collect all monetary inducement but vote your conscience for Ekwueme', for the televised balloting system made it impossible to know for whom votes were cast.[62] A journalist mused:

> Anyone who wants to be president has to grit his teeth and get his hands dirty occasionally and mix with bad company from time to time.
> ... I sincerely believe that Obasanjo has some laudable aims, a fundamentally decent personality and an above-average track record.... He should not be underestimated by those who naively believe that only saints should stand for election. In today's Nigeria, a saint would not have stood a chance.[63]

Obasanjo had, however, made other preparations. Before the poll he persuaded Nwobodo to pursue his candidacy, thereby taking south-eastern votes away from Ekwueme. At the same time he induced Abubakar Rimi of Kano - the only northern candidate – to abandon his campaign and support Obasanjo. Rimi's supporters carried placards reading, 'Obasanjo for President, Rimi for Vee-Pee.'[64] When the convention opened, Obasanjo, dressed with deliberate simplicity, arrived at the arena before Ekwueme and then halted his rival's triumphal circuit on the grounds that campaigning was banned within the stadium. Each of the seven surviving aspirants spoke briefly, in alphabetical order. Ekwueme stressed his unique democratic experience. Obasanjo, speaking last – and when he could be heard above the jeers of Ekwueme's supporters – replied that his experience was in the first rather than the second position, that he had succeeded in the past, and that he would do so again. Then the voting began, mostly by candlelight because of a power cut, and lasted from 10.45 p.m. to 4.40 a.m. 'Obasanjo sat spread on the chair like a sultan.' Stella, who accompanied him through much of the campaign, sat beside him keeping a tally. Spectators 'shivered and dozed intermittently'. Once the public count began, it was soon clear that Obasanjo was winning. When the result was announced at 10.10 a.m., he had 1,658 votes against 521 for Ekwueme and 260 for the other candidates. Commentators reckoned that he had won the mass of northern and south-western votes, just over half from the delta region, and a proportion from the south-east. Some had seen the convention as a contest between generals and politicians. In reality, it had displayed both the continuing power of the northern constituency and the emerging power of the PDP governors, who had with only one exception supported Obasanjo. As so often in his career, his assessment of power had been immaculate.[65]

In his acceptance speech, Obasanjo pledged to 'devote all my energy and all I possess in my power to serve the people of Nigeria and humanity'. He rejoiced that his military background had not stood against him, 'as if it were a crime to have chosen a profession with the potential for supreme sacrifice for one's nation'. 'After my release from prison', he recalled,

> counsel of caution and withdrawal from public life sounded so sweet to my ears. Yet, there comes a time in the life of a patriot, when abdication would amount to a betrayal ...
> Thus, I came out of retirement to re-establish the traditions and structures of good governance that had broken down ...
> The task ahead is to pick up from where we stopped in 1979 and forge ahead ...
> Let us work together as one united family so that we can realise for our potentially great nation its manifest destiny. Nigeria has no business with poverty.[66]

Unity was now the issue. The PDP's domination of state and legislative elections seemed to guarantee that the presidential contest would be less demanding than securing the nomination, but that depended on Ekwueme. His defeat was traumatic for many of his Igbo followers, who had seen an Ekwueme presidency – already denied them in 1987 – as their long-awaited restoration to equality within the Nigerian state. In the immediate aftermath of the convention, some muttered of a new Biafra. More had warned that Igbo voters might turn against the PDP. If they did, and if the APP and AD put up an agreed candidate, there was every chance of defeating Obasanjo.[67] Yet Ekwueme had made clear his loyalty to the party he had helped to found. Despite criticism for his failure by younger Igbo leaders, not only did he support Obasanjo, but he chaired the General's fund-raising dinner, receiving a standing ovation. Obasanjo offered him the presidency of the Senate, which was not his to give, but Ekwueme – perhaps unfortunately – thought it inappropriate for a former vice-president. Yet his personal loyalty to the PDP did not guarantee the votes of the much-divided Igbo. Their main ethnic organisation, Ohanaeze Ndigbo, urged them to oppose Obasanjo.[68]

The victor's other immediate priority after the convention was to choose his vice-presidential running mate. This had to be a northerner. The PDP chairman, Solomon Lar, and other leaders urged the case of Abubakar Rimi, a party founder and former radical governor of Kano who may well have believed that his deal with Obasanjo had ensured his selection. Yet, as Anenih pointed out, the belligerent and intensely ambitious Rimi would have been an impossible deputy. Obasanjo told Lar that any agreement with Rimi must be broken. By some accounts his own preference might have been a senior northern politician such as Adamu Ciroma or Bamanga Tukur, but a vice-president of such seniority and regional standing could also have been a source of difficulty. Moreover, Obasanjo was under pressure from his early supporters in the PDM to choose their leader, Atiku Abubakar, who had perhaps made the greatest contribution to Obasanjo's campaign. Self-made, wealthy, politically adept, unassuming, and popular, Atiku had the added advantage of youth to disable him from challenging Obasanjo's leadership while acting as a bridge to the next generation. Obasanjo, always insistent on the authority of age, reportedly outlined the relationship he wanted and asked Atiku, 'Are you prepared to take orders from me?' Reassured, Obasanjo told him to go and inform the party leaders that he had been selected. 'Obasanjo has executed a coup,' Lar complained.[69]

The presidential election took place on 27 February 1999, only twelve days after the PDP convention. Obasanjo's sole opponent was Olu Falae, the Yoruba economist selected by the AD but technically standing for the APP, which nominated Umaru Shinkafi as a strong northern running mate. This alliance, seen by the parties as their only chance of success, caused some aspiring APP candidates to defect to the PDP, notably Dr Olusola Saraki, the political overlord of Kwara State. In other circumstances, Falae could have been a formidable candidate, but with the backing of parties that agreed only on wanting a civilian government, with little money, and with a campaign that began less than a month before the vote, Falae had reason to describe himself as David challenging Goliath.[70] Obasanjo and Atiku, by contrast, had a functioning campaign machine, substantial funds, and the use of three aeroplanes; between them they toured the entire country 'with an almost feverish zeal', starting at Maiduguri and meeting again at Lagos. Two days before the vote, Obasanjo and his wife even received a triumphant reception into Ibadan from the local rivals of the Afenifere establishment, with the candidate dancing and singing to traditional music in the manner that had become part of his electioneering style.[71]

By Nigerian standards, the election was relatively orderly, although only about one-quarter of the eligible electorate voted. A survey in January 2000 found that 72% of respondents thought it had been conducted fairly. The chief abuse took place long before election day when 57 million voters were registered, probably about 15 million more than existed.[72] Rigging was most blatant in the delta region, as was to become the norm in subsequent elections. Bayelsa State reported a 123% turnout. The PDP vote in Rivers State was more than double that in the state governorship election, while the joint returns for the other two parties fell by 73%.[73] In one location there,

> the presiding officer at the poll and the two party agents – one from the APP – were busy thumb-printing as many PDP votes as they could stuff into the ballot box. When I inquired as to what they were doing, they smiled politely, laughed, and continued their business. Waiting in line to vote were three 12-year-old boys. I asked one how old he was. He smiled at me sheepishly. 'Thirty-five, sir,' he replied. And he had a registration card to prove it.[74]

A journalist described the election as 'free and fair rigging,' meaning that each party exaggerated the vote where it was strong, so that the overall result was reasonably accurate. Anxious not to give the military an excuse to stay, the 12,000 election observers generally expressed content, pleased that there had at least been no violence. Only Jimmy Carter's monitoring organisation reported that the disparity between voters observed and results reported rendered it 'not possible for us to make an accurate judgment about the outcome'.[75]

Yet not even Carter can have doubted that Obasanjo had won, and in a most remarkable way. The official tally gave him 63% of the votes. He had lost all six states in his Yoruba homeland (although gaining 30% of votes in his own Ogun State) and four states in the far north where the APP was strong. The rest of the country was his: a president, perhaps unique in Africa, who was not without honour except in his own region. His success in thirteen states of the North and Middle Belt was the core of his victory, much helped by Saraki's defection that gave him Kwara and Kogi. But he had also won all six states in the delta region (the South-South) and all five south-eastern states, where fears of Igbo revenge proved groundless and Ekwueme's Anambra State voted 76% for Obasanjo.[76] 'I am overwhelmed by the magnitude of the mandate which clearly cuts across ethnic, regional, religious and even partisan lines,' he declared. 'I regard the result of this election as a mandate from the people of Nigeria and a command from God Almighty that I should spare no effort in rebuilding this nation.... Let us now join hands and work together to make Nigeria great again.'[77]

The road was not yet entirely clear. While some of Falae's supporters in Yorubaland attacked police stations, the candidate himself, after hesitation, challenged the election result in court, only to drop what was clearly a hopeless case.[78] More dangerously, there were rumours that senior military officers who had reason to fear Obasanjo's revenge were pressing Abdulsalami to remain in power, which he refused, or at least to leave the heads of the three services in office when the remainder of the junta retired, much as Abacha had survived Babangida's departure – and this Abdulsalami thought it wise to do.[79] The revised 1979 constitution under which Nigeria was to be governed was made public only one day before power was transferred, arousing suspicions that the junta had delayed it until sure that supreme military command would be in acceptable hands. Two weeks earlier, rumours that Obasanjo had been assassinated had triggered youth riots in Lagos and Abeokuta.[80]

Meanwhile, the President-elect visited eighteen foreign capitals and undertook a 'thank you' tour of the country. On 16 May 1999 he moved into the presidential complex at Aso Rock, after thought of first exorcising it.[81] Three years before, a leading political scientist had questioned 'whether anyone at all can rule Nigeria successfully.'[82] Obasanjo showed no such doubts. 'This time a man is taking over who is not a novice', he told an interviewer. 'I've run government before. There is no Nigerian who has the international connections and the experience that I have. I am as at home with the military as I am with civilians. It wasn't like that before.'[83]

Obasanjo was ready to take on Nigeria.

NOTES

1. *This Day*, 18 January 2004; Anyaoku, *Inside story*, pp. 179–80.
2. *Guardian*, 3 July 1998.
3. *Tell*, 20 July 1998, p. 15.
4. *New Nigerian*, 12 July 1998; *Guardian*, 9–10 July 1998. The Oputa Panel blamed Abiola's death on his incarceration but suspected that Abdulsalami's government knew more about it than it had revealed. See Nigeria: Human Rights Violations Investigation Commission, 'Report', vol. 7, p. 69.
5. *New Nigerian (weekly)*, 27 June 1998; *Tell*, 25 January 1999, pp. 17–19; *West Africa*, 3 August 1998, pp. 624–6.
6. *Nigerian Tribune*, 19 June 1998.
7. *Daily Champion*, 27 March 2007; *Tell*, 30 November 1998, p. 9; Adinoyi Ojo Onukaba, *Atiku: the story of Atiku Abubakar* (Abuja, 2006), p. 307.

8. *New Nigerian*, 18 August 1998.
9. Adinoyi Ojo Onukaba, *Atiku*, pp. 306–7; *Nigerian Tribune*, 14 February 2003; *Newswatch*, 27 March 2000, p. 13; *Guardian*, 3 July 1998; *Tell*, 13 July 1998, pp. 17–18, and 19 October 1998, pp. 12–13.
10. *Newswatch*, 31 August 1998, p. 23.
11. Sumaila I. Umaisha, 'To your tribes, O politicians', *New Nigerian (weekly)*, 15 August 1998.
12. *Newswatch*, 7 September 1998, pp. 24–5, 2 November 1998 pp. 24–6, 7 December 1998 p. 28, and 21 December 1998, p. 12.
13. For the texts, see *Newswatch*, 15 June 1998, pp. 20–6.
14. *New Nigerian*, 31 August, 17 September, and 15 December 1998; *This Day*, 15 January 1999; *Newswatch*, 20 December 1999, p. 42; Adigun Agbaje, Adeoku Akande, and Jide Ojo, 'Nigeria's ruling party: a complex web of power and money', *South African Journal of International Affairs*, 14, 1 (Summer 2007), 82–5.
15. *Newswatch*, 17 August 1998, pp. 8–15.
16. *New Nigerian*, 3 and 15 September 1998; Adewale Niyi Adebanwi, 'Structure and agency in a cult of power: a study of the Yoruba power elite', Ph.D. thesis, University of Cambridge, 2008, pp. 144–5.
17. *New Nigerian*, 19 September 1998; *Weekly Trust*, 18 September 1998.
18. *New Nigerian*, 20 November 1998.
19. *Newswatch*, 10 July 2000, p. 14.
20. *Times*, 17 February 1999.
21. *Africa Confidential*, 11 September 1998, p. 1.
22. *Newswatch*, 4 April 1994, p. 24.
23. *Tell*, 22 February 1999, p. 25.
24. *Tell*, 19 October 1998, p. 13; *Newswatch*, 23 November 1998, p. 13.
25. *New Nigerian (weekly)*, 10 October 1998.
26. *New Nigerian*, 17 and 20 September 1998; *Tell*, 19 October 1998, p. 18.
27. *New Nigerian*, 12–13 September 1998; *Weekly Trust*, 18 September 1998.
28. *Newswatch*, 13 May 2002, pp. 61–2; *Tell*, 19 October 1998, pp. 13, 17; *This Day*, 16 February 2003.
29. *Tell*, 19 October 1998, p. 11; *Africa Research Bulletin (Political)*, October 1998, p. 13286, and November 1998, p. 13322.
30. *Newswatch*, 16 November 1998, p. 20.
31. *New Nigerian*, 4 December 1998.
32. Quoted in Ukeje Jonah Nwokeforo, *Obasanjo's presidency and King David's rule (overwhelming similarities)* (Ibadan, 2006), p. 45.
33. *This Day*, 24 February 1999.
34. Ibid.; *Guardian*, 24 February 2008; *Hotline*, 1 August 1999, p. 15; Adinoyi Ojo Onukaba, *Atiku* , pp. 305, 307, 316.
35. *New Nigerian*, 13 November 1998; *This Day*, 16 January 1999 and 1 July 2000; *New Nigerian (weekly)*, 26 December 1998; *Newswatch*, 30 October 2000, p. 17.
36. *Africa Research Bulletin (Political)*, January 1999 p. 13398, and March 1999, p. 13472.
37. For this analysis, see Richard L. Sklar, 'Unity or regionalism: the nationalities question', in Robert I. Rotberg (ed.), *Crafting the new Nigeria: confronting the challenges* (Boulder, 2004), pp. 39–41.
38. *Newswatch*, 21 December 1998, p. 13.
39. *New Nigerian*, 18 October and 17 December 1998; *This Day*, 10 January 1999 and 8 October 2000; Adinoyi Ojo Onukaba, *Atiku*, pp. 314–15.
40. Akin Adeoya, 'Obasanjo: the rubbishing of a mega brand', *This Day*, 16 January 1999.
41. *This Day*, 19 April and 16 February 1999.
42. *Tell*, 9 November 1998, p. 28; *Weekly Trust*, 13 August 1999; Asonzeh Franklin-Kennedy Ukah, 'The Redeemed Christian Church of God (RCCG), Nigeria: local identities and

global processes in African pentecostalism', Ph.D. thesis, University of Bayreuth, 2003, p. 198; Matthews A. Ojo, 'Pentecostal movements, Islam and the contest for space in Northern Nigeria', *Islam and Christian-Muslim Relations*, 18 (2007), 186.

43. *This Day*, 1 and 10 February 1999.
44. *This Day*, 1 February 1999.
45. *This Day*, 16 and 19 January and 4 February 1999; *Guardian*, 29 March 2008.
46. *Guardian*, 5 November 2002; *Newswatch*, 8 February 1999, pp. 10–13; *This Day*, 24 January 1999.
47. *This Day*, 15 February 1999.
48. Alex I. Ekwueme, *Whither Nigeria? Thoughts on democracy, politics and the constitution (1992–2000)* (Enugu, 2002), Chs. 1–3; *Weekly Trust*, 5 June 1998.
49. *Source*, 1 March 1999; *Tell*, 8 February 1999, pp. 24–6, and 22 February 1999, pp. 20–1, 25.
50. *Guardian*, 11 November 2002.
51. Arthur Nzeribe, *Ndigbo and Obasanjo: fallacy of the hatred theory* (Enugu, 2002), p. 2.
52. Maier, *This house*, p. 30.
53. *This Day*, 3 February 1999; *Newswatch*, 15 February 1999.
54. *This Day*, 3 and 7 February 1999.
55. Tieku, 'Exploring', p. 259; 'Funmi Olonisakin, *Peacekeeping in Sierra Leone: the story of UNAMSIL* (Boulder, 2008), p. 32; Obasanjo, 'The country of anything goes'; *This Day*, 3 March 1999; below, p. 218.
56. *This Day*, 16 January 1999; *West Africa*, 3 August 1998, p. 602; *Africa Research Bulletin (Political)*, January 1999, p. 13399; *New Nigerian*, 4 December 1998.
57. Ademiluyi, *From prisoner to president*, p. 228; *This Day*, 14 January 1999.
58. *Weekly Trust*, 26 February 1999; *This Day*, 7 February 1999.
59. *This Day*, 16 April 2000. Other accounts of the document and the meeting vary in detail: *This Day*, 18 July 2000 and 5 October 2002; Ademiluyi, *From prisoner to president*, pp. 201–3. Obasanjo (in *West Africa*, 14 October 2002, p. 19) said only that he did not sign the original document.
60. *This Day*, 4, 7, and 13 February 1999; *Insider Weekly*, 3 June 2002, p. 25. Numbers quoted varied greatly: 2,439 votes were eventually cast.
61. *This Day*, 7 February 1999. This was based on guesswork, not a poll.
62. For accounts of the convention, see *This Day*, 12–16 February 1999; *Newswatch*, 1 March 1999, pp. 13–19; *Tell*, 1 March 1999, pp. 17–24.
63. *This Day*, 27 February 1999.
64. *Newswatch*, 1 March 1999, p. 15.
65. *West Africa*, 1 March 1999, p. 90; *This Day*, 17 February 1999.
66. *Tell*, 1 March 1999, p. 22.
67. *This Day*, 3 February 1999 and 18 February 2001; Ademiluyi, *From prisoner to president*, p. 232.
68. *This Day*, 1, 24, and 25 February 1999; Tony Amadi, *Power and politics in the Nigerian Senate* (Garki Abuja, 2005), pp. 15–17.
69. *This Day*, 19 May and 18 August 2001, 2 September 2005; Adinoyi Ojo Onukaba, *Atiku*, p. 320.
70. *This Day*, 4 and 26 February 1999; *Tell*, 15 March 1999, p. 25.
71. *This Day*, 19, 26, and 27 February 1999.
72. *Newswatch*, 10 May 1999, p. 6; Peter Lewis and Etannibi Alemika, 'Seeking the democratic dividend: public attitudes and attempted reform in Nigeria', Afrobarometer Working Paper no. 52, October 2005, p. vii, http://www.afrobarometer.org/papers/AfropaperNo52–17nov06.pdf (accessed 19 August 2007); Darren Kew, '*Democrazy – Dem Go Craze, O*: monitoring the 1999 Nigerian elections', *Issue*, 27, 1 (1999), 30.
73. *Africa Confidential*, 5 May 1999, p. 2; *This Day*, 2 March 1999.
74. Kew, '*Democrazy*', p. 31.

75. *This Day*, 3 March 1999; Commonwealth Observer Group, *The National Assembly and presidential elections in Nigeria, 20 and 27 February 1999* (London, 1999), pp. vii, 27, 43; Carter Center, 'Observing the 1998–99 Nigeria elections: final report' (Atlanta, 1999), p. 12, http://www.cartercenter.org/documents/1152.pdf (accessed 26 December 2007).
76. *This Day*, 1–2 March 1999; *Newswatch*, 8 March 1999, pp. 9–10.
77. *Tell*, 15 March 1999, pp. 26–7.
78. *Obanta Newsday*, July 1999, p. 40; *Africa Research Bulletin (Political)*, March 1999, p. 13472.
79. *Tell*, 8 March 1999, pp. 14–17, and 26 April 1999, p. 22.
80. *Tell*, 3 May 1999 and 31 May 1999, p. 34.
81. *This Day*, 8 April and 7 May 1999, 9 July 2000.
82. Jeffrey Herbst, 'Is Nigeria a viable state?' *Washington Quarterly*, 19, 2 (Spring 1996), 154.
83. *This Day*, 24 May 1999.

Part IV

The First Presidential Term
(1999–2003)

15
Containing conflict

On 29 May 1999 – Democracy Day, as he later named it – Obasanjo took the presidential oath in Eagle Square, Abuja, in the presence of Nelson Mandela, heads of state and dignitaries, and the Nigerian public. In his inaugural address, he described himself as 'a man who has walked through the valley of the shadow of death'. His task, he said, was to restore the morale, the state, and the economy ravaged by fifteen years of military rule:

> I am not a miracle worker. It will be foolish to underrate the task ahead. Alone, I can do little. You have been asked many times in the past to make sacrifices and to be patient. I am also going to ask you to make sacrifices, and to exercise patience.... This time, however, the results of your sacrifice and patience will be clear and manifest for all to see ...
>
> I am determined, with your full cooperation, to make significant changes within a year of my administration.[1]

He then outlined an unwieldy list of eighteen priorities, headed by attacks on corruption and cynicism, resolution of the crisis in the oil-producing Niger Delta, reduction of military commitments in Liberia and Sierra Leone, reprofessionalisation of the armed forces, harmonious cooperation with the legislature and judiciary, and, above all, 'to rekindle confidence amongst our people. Confidence that their conditions will rapidly improve and that Nigeria will be great and will become a major world player in the near future.' It was a sober, somewhat graceless, but purposeful speech by a man conscious of the task awaiting him.

Alert to popular expectations, and perhaps imitating Murtala's successful example, Obasanjo launched his presidency with a whirlwind of activity. Barely two hours after inauguration he removed the service chiefs whom Abdulsalami had left in post, replacing them by men from minority groups who had never held political office.[2] During the next two months he retired some 200 further officers, including all 93 who had held political positions. Although this angered northern conservatives accustomed to predominance within the military, it avoided the mistake that had allowed Shagari to be ousted by officers with political experience. It also demonstrated to surviving officers that political intervention jeopardised military careers and it created promotion opportunities for non-political officers, often from minority groups or the Yoruba. The government also brought the Defence Ministry under more direct control by moving it from Lagos to Abuja.[3] Obasanjo's success in depoliticising the army was probably his greatest achievement. No-one else could have done it.

The next priority was to form the new government. Obasanjo had already ensured himself the services of three trusted former generals: Aliyu Gusau, the security expert who had headed his election campaign and now became National Security Adviser; Abdullahi Mohammed, who had created the National Security Organisation in 1976 and became Chief of Staff; and Danjuma, his former colleague and recent financial backer, who was with difficulty persuaded to become Minister of Defence. Danjuma also headed a Presidential Policy Advisory Committee that drafted a programme for the presidency and allocated offices to the six geopolitical zones in accordance with the federal principle.[4] The constitution required Obasanjo to appoint at least one minister from each of the 36 states. He asked the PDP to suggest three names from each state, but disregarded many suggestions. His eventual team, containing 49 ministers and deputies, was largely shaped by political considerations.

Although Obasanjo had refused an undertaking to appoint northerners to certain key ministries, in fact he did so, except by retaining the Ministry of Petroleum Resources for himself. Adamu Ciroma became Minister of Finance to represent the northern political establishment. Another experienced but more surprising appointment was Bola Ige, the unsuccessful candidate for the AD's presidential nomination, a longstanding friend chosen as a step towards a government of national unity, a means of dividing the opposition, and a bid for Yoruba support. With Danjuma and Ciroma, he was one of the three ministers from whom Obasanjo did not demand an undated letter of resignation.[5] The ministries were equally divided between North and South, but there was some geographical bias towards Yorubaland and a distinct bias towards Christians, both of which angered northern critics. Obasanjo later said that he had known only four or five of the ministers when appointing them.[6] Few were technocrats of the kind generally favoured in a presidential system. The cabinet as a whole was widely considered too old, conservative, mediocre, political, and lacking in expertise, especially in the economic field. Its inadequacies partly explained the regime's disappointing performance, although the president was reputed to dominate his cabinet and take all major decisions.[7]

Ministries were not the only offices to be filled. A key appointment was the head of the State Security Service, Colonel Kayode Are, a protégé of Aliyu Gusau from Obasanjo's Owu section of Abeokuta. The President's personal staff came to embrace sixteen special advisers and forty special assistants.[8] Two of particular consequence were Phillip Asiodu, a former Super Permsec restored as Special Adviser on Economic Affairs and widely seen as the spokesman for IMF policies within the government, and Rilwanu Lukman, former Secretary-General of OPEC, who became Special Adviser on Petroleum Affairs.[9] Alongside these policy-makers were personal aides like Otunba Fasawe, his fund-raiser and business manager; Andy Uba, Stella Obasanjo's brother-in-law, who had befriended Obasanjo in America and now, as Special Assistant on Domestic Matters, 'wakes me up and watches me till I sleep'; several young sons of powerful public figures; and a penumbra of successful businessmen.[10]

Aso Rock was a court. The day began with prayers for family and personal staff in the chapel that Obasanjo constructed next to his residence. By 7.30 a.m. or earlier the daily routine of interviews and meetings was under way. It seldom ended before 6 p.m. 'He will not leave a file unattended before calling it a day', wrote an exhausted journalist. After a heavy late evening meal of cherished Yoruba food, further discussions might follow, for Nigerian politicians notoriously made decisions by night and implemented them by day. At midnight a long-suffering A.D.C. might be required to play (and lose) at the squash court. Obasanjo slept little and badly. In his mid sixties he regularly worked 18–20 hours a day with the same abrasive vitality that had energised Ota Farm. 'His aides say he lives, breathes and sleeps Nigeria and that he is so obsessed with transforming the country that he sometimes forgets that things could not be done with the same military fiat he is used to.'[11]

Despite his long-term plans, Obasanjo's presidency was immediately engulfed in social conflict released by the transition from military to democratic rule. Although his second term of office would become a time for navigation towards planned objectives, the first was a time for seamanship, for keeping the ship afloat, for not presiding over national disintegration as Nigeria's Gorbachev, in a parallel much prophesied at the time.[12] One observer reckoned that 1,000 Nigerians died in episodes of public violence during Obasanjo's first hundred days. Others put the figure for the first four years at over 10,000. Obasanjo rejected that figure, but he was appalled by the violent disorder around him.[13] 'When we came into office in 1999', he recalled six years later, 'the challenge was how to hold Nigeria together. Dozens of iconoclastic, extralegal, and violent organizations dotted the political landscape. At that time the Nigerian State was unsteady, uncertain, weak and badly delegitimated.'[14]

There were many reasons for this violence. Much was urban and related to the massive growth of towns, the collapse of their facilities, and the struggle for economic opportunity and employment, especially among the young, for as a result of rapid population growth, some 28% of Nigerians in the mid 1990s were aged between 10 and 24. Population growth also underlay much rural unrest, which was no longer peasant protest against taxation or crop prices – both of which now escaped government control – but was competition for increasingly scarce land. Conflict had been exacerbated by structural adjustment policies that reduced the resources open for competition, weakened the state's capacity to contain discontent, and encouraged ethnic and religious groups to mobilise in defence of their interests.[15] Sixteen years of military rule had eroded local institutions, robbed the country of effective political parties to moderate conflict, and encouraged violent response to military violence.[16] Always suspicious of rivals, the military had denied resources to the national police and reduced their numbers to no more than 120,000 for the whole country in 1999, a number Obasanjo was to double by 2003 and raise to 325,000 by 2007. Ineffective, badly paid, corrupt, brutal, the least trusted of all public institutions, the police also faced during the 1990s an influx of smuggled and easily handled firearms. State governors demanded power to create their own police forces, which the federal authorities feared might become private armies.[17]

While Obasanjo inherited these sources of violent conflict, the restoration of democracy exacerbated them. Military rule and economic decline had left many groups anxious to renegotiate their position within the Nigerian state. The most articulate were the Yoruba politicians of Afenifere, whose leader spoke of 'the Yoruba nation' becoming 'a self-governing autonomous nation within either a reconstituted Federal Nigerian Union or a reconstituted Federal Pan African Union'.[18] Their Igbo counterparts in the less strident Ohanaeze Ndigbo demanded the conversion of Nigeria into a confederation of regions or zones with separate armies and police forces and the control of all resources within their territory, a demand made even more strongly by organisations in the Niger Delta whose resources included the oil wells. By contrast, it was now the far north, heavily dependent on a share of oil revenue, that defended a unitary Nigeria against 'the new secessionists'.[19] 'If they [the Yoruba] declare Republic of Oduduwa today, we shall go to war to keep Nigeria one', the chairman of the Arewa [Northern] People's Congress warned in January 2000. Nigerians, an analyst explained, 'are in a state of relationship fatigue. They are fed up with one another.'[20]

Beneath this conflict among major regions, the restoration of electoral competition fostered communal rivalries and encouraged previously repressed minorities to assert claims. While a civilian government was loath to deploy troops, elected politicians were less able than traditional or military authorities to restrain local demands. One observer compared the struggle to establish positions in the new political order to the violence that accompanied the end of apartheid. For many Nigerians, Obasanjo's regime was itself illegitimate, either because it did not meet religious prescriptions or because it was elected under a constitution foisted on the country by the military. That constitution, in turn, increased the revenues and powers of state governors, encouraging several to pursue contentious independent agendas.[21]

This turmoil would dominate Obasanjo's first term and extend in one particularly intractable case throughout his presidency. Yet his partial containment of the turmoil, despite the heavy cost in lives, was perhaps one the four major achievements of his presidency, ranking with his control of the military, his role in the creation of the African Union, and his liquidation of Nigeria's external debt. Although he acted pragmatically in each conflict situation, a pattern emerged. As a cautious soldier with much experience of violence, Obasanjo recognised the limited resources at his disposal and the restrictions on his power. Ruling 120 million people with 120,000 doubtfully effective policemen, his only real power lay in the army, which he was most reluctant to use, especially against the largest ethnic groups, not only because he knew its destructive capacity but because he feared to give his regime a military image and knew from experience thirty years earlier in Ibadan how deeply soldiers resented being used as surrogate policemen. Consequently, he sought to avoid intervention, especially in local conflicts better left to state authorities, for although the federal structure of 36 states bred localised conflict, it also ensured that most remained localised.[22] If a state governor had to request military assistance, Obasanjo authorised it, but he generally waited for a request. He intervened more forcibly if a crisis threatened the federation itself. That happened chiefly in four cases: when violence in oil-producing areas endangered the economy; when Yoruba vigilantes, mainly in Lagos, attacked northerners on a scale threatening political relations between North and South; when Igbo extremists revived the dream of Biafran secession; and when the police or military suffered casualties that might endanger their loyalty if unavenged. These situations did not include the threat to national unity from the decision by northern states to adopt Sharia law, where Obasanjo saw the danger to lie in intervention rather than abstention. His strategy offended purists because it generally involved a political compromise with illegality and did not necessarily give priority to minimising loss of life or punishing perpetrators of violence. Throughout his career, Obasanjo gave priority to politics over law and to results over procedures. An opinion survey found his approach widely favoured.[23]

The area of most acute conflict, highlighted in Obasanjo's inaugural address, was the Niger Delta, the 70,000 sq.kms of creeks, swamps, and patches of agriculture supporting Nigeria's oil industry and some 25 million people speaking scores of languages and dialects. Until the civil war began in 1966, these relatively small communities had generally valued central government protection against their more numerous Igbo neighbours. The war had disrupted that alliance and precipitated armed dissidence when Ijaw youths dynamited the first oil well in 1966 and declared a Niger Delta People's Republic. In the mid 1990s, the main conflict in the region was between the Ogoni people and the Shell oil company, culminating in Shell's abandonment of the Ogoni area and the execution of the Ogoni leader, Obasanjo's friend Ken Saro-Wiwa.[24] By the time Obasanjo took office, however, the focus had shifted back to the more numerous Ijaw. Late in 1998 they had closed down one-third of Nigeria's oil production and created the Ijaw Youth Council, which issued the Kaiama Declaration asserting that 'All land and natural resources (including mineral resources) within the Ijaw territory belong to Ijaw communities', demanding the 'withdrawal from Ijawland of all military forces of occupation and repression by the Nigerian State', and agreeing 'to remain within Nigeria but to demand and work for self-government and resource control for the Ijaw people'. The declaration was followed by a protest march dispersed by gunfire. Abdulsalami's government declared a state of emergency and moved in military reinforcements.[25] When Obasanjo visited the Delta during his campaign tour in January 1999, Ijaw youths met him with hostility, believing, mistakenly, that his Land Use Decree of 1978 had robbed them of their oil.[26]

Obasanjo concluded that the first priority was a development plan for the region, but on the day after his inauguration further violence erupted in Warri, an oil town long disputed between Ijaw, Itsekiri, and Urhobo inhabitants. Fighting with weapons that included bazookas and Kalashnikovs caused several hundred deaths.[27] Visiting the region ten days later, Obasanjo had a successful meeting with elders, again promising a development plan, but clashed once more with Ijaw youths. 'You want to threaten me? You can't', he declared, challenging one leader, 'Can you fight? *See im face like Ijaw man face*'. The youths laughed and Obasanjo told them, 'I totally, absolutely reject your presentation. But the door is open for dialogue and discussion.' Turning back to the elders, he said, 'You have failed to pull them by their ears. We are in danger of having anarchy being unleashed by our youths.' Two days later the Ijaw Youth Council declared Nigeria a 'failed state' and demanded a sovereign national conference.[28] In September 1999, they closed down the newly established and immensely expensive liquefied natural gas plant at Bonny. Still claiming 'that the Niger Delta problem was one of neglect and injustice not a secessionist threat', Obasanjo now added that it was necessary to 'differentiate genuine protests from criminality'. In November he sent two army battalions to apprehend youths who had murdered policemen at the Delta town of Odi. Hopes of conciliation were fading.[29]

The development plan made slow progress. Early in July 1999, Obasanjo sent the National Assembly a bill to create a Niger Delta Development Commission to formulate and implement such a plan, but regional representatives saw this as a means of taking power and funds out of local hands. After six months' debate the Assembly redrafted the measure to give itself the power to approve the Commission and to make its funding additional to the revenue routinely allocated to the states. Alarmed at the cost and the challenge to his executive authority, Obasanjo threatened to veto such a bill. The Assembly threatened to override him. During 2000, the bill passed backwards and forwards between presidency and legislature as

Obasanjo refused to implement it without amendment. Not until December 2000 was the Commission inaugurated.[30]

Meanwhile violence in the Delta grew. On one side, oil companies and state governors with increasing oil revenues subsidised militant groups, known as 'cults', to protect their interests. These cults may first have been employed in the rigged election in Rivers State in 1999. Thereafter, the two most powerful cult leaders, Ateke Tom and Asari Dokubo, reinforced their positions by tapping pipelines and exporting the oil – 'bunkering', as it was known – to finance the purchase of ever more sophisticated weapons. At the same time, community resentment of neglect and environmental pollution escalated into widespread occupation of oil installations.[31]

Obasanjo found no answer to the explosive combination of community protest, ethnic rivalry, easy money, and criminal violence amidst the uniquely difficult delta environment, but could only hope that planned development might in the long term remove the causes of violence. A parallel threat existed in the young vigilantes who had long policed and protected Nigerian towns but had organised on a new scale and with new political purposes in response to Abacha's repression and the restoration of democracy. Their most dangerous organisation was the Oodua People's Congress (OPC), a Yoruba body founded in Lagos in August 1994 by Frederick Fasehun, a medical doctor. A reaction against the annulment of Abiola's presidential election, it was initially designed to secure his installation, defend the Yoruba against the military regime, and unite them to resist any similar future disaster, but its political objectives expanded to demand a sovereign national conference to restructure Nigeria as a confederation of ethnic units. When Fasehun was gaoled in 1996, leadership was taken by a younger militant, Ganiyu Adams, who recruited artisans, unskilled workers, and unemployed urban youths, although the organisation also had many educated Yoruba supporters.[32] When democratic politics returned in 1998–9, Fasehun initially supported Obasanjo 'because of his facial tribal marks', but Adams urged disruption of the elections and led his followers into vigilantism, often with more or less covert support from state governors.[33] In Lagos, by early 1999, the OPC was virtually at war with the police. In July it was involved in fighting with economic rivals among northern immigrants in Shagamu, the first of several bloody ethnic conflicts in Yoruba towns during the next three years. The Shagamu fighting led to retaliation against Yoruba in Kano.[34] Visiting both towns, Obasanjo 'was shocked by what he saw' and blamed enemies of his administration. Under northern pressure to curb the OPC, he responded to renewed attacks on Hausa traders in Lagos in November 1999 by ordering the police to shoot on sight any OPC member who resisted arrest and by threatening to impose a state of emergency in the city if its governor did not restore control.[35] Late in 2000 he banned OPC and ordered the arrest of its leaders. In February 2002, troops were needed to quell further fighting in Lagos.[36] Two months later Obasanjo proposed legislation to proscribe ethnic associations judged to promote violence, but the National Assembly rejected it as a potential weapon of executive tyranny. Thereafter, however, the level of violence declined, although the two OPC factions continued to fight one another. One reason for the decline, along with harsh reprisals by the police and military, was probably that Obasanjo's growing political rift with the North rallied Yoruba behind him. At the election in 2003 both OPC factions would support him.[37]

Obasanjo's repression of the OPC was a response not only to its violence but to the danger it posed to Nigeria's political unity. He responded more hesitantly to vigilante groups in south-eastern cities, where local issues predominated and the vigilantes had no distinctly political agenda.[38] The Bakassi Boys, as they were known, were organised in late 1998 by the shoemakers of Aba (in Abia State) to fight criminal gangs, which they did with ferocity and such success that they were invited into other towns in Abia and then Anambra States, whose governors had turbulent urban populations, enlarged shares of oil revenues, but no disciplined forces except the undermanned federal police. Governor Orji Uzor Kalu of Abia converted a group of Bakassi Boys into the Abia State Vigilante Service in July 2000. A month later his counterpart in Anambra, Chinwoke Mbadinuju, formed a similar Anambra State Vigilante Service, equipped it with arms, uniforms, and transport, and used it as effectively his private army in the state's internecine political struggles.[39] At this stage the Bakassi Boys were sufficiently popular for the main Igbo ethnic organisation, Ohanaeze Ndigbo, to send a delegation, including the eminently respectable Ekwueme, to dissuade government from banning them. The popularity continued into 2001 and there was pressure on other south-eastern governors to establish similar groups. Some governors were reluctant, police commanders were generally hostile, and Obasanjo made known his opposition but hesitated to interfere where the vigilantes had popular support and state authorisation.[40]

By January 2002, however, the Bakassi Boys were estimated to have killed over 2,000 people and their brutality – especially their horrific method of public execution – was swinging opinion against them. Refused legislation authorising him to ban militias, Obasanjo ordered the tough mobile police to break up the organisation.[41] Yet the demand for vigilantes remained. During his second term, the Bakassi Boys reappeared in Abia and Anambra, with the governors' support, and were again suppressed by federal forces.[42]

In contrast to their ambivalence towards the Bakassi Boys, the authorities, after initial hesitation, took a more hostile stance towards another Igbo organisation that emerged during the return to civilian rule: the Movement for the Actualisation of the Sovereign State of Biafra (MASSOB). Launched late in 1999 by the lawyer Ralph Uwazuruike as an openly secessionist organisation, but proclaiming itself non-violent, it gained prominence in May 2000 when Uwazuruike raised the Biafran flag to the strains of the Biafran anthem in the market at Aba, before escaping on a motorcycle. MASSOB was denounced by Ohanaeze Ndigbo and other Igbo ethnic organisations, but it drew strength from their disunity and ineffectiveness, from a widespread Igbo sense of marginalisation, and from the support of Igbo too young to have experienced the civil war. During Obasanjo's first term, his government largely ignored MASSOB's challenge, but in August 2004 the organisation displayed unexpected strength on Biafra Day. The federal attorney-general then denounced the movement as treasonable, Uwazuruike was arrested, and his followers became locked in violent competition for urban predominance with the police and the various armed bodies controlled by state governors. Like the OPC, with which it began to cooperate, MASSOB's threat to Nigeria's political integrity attracted state repression.[43]

These challenges to the national unity that Obasanjo, as president, had a particular responsibility to defend tended to reinforce his centralising instinct. They led him to reject all demands for a Sovereign National Conference, insisting that its composition would be impossible to determine – the number of ethnic 'nationalities' present at an unofficial conference in December 1998 had been variously estimated at between 5 and 112[44] – and that constitutional amendment must follow constitutional procedures. Forced by the threat of action in the Supreme Court to comply with the constitutional requirement that at least 13% of oil revenue should be allocated to oil-producing states, he sought to confine this to onshore oil and rejected demands for 'resource control', by which states would retain all locally generated revenue and merely pay tax on it to the federal government.[45] Yet Obasanjo had overseen the drafting of the constitution that made Nigeria the continent's most successful federation. His awareness of the federal structure's value in accommodating cultural differences was clear from his response to the conflicts that racked the North during the first years of his presidency.

These conflicts were rooted in the region's fragmentation into numerous states, the challenge to its traditional rulers by young administrators and businessmen (often educated at Ahmadu Bello University), and the spread of popular education that subjected Islam to the same democratising pressures that produced Pentecostal Christianity, opening the Muslim community to scripturalist versions of the faith[46] at the same time as improved communications exposed it to currents of thought in the wider Islamic world and 'power shift' to the South highlighted the economic backwardness of northern society. The result was theological and institutional ferment, sectarian disunity, and a missionary impulse expanding southwards into hitherto un-Islamised areas of the Middle Belt, where it met a similar Christian missionary impulse pressing northwards. In 1987, the first violent clash between followers of the two evenly balanced religions took place at Kafanchan in southern Kaduna State.[47]

This was the ferment from which the issue of Sharia law re-entered politics shortly after Obasanjo's inauguration. In order to preserve the unity of the northern region, the implementation of Sharia law there had been restricted at independence to civil cases between Muslims. Criminal cases were governed by a criminal code derived from the Sharia but without elements that modernisers thought outdated. This offended purists. In 1999, the All People's Party governorship candidate in the far northern Zamfara State, Ahmed Sani, won a closely fought election after promising to implement Sharia fully in the criminal as well as civil sphere. To do so, he took advantage of a loosely drafted clause in the new constitution that allowed a state to extend the jurisdiction of its Sharia courts.[48] On 19 September 1999, he announced the new measures amidst great excitement. They included rigid segregation of the sexes, prohibition of immoral acts such as prostitution and the consumption of alcohol, and the imposition of Koranic punishments for certain offences. Among the first victims were a man whose hand was amputated for cattle theft and an unmarried mother sentenced to 100 lashes after claiming that she had been raped.[49] A uniformed force of *hisba* vigilantes enforced the legislation when federal police refused. The governor was careful to exclude Christians from his legislation and to preserve the existing civil courts, insisting that he was acting constitutionally.[50]

A study by human rights activists in February 2000 concluded that although Zamfara had become plainly an Islamic state, with only a small Christian minority, its atmosphere was less repressive than was generally supposed.[51] By then, however, expectations and fears were spreading through less homogeneous states. Tension was highest in Kaduna, where over one-third of the population were Christians.[52] Early in November 1999, Christians in Kaduna demonstrated against the adoption of Sharia law in Zamfara. In reply, Muslims demonstrated to demand that Kaduna follow the same path. While Governor Makarfi struggled to preserve the peace, an anti-Sharia march on 21 February led to fighting and mutual slaughter that spread

190

to neighbouring towns and caused some 1,295 identifiable deaths before the army restored order. When bodies of Igbo victims returned to Aba and other southeastern towns, revenge mobs killed over 300 northerners.[53]

After seeing for himself that 'Kaduna has overnight been turned into a battle-field', Obasanjo summoned the Council of State, an advisory body composed of former heads of state and chief justices together with incumbent governors. What took place was disputed. Vice-President Atiku first met separately with the governors and apparently reported to the full council that they had agreed to suspend the implementation of Sharia and return to the *status quo ante*. Obasanjo then announced that the Council had unanimously approved this. Ahmed Sani, who was reported to have walked out of both meetings, promptly denied that there was any question of suspending Sharia, General Buhari denied that the Council had even considered Sharia, and ex-President Shagari (who had not attended) denied that the Council had any authority in the matter. During the following months, Kaduna was in effect partitioned between the two religious groups.[54]

The fiasco at the Council of State illustrated the delicacy of Obasanjo's position, if not great delicacy in handling the issue at that meeting. Christian opinion throughout Nigeria was fiercely hostile to recognition of Sharia penal law, holding that its punishments were barbaric, its treatment of women was unjust, its aim was to destabilise a southern president, and its recognition would contravene the constitutionally guaranteed secularity of the state – the last point being mistaken, since the constitution stated rather than neither the federal nor a state government might adopt any religion as state religion.[55] Ahmed Sani insisted that he was observing that requirement in Zamfara. His critics denied it, demanding that Obasanjo should seek a ruling from the Supreme Court. Both houses of the National Assembly urged this.[56]

Obasanjo was unmoved. He had tried unsuccessfully to dissuade Ahmed Sani from implementing his plans in Zamfara. One report claimed that northern ministers had walked out of a meeting of the Federal Executive Council when it was suggested that the government should coerce Zamfara State by force.[57] The President's first public comments were made in the United States in late October 1999, but there were conflicting accounts of what he said. According to one, he 'said that the 1999 constitution recognises Nigeria as a secular state but that the country being a federation, the same constitution allows any state that desires Sharia to adopt it', adding, however, that he thought the issue would soon 'fizzle out'.[58] Other reports, however, claimed that he had described Sharia as unconstitutional, and these were widely repeated.[59] Perhaps he was confused by the complexity of the issue, as many were, but as the controversy developed he clarified his position. Asked in February 2002 why he tolerated Sharia, he replied, 'Because under the constitution, Nigeria is a multi-religious nation in which states can draw up their own legal code.' Two months later he contradicted the attorney-general's statement that the Sharia code's punishments were unconstitutional, much as he personally condemned them.[60] He continued, however, to distinguish 'genuine Sharia', the moral code of Islam that he admired and said had long been in force in the North, from 'political Sharia', the emotive campaign that he believed to be directed against his regime and inevitably ephemeral. 'I believe that the emotion and the politics will go away but the religious aspects of Sharia will stay', he explained in August 2000.[61]

This was no doubt an oversimplification, but it enabled Obasanjo to counsel toleration while condemning the carnage at Kaduna. He knew that northern leaders like Ahmed Sani had no wish to disrupt a federation from which their region received much-needed revenue. Nor did they wish to alienate further the Christian areas of the Middle Belt, from which Obasanjo's regime drew much support, both electoral and military. Not only did the constitution deter him from interfering in the religious affairs of the northern states, but those affairs, unlike the Sharia Appeal Court crisis of 1978, did not threaten the structure of the federation unless extremists on one side or the other insisted on doing so. For this reason, Obasanjo was anxious, as always, to treat the issue as political rather than constitutional, and above all to avoid taking it to the Supreme Court. Lawyers debated whether the government could do so without taking a position for or against the constitutionality of Sharia.[62] More important, an application to the Supreme Court might not only split the court, which was carefully balanced between Muslim and Christian judges, but would not convince the unsuccessful party and would probably not be obeyed by it. Ahmed Sani stated early in 2000 that not even the Supreme Court could stop him implementing the Sharia. As Obasanjo commented, it was a no-win situation. The Nigerian Bar Association supported his anxiety not to endanger the court. So did the court itself, which skilfully avoided Sharia cases.[63]

Obasanjo's response to Sharia was bitterly criticised in the South as 'an *ostrich* style of leadership' displaying 'total lack of courage'. Northern extremists taunted, 'Since he has described the Shari'ah as unconstitutional, why hasn't he done anything about it? Or is he afraid?'[64] In reality, he had the courage to appear weak and the wisdom to do nothing – often the most difficult thing for a politician to do. Speaking after his retirement, he said that Sharia 'was the biggest challenge he ever faced as a leader … its introduction would have set the country on fire if not for the mature way it was handled.'[65]

The immediate cost, however, was further conflict. Following Zamfara's lead, another four northern states adopted Sharia penal law during 2000 and seven during 2001, generally in response to popular demand.[66] In Kano, for example, angry crowds obliged Governor Kwankwaso to declare Sharia to be binding on everyone in the state (much to Obasanjo's displeasure), a *hisba* organisation was established outside the governor's control, and a zealot defeated Kwankwaso at the next election.[67] The heightened tension led to a sequence of violent incidents in several northern states. In October 2001, for example, Nigeria's support for American bombing of Afghanistan led demonstrators in Kano to take revenge on hapless Igbo residents, killing some 200 before the army restored control. Obasanjo was booed when he visited the city two days later.[68] In November 2002, Kaduna suffered again when a derogatory newspaper reference to the Prophet sparked three days of fighting between Muslims and Christians in which some 215 died. Obasanjo once more visited the city and promised to punish the perpetrators, but nothing was done.[69] Meanwhile a new focus of conflict had emerged further south in Plateau State, where there was longstanding tension between the indigenous majority, often recent converts to a militantly fundamentalist Christianity, and immigrant Muslim trading groups from the north, a tension focused especially on the control of towns and fear that the immigrants might seek to introduce Sharia law. In September 2001 a minor incident sparked a week of fighting in the state capital, Jos, interrupted and intensified by news of al-Qaeda's attack in New York. Some 500 people were killed before the army gained control.[70] Obasanjo visited the city to express shock and urge reconciliation, but the violence spread further into the countryside, where at least 1,000 people died in fighting between 'indigenes' and 'settlers' before the President declared a state of emergency in May 2004, suspended the Christian-biased and ineffective state government, and installed six months of military rule that restored a degree of order.[71]

An international organisation that investigated the crisis in Plateau State condemned the 'culture of impunity' that it believed Obasanjo had followed throughout these ethno-religious disturbances:

> The conflicts in Plateau State and Kano in 2004 have illustrated the grave consequences of the Nigerian government's persistent neglect of communal tensions and of its failure to take action to prevent longstanding grievances from turning into violence…. Had the government acted much earlier or, notably by bringing to justice those responsible for the violence, hundreds of lives might have been saved.[72]

Obasanjo, who had much experience of violence and peacemaking and knew the limited forces at his disposal, held a different opinion, more consistent with the widespread African notion that the chief purpose of justice was to restore harmony. 'It is my view', he wrote, 'that the prolonged nature of the conflict in Plateau State and the extensive number of alleged perpetrators of violations in the course of these conflicts makes the combination of truth, forgiveness, reprieve, amnesty and reconciliation a more desirable option, in the first instance, to retributive criminal justice.' He might have added that attempts by earlier regimes to hunt out perpetrators had sometimes led to further rioting.[73] In retrospect, too, the Plateau disturbances of 2004 were the peak of ethno-religious conflict. Sporadic violence continued in the state, and less often elsewhere, but Obasanjo's prediction that the conflict surrounding Sharia law would lose intensity was largely correct. Opinion surveys showed that between 2001 and 2007 support for Sharia increased among people of all religious communities, in both Sharia-enforcing and other states, especially among poorer and middling economic groups. 'Perhaps Nigerians have learned to live with Sharia', the researcher concluded.[74]

Obasanjo may also have reflected on two occasions when he had exerted the force at his command and had suffered almost universal condemnation. Late in 1999 the police in Yenagoa, capital of Bayelsa State in the Niger Delta, expelled from the town a youth gang, the Asawana Boys, who had been employed as party thugs during the 1999 election. They took refuge in their leader's hometown, Odi.[75] Either because the gang terrorised the community or because they were rumoured to be planning to attack OPC militants in Lagos, a small force led by a Yoruba police officer was sent to investigate. The Asawana Boys kidnapped, tortured, and killed them. Obasanjo instructed the governor to apprehend those responsible. When he reported that he could not do so, Obasanjo handed the mission over to the army, with, according to his press secretary, 'clear, specific and unambiguous instructions: dislodge perpetrators of violence, restore law and order and apprehend suspected murderers'.[76]

A force variously reported at between 300 and 2,000 reached Odi on 20 November 1999 in armoured personnel carriers, apparently with some heavy weapons. What happened next was disputed. The Army Chief of Staff said they were ambushed at the entrance to the town and met serious resistance within it.[77] Others said there was a brief exchange of fire before the military cleared the town and then spent several days destroying everything within it except the bank, Anglican church, and health centre. Graffiti left on the walls included 'We will kill all Ijaws, by soldier' and 'The governor has given us the right to destroy everything.'[78] The government stated that 43 people died. A local NGO put civilian deaths at 2,483.[79] 'Odi is our

Guernica', Wole Soyinka declared.[80] It haunted Obasanjo for the rest of his presidency. He told a delegation of survivors that the destruction was 'regrettable' and 'avoidable'. Visiting the ruined town in March 2001, he said the soldiers had 'gone beyond their brief': 'only a sadist could have ordered the destruction of Odi.' But he refused to pay compensation, rebuild the town (although the Niger Delta Development Commission did so), apologise, or condemn the soldiers concerned. Questions about the incident infuriated him.[81] Unless the military records are unusually frank, there may never be agreement on exactly what happened, but the incident probably bore out an army commander's earlier warning to President Shagari that it was almost impossible to stop soldiers killing those who killed their comrades.[82] The contrast with the soldiers' excellent behaviour in Plateau State, where they had no comrades to avenge, reinforced the point. In refusing to condemn his troops, Obasanjo may have considered the possible impact on military attitudes to the civilian regime at this relatively early point in its existence. The most powerful lesson of Odi must have been the danger of using the only substantial weapon in his armoury.

That lesson was reinforced less than two years later at Zaki-Biam, a village on the border between Benue and Taraba states in a region long disputed between the Jukun and Tiv peoples, both with strong military traditions. In October 2001 nineteen soldiers sent to keep the peace in the area were surrounded by Tiv militiamen, who were themselves mainly ex-soldiers. The troops were taken to Zaki-Biam, declared to be Jukun militiamen in uniform, and very brutally killed. Amidst intense anger in the army, so it was alleged, Obasanjo reportedly declared, 'Those who killed my soldiers must be fished out.'[83] He rounded on a journalist: 'You don't expect me to hold my hands and do nothing because tomorrow neither soldiers nor policemen will go anywhere I send them.'[84] Although his spokesman claimed that he had ordered 'minimum force', the army rounded up and massacred perhaps 250–300 men in half a dozen villages. Vice-President Atiku admitted that 'things went out of hand'. Obasanjo, after initially parrying questions, apologised for 'an excessive use of force and loss of civilian lives' when he visited the region a year later.[85]

Observers commented that such military violence 'is becoming a nationwide trend', but that was not true. Rather, as Obasanjo said at the time of the Zaki-Biam controversy, 'We must utilise military force only when all else has failed. That is my own principle and philosophy.'[86] Any incident of violence was likely to draw blame upon him. This happened in January 2002, when an ammunition dump at the Ikeja barracks on the outskirts of Lagos exploded and perhaps a thousand people died, many of them in the ensuing panic. Hastening to the scene and apparently unaware of the casualties, he was taunted by the angry crowd, 'President, go inside', and replied furiously, 'Shut up. I took the opportunity of being here to see what could be done. I don't have to be here.' He later apologised, but his critics made much of the incident.[87]

A later historian wrote that Obasanjo's regime 'drifted uneasily between anarchy and tyranny. It either used too little or too much force to manage religious, resource and ethnic conflicts.'[88] This was true, but the reason for it was that either too little or too much force was what it had at its command. Moreover, there was progress. Asked in May 2001 what he had achieved during his first two years, Obasanjo replied, 'Nigeria is still one.' Even his critics recognised that levels of violence and disorder were declining. Those like Olu Falae who had claimed that agitation for ethnic self-actualisation and a sovereign national conference was bound to grow were proved wrong: it diminished and the country's stability increased.[89] Much of this, as Babangida observed, was due to Obasanjo's experience and strength of character:

> If it hadn't been an Obasanjo sitting down there, if not him, he would have been intimidated to the point of throwing in the towel. Intimidation from the media or the society or from critics. Intimidation. Conference of nationalities would have overwhelmed him. The Niger Delta crisis would have … I don't think he loses his sleep [over the Sharia issue], because he is strong, and that is what we need for this time, for this period.[90]

Paradoxically, this strength had shown itself most fully in inaction: in a refusal to call a national conference or place Sharia before the Supreme Court or seek legal retribution against perpetrators of mass violence. In terms of human rights, too, Obasanjo's first administration enlarged the freedom of ordinary Nigerians. 'Everyone's liberty is allowed as enshrined in the constitution', he told an American audience in 2002. 'Our people are free. They have never been freer. We have no political prisoners, no detainees. Our press is free. Some would say, too free.' Certainly the freedom of the press included a freedom to abuse the president that would have been remarkable anywhere and was seen by one observer as the practical form of the anticipated democracy dividend.[91] Obasanjo imposed a virtual moratorium on capital punishments,[92] although he achieved little by way of prison reform, chiefly because of the appalling delays of Nigeria's investigative and judicial system: in February 2008, 25,789 of the country's 38,252 prisoners were reported to be on remand.[93] Nor was there much progress in checking the brutality by which the overburdened police tried to exert a degree of authority, for torture of suspects was 'widespread and routine' and between January 2000 and February 2004 the police killed 7,198 'suspected armed robbers'.[94]

By the end of his first term of office, Obasanjo had weathered much of the ethnic and religious conflict that accompanied the return of civilian rule. It was one of his most valuable services to his country. But it had forced him to concentrate on damage limitation and distracted him from his intended priority: to rebuild Nigeria's economy.

NOTES

1. 'President Obasanjo's inaugural address to the nation – May 29, 1999', http://www.dawodu.com/obasl.htm (accessed 27 October 2008). I am grateful to Marilyn Glanfield for locating this.
2. *Newswatch*, 14 June 1999, p. 13.
3. *This Day*, 11 June, 10 July, and 11 September 1999; Johannes Harnischfeger, *Democratization and Islamic law: the Sharia conflict in Nigeria* (Frankfurt, 2008), pp. 120–1; *Africa Confidential*, 8 July 2005, p. 3.
4. *Africa Research Bulletin (Political)*, June 1999, p. 13578; *Tell*, 7 June 1999, p. 23.
5. *This Day*, 5 and 7 June 1999, 17 April 2000; *Newswatch*, 12 July 1999, pp. 16–17.
6. *Tell*, 27 September 1999, p. 27; *Weekly Trust*, 2 September 1999; *Vanguard*, 13 February 2007.
7. Pat Utomi, *To serve is to live: autobiographical reflections on the Nigerian condition* (revised edition, Ibadan, 2002), pp. 293–6; *This Day*, 8 June and 4 July 1999, 10 June 2001.
8. *Weekly Trust*, 2 July 1999; *This Day*, 30 June 2001.

9. *This Day*, 27 December 1999; John N. Paden, *Faith and politics in Nigeria: Nigeria as a pivotal state in the Muslim world* (Washington DC, 2008), pp. 44–5.
10. *This Day*, 10 June 2001; *Guardian*, 18 February 2007.
11. *Newswatch*, 11 December 2000, pp. 8–17; *Guardian*, 15 April 2002.
12. Festus Eriye in *This Day*, 19 March 2000.
13. *African Confidential*, 27 August 1999, p. 2; Lewis and Alemika, 'Seeking the democratic dividend', p. 2; *This Day*, 18 September 2002.
14. Obasanjo, *Standing tall*, p. 137.
15. Charles Gore and David Pratten, 'The politics of plunder: the rhetorics of power and disorder in southern Nigeria', *African Affairs*, 102 (2003), 216; *Guardian*, 5 July 2007; Attahiru Jega (ed.), *Identity transformation and identity politics under structural adjustment in Nigeria* (Stockholm, 2000), esp. pp. 20, 25, 62, 81, 107.
16. Rotimi T. Suberu, 'Religion and politics: a view from the South', in Diamond et al., *Transition*, p. 419; Tunde Babawale (ed.), *Urban violence, ethnic militias and the challenge of democratic consolidation in Nigeria* (Lagos, 2003), p. x.
17. Rotimi T. Suberu, 'Can Nigeria's new democracy survive?' *Current History*, May 2001, p. 209; Obasanjo, *Standing tall*, p. 79; Alice Hills, 'The dialectic of police reform in Nigeria', *Journal of Modern African Studies*, 46 (2008), 217; Practical Sampling International, 'Summary of results: round 3 Afrobarometer survey in Nigeria, 2005' (2007), p. 22, http://www.afrobarometer.org/Summary%20of%20Results/Round%203/nig-R3S0R-24jan07-final.pdf (accessed 26 August 2007); Godwin Onuoha, 'Contextualising the proliferation of small arms and light weapons in Nigeria's Niger Delta: local and global interactions', *African Security Review*, 15, 2 (2006), 108–14.
18. *Weekly Trust*, 27 October 2000.
19. *Weekly Trust*, 31 March 2000; J.O. Irukwu, *Nation building and ethnic organisation: the case of Ohanaeze in Nigeria* (Ibadan, 2007), p. 121; Ben Naanen, 'Oil-producing minorities and the restructuring of Nigerian federalism: the case of the Ogoni people', *Journal of Commonwealth and Comparative Politics*, 33 (1995), 60–2.
20. *Weekly Trust*, 14 January 2000; Isaac Olawale Albert, 'The myth, reality and challenges of Nigeria's reconciliation with *Ndigbo*', in Osaghae et al., *Nigerian Civil War*, p. 321. Oduduwa was the legendary Yoruba ancestor.
21. Obasanjo, *Standing tall*, p. 141; Festus Eriye in *This Day*, 2 June 2000; David Pratten, 'Introduction: the politics of protection: perspectives on vigilantism in Nigeria', *Africa*, 78 (2008), 5.
22. Rotimi Suberu, 'Federalism and the management of ethnic conflict: the Nigerian experience', in David Turton (ed.), *Ethnic federalism: the Ethiopian experience in comparative perspective* (Oxford, 2006), p. 67.
23. Afrobarometer, 'Violent social conflict and conflict resolution in Nigeria', Afrobarometer briefing paper no. 2 (2002), p. 4, http://www.afrobarometer.org/papers/AfrobriefNo2.pdf (accessed 26 August 2007).
24. J. Shola Omotola, 'Dissent and state excesses in the Niger Delta, Nigeria', *Studies in Conflict and Terrorism*, 32 (2009), 129–30; Isaac Boro, *The twelve-day revolution* (ed. T. Tebekaemi, Benin City, 1982); Civil Liberties Organisation, *Ogoni: trials and travails* (Lagos, 1996).
25. *This Day*, 16 January 1999; *Tell*, 18 January 1999, pp. 20–1; Augustine Ikelegbe, 'The perverse manifestation of civil society: evidence from Nigeria', *Journal of Modern African Studies*, 39 (2001), 12–13.
26. *This Day*, 9 February 1999.
27. *Newswatch*, 25 January 1999, p. 22, and 21 June 1999, pp. 18–22; *This Day*, 31 May 1999.
28. *Newswatch*, 28 June 1999, pp. 21–2.
29. *This Day*, 24 September and 1 November 1999; *Tell*, 8 November 1999, p. 14; below, p. 260.

30. *This Day*, 29 August 1999 and 6 January 2000; Obe, *New dawn*, vol. 2, pp. 211–12.
31. Human Rights Watch, 'Rivers and blood: guns, oil and power in Nigeria's Rivers State', Human Rights Watch briefing paper (2005), http://hrw.org/backgrounder/africa/nigeria0205/nigeria0205.pdf (accessed 23 September 2007); Terisa E. Turner and Leigh S. Brownhill, 'Why women are at war with Chevron: Nigerian subsistence struggles against the international oil industry', *Journal of Asian and African Studies*, 39 (2004), 64–76. See further below, p. 260.
32. Fasehun, *Frederick Fasehun*, pp. 160–1, 228–9, 244; Gani Adams, 'Politics and agenda of ethnic militias: the case of OPC', in Babawale, *Urban violence*, p. 100; Insa Nolte, 'Ethnic vigilantes and the state: the Oodua People's Congress in south-western Nigeria', *International Relations*, 21 (2007), 219–23; Wale Adebanwi, 'The carpenter's revolt: youth, violence and the reinvention of culture in Nigeria', *Journal of Modern African Studies*, 43 (2005), 348–59.
33. *This Day*, 8 December 1999; Adebanwi, 'Carpenter's revolt', pp. 343–4; Fourchard, 'New name', p. 43.
34. *Newswatch*, 22 March 1999, pp. 29–30; *This Day*, 25 July and 3 August 1999; Insa Nolte, *Obafemi Awolowo and the making of Remo: the local politics of a Nigerian nationalist* (Edinburgh, 2009), pp. 243–5.
35. *Newswatch*, 30 August 1999, p. 23; *This Day*, 26 November 1999; *Tell*, 31 January 2000, pp. 14, 31.
36. *Source*, 30 October 2000, pp. 10–15; *This Day*, 5 February 2002.
37. *Guardian*, 12 April and 1 November 2002; *This Day*, 19 April 2000, 21 October 2005; Nolte, 'Ethnic vigilantes', p. 227.
38. Human Rights Watch, 'The Bakassi Boys: the legitimization of murder and torture' (2002), p. 38, http://www.hrw.org/reports/2002/nigeria2/nigeria0502.pdf (accessed 30 October 2008).
39. Ibid., pp. 2, 9–11; Kate Meagher, 'Hijacking civil society: the inside story of the Bakassi Boys vigilante group of south-eastern Nigeria', *Journal of Modern African Studies*, 45 (2007), 89–106.
40. Ifeanyi Onyeonoru, 'Insecurity and the Bakassi Boys operation in eastern Nigeria', in Laurent Fourchard and Isaac Olawale Albert (ed.), *Sécurité, crime et ségrégation dans les villes d'Afrique de l'ouest du 19e siècle à nos jours* (Paris, 2003), p. 379; *This Day*, 4 August 2000 and 15 May 2001; Meagher, 'Hijacking', p. 108.
41. Harnischfeger, *Democratization*, p. 172; Meagher, 'Hijacking', p. 109; *Tell*, 19 August 2002, p. 36.
42. Meagher, 'Hijacking', pp. 109–10; *Daily Champion,* 8 December 2007.
43. *Newswatch,* 13 December 1999 p. 23, 5 June 2000 pp. 40–1, 21 November 2005 pp. 13–17, 19 December 2005 p. 32, and 3 July 2006 pp. 54–5; *This Day*, 3 September 2004; Kenneth Omeje, 'The ethno-cultural bogey and revival of centrifugal Ibo nationalism in Nigeria', *Journal of Social Development in Africa*, 23, 1 (January 2008), 97–104.
44. *Weekly Trust*, 25 December 1998.
45. Rotimi T. Suberu, 'The Supreme Court and federalism in Nigeria', *Journal of Modern African Studies*, 46 (2008), 462–5; *This Day*, 23 January 2002, 12 December 2002, and 18 February 2004; *Newswatch*, 4 April 1994, p. 24.
46. See, for example, Ousmane Kane, *Muslim modernity in postcolonial Nigeria* (Leiden, 2003).
47. Falola, *Violence*, pp. 179–92.
48. Jamil M. Abun-Nasr, 'Zur politischen Bedeutung der Berufungsgericht für die Muslime in Nigeria', *Die Welt des Islams*, 28 (1988), 51–3; Murray Last, 'The search for security in Muslim Northern Nigeria', *Africa*, 78 (2008), 60; Ostien in Soares, *Muslim-Christian encounters*, p. 249.
49. *This Day*, 6 October 1999, 25 March 2000, 2 February 2001; *Weekly Trust*, 8 October 1999.

50. Last, 'Search', pp. 51–3; *Weekly Trust*, 12 November 1999; *Hotline*, 14 August 1999.
51. *This Day*, 16 February 2000. For contrary evidence,. see *Newswatch*, 15 October 2001, p. 29.
52. Nigeria: Federal Office of Statistics, *Report of Nigeria living standards survey 2003/2004* (Abuja, 2004), p. 84.
53. *This Day*, 2 November 1999, 21 December 1999, 1 March 2000, 6 October 2001.
54. *This Day*, 1–3 and 9 March 2000; *Newswatch*, 13 March 2000, pp. 24, 27; Larry O. Enukara, 'Managing ethno-religious violence and area differentiation in Kaduna metropolis', in Yakubu et al., *Crisis*, vol. 2, pp. 625–30.
55. See above, p. 90.
56. *This Day*, 24 and 29 February and 1 March 2000.
57. *Newswatch*, 8 November 1999, p. 34, and 28 February 2000, p. 42; *Source*, 15 November 1999, p. 18.
58. *This Day*, 1 November 1999.
59. *This Day*, 2 and 28 November 1999; *Tell*, 15 November 1999, p. 18.
60. Robin Lustig, 'Obasanjo gives as good as he gets', 16 February 2002, http://news.bbc.co.uk/1/hi/world/africa/1824724.stm (accessed 15 September 2008); *West Africa*, 6 May 2002, p. 9.
61. *This Day*, 4 August 2000.
62. *This Day*, 13 March 2000; Andrew Ubaka Iwobi, 'Tiptoeing through a constitutional minefield: the great Sharia controversy in Nigeria', *Journal of African Law*, 48 (2004), 152–63.
63. *Newswatch*, 20 March 2000, p. 27; *This Day*, 22 March and 2 April 2000; *West Africa*, 20 March 2000, p. 18; Suberu, 'Supreme Court', p. 477.
64. Victor E. Dike, *Nigeria and the politics of unreason: a study of the Obasanjo regime* (London, 2003), p. 48; *Newswatch*, 13 March 2000, p. 29; *Hotline*, 26 December 1999.
65. *Punch*, 9 February 2009.
66. *West Africa*, 8 April 2002, p. 14.
67. Susan A. O'Brien, 'La charia contestée: démocratie, débat et diversité musulmane dans les "états charia" du Nigeria', *Politique Africaine*, 106 (2007), 58–65; *This Day*, 28–29 June 2000; Fatima L. Adamu, 'Gender, *hisba* and the enforcement of morality in Northern Nigeria', *Africa*, 78 (2008), 140.
68. *Tell*, 29 October 2001, pp. 32–6, and 5 November 2001, p. 51.
69. Human Rights Watch, 'The "Miss World riots": continued impunity for killings in Kaduna' (2003), http://www.hrw.org/reports/2003/nigeria0703/nigeria0703.pdf (accessed 30 September 2007).
70. Human Rights Watch, 'Jos: a city torn apart' (2001), http://www.hrw.org/reports/2001/nigeria/nigeria1201.pdf (accessed 30 September 2007); Adam Higazi, 'Violence urbaine et politique à Jos (Nigeria), de la période coloniale aux élections de 2007', *Politique Africaine*, 106 (2007), 69–91.
71. Adam Higazi, 'Social mobilization and collective violence : vigilantes and militias in the lowlands of Plateau State, Central Nigeria', *Africa*, 78 (2008), 107–35; Human Rights Watch, 'Revenge in the name of religion: the cycle of violence in Plateau and Kano States' (2005), pp. 1–40, http//hrw.org/reports/2005/nigeria0505/nigeria0505text.pdf (accessed 30 September 2007); below, p. 261.
72. Human Rights Watch, 'Revenge', p. 73.
73. Ibid., p. 45; Falola, *Violence*, p. 209.
74. Taiye O. Adewuyi, 'Spatial and temporal analysis of ethno-religious conflicts in Northern Nigeria', in Yakubu et al., *Crisis*, vol. 1, pp. 298, 301; Matthew Kirwin, 'Popular perceptions of Shar'ia law in Nigeria', Afrobarometer briefing paper no. 58 (2009), pp. 5–10, http://www.afrobarometer.org/papers/AfrobriefNo58.pdf (accessed 16 May 2009).
75. Major accounts of this incident are: Human Rights Watch, 'The destruction of Odi and rape in Choba, December 22, 1999', Human Rights Watch background report,

December 1999, http://www.hrw.org/press/1999/doc/nibgl299.htm (accessed 23 September 2007); Edem Effiong, 'The Odi killings', in World Organisation Against Torture, 'Hope betrayed? A report on impunity and state-sponsored violence in Nigeria' (2002), pp. 69–82, http://www.omct.org/pdf/Nigeriareport0802.pdf (accessed 12 October 2008).

76. *This Day*, 1 December 1999. Effiong's account claims the troops were ordered to shoot anything that moved. See also *Insider Weekly*, 21 July 2003, pp. 21–2.
77. Malu in *Newswatch*, 17 June 2002, p. 53. See also *Source*, 6 December 1999, p. 20.
78. Environmental Rights Action, *A blanket of silence: images of the Odi genocide* (n.p., 2002), pp. 13, 18–20.
79. Ibid., p. 7.
80. *This Day*, 26 January 2000.
81. *This Day*, 30 December 1999; Environmental Rights Action, *Blanket of silence*, p. 9; *Newswatch*, 9 April 2001, p. 39; *Post Express*, 21 September 2002.
82. Shagari, *Beckoned*, p. 324.
83. *Tell*, 5 November 2001, pp. 35–43, and 21 January 2002, p. 33.
84. Ukoha Ukiwo, 'Political anxiety and violence in Nigeria: the politicisation of Bakassi Boys in Eastern Nigeria', in Babawale, *Urban violence*, p. 142.
85. *Africa Research Bulletin (Political)*, November 2001, p. 14642; Ijeoma Nwachukwu and Isioma Ojugbana, 'The Benue killings', in World Organisation Against Torture, 'Hope betrayed?' pp. 156, 164; Philip C. Aka, 'Nigeria since May 1999: understanding the paradox of civil rule and human rights violation under President Olusegun Obasanjo', *San Diego International Law Journal*, 4 (2003), 254; *Post Express*, 19 October 2002.
86. *Guardian*, 28 October 2001.
87. *Newswatch*, 11 February 2002, pp. 45–8; *Guardian*, 31 January 2002, quoted in Dike, *Nigeria*, p. 162.
88. Adekeye Adebajo, 'Hegemony on a shoestring: Nigeria's post-Cold War foreign policy', in Adebajo and Mustapha, *Gulliver's troubles*, p. 6.
89. *Guardian*, 18 May 2001; Democratic Socialist Movement, *Nigeria: civil rule in danger* (Lagos, 2002), p. 15; Falae, *Way forward*, p. 130.
90. *Newswatch*, 10 July 2000, p. 21.
91. *Guardian*, 22 June 2002; *This Day*, 24 June 2000.
92. *Newswatch*, 15 February 2009, reported that Amnesty International had identified at least 22 during the previous decade. For Obasanjo's wish to eradicate them, see *Daily Trust*, 1 August 2003.
93. *Punch*, 23 June 2008.
94. Human Rights Watch, '"Rest in pieces": police torture and death in custody in Nigeria' (2005), p. 1, http://www.hrw.org/sites/default/files/reports/nigerian0705.pdf (accessed 26 December 2008); Bronwen Manby, 'Principal human rights challenges', in Rotberg, *Crafting*, p. 184.

16
Salvaging the Economy

During the twenty years since Obasanjo had left power in 1979, some 75 million Nigerians had been born and 25 million had died.[1] Total population numbers were contentious but may have increased between 1979 and 1999 from about 70 million to 120 million.[2] A continuing high birthrate more than compensated for child mortality 60% higher than the average in low-income countries.[3] When Obasanjo took office in 1999, half of all Nigerians were no more than seventeen years old.[4] The problems facing the regime can be understood only against this demographic background.

A major reason for high mortality was deplorable public health services, which the World Health Organisation ranked 187th among its 191 member states in 2000–1.[5] During the 1990s public health expenditure had absorbed about 0.2% of GDP, the lowest proportion in the world, equalled only by Myanmar. In 1998 only an estimated 35% of the population had access to modern health services, some 80% of which were located in the South.[6] The proportion of children aged 12–23 months who were fully immunised fell between 1990 and 1999 from 30 to 17%. In the latter year, 46% of children were judged to be malnourished.[7] Obasanjo's regime more than doubled the proportion of federal expenditure allocated to health and launched a new primary health care campaign, appropriating local government funds with the aim of building a clinic in each of the 774 local government areas.[8]

The most urgent health problem facing the new government was the AIDS epidemic. First diagnosed in Nigeria in 1985, HIV was recognised as a major health risk six years later, but the national programme formulated then was aborted by the indifference of Abacha's regime. In 1996 Nigeria had twice as many HIV-positive people as Uganda but spent only 5% of Uganda's AIDS budget.[9] Obasanjo had been quick to recognise the epidemic's danger and his election in 1999 coincided with a new urgency aroused by a survey at ante-natal clinics suggesting that 5.4% of those attending were infected, thereby exceeding the 5% figure at which a mass epidemic on the southern African scale was feared to be inevitable. An American intelligence report predicted that by 2010 prevalence would have increased to 18–26%. One of Obasanjo's first actions after election was to demand a situation report. He then appointed a Presidential Committee on AIDS, under his chairmanship, and a National Action Committee to prepare and implement an emergency plan for the period 2000–3. This stressed publicity, training, counselling, testing, and control of blood products.[10] In January 2002, once cheap antiretroviral drugs became avail-

200

able, the government launched a small programme that was extended in subsequent years, with massive external funding, to treat some 170,000 patients at the end of 2007, although that was only 25% of those needing treatment.[11] Rather than adult prevalence rapidly increasing, the first national survey in 2007 showed it to be only 3.6%. Some doubted this figure, but a public opinion survey in 2003 rated the government's handling of the AIDS epidemic as its most satisfactory performance.[12]

A second reason for high mortality was poverty. As Obasanjo insisted, Nigerians vastly exaggerated their country's wealth, especially its wealth from oil, which even at the high prices of 2002 earned only $129 per Nigerian per year – less than a quarter of Angola's figure – because Nigeria's population was so large. Measured at purchasing power parity, Nigerian income per person was only half the sub-Saharan average at that time.[13] Very unreliable figures released two days before Obasanjo's inauguration suggested that during the previous twenty years the proportion of the population earning less than 66% of average national income had more than doubled.[14] He reacted with a hasty scheme to pay N3,500 (about $35) a month to 200,000 people, evenly distributed among the states, to undertake routine tasks like sweeping and mending roads. This 'generated a deluge of accusations of shoddiness and corruption' before it was replaced by a National Poverty Eradication Programme focused on youth employment, rural infrastructure, social welfare services, and conservation.[15] This probably had some limited impact, but Obasanjo retained a rural Yoruba view of able-bodied poverty as an avoidable consequence of idleness. In 2004 he declared 'that there is no poverty in Nigeria, that in the rural areas, especially the rural areas, nobody wakes up without knowing where his next meal would come from.'[16]

Urban poverty was certainly more conspicuous. Town populations were still growing at over 5 per cent per year, with 43% of Nigerians living in towns of over 20,000 people in 1999.[17] The population of Lagos State (effectively the city and its suburbs) increased from 5,725,116 in 1991 to 9,113,605 in 2006. Overcrowding in the city may have worsened slightly between 1973 and about 2002 from 3.5 to 3.8 persons per room. Obasanjo called it a jungle city, unfit for human occupation.[18] Surveys in 2001 and 2003 found that some 20% of adult Nigerians were unemployed and actively seeking work. Unemployment was especially common among secondary school leavers, but the government's attempts to create employment for them were frustrated by lack of funds.[19] Unemployment certainly contributed to high levels of violence and fear. In 2001, nearly 40% of those surveyed countrywide felt unsafe in their homes, 25% had suffered a crime, and 75% reported violent conflict in their communities.[20]

Such were the problems facing the new president. To meet them and to make Nigerian the great country that he believed it could become, he had first to restore the economy, which one adviser compared to 'a post-conflict economy' such as she had seen in Kampuchea.[21] In a telling comparison, whereas in 1965 Nigeria's per capita GDP had slightly exceeded that of Indonesia – a similarly populous oil-producing state – in 2000 the Nigerian figure was less than 20% of Indonesia's.[22] The estimated $350 billion (at 1995 prices) that the Nigerian state had earned from oil during the intervening 35 years had not improved the people's average wealth, which had probably slightly declined.[23] Since 1979 the currency had lost over 99% of its value against the American dollar. Inflation had averaged nearly 30% per year during the 1990s and contributed largely to the growth of poverty. The level of external debt was disputed but was in the region of $30 billion, roughly 75% of

GNP.[24] By comparison, it has been estimated that between 1970 and 1996 nearly three times as much ($86.76 billion) had been exported from Nigeria, although not necessarily by Nigerians.[25] One consequence was a very low level of investment. In 1999 gross capital formation was only 5.4% of GDP, almost entirely in the oil sector.[26] Agricultural production had held up relatively well, but the contribution of manufacturing to GDP had fallen between 1980 and 1999 from 8.4 to 5.5%. In the latter year only an estimated 32% of manufacturing capacity was utilised.[27] One reason was a bungled entry into the World Trade Organisation that exposed Nigeria's textile industry to imported competition and halved its output during the 1990s. Another was the decay of infrastructure, especially electricity supply and transport. The railway system had lost most of its traffic and the national air and shipping lines had virtually ceased to exist.[28]

Analysts gave many different reasons for this economic failure. Some blamed Nigeria's ethnic divisions and fractious politics, which prevented the stability and consistent policy direction that development required. Many pointed to oil market fluctuations, which gave Nigeria one of the most volatile economies in the world, and to the perverse effects of oil dependence, which discouraged other forms of enterprise while encouraging governmental extravagance, rent-seeking, corruption, and rural neglect.[29] Others held that most of Nigeria's oil revenue had simply been wasted, either because the country lacked the institutions needed to absorb and utilise such revenues efficiently or because the development strategies adopted had been mistaken.[30] Industrialists blamed especially the country's hostile business environment, which required enterprises to invest heavily in power, transport, water, and other services that elsewhere were publicly provided.[31] Some economists denounced the state-dominated programme of heavy industrial and infrastructural investment pursued by regimes headed by Gowon, Obasanjo, and Shagari. Others blamed either Babangida's structural adjustment programme or his abandonment of it.[32] Many, in the aftermath of Abacha's death, denounced the late dictator's fluctuations of policy between state control and liberalisation, his continued military expenditure, his negligent administration, and his grotesque personal corruption.[33]

Obasanjo's attempt to grapple with these economic problems during his first presidential term was a failure. On taking office, he launched an 'economic rescue programme' designed to halve poverty and achieve 6–10% annual growth within four years. Moving away from his state-centred strategy of the 1970s, he ruled that the private sector was to lead growth, with government providing an enabling environment. Specific goals were to create five million jobs; foster agriculture, small enterprises, and house building; re-introduce universal basic education; and expand rural electrification, water supplies, and health facilities.[34] Despite criticism, the government also invited the IMF to review the economy and the resources needed to restore it. The two parties agreed on the need to fight corruption, achieve macroeconomic stability, gradually privatise state enterprises, regularise revenue allocation, and resolve the problems of the Niger Delta. The government resisted IMF pressure to abolish the subsidy on petrol prices and to float the naira, believing both would threaten stability, but in January 2000 the IMF made available a $1 billion stand-by loan, which enabled the government to enter debt rescheduling negotiations with its creditors.[35]

Yet just as Obasanjo's long-term plans were interrupted by ethnic and religious conflict, so the immediate economic problem in May 1999 was an economy 'in freefall', as the *Economist* magazine described it.[36] Late in 1998, owing to an Asian economic crisis, the world price of oil had fallen to $9 per barrel, its lowest price for 25 years. By May 1999 it had risen again to $16, but the price collapse had caused an unsustainable budget deficit, provoked further devaluation, increased inflation and interest rates, and created a foreign exchange crisis. Between January and May 1999, Nigeria's foreign reserves fell from $7.1 billion to $3.75 billion, with the help, it was believed, of corruption by the departing military.[37] Obasanjo's immediate priorities were therefore to prepare a supplementary budget to reduce expenditure by 20%[38] and to launch an attack on the corruption to which he, like most Nigerians, attributed much of the country's economic failure.

One of Obasanjo's first actions on taking office was to suspend all contracts and appointments made by Abdulsalami's government during 1999. The commission that investigated them recommended the cancellation of 1,684 of 4,072 contracts, 755 of 768 national awards, 19 of 576 licences, 107 of 111 approvals, and 50 of 807 appointments.[39] The most notorious military corruption, however, was Abacha's. The exact amount that he stole from the state is unknown, but it probably exceeded $3 billion.[40] His most spectacular fraud, in collaboration with other officials, was first to purchase for $500 million the $2.5 billion debt that Nigeria owed Russia for the Ajaokuta steelworks, then to pay himself the full sum from the Nigerian treasury. He also exploited the oil industry, including the $190 million that Elf Aquitaine admitted paying him.[41] Most was deposited in some 150 Western bank accounts. Recovering it was complicated and frustrating, but by May 2009 some $1.9 billion had been regained and the location of another $700 million was known.[42]

Although Obasanjo had been suspected of corruption when military head of state, nothing had been proved against him and he had certainly not exploited all the opportunities open to him. Out of office, he had become a fervent public critic of corruption, chairman of Transparency International's advisory panel, and an advocate of imitating Hong Kong's model of 'an anti-corruption agency that will have power to search, to seek and to recover both internally and externally'.[43] He presented his Anti-Corruption Bill to the National Assembly only a few days after taking office. Providing, among other things, for investigation of any officer apparently living above his means, it aroused fierce opposition as a weapon of potential tyranny:

> Not a worse military dictator would have thought of such a terrible anti-human rights and totalitarian bills where the property of citizens could be sold without warrant and without court order. Or their houses forcefully broken into and their property sold in their absence. Or their letters opened, telephone tapped and their houses searched in their absence, so that something could be planted to implicate them. No worse bill has ever been contemplated in Nigeria since independence.[44]

While Obasanjo 'agonised' and relations between the two branches of government soured, the National Assembly spent the next nine months formulating amendments designed to reduce the commission's powers, remove it from the president's political control, and provide machinery to investigate and indict the president and state governors. Obasanjo signed a compromise law on 13 June 2000 and inaugurated the Corrupt Practices and Other Related Offences Commission on 29 September. It prosecuted 39 cases during his first term. Among those it indicted was the Governor of Bayelsa State.[45] Yet it did not secure the conviction of any public official before the National Assembly emasculated it further in retaliation for investigating leading legislators. Dissatisfied with the commission's performance, Obasanjo inaugurated an additional Economic and Financial Crimes Commission in March 2003.[46]

The President claimed that his attack on corruption had broken the conspiracy of silence hitherto surrounding it among office-holders. His repeated insistence on his own honesty and his reported dismissal of a minister for accepting bribes probably did make corruption more discreet than it had been under Babangida and Abacha, but there is little reason to think that it became less widespread. In 2000 Transparency International declared Nigeria the most corrupt country in the world. A survey two years later found that almost all Nigerian firms paid bribes in some form.[47] At one extreme, an American oil firm was alleged to have paid Nigerian officials over $180 million in bribes to obtain the $6 billion contract to build a liquefied natural gas plant at Bonny, a task that the company was fully qualified and competitive to undertake.[48] At the other extreme, Obasanjo's regime did nothing to check the low-level corruption, commonly at state and local government level, that was the bane of ordinary Nigerians: policemen pocketing bribes at roadblocks, teachers demanding 'settlement' before granting school places, or nurses extorting payment from their patients.[49] As the regime's inability to tackle corruption became clear, so its public approval rating in this area fell between 2000 and 2003 from 64% to 24%. Potential investors agreed. 'Corruption has so distorted Nigeria's business and investment climate,' the London *Times* wrote in 2003, 'that only the brave or those already tainted would think of doing business there.'[50]

Obasanjo claimed that an important means of attacking corruption was to liberalise the economy in order to reduce the opportunities for rent-taking by officials. Always sensitive to the dominant economic orthodoxy of the moment, he recognised, like other African leaders of this period, that he could not openly contest the 'Washington consensus' of fiscal discipline, free markets, and privatisation. 'I am a believer in market efficiency', he declared in 2001, 'having witnessed, personally and as twice Head of State of my country, how public sector mismanagement can destroy and reverse the fortunes of a nation.' Like many converts, however, Obasanjo also had a hankering after old ways. 'Though he professes trust of markets,' the economist Pat Utomi observed, 'his nature, his exposure and his passionate commitment to saving Nigeria himself inclines him to believing in government as the great source of moving society forward.'[51] Obasanjo would retain this ambivalence until the end of his career. Moreover, his regime embraced many economic viewpoints, from the market liberalism of Phillip Asiodu and the Central Bank to the economic nationalism of northern leaders like Adamu Ciroma and the lingering socialism of many legislators and trade unionists.[52] The result was much confusion of policy. 'There does not seem to be any cohesion in the management of the economy', the Lagos *Guardian* complained in June 2001. 'There are just too many players from the Vice President to ministers to advisers to the Central Bank each exerting their own influence.'[53] Above all, Obasanjo had not yet assembled a group of skilled economists to replace the Super Permsecs of the early 1970s. In a revealing incident while visiting Washington just before taking office, he was nonplussed when the American Treasury Secretary asked him to introduce his economic team.[54]

On the surface, Obasanjo continued to enjoy his legendary good fortune. From its rock-bottom price of $9 per barrel shortly before his election, oil rose in response to the second Gulf War crisis to a peak of $37 in late 2000 and continued at high levels for the rest of his presidency.[55] In 2000 the industry employed only some 100,000 people but provided 98.7% of Nigeria's export earnings. Of these the

Nigerian state took some 80–90%, compared to an average of only about 50% in West Africa generally.[56] The government also planned to increase output from the current two million barrels per day to three million by 2003 and four million by 2010, abandoning its old-fashioned joint venture agreements with the oil companies, by which the government had to provide a share of development capital that it had difficulty in raising, in favour of production sharing contracts, by which the companies would provide all the capital in return for a larger share of output. The additional production would come from the first deepwater offshore fields, discovered in 1996 and developed from 2000.[57] Even more promising were the prospects for liquefied natural gas, which was first exported in October 1999 from the plant at Bonny, designed to became the largest industrial project ever undertaken in Africa. Obasanjo hoped that by 2003 gas exports would rival the value of oil.[58]

Aided by rising oil prices, Obasanjo's supplementary budget of August 1999 temporarily reduced expenditure, converted a looming deficit of 8% of GDP into a near annual balance, reduced inflation to 8%, added some 70% to the foreign reserves by February 2000, and checked the fall of the naira. GDP grew by 2.8% during 1999, almost equalling population growth.[59] In November 1999, however, with oil prices still increasing, Nigerians demanding a 'democracy dividend', and the IMF watching him intently, the hankering to spend windfall profits proved as irresistible as in the 1970s. Obasanjo's 'People's Budget' for 2000 proposed to increase expenditure by 38%, reduce import duties on many raw materials and essential goods, abolish taxes on agricultural inputs, finance universal basic education, and spend heavily on police, health, electric power, steel production, and poverty reduction. The National Assembly added another N100 billion ($1 billion) to the proposed expenditure. Although the government was already struggling to absorb a threefold increase in the minimum wage of public servants decreed by Abdulsalami, Obasanjo courted labour support by announcing a further doubling of the minimum wage at a trade union rally on May Day 2000. 'At no time in our country's history', he declared at this time, 'have we been as well placed as we are today, to take the decisive and positive steps that will transform Nigeria into what God destined it to be – a land of opportunity, equity, progress and prosperity for all.'[60]

The economy almost immediately overheated. The Economist Intelligence Unit estimated annual inflation at 19% in 2001. Between 1999 and 2002 the naira lost about 20% of its free market value. A government theoretically dedicated to liberalisation increased its expenditure as a share of GDP from 29% in 1997 to 50% in 2001.[61] In July 2000 the IMF had warned that government was overspending and should save its windfall oil profits. A year later the Central Bank added its demand for a tighter control on spending. It repeated the warning in 2002.[62]

At the same time that Obasanjo was learning that Nigeria could not spend its way to rapid recovery, he was also learning the difficulty of rehabilitating its units of production. Among these, he focused first on the downstream sector of the oil industry and the supply of petroleum. In 1999 Nigeria had four oil refineries, all state-owned and built between 1965 and 1989. Their nominal capacity was 445,000 barrels per day. Nigeria's consumption was about 300,000 barrels per day, but because the refineries were old and ill-maintained, their output was commonly well below consumption needs.[63] The balance had to be imported at international prices, which successive governments subsidised. The IMF regarded abolition of this subsidy as a priority in displaying the financial probity needed for debt relief.

Yet repeated attempts since 1986 to reduce or remove the subsidy had been resisted violently by southern townsmen concerned with transport costs and the price of kerosene for cooking. One such protest had given Abacha the opportunity to depose Shonekan. Subsidising petrol also encouraged wasteful use, benefited the rich (who used more of it), enriched smugglers who transported it to neighbouring countries with higher prices, and deterred investors from building refineries or buying the existing ones, which were anyway unattractive because three were in the turbulent Niger Delta. Whenever a refinery or the importing or distribution system broke down, long queues formed outside petrol stations, an infuriating experience in an oil-producing country.[64]

Obasanjo was determined to abolish the petrol subsidy by raising prices (currently N20 per litre) to commercial rates, but that was to challenge the labour movement, which, with the restoration of democracy, had resurfaced as the Nigerian Labour Congress (NLC) under the presidency of Adams Oshiomhole, an astute and dedicated trade unionist opposed to economic liberalisation. After sharing a platform with Oshiomhole in May 2000 to announce the doubling of the government's minimum wage, Obasanjo raised the petrol price to N30 per litre with virtually no prior consultation, doubtless for fear of provoking panic buying and hoarding. The NLC called a general strike from 8 June. After meeting the union, Obasanjo reduced the price to N25, probably expecting the compromise to be acceptable. He had underestimated public anger. Even the PDP denounced the price increase, leading Obasanjo to talk of returning to his farm, until Atiku dissuaded him. Oshiomhole, holding that the solution was for the government to make the refineries work or build new ones and refine Nigerian oil obtained at local cost, continued the strike. It ended at 4.00 a.m. on 13 June with an agreed price of N22. 'Take a naira or two', boasted Oshiomhole, now a popular hero. 'Obasanjo's fuel fiasco' damaged more than the President's esteem; it established him in the public mind, for the first time, as an enemy of the poor.[65]

As targets of public anger, petrol queues were rivalled by power cuts. Nigeria's electricity system had suffered even more than its refineries from nearly two decades of military neglect. Whereas budgetary allocations to the power sector during Obasanjo's military regime between 1976 and 1979 had averaged $271 million per year, the average between 1990 and 1999 had been $12 million. No power station or transmission line had been built during that decade, despite population growth and urbanisation.[66] At Obasanjo's inauguration in May 1999, some 30% of households had access to electricity. The installed public generating capacity was 5,876 megawatts (MW), but only 1,600MW was being produced. Peak demand was variously estimated at 2,200–3,000MW.[67] Aging distribution lines increased the breakdowns that interrupted industrial production and made Nigeria the world's largest market for private generators. Commercial firms provided about 66% of their own electricity, at about three times the public price, some not even bothering to connect their factories to the national grid. Almost all regarded power supply as the greatest single obstacle to growth.[68] In addition, although electricity was heavily subsidised, only half of it was paid for and the Nigerian Electrical Power Authority (NEPA) was owed huge sums in unpaid bills, to which might be added many townspeople who had tapped into power lines illegally.[69]

Misled by his officials, the elderly Bola Ige, who had chosen the Ministry of Power and Steel, vowed to halve power cuts within six months. Instead Obasanjo removed him after a year and appointed a technical board to rehabilitate existing installations where possible, encourage independent power producers to instal emergency plants, and prepare NEPA for privatisation, promising to raise output to 4,000MW by the end of 2001.[70] Although theoretical capacity did reach that level, repeated breakdown of worn-out equipment reduced average output during 2003 to about 2,400MW. Budgetary allocations rose to $225 million in 2000 and $447 million in 2001.[71] Late in 2001 Obasanjo opened the first new power station for twelve years. Contracts for four more were finalised during 2002, designed to use the natural gas that Nigeria currently burned away uselessly.[72] A long-term plan based on the same fuel source was also developed, but privatisation was still impracticable and discussion of it deterred public investment.[73] As Obasanjo's adviser later admitted, it took the regime five years to understand the power sector and devise a workable strategy for it.[74]

The iron and steel industry was in even worse condition. Construction of the giant integrated steelworks at Ajaokuta had been delayed repeatedly by lack of funds. By 1999 the first phase was said to be 98% complete, but the unfinished elements included the blast furnace and almost all the transport network to supply it. It had cost nearly N1,000 billion ($10 billion), had some 4,500 workers on its payroll, had produced only a tiny quantity of metal in time for the 1983 election, and was reckoned to need another N200 billion ($2 billion) to put it into operation. In the meantime the completed sections rusted quietly in the sun.[75] Like all his predecessors, Obasanjo vowed to complete the project, but he refused to spend new money on it until the completion of a technical audit, following which the complex would be prepared for privatisation. By 2003 the government was close to signing a contract with an American company to rehabilitate and complete the project and run it for ten years. Privatisation was also the hoped-for fate of the smaller Delta Steel Plant, which had been virtually moribund since 1996.[76]

Privatisation was the panacea of Obasanjo's new government, adopted with the same lack of discrimination – although probably not the same enthusiasm – as state ownership twenty years before. Despite earlier privatisation under Babangida, in 1999 the federal government still owned 588 public enterprises. They contributed at least 40% of GDP, but none made a true profit, they accounted for over 55% of the external debt, and they imposed an annual burden of N200–300 billion ($2–3 billion) on the economy.[77] In July 1999 Obasanjo inaugurated a National Council on privatisation, headed by Vice-President Atiku, and outlined a three-stage programme to sell first its portfolio of quoted stocks (chiefly in cement, banking, and oil marketing companies), then enterprises in competitive markets (including hotels and paper, sugar, fertiliser, and vehicle assembly plants), and finally (and perhaps only partially) the major utilities: electricity, telecommunications, airways, and refineries. The objective would be to spread ownership as widely as possible among Nigerians without losing operating expertise. The government rejected World Bank pressure to privatise the oil industry.[78]

The first phase, with competitive bidding, began in December 1999 and quickly ran into two difficulties: local opposition to the acquisition of assets by Nigerians from other regions (notably the Benue Cement Company by the Kano-based entrepreneur, Aliko Dangote) and suspicion that those controlling the divesture were themselves acquiring assets through 'fronts'. Nevertheless, progress was made with the first two stages of privatisation, although too slow to satisfy Obasanjo's impatience.[79] The major problem was the utilities, with their antiquated equipment, sprawling distribution networks, and parlous finances. For example, the Nigerian

Telecommunications Corporation (NITEL), the monopoly operator of Nigeria's notorious telephone system, was reported to have over N40 billion ($400 million) missing from its pension fund. It was, nevertheless, the first utility to find a buyer willing to purchase 51% of its equity, in November 2001, only for the sale to collapse four months later when the bidder failed to raise the money. By the end of Obasanjo's first term, two other deals, for the fertiliser company and a moribund aluminium smelter, had fallen through for the same reason. Ajaokuta seemed to have found a bidder, but nobody wanted the oil refineries, while the electricity system was not remotely ready for privatisation. The programme had been partially successful, but the obstacles remaining helped to explain the increasing desperation with which Obasanjo would approach the issue during his second term.[80]

An opinion survey in 2000 found that only 35% of Nigerians favoured privatisation. On the larger question of preference between a market-oriented economy and more state involvement, opinion in 2001 was split down the middle. Nigerians keenly supported private property rights (85% in 2001) and a majority (although not in the North) believed that people should be free to earn as much as they could, but there was also a strong feeling that the government should regulate markets and be the main provider of services and jobs. In 2000 only 40% were familiar with structural adjustment, but a majority felt that economic reforms benefited only a fortunate minority. Some 49% said the government should change its economic policies. Yet Nigerians were not only resilient but remarkably optimistic about their own economic prospects.[81] The proportion who said they accepted present hardships for the future benefits they would bring rose between 2000 and 2001 from 45% to 65% and was still at 53% in 2003.[82] The investigators concluded in 2001 'that if the Nigerian government decides to persist with policies of economic liberalization, it can do so without evoking a popular backlash.'[83] If Obasanjo knew of this, it may have encouraged him. If the findings had been otherwise, they would certainly not have changed his course.

That course had severe costs. Its worst victim was manufacturing industry. Obasanjo had hoped to increase its contribution to GDP from 5.5% in 1999 to 12% in 2003, but in fact it remained at 5–7%, although of a larger GDP owing to the intervening increase in oil prices.[84] Official figures claimed that industrial capacity utilisation rose between 1999 and 2003 from 29–36% to 50–60%, but since there was no significant increase in real output, this probably indicated a reduced estimate of capacity, perhaps especially in the textile industry where output continued to decline and there was a drastic reduction in enterprises and employment. Electricity supply problems, World Trade Organisation rules, and competition from imported (often smuggled) goods contributed to this, especially after China joined the WTO in December 2001.[85] Obasanjo declared early in his presidency that light industry must be rehabilitated even if it meant contravening WTO rules, so that the IMF criticised the government's continuing industrial protection,[86] but indigenous industry stagnated and was not compensated by success in attracting foreign investment, except in the oil and gas industries, because manufacturers, unlike oil companies, could not afford to construct their own supporting infrastructure.

The determined optimism of Obasanjo's mid-term economic report in May 2001 met scepticism among Nigerians but more encouragement from international observers, the World Bank's resident representative commenting that 'much more has happened for the good in the past two years than had happened in the previous ten years or so.'[87] There were some grounds for optimism. For the first time, Obasanjo had assembled a team of younger Nigerians with the skills and experience to manage the economy, recruiting them astutely from expatriate Nigerians less likely to be captured by local interest groups. The central figure was Ngozi Okonjo-Iweala, an American-trained economist who had spent eighteen years with the World Bank, working in West Africa, the Middle East, and East Asia. In 2000 she took leave of absence to become Obasanjo's Economic Adviser, head the Economic Policy Coordinating Committee, and set up a Debt Management Office – run by another World Bank official, Mansur Muktar – which would prepare for the anticipated negotiations. 'It is going to take some time to rebuild', Okonjo-Iweala insisted in August 2000, '… it is going to take us two to three years to lay the foundation for the economy to begin to take off.' In the meantime, Nigerians had to be patient:

> There is a time when you can not really afford too much politics and where you have to put economists to do the job first. Get the people who can get you out of the doldrums. And when they have done that, you can then put other people, but this is only when the nation has been set on a path that is irreversible … then you can afford to play.[88]

Another member of the new team – and another member of the Redeemed Christian Church of God – was Obiageli Ezekwesili, also American trained and recruited from Transparency International as Special Assistant for the Budget, with the task of setting up a Budget Monitoring and Price Intelligence Unit (generally known as the Due Process Unit) to purge government contracts of waste and corruption. Between 2001 and 2003 the unit was said to have saved N60 billion (nearly $500 million).[89]

The economic team emphasised especially the damage that the economy had suffered from fluctuating oil prices. The IMF had pressed this point on Obasanjo early in his presidency. His budgets made some provision against it by estimating revenue according to a benchmark oil price set somewhat below the expected price. Any revenue above that was to be paid into a stabilisation fund that became known as the Excess Crude Account, available to supplement revenue when the oil price was low.[90] In itself, however, this was no guarantee against the overspending seen in 2000–1. The economic team insisted that strict adherence to such a 'fiscal rule' was essential to economic stability.[91] Yet the strategy also had political implications, as politicians quickly realised, for the Excess Crude Account could and did become a discretionary fund in executive hands, much like those operated by Babangida and Abacha. Moreover, the constitution required that federal revenues should be shared among the federal, state, and local governments. Conflict was inevitable if a president claimed that the Excess Crude Account, being a reserve fund, should not be distributed. As Ezekwesili commented, 'By the time that the financial team appreciated that the government could not continue to spend all of its revenues, it was difficult to explain the situation to the state governors who resented federal control.'[92] Nevertheless, decoupling the economy from the oil market was an essential step towards recovery.

There were also more tangible steps during the latter part of Obasanjo's first term. Agriculture, still the core of the economy, showed modest but steady growth, averaging an annual 6.1% increase in production between 2001 and 2005.[93] OPEC quotas restricted oil production to about two million barrels per day, rather than the three million that Obasanjo desired, but the industry entered a new phase when the first deepwater oil was pumped in April 2003. A third unit was added to the liquefied natural gas plant at Bonny, two more were planned, and negotiations to construct a second plant in the Delta at Brass neared completion.[94] In January 2002, when Obasanjo partially deregulated the downstream oil sector and raised the petrol price from N22 to N26 per litre, the NLC's predictable general strike collapsed when the courts declared it illegal.[95]

The most remarkable economic success of the new millennium came not from the massive equipment of the oil industry but from the pocket-sized mobile phone. Whereas in 1999 only about half of NITEL's 400,000 land lines worked and Nigeria had the lowest telephone density to population in the world apart from Mongolia and Afghanistan, by the end of 2004 over 7,000,000 Nigerians were cell phone subscribers. The new technology, pioneered largely by South African firms, accelerated business activity, created a mass of jobs in call centres, became a means of status competition, and facilitated both political organisation and rioting. Obasanjo managed the innovation skilfully and took the credit for it.[96] It had a parallel in another success story: the cheap *okada* motorcycle taxis that carried passengers through the traffic jams of Nigerian cities. The mass of small-scale manufacturing enterprises in the south-east, producing anything from shoes to motor parts, were a third example of the scale of operation that worked best in Obasanjo's Nigeria and deserved more attention than he gave it. The Nollywood video industry was a fourth.[97]

A popular enterprise to which Obasanjo was profoundly committed was universal primary education, which he believed 'would break the cycle of poverty for individuals and every community'.[98] His introduction of it in 1976 had greatly increased enrolment, but after 1979 the programme decayed under the pressure of population growth, pupil numbers, and financial decline, especially because the new federal constitution made it the responsibility of state and local governments. Although many different figures were quoted, a household survey in 1995 found that 63% of children aged 6–11 were enrolled in primary schools. Four years later Obasanjo launched a programme of universal basic education, compulsory for all children aged 6–15, recognising that it would take time to implement.[99] That caution was justified, for although in 2003 the government claimed that some 76% of children of primary age were at school, household survey data showed no change since 1995. By 2007 some 8–10 million school age children – especially rural girls from poor families – were still not at school, with proportions in the North said to be the highest in the world. Although there were areas of real progress, the quality of education was often poor.[100]

As a whole, economic growth during Obasanjo's first term was disappointing, only keeping pace with the growth of population and falling slightly from 3.5% per year in 2001 and 2002 to 3.0% in 2003.[101] This scarcely satisfied Nigerian expectations at a time of relatively high oil prices. In December 1999, 84% of those interviewed had expressed satisfaction with Obasanjo's performance, a figure that had fallen to 72% by 2001. In September 2003 (after the election of that year) it was only 39%.[102]

The President, too, had reason for dissatisfaction. His most cherished goal, to negotiate debt reduction, had not been achieved. The amount of debt was itself disputed: in August 2001 Nigeria put it at $28.42 billion, of which $22.04 billion was owed to the governments of developed countries who made up the so-called Paris Club, the largest creditor being Britain. The rest was owed to commercial (London Club) or multilateral creditors. During Obasanjo's first term, the budget generally provided about $1.5 billion per year for debt service, which was barely half of the sum due, so that the external debt continued to increase, reaching $35.9 billlion in 2004.[103] Even $1.5 billion was three times the federal education budget and nine times the federal health budget in 2000, so that Obasanjo could insist in almost every speech to international audiences that Nigeria's debts were unpayable and endangered both its economy and democracy.[104]

The creditors were not impressed. Canada, Italy, and the United States cancelled Nigeria's debts, but they were small.[105] The major creditors insisted that Nigeria was too well endowed to be entitled to substantial debt cancellation. Instead, they would consider only rescheduling and made that dependent on the government meeting conditions laid down by the IMF.[106] The standby credit secured in January 2000 permitted negotiations with the Paris Club and a rescheduling that fixed annual service payments at $1.7 billion. It did not grant any debt remission.[107] Further concessions required continued IMF approval, but in 2001 Nigeria failed to meet its numerous conditions.[108] Obasanjo expressed his frustration at a United Nations Conference on Financing for Development in March 2002:

> Since coming into office, almost three years ago, I have tirelessly toured the world, and especially donor nations, with one overriding objective: to obtain tangible relief from the crushing debt overhang burden built up in two decades of mismanagement and corruption. I was encouraged to do so by many world leaders, from whom I obtained sympathetic statements and promises of support for Nigeria's new dawn of democracy. Today, I must be candid with all of you: despite warm words of encouragement and sympathy, I have been unable to obtain even a single cent of debt relief that could be re-allocated for the crying needs of my people.[109]

As he spoke, the National Assembly increased proposed expenditure in the 2002 budget and Nigeria withdrew from IMF monitoring, rather than see the IMF withdraw it for failure to meet what Ciroma called its 'narrowly defined macro-economic targets'. 'Because of political fragility and since Nigerians are new to the practice of democracy', he added, 'the government needs to come up with approaches for securing the support of a majority of the National Assembly and the people of Nigeria on its macroeconomic targets.'[110] This drew nationalist applause, but it was a tactical step that alarmed both Nigerian professionals and Western creditors.[111] Formal ties with the IMF were renewed on 1 October 2002, but the two sides agreed to suspend discussion of debt relief until after the elections in April 2003.[112] In this, the centrepiece of his economic strategy, Obasanjo's first term had failed.

NOTES

1. World Bank, *World development report*, 1990, p. 230, quoted a birthrate of 47 per thousand and a death-rate of 15 per thousand in 1988.
2. Ibid., 2000/1, p. 279, estimated the population in 1980 at 71,100,000 and in 1999 at 123,900,000. The 1991 census (probably an undercount) showed 88,992,220; that of 2006 showed 140,431,790. See Nigeria: National Population Commission, *1991 population census of the Federal Republic of Nigeria: analytical report at the national level* (Abuja, 1998), p. 25; *Newswatch*, 15 March 2009.

3. Ngozi Okonjo-Iweala and Philip Osafo-Kwaako, 'Nigeria's economic reforms: progress and challenges' (2007), p. 6, http://www.brook.edu/views/papers/20070323okonjo-iweala.htm (accessed 25 December 2007).
4. Phyllis J. Kanki and Oluroji Adeyi, 'Introduction', in Oluroji Adeyi, Phyllis J. Kanki, Oluwole Odutolu, and John A. Idoko (ed.), *AIDS in Nigeria: a nation on the threshold* (Cambridge MA, 2006), p. 9.
5. *Guardian*, 23 July 2001.
6. World Bank, *World development report*, 2000/1, p.287; Ernest Massiah, 'Determinants of STD/AIDS treatment behaviour in Northern Nigeria', *Scandinavian Journal of Development Alternatives and Area Studies*, 19, 2–3 (2000), 61.
7. 'National economic empowerment and development strategy (NEEDS)', in Hobson E. Nnebe (ed.), *Policies of the Federal Republic of Nigeria; the Obasanjo years (1999–2007)* (3 vols, Kaduna, 2006), vol. 2, p. 319; Economist Intelligence Unit, 'Country profile: Nigeria', 2001 (electronic resource).
8. Sally Hargreaves, 'Time to right the wrongs: improving basic health care in Nigeria', *Lancet*, 359 (2002), 2031; Economist Intelligence Unit, 'Country profile: Nigeria', 2008; *Newswatch*, 25 January 1999, p. 21; *Nigerian Tribune*, 29 January 2008.
9. Abdulsalami Nasidi and Takena O. Harry, 'The epidemiology of HIV/AIDS in Nigeria', in Adeyi et al., *AIDS*, p. 18; Great Britain: House of Commons: Session 2000–01: International Development Committee, *Third report: HIV/AIDS: the impact on social and economic development (HSC.354)* (2 vols, London, 2001), vol. 1, p . lxix.
10. Olusegun Obasanjo, 'Africa in the 1990s: the challenges of economic reform', in Olusegun Obasanjo and Hans d'Orville (ed.), *The leadership challenge of economic reforms in Africa* (New York, 1991), p. 9; Kanki and Adeyi in Adeyi et al., *AIDS*, p. 8; Daniel J. Smith, 'HIV/AIDS in Nigeria: the challenges of a national epidemic', in Rotberg, *Crafting*, p. 201.
11. Gilbert Kombe, David Galaty, and Chizoba Nwagbara, 'Scaling up antiretroviral treatment in the public sector in Nigeria: a comprehensive analysis of resource requirements' (2004), p. 4, http://www.phrplus.org/Pubs/Tech037-fin.pdf (accessed 15 July 2004); *Punch*, 19 December 2007; UNAIDS, *Report on the global AIDS epidemic 2008* (Geneva, 2008), p. 134.
12. UNAIDS, 'AIDS epidemic update, December 2009', p. 19, http://data.unaids.org/pub/Report/2009/2009_epidemic_update_en.pdf (accessed 6 December 2009); Lewis and Alemika, 'Seeking', p. 6.
13. Todd Moss, Scott Standley, and Nancy Birdsall, 'Double-standards, debt treatment, and World Bank country classification: the case of Nigeria', Center for Global Development working paper no. 45 (2004), http://www.cgdev.org/content/publications/detail/2741.pdf (accessed 4 March 2009); World Bank, *World development report*, 2004, p. 253.
14. Nigeria: Federal Office of Statistics, *Poverty profile for Nigeria 2004* ([Abuja] 2005), pp. 6–7, 21–4; Simon Appleton, Andrew McKay, and Babatunde Adewumi Alayanda, 'Poverty in Nigeria', in Paul Collier, Chukwuma C. Soludo, and Catherine Pattillo (ed.), *Economic policy options for a prosperous Nigeria* (Basingstoke, 2008), pp. 335–7, 368.
15. Chukwuemeka K. Okoye and Onyukwu E. Onyukwu, 'Sustaining poverty reduction efforts through inter-agency collaboration in Nigeria,' in Kenneth Omeje (ed.), *State-society relations in Nigeria: democratic consolidation, conflicts and reforms* (London, 2007), pp. 184–6.
16. Nigeria: Federal Office of Statistics, *Poverty profile for Nigeria 2004*, p. 25; *Newswatch*, 29 November 2004, p. 54.
17. World Bank, *World development report*, 2000/1, p. 277.
18. Nigeria: National Population Commission, *1991 population census*, p. 29; *Newswatch*, 15 March 2009; Ogunpola and Ojo in Nigerian Economic Society, *Poverty*, p. 115; Ademola Ariyo, *NEPAD City Programme: profile of Lagos City, Nigeria* (Lagos, 2004), p. 75; *Source*, 7 May 2001, p. 7.

19. Lewis and Alemika, 'Seeking', p. 25; Nigeria: Federal Office of Statistics, *The Nigerian household 1995* (Lagos, 1996), p. 13; Magnus Kpakol, 'Poverty eradication efforts', in Hassan Saliu, Ebele Amali, and Raphael Olawepo (eds), *Nigeria's reform programme: issues and challenges* (Ibadan, 2007), pp. 454–5.

20. Peter Lewis, Etannibi Alemika, and Michael Bratton, 'Down to earth: changes in attitudes towards democracy and markets in Nigeria', Afrobarometer paper no. 20 (2002), p. 6, http://www.afrobarometer.org/papers/AfropaperNo20.pdf (accessed 12 August 2007).

21. Ngozi Okonjo-Iweala in *This Day*, 7 August 2000.

22. Lewis, *Growing apart*, p. 183.

23. Sala-i-Martin and Subramanian, 'Addressing', p. 4.

24. *This Day*, 11 May 1999; Okonjo-Iweala and Osafo-Kwaako, 'Nigeria's economic reforms', p. 7; World Bank, *World development report*, 2000/1, p. 315.

25. James K. Boyce and Léonce Ndikumana, 'Is Africa a net creditor? New estimates of capital flight from severely indebted sub-Saharan African countries, 1970–96', *Journal of Development Studies*, 38, 2 (2001), 43–6.

26. Economist Intelligence Unit, 'Country profile: Nigeria', 2001.

27. Victoria Kwakwa, Adeola Adenikinju, Peter Mousley, and Mavis Owusu-Gyamfi, 'Binding constraints to growth in Nigeria', in Collier et al., *Economic policy options*, p. 15; Central Bank of Nigeria, *Changing structure*, p. 69.

28. Adeola F. Adenikinju, 'African imperatives in the new world trade order: country case study of the manufacturing sector in Nigeria', in E. Olawale Ogunkola and Abiodun S. Bankole (ed.), *Nigeria's imperatives in the new world trade order* (Nairobi, 2005), pp. 137, 139, 146; Obasanjo, *Standing tall*, p. 192; Obe, *New dawn*, vol. 2, p. 141.

29. Peter M. Lewis, 'Getting the politics right: governance and economic failure in Nigeria', in Rotberg, *Crafting*, pp. 99, 105–6; Okonjo-Iweala and Osafo-Kwaako, 'Nigeria's economic reforms', pp. 8–9; Soares de Oliveira, *Oil and politics*, pp. 33–7.

30. Paul Collier, 'International experience of aid and debt strategies: implications for Nigeria', in Ngozi Okonjo-Iweala, Charles C. Soludo, and Mansur Muktar (ed.), *The debt trap in Nigeria: towards a sustainable debt strategy* (Trenton, 2003), pp. 230–1; Sala-i-Martin and Subramanian, 'Addressing, pp. 1–17.

31. Kwakwa and others in Collier et al., *Economic policy options*, pp. 30–9.

32. Sala-i-Martin and Subramanian, 'Addressing', pp. 16, 39; Osaghae, *Crippled giant*, pp. 196–207; Moser et al., *Nigeria*, Ch.6.

33. Economist Intelligence Unit, 'Country profile: Nigeria', 2001.

34. Nigeria, *Obasanjo's economic direction 1999–2003* (Abuja, 2000), pp. 7–12.

35. *This Day*, 1 August 1999; *Weekly Trust*, 7 January 2000.

36. Quoted in *This Day*, 24 May 1999.

37. *This Day*, 11 May and 5 June 1999; *Petroleum Economist*, June 1999, p. 58; *Newswatch*, 31 May 1999, pp. 7–11; *Tell*, 10 May 1999, pp. 20–2.

38. *Tell*, 9 August 1999.

39. *This Day*, 29 July 2001.

40. *Guardian*, 21 May 2009; *This Day*, 21 May 2009.

41. *This Day*, 21 June 1999; *West Africa*, 11 November 2002, p. 25.

42. *Tell*, 8 March 2004, p. 3; *Guardian*, 21 May 2009.

43. *Weekly Trust*, 8 January 1999.

44. Wada Nas in *Weekly Trust*, 13 August 1999.

45. Obe, *New dawn*, vol. 2, pp. 115–17, and vol. 3, p. 385; *Insider Weekly*, 3 February 2003, p. 18.

46. Reuben Abati (ed.), *The whole truth: selected editorials of* The Guardian *(1983–2003)* (Lagos, 2004), p. 199; *Nigerian Tribune*, 27 February and 25 March 2003.

47. *West Africa*, 30 June 2003, p. 10; *Weekly Trust*, 30 June 2000; *This Day*, 14 September 2000; Okonjo-Iweala and Osafo-Kwaako, 'Nigeria's economic reforms', p. 17.

48. See the indictment in *Guardian*, 15 March 2009; below, p. 256.
49. Daniel Jordan Smith, *A culture of corruption: everyday deception and popular discontent in Nigeria* (Princeton, 2007), Ch.2.
50. Peter Lewis and Michael Bratton, 'Attitudes to democracy and markets in Nigeria', Afrobarometer paper no. 3 (2000), p. 16, http://www.afrobarometer.org/papers/AfropaperNo3.pdf (accessed 27 July 2007); Lewis and Alemika, 'Seeking', p. xi; *Times*, 19 April 2003.
51. Obe, *New dawn*, vol. 3, p. 134; Utomi, *To serve*, p. 289.
52. Central Bank of Nigeria, *Changing structure*, pp. 2, 61; *Weekly Trust*, 4 September 1998; above, p. 211.
53. *Guardian*, 11 June 2001.
54. *This Day*, 19 April 1999.
55. *This Day*, 5 October 2000.
56. *Economist*, 15 January 2000; *This Day*, 17 July 2001; Kenneth Omeje, *High stakes and stake holders: oil conflict and security in Nigeria* (Aldershot, 2006), pp. 48–9; Soares de Oliveira, *Oil and politics*, p. 83 n.86.
57. Nigeria, *Obasanjo's economic direction*, p. 33; *Petroleum Economist*, May 1999 p. 3, November 1999 p. 42, January 2000 p. 43, February 2000 p. 39.
58. *Petroleum Economist*, November 1999, p. 38; *This Day*, 28 July 1999.
59. *West Africa*, 11 September 2000, p. 28; *This Day*, 14 January 2000, 10 April 2000, 17 July 2001.
60. *This Day*, 25 November 1999; Obasanjo, *Selected speeches*, pp. 23–5; *Newswatch*, 29 March 1999 p. 21, 1 May 2000 pp. 10–17, 15 May 2000 p. 32; Obe, *New dawn*, vol. 2, p. 27.
61. *Newswatch*, 8 July 2002, p. 57; Economist Intelligence Unit, 'Country profile: Nigeria', 2003; *West Africa*, 30 September 2002, p. 16; 'National economic empowerment and development strategy', in Nnebe, *Policies*, vol. 2, p. 257.
62. *This Day*, 5 July 2000 and 17 July 2001; *Guardian*, 26 June 2002.
63. Khan, *Nigeria*, pp. 139–42; *Newswatch*, 4 January 1999, p. 10.
64. *This Day*, 1 August 1999; Khan, *Nigeria*, pp. 128–9; above, p. 144; *Newswatch*, 4 June 2001, p. 26.
65. Osedebamu Isibor, 'How Aso Rock managed the crisis', *This Day*, 17 June 2000; Obiora Chinedu Okafor, 'Remarkable reforms: the influence of a labour-led socio-economic movement on legislative reasoning, process and action in Nigeria, 1999–2007', *Journal of Modern African Studies*, 47 (2009), 246; *Tell*, 8 January 2001.
66. Olukoju, '"Never expect power always"', p. 64; 'National economic empowerment and development strategy', in Nnebe, *Policies*, vol. 2, p. 287.
67. Nigeria, *Obasanjo's economic direction*, pp. 55–6; *Newswatch*, 12 July 1999, p. 33; *This Day*, 26 April 1999.
68. *This Day*, 30 September 2000; Adeel Malik and Francis Teal, 'Towards a more competitive manufacturing sector', in Collier et al., *Economic policy options*, pp. 250–1; Adenikinju in Ogunkola and Bankole, *Nigeria's imperatives*, p. 146.
69. J. Ikeme and Oban John Ebohan, 'Nigeria's electric power sector reform: what should form the key objectives?' *Energy Policy*, 33 (2005), 1216.
70. Olukoju, '"Never expect power always",' pp. 61–2; *This Day*, 14 May 2000; Sanusi and Martins-Kuye to Köhler, 20 July 2000, http://www.imf.org/external/np/loi/2000/nga/01/index.htm (accessed 30 November 2008); *Guardian*, 26 June 2001.
71. P.V.S.N. Tallapragada and B.S. Adebusuyi, 'Nigeria's power sector: opportunities and challenges', in Collier et al., *Economic policy options*, p. 309; Olukoju, '"Never expect power always"', p. 64.
72. *Newswatch*, 12 November 2001, p. 58; *Guardian*, 21 November 2002.
73. *Guardian*, 23 April 2002.
74. *Punch*, 19 March 2008.

75. Central Bank of Nigeria, *Changing structure*, p. 76; *Newswatch*, 6 March 1995, pp. 15–21; *This Day*, 27–28 September 2000.
76. *This Day*, 1 December 1999 and 31 December 2000; Sanusi and Martins-Kuye to Köhler, 20 July 2000 (above, n. 70); Economist Intelligence Unit, 'Country profile: Nigeria', 2004.
77. *This Day*, 10 May 1999; Irene N. Chigbue, 'Privatizing the national economy: the journey so far', in Saliu et al., *Nigeria's reform programme*, pp. 422–7.
78. Nigeria, *Obasanjo's economic direction*, p. 47; *This Day*, 28 July 1999; *Africa Confidential*, 14 April 2000, p. 4.
79. *Tell*, 10 April 2001, p. 66, and 21 May 2001, p. 27.
80. *Tell*, 21 May 2001, p. 27; Economist Intelligence Unit, 'Country profile: Nigeria', 2002–4; below, p. 275.
81. Lewis and Bratton, 'Attitudes', pp. 12–15, 17–18; Lewis et al., 'Down to earth', pp. 5–6, 32.
82. Lewis and Alemika, 'Seeking', p. 24.
83. Lewis et al., 'Down to earth', p. 54.
84. Kwakwa and others in Collier et al., *Economic policy options*, p. 15; Nigeria, *Obasanjo's economic direction*, p. 23; 'National economic empowerment and develoment strategy', in Nnebe, *Policies*, vol. 2, p. 328.
85. 'National economic empowerment and development strategy', in Nnebe, *Policies*, vol. 2, pp. 211, 235; Malik in Collier et al., *Economic policy options*, p. 263; *This Day*, 29 May 2001.
86. *Weekly Trust*, 11 June 1999; International Monetary Fund, 'Nigeria: staff report for the 2004 Article IV Consultation', 22 June 2004, p. 14, http://www. imf.org/external/pubs/ft/scr/2004/cr04239.pdf (accessed 21 December 2008).
87. Obe, *New dawn*, vol. 3, pp. 19–28; *Guardian*, 29–30 May 2001.
88. *This Day*, 7 August 2000.
89. Obasanjo, *Standing tall*, p. 78.
90. *This Day*, 8 August 2000; Sanusi and Martins-Kuye to Köhler, 20 July 2000 (above, n. 70).
91. *Tell*, 2 December 2002, p. 54.
92. *This Day*, 12 August 1999; Deborah L. West, 'Governing Nigeria: continuing issues after the elections' (2003), p. 12, http://www.ciaonet.org/wps/wed04/wed04.pdf (accessed 30 September 2007).
93. Economist Intelligence Unit, 'Country profile: Nigeria', 2008.
94. *Petroleum Economist*, June 2003, pp. 27–8, and April 2002, p. 40; *Newswatch*, 17 November 2003, pp. 28–9.
95. *Newswatch*, 14 January 2002, p. 44, and 28 January 2002, pp. 31–4.
96. Nigeria, *Obasanjo's economic direction*, p. 66; Ebenezer Obadare, 'Playing politics with the mobile phone in Nigeria: civil society, big business and the state', *Review of African Political Economy*, 107 (2006), 97, 100; Daniel Jordan Smith, 'Cell phones, social inequality, and contemporary culture in Nigeria', *Canadian Journal of African Studies*, 40 (2006), 496–523; Adekeye Adebajo, 'South Africa and Nigeria in Africa: an axis of virtue?' in Adekeye Adebajo, Adebayo Adedeji, and Chris Landsberg (ed.), *South Africa in Africa: the post-apartheid era* (Scottsville, 2007), p. 230; Aliyu Mohammed, 'Crises and conflict management in Nigeria', in Yakubu et al., *Crisis*, vol. 1, p. 23.
97. Forrest, *Advance*, Chs. 6 and 7; Akin Adesokan, 'Practising "democracy" in Nigerian films', *African Affairs*, 108 (2009), 604.
98. *Newswatch*, 25 January 1999, p. 21.
99. *This Day*, 1 October 1999; Shagari, *Beckoned*, p. 309; Nigeria: Federal Office of Statistics, *Nigerian household 1995*, p. 7.
100. 'National economic empowerment and development strategy', in Nnebe, *Policies*, vol. 2, p. 235; Nigeria: National Bureau of Statistics, *General household survey report 1995–*

2005 (Abuja, 2007), p. 24; *Guardian*, 27 September 2007; *Nigerian Tribune*, 7 October 2008; Human Rights Watch, 'Chop fine: the human rights impact of local government corruption and mismanagement in Rivers State, Nigeria', January 2007, pp. 1, 3, 12–13, 32–3, http://hrw.org/reports/2007/nigeria0107/nigeria0107web.pdf (accessed 29 August 2007).

101. http://www.indexmundi.com/g/g.aspx?v=66+c=ni+l=en (accessed 4 August 2009).
102. Lewis and Bratton, 'Attitudes', p. 4; Lewis and Alemika, 'Seeking', p. vii.
103. Okonjo-Iweala et al., *Debt trap*, pp. 5–8; Okonjo-Iweala and Osafo-Kwaako, 'Nigeria's economic reforms', p. 11.
104. Sanusi and Martins-Kuye to Köhler, 20 July 2000 (above, n. 70); *This Day*, 23 September 1999.
105. *Africa Contemporary Record*, 1998–2000, p. B189; *This Day*, 23 November 2000.
106. *This Day*, 31 July 2001; *Guardian*, 18 May 2001.
107. Economist Intelligence Unit, 'Country profile: Nigeria', 2002.
108. Moss et al., 'Double-standards'.
109. Obe, *New dawn*, vol. 3, pp. 244–5.
110. *Guardian*, 6 March 2002.
111. *Guardian*, 8 March 2002, 30 April 2002, 24 June 2002.
112. *Guardian*, 22 June 2002; Economist Intelligence Unit, 'Country profile: Nigeria', 2003; Lewis, *Growing apart*, p. 250.

17
Restoring International Relationships

One major task – and one major success – of Obasanjo's first presidential term was to restore Nigeria's international reputation, damaged by Abacha's years of repression and isolation, and to regain the prominent role in continental affairs that the country had played when Obasanjo had been its military leader. He realised that his personal experience as a victim of repression was an asset to be exploited. 'This is a country that has been isolated, this is a country that needs to come into the mainstream of the international community,' he explained, 'and … you don't sit at home to do that, you need to go round and say well look, we have a new Nigeria and I'm the epitome of other new Nigeria.'[1] The need to secure debt relief was a further reason to seek maximum international exposure. Even before his inauguration, Obasanjo visited over twenty foreign countries in every continent except Australia, making a special point of South Africa, the United States, France, and Britain. By October 2002 he had travelled to 92 countries as President, spending more than a quarter of his first term out of the country, a display of energy that brought him much domestic criticism and little immediate profit in terms of debt relief or foreign investment, but would eventually have its reward. Throughout his tenure he was essentially his own foreign minister, leaving little to the enlightened but relatively inexperienced Sule Lamido.[2]

During his twenty years out of power, Obasanjo had recognised that decolonisation and the Cold War had been replaced by problems arising from Africa's marginalisation, economic decline, state weakness, and civil strife within an increasingly globalised context. Allying himself with the optimistic mood of the new South Africa, his foreign policy during his first presidential term focused on creating an African Union that could meet continental problems, make the African state system work, and perhaps eventually replace that system by larger regional or continental units. Together with the survival of Nigeria as a state, this was his most important lifetime contribution. In addition, he devoted much energy to mediating in African disputes, which had multiplied since the end of the Cold War. Unlike his military predecessors and his own early foray into Angolan affairs, a more experienced Obasanjo set little value on displays of national vanity or the emotional satisfaction offered by anti-colonial campaigns. Recognising Nigeria's economic weakness, he was anxious rather to reduce its external commitments and to act whenever possible through multilateral institutions.[3]

This was clear in his handling of his most immediate international problem:

Nigeria's military involvement in Liberia and Sierra Leone. The Liberian war seemed in May 1999 to be over. Nine years earlier, Babangida had sent Nigerian troops there as the bulk of an ECOWAS Monitoring Group (ECOMOG) to end a war between President Samuel Doe's regime and rebels led by Charles Taylor, who became Nigeria's chief adversary. In 1997, with Doe dead and Taylor controlling much of the country, the Nigerians were obliged to accept a presidential election in which Taylor won 75% of the votes. Nigerian troops left Liberia in 1998, but Taylor's regime was far from secure,[4] and in the meantime ECOMOG's use of Freetown as a base had involved it in a similar war in Sierra Leone, where it restored President Kabbah to power in February 1998 and then attempted to take control of the interior from the rebel Revolutionary United Front (RUF), an attempt that failed in December 1998 and was followed by renewed and violent fighting for control of Freetown during January 1999.[5]

By this time both the army and Nigerian public opinion were heartily sick of the war, which (in the two countries together) had cost about $8 billion and over a thousand Nigerian lives.[6] Withdrawal from Sierra Leone once stability was achieved was a major promise during Obasanjo's election campaign in 1999. Shortly after taking office in May 1999, he ordered planning for a phased withdrawal. In July, with American and British aid, he coerced Kabbah and the RUF into a coalition government. A month later he announced that he would withdraw 3,000 of Nigeria's 12,000 troops from Sierra Leone each month, while offering to allow some to remain as part of a peacekeeping force controlled and financed by the United Nations.[7] 'The time has come', he told the UN General Assembly in September,

> for the Security Council to assume its full responsibility, specifically in Sierra Leone and other flash points in Africa. For too long the burden of preserving international peace and security in West Africa has been left almost entirely to a few states in our subregion … Nigeria's continued burden in Sierra Leone is unacceptably draining Nigeria financially. For our economy to take off, this bleeding has to stop.[8]

Under urgent pressure not to leave a power vacuum, Obasanjo suspended the withdrawal until a UN force was formed in April 2000, with some 4,000 Nigerian troops serving at UN expense. Once this force was in place, Obasanjo, with his habitual emphasis on state authority, insisted that it must re-establish the government's full control of the country. He had his way. During 2001–2 the force supervised the disarmament of the RUF. The last UN troops withdrew in 2005.[9]

Yet violence had meanwhile returned to Liberia. In 1999 rebels hostile to Taylor crossed the border from Guinea and fought their way towards the capital. By February 2002 they were scarcely 30 kilometres from it. Obasanjo – never squeamish in dealing with power-holders, however brutal – had cultivated relations with Taylor because of his influence with the RUF in Sierra Leone. As Taylor's hold on Monrovia weakened, Obasanjo averted a fight to the death by enabling him to take sanctuary in Nigeria in August 2003.[10] While fresh elections installed a new government in Liberia under Ellen Johnson-Sirleaf, Taylor lived in restriction near the eastern Nigerian town of Calabar. Human rights groups in Africa and the West demanded that he should face trial for war crimes and the United States threatened to cut aid to Nigeria unless he was handed over. Obasanjo initially resisted the pressure. 'We must tell the world we are a country of honour,' he declared. 'If we say come here we'll give you security we should be able to do so.'[11] But he added that he would hand Taylor over at the request of an elected Liberian president. This shifted the pressure to Johnson-Sirleaf, who eventually made the request. At this point, it appears, Obasanjo – despite his denials – sought to justify his breach of faith by helping Taylor to 'escape' towards the border, where he was arrested at Maiduguri and delivered to the war crimes tribunal in March 2006, one week before Obasanjo visited President Bush in Washington.[12]

Nigerian troops re-entered Liberia when Taylor left in August 2003, but they passed to UN command two months later and Obasanjo maintained his determination to avoid further military commitments. In 1999 he had refused to participate in an unsuccessful ECOMOG intervention during civil war in Guinea-Bissau. Three years later he gave the same response to a request to send peacekeeping troops to Côte d'Ivoire.[13] Not only were such interventions unpopular with the Nigerian public, but the failure to achieve swift success in Liberia and Sierra Leone had revealed major deficiencies of training, equipment, discipline, and morale within the military.[14] Obasanjo was anxious to retrain and reprofessionalise the army – in June 2001 he angered it by declaring that it was not in a condition to resist an invasion[15] – and for this he turned to the United States, which relied on Nigeria to maintain order in the oil-rich Gulf of Guinea. To be retrained by Americans for the peacekeeping duties that Nigerian troops had been performing for the last decade was galling to many officers and led to the forced retirement of the protesting Army Chief of Staff, but Nigeria became the chief African recipient of American military assistance.[16] Together with Nigerian oil exports, American support for debt relief, and a mutual interest in the success of Nigeria's new democratic order, the military relationship provided the basis for the close ties Obasanjo formed with President Clinton, who visited Abuja in August 2000 and assured the National Assembly that by its peacekeeping efforts, Nigeria was 'building the record of a moral superpower.'[17] This relationship survived both the advent of President Bush, to whom Obasanjo paid a successful visit in May 2001, and al-Qaeda's attack on New York, when the Nigerian government supported the American retaliation against Afghanistan, despite violent protests in northern cities.[18] When the American government prepared to invade Iraq in 2003, however, Obasanjo joined with the presidents of South Africa and Senegal in a letter of warning to which the Americans responded by withdrawing their military assistance. Obasanjo's initiative in removing Taylor from Monrovia then helped to restore relations.[19]

Anxiety to rebuild Nigeria's international position and to win the sympathy of its largest creditor encouraged Obasanjo to cultivate closer ties with Britain than had been possible during his military tenure twenty years earlier. He attended his first Commonwealth Conference in November 1999 and hosted the conference in December 2003, receiving an honorary knighthood from the British Queen.[20] Britain had meanwhile asked him to mediate in its bitter dispute with President Mugabe of Zimbabwe.[21] This arose when Britain ceased to finance purchases of land from white settlers, on the grounds that it was being allocated to political cronies rather than the landless. Mugabe replied by encouraging supposed veterans of Zimbabwe's liberation war to occupy white farms by force.[22] During 2000–1, Obasanjo, in association with President Mbeki of South Africa, mediated two agreements that failed to check the violence, now increasingly between Mugabe's regime and the opposition Movement for Democratic Change (MDC).[23] To avert an open split at a forthcoming Commonwealth Conference, Obasanjo, Mbeki, and Prime Minister Howard of Australia were appointed in March 2002 as a 'troika' to handle the dispute, with Obasanjo trying to hold a balance between his sharply opposed colleagues. Together with Mbeki, he made three visits to Zimbabwe, seeking by quiet diplomacy, but without success, to persuade the elderly Mugabe either to retire or to form a power-sharing government with the MDC.[24] The partnership with Mbeki finally broke down at the Abuja Commonwealth Conference of December 2003, when Obasanjo, as host, feared a white boycott of the meeting, insisted that the suspended Mugabe must not attend, and defeated Mbeki's attempt to oust the Secretary-General on the grounds of bias.[25]

The two leaders' intervention suggests how pivotal they were to African affairs during Obasanjo's first term and how charged but potentially creative was their interaction.[26] Heading the two dominant states of sub-Saharan Africa, both understood that the end of the Cold War and the political and economic marginalisation of the continent had created a leadership vacuum that they could fill. As Obasanjo put it at a state banquet for Mbeki in October 2000, 'Our location, our destiny and the contemporary forces of globalisation have thrust upon us the burden of turning around the fortunes of our continent. We must not and cannot shy away from this responsibility.'[27] Yet, twinned as they were, they were remarkably different men: Mbeki cerebral and almost inhumanly composed, Obasanjo calculating but explosive; Mbeki schooled in exile politics, Obasanjo in civil war; Mbeki dedicated to surfing the internet, Obasanjo to preaching the Word. Sometimes at odds, they nevertheless needed one another. Obasanjo had believed since his visit in 1986 that South Africa's industrial wealth could transform the continent's economic future. Mbeki knew that South Africa's racial history denied it a legitimacy in African eyes that cooperation with Nigeria might supply. They had known one another since the late 1970s, when Obasanjo, as head of state, had welcomed Mbeki as the ANC's representative in Lagos.[28] Obasanjo appears, also, to have taken the initiative in renewing their relationship, after both had taken office in 1999, by encouraging South Africa to engage in peacekeeping operations, initially in the Democratic Republic of the Congo.[29] Attending a meeting of the Southern African Defence Community in August 1999, he suggested that the organisation should cooperate with ECOWAS. In October, the two countries established a South African-Nigerian Bi-National Commission that met six times during the next five years to discuss economic and other forms of cooperation.[30] And the synergy between the two leaders set in train two initiatives of greater significance.

One was the creation of the African Union. Its impetus came from three main directions. One was widespread dissatisfaction with the Organisation of African Unity (OAU), which had achieved its main goal of liberating the whole of colonial Africa but was manifestly unequipped either to check the continent's economic decline or – thanks to the OAU's rigid dedication to national sovereignty – to intervene in the internal crises of African states such as the Rwandan genocide of 1994.[31] The second impetus was Obasanjo's initiative, at his first OAU summit as Nigerian president in Algiers in July 1999, to resubmit the Kampala Document of 1991, which stressed that Africa's economic development depended on cooperative action to establish security, democracy, and good governance within the continent. The OAU had hitherto sidelined the document. The Algiers meeting received it and subsequent summits at Sirte in September 1999 and Lomé in July 2000 incorporated it into OAU structures, thereby affirming a collective interest in the internal affairs of member states.[32] The Sirte meeting also provided the third impetus towards the formation of the African Union. It was called by the Libyan leader, Muammar

Gaddafi, in an attempt to reassert his influence in African affairs. He astonished the assembled heads of state by proposing immediate agreement to a United States of Africa with a five-year presidency and a common army and currency. Mbeki and Obasanjo accepted the need to replace the OAU but opposed the extravagance of Gaddafi's proposal, Obasanjo urging instead that the model for the African Union should be the European Union rather than the United States. This was the pattern eventually agreed at Sirte. The subsequent Lomé summit approved the act constituting the new organisation.[33]

Despite this caution, the African Union was a most ambitious organisation. The Constitutive Act provided for the creation of eighteen new organs, including a chairman (initially Mbeki), a permanent Commission, an Executive Council, a Peace and Security Council (Obasanjo's particular concern), a peacekeeping force, a court of justice, a central bank, and a parliament consisting of five members from each constituent state, the last being a major concession by Nigeria, which had originally wished for representation partly by population. Nigeria and South Africa also attempted to secure permanent, veto-wielding membership of the Peace and Security Council, but other members refused.[34]

The Union had two especially novel features. One, accepted by the Algiers summit at the initiative of Obasanjo and Mbeki, was to refuse membership to future regimes established by military means, a provision that by 2003 had been applied to Comoros, Côte d'Ivoire, and Guinea-Bissau.[35] The other was a specific right of collective intervention in the affairs of member states 'in respect of grave circumstances, namely war crimes, genocide and crimes against humanity', or (by a later amendment at Gaddafi's instance) 'serious threat to legitimate order'. The Constitutive Act was the first international treaty to recognise a right of intervention for humanitarian purposes, although lack of clarity concerning the mechanism for implementing the provision was to be one important weakness of the Union.[36]

Obasanjo was a major founder of the African Union. He contributed less to the second important initiative of the period, the New Partnership for African Development (NEPAD), a policy document drafted mainly by Mbeki and his staff but revised and adopted by African Union institutions. It arose from discussions of debt relief in July 2000 between Mbeki, Obasanjo, and President Bouteflika of Algeria, acting on behalf of the OAU, and the developed countries known as the G8. When the African leaders promised economic responsibility and good governance in return for debt remission – a bargain Obasanjo had suggested in 1993 – the G8 demanded a 'workable plan as the basis of the compact'. NEPAD was the response.[37] Its chief significance was to commit its signatories to a partnership with the developed countries based on the neo-liberal economic orthodoxies of the IMF and the World Bank that Mbeki and Obasanjo had formally accepted for their own countries, which was doubtless why it enjoyed greater favour from the international institutions than earlier African economic initiatives.[38] For Obasanjo, the chief reason for supporting the programme vigorously (he became chairman of its implementation committee) was probably its utility as a bargaining tool in his relentless search for debt relief, which took him and Mbeki to four further G8 meetings in 2001–4, without any substantial success in securing either relief or development aid.[39]

During Obasanjo's first presidential term, these continental preoccupations overshadowed the regional issues that concerned ECOWAS, which remained divided between its Anglophone and Francophone members – Obasanjo and President Wade of Senegal were on poor terms – and made little progress towards monetary union or other forms of economic integration.[40] More was achieved in dividing up the disputed waters of the Gulf of Guinea and the oil reserves beneath them, especially through a highly advantageous deal that Obasanjo imposed in August 2000 on the tiny islands of São Tomé e Príncipè. This drew a maritime border between the islands and Nigeria, creating a Joint Development Zone on São Tomé's side of the border in which Nigeria would enjoy 60% of the oil. Obasanjo also gave strong support to Nigerian concerns with interests in the area, headed by Sir Emeka Offor's Chrome Oil. Other boundary definitions were made with Equatorial Guinea and Gabon.[41]

Nevertheless, the Gulf region also presented Obasanjo's most difficult problem at the end of his first term. The Bakassi Peninsula was some 1,000 square kilometres of mangrove swamps and islands on Nigeria's eastern border with Cameroun. In precolonial times, it had housed fishing villages linked westwards to Calabar. The Berlin Conference of 1885 allocated it to Britain. The British ceded it to German Kamerun in 1913, but war intervened and the agreement was not ratified. The area remained under British control until 1961, when the southern British Cameroons voted to join Cameroun rather than Nigeria. Nigerian troops occupied the peninsula while encircling Biafra during the civil war. Cameroun then demanded its cession, with its implications for offshore oil reserves. Gowon agreed to this in 1975, but he was ousted, the Supreme Military Council refused to ratify the agreement, and Murtala renounced it. When Obasanjo tried to reopen the issue in 1977, Cameroun refused. One border clash in 1981 led to threats of war. Another, in 1994, caused the French government to move paratroops to Cameroun and the government there to submit the case to the International Court of Justice. Abacha refused to recognise the court and tension mounted, but Obasanjo had more concern for international propriety and agreed to accept its judgment. In October 2002 the court found in favour of Cameroun, citing the OAU's principle of the inviolability of colonial boundaries.[42]

With the people of the peninsula anxious to remain Nigerian and public opinion fiercely hostile to cession, Obasanjo – a committed internationalist, once a potential UN Secretary-General, and now agitating for permanent membership of the Security Council – handled the crisis with great care. He ordered official silence, consulted the Council of State and the Cabinet, promised not to cede Nigerian territory, announced that the government would both pursue peace and protect the welfare of the peninsula's Nigerian inhabitants, and asked Secretary-General Kofi Annan to intervene in the interest of their wellbeing.[43] While Cameroun complained at the delay, Annan persuaded both sides to withdraw troops from the peninsula and accept a mixed commission to defuse tension. The commission decided to demarcate the entire length of the boundary between the two countries. As Obasanjo prepared for his re-election contest in April 2003, the Bakassi issue stood in abeyance.[44]

NOTES

1. *Newswatch*, 30 October 2000, p. 19.
2. *Newswatch*, 24 April 1999, p. 26, and 10 March 2003, p. 34; *Post Express*, 1 October 2002; *Daily Trust*, 25 July 2003; *West Africa*, 8 July 2002, p. 7; Jean-Francois Médard, 'Crisis, change and continuity: Nigeria-France relations', in Adebajo and Mustapha, *Gulliver's troubles*, p. 328.

3. *Newswatch*, 13 September 1999, p. 26; Chris Landsberg, 'An African "concert of powers"? Nigeria and South Africa's construction of the AU and NEPAD', in Adebajo and Mustapha, *Gulliver's troubles*, p. 209.
4. Adebajo, *Liberia's civil war*, Chs 10 and 11.
5. R.A. Adeshina, *The reversed victory (the story of Nigerian military intervention in Sierra Leone)* (Ibadan, 2002), Chs. 3–10; David Keen, *Conflict and collusion in Sierra Leone* (Oxford, 2005), Ch.13.
6. *This Day*, 9 March and 26 September 1999.
7. *This Day*, 11 March 1999; Adebajo, *Building peace*, pp. 97–100.
8. Adebajo, *Building peace*, p. 90.
9. Olonisakin, *Peacekeeping*, pp. 43–7, 111; *This Day*, 10 June 2000; Keen, *Conflict*, pp. 267–8.
10. Adebajo, *Liberia's civil war*, pp. 234–8; Adekeye Adebajo, 'Mad dogs and glory: Nigeria's interventions in Liberia and Sierra Leone', in Adebajo and Mustapha, *Gulliver's troubles*, pp. 179–80.
11. *This Day*, 23 July 2004.
12. This account is based on *New African*, 451 (2006), 13–23. For Obasanjo's denial, see *Times*, 30 March 2006. For Taylor's account, see *This Day*, 11 November 2009.
13. Adebajo in Adebajo and Mustapha, *Gulliver's troubles*, p. 196.
14. Adeshina, *Reversed victory*, pp. 94, 138–42, 160.
15. *This Day*, 24 and 29 June 2001.
16. Gwendolyn Mikell, 'Players, policies and prospects: Nigeria-US relations', in Adebajo and Mustapha, *Gulliver's troubles*, p. 286.
17. *This Day*, 27 August 2000.
18. *Africa Confidential*, 8 May 2001, p. 6; *Newswatch*, 29 October 2001, p. 38; above, p. 192.
19. *Nigerian Tribune*, 17 March 2003; *Africa Research Bulletin (Political)*, March 2003, pp. 15249–50; *Daily Trust*, 1 September 2003.
20. *This Day*, 16 November 1999; *Times*, 4 December 2003.
21. *This Day*, 12 April 2000.
22. Jocelyn Alexander, *The unsettled land: state-making and the politics of land in Zimbabwe 1893–2003* (Oxford, 2006), pp. 184–5.
23. *Times*, 4 April 2000 and 6–8 September 2001; *This Day*, 25 May 2000; *Sunday Times* (London), 5 November 2000.
24. *Times*, 1 December 2000, 20 March 2002, and 5 May 2003.
25. Adebajo in Adebajo et al., *South Africa in Africa*, p. 233; *Times*, 17 September and 9 December 2003; *Mail and Guardian*, 9 January 2004.
26. For the relationship, see esp. Chris Landsberg, 'Pax Pretoriana vs. Pax Nigeriana', in Centre d'Etude d'Afrique Noire, *L'Afrique politique 2000* (Paris, 2000), pp. 112–15.
27. Adebajo in Adebajo et al., *South Africa in Africa*, p. 227.
28. Gevisser, *Thabo Mbeki*, pp. 370–7.
29. *Africa Research Bulletin (Political)*, June 1999, p. 13591; Landsberg in Adebajo and Mustapha, *Gulliver's troubles*, p. 209.
30. *This Day*, 18 August 1999; Adebajo in Adebajo et al., *South Africa in Africa*, pp. 227–8.
31. Timothy Murithi, *The African Union: pan-Africanism, peacebuilding and development* (Aldershot, 2005), pp. 3, 29.
32. Olusegun Obasanjo, 'Preface', in Francis M. Deng and I. William Zartman, *A strategic vision for Africa: the Kampala movement* (Washington DC, 2002), pp. xiv-xvi; Murithi, *African Union*, pp. 118–19; above, p. 130.
33. Tieku, 'Explaining', pp. 260–5; Landsberg in Adebajo and Mustapha, *Gulliver's troubles*, p. 207; *Newswatch*, 13 August 2001, p. 36.
34. Chris Landsberg, 'South Africa and the making of the African Union and NEPAD:

Mbeki's "progressive African agenda"', in Adebajo et al., *South Africa in Africa*, pp. 200–1; Obe, *New dawn*, vol. 2, p. 281.

35. Adebajo in Adebajo and Mustapha, *Gulliver's troubles*, p . 22 .
36. Evarist Baimu and Kathryn Sturman, 'Amendment to the African Union's right to intervene: a shift from human security to regime security', *African Security Review*, 12, 2 (2003) (electronic resource).
37. Jimi O. Adesina, 'Towards a political economy of African development discourse', in Malinda S. Smith (ed.), *Beyond the 'African tragedy': discourses on development and the global economy* (Aldershot, 2006), pp. 57–9; above, p. 129.
38. Adebayo Adedeji, 'From Lagos to NEPAD', *New Agenda*, 33 (2002), 34–40.
39. Landsberg in Adebajo and Mustapha, *Gulliver's troubles*, p. 213; *Africa Research Bulletin (Political)*, June 2002, pp. 14882–3.
40. Lewis, *Growing apart*, p. 53.
41. Jedrzej George Frynas, Geoffrey Wood, and Ricardo M.S. Soares de Oliveira, 'Business and politics in São Tomé e Príncipè: cocoa monoculture to petro-state', *African Affairs*, 102 (2003), 62–80.
42. Richard Cornwell, 'Nigeria and Cameroon: diplomacy in the Delta', *African Security Review*, 15, 4 (2006), 48–55.
43. *Post Express*, 11–12 and 22–25 October 2002; *Tell*, 17 November 2003, p. 33.
44. *Guardian*, 17 November 2002; *Africa Research Bulletin (Political)*, September 2002 p. 14995, November 2002 pp. 15070–1, December 2002 pp. 15106–7.

18
President and Politicians

Although sectional conflict and economic recovery were Nigeria's chief domestic problems during Obasanjo's first presidential term, the foreground of public life was occupied by a struggle between executive and legislature. The division of power between them, with the restraint and compromise it was designed to foster, was the core of the constitution whose drafting Obasanjo had overseen in 1976–9. Nigerians familiar with the parent American system assured their compatriots that conflict between the two branches of government was healthy and predictable.[1] In Nigerian circumstances, however, it was particularly abrasive. This was partly due to what Obasanjo once called Nigerians' 'unusual love for grandeur',[2] inherited from honour cultures. 'The first term from 1999 was characterised by the typical Nigerian over-assertiveness, of one side trying to establish dominance over the other,' an experienced senator reflected. 'It is fair to say that the problem was the operators, not the constitution, not the environment.'[3] Yet it was not only the operators. The architects of the constitution had intended that while the legislature would prevent abuse of power by the executive, shared membership of a majority party would ensure the conduct of government. Shagari suffered the consequences of this optimistic assumption when his lack of a party majority left him no safeguard against abuse of power by the legislature.[4] Obasanjo was determined to avoid Shagari's fate by dominating the legislature. For that he had the advantage of a large party majority, but now it was a party without policy or discipline.

Obasanjo's determination to dominate matched his military training, his experience as a military ruler, his supreme assurance of his own vocation, his passionate concern for national revival and development, and his long-standing contempt for politicians, whom he openly described as 'legislooters'.[5] Although a committed democrat, as he repeatedly insisted, it was in the narrow sense of believing that the country's leaders were better chosen and removed by election than by the gun. For Obasanjo, as a legislator remarked, 'democracy starts and ends with winning elections.' 'He wanted democracy without the interference of the people or their elected representative in how he governed them', a journalist added. 'That's the democracy of the barracks.' Certainly Obasanjo believed that democracy hindered development.[6] He also feared that it might threaten national unity, which, for one who belonged to the independence generation and had fought the civil war, was still the overriding concern, whereas many younger Nigerians gave equal weight to participatory democracy and civil rights. Asked which was the more important, economic development or democracy, in 1973 some 62% of university students had said development, but by 1995 some 61% said democracy.[7]

At the age of 62, Obasanjo was out of sympathy with most members of the new National Assembly. According to one survey, 78% of them were university graduates.[8] A number had been educated in the USA and understood a presidential system better than the president. Others – including his chief adversary, Ghali Umar Na'Abba – had belonged to the student generation that had opposed his educational policies in the late 1970s. Many members of the House of Representatives were even younger, for their average age was 37. Senators were generally older, although their president for most of Obasanjo's first term was chosen at the age of 39.[9] Deeply attached to Yoruba notions of gerontocracy, Obasanjo habitually referred to the Representatives as 'boys', accused them of having 'power without knowledge or experience', and infuriated them by his patronising manner.[10] Significantly, vocal criticism of him came less from Yoruba members of opposition parties than from his own PDP members, drawn either from Igbo society, where deference for age was less marked, or from northerners like Na'Abba, often educated at Ahmadu Bello University, who had already seized much regional leadership from less-educated elders. A journalist claimed that Obasanjo's mistake was not to have cultivated the more reasonable legislators.[11] It was a fair criticism, but for the President it would have been unthinkable to 'cultivate' men young enough to be his sons. Generational conflict was a major element in the politics of Obasanjo's presidency.

Yet more important was the conflict between national and local interests. Obasanjo had no regional constituency. His instincts were Yoruba, but his mind and loyalties were truly Nigerian. By contrast, every member of the National Assembly had been elected by a geographical constituency and it is unlikely that any – except perhaps representatives from Abuja and one or two other cities – was other than an 'indigene' of that constituency. Their voters were overwhelmingly local people who chose representatives less to participate in making national policy than to bring the largest possible share of the national cake to the constituency. 'Without performing you cannot go back to the people, for if you do they would stone you', a politician explained. 'This is at the back of every politician's mind and ignoring this fact means forfeiting any chances of running for a second term.'[12] These considerations governed much of the legislators' behaviour, especially their eagerness to inflate government expenditure at the risk of financial instability and the displeasure of Obasanjo, the IMF, and the Paris Club.

Legislators were also desperate for money and other forms of patronage. As Obasanjo had learned – but was unwilling to concede to others – Nigerian politics was extremely expensive, partly because the country was so big and populous. An activist in Delta State – perhaps an especially costly area – reckoned in 2003 that a seat in the House of Representatives might cost about N15 million (over $100,000) if one were well known, perhaps N20–25 million if not.[13] A governorship might cost $2 million or more, as one successful candidate confirmed.[14] Candidates, rather than their parties, were expected to raise most of the money. Most legislators were probably deeply indebted – in financial and other terms – before they reached Abuja. As a Senate President put it, 'Membership of the National Assembly is an investment because most of us sold our houses to get to the Senate … but it is the ability to recoup whatever you spent legitimately that is the problem.'[15] The expectations from politicians were immense: 'They torment you with demands because they voted for you.'[16] Such expectations made the temptations to corruption almost irresistible and many politicians regarded it as legitimate, at least within limits. 'We all worked hard and spent a lot of money to achieve power and put Obasanjo there', one PDP member explained. 'So he should not take our gari [food] from our mouths.'[17] Moreover, Nigerian politics was a dangerous and dirty business that attracted adventurers as much as it deterred the respectable.

In Obasanjo's eyes, the legislature's parochial, mercenary, and irresponsible behaviour was compounded by its failure to contribute positively to law-making. In its first two years the new National Assembly approved only fourteen bills, almost all initiated by the executive. Yet this was scarcely surprising, given that few members had legislative experience and the House of Representatives, at its inauguration, possessed four typewriters for its 360 members.[18] The legislators, in turn, saw it as a major priority to prevent the arrogant and wilful president from distorting the democratic constitution. 'He runs the government of the federation in a typical military fashion without respect for constitutional provisions', a northern representative said after less than two months experience of Obasanjo, adding, 'We pray we are not replacing military dictatorship with civilian autocracy.'[19]

Unable to rely on party loyalty, Obasanjo resorted to cruder methods to control the National Assembly. His constitutional power to draft the budget gave him a degree of control over the legislature's finances, which became a subject of conflict between them. Although a strident critic of Nigeria's 'money politics', he appears to have turned a blind eye when his agents resorted to bribery in what he judged to be the national interest. Early in 2007 senators discovered that their chamber was equipped with closed-circuit monitoring cameras.[20] The President disparaged legislators in public, welcomed attacks upon them by trade unionists and other critics, and mobilised auditors, policemen, and anti-corruption officers to harass them. Occasionally, he blatantly defied the law and constitution.

Yet it was only gradually that Obasanjo learned the most effective way to control legislators, which was to control their re-election. As 2003 neared, opposition within the National Assembly evaporated. Few of its former leaders returned to Abuja after the voting. To secure re-election, PDP legislators had first to win nomination at party primary elections in which most voters were dependents and nominees of state governors, whose control of funds and patronage made them the key figures in local politics. Obasanjo had learned the governors' power during his campaign for nomination. He cultivated them assiduously during his presidency and possessed much leverage over them through his control of development projects, the police, and the possible declaration of a state of emergency, in addition to the governors' need for the support of party headquarters in seeking their own re-election. In the contest between federal executive and legislature, Obasanjo's allies were the state executives. The threefold structure of federation, state, and local government bred a political system in which mobilisation of resources at one level was the key to power at another.[21] Obasanjo's domination of Nigerian politics depended on mastery of this process.

The struggle between executive and legislature began as soon as the National Assembly met in May 1999. The election of a young member from Kano, Saliyu Buhari, as Speaker of the House of Representatives was initially uncontroversial, but when he was found to have falsified his age and qualifications, the House gave Obasanjo no chance to interfere before replacing the Speaker with Ghali Umar Na'Abba, a 40-year-old Kano businessman with a political science degree from ABU who had been a member of the G34 opposition to Abacha and was a protégé of

Abubakar Rimi, whom Obasanjo had made his most virulent political enemy.[22] Similarly, Obasanjo's intervention to secure the election of the amenable Evans Enwerem as Senate President, rather than the popular Chuba Okadigbo, created an immediate breach with many senators and left Okadigbo in a position to make Enwerem's position untenable.[23]

The President's initial legislative programme was equally controversial. His anti-corruption bill was seen as draconian and was consigned to a long process of amendment, as was his bill to create the Niger Delta Development Commission. There was delay in approving some of his ministers.[24] But the critical confrontation came on 28 July, when he met the Assembly to submit a revision of the 1999 budget to check governmental overspending. Meeting the two houses jointly in the Representatives' chamber, Obasanjo first breached protocol by taking the chair, then, after making his presentation, he tactlessly asked the senators, who considered themselves the senior house, to leave while he held a discussion with the representatives. These he offended by saying that the government would refurbish their accommodation rather than give them the money to do so, lest they should use it instead to pay their election debts. When they replied by complaining of the inadequacy of their working facilities, Obasanjo lost his temper, stormed out, and marched uninvited into the midst of an equally angry meeting of the Senate. Ordering the gallery to be cleared, he sought to mend his fences with the senators, but in the meantime the representatives threatened not to consider the budget until he apologised for his behaviour. Next day the Senate, on Okadigbo's motion, rejected the amended budget.[25]

The incident left lasting bitterness. 'He shall address us not as headmaster to his pupils', one representative fumed.[26] Na'Abba declared that Obasanjo 'must undergo a process of education on how to behave like a democrat', and insisted that the National Assembly would control the furnishing of its members' quarters.[27] Obasanjo, who had already reduced the members' allowances for that purpose, complained on television that the legislature had not passed a single bill during its first two months. Oshiomhole led 3,000 workers to the Assembly to protest at its extravagance.[28]

The dispute gradually focused on two issues. One was the size of the supplementary budget. Obasanjo had proposed a capital expenditure of N54.7 billion, which the Assembly wished to raise to N82.3 billion, including a sum for its own projects, to be met by raising the benchmark price of oil used in calculating anticipated revenue. This raised economic, political, and constitutional issues. Anxious to negotiate an agreement with the IMF, Obasanjo wanted to restrain government spending, check inflation, insulate the budget from fluctuating oil prices, and perhaps, by paying the balance of revenue into the Excess Crude Fund, to create an extra-budgetary account for use at his own discretion – or so representatives feared.[29] Legislators, by contrast, were anxious to impress their constituents by expanding public expenditure, especially if they could claim personal responsibility for it. Elsewhere in the world, legislatures generally sought to check expenditure that must be met by unpopular taxation, but in an economy based on oil revenues the budgetary process was inverted. This raised constitutional issues. Obasanjo insisted that the constitution specified that the President must prepare all estimates of expenditure and 'does not, in my view, permit the National Assembly to incorporate its own expenditure or projects into the bill in excess of what the Executive seeks approval for.'[30] Legislators replied 'that all funds belonging to the federation cannot be spent

228

except in the manner prescribed by the National Assembly.'[31] They also insisted that the President was obliged to spend all the money and execute all the programmes specified in the annual Appropriation Act. Obasanjo denied this, claiming that he could execute only the programmes for which revenue could be found and executive capacity existed – which meant, in practice, the programmes he had included in his original budget. In the United States, the executive's refusal to spend all money appropriated (known as impoundment) became a major issue only during the 1970s under Richard Nixon, but in Nigeria it had been an issue even in Shagari's presidency, owing to the nature of the oil economy and the dynamics of Nigerian politics, and was to remain an issue under Obasanjo's successor.[32] The only way to resolve the dispute was for the two branches of government to discuss the budget before it was submitted to the National Assembly, but relations between them in late 1999 scarcely permitted this.

The second focus of dispute was the Senate presidency. Obasanjo's brusque treatment of the institution on 28 July had humiliated Enwerem and given Okadigbo and his many supporters the opportunity to mobilise against him. Like Buhari, he was accused of falsifying his age and qualifications, as well as incompetence. In October he survived an attempted impeachment, allegedly thanks to presidential funds, but eventually even his fellow senators from the south-east turned against him, Obasanjo withdrew his support, and he was ousted on 18 November by 90 votes to 2.[33] Okadigbo was unanimously elected to replace him, promising 'to restore the dignity of the Senate ... and to co-operate with the government of President Obasanjo, stressing that the era of confrontation was over'.[34]

That was far from true, but in the meantime Obasanjo was embroiled in another political controversy. He was determined to gain control of the PDP apparatus and use it to discipline party members and push legislation through the National Assembly. This meant breaking the power of the notables – the Aborigines, as they were sometimes known – who had founded the party in 1998.[35] His first target was the chairman, Solomon Lar, who was over seventy, was accused of inefficiency, and was at odds with the President on numerous issues. Lar agreed to retire at a party convention fixed for November 1999.[36] Since all major offices were 'zoned' to specific regions, he had to be succeeded by another chairman from the Middle Belt. There were two main candidates: Sunday Awoniyi, a northern Yoruba from Kogi State and a PDP founder who had formerly lost the chairmanship to Lar, and Barnabas Gemade, a more recent party member from Benue State who had supported Abacha's political ambitions.[37] To choose the independent-minded Awoniyi, who had backed Ekwueme for the presidential nomination, would leave the Aborigines in control. Obasanjo mobilised his agents, notably Atiku, Anenih, and other PDM fixers. They produced a list of favoured candidates for all the 26 offices to be filled at the convention. Both sides were said to have spent lavishly. Atiku, as usual, collaborated with the governors who controlled delegates. The voting was so chaotic that Awoniyi and other notables begged that it should be stopped, but when it ended, all 26 contestants on Anenih's list were declared elected, Gemade by 1,828 votes against Awoniyi's 985.[38] The National Electoral Commission commented that the convention 'fell short of the level of transparency expected from a democratic process'.[39] Awoniyi stormed out, Ekwueme 'called on the elders of the party to meet soon to save the party', and Obasanjo declared that 'The founding team of our great party, the PDP, have given their best, but as is natural in human affairs, many of them must now yield their places to a new set of elected leaders.... He called on the party's new executive to initiate codes of discipline that would forge a cohesion between the government, the party and the legislature.'[40] Attempts at reconciliation failed. During the following years many Aborigines left or were expelled from a party that they complained had forsaken its democratic ideals.[41]

Nor did the convention encourage cohesion between executive and legislature. During December 1999, the Senate refused to discuss the budget for 2000 until Obasanjo explained his failure to implement that for 1999. The House of Representatives considered impeaching the President over the army's destruction of Odi and various financial irregularities. Obasanjo's allies among the representatives tried unsuccessfully to impeach Na'Abba, whose elevated view of his office and extravagance in exercising it earned him the hostility of less favoured members.[42] Further threats of impeachment flew backwards and forwards during the following months, while the National Assembly emasculated Obasanjo's anti-corruption bill and inflated the budget for 2000 until the IMF threatened to veto debt rescheduling talks, to which Okadigbo replied that it could 'go to hell'.[43] He was mired in rumours of corruption and rivalries for patronage-controlling committee chairmanships, needing an unanimous vote of confidence from the House of Representatives in April 2000 to protect him from impeachment.[44] By contrast, Na'Abba, despite his extravagance and pretension, was gathering support as leader of the younger, ambitious representatives who saw the formulation of policy as their responsibility, with the President as its executor. 'Our generation is angry with what happened in the past', Na'Abba explained. 'Those people who are responsible for what Nigeria went through, are still very much around – and some of them are in government.'[45] In February he published an eleven-point 'Contract with Nigeria'. In June he set out a legislative programme for the next session, including reforming the tax system, humanising the prison service, and abolishing the death penalty.[46]

Another chance to oust Okadigbo came in August 2000, when the Clerk to the National Assembly revealed that, among other forms of misappropriation, the Senate President had awarded himself $370,000 to buy furniture, and $220,000 as a Christmas bonus. He was impeached by 81 votes to 14 and replaced by Anyim Pius Anyim, an equable Igbo lawyer whose attention to senators' interests reduced them to docility for the next two years.[47] The larger and younger House of Representatives was less amenable. Obasanjo's determination to remove Na'Abba was sharpened during President Clinton's brief visit to Nigeria later in August, an important moment for Obasanjo in restoring Nigeria's reputation and his own standing as an international statesman. He did not accompany his guest to the National Assembly, where Na'Abba's observation that Nigeria must learn to respect the constitution and the separation of powers won an ovation in which Clinton joined.[48] At a state banquet that evening, Obasanjo remarked, 'Our politics is a boisterous one. So you will see people with loud mouth. However, no insult or intercession will stop me from working with every arm of government.' Clinton replied that America too had its 'creative tension'. Na'Abba's remark was an insult that Obasanjo would never forgive in a man twenty years his junior.[49]

'Only one man, heading one institution, stands between President Olusegun Obasanjo and total dominance of the Nigerian political scene. The man is Alhaji Ghali Umar Na'Abba', an opposition newspaper declared in September 2000.[50] Yet Na'Abba was vulnerable. He lived, travelled, and behaved like a prince.[51] The investigation that ruined Okadigbo also made damaging accusations against the Speaker. His standing in the House was sufficient to win him a vote of confidence, but his opponents maintained their pressure. The police and the Code of Conduct Bureau investigated his financial conduct, the NLC threatened 'practical' action if the representatives did not submit to enquiry, and Obasanjo's agents were reported to be offering each member a million naira (nearly $10,000) to impeach the Speaker.[52] 'Every child on the street knows who is paying the members, labour and students to issue threats and lay a siege on the House', Na'Abba's spokesman declared.[53]

The President was said to believe that he had nearly the two-thirds of votes needed for impeachment when, on 31 October 2000, 'to the amazement and embarrassment of watchers', the chairman of the House's anti-corruption committee deposited N4 million (nearly $40,000) in notes on the table beside the mace, claiming that it had been given to eight members in return for undertakings to support Na'Abba's impeachment, allegedly by the presidential liaison officer to the House, who was said to be acting on behalf of Obasanjo's loyal and wealthy supporter, Governor Odili of Rivers State, although both denied it. Some 37 other members claimed to have received similar offers. The House promptly rejected by 182 votes to 76 a proposal to investigate Na'Abba's corruption.[54] A panel headed by Ekwueme concluded that money might indeed have changed hands, but exonerated Obasanjo, Atiku, and Odili.[55] Na'Abba himself later claimed that the presidency had offered him huge sums for his compliance.[56]

Obasanjo made a tactical retreat. On 9 November, he presented his 2001 budget to the National Assembly, stressed the need for executive and legislature to work together, and received warm applause. Learning from experience, the government had already discussed the budget extensively with legislators. It was approved within six weeks, although with the addition of N500 million (nearly $5 million) for each of the 109 senatorial districts to finance 'constituency projects' determined by their representatives in the National Assembly.[57] In consequence, the early months of 2001 formed a political interlude between the two halves of Obasanjo's first term. In the eyes of the general public - although probably not of the political elite - he had had the better of his dispute with the National Assembly. In a public opinion survey during August 2001, 72% of those interviewed assessed him favourably and 82% said they trusted him (down from 90% early in 2000). By contrast, only 45% approved the performance of their representatives to the National Assembly, State Assembly, and local council. Some 67% trusted the National Assembly 'a little' or more. Few had any contact with their elected representatives and 86% thought they seldom if ever looked after people like themselves.[58]

The political temperature rose again in mid 2001, initially over Obasanjo's refusal to finance the constituency projects that legislators had added to the budget. 'We had nothing to take home,' one Representative later complained.[59] The chief reason for tension, however, was awareness of the approaching election scheduled for April 2003. Within the PDP, attention focused again on the chairmanship, with a widespread feeling, shared by Obasanjo, that Gemade had not given the party the drive and discipline it needed. Gemade tried to prevent the holding of a national convention, but Obasanjo and his agents insisted on it. At Abuja, in November 2001, they replaced the chairman by a former minister, Audu Ogbeh. To the anger of the party's founders, the choice was made not by election but by 'consensus', which meant in effect nomination by a leadership clique headed by Obasanjo, who used the opportunity to arrogate to himself a non-existent role as party leader and to outline a new pattern of dominant party politics:

The Party Chairman has to work with the President in a manner that there can be no question as to who has the mandate to govern the country. Therefore there can be no ... room, for those who regard the national executive, together with the Party Chairman, as alternative executive authority of the nation that can oppose the elected government.

Either you are a loyal and disciplined party member and obey the party regulations and seek redress through appropriate party channels, or you are not with us...The cardinal element of such an organisation is discipline ...

Political analysts are beginning to reckon with the probability of PDP becoming the only viable party organisation in the country ... PDP will not – and should never – take advantage of its power in a manner that may appear to suppress views that are different, and by extension, appear to be moving the country towards a one-party State.... If we in PDP use our success democratically, and we faithfully abide by the relevant provisions of the constitution, we will see political organisations come and go.[60]

Obasanjo had long feared the divisive potential of a multi-party system, but he had also recognised during the 1990s that one-party states were no longer viable. The PDP's electoral success offered a middle way, already pioneered in South Africa by the ANC and in several other African countries: the dominant party that embraced most of the population, represented national unity, won national elections, and enjoyed a virtual monopoly of patronage, but allowed dissenting groups to organise and compete. At the Abuja convention, Obasanjo pointed the PDP firmly in this direction.[61]

The President's dealings with the legislature almost immediately offered him another opportunity to shape the political system. During 2001 the main legislation under consideration was an Electoral Bill to regulate the 2003 election. Civil society groups and others were demanding, in the interests of democracy, that party registration should be made easier than in had been in 1999, or even that registration should be automatic, whereas Obasanjo was anxious to prevent a divisive proliferation of parties, especially perhaps by dissidents from the PDP.[62] After much debate, the National Assembly approved a bill specifying that a party seeking to contest election must demonstrate its federal character by sponsoring candidates for at least 15% of seats in at least two-thirds of states. Obasanjo immediately wrote back to Na'Abba suggesting an amendment requiring such a party first to *win* at least 15% of seats in two-thirds of states in a local government election. This would have prevented any new party from contesting the federal and state elections in 2003 and might also have excluded the Alliance for Democracy. Na'Abba replied that it was too late to make any such amendment, but at his suggestion the President wrote to the National Assembly, which was in recess, suggesting that a conference of the two houses, such as commonly harmonised their draft bills, should insert the necessary clause. Anyim (the Senate President), Na'Abba, and other leaders met with Obasanjo. What took place was much disputed. According to Na'Abba, 'Obasanjo said we could do the amendment and call it the printer's devil.' Obasanjo insisted that the change (which specified 10% rather than 15%) was made entirely by the National Assembly leaders. Na'Abba denied any part, but Anyim insisted that the Speaker had known what was being done, as he had himself, believing it to be legal and in the national interest. Obasanjo signed the amended bill.[63]

When published, the Act angered those who wanted to liberalise party formation and legislators who insisted that any alteration made at the harmonisation stage had to be referred to each house of the National Assembly for final approval. Both houses repealed the insertion and the Supreme Court eventually ruled that any party was free to contest election.[64] The incident seriously damaged Obasanjo's reputation and revived his antagonistic relations with the legislature, especially with Na'Abba.[65]

At this moment in January 2002, Obasanjo asked the Speaker for details of representatives' earnings, ostensibly for budgetary purposes. When Na'Abba refused, the President suspended payment to members. Rather than fostering dissatisfaction with their leader, this angered the House, which resolved to investigate Obasanjo's entire term of office, especially his compliance with Appropriation Acts, and was reported to be taking initial steps towards impeachment, as Na'Abba later confirmed. There was talk of the Speaker running for the presidency in 2003 with House support.[66] In May 2002 he survived yet another attempt to oust him on grounds of financial impropriety, winning instead a standing ovation after declaring that 'democracy cannot flourish under Olusegun Obasanjo….We are dealing with a situation whereby the president feels he is more important than the party.'[67] An attempt to impeach Obasanjo in the Senate collapsed in June for lack of support, after Senate President Anyim had reportedly been threatened with expulsion from the PDP.[68] In the meantime the National Assembly increased Obasanjo's capital budget for 2002 from N297 billion ($2.5 billion) to N486 billion ($4.0 billion) and overrode his veto, thereby precipitating the government's breach with the IMF.[69]

The conflict now moved towards a climax. On 13 August 2002, the House of Representatives resolved to call on Obasanjo to 'resign honourably … within two weeks from the date of this motion or face impeachment', on account of 'monumental inadequacies, ineptitude, persistent disrespect for the rule of law and obvious corruption being perpetrated in the presidency, which exposes the President's inability to steer the ship of state'.[70] Interviewed, Na'Abba accused Obasanjo of moving like Hitler, step by step, towards 'a civilian dictatorship'. Conservative northern notables gave the Speaker their support. Obasanjo dismissed the ultimatum as 'a joke taken too far'.[71] His allies mobilised support. Finance Minister Ciroma called the threat 'a blackmail move against Obasanjo for his prudent utilisation of public funds'. The PDP Working Committee summoned party members of the House and ordered them to withdraw the impeachment motion or leave the party.[72] At a meeting between Obasanjo and PDP governors, the motion was attributed to a 'conspiracy of some retired generals in collaboration with some foreign governments and medias', seeking, according to Obasanjo, to terminate democracy. Suggestions included charging those responsible with treason, organising mass solidarity visits to support the President, and offering a 're-election bonus' to legislators who opposed impeachment.[73] Oshiomhole threatened that workers would storm the National Assembly if Obasanjo was impeached. In Yorubaland, Afenifere denounced the demand for resignation. The Ogun State branch of the PDP described it as a 'coup by the North against the South-West', and the Oodua People's Congress threatened to break up the country if impeachment went ahead.[74] Some Christians were reported to see it as a Muslim plot. Ohanaeze Ndigbo denounced the motion as 'most irresponsible'.[75] In Na'Abba's constituency in Kano, Obasanjo asked the emir to intervene on his behalf and the PDP chairman warned of ethnic pogroms if impeachment took place.[76]

The legislators were determined to proceed. At the end of August the Senate resolved by 77 votes to 6 to liaise with the House in investigating Obasanjo's non-compliance with appropriation acts. As the date of the ultimatum expired, Vice-President Atiku and others sought to mediate, while the President himself was reported to be increasingly worried and conciliatory.[77] On 3 September, the

House of Representatives issued the list of Obasanjo's seventeen alleged constitutional breaches forming the case against him. The most weighty were his refusal to implement budgets fully; various unbudgeted expenditures; maintaining illegal dedicated accounts (presumably the Excess Crude Account); failure to pay the full 13% of revenue to oil-producing states; personally exercising the functions of the Minister of Petroleum Resources; and his use of the army at Odi and Zaki-Biam.[78] Four days later, Obasanjo published a characteristically thorough, point by point reply, describing it as an educational exercise rather than a constitutional duty.[79] He insisted that none of the charges against him was of a kind to justify impeachment. All were false or mistaken. 'A budget', he explained, 'is an indicative plan which can only be implemented to the extent that resources are available.' He claimed to have implemented 52% of the capital budget in 1999, 70% in 2000, and 66% in 2001. Taken as a whole, it was an impressive and convincing reply, with perhaps two exceptions. He did not justify the Excess Crude Account, perhaps holding that it was not a dedicated account as normally defined. And although he claimed the sole constitutional right to use the army within Nigeria when necessary, he did not defend the manner in which the troops had acted at Odi and Zaki-Biam.

Whether Obasanjo's response influenced political opinion is unknown, but by mid September – and probably from the beginning of the crisis – majority feeling was clearly that impeachment was too dangerous to proceed with, as an opinion poll suggested.[80] On 10 September, for example, Emeka Anyaoku, former Secretary-General of the Commonwealth, called for a truce because the issue was 'evoking primordial instincts of ethnicity' at 'great peril to the continued peace and corporate existence of our country,' which could not be justified only months before an election.[81] The Representatives, however, remained defiant. At a caucus meeting, a motion accusing Obasanjo 'was received with an ovation that nearly brought down the roof'. Over 90% of those present were said to have scrambled to sign it. One leading advocate of impeachment claimed that the necessary two-thirds majorities in favour of it existed in both the House and the Senate.[82] A month later, at a meeting of PDP leaders designed to bring about reconciliation, Obasanjo was criticised on all sides and denounced by Na'Abba: 'I will tell you that you, Mr President, is [sic] the problem in the PDP. You claim to be a messiah and you have become arrogant to the extent that you have sidelined all the people who contributed to your victory in 1999.' Several speakers urged Obasanjo to abandon thought of a second term of office. 'While people spoke one after another, looking at the president in the face, and accusing him of failing woefully, the president sat speechless', a journalist was told. At the end he 'pleaded for forgiveness': 'if anybody has done anything wrong, everything ends on my desk as the President of the country.'[83] It was a humiliation he would neither forget nor forgive.

Yet the pressure on the Representatives was growing. A PDP panel cleared Obasanjo of all the charges against him. The President chose this moment to reveal that he had refused before his nomination to sign a pact guaranteeing powerful offices to the North, angering Afenifere and causing Middle Belt leaders to complain that it had been a dirty political intrigue.[84] Moreover, agents were working assiduously on individual legislators with threats and promises. Several were warned that anyone signing an impeachment motion would be denied PDP renomination, although Na'Abba commented that unless Obasanjo were first removed there would in any case be no fair election.[85] The final blows to the impeachment campaign appear to have come through mediation by former heads of state and by pressure on the Senate and its President that eroded the potential two-thirds majority there. The proposal was abandoned early in November.[86]

All eyes were now on the elections due in April 2003. Their approach swung the balance of power decisively away from legislators and towards executives, both the President and especially the state governors, with their control of local patronage and votes. The most conspicuous victims of this process were the leaders of the two houses of the National Assembly. Anyim Pius Anyim had presided over a largely quiescent Senate, but he had gained Obasanjo's enmity during the dispute over the Electoral Bill, by allowing the Senate to give initial support to impeachment, and by leading the move late in 2002 to emasculate the Independent Corrupt Practices Commission.[87] Equally important, Anyim was in competition with Governor Sam Egwu, an early Obasanjo loyalist, for predominance in Ebonyi State, a contest rooted in rivalry between Anyim's better educated southern portion of the state and Egwu's more populous section.[88] Following Anyim's election as Senate President, his interventions in state affairs led to violent disputes within the PDP. Party headquarters tried initially to resolve the conflict, but Egwu's control of party congresses enabled him to oust Anyim's supporters. Then the escalating conflict between the National Assembly and the presidency swung the party leadership behind Egwu.[89] In October 2002, Anyim announced that he would not seek re-election to the Senate, although insisting that this was not due to the erosion of his local popularity: 'my constituency is very much intact.' It was at least a tactical retreat. Seven years later Anyim and Egwu were still in competition.[90]

That left Na'Abba. Obasanjo had made no secret of his determination to destroy him.[91] The opportunity lay in the complicated political rivalries of Kano State, where control of the PDP was disputed between the governor, Rabiu Kwankwaso, an Obasanjo loyalist, and one of his predecessors, Abubakar Rimi, whom Obasanjo had made his most bitter political enemy. Na'Abba was Rimi's protégé and had vowed to leave the PDP if Obasanjo remained its presidential candidate, but as the election approached, he back-tracked and was re-adopted for his Kano Central constituency. The irreconcilable Rimi, however, supported the ANPP governorship candidate against Kwankwaso. Na'Abba was suspected of conniving with him. Three days before the election, the PDP suspended Na'Abba for 'anti-party activities' and Kwankwaso swung the party machine against him. With the PDP divided, Kwankwaso lost the governorship and Na'Abba lost his National Assembly seat.[92] His national political career collapsed as meteorically as it had begun. The lesson was there for the next generation of legislators.

NOTES

1. Bolaji Akinyemi in *This Day*, 30 August 1999.
2. *Daily Times*, 2 January 1978.
3. Jubril Aminu in *Newswatch*, 19 June 2006, p. 56.
4. Above, p. 103; Shagari, *Beckoned*, p. 199.
5. Utomi, *To serve*, p. 306.
6. *Newswatch*, 19 July 1999, p. 9; *Daily Trust*, 25 July 2003; Obe, *New dawn*, vol. 3, p. 341.
7. Lewis and Bratton, 'Attitudes', p. 3.
8. *Tell*, 14 February 2000, p. 50.

9. *Newswatch*, 11 September 2000, p. 22; *This Day*, 11 August 2000.
10. *This Day*, 17 August 2002; *Africa Research Bulletin (Political)*, February 2000, p. 17877.
11. *Tell*, 2 September 2002, p. 3.
12. Governor Abubakar Audu of Kogi in *West Africa*, 17 June 2002, p. 13.
13. Darren Kew, 'The 2003 elections: hardly credible, but acceptable', in Rotberg, *Crafting*, pp. 142–3.
14. *Daily Trust*, 22 July 2003.
15. Isaac Olawale Albert, 'A review of the campaign strategies', *Journal of African Elections*, 6, 2 (October 2007), 73; *This Day*, 30 December 2001.
16. Audu Ogbeh, quoted in *West Africa*, 21 April 1986, p. 823.
17. *Tell*, 29 May 2000, p. 21.
18. *Tell*, 13 May 2002; *Hotline*, 5 September 1999.
19. *Newswatch*, 19 July 1999, p. 9.
20. Nwabueze, *How Obasanjo subverted law*, p. 144.
21. The models for this analysis are F.G. Bailey, *Stratagems and spoils: a social anthropology of politics* (Oxford, 1970); John Gallagher, Gordon Johnson, and Anil Seal (ed.), *Locality, province and nation: essays on Indian politics 1870 to 1940* (Cambridge, 1973).
22. *This Day*, 13 and 24 July 1999; *Newswatch*, 8 January 2001, p. 23.
23. Amadi, *Power and politics*, pp. 17–20; *This Day*, 16 July 1999.
24. Above, pp. 187, 203; *This Day*, 13 July 1999.
25. *This Day*, 28–29 July and 1 August 1999.
26. *This Day*, 3 August 1999.
27. *Hotline*, 5 September 1999; *This Day*, 25 August 1999.
28. *This Day*, 12 and 15 August 1999; *Newswatch*, 23 August 1999, p. 22.
29. *This Day*, 2 September 1999.
30. Obasanjo, *Selected speeches*, vol. 2, p. 192. See also Nwabueze's view in *This Day*, 17 May 2000, and the criticism in *This Day*, 22 May 2000.
31. Na'Abba in *Punch*, 16 November 2008.
32. Arthur M. Schlesinger Jr., *The imperial presidency* (new edition, Boston, 1989), pp. 235, 238, 398; Shagari, *Beckoned*, p. 255; *This Day*, 15 July 2009.
33. *This Day*, 24 October and 5 and 19 November 1999.
34. *Africa Research Bulletin (Political)*, November 1999, p. 13759.
35. *Guardian*, 1 August 2007.
36. *This Day*, 31 March 1999; *Tell*, 8 November 1999, pp. 18–19.
37. *Guardian*, 14 December 2007; Okoi-Uyouyo, *Yusufu*, p. 141
38. *This Day*, 21–22 November and 15 December 1999.
39. *Tell*, 3 January 2000, p. 23.
40. *This Day*, 24 November 1999; *Newswatch*, 6 December 1999, p. 29.
41. *Guardian*, 1 June 2001.
42. *This Day*, 1, 5, and 10–17 December 1999; *Newswatch*, 27 December 1999, pp. 26–7.
43. *This Day*, 23 April and 8 May 2000.
44. *This Day*, 15 and 27 April and 3 May 2000.
45. *This Day*, 27 February 2000.
46. *This Day*, 22 February and 18 June 2000.
47. *This Day*, 9 and 23 August 2000, 4 September 2002.
48. *Newswatch*, 8 January 2001, pp. 22–3; *This Day*, 27 August 2000; *Weekly Trust*, 1 September 2000.
49. *This Day*, 27 August and 28 October 2000.
50. *Weekly Trust*, 1 September 2000.
51. *Tell*, 14 August 2000, p. 23.
52. *This Day*, 5 August and 7, 14, and 25 October 2000.
53. *This Day*, 24 October 2000.

54. *This Day*, 1, 5, and 14 November 2000; *Tell*, 20 November 2000, pp. 20–2; *Weekly Trust*, 3 November 2000 (giving the vote as 192 against 76).
55. *This Day*, 17 and 22 December 2000.
56. *Guardian*, 25 May 2007.
57. *This Day*, 10 November and 13 and 20 December 2000.
58. Lewis et al., 'Down to earth', pp. 4, 16; Lewis and Alemika, 'Seeking', p. vii.
59. *This Day*, 12 July 2001; *Post Express*, 3 September 2002.
60. Obe, *New dawn*, vol. 3, pp. 171–4. See also *This Day*, 18 November 2001; *Newswatch*, 20 November 2001, pp. 15–19; *West Africa*, 26 November 2001, pp. 19–20.
61. See Toyin Falola (ed.), *African politics in postimperial times; the essays of Richard L. Sklar* (Trenton, 2002), p. 407.
62. *This Day*, 1 June 2001 and 4 January 2002; *Newswatch*, 24 September 2001, pp. 16–17.
63. *This Day*, 29–30 December 2001; *Newswatch*, 14 January 2002, pp. 21–7, and 10 February 2003, p. 55; *Insider Weekly*, 17 June 2002, p. 3.
64. *This Day*, 13 December 2001; *Newswatch*, 14 January 2003, pp. 28–9.
65. *This Day*, 17 August 2002; Nwabueze, *How Obasanjo subverted law*, p. 334.
66. *This Day*, 15–16 February 2002, 3 and 10 March 2002; *Newswatch*, 11 March 2002, pp. 43–50; *Nigerian Tribune*, 2 March 2003.
67. *Newswatch*, 27 May 2002, pp. 43–7.
68. *Newswatch*, 1 July 2002, p. 41, and 15 July 2002, pp. 12–13.
69. See above, p. 211.
70. *This Day*, 14 August 2002.
71. *This Day*, 18 and 23 August and 8 September 2002.
72. *This Day*, 17–18 and 21 August 2002.
73. *This Day*, 19 August 2002.
74. *Post Express*, 6 September 2002; *This Day*, 21 August 2002; *West Africa*, 16 September 2002, p. 4.
75. *West Africa*, 14 October 2002, p. 19, and 26 August 2002, p. 16.
76. *Newswatch*, 2 September 2002, p. 13; *This Day*, 18 August 2002.
77. *This Day*, 28 and 31 August 2002; *Post Express*, 4 September 2002.
78. Texts in *This Day*, 5 September 2002; *West Africa*, 16 September 2002, pp. 10–11.
79. *Post Express*, 16 September 2002; *West Africa*, 30 September 2002, pp. 12–18.
80. *Post Express*, 15 September 2002.
81. *This Day*, 11 September 2002.
82. *This Day*, 15 September 2002; *West Africa*, 16 September 2002, p. 14.
83. *This Day*, 16 October 2002; *Post Express*, 16 October 2002; *Newswatch*, 28 October 2002, p. 44.
84. *Post Express*, 27 September and 13 October 2002; *This Day*, 22 January 2006.
85. *Post Express*, 6 and 18 September 2002.
86. *Guardian*, 2 November 2002; *Newswatch*, 18 November 2002.
87. *This Day*, 26 October 2002; *Guardian*, 20 November 2002.
88. *This Day*, 3 October 2001; *Guardian*, 11 June 2002.
89. *This Day*, 15 January and 9 and 15 July 2002.
90. *Nigerian Tribune*, 26 September 2009.
91. *This Day*, 17 August 2002.
92. *This Day*, 8 September 2002; *Newswatch*, 16 April 2001, p. 49; *Guardian* , 30 June 2002; *Nigerian Tribune* , 16, 18, and 22 February and 2 March 2003; A. Carl LeVan, Titi Pitso, and Bodunrin Adebo, 'Elections in Nigeria: is the third time a charm?' *Journal of African Elections*, 2, 2 (2003), 42; *Tell*, 28 April 2003, p. 5.

19
Re-election

The constitution limited presidents and state governors to two four-year terms of office. There was no limitation for legislators. Nigerian politicians began to prepare for the next election on the day after the last one. By September 1999, less than six months after Obasanjo's initial victory, a shadowy group called Forum 37 was in being to ensure his re-election in 2003, with Vice-President Atiku as grand patron. The organisers, it was said, were 'cashing in on the high performance rating of the administration and the mass support being enjoyed by it from most Nigerians'.[1]

Obasanjo was initially very popular. The restoration of democracy after sixteen years of military rule raised high – indeed, unrealistic – expectations. In January and February 2000, after about nine months of Obasanjo's administration, the American-financed Afrobarometer organisation carried out the first of four rounds of public opinion polls conducted during Obasanjo's presidency. Some 90% of those interviewed disapproved of military rule, 81% supported democracy, 84% were satisfied with the democracy existing in Nigeria, and 81% believed they could choose leaders who would improve their lives. A similar proportion, 81%, rated the government's performance as good or very good, while 90% said they trusted the president.[2] His military purge, his attack on corruption, and his obvious energy and determination all won respect. 'President Obasanjo still commands popular acclaim' at the end of his first year in office, a journalist wrote, adding, however, that 'he has lost the critical acclaim.'[3]

The emerging political criticism was strongest in the North, where Obasanjo had won his crucial electoral support. The retirement of mainly northern 'political' officers, the alleged Christian and Yoruba bias in his cabinet, and the OPC attacks on northerners in Lagos aroused anger even among many who had supported his campaign. Obasanjo's 'main objective', an extremist warned, 'is to fling Hausa-Fulani supporters of his presidential ambition on to the dunghill of political extinction and irrelevance.'[4]

Politicians from the Middle Belt and the Niger Delta, which had profited from Obasanjo's military appointments, viewed his early regime more warmly, but Igbo leaders in the south-east saw little to allay the sense of marginalisation they had felt since the civil war. They, too, counted the ministries (three of twenty-two, it was claimed) and permanent secretaryships (one of seventy-two) allocated to them. They complained, with justice, that new federal institutions were not located in their region.[5] They were angered when Obasanjo first denied Okadigbo the Senate presidency and then manoeuvred him out of it. 'As far as I'm concerned', Obasanjo insisted, 'the civil war ended in 1970', but many easterners did not believe him: 'Obasanjo's anti-Eastern agenda is so ingrained in him that I suspect he implements it unconsciously.'[6]

Alongside regional discontents went the widespread feeling that Obasanjo's ministers were too numerous, old, corrupt, political, and incompetent. In November 2000, 47 prominent people aged under 50 formed a National Integration Group to press for a transfer of power to their generation. They included Anyim and Na'Abba, at least fourteen state governors, the industrialist Aliko Dangote, and the trade unionist Adams Oshiomhole.[7] Perhaps partly in response, Obasanjo replaced ten of his ministers in January 2001 and another four in June, although he retained several older men of political weight, including Danjuma, Ciroma, Ige, and Anenih.[8] Repeated conflict with the National Assembly damaged the President's standing, as, perhaps more severely, did his mishandled attempt to reduce the petrol subsidy. It was indeed in the economic field that popular dissatisfaction with the regime first became widespread. A poll of 1,550 respondents in November 2002 was evenly divided over whether the President should enjoy a second term.[9]

Regional discontents crystallised into a belief that Obasanjo was favouring his own Yoruba people, although they had voted against him:

> The moment he got the Presidency, he allowed himself to be hijacked by Afenifere, the Yoruba tribal irredentists who see themselves as the best of mankind....The idea is to let Yorubas get as much as possible before the eventual breakup.... All these Afenifere insolence is about making an issue of 2003 election; if Obasanjo doesn't get a second term they will opt out of Nigeria.[10]

To support this analysis, critics pointed to Yoruba over-representation in positions of power (especially the President's security apparatus), the OPC's ethnic arrogance, and the remarkable swing of Yoruba opinion towards the new regime. In 1999 Obasanjo had received only 20% of the votes in the six Yoruba states,[11] but in May 2000 some 80% of people interviewed there replied that they would vote for him in an immediate election, against a maximum of about 65% in any other region.[12]

Politicians scrambled to adjust themselves to a swing that transformed the political scene. For Obasanjo himself, victory in his own region would not only compensate for his declining support in the North but would strengthen his position within the PDP and indicate an acceptance by his own people hitherto denied him.[13] For his opponents in the Alliance for Democracy (AD) who currently controlled Yorubaland, the swing of opinion accompanied a split in December 1999 between those loyal to the ethnic leadership of Afenifere and those (including Bola Ige) anxious to free the party to canvass support elsewhere in the country. The Electoral Commission recognised Ige's faction as the official party leadership.[14] Obasanjo reinforced the attack on Afenifere by encouraging the formation, late in 2000, of a rival Yoruba Council of Elders, which embraced not only opponents of Awolowo's former dominance of Yoruba politics but some of his closest disciples, including L.K. Jakande, previously Governor of Lagos. In August 2001 the Council declared support for Obasanjo's re-election.[15] Two months later he conducted a fund-raising ceremony and made a tactful donation of N200,000 (nearly $2,000) to complete the hospital that Awolowo had planned at his Ikenne home.[16] By then, an Obasanjo Solidarity Forum was campaigning vigorously in Yorubaland, while both branches of the

Oodua People's Congress, which had opposed Obasanjo's election in 1999, now threatened vengeance against his opponents in the National Assembly.[17]

The key question was whether the PDP should confine its campaign in Yorubaland to the presidential contest, seeking AD support for Obasanjo while leaving the incumbent AD governors and legislators in office, or whether it should seek a complete dominance of regional politics at the 2003 elections. Bola Ige, caught between his leading role in the AD and his position in Obasanjo's cabinet, naturally urged the former course. Others insisted that the PDP must gain control at all political levels, especially in local government, because (as in 1999) its representation there would determine the number of Yoruba delegates to vote for Obasanjo at the PDP's nominating convention.[18] Obasanjo cleverly allowed this question to remain unresolved. Afenifere, equally, refused to decide whether or not to support his candidacy, despite his attempt to persuade its elderly leaders to back him, but they had no alternative presidential candidate and could only hope to divide the Yoruba vote.[19] Gradually the dynamics of political competition settled the issue. Torn between the two parties, Ige was about to resign from the cabinet when, in December 2001, he was the victim of a professional murder under circumstances that have never been explained.[20] Two months later the incumbent AD governors in the region resolved to reunite the party and refuse any state governorship to the PDP at the election, but they were challenged by relatively young businessmen and professionals, such as Gbenga Daniel in Ogun and Segun Agagu in Ondo, who were eager to gain power on a PDP-Obasanjo ticket. Both parties were divided on whether they wanted to compromise.[21] Opaque negotiations during mid 2002 produced no clear agreement, the AD governors later claiming, and Obasanjo denying, that the PDP undertook not to put up governorship candidates if the AD did not contest the presidency.[22] Meanwhile the impeachment crisis of August 2002 further consolidated Yoruba support behind the President. Shortly before the election, AD leaders made clear their backing for him.[23] Ironically, as so often, it was his fate, as the enemy of ethnicity, to demonstrate the continuing power of Yoruba ethnicity.

According to the press, by October 2000 Obasanjo had told Anenih that he wanted a second term. Two months later, Anenih declared that there would be no vacancy for a president in 2003. Publicly, however, Obasanjo denied that he had even considered the question.[24] Critics urged him to take the 'Mandela option' by handing over to a younger man after a single term, although Mandela was a full decade older. The cautious Obasanjo was more concerned to be sure that if he stood, he would win. The growing evidence of Yoruba support must have encouraged him. By January 2002 there were at least five bodies campaigning on his behalf, but he did not announce his candidacy for the PDP nomination until April, after three bus-loads of politicians had urged him to run. He made the announcement at a televised carnival of the political elite in the International Conference Centre at Abuja. 'Service is still my only purpose', he declared. 'Service to Nigeria, service to humankind, and service to God.' 'The capacity crowd … rose and roared in appreciation.'[25]

Yet re-election demanded more than loyal cheers. In 2003, more than ever, it demanded the support of state governors and the votes they controlled, for the restoration of democracy in 1999 meant that almost all state governors were also seeking re-selection, with all the power of incumbency they enjoyed. During April 2002, the bulk of PDP governors were reported to be offering support for Obasanjo in return for a promise of re-selection for themselves.[26] No deal was made at that time, perhaps because it would have driven other gubernatorial aspirants into opposition parties. As a result, during the next six months, as Obasanjo's conflict with the National Assembly escalated, his authoritarianism became increasingly apparent, and his popularity ratings fell, several governors began to contemplate alternative presidential candidates. This was especially true of the governors of Niger Delta states, angered by the President's refusal – endorsed by the Supreme Court – to allocate them 13% of revenues from offshore oil.[27] In November 2002, as the date of the PDP's presidential nominating convention neared, Governor Ibori of Delta State hosted 15 of the 21 PDP governors at a meeting where a large majority reportedly agreed to seek a new candidate. The party chairman failed to dissuade them and informed Obasanjo.[28] For many governors, this may well have been a renewed attempt to bargain for their own re-selection, not least because the Independent Corrupt Practices Commission was investigating allegations against eleven governors, who remained immune from prosecution only while in office.[29] Anenih announced at this time that the PDP would re-select all its governors, but this infuriated other aspirants and was disowned by Obasanjo and Ogbeh.[30]

One possible alternative to Obasanjo was Vice-President Atiku. The relationship between a president and his deputy was inevitably tense, especially with so domineering a leader as Obasanjo, but on the surface the two had worked well together, although they were not personally close. The Vice-President had a distinct constitutional role as Chairman of the National Economic Council. Obasanjo also gave him charge of privatisation and relied heavily on him in dealings with the North, especially during the Sharia crisis. Atiku behaved with loyalty and discretion, risking his popularity by trying to restrain Muslim zealots while making clear his personal commitment to Sharia law.[31] Beneath the surface, however, the relationship became increasingly difficult. Atiku's northern support and his leadership of the PDM faction gave him a powerful position within the ruling party and especially among the governors, many of whom belonged to the PDM and saw Atiku as a man of their own generation with whom they could do business more easily than with the patronising and temperamental Obasanjo. This independent power alarmed not only the President and the military men around him but rival political operators like Anenih.[32] Tension was especially high during the impeachment crisis, when Obasanjo's aides assured him that Atiku – the natural beneficiary of a successful impeachment – was covertly encouraging and financing the campaign.[33] The President also believed – as did many – that Atiku had taken corrupt advantage of the privatisation process, that he lay behind suggestions that Obasanjo should follow the 'Mandela option', and that he encouraged northern campaigns to make himself a presidential candidate in 2003, an entirely feasible possibility that was sponsored in part by the PDP's opponents.[34] When Atiku appeared to take it for granted that he would be Obasanjo's running-mate, the President declared his own candidacy without mentioning him.[35] Obasanjo remedied this a few days later, after Atiku had said that he would rather run with Obasanjo than against him and several governors had warned that if Atiku was dropped they might in turn drop Obasanjo.[36] As the convention approached, however, Atiku remained a possible candidate. So did the seventy-year-old Alex Ekwueme, an embittered but reluctant candidate persuaded by the party's Aborigines to enter the contest only three weeks before the convention, saying that he would not have done so if Nigeria had possessed a president who heeded advice.[37]

The many different accounts of intrigue at the PDP convention of January 2003 make a firm reconstruction impossible, but it appears that by repeating their reservations about Obasanjo's candidacy and discussing the alternatives of an Ekwueme-Atiku ticket or an Atiku presidency, the governors secured assurances of re-selection from the party leaders in return for undertakings to back Obasanjo at the convention (although in one case the leaders reneged on this).[38] At the same time, Atiku, who had been warned that Obasanjo might drop him, told an interviewer that he had not decided between Obasanjo, Ekwueme, or his own candidacy. This obliged Obasanjo's camp to repeat its assurances to him, while Atiku persuaded the governors that it would be demeaning for him to switch to Ekwueme and against the national interest to contest the presidency in 2003 as a northerner.[39] Matters were finalised at a meeting at which, according to Ibori's account, 'Atiku told the President in the presence of the governors that he was known to be very dictatorial, vindictive and unforgiving. The President appealed to the governors to support him and assured both the governors and the party leadership that if he was allowed to continue for the second term, he would adopt a more democratic approach.'[40] Legend had it that the President prostrated himself before his deputy in the governors' presence. That was singularly unlikely and Atiku denied it, but that did not save Obasanjo from his enemies' taunts: 'It was his running-mate that picked him.'[41] Atiku would pay for that.

When the full convention met under television lights, the decision had already been made and the voting was immaculate. Obasanjo received 2,642 votes, Ekwueme 611, Rimi 159, and Gemade 17. Obasanjo described his victory as 'the Lord's doing'. Ekwueme denounced it as a charade.[42]

Ekwueme's anger was shared by the one PDP governor denied reselection, Chinwoke Mbadinuju of Anambra, who was at odds with Sir Emeka Offor, the self-made oil tycoon who contributed generously to PDP funds. Offor was determined to oust the governor and had the support of Anambra's elite, for previous governors had ruined Anambra's finances and Mbadinuju could not pay its teachers and civil servants for months at a time, during which they went on strike.[43] The governor allegedly used the support of the Bakassi Boys. He also had effective control of the local PDP machine. Late in 2002, he won re-nomination at three successive party conventions, the first two being annulled by headquarters. Finally Obasanjo intervened to veto the governor's candidacy, ostensibly because of his poor performance in office. Mbadinuju stood instead for an opposition party and lost.[44]

'Godfathers' like Offor were central figures in the election of 2003, thanks to the great expense of Nigerian politics.[45] Some state governors, such as Peter Odili of Rivers and Chimaroke Nnamani of Enugu, had been able to use the wealth and power of their office to free themselves from the financiers who had backed them in 1999, thereby securing Obasanjo's support. Where a godfather retained effective local control, however, the President had no inhibition in allying with him, sometimes earning himself the title of godfather of godfathers. This was the case in Kwara State, which Olusola Saraki delivered to Obasanjo in 2003 as he had delivered it in 1999, while at the same time inserting his son into the governor's office.[46] It was also the case in Oyo State, where the dominant Ibadan city had long been controlled by street politicians whose methods were the despair of the local elite of Christian modernisers. Like his colleague and political precursor, Shehu Musa Yar'Adua, Obasanjo knew that 'you cannot get to the grassroots level without passing through an acceptable leader of the people' and that 'there was a big difference between those who could win elections and those who could govern.'[47] Like

242

Yar'Adua, therefore, Obasanjo found the spearhead for his assault on Yorubaland in the man who could win elections in Ibadan, the 79-year-old Lamidi Adedibu, the most notorious of Nigeria's city bosses.[48] Adedibu, a Muslim like most of Ibadan's people, had two years of secondary education before entering local politics in 1951 and doing business as a 'political contractor'.[49] In return for payment, in cash and patronage opportunities, Adedibu provided not only voters but, more important, votes, with the networks, thuggery, and rigging needed to ensure them. The cash and patronage were then distributed, chiefly as food, to the crowds that thronged his compound:

> He held court sprawled across a large chair underneath a tin roof adjacent to his car park which was crowded with a long line of would-be supplicants. Adedibu's every word brought nods or cheers from those who crowded around to listen, and several people who walked across his field of vision immediately prostrated themselves as a gesture of deference when he glanced up in their general direction.[50]

Adedibu's most striking political success had been to deliver Oyo State to Yar'Adua during the abortive presidential campaign of 1992, despite opposition from strong Yoruba candidates. In 1999, he made the mistake of backing the APP, but as soon as Obasanjo emerged as victor, Adedibu offered his services, claiming that it was a religious duty to support the government of the day. By 2001 he was mobilising for the PDP.[51] 'In as much as Alhaji Lamidi Adedibu's kind of politics brings results,' Obasanjo declared after his retirement, 'I will continue to be his political disciple.'[52] In 2003 it did bring results, both for Obasanjo and for the PDP's governorship candidate, Rasheed Ladoja, a wealthy businessman and PDP founder who utilised Adedibu's electoral support: 'He said "Rashidi, what is it that you want?" I said I wanted to be governor. He said he would like to work with me and that there are certain things that they do in politics which I won't be able to do…. So, I said no problem.'[53]

The Ibadan model found echoes elsewhere in Yorubaland in 2003, especially in Ekiti State, where a young Ibadan businessman, Ayo Fayose, popularised himself by supplying water and drugs to voters before defeating rivals drawn from the state's educated elite, thereby earning their loathing and Obasanjo's support.[54] Yet the PDP in Yorubaland was not merely a 'ragtag army of former outsiders', as one opponent claimed.[55] Of its governorship candidates, Ladoja, Daniel, and Agagu were all relatively young and successful men impatient with Afenifere's introverted gerontocracy and eager, like the President, to draw the Yoruba back into the heart of national politics. Obasanjo was to claim this as one of his main achievements.[56]

The President did not fight his campaign of 2003 on issues. He fought in part on his record, claiming progress in telecommunications, electricity generation, primary schooling, industrial wages, and Nigeria's international standing.[57] He promised continuity and stability. He remained the best security against a return to military rule. He embodied Nigerian unity and the authority of the state, in so far as any individual could do so. As in 1999, he campaigned with such vigour that observers wondered what drove him.[58] In addition, he headed the only party with a national coverage and organisation and with the resources to mount a national campaign. Money remained central to Nigerian politics. Two years after the election, 26% of those questioned in an opinion survey said that they had been offered something for their vote.[59] Probably it was normally something quite small – four years later,

N200 ($2) was sometimes mentioned as the price of a vote[60] – but the major costs of electioneering were staff salaries, entertainment, travel, and publicity. The main PDP fund-raising dinner in Abuja was variously reported to have collected between N1 billion and N2.5 billion ($8–20 million), mostly from its businessmen-financiers (Dangote, Offor, Otedola, Adenuga, 'Atiku and friends') plus N10 million from each PDP governor, probably taken directly from public funds, and a pledge of another N2 billion from 'Corporate Nigeria', organised through the Stock Exchange.[61] The fees charged to aspirants for nomination (N5 million for president, N1 million for senators, and so on) may have brought the PDP another N1 billion. Governors of oil-producing states also commanded huge resources: Odili was said to have raised N1.4 billion for his re-election in Rivers State, while in Delta State, Ibori – popularly known as the Sheikh – was reported to have received N1 billion from five subscribers within fifteen minutes.[62] When Obasanjo met the new National Assembly in June 2003, he asked them to consider how the expense of elections could be restrained.

Opposition parties could not match these resources, nor could any of them present a presidential candidate with Obasanjo's claim to nationwide stature. The AD gave him its somewhat grudging support and confined itself to contesting governorship and legislative offices, mainly in the south-west. The former APP, now renamed the All Nigeria People's Party (ANPP), provided the chief opposition but was acutely short of funds and remained divided over whether to present a southern or northern candidate. The division delayed its registration and caused its convention to be postponed five times before the northern governors took control and chose Muhammadu Buhari, the authoritarian military head of state from 1983 to 1985, as its candidate. His outspoken support for Sharia law and avowed distaste for politics were thought by some to make him unelectable. With no hope of support in Yorubaland, Buhari looked for an Igbo running-mate and chose Okadigbo, who had abandoned the PDP after his ousting as Senate president.[63] Hopes of Igbo support, however, were dimmed by another contestant, the former Biafran leader, Emeka Ojukwu, representing the newly-registered All Progressive Grand Alliance (APGA), responding to vocal demands for an Igbo president, and hoping to imitate Yoruba success by reasserting his people's place in national politics.[64] The APGA was the only significant contender among seventeen new parties that contested the presidency after the Supreme Court facilitated party registration.

The 'battle of the generals,' as the impending three-way contest for the presidency was dubbed, aroused many fears that it might revive the regional and religious animosities of the First Republic and end similarly in military intervention.[65] Certainly, in the first election organised by a civilian government for twenty years, the competition to rig the elections before polling day was much greater than in 1999. Obasanjo had obstructed preparations by delaying the release of funds to the Independent National Electoral Commission (INEC). The voters' register was especially unreliable: 18% of potential voters interviewed two years later said they had not been registered, although the list contained the improbably large number of 60.8 million voters in a population of some 130 million. INEC's chairman admitted that 'the exercise was marked by multiple registration, under-aged registration, registration of aliens and possibly, the registration of the dead.' [66] In Lagos the police reportedly found 5 million false voters' cards. Unwilling to recruit the necessary 600,000 electoral officials from government employees because they might be controlled by state governors, INEC adopted the curious alternative of inviting political parties to nominate them.[67] Predictably, rigging was most intense in Rivers State, which also saw the most sensational murder, the shooting of Governor Odili's estranged godfather, Marshall Harry, while he was organising the launching of Buhari's campaign. Estimates of deaths during the entire electoral process ranged from 73 to over 100.[68]

Nevertheless, by Obasanjo's account, 12 April 2003 'saw the people of Nigeria turning out in record numbers to freely, transparently and fairly make their choice' of National Assembly members. Of the 346 seats in the House of Representatives, PDP won 213, ANPP 95, AD 31, and other parties 7.[69] The presidential and gubernatorial elections took place a week later. Turnout was 60% and voting was generally unexpectedly peaceful, the voters 'enthusiastic and vigilant'.[70] The main exceptions were parts of Rivers and Bayelsa States, where one monitoring group described the elections as 'low intensity armed struggle.' Rivers reported a 96% turnout and a 93% majority for Obasanjo, while Brass constituency in Bayelsa achieved both a 100% turnout and a 100% PDP vote.[71] Fraud, as distinct from violence, was reported by European Union observers in 13 of the 36 states. It was especially prevalent in Igboland, where one opinion poll before the election had shown a slight lead for Ojukwu but the election results recorded massive victories engineered by PDP governors.[72] 'In Enugu State, in the full view of international observers, a gang drove in a bus and made away with the ballot boxes before counting could start.' The successful PDP candidate for Anambra's troubled governorship later admitted that he knew he had not won. Obasanjo's home state, Ogun, recorded 747,296 votes in the gubernatorial election and 1,365,367 in the simultaneous presidential poll, with Obasanjo gaining 99.92% of the latter.[73]

The final result of the presidential poll gave Obasanjo 61.94% of the votes, Buhari 32.19%, and Ojukwu 3.29%.[74] Obasanjo's victory was certainly inflated, especially at Ojukwu's expense, but would probably have taken place even without the rigging. The PDP had hoped to win half of the six Yoruba states but in fact won all save Lagos. Obasanjo gained nearly 89% of votes in the south-west and won all other southern states, while the ANPP claimed seven states in the far north, taking Kano from the PDP – allegedly because *hisba* vigilantes protected the ballot boxes against tampering – but leaving it in control of twelve other northern states.[75] For Obasanjo, the reincorporation of the Yoruba into mainstream politics was a victory, but the alienation of the far north – the bulk of the Sharia states – was a compensating defeat, for it meant that Nigeria was not yet a dominant party state. As he commented, the election had replaced ethnicity by religion as the chief dividing line in politics.[76] Similarly, for a civilian government to have conducted a nationwide election was, in Nigerian terms, a victory. The compensating defeat was the manner of that victory. The reports of the more than 40,000 election observers illustrated this ambivalence. The most critical came from the Nigerians of the Transition Monitoring Group:

> While some of the governors would have won their elections with slim majorities, they proceeded to use state machinery to allocate obscene number of votes to themselves. While the President might have won his election with [a]simple majority of votes, his campaign moguls and hired mercenaries did not want to leave anything to chance. In the end we have an election that we are not sure reflects the genuine wish of the Nigerian people.[77]

European Union monitors were also sharply critical, focusing on the most abusive areas. 'In Enugu, Delta, Rivers, Cross River, Edo, Imo and Abia,' they reported, 'it

245

is doubtful that any credible elections took place.'[78] The Commonwealth Observer Group, by contrast, exphasised their positive impression

> that in most of Nigeria, despite significant challenges, a genuine and largely successful effort was made to enable the people to vote freely and that in most of the country conditions were such as to enable the will of the people to be expressed. However, there were parts of Nigeria in which many Nigerians were denied the right to participate in an authentic democratic process.[79]

Perhaps the *Economist* magazine summarised it most succinctly: 'The poll was dirty, but the more popular man won.'[80]

That was also the view of the courts. The roughly 1,600 elections held in April and May 2003 gave rise to nearly 900 legal challenges.[81] Both Ojukwu and Buhari contested Obasanjo's victory. Ojukwu's suit was quickly dismissed, but Buhari's provoked over two years of legal wrangling before the Supreme Court rejected it in July 2005 on the grounds that the election result was substantially fair.[82] Asked why there were so many allegations of rigging, the President replied blandly, but with a degree of truth, that Nigerian culture always attributed misfortune to other people's malice.[83]

The important verdict, however, was that of the people. In January 2000, when the Afrobarometer opinion pollsters had asked their carefully balanced sample of Nigerians whether the presidential election of 1999 had been conducted fairly, 72% had answered in the affirmative. Asked the same question about the 2003 election, in October of that year, only 40% thought it had been fair. Positive responses in 2003 ranged from 58% in the north-eastern zone (Atiku's homeland) and 57% in the south-west (Obasanjo's) to only 12% in the south-south, where rigging and violence had been worst, and 10% in the south-east, where Ojukwu was widely thought to have been robbed. The role of the election in further alienating the people of the Niger Delta was to be especially important.[84]

In a wider perspective, experience of the election does not seem to have done serious damage to Nigerian belief in democracy, which was declining naturally but fairly steadily from the unrealistic hopes of 1999. In 2000, 81% preferred democracy to any other kind of government; in 2001, 71%; in 2003, 68%; and in 2005, 65%. Between 2001 and 2003, however, preference for democracy declined especially in the south-south (from 77% to 59%) and the south-east (from 89% to 65%).[85]

Responses changed radically, however, when those interviewed were asked whether they were very or fairly satisfied with the current working of Nigerian democracy. In 2000, a very high 84% had answered positively. This had fallen by 2001 to a more realistic 57%. In 2003 it fell still further to only 35%. It would be wrong to attribute this only to the election, for it doubtless also expressed many other reasons for dissatisfaction. Yet that the election was a major – probably *the* major – reason for dissatisfaction was suggested by the radical decline in positive responses between 2001 and 2003 in the south-south (from 45% to 14%) and the south-east (from 51% to 12%). Asked if they now enjoyed more political voice than under military rule, 60% of Nigerians had answered yes in 2001, but only 41% in 2003.[86]

Obasanjo made a grave political mistake to dismiss dissatisfaction with the election so glibly. His age and experience focused all his concern on the achievement of national unity and development. In pursuit of those vital goals, democracy had for him only an instrumental value. By contrast, for the next generation of Nigerians (the average age of Afrobarometer respondents was 28–9) the free and fair operation of democracy was important in itself, perhaps for some as important as unity or development, and more fragile than either. Obasanjo's age, dedication, and self-righteousness had prevented him from making that adjustment. The result was seen when Nigerians were asked another question: did they approve or strongly approve of their President's performance? Again the answers presumably expressed a range of experiences of the past four years. Yet whereas in 2001 some 72% had approved of Obasanjo's performance, in 2003 only 39% did so. Moreover, the proportions approving in 2003 were again exceptionally low in the south-east (17%) and the south-south (only 9%). Back in January 2000, eight months after he took office, 70% of people in the south-south had expressed approval of their President. At that time 30% of Nigerians had said they trusted Obasanjo a lot. In October 2003, only 3% said they trusted him 'a very great deal'.[87] As he entered his second term of office, Obasanjo carried a damaging burden of mistrust.

NOTES

1. *This Day*, 25 September 1999.
2. Lewis and Bratton, 'Attitudes', pp. 6–7, 10–11; Lewis and Alemika, 'Seeking', p. vii.
3. *This Day*, 21 May 2000.
4. Usman Balarabe, 'Obasanjo: the mask has fallen', *Weekly Trust*, 27 August 1999.
5. *Weekly Trust*, 12 November 1999; Alli, *Federal Republic*, p. 66; *This Day*, 20 September 1999.
6. *This Day*, 5 and 20 September 1999.
7. *This Day*, 13, 18, and 25 November 2000.
8. *Newswatch*, 12 February 2001, pp. 16–17; *This Day*, 13 June 2001.
9. *Guardian*, 14 November 2002.
10. *This Day*, 4 January 2001.
11. LeVan et al., 'Elections', p. 42.
12. These are rough estimates from figures in *This Day*, 28 May 2000.
13. Reuben Abati, 'Obasanjo: a psychoanalysis', *Guardian*, 8 June 2001.
14. *Newswatch*, 24 January 2000, pp. 32–3; *This Day*, 7 January 2001.
15. *This Day*, 7 January and 13 August 2001.
16. *Guardian*, 19 October 2001; Nolte, *Obafemi Awolowo*, p. 252.
17. *This Day*, 1 July 2001; Insa Nolte, '"Without women nothing can succeed": Yoruba women in the Oodua People's Congress (OPC), Nigeria', *Africa*, 78 (2008), 89.
18. *This Day*, 10 March 2001; Olusegun Agagu, *Towards 2003: year of destiny* (n.p., n.d.), p. 9.
19. *This Day*, 21 December 2001 and 14 March 2002.
20. *This Day*, 24 December 2001; *Tell*, 5 May 2003, p. 5.
21. *This Day*, 17 and 22 February and 19 May 2002.
22. *This Day*, 22 July 2002 and 5 April 2003; Kew in Rotberg, *Crafting*, p. 147.
23. *This Day*, 14 March 2003.
24. *This Day*, 8 October and 11 and 31 December 2000.
25. Obe, *New dawn*, vol. 3, p. 256; *Tell*, 6 May 2002, p. 36.
26. *Guardian*, 14 April 2002.
27. *Nigerian Tribune*, 1 January 2003.
28. Ibori's account is in *Guardian*, 26 September 2009.
29. Kew in Rotberg, *Crafting*, p. 145.

30. *Tell*, 9 December 2002, pp. 38–9.
31. *Guardian*, 5 April 2002.
32. *This Day*, 18 August 2001 and 16 May 2002.
33. *Tell*, 9 September 2002, p. 22, and 30 September 2002, pp. 26–7.
34. *Newswatch*, 17 September 2001, pp. 30–2; *Tell*, 15 July 2002, p. 18; *Guardian*, 19 April 2002.
35. *Guardian*, 16 April 2002; *Newswatch*, 6 May 2002, pp. 17–19.
36. *This Day*, 4 May 2002.
37. *This Day*, 20 October 2002 and 26 January 2003.
38. *Nigerian Tribune*, 3 January 2003.
39. *Nigerian Tribune*, 1 January 2003; *This Day*, 5 and 16 January 2003; *Newswatch*, 24 February 2006, p. 18; Atiku in *Newswatch*, 4 December 2006, pp. 19–20.
40. *Guardian*, 26 September 2009.
41. *Newswatch*, 20 February 2006, p. 18; *Guardian*, 24 February 2008; Atiku in *Newswatch*, 4 December 2006, p. 2; Wale Adebanwi, 'Obasanjo, Yoruba and the future of Nigeria', http://www.odili.net/news/source/2003/ feb/16/220.html (accessed 15 December 2008).
42. *This Day*, 6–7 and 20 January 2003.
43. *Newswatch*, 28 June 1999, pp. 30–1, and 6 May 2002, pp. 31–2; *This Day*, 1 August 2002.
44. Above, p. 189; *This Day*, 6 February and 13 December 2003, 12 January 2006; *Daily Champion*, 3 December 2006.
45. For analysis of this phenomenon, see Steve Nwosu, 'When the falcon no longer hears the falconer', *This Day*, 16 April 2001.
46. *Newswatch*, 9 July 2001, pp. 21–3; *This Day*, 5 and 21 April 2003.
47. Ayokunle Olumuyiwa Omobowale and Akinpelu Olanrewaju Olutayo, 'Chief Lamidi Adedibu and patronage politics in Nigeria', *Journal of Modern African Studies* , 45 (2007), 433; Farris and Bomoi, *Shehu Musa Yar'Adua*, p. 202.
48. For this political pattern, see Sklar, *Nigerian political parties*,Ch.7; Kenneth W.J. Post and George D. Jenkins, *The price of liberty: personality and politics in colonial Nigeria* (Cambridge, 1973).
49. The phrase comes from Kolapo Idola in *Newswatch*, 6 June 1994, p. 18.
50. Human Rights Watch, 'Criminal politics: violence, "godfathers" and corruption in Nigeria' (2007), pp. 52–3, http://www.hrw.org/en/reports/2007/10/08/criminal-politics (accessed 10 October 2010). See also the vivid description by Olusegun Adeniyi in *This Day*, 4 January 2006.
51. *Newswatch*, 30 May 1994; *Nigerian Tribune*, 16 December 2006; *Weekly Trust*, 8 October 1999; *This Day*, 23 December 2001.
52. *Nigerian Tribune*, 3 February 2008.
53. *Vanguard*, 26 November 2006.
54. *Guardian*, 18 May 2001; *Nigerian Tribune*, 30 March 2003; *Source*, 2 February 2004, pp. 12–16.
55. Waziri Adio in *This Day*, 20 April 2003.
56. *This Day*, 1 August 2004.
57. Election address in *This Day*, 14 February 2003.
58. *Nigerian Tribune*, 11 March 2003.
59. Practical Sampling International, 'Summary', p. 26.
60. N.D. Danjibo and Abubakar Oladeji, 'Vote buying in Nigeria: an assessment of the 2007 general elections', *Journal of African Elections*, 6, 2 (2007), 180–200.
61. *This Day*, 25 January 2003; *Nigerian Tribune*, 18 January 2003; *Tell*, 31 March 2003, pp. 30–1.
62. *This Day*, 1 December 2002 and 6 March 2003.
63. *This Day*, 28 July 2002 and 1 April 2003; *Nigerian Tribune*, 14 March 2003.
64. *Newswatch*, 1 April 2002, p. 30, and 10 February 2003, pp. 14–15.

65. *This Day*, 9 and 19–20 January 2003; *Newswatch*, 20 January 2003, p. 10.
66. Kew in Rotberg, *Crafting*, p. 148; Practical Sampling International, 'Summary', p. 11; Dele Seteolu, 'The electorate, voting behaviour and the 2003 general elections', in Remi Anifowose and Tunde Babawale (ed.), *2003 general elections and democratic consolidation in Nigeria* (Lagos, 2003), p. 148; *This Day*, 23 January 2003.
67. *This Day*, 17 January 2003; Alaba Ogunsanwo, 'Keynote address', in Anifowose and Babawale, *2003 general elections*, p. 15.
68. Kew in Rotberg, *Crafting*, p. 151; *This Day*, 23 June 2003; Human Rights Watch, 'Rivers and blood', pp. 4–5.
69. Obasanjo, *Standing tall*, p. 1; Peter M. Lewis, 'Nigeria: elections in a fragile regime', *Journal of Democracy*, 14, 3 (2003), 143.
70. Commonwealth Observer Group, *The National Assembly and presidential elections in Nigeria, 12 and 19 April 2003* (London, 2006), p. 29; Kew in Rotberg, *Crafting*, pp. 139, 157.
71. Human Rights Watch, 'Nigeria's 2003 elections: the unacknowledged violence' (2004), p. 6, http://www.hrw.org/reports/2004/nigeria0604/nigeria0604.pdf (accessed 30 September 2007); Kew in Rotberg, *Crafting*, p. 161; *This Day*, 1 November 2003.
72. *Times*, 23 April 2003; Kew in Rotberg, *Crafting*, pp. 151–4.
73. *West Africa*, 28 April 2003, p. 10; *This Day*, 16 December 2004; Kew in Rotberg, *Crafting*, p. 160.
74. *West Africa*, 28 April 2003, pp. 7–8.
75. LeVan et al., 'Elections', p. 43; *Newswatch*, 5 May 2003, p. 20; Tahir Haliru Gwarzo, 'Activities of Islamic civic associations in the northwest of Nigeria: with particular reference to Kano State', *Afrika Spectrum*, 38 (2003), 302.
76. *West Africa*, 30 June 2003, p. 9.
77. *Daily Trust*, 1 September 2003.
78. *Newswatch*, 19 May 2003, pp. 39–40.
79. Commonwealth Observer Group, *National Assembly and presidential elections*, p. vi.
80. Quoted in Last, 'Governing Nigeria', p. 1.
81. Obasanjo, *Standing tall*, p. 49.
82. *Daily Trust*, 23 July 2003; *This Day*, 3 July 2005.
83. *West Africa*, 30 June 2003, p. 9.
84. Lewis and Alemika, 'Seeking', pp. vii, 43.
85. Lewis, 'Performance', p. 3; Lewis and Alemika, 'Seeking', p. 41.
86. Lewis, 'Performance', p. 4; Lewis and Alemika, 'Seeking', pp. 15, 41.
87. Lewis, 'Performance', p. 6; Lewis and Alemika, 'Seeking', pp. vii, 44; Lewis and Bratton, 'Attitudes', p. 33; Lewis et al., 'Down to earth', p. 16.

Part V

The Second Presidential Term (2003–7)

20

The Imperious Presidency

When Obasanjo renewed his presidential oath on 29 May 2003, he was at the peak of his power. Whereas his initial election in 1999 had largely been arranged for him by political sponsors, his victory in 2003 was essentially his own, especially his triumph among his Yoruba people. He now dominated the party and the country. Less preoccupied by separatism and violence in all corners of the land, he could hope in his second term to move from seamanship to navigation, from merely keeping Nigeria afloat to giving a lasting trajectory to the country and the continent.

He had no doubt what that direction should be. He remained a patriot dedicated to the 'Nigerian project', impatient of fashionable scepticism with the African nation-state and of those wishing to take Nigeria to pieces and reconstruct it according to their various fancies. 'The measure of patriotism and dedication to common and collective good', he declared in his Independence Day broadcast on 1 October 2003, 'is not to become pessimistic and cynical, but to join hands to work hard for the nation, the community, family and individual. That is how to build a nation.'[1] 'The task ... of making Nigeria great'[2] required also a resolute commitment to the programme of economic reform and liberalisation that had begun to take shape during his first term. In pursuit of these goals, at the age of 66 and to the alarm of his doctors, Obasanjo still worked relentlessly, exhausting his staff, pestering them with enquiries at all hours of day or night, overawing them by his range of knowledge, seeking always to energise a country and a government that were exceptionally difficult to move.[3] Observers noted how the tempo of life in Abuja relaxed when the President was out of town, which was often, because in addition to assiduous touring of Nigeria he undertook heavy international duties, especially as Chairman of the African Union during 2004, when he spent 189 days outside Nigeria.[4]

Despite his years in power and his friendships with the great, Obasanjo had not lost his common touch. He no longer dressed like a farmer, but rather in a seemingly endless variety of Nigerian robes that gave dignity to his stature and corpulence and won the admiration of the crowds, for Nigerians, as he once boasted, could count themselves among the best dressed people on earth.[5] He did not waste his time, as he would have seen it, identifying with the spectators at national football matches, but he could address the people in their own languages and idioms. He was earthy, witty, apparently ageless:

> He could dance with the masses at political rallies, stop by the roadside and buy roasted corn; remove his agbada in public and settle down to a physical combat if anyone chal-

lenged him (nobody dared). He had no aristocratic airs, and he spoke straight from the heart. He was a mythical personality in the people's imagination, and they had so many sobriquets for him: OBJ, Baba Iyabo, Ebora Owu. His relationship with women was even a major topic of interest, and a source of curious admiration. He was generally regarded as an alpha male, in a society where a capacity for fun is admired, Obasanjo was seen as a 'correct guy'.[6]

Yet power had left its marks. During his second term, he grew increasingly authoritarian, impetuous, and unscrupulous. Power had accentuated the patriarchalism of his rural Yoruba upbringing, until he patronised not only unruly students or legislators but younger international statesmen.[7] He remained a man of military instincts and volcanic temper, capable, even as president, of seizing a whip to flog those who offended him on public occasions.[8] 'An angry Obasanjo is not a pretty sight',[9] a journalist remarked. As his severest critic, Wole Soyinka, saw acutely, the President's modest birth and upbringing had made him 'a study in the outer limits of compulsive rivalry', a man whose determination to win at all costs and no matter how long it took had been strengthened by his sense of providential mission.[10] 'I enjoy critics but I don't listen to them', he declared. 'What matters to me is my God, my goal and my work.'[11] His conviction made him intolerant of contradiction – he said that he could not allow a man talking nonsense to complete his sentence[12] – and ruthless in disposing of those who had served his purpose. His notorious ingratitude was in part a self-made man's anxiety to avoid indebtedness, but it was also a principled determination not to show undue favour to those who might make interested claims upon him, much as he discouraged such claims by his family and his Egba tribesmen. Obasanjo was above all a man of contradictions and unpredictability. Reporters who interviewed him, it was remarked, related their impressions like blind men describing an elephant.[13]

In no field was this more apparent than in his attitudes towards corruption. Nigerians were obsessed with the subject and Obasanjo was inevitably surrounded by allegations. He denied them vigorously and absolutely as what he once called 'unsubstantiated coffee shop rumours'.[14] 'I am the only leader in Nigeria that has [been] investigated and cleared by the anti-corruption bodies', he told an interviewer two years after leaving office. 'I do not say that people in my government were not corrupt. But I'm not corrupt.' The chairman of the Economic and Financial Crimes Commission (EFCC) confirmed this.[15] Obasanjo blamed the allegation on the envy and cynicism so damaging to the country:

> When I was growing up in the forties and people saw a man in a new car or dress or they passed by a new house, they would pray for the owner and pray that they might have one like him. Today whether you are in the private or public sector, every new thing you acquire is suspect and tended to be seen as the product of corruption and ill-gotten wealth. There seems to be no distinction made in the ordinary people's perception between honest living and acquisition To them the saint and the Satan are the same. It is a dangerous class reaction. Dictatorial misrule and bad government change the people and society for the worse.[16]

In reality, the change he lamented was probably due chiefly to the oil economy, which severed the connection between work and wealth, fostering the belief that substantial riches must be illegitimate.[17] These attitudes compound the difficulty of assessing whether and how Obasanjo was corrupt that results from the sensitivity of the subject, the inevitable obscurity of the evidence, and the fact that many investigations were still in progress after his retirement. Nevertheless, the issue is so important to an assessment of the man that it cannot be ignored.

Two general points emerge. First, Obasanjo's attitude towards corruption, like that of most people exposed to the temptation, was personal and complicated, certainly more complicated than his public posture on the issue. That did not make him a hypocrite; it merely meant that corruption is exceedingly difficult to define and delimit. Second, his attitudes and behaviour relaxed somewhat over time, in response, it will be suggested, to the behaviour of those around him and the problems requiring his attention.

In his career before becoming president, Obasanjo, like any powerful Nigerian, was often suspected of corruption, but no hard evidence was produced or has subsequently appeared, although he was clearly an astute and acquisitive businessman. He was also willing to help valued associates, as he did, for example, after leaving office in 1979, when aiding Andrew Young to negotiate a contract for an American firm to build a fertiliser plant in Nigeria, thereby strengthening a connection that Obasanjo had good reason to think was to Nigeria's advantage. During Obasanjo's presidency, Young's firm also handled Nigeria's public relations in the United States for a substantial fee.[18]

As a private citizen, Obasanjo campaigned vigorously against corruption. He continued the campaign during his first presidential term, securing the creation of the Independent Corrupt Practices Commission and then, when this proved inadequate, the Economic and Financial Crimes Commission, which received many of the powers of investigation, arrest, and prosecution denied to its predecessor and was headed by Nuhu Ribadu, an austere and ruthless young police lawyer trained at ABU. Ribadu began with a successful campaign against '419' advance-fee fraud, investigated the banking sector, had his first coup by gaoling the Inspector-General of Police for stealing $98 million of public money, and went on to pursue the state governors of Bayelsa, Plateau, and Ekiti. When most governors were due to hand over to successors in May 2007, seven were absent for fear of arrest by the EFCC once they lost their executive immunity. By then the Commission had secured nearly 300 convictions.[19] It had 'exploded the myth of the untouchable "big man"' and earned Obasanjo's regime much credit. An Afrobarometer poll in 2005 that showed growing hostility to the regime nevertheless praised its efforts against corruption. Transparency International, having ranked Nigeria the most corrupt country in the world in 2000, placed it at 149 among the 180 countries assessed in 2007.[20]

Ironically, Obasanjo's personal reputation for opposition to corruption moved in the opposite direction. It was generally high during his first presidential term. He declared his assets on taking office, although privately, as was perhaps inescapable for a polygynist with a fractious family. He was reported to have assembled his family, warned them not to take advantage of his name, and instructed cabinet members not to extend patronage to them.[21] He placed his shareholdings and business interests in a blind trust, Obasanjo Holdings Limited, over which he had in principle no control while he remained in office. The businessman Otunba Fasawe was reported to live in the presidential complex at Abuja and to represent Obasanjo's business interests.[22] These precautions helped to protect the President's reputation. Segun Agagu, his Minister of Power and Steel, affirmed in June 2002 that in three years he had never known Obasanjo to hint at corruption. The *Nigerian Tribune*, which had criticised Obasanjo relentlessly after 1979 but had now become supportive, described him shortly before the election of 2003 as one of only two 'stainless characters' among PDP leaders.[23]

Yet there were hesitations. Some wondered how the President had so quickly restored the fortunes of his Ota farm after it had decayed during his years in gaol.[24] Others questioned the sources of his campaign funding and his party's finances. Rumours were growing of the bribery scandal surrounding the liquefied natural gas plant at Bonny. The individual recipients of the more than $180 million kickback on that deal were not named and the bulk appears to have been paid before Obasanjo took office, but the American indictment claimed, for example, that in August 2002 a pilot's briefcase containing $1 million in $100 bills was handed over at an Abuja hotel 'for the benefit of a political party in Nigeria', at a time when there was only one political party worth corrupting. Whether Obasanjo was aware of such dealings is unknown, but they were part of the milieu in which he worked.[25] Other funds operated by the President's associates were alleged to act as conduits to the PDP.[26] There were many accounts of attempts by presidency agents to suborn the National Assembly. The most damaging allegation involving Obasanjo personally during his first term sought to implicate him, together with Vice-President Atiku, in a scheme to misuse their power to acquire rights over an oil block (OPL 245) containing unexpectedly rich reserves.[27] The President's association with Atiku may have explained an item discovered by American investigators in the accounts of the Siemens corporation, which allocated $172,000 for the purchase of watches for 'P. and V.P.', identified by the investigators as 'likely referring to the President and Vice President of Nigeria,' although there is no evidence that such gifts reached either.[28] As this example suggests, the truth of these allegations is generally impossible to determine. The point, however, is that Obasanjo, as President, was operating in a milieu of very wealthy men whose principles were not necessarily those of Transparency International.

That was also true, at a more modest level, of his family circle. His official wife, Stella, had stood by him before and after his imprisonment, participated in his initial presidential campaign, and acted more as a First Lady than her husband had intended until her death, following an operation, in October 2005, an event that deeply affected Obasanjo and probably drove him – after a single day of mourning – to take refuge more than ever in his work.[29] Warm-hearted and free-spending, Stella had launched a charity for handicapped children that was alleged to depend heavily on donations drawn ultimately from public funds. When eight members of her family were listed among those given options on government houses in Lagos, Obasanjo sacked the minister responsible, who later claimed to have acted on his handwritten instructions.[30] Further, one of Stella's sisters was married to Andy Uba , Obasanjo's aide, who was one of several close associates enjoying advantageous positions in the oil industry, was to be detected by American authorities importing undeclared funds into the United States on the presidential plane, and was to conduct a notoriously corrupt governorship campaign in Anambra in 2007.[31] As Obasanjo moved into his second term, the restraint he had sought to impose on his family weakened further. His son Gbenga, although alienated from his father, reportedly tried to use the connection to advance his business interests. A daughter became the subject of an EFCC investigation.[32]

Evidence of favours also multiplied during Obasanjo's second term. The House of Representatives later published a list of organisations to which the regime had granted import duty waivers or concessions, including several with known ties to the presidency.[33] There were many allegations of favouritism in the award of oil contracts and licences over which the President retained personal control as Petroleum Minister. 'Why should Wabara be taking bribes when I gave him an oil block?' Obasanjo is alleged to have commented when the Senate President was indicted in 2005. Accusations that Obasanjo had misappropriated large sums from the Petroleum Development Trust Fund were rejected by a Senate investigation, although it became clear that he had sanctioned expenditure before seeking the necessary authorisation.[34]

The most controversial and revealing exercise of presidential favour during the second term was the creation in November 2004 of the Transnational Corporation (Transcorp) by a group of business people, some of whom – including Aliko Dangote – had close links with the presidency. Obasanjo formally launched Transcorp's operations in a ceremony at State House in July 2005, simultaneously allocating the company four oil blocks and licences for various new enterprises. Obasanjo Holdings Limited was reported to have bought 200 million shares in the corporation at well below the eventual market price, financing the purchase by bank loans.[35] Transcorp described itself as 'Nigeria's own conglomerate which will mobilise local and international capital for investment in world class promotion facilities sited in Nigeria and managed by Nigerians.' The model was said to be a Korean *chaebol*, a private corporation closely integrated into national development policy.[36] Transcorp's first two acquisitions were public enterprises for which the government had failed to find private buyers: the Nicon Hilton Hotel in Abuja and Nigerian Telecommunications Limited (NITEL), an ailing concern in which Transcorp bought 51% of the equity. It also participated in a consortium that in the last days of Obasanjo's presidency bought two oil refineries that he had been trying to privatise for several years. The implication is that Transcorp was designed to facilitate the privatisation programme at the heart of the government's economic strategy, while keeping national assets in Nigerian hands. It never declared a dividend during Obasanjo's presidency.[37]

The criticism surrounding Transcorp extended also to Obasanjo's role in May 2005 in presiding at a fund-raising ceremony to finance the Olusegun Obasanjo Presidential Library, a scheme modelled on American precedents but without the federal financing they enjoyed. The N6 billion ($46 million) reported to be promised at the ceremony came not only from firms and businessmen but also in N10 million contributions from each of the 36 state governors, which Soyinka denounced as 'executive extortion' and Ribadu thought undesirable so long as Obasanjo held office. The occasion's organisers, led by the respected businessman Christopher Kolade, insisted that Obasanjo had no personal role in the project and would not benefit financially from an institution of public value, but many felt that Nigeria had more urgent priorities than presidential libraries.[38]

This account has illustrated the complexity of Obasanjo's attitude towards corruption. There is no suggestion that he could be bribed or that he would demean himself by bribing others on his own account. Nor did he dispense lavish largess like his counterparts in Gabon and the Democratic Republic of the Congo, for which he was too close-fisted. In public affairs he carefully kept within the letter of the law, as in turning over his affairs to a trust, distancing himself from the library project, or returning an auditor's report on the NNPC with a demand that the auditors trace a missing $250 million, for otherwise people 'would say it is Obasanjo who has stolen [it]'.[39] (The sum proved not to be missing.) He may have avoided knowing that the PDP accepted kickbacks, although many believed that they financed his election campaigns in 2003 and 2007. Yet he was convinced that his Vice-President was corrupt. He failed to act on an EFCC report detailing corruption by Bode George, the chief organiser of his 2003 election victory in Yorubaland, although the charges later resulted in a two-year prison sentence.[40] Obasanjo cannot have been unaware that his political agents were suspected of bribing legislators, that many of his close associates were taking advantage of their positions, and that his personal finances were in hands less discriminating than his own.[41] He became a wealthy man during his presidency, although not as wealthy as a President of Nigeria might have become. Nor, remarkably, was it ever suggested that he invested any part of his wealth outside Nigeria, and it is striking that even his most controversial actions, such as the Transcorp investment and the library project, were arguably in the national interest. Obasanjo was no saint, but he was a patriot. Indeed, his patriotism was so compelling that it could on occasion override his scruples. As he grew older, more entrenched in power, and more inured to criticism, he became more convinced of his own righteousness and less careful of his public reputation. He was less sensitive to corruption during his second presidential term than at earlier stages in his career, just as he was less sensitive to political opinion, less scrupulous in his use of power, and less respectful of the law, but he did not neglect what he believed to be his duty to Nigeria.

Nevertheless, many heard his inaugural address in May 2003 with anxiety. Balarabe Musa, perhaps the most principled of Nigerian radicals, warned next day that 'We are entering into a dangerous phase of fascism and police state.' A few months later, another veteran politician, Anthony Enahoro, expressed a widespread fear that Nigeria was moving towards a civilian dictatorship of the kind that the Constitution Drafting Committee of 1976 had sought to avert by balancing legislature against executive, only for the mass unseating of legislators during the 2003 elections to demonstrate its ineffectiveness.[42] 'We are having something like an emperor, something very imperial now about Obasanjo', a lawyer observed in 2004. 'You can see it in his carriage, in the way he speaks on every matter.'[43] The constitutional lawyer, Ben Nwabueze, agreed. Following Obasanjo's electoral success in 2003, he wrote,

> He became ever more dictatorial and ever more intolerant of differing views. His entire posture became, in short, that of a dictator, with the extreme arrogance inseparable from autocratic power. The traits of dictatorship inherent in his personality and implanted in him by his military antecedents began to assume and manifest themselves in a more marked form.[44]

There were two problems with Nwabueze's analysis. One was that it neglected those areas in which Obasanjo did not display authoritarian tendencies, notably in the extreme freedom of the Nigerian press and the large degree of liberty that Nigerians enjoyed throughout his presidency, only slightly reduced towards the end of his second term by the arrest of a few extremists from the Niger Delta and the MASSOB secessionist movement, who were detained for their political activities rather than their beliefs. Obasanjo enjoyed power, but he exercised it with restraint and entirely without the cruelty of a dictator. The other problem with Nwabueze's legalistic analysis was that it did not explain why Obasanjo's administration became more authoritarian during his second term – as it did – except by picturing 'a ravenous President hungry to aggregate power to himself.'[45] As will be seen, the chief reason was the President's anxiety – probably his exaggerated anxiety – to ensure that after his departure, Nigeria should not again experience the disaster that had followed his earlier withdrawal from power in 1979.

The new administration of May 2003 was more purposeful than its predecessor. Obasanjo offended the PDP by saying that this time his ministers were of his own choosing.[46] He appointed a somewhat younger and more technocratic cabinet, with Okonjo-Iweala as Minister of Finance and other members of the economic team stationed at key points in the bureaucracy. There were posts for defeated loyalists such as former Governor Kwankwaso of Kano, the new Minister of Defence. With Lukman no longer acting as his Special Advisor, the President's personal administration of the Petroleum Ministry became increasingly authoritarian and idiosyncratic. He was also determined to assert his authority over the new National Assembly. Opening its session on 5 June in his most belligerent style, he urged it to consider the radical turnover of its membership – nearly three-quarters of senators and over two-thirds of representatives were newcomers – as a rejuvenation. Experience with the previous assembly, he said, had been at best 'a learning curve'. The new body must observe the principle of party discipline. Referring to control of budget implementation, he decreed:

The definition – and the use – of the instrument of 'oversight function' to mean attempts to extort and blackmail, will simply not work. Furthermore, impeachment, or even the threat of it, as a means of arms-twisting and not as a result of some patent constitutional breach on the part of the executive, will destabilise not only the President, but the entire country, whilst making a mockery of our notion of democracy and democratic processes. And let me say it here and now, this executive will not succumb to blackmail, threats or intimidation, under any circumstance.[47]

As in 1999, Obasanjo interfered vigorously in the election of the assembly's leaders. The chosen Speaker, Aminu Masari, was a loyalist recommended by the Governor of Katsina State, Umaru Yar'Adua, the brother of Obasanjo's former colleague. For the Senate presidency, PDP leaders persuaded unwilling senators to accept Adolphus Wabara, although he had originally lost the PDP nomination in his constituency, had been reinstated and then lost the Senate election, and had finally been declared its winner by a court only one day before his choice as Senate President. Wabara had a modest view of his role and a long record of loyalty to Obasanjo, but he almost immediately became a target for accusations of corruption, meanness, authoritarianism, and subservience to the executive. Masari, similarly, was soon threatened by impeachment by representatives desperate for salaries and allowances that Obasanjo delayed paying them.[48]

The President's control over the military still appeared firm, despite recurrent rumours of conspiracy. After initially retiring all officers who had held political posts, he had faced a challenge in April 2001 when the outspoken Army Chief of Staff, General Malu, had objected to retraining of the army by American advisers and to drastic cuts in military expenditure. Malu and the other service chiefs had been replaced.[49] He remained a vocal critic – on one occasion he publicly regretted that he had not staged a coup d'état against Obasanjo[50] – but the new generation of senior officers, mostly from minority ethnic groups, were strongly apolitical. 'We have finished with getting involved in governance and politics of the nation', declared General Alexander Ogomudia, the army's first full general never to have held a political post, a point Obasanjo celebrated when promoting him.[51] Beneath the surface, however, there was much military discontent, especially over poor pay and living conditions and the loss of status by soldiers generally and northern officers in particular. It found expression in the army's action at Zaki-Biam and in a succession of rumoured coup plots, the most circumstantial being, first, talk of overthrowing Obasanjo at the time of his re-inauguration, which led to several dismissals and elaborate security precautions at the ceremony,[52] and, second, an extraordinary allegation in April 2004 that Abacha's former security chief, Hamza al-Mustapha, from his cell at Kirikiri Prison, had masterminded a plot to shoot down the President's helicopter with a Stinger missile – an allegation that a court eventually dismissed for lack of evidence.[53] Obasanjo was the last man to be disconcerted by rumours of coup plots, but they were part of the context within which he governed.

The major disorder throughout Obasanjo's second term took place in the oil-rich Niger Delta, where the violence that had largely died away elsewhere in the country continued and was exacerbated by the corrupt elections of April 2003, when politicians again recruited and armed cult groups as political thugs. The PDP government of Rivers State, for example, was said to have paid gang leaders up to N10 million ($77,000) to prevent people from voting.[54] In the wake of the election, Obasanjo was obliged to order a Joint Task Force from the various armed services into the region. Its initial role was to stop community unrest and ethnic conflict for control of Warri, but during May 2004 its focus shifted to Port Harcourt, where the two most powerful cult groups, led by Asari Dokubo and Ateke Tom, were fighting for control. After hundreds of deaths, an attack by helicopter gunships on Asari Dokubo's headquarters led him to threaten all-out war against Nigeria and the oil installations from 1 October, which drove the world price over the $50 per barrel mark.[55] Under international pressure, Obasanjo used peace activists to bring both cult leaders to Abuja, where they ostensibly agreed to cease fighting and disband their forces. At the same time the Niger Delta Development Commission outlined its elaborate master plan, eventually estimated to cost some $50 billion.[56]

After a brief lull, fighting in the Delta resumed in mid 2005, when armed youths freed the inmates from Port Harcourt gaol and northern opposition to demands for local control of oil resources provoked Asari Dokubo to demand the break-up of Nigeria. Obasanjo ordered his arrest on a charge of treasonable felony.[57] This weakened his following, but a new umbrella body emerged, the Movement for the Emancipation of the Niger Delta (MEND), which combined criminality with more sophisticated military tactics and publicity. Its stated aim was not to dismember Nigeria but to destroy the government's capacity to export oil until control of the resource was transferred to Delta people. During 2006 MEND sabotaged oil installations, attacked and kidnapped workers, and launched the first assaults on offshore facilities and the vulnerable natural gas infrastructure. Attempts to blunt this campaign by substantial development works, oil concessions granted to Delta youths, and eventually Asari Dokubo's release in June 2007 – all accompanied by sporadic military action – had little impact on a determined and well-armed leadership.[58] Obasanjo believed that regional resource control would threaten Nigeria's survival and that the militants were primarily criminals. He put his faith in the development plan, arguing that militancy would disappear only when youths found it more profitable to acquire skills and jobs. In the meantime, when he left office, some 900,000 barrels of oil per day – nearly one-third of Nigeria's production capacity, worth over $61 million – was inaccessible owing to actual or threatened violence.[59]

The scale of violence in the Niger Delta made federal intervention inescapable. Elsewhere, a major element in the critique of Obasanjo's 'dictatorship' was the accusation that, as a military centraliser, he was an enemy of federalism and a subverter of the constitution. Of the three major instances quoted against him, the most convincing was his treatment of Lagos, where in 2003 the assertive AD governor, Bola Tinubu, added 37 new local government areas to the existing 20.[60] To acquire legal force, this needed the approval of the National Assembly, while Obasanjo, who opposed the multiplication of local government areas because it undermined fiscal discipline and made them too small to be efficient, decided to make an example of Lagos (which the PDP hoped to win at the next election) by cutting off all its local government funding. Tinubu appealed to the Supreme Court, which ruled in December 2004 that the President had no such power and ordered him to restore the funding immediately. Obasanjo released only part of it, which the Chief Justice condemned as 'a clear contempt of the Supreme Court'. It earned the President widespread condemnation as the most blatant of several cases in which he defied court orders, professedly in the public interest.[61] His successor paid Lagos its arrears and promptly faced the problem of local government proliferation.[62]

'As far as President Obasanjo is concerned', Nwabueze wrote, 'the State Governors are only his agents and subject to his direction', rather than the executive heads of distinct constitutional entities.[63] The President viewed local governments in the same way, intervening to pay their teachers directly from their revenues or to appropriate their funds to build health care centres on their behalf. Obasanjo may have had a common touch, but he had little confidence in the capacity of Nigerians to run their own affairs without central supervision. Yet Nwabueze was wrong to think that Obasanjo intervened from a crude lust for power. He intervened from a sense of responsibility, because state governors, local government councillors, and Nigerians of all kinds on occasion conducted their affairs disastrously and the President felt a duty to ensure good government throughout the federation.

This was the situation in the second of Obasanjo's most contentious interventions, during the Plateau State crisis of 2004, when at least 1,000 people died in violence between 'indigenes' and 'settlers'.[64] On 18 May 2004, he declared a state of emergency in Plateau, with the subsequent endorsement of the National Assembly, suspended the young Governor Dariye and the State Assembly, and imposed six months of military rule. Obasanjo blamed the crisis chiefly on Dariye. 'As at today', he declared, 'there is nothing on ground and no evidence whatsoever to show that the State Governor has the interest, desire, commitment, credibility and capacity to promote reconciliation, rehabilitation, forgiveness, peace, harmony and stability. If anything, some of his utterances, his lackadaisical attitude and seeming uneven-handedness over the salient and contending issues present him as not just part of the problem, but also as an instigator and a threat to peace.'[65] Although many people in Plateau agreed with that assessment, many others did not, especially among the embattled Christian community and the state legislators. Moreover, although Obasanjo certainly had the power to declare an emergency, lawyers, civil rights activists, and dedicated federalists questioned his power to suspend a governor or state assembly, an issue never satisfactorily settled by the courts.[66] As the period of military rule in Plateau State ended, Obasanjo sought to prevent Dariye returning to office, using against him charges, brought by the British police, of attempting to launder some £3 million of misappropriated funds in London. Dariye jumped bail and returned to Nigeria, where the courts ruled that as a governor he was immune from prosecution. The State Assembly refused to remove his immunity by impeaching him. During 2006 the EFCC arrested state legislators who opposed impeachment and obliged six of the remaining eight to vote it, although the courts overruled this and Dariye returned to office in April 2007, only a month before his governorship expired.[67]

Obasanjo's intervention in Plateau State clearly exceeded the law. In his opinion, Dariye was unfit to continue as governor. Obasanjo preferred good government to what he regarded as legalism. His decision in his third contentious intervention, in Ekiti State in 2006, appears to have followed the same calculation, although the circumstances were different. The young Governor Ayo Fayose had won Ekiti for the PDP in 2003 by a populist campaign of largesse that aroused the hostility and contempt of the local elite. A later governor described Fayose's supporters as the 'dregs of the society'.[68] He kept open house in the governor's residence, sacked many senior officials, launched a host of projects, and continued to distribute largesse in all directions. When Obasanjo visited the state in 2005 he praised the governor's development achievements and 'the people-oriented government being run in the state.' In August 2006, however, escalating violence culminated in the murder of a rival for the PDP nomination. Suspicion inevitably focused on the governor.[69] A month later the EFCC informed the State Assembly of investigations raising charges of fraud and corruption against Fayose and other senior members of the state government. Obasanjo was said to have told him to announce that he would not seek re-election in 2007. When he refused, the Assembly was pressured into impeaching him, but did so in an illegal manner. Fayose went into hiding, his former deputy proclaimed himself governor, and in October 2006 Obasanjo declared a state of emergency under a military administrator, for fear, as he claimed, of impending anarchy.[70] Only after heated debate did this gain the grudging endorsement of the National Assembly, for many feared that the President's action was part of a plot to extend his own tenure beyond 2007. When Obasanjo tried to renew the emergency six months later to cover the election period, the National Assembly refused.[71]

As these examples suggest, Obasanjo generally interfered in local politics only when he was drawn into them, either by the threat of disorder or by disputes involving the regional politicians on whom he relied for electoral support. The most notorious of these disputes during his second term took place in Anambra State. When Governor Chinwoke Mbadinuju was denied reselection by the PDP in 2003, a majority of the state's voters probably chose an APGA candidate, as the courts decided three years later, but at the time both the governorship and all but one of the legislative seats were awarded to PDP candidates sponsored by a rich and unsophisticated local businessman named Chris Uba, an early PDP financier and brother of Obasanjo's close assistant, Andy Uba.[72] Uba required his candidate for governor, a doctor named Chris Ngige, to sign an IOU for N3 billion, an undated letter of resignation, and a quasi-business 'contract' containing a vow of 'absolute loyalty', promising Uba the control of all important appointments and contracts, and empowering him to 'avenge himself in the way and manner adjudged by him as fitting and adequate' if Ngige reneged on the deal. Uba also pressed Ngige and probably most legislators to swear oaths of loyalty to him at the local Okija shrine.[73] Once in office, Ngige, a founder of PDP and protégé of Alex Ekwueme, proved recalcitrant. As Uba complained, 'The problem is the immunity the governors are having … you spend your money to bring them into power and they say, "Go to hell". It should be just like, you invest in a bank and then you have power to make some decisions because of your controlling shares.'[74] In July 2003, Uba instructed the compliant local police chief to abduct Ngige at gunpoint, presented the letter of resignation to the State Assembly (whose Speaker was Uba's sister) and had Ngige replaced by his deputy. Ngige managed to telephone a political ally, Vice-President Atiku, who ordered the police to release him.[75]

During the subsequent uproar, Obasanjo interviewed the two protagonists:

> I got the real shock of my life when Chris Uba looked him [Ngige] in the face and said 'You know you did not win the election' and Ngige answered him 'Yes. I know I did not win.' Chris Uba went further to say to Ngige 'You don't know in detail how it was done.' I was horrified and told both of them to leave my residence.[76]

According to another account, Ngige told the President, 'The results of our elections were written on the same table.'[77] Obasanjo, the born-again Christian, may have been horrified by the involvement of the Okija shrine, for he apparently instructed the police to clean it up and may have extended the order to other cult centres.[78] Contemptuous of Ngige, tolerant of godfathers who delivered elections, at odds with both Ekwueme and Atiku, and allegedly anxious not to embarrass Andy Uba, Obasanjo had reason to want the issue buried and was reportedly angry when PDP headquarters expelled Chris Uba from the party. Conflict over how to handle the situation simmered throughout 2004 and peaked in November when armed thugs, believed to be in Chris Uba's pay, invaded the Anambra state capital, destroying the governor's office and the state broadcasting headquarters while the police looked on.[79]

This incident transformed a local conflict into a power contest in Abuja. Although Audu Ogbeh had been Obasanjo's nominee as chairman of the PDP in 2001, he was an upright and strong-minded man who regretted the influence of godfathers like Chris Uba in the party and sympathised with the founding Aborigines who resented Obasanjo's capture of their creation. Ogbeh was also rumoured to favour Atiku's candidacy in 2007, which the President was probably already determined to prevent, and he was an open critic of the liberalisation strategy advocated by Obasanjo's unpopular economic team.[80] Ogbeh now warned Obasanjo that events in Anambra threatened to discredit the party and invite military intervention. 'On behalf of the People's Democratic Party,' he wrote, 'I call on you to act now and bring any, and all criminal, even treasonable, activity to a halt.' The letter, copied to Atiku and the Speaker of the House of Representatives, leaked to the press. Six days later, Obasanjo wrote a furious reply, claiming that Ogbeh had 'finally, at least in writing, decided to unmask and show your true colour'. The President insisted that he had acted properly in Anambra, whereas Ogbeh had failed to resolve the conflict within the local party. 'I have taken judicial note', he added, 'of the ominous comparisons you made between a government … that was overthrown in a coup d'état and this present administration.'[81] At two meetings of the party's National Executive Committee, the President failed to muster enough support to dismiss Ogbeh, but on 4 January 2005, Obasanjo told the chairman that he must resign because they could not work together. 'Maybe I am too much of an idealist,' Ogbeh reflected.[82]

Obasanjo now asserted his full authority over the party. Without calling the required convention, he engineered Ogbeh's replacement by Colonel Ahmadu Ali, the former military doctor who, as the domineering Commissioner for Education, had been the target of student riots in 1978 and had most recently coordinated Obasanjo's election campaign in 2003.[83] At the same time the party rules were changed to give the President greater control of party officials, the senior office holders were replaced, and a purge of the party apparatus at state level began. By June 2006, fewer than half a dozen of the G34 pioneers were still active party members. 'What comes out of the PDP Secretariat is akin to statements from military barracks', a journalist complained.[84]

'The PDP of Obasanjo's second term,' wrote perceptive observers, 'has been transformed into an instrument of presidential power and supremacy.'[85] The regime reminded contemporaries of America's 'imperial presidency', when Richard Nixon had concentrated power and decision-making within the White House.[86] Yet not only was power within the PDP concentrated at Aso Rock, but the party itself, except in the seven ANPP states in the far north, was a dominant party in a sense that the United States had not seen in the twentieth century: a party that permitted organised political opposition but monopolised effective power. Obasanjo's presidency was not imperial; it was imperious, seeking to extend power outwards through the party apparatus to foster unity and development. Yet the PDP was not a dominant party in the same sense as the Indian National Congress after independence or the African National Congress of South Africa, because it was not rooted in a successful nationalist movement and could not claim the instinctive loyalty and moral authority that conferred. And that was the problem, for a party so little rooted in the society could scarcely act as the agent of mobilisation and development that Obasanjo had envisaged in 1989.[87] The PDP dominated Nigeria but could not change it.

NOTES

1. *Tell*, 13 October 2003, p. 23.
2. Obasanjo, *Standing tall*, p. 10.
3. *Tell*, 13 October 2003, p. 21.
4. *Guardian*, 15 November 2002; *Punch*, 29 May 2007.
5. Obe, *New dawn*, vol. 2, p. 125.
6. Reuben Abati in *Guardian*, 1 June 2007.
7. See below, p. 283.
8. *This Day*, 29 October 2000; *Insider Weekly*, 21 July 2003, p. 21.
9. *Guardian*, 15 January 2007.
10. Soyinka, *You must set forth*, p. 219.
11. Quoted in *Nigerian Tribune*, 14 March 2007.
12. *Punch*, 27 May 2007.
13. *Nigerian Tribune*, 19 January 2008; *Tell*, 13 October 2003, p. 24; *Newswatch*, 14 November 1994, p. 18.
14. Paden, *Faith and politics*, p. 72.
15. *This Day*, 20 March 2009; *Vanguard*, 26 February 2007; *Guardian*, 23 March 2007.
16. Obasanjo, *This animal*, p. 203.
17. Karin Barber, 'Popular reactions to the petro-naira', *Journal of Modern African Studies*, 20 (1982), 434–7, 448.

18. *Sunday Sketch*, 9 December 1979; *Guardian*, 6 June 2001.
19. *This Day*, 30 August 2003, 25 November 2005, 28 September 2006; Kenneth Omeje, 'Reappraising contemporary political developments in Nigeria', in his *State-society relations*, p. 15; Ribadu's statement in http://www.saharareporters.com (accessed 19 May 2009).
20. *Guardian*, 1 September 2006; Practical Sampling International, 'Summary', pp. 23, 31–2; Transparency International, *Global corruption report 2008* (Cambridge, 2008), p. 301.
21. *This Day*, 3 August 1999; *Weekly Trust*, 30 June 2000; *Newswatch*, 4 February 2008, p. 15.
22. *Newswatch*, 4 September 2006, p. 53; *Weekly Trust*, 30 June 2000; *Insider Weekly*, 10 March 2003, p. 24.
23. *Guardian*, 22 June 2002; *Nigerian Tribune*, 12 March 2003.
24. Nwabueze, *How Obasanjo subverted law*, pp. 401–2; *Daily Telegraph*, 20 May 2006.
25. The indictment was printed in *Guardian*, 15 March 2009. See also *Guardian*, 30 November 2004 and 7 June 2009.
26. Nwabueze, *How Obasanjo subverted law*, pp. 403–5.
27. *Insider Weekly*, 3 March 2003, pp. 23–7, and 10 March 2003, pp. 19–25.
28. Securities and Exchange Commission complaint against Siemens Aktiengesellschaft, 12 December 2008, http://www.sec.gov/litigation/complaints/2008/comp20829.pdf (accessed 27 December 2008); *Punch,* 27–8 December 2008.
29. *Newswatch*, 7 November 2005, pp. 11, 26–31, 58–68; Nwokeforo, *Obasanjo's presidency*, p. 150.
30. *Weekly Trust*, 2 June 2000; *Newswatch*, 18 April 2005, pp. 12–14; *This Day*, 25 March 2009.
31. Alex Vines, Lillian Wong, Markus Weimer, and Indira Camros, 'Thirst for African oil: Asian national oil companies in Nigeria and Angola', Chatham House report, August 2009, pp. 13–17, http://www.chathamhouse.org.uk/files/14524_ro809_africanoil.pdf (accessed 24 August 2009); *Newswatch*, 17 April 2006, p. 15; *Africa confidential*, 2 November 2007, p. 2; Human Rights Watch, 'Criminal politics', pp. 74–7.
32. *Newswatch*, 4 February 2008, pp. 16–18, and 21 March 2008, p. 23.
33. *Punch*, 9 March 2009.
34. Soares de Oliveira, *Oil and politics*, p. 151 n. 107; Sam O. Agbalino, 'An appraisal of the oil sector reforms', in Saliu et al., *Nigeria's reform programme*, p. 229; *Guardian*, 18 March 2007.
35. *This Day*, 9 August 2006; Nwabueze, *How Obasanjo subverted law*, pp. 394–6; Anas A. Galadima, 'Corruption charges and questions trail Obasanjo's shares in Transcorp' (2006), http://www.usafricaonline.com/obasanjo.transcorpdeal.html (accessed 30 November 2008).
36. *This Day*, 9 August 2006; *Punch*, 12 June 2007.
37. Omeje, *State-society relations*, pp. 16–17; *Tell*, 30 May 2007; *Guardian*, 25 April 2008.
38. *Guardian*, 14–15 May 2007; *This Day*, 25 May 2005; Nwabueze, *How Obasanjo subverted law*, pp. 391–4.
39. *Guardian*, 4 May 2006.
40. *Guardian*, 27 October 2009; Nosa Osaigbovo in *Nigerian Tribune*, 9 November 2009.
41. See Omoyole Sowore, 'Obasanjo and Atiku war: Fasawe is the first casualty', 25 May 2005, http://www.nigeriavillagesquare.com/articles/omoyole-sowore.html (accessed 25 December 2009).
42. *This Day*, 30 May and 7 November 2003.
43. *Tell*, 30 August 2004, p. 16.
44. Ben Nwabueze, *How President Obasanjo subverted Nigeria's federal system* (Ibadan, 2007), pp. xxxi–xxxii.
45. Ibid., p. xxvi.

46. *This Day*, 17 December 2004.
47. Obasanjo, *Standing tall*, pp. 14–16.
48. *Newswatch*, 16 June 2003 pp. 21–9, 30 June 2003 pp. 25–34, 5 September 2003 pp. 34–5, and 24 November 2003 pp. 29–30; Amadi, *Power and politics*, pp. 29–30.
49. *Newswatch*, 7 April 2001, pp. 9–11.
50. *Nigerian Tribune*, 27 July 2007.
51. *This Day*, 30 August 2001; *Newswatch*, 23 June 2003, p. 45.
52. *Tell*, 4 August 2003, pp. 18–20.
53. *Guardian*, 12 April 2008.
54. Human Rights Watch, 'Criminal politics', p. 36.
55. *Africa Research Bulletin (Political)*, August 2003, pp. 15423–4, and October 2004, p. 15962; Turner and Brownhill, 'Why women', pp. 64, 76; Human Rights Watch, 'Rivers and blood', pp. 11, 18–19.
56. *Newswatch*, 18 October 2004, pp. 13–17; *This Day*, 13 October 2004 and 23 March 2007.
57. *Newswatch*, 4 July 2005, pp. 12–13, 5 September 2005, pp. 12–18, and 17 October 2005, pp. 14–15.
58. International Crisis Group, 'The swamps of insurgency: Nigeria's delta unrest', Africa Report no. 115 (2006), pp. iii, 2, http://www. ciaonet.org/pbei/icg/icg016/icg016.pdf (accessed 27 August 2007); *Guardian*, 27 January 2008; *Petroleum Economist*, September 2007, p. 20; *Vanguard*, 23 June 2007.
59. International Crisis Group, 'Swamps of insurgency', pp. ii, 2; *Tell*, 10 May 2007; *Nigerian Tribune*, 28 May 2007.
60. Suberu, 'Supreme Court', pp. 471–2; Nwabueze, *How Obasanjo subverted Nigeria's federal system*, pp. 47–8.
61. *Guardian*, 11 December 2004; *Nigerian Tribune*, 10 April 2007; *This Day*, 14 December 2005.
62. *Guardian*, 24 July 2007 and 27 July 2009.
63. Nwabueze, *How Obasanjo subverted Nigeria's federal system*, p. xxvii.
64. See above, p. 192.
65. Quoted in Human Rights Watch, 'Revenge', p. 40.
66. Nwabueze, *How Obasanjo subverted Nigeria's federal system*, p. 231.
67. Ibid., Chs. 9–12; *This Day*, 6 October 2006; *Vanguard*, 17 November 2006; *Guardian*, 9 March and 1 May 2007.
68. *Nigerian Tribune*, 25 January 2008; above, p. 243.
69. *This Day*, 21 June and 31 December 2003, 26 June and 15 October 2004, 23 April 2005; *Nigerian Tribune*, 7 October 2006.
70. *This Day*, 21 September 2006; *Nigerian Tribune*, 7 October 2006; *Newswatch*, 30 October 2006, p. 18.
71. *Guardian*, 26–7 October 2006 and 25 April 2007. See also Nwabueze, *How Obasanjo subverted Nigeria's federal system*, Ch.13.
72. Above, p. 184; *This Day*, 4 and 13 July 2003, 15 March 2006; *Newswatch*, 19 May 2003, pp. 29–31.
73. Human Rights Watch, 'Criminal politics', pp. 113–22; Smith, *Culture of corruption*, pp. 125–34, 160–1.
74. Human Rights Watch, 'Criminal politics', p. 71.
75. *Newswatch*, 28 July 2003, pp. 45–57.
76. Obasanjo to Ogbeh, 12 December 2004, in *This Day*, 16 December 2004.
77. *Insider Weekly*, 29 December 2003, p. 21.
78. *Source*, 23 August 2004, p. 22; Anwunah, *Nigeria-Biafra war*, pp. 358–60.
79. *Newswatch*, 1 September 2003, pp. 48–9; Felix Ubah, *Anambra political crises ... eye-witness account* (Enugu, 2005), p. 22.
80. *This Day*, 7 November and 14 December 2003; *Tell*, 5 July 2004, p. 20.

81. *Guardian*, 13 December 2004; Smith, *Culture of corruption*, pp. 233–40.
82. *This Day*, 17 December 2004, 8 and 11 January 2005; *Newswatch*, 24 January 2005, pp. 13–16.
83. *This Day*, 3 March 2005.
84. *Newswatch*, 27 June 2005, p. 20; *Guardian*, 10 June and 10 October 2006; *This Day*, 8 December 2005 and 27 September 2006.
85. Richard L. Sklar, Ebere Onwudiwe, and Darren Kew, 'Nigeria: completing Obasanjo's legacy', *Journal of Democracy*, 17, 3 (2006), 111.
86. Dare Babarinsa in *Tell*, !0 May 2004, p. 5; Schlesinger, *Imperial presidency*, p. 232.
87. Obasanjo, *Constitution*, pp. 81–3.

21
Economic Reform

Four issues dominated Obasanjo's second presidential term: economic reform leading on to debt relief, a new attempt to use oil resources to modernise national infrastructure, implementing the principles of the new African Union, and controlling the outcome of the 2007 election. Economic policy was certainly more successful than during his first term. The core of his reform programme was a National Economic Empowerment and Development Strategy (NEEDS),[1] which itself grew out of a National Economic Agenda (2003–2007)[2] prepared towards the end of his first term as the draft of the Poverty Reduction Strategy Paper that the IMF required from governments before entering negotiations. Its preparation was mainly the work of Obasanjo's Chief Economic Adviser, Charles Soludo, an economist from the University of Nigeria who had been a consultant to the IMF and the World Bank, working under the supervision of the Economic Management Team headed by Okonjo-Iweala. During the second half of 2003 and early 2004, their draft was discussed with Nigerian economists and interested groups, whose input is obscure, before the President launched NEEDS as official policy on 29 May 2004, taking the political responsibility for it because he believed that successful implementation of inevitably unpopular policies required the technocrats to be sheltered from political pressures.[3]

NEEDS blamed Nigeria's failure to achieve development since the mid 1970s, despite oil export earnings of about $300 billion, on 'decades of corruption and mismanagement especially during the military administrations. The old development models of import substitution industrialization ... and statism whereby government assumed the dominant role as producer and controller in the economy produced perverse incentives, inefficiencies and waste.'[4] The modest economic growth achieved since 1999 had not been enough to prevent poverty from worsening. The fundamental mistake was to allow the volatile oil market to dictate budgetary expenditure:

> Past governments allowed oil income to influence spending: when income was high, spending was high, while drops in oil prices were treated as temporary. Together with poor coordination between federal and state governments in budgeting and expenditure, this practice led to spiralling debt. Today all tiers of government spend far more than they earn: the deficit for the past five years alone amounts to more than Nl trillion. With external and domestic debt of 70% of GDP, current revenue is largely eaten up just by debt service.[5]

The answer, as the government had recognised during Obasanjo's first term, was to adopt a fiscal rule: to base the annual budget on a relatively low average oil price and invest any surplus earnings to provide a cushion against bad years, so that what was constructed in times of prosperity need not decay during stringency, as in the past.

Along with these measures to stabilise the economy, NEEDS proposed three priority strategies: to foster private enterprise through privatisation and liberalisation, confining the state to the provision of essential services and regulation; to restrict government 'to make it smaller, stronger, better skilled, and more efficient at delivering essential services'; and to reduce poverty and increase empowerment through job creation and expenditure on health, education, and other social services.[6] Together, these strategies aimed to increase the annual growth of real GDP to 7% by 2007; to reduce annual inflation below 10%; to increase industrial capacity utilisation to 70%; and to create 7 million new jobs.[7] The emphasis on strategy and economic management contrasted with the lists of investment projects that had composed the development plans of the 1970s.

This programme immediately provoked opposition. Left-wing intellectuals and the Nigerian Labour Congress dismissed it as the 'warmed-over remains of the IMF/ World Bank fare on which Nigeria has been fed since 1986 with disastrous consequences'. Obasanjo's northern critics saw it as a plan to sell off national assets to the Yoruba. Some officials damned the 'economic dream team' as intellectuals with no experience of government. There were rumours of military discontent.[8] The President, however, had no time for 'grandstanding strategies that rely on ideologies, methods, languages and ideas of the past that have been transcended all over the world'.[9] His 2004 budget, presented in December 2003, adopted a fiscal rule, narrowed the proposed deficit, reduced capital spending, and focused expenditure on job creation and poverty reducing services.[10] During the last quarter of 2003 and the first four months of 2004, some $1.3 billion of oil revenue was added to the reserves. The IMF was delighted by this 'clear break in Nigeria's macroeconomic management ... broadly consistent with the recommendations' that the Fund had made in 2002. It agreed to monitor the programme in the manner that might bring the approval needed for debt reduction negotiations.[11] The outstanding questions were whether the regime could carry through so many simultaneous changes, whether it could hold to this politically difficult course, whether the strategy could foster positive growth, and whether Obasanjo's innate belief in individual enterprise would prevail over his equally innate impatience for large-scale development.

Over the next three years, the government did largely hold to its macroeconomic strategy. Despite pressures from the National Assembly and threats of impeachment if the budget was not fully implemented, the fiscal rule was maintained and the foreign reserves rose from $7.5 billion in November 2003 to almost $45 billion in October 2006. As Obasanjo explained, 'Now, we don't eat it all, even though some people keep pressurizing us to eat it all.'[12] In addition, he maintained the Excess Crude Account, illegally, and used it for major capital expenditure on power stations, liquefied natural gas installations, and other projects, arguing that the state and local governments, with which the money should constitutionally have been shared, lacked the capacity to use it productively. The federal structure was indeed a major obstacle to financial prudence, as it was to accountability and efficient delivery of social services. The government tried to exert some restraint through a Fiscal Responsibility Bill imposing fiscal rules on state budgets, to the fury of dedicated federalists, and by publishing the sums allocated to each state, which provoked death threats to Okonjo-Iweala. None of this, however, checked the pervasive waste and corruption at state level, for which the governors of some oil-rich delta states were especially notorious.[13]

The regime was more effective in carrying out the federal government reforms outlined in the NEEDS programme. Against much resistance, some 35,700 federal civil servants were retrenched, various perquisites were replaced by equivalent additions to salaries, overall salaries were increased substantially, and a new contributory pension scheme was introduced.[14] Most striking was the reform of the hitherto unstable banking system that Soludo carried through, again against fierce opposition, especially from the North, after he was transferred to head the Central Bank in 2004. By raising a bank's required minimum capital from N2 billion ($15 million) to N25 billion ($192 million) the 89 banks were forced to consolidate into 25 more secure institutions with some capacity to foster economic development, although also with more capacity to misuse their resources. Lending to the real sector increased by 40%. Between 2004 and 2007, the number of Nigerians with bank accounts rose from 13 million to over 44 million.[15]

One major success of the NEEDS strategy was to reduce annual inflation from 11% in 2003 to only 6.4% in June 2007, well below the 9% that the programme had targeted. It was accompanied by an exchange rate stability between 2003 and mid-2007 (at about N128–9 to $1) that was remarkable in the context of the previous twenty years of devaluation.[16] Most important, from Obasanjo's viewpoint, macroeconomic stability and the building of foreign reserves created an opportunity to secure the relief from Nigeria's foreign debt that had become an obsessive goal of policy. Okonjo-Iweala conducted most of the complex negotiations.[17] Early in 2005, Nigeria owed $34 billion to foreign creditors, chiefly the governments making up the Paris Club.[18] The Club was not prepared to remit up to two-thirds of the debt, its rule for the poorest countries, because the World Bank did not classify Nigeria as a country to which loans could be made only on concessional terms by its International Development Agency (an 'IDA-only' country). In November 2004, however, the American government persuaded the Paris Club to grant 80% debt relief to Iraq, then under American occupation. Nigerian negotiators and international supporters of the Obasanjo regime used this blatant double standard to strengthen their case in persuading the World Bank to reclassify Nigeria as IDA-only.[19] Finance ministers of the G8 industrialised countries then gave their support to debt relief, and the Paris Club, meeting in June 2005, somewhat reluctantly agreed to an ingenious proposal, broadly on lines suggested by the Center for Global Development in Washington, by which Nigeria paid its outstanding arrears of $6.4 billion, had $16 billion (two-thirds of the remainder) written off, and bought back the remaining $8 billion of debt for $6 billion, thus in all paying $12.4 billion to cancel a debt of $30.4 billion.[20] The money came from the Excess Crude Account. The agreement was finalised in October when the IMF certified its approval of the operation of the NEEDS programme. The smaller debt to commercial creditors forming the London Club was settled in March 2007, leaving only a debt of $2.6 billion to the World Bank, largely owed by state governments, and a large and rapidly growing internal debt, estimated in March 2007 at N1,870 billion (nearly $15 billion).[21] 'God has granted us success in a near miraculous way', Obasanjo rejoiced, urging his critics 'to abandon their cynical and backward looking attitudes and begin to see the Nigerian cup as half-full rather than half-empty'.[22]

Debt relief was made possible by the high price of oil. The NEEDS programme had a clear strategy for the industry. By 2007, it hoped to double existing output

270

to about 4 million barrels per day, securing a higher OPEC quota by identifying new reserves in the deepwater offshore fields that were the main expansion areas. The strategy assumed a stable oil price of about $22–3 per barrel throughout the period.[23] In reality, the price rose throughout Obasanjo's second term, reaching $42 in July 2004 and $68 when he left office in May 2007, before climbing to a record $147 in July 2008.[24] Nevertheless, there was no increase in production, which averaged 2,150,000 barrels per day in 2003 and 2,168,000 in 2007. One reason for this was the production quota imposed on Nigeria by its membership of OPEC, whose members held up prices at the expense of supplying a diminishing share of world production. Another reason was the disappointingly slow development of deepwater production, especially when compared with the rapid progress of the parallel industry in Angola. Although deepwater oil began to flow in April 2003, the difficulties and costs of development exceeded expectations, so that when Obasanjo left office in May 2007 only two large deepwater fields were in operation.[25] Obasanjo was anxious to increase Nigerian participation in all branches of the industry, but it was still less than 20% in 2007. His proposal in 2005 that producing firms should be required to refine half their crude output in Nigeria came to nothing.[26] Although immensely profitable in revenue terms, the industry remained frustratingly dependent on the export of crude oil by the great international companies.

Despite the first attempts to sabotage gas installations, the development of the massive liquefaction plant at Bonny continued smoothly and profitably, its sixth element entering production in 2007, bringing total output to 22 million tonnes per year. During Obasanjo's presidency, Nigeria's total gas production had roughly trebled and the expectation, with other liquefaction plants under construction, was that gas exports would earn Nigeria more than oil by the end of the decade.[27] Pipelines to other African countries were still inoperative, however, and Obasanjo's enthusiasm for investment in gas exports, predicated on a lack of internal demand and the spectacle of vast quantities wasted by flaring, had committed so much gas to Western export contracts that it obstructed the development of the electrical generating capacity that Nigeria desperately needed.[28]

Oil and gas provided nearly one-third of Nigeria's GDP. Agriculture's contribution was almost exactly the same. The NEEDS programme had projected that output would grow at 6% per year and the value of imported food would fall from about 10% to 5% of all imports by 2007. These targets were almost exactly met: output grew at 6–8% and imports fell to 7% of total imports in 2006. Expansion, however, was achieved mainly by extending cultivation into less fertile land, with declining average yields per hectare. There was little sign in this period of more intensive development.[29]

Industry remained the great weakness of the economy, despite an ambitious target to increase output by 20% per year.[30] The only spectacular success continued to be the expansion of mobile telephones, in which over $12 billion was invested between January 2001 and October 2008. By the latter date there were 59 million active lines, the highest density per head in Africa.[31] A petrochemical industry, long projected, did not appear. Motor assembly and manufacture did not develop. Both the Ajaokuta steelworks and the Delta Steel plant at Aladja were sold on controversial terms to an Indian firm that failed to bring them into production.[32] According to the Auditor-General, Obasanjo's regime spent N86.29 billion (about $675 million) on the rehabilitation of the railway system, with as yet little result.[33] Road building and maintenance were subjects of intense public criticism.[34] In 2009 the Manufacturers Association of Nigeria claimed that 820 firms had been forced out of business during the previous eight years.[35]

The chief obstacle to industrial development and the chief source of public discontent remained the deficient supply of electricity. Obasanjo's economic team recognised this, estimating that per capita consumption in Nigeria was about 82 kilowatts (an overestimate) compared with 456 kilowatts elsewhere in sub-Saharan Africa. 'Simply providing more and more reliable power', they wrote, 'could triple the amount Nigerian industries produce by 2007.' They set a target of 10,000MW to be generated by 2007. Part of the strategy was to break up the unwieldy Nigerian Electrical Power Authority (NEPA), privatise most of its component parts, and encourage further private investment.[36] The legislation to permit this passed in 2005, but by then it had become clear that the construction of new power stations could not be left to private capital so long as electricity was supplied at subsidised, below-cost prices. Instead the government returned to direct state investment. Four thermal power stations fired by natural gas were already under construction in the south. Obasanjo commissioned the first of these shortly before he left office in 2007. The new National Integrated Power Project of 2005 consisted of building seven further stations of the same type, one in each of the seven delta states.[37]

This was a far sighted programme, but it was characteristically ambitious and raised problems of coordination, of the kind that had dogged the Ajaokuta steel plant, that Nigerian governments were especially bad at resolving.[38] Since the minimum gestation period for a power station was about three years, Obasanjo brushed aside constitutional niceties, financed the programme from the Excess Crude Account rather than the normal budgetary process, and waived some of the time-consuming due process procedures that normally scrutinised contracts.[39] Amid the problems of the Niger Delta, several contractors had difficulty securing local agreement to construction sites. After the normal delay in importing gas turbines, there was much difficulty in transporting them to the sites, so that in April 2008, according to the minister formerly responsible, 21 gas turbines costing over $300 million were still rusting at Nigerian ports. He also reported that some 2,000MW of installed generating capacity was then standing idle for lack of gas to drive the turbines, for gas supply required construction of pipelines through the hostile natural and political environment of the delta and also had to compete with the very profitable export of liquefied natural gas on 25-year contracts.[40]

When Obasanjo left office in May 2007, average output of electricity was not the promised 10,000MW but between 3,000 and 3,500MW, or roughly twice what it had been when he was elected in 1999. Estimated demand in 2006 was about 8,000MW.[41] The President claimed, with justice, that he had 'pursued the issue of power, which had been previously neglected for 20 years, with high dedication, commitment, prudence, utmost integrity, aggressiveness and diligence required and the best judgment and in the best interest of the nation'.[42] Yet he had also taken so long to formulate an effective programme that he could not complete it during his tenure.

A survey towards the end of Obasanjo's presidency found that manufacturers themselves generated about 72% of the electricity they used. They regarded this as the most serious obstacle to doing business in Nigeria, followed by the difficulty of securing credit (with very high interest rates), the volatility of the economy, and difficulties in the supply of imported inputs. These obstacles were largely responsible for a disappointing level of foreign investment (except in oil and gas), which was less than remittances to Nigeria from its citizens living abroad, where much of the country's wealth was held.[43] Early in 2007, Michelin abandoned operations in Nigeria, with the loss of 1,200 jobs, blaming the hostile business environment. Dunlop soon followed, finding local production unable to compete with imports.[44] Closures allegedly reduced textile factories from 170 in the early 1980s to only 26 in 2007, although other accounts suggested a less dramatic decline.[45] In contrast to the ambitious projections of the NEEDS programme, the contribution of manufacturing to GDP appears to have remained static throughout Obasanjo's presidency at 4–5%, one of the lowest rates in Africa.[46]

In this context, Obasanjo searched eagerly for industrial entrepreneurs. Always impressed by largeness of scale, he took as his model the career of Aliko Dangote, named by *Forbes* magazine in 2008 as the continent's richest African.[47] Related to the great Dantata trading family of Kano, Dangote was educated at the Azhar university in Cairo, began as a petty trader, and then, in 1980, was lent N500,000 (about $900,000) to establish himself in business. He claimed to work 18–20 hours a day. From importing sugar, rice, and salt he diversified into transport, property, banking, and oil, before abandoning trade and concentrating after 1997 on processing and manufacturing, especially flour-milling, sugar-refining, and cement-making, the last becoming his most important enterprise. 'I believe that anybody who is into trading only is not adding value to the economy', he said in 1999. 'There is no way the country can develop, unless you have an industrial base … Industries don't have enough support.'[48] Obasanjo wholeheartedly agreed. Opening a new Dangote cement plant in 2007, he said that Nigeria needed more industrialists, not more traders: 'If after 50 years of our cement business in Nigeria we could not get it right and under four years Dangote has gotten it, we have to support him.'[49] And Obasanjo certainly supported him, banning the importation of bagged cement, ordering the closure of a newly-built bagging plant, and insisting that such plants should be operated only by firms that had already invested in cement production in Nigeria.[50] Because existing local production could not meet demand, cement prices, construction costs, and rents rose to levels that led Obasanjo's successor to relax the protective measures.[51] Dangote suspended further investment. 'Under the prevailing environment, it will be better to cut down on investing in the country and simply import', he explained. 'When the government is ready to provide electricity, water, roads, and other infrastructure, we'll be more than willing to reconsider our strategy, but right now it is no longer worth our while to invest in a climate that fails to protect its manufacturing sector.'[52]

Dangote was the largest contributor to Obasanjo's campaign funds and a member of his inner circle. In November 2008 the industrialist undertook to give the PDP all the cement needed to build a new headquarters.[53] Party and presidency had similar ties with Mike Adenuga (an associate of Vice-President Atiku, active in oil, telecommunications, and banking), Femi Otedola (oil and gas), Emeka Offor (oil), and a number of successful bankers. 'Obasanjo showed no empathy to the poor Nigerians', a critic complained. 'He was more willing to protect his privileged businessmen friends than the nation.'[54] There was truth in this: Obasanjo was willing to sacrifice immediate popular welfare – cheaper cement or cheaper petrol – to what he believed to be the interests of Nigeria's long-term development. But that did not simply mean supporting the rich against the poor; it meant attempting to extricate Nigerian capitalism from the purely commercial, comprador role to which left-wing critics had long believed it was condemned by the country's place in the world economy. As the stagnation of manufacturing demonstrated, however, the attempt was largely unsuccessful. One Dangote did not make an industrial revolution.

Nevertheless, the 'long-term capitalist dynamic' that Tom Forrest observed in Nigeria during the 1990s accelerated during Obasanjo's presidency.[55] It could be seen in the diversification of business interests; in the remarkable expansion of banking and bank accounts; in the partial revival of the middle class, indicated by an increased purchase of motor cars between 1999 and 2003 from 103,000 to 340,000;[56] in the popularity of churches preaching the prosperity gospel; in the reduction of social mobility as educational institutions fell behind those of Western countries to which only the rich had access;[57] in the 'wide gap [that] exists between urban and rural women, between the elite on the one hand, and the working class and peasantry on the other', which robbed female politicians of the support needed for effective action;[58] and in the growing political prominence of the wives and children of senior male leaders. It could also be seen in more subtle forms, notably in the 'reciprocal assimilation of elites',[59] as successful businessmen and retired generals and permanent secretaries filled 'traditional' chieftainships, state political offices, and the mass of commercial and statutory boards, forming a single ruling class.

The most striking example of the penetration of capitalism was in university education. By 1999, when Obasanjo was first elected, the publicly financed, residential university pattern bequeathed by the British was collapsing in the face of student numbers and inadequate finance. Between 1982–3 and 2005, the number of universities increased from 24 to 80 and their student enrolment from 92,116 to 724,856.[60] The result was appalling overcrowding and lack of facilities: Plateau State University opened, briefly, in 2007 with 500 students but no library or permanent staff. Initially, students responded with militant protest, but after their union was banned in 1978 and again in 1986, most sought support instead in religious organisations or secret 'cult' groups that caused some 200 student deaths between 1996 and 2005.[61] The Academic Staff Union of Universities preserved its militancy more effectively, striking for a total of over 21 months between 1999 and 2007.[62] Obasanjo called it 'an obstacle against academic excellence'.[63]

Nigeria's universities had long exasperated the President. His response was the University Autonomy Act of 2003, which freed universities to choose their own officers and charge non-academic fees while requiring them to seek funding from private sources and their students. 'The courses taught at universities will be changed to reflect the priority demands of the economy', the NEEDS programme declared. 'Wages will be linked to performance, and students will be exposed to mobilization and reorientation campaigns that emphasize the critical importance of hard work, discipline, and selfless service.' By 2007 every university was supposed to have a Centre of Entrepreneurial Studies.[64] The new model was to be American rather than British. By 2008 Nigeria had 33 recognised private universities, along with 27 federal and 34 state institutions, plus 36 illegal 'universities' said to have some 81,000 students.[65] Several private universities were owned by religious organisations and depended heavily on wealthy philanthropists. On his installation as Chancellor of Nigeria's first Islamic University, at Katsina, the Kano businessman Aminu Alhassan Dantata gave it a billion naira (about $8 million).[66] Igbinedion University in Benin was founded and named after a local business family that also provided the state governor. The financing of students, a traditional and much admired form of philanthropy, also flourished in this expanding capitalism. Emmanuel Iwuanyanwu,

274

an Igbo press baron and presidential aspirant, was said in 2007 (by his own news-paper) to have assisted over 10,000.[67]

Public opinion linked this concentration of wealth especially to the privatisa-tion programme that Obasanjo had pursued throughout his presidency and had made central to the NEEDS strategy, especially because the government's search for a 'core investor' to take the largest stake and management responsibility in a privatised enterprise tended to favour the wealthy.[68] During Obasanjo's first term, the government had sold most of its interests in banks and enterprises operating in competitive markets, but had made little progress with the major utilities, which were commonly antiquated and unprofitable. That remained the case until the end of 2004, when the President appears to have lost patience and encouraged the formation of Transcorp, whose acquisition of NITEL was probably intended to provide a model.[69] If so, the initiative failed. One successful privatisation in 2005 was the sale of the National Fertiliser Company,[70] but otherwise Obasanjo's efforts at privatisation became increasingly desperate during his last two years in office, giving the impression that he was determined to rid the public sector of unworkable encumbrances. During 2005, he sold Ajaokuta and Delta Steel on terms that his successor cancelled,[71] as he also suspended the first steps taken to privatise sections of the electric power industry and revoked the sale of two oil refineries to a consortium of Dangote, Femi Otedola's oil company, Transcorp, and the Rivers State govern-ment, a deal completed in the last days of Obasanjo's presidency.[72] Denounced at the time as 'illegal auctioning of our national patrimony to his cohorts for a pittance',[73] it was more probably a last attempt to make the enterprises work.

These desperate attempts at privatisation were paralleled by the other major entrepreneurial initiative of Obasanjo's second term: his attempt to use Nigeria's oil resources to entice Asian governments to participate in the renewal of Nigeria's infrastructure.[74] The President had long been exasperated by the international oil companies that were eager to export Nigeria's oil and gas but refused to invest in enterprises such as oil-refining or in infrastructural developments that were not essential to their own core businesses. During 2004, as dramatic economic growth in China, India, and South Korea created an international scramble for oil, Obasanjo's characteristic alertness to the global context led him to offer Asian national oil companies 'rights of first refusal' to explore and develop oil blocks in return for undertakings to invest capital and technology in Nigerian infrastructure. In three licensing rounds between 2005 and 2007, 26 blocks were offered and 8 were accepted. In return, the Asian firms, with government backing and technical partners, agreed to undertake projects with an overall value of about $20 billion. The Chinese undertook to rebuild the Lagos-Kano railway, invest heavily in the Kaduna refinery, and construct a hydroelectric complex on the Mambilla Plateau inspired by Obasanjo's admiration for China's Three Gorges project. Indians agreed to built a large refinery and power plant and to study the feasibility of a railway from Lagos to the Niger Delta. South Koreans promised a gas pipeline from Ajaokuta to northern cities, gas-fired power stations in Abuja and Kaduna, and the renewal of the Port Harcourt-Maiduguri railway. Malaysians and Taiwanese also gave preliminary undertakings. It was a reversion to the strategy of massive infrastructural investment that had characterised Obasanjo's military rule and had been overlain, but never truly supplanted, by his overt conversion to the Wash-ington consensus. During his last months in office he tried to set things moving by a number of hasty decisions, releasing a mobilisation fee for the Chinese railway plan and awarding the first phase contract for the Mambilla scheme, although there had been no feasibility study.

When Obasanjo left office in May 2007, nothing of these plans was yet visible on the ground, but the difficulties were increasingly obvious. The viability of the projects (especially the railways) was often uncertain. The agreements had no binding provisions regulating the relative timing of the oilfield and infrastructural developments, so that the Indians, for example, intended to invest in infrastructure only after their oil began to flow. The infrastructural estimates were often inflated and the financial details opaque, disputed, and burdensome to Nigeria. Suspicions proliferated of kickbacks to finance Obasanjo's political schemes and line his agents' pockets. The Asian firms realised that they had plunged into a political and business environment they did not understand. 'We salivated in anticipation of what could be off the shores of Nigeria', an Indian Petroleum Minister remembered. Obasanjo's ambition and drive had once more outrun Nigeria's managerial capacity.

The last Afrobarometer opinion survey of Obasanjo's presidency, in 2005, revealed widespread public dissatisfaction with the effects of economic reform. Some 78% of respondents thought the government's economic policies hurt most people and benefited only a few. Asked about changes over the previous five years, 66% thought that the availability of goods had declined, 75% that jobs had become scarcer, and 81% that the gap between rich and poor had widened. Yet Nigerians remained resolutely optimistic – 69% expected to be more satisfied with their life prospects in a year's time – and the proportion who favoured accepting present hardships for the future benefits they would bring had risen since 2003 from 53% to 60%. Asked to specify the country's leading national issue, opinions focused on two of equal weight: unemployment and poverty. The NEEDS programme's dream of creating seven million new jobs had remained a dream. In 2008 the World Bank estimated the unemployment rate at 20%, with no less than 60% among youths. Complaints of poverty focused especially on the effects of inflation, only 9% of respondents expressing satisfaction with the government's performance on this score.[75]

As during the previous twenty years, popular discontent crystallised in resistance to increased fuel prices. Nigeria's worn-out refineries produced less than 20% of fuel needs at the beginning of Obasanjo's second term, seldom achieved 50% thereafter, and were producing nothing at all when he left office, owing to maintenance closures and vandalisation of supply lines. Nigeria had to import refined petrol at international prices that rose continually. As Oshiomhole of the NLC pointed out, the rising oil prices that swelled the foreign reserves were a disaster for the workers.[76] While they demanded continued subsidies, Obasanjo insisted that 'No one in their right mind will set up a refinery to sell at a subsidised price', and was determined not to burden the treasury with new state-owned refineries.[77]

Faced with this impasse, the issue once more overflowed into the streets. Obasanjo had warned that, if elected, he would raise petrol prices. When he immediately increased them from N26 to N40 per litre, the NLC called a general strike from 30 June 2003 that lasted eight days – during which the police shot at least a dozen demonstrators in Lagos – until the two sides compromised on a price of N34.[78] The agreement divided labour leaders and determined Obasanjo to launch a sustained attack on the NLC. In September, he removed all restrictions on petrol prices, while continuing to subsidise them. While the price rose to N40 and police arrested union members picketing petrol stations, Obasanjo accused the NLC of trying to behave like a parallel government[79] and sent the National Assembly a bill that would allow the Minister of Labour to register any number of union federations, abolish check-off dues unless unions entered non-strike agreements, and prohibit strikes without the approval of members voting by secret ballot, claiming that these measures would democratise the labour movement.[80] Throughout 2004, the bill was debated back and forth in the Assembly, Oshiomhole threatened strike action, the courts declared political strikes illegal, and the petrol price drifted upwards. In March 2005, Obasanjo signed a somewhat less draconian Trade Union Act, permitting the formation of federations other than the NLC, permitting check-off dues only if workers contracted in, restricting strikes to labour issues, outlawing them in essential services, and requiring a majority vote by union members before striking.[81] He was now ready for at least a temporary truce and froze the price of fuel through 2006, but he increased it to N75 only days before leaving office, perhaps thinking it better to take the blame than leave it to his successor.[82]

Some months before Obasanjo left office, the economic team that had crafted the NEEDS programme disintegrated. Soludo remained at the Central Bank, but the strong-minded Okonjo-Iweala, with whom Obasanjo's relations had never been easy, was transferred from Finance to Foreign Affairs in June 2006 and resigned in August.[83] Ezekwesili was also moved to Education in June 2006 and resigned a year later.[84] Both took senior posts with the World Bank. They were proud of their achievement. 'Viewed against the backdrop of its economic performance since the 1980s', Okonjo-Iweala claimed in 2007, 'Nigeria has clearly turned a corner.'[85] Soludo agreed that through the NEEDS strategy,

> a successful programme of economic liberalization has been put in place; inflation is coming down; significant privatization gains have been recorded; the banking sector has undergone an internationally acclaimed consolidation; growth is looking up; and the country is no longer a debtor nation.[86]

The IMF, too, celebrated the broad success of its favoured policies in achieving macroeconomic stability and ensuring that an oil boom at last had a positive rather than destructive economic impact.[87] Annual GDP growth had ranged between 7.1% in 2004 and 5.3% in 2007, averaging about twice as much as during Obasanjo's first term.[88] Although critics attributed this almost entirely to increasing oil and gas prices, growth in the non-oil sector slightly exceeded the general growth of GDP, suggesting that oil revenues were at least stimulating the wider economy.[89]

Yet many problems remained untouched, as Okonjo-Iweala admitted. She listed the need for accountability at state and local levels, employment generation, an improved business climate, infrastructural investment, solutions to Niger Delta unrest, better social spending, and legislation to institutionalise current reforms.[90] Detached observers highlighted four areas of particular failure: continuing high levels of corruption; wasteful and ineffective expenditure on infrastructure; inadequate service delivery of electricity, roads, education, health, and social welfare; and especially the failure to extend the benefits of economic reform to the 92% of Nigerians who still lived on less than two dollars a day.[91]

NOTES

1. Nigerian National Planning Commission, 'Meeting everyone's needs: national economic empowerment and development strategy' (2 vols, 2004), http://www.imf.org/external/pubs/ft/scr/2005/cr05433.pdf (accessed 21 September 2007), reprinted in Nnebe, *Policies*, vol. 2, Ch.5.
2. Published in *Post Express*, 29 October 2002.
3. Soludo in *Newswatch*, 17 April 2006, p. 16.
4. Nnebe, *Policies*, vol. 2, p. 230.
5. Nigerian National Planning Commission, 'Meeting everyone's needs', vol. 1, p. xiv.
6. Ibid., pp. x–xi.
7. Ibid., pp. xvi–xxiv.
8. *This Day*, 21–2 September 2003; *Weekly Trust*, 2 August 2003; *Tell*, 17 May 2004, p. 21; *Africa Confidential*, 19 December 2003, p. l.
9. Obasanjo, *Standing tall*, p. 185.
10. Ibid., pp. 76–91.
11. International Monetary Fund, 'Nigeria: staff report for the 2004 Article IV Consultation' (22 June 2004), pp. 13, 4: http://www.imf.org/external/pubs/ft/scr/2004/cr04239.pdf (accessed 21 December 2008).
12. *This Day*, 6 May 2005; Nnebe, *Policies*, vol. 1, p. 46; Obasanjo, *Standing tall*, p. 81; *Nigerian Tribune*, 8 April 2007.
13. Nwabueze, *How Obasanjo subverted Nigeria's federal system*, pp. 79, 84; *Tell*, 5 April 2004, p. 23; Human Rights Watch, 'Chop fine', pp. 2–5.
14. Okonjo-Iweala and Osafo-Kwaako, 'Nigeria's economic reforms', p. 14; *Tell*, 10 May 2007.
15. Charles Soludo, 'The banking sector reforms', in Saliu et al., *Nigeria's reform programme*, ch. 12; *Tell*, 10 May 2007; *Guardian*, 21 July 2008.
16. *Tell*, 12 July 2004, p. 42; *This Day*, 2 August 2007.
17. The following account is taken largely from Thomas M. Callaghy, 'The search for smart debt relief: question of when and how much', in Richard Joseph and Alexandra Gillies (ed.), *Smart aid for African development* (Boulder, 2009), pp. 93–8.
18. *This Day*, 19 March 2005; IMF, 'Nigeria: staff report', p. 60.
19. Moss et al., 'Double-standards'.
20. Todd Moss, 'Resolving Nigeria's debt through a discounted buyback' (April 2005), http://www.cgdev.org/files/3223_file_NoteNigeriaBuyback.pdf (accessed 4 March 2009).
21. *Daily Champion*, 6 April 2007; *Guardian*, 26 January and 5 March 2007.
22. Obasanjo, *Standing tall*, pp. 25–6.
23. Nnebe, *Policies*, vol. 2, pp. 251, 307–8.
24. *This Day*, 23 July 2004; *Nigerian Tribune*, 17 May 2007; BBC news, 26 July 2008.
25. *Petroleum Economist*, November 2003 p.2, June 2004 p. 48, May 2005 p. 9, May 2008 p. 20, June 2008 p. 47.
26. *Guardian*, 21 August 2007 and 8 May 2008.
27. *Petroleum Economist*, May 2008, p. 19, and April 2009, p. 12; *Nigerian Tribune*, 28 May 2007.
28. *This Day*, 11 September 2007; *Newswatch*, 17 November 2003, pp. 28–9; *Guardian*, 18 March and 5 August 2008.
29. Nigeria: Federal Office of Statistics, 'Poverty profile', p. 4; Nnebe, *Policies*, vol. 2, pp. 232, 297; *Guardian*, 20 January 2007; Economist Intelligence Unit, 'Country profile: Nigeria', 2008; Kwakwa and others in Collier et al., *Economic policy options*, pp. 14–15.
30. 'National industrial policy' (2001), in Nnebe, *Policies*, vol. 2, p. 22.
31. *This Day*, 9 June 2009.
32. *This Day*, 20 June 2007.

33. *Nigerian Tribune*, 25 June 2008.
34. *Guardian*, 21 April 2008.
35. Okonjo-Iweala and Osafo-Kwaako, 'Nigeria's economic reforms', p. 6; Nigerian National Planning Commission, 'Meeting everyone's needs', vol. 1, pp. xviii–xix, xxv.
36. Obasanjo, *Standing tall*, pp. 202, 226, 228, 231.
37. See the evaluation by Ambrose Okiya in *This Day*, 22 February 2009.
38. *Guardian*, 18 and 28 March and 14 June 2008; *Newswatch*, 31 March 2008, pp. 16–22.
39. *Guardian*, 26 March 2008; *This Day*, 3 April 2008.
40. Tallapragada and Adebusuyi in Collier et al., *Economic policy options*, p. 309; *Guardian*, 29 June 2007; Chigbue in Saliu et al., *Nigeria's reform programme*, p. 436.
41. *Nigerian Tribune*, 14 October 2008.
42. Collier et al., *Economic policy options*, pp. 7–8, 21, 306; Economist Intelligence Unit, 'Country profile: Nigeria', 2004 and 2006.
43. *Nigerian Tribune*, 1 April 2007; *This Day*, 22 June 2009.
44. *Nigerian Tribune*, 1 April 2007; *Guardian*, 15 November 2006.
45. Kwakwa et al., in Collier et al., *Economic policy options*, p. 15; *Vanguard*, 9 August 2007.
46. *This Day*, 7 January 2008. For his biography, see *Newswatch*, 21 April 2008, pp. 14–19.
47. *This Day*, 7 August 1999.
48. *This Day*, 13 May 2007.
49. *Tell*, 22 August 2006.
50. *This Day*, 1 January 2008; *Guardian*, 17 June 2008.
51. *This Day*, 13 December 2008. Obasanjo's policy was restored a year later: *Nigerian Tribune*, 21 October 2009.
52. *This Day*, 15–16 November 2008.
53. *This Day*, 29 January 2008.
54. Forrest, *Politics*, p. 1.
55. *This Day*, 30 May 2004.
56. Reuben Abati in *Guardian*, 2 January 2007.
57. Charmaine Pereira, 'National Council of Women's Societies and the state, 1985–1993', in Jega, *Identity transformation*, p. 119.
58. Jean-François Bayart, *The state in Africa: the politics of the belly* (trans. M. Harper and C. and E. Harrison, London, 1993), Ch.6.
59. *West Africa*, 15 October 1984, p. 2100; Economist Intelligence Unit, 'Country profile: Nigeria', 2008.
60. Human Rights Watch, 'Criminal politics', p. 24.
61. *This Day*, 3 August 2009.
62. *Newswatch*, 31 December 2001, p. 21.
63. Nigeria National Planning Commission, 'Meeting everyone's needs', vol. 1, pp. xvi–xvii; Peter Okebukola, 'The educational sector reforms', in Saliu et al., *Nigeria's reform programme*, p. 84.
64. *Punch*, 19 October 2008; *Nigerian Tribune*, 9 January 2009.
65. *This Day*, 28 October 2007.
66. *Daily Champion*, 4 September 2007.
67. Ayodele Jimoh, 'Introducing Nigeria's reform program', in Saliu et al., *Nigeria's reform programme*, p. 10.
68. See above, p. 207.
69. *This Day*, 7 January 2009.
70. See above, p. 208.
71. *Guardian*, 7 September 2007; *This Day*, 1 August 2007.
72. *Guardian*, 23 June 2007.
73. This account is based on Lillian Wong, 'Asian national oil companies in Nigeria', in Vines et al., 'Thirst for African oil', part 1.

74. Practical Sampling International, 'Summary', pp. 4, 7, 30–1, 37; *Nigerian Tribune*, 22 May 2008.

75. *Africa Confidential*, 23 January 2004, p. 7; *Newswatch*, 19 September 2005, p. 50; *Guardian*, 2 January 2009; *This Day*, 29 June 2007.

76. *Newswatch*, 21 June 2004, p. 19.

77. *Times*, 4 July 2003; *Newswatch*, 8 March 2004, p. 37.

78. *Daily Trust*, 1 August 2003; *This Day*, 29 June and 8 July 2003; *Newswatch*, 21 July 2003, pp. 42–5, 54; Turner and Brownhill, 'Why women', pp. 73–6.

79. *Newswatch*, 10 November 2003, p. 59; *This Day*, 14 October 2003; IMF, 'Nigeria: staff report', p. 11 n. 6.

80. *Newswatch*, 17 November 2003, pp. 24–5.

81. *This Day*, 31 March 2005; Okafor, 'Remarkable reforms', pp. 251–6; J.N. Olanrewaju, 'Labour aspects of the reform programme', in Saliu et al., *Nigeria's reform programme*, pp. 164–5.

82. *Guardian*, 24 June 2007 and 6 February 2008.

83. *Guardian*, 20 July 2003; *Newswatch*, 21 August 2006, pp. 32–3, and 9 October 2006, p. 23.

84. *Africa Confidential*, 23 June 2006, p. 8; *Nigerian Tribune*, 1 June 2007.

85. Okonjo-Iweala and Osafo-Kwaako, 'Nigeria's economic reforms', p. 25.

86. Soludo in Collier et al., *Economic policy options*, p. xvi.

87. *Daily Champion*, 29 June 2007; *This Day*, 18 February 2008.

88. http://www.indexmundi.com/g/g.aspx?v=66+c=ni+l=en (accessed 2 August 2009).

89. Lewis, *Growing apart*, pp. 270–1; Alexandra Gillies, 'Obasanjo, the donor community and reform implementation in Nigeria', *The Round Table*, 96 (2007), 575.

90. Okonjo-Iweala and Osafo-Kwaako, 'Nigeria's economic reforms', pp. 21–5.

91. Omeje, *State-society relations*, pp. 11–20; Gillies, 'Obasanjo', p. 576.

22
Africa's Elder Statesman

During his second presidential term, Obasanjo's priority in international affairs was no longer to restore Nigeria's reputation or create new continental institutions, but rather to strengthen those institutions, to use them and his own international standing to resolve conflict and foster democracy and development, and to free Nigeria from its burden of foreign debt. At the peak of his influence in 2005, he was chairman of the African Union (from July 2004 to January 2006), the NEPAD Heads of State and Government Committee, the Group of 25, and the Commonwealth – an array of posts that irritated other African leaders.[1] His extraordinary energy enabled him to conduct all these duties conscientiously – he was an unusually active chairman of the African Union and the Commonwealth[2] – while also presiding imperiously over his own turbulent country and personally conducting much of its foreign policy, the Foreign Minister for most of the period being a career diplomat.

Obasanjo was no longer yoked to President Mbeki: the divide between them that had opened during 2003 over Zimbabwe widened markedly during the next two years. Nor, once debt relief was secured in 2005, was Nigeria still a supplicant to the Western industrial powers. Rather, it was an aspiring regional power in its own right, dominating the Gulf of Guinea, whose oil reserves made it the one region of tropical Africa that was of more than marginal importance to the rest of the world.[3] Looking westwards, Nigeria was an increasingly important ally of the United States, supplying some 12% of American oil imports, supporting a large Muslim population, and acting as a key peacekeeper throughout sub-Saharan Africa.[4] Looking eastwards, Nigeria's oil resources enabled it to engage with the forces of Asian economic growth that were creating a new international order to replace the brief hiatus of American hegemony. Obasanjo visited China four times between 2001 and 2006, the year when China overtook Britain as Africa's third largest trading partner (behind the United States and France) and bought its first major stake in Nigerian oil. From these and other Asian travels came Obasanjo's optimistic oil-for-infrastructure deals.[5]

Earlier in his second term, the President spent much time attempting to prevent or reverse military interventions that now disqualified regimes from membership of the African Union. The first took place in the tiny island state of São Tomé e Príncipe, where Nigeria had important oil interests. When military officers, dissatisfied with these arrangements, deposed President Menezes while he was visiting Nigeria during July 2003, Obasanjo personally took him back to the island and ended the coup by threatening military action, taking the opportunity to strengthen his personal control of the islands' oil resources.[6] Two months later, Guinea-Bissau's army also ousted its president and Obasanjo intervened, this time persuading the soldiers to appoint a team of technocrats to hold elections.[7] In January 2005, he led moves to prevent Lieutenant Yahya Jammeh, the Gambia's military leader, from becoming the chairman of ECOWAS.[8] A month later he intervened forcibly but less effectively when President Eyadema of Togo died and his fiercely loyal army ignored the constitutional requirement for elections and installed his son Faure as his successor. ECOWAS and the African Union suspended Togo and Obasanjo persuaded Faure to stand down while an election was held, but the Nigerian President failed to engineer a government of national unity and Faure won 61% of votes in an election that was scarcely free and fair but may have returned the more popular candidate.[9] Mauritania, too, was suspended from the African Union in August 2005 until incoming soldiers organised elections.[10]

A more difficult situation arose in Côte d'Ivoire, where civil war in 2002–3 split the country between north and south, with French peacekeeping troops stationed between them. Warned by experience in Liberia and Sierra Leone, Obasanjo refused to commit Nigerian soldiers. For the next four years, France, ECOWAS, and the African Union tried to negotiate a reconciliation government against the opposition of armed extremists on both sides. For this purpose, Obasanjo turned to Mbeki, but his diplomacy was unsuccessful and widened the gulf between the two men. Côte d'Ivoire remained divided to the end of Obasanjo's presidency, although a peace agreement signed at Ouagadougou in 2007 brought a degree of reconciliation.[11]

Other areas of tension also distanced Obasanjo from Mbeki. Once the Nigerian President became chairman of the African Union in mid 2004, the organisation became increasingly critical of President Mugabe's human rights record in Zimbabwe, whereas Mbeki persevered with his quiet but equally ineffective diplomacy.[12] A more serious conflict arose over competition for permanent seats on the expanded UN Security Council, an ambition, harboured by Nigeria since at least 1991, that was revived in 2004 when a panel appointed by Secretary-General Annan suggested expanding the body to 24 members, with two permanent and four non-permanent seats for Africa. The general expectation was that Egypt would hold one African permanent seat while the other was contested between Nigeria and South Africa. In the competition that followed, Obasanjo lobbied energetically, stressing Nigeria's population, peacekeeping record, and claim to be the world's most convincing representative of black people. Mbeki could point to South Africa's economic strength and its efforts to achieve racial harmony. With the African Union divided and many similar rivalries in other continents, the General Assembly failed to reach agreement in September 2005 and the issue fell into abeyance, leaving a residue of bitterness between the African candidates.[13] The industrial powers' preference for South Africa was made clear in 2006 when Mbeki was invited to the G8 meeting but Obasanjo was not.[14] The South Africa-Nigeria Bi-National Commission did not meet during 2005 or 2006.[15]

Obasanjo's chief concern as chairman of the African Union was the deteriorating situation in the Darfur region of Sudan.[16] Power in Sudan was concentrated in Khartoum and the Nile Valley. Darfur, in the remote west, was neglected, repeatedly disturbed by the overspill of violence from civil war in neighbouring Chad, and divided by competition for resources between its 'African' and 'Arab' inhabitants – a distinction more of claimed ancestry than race or lifestyle. Rebellion by

African groups began in 2001. To repress it, the government supplemented its army by mobilising Arab militias, known as Janjawiid, whose chief leader said he had orders 'to change the demography of Darfur and empty it of African tribes'.[17] As destruction and famine escalated, the African Union negotiated a notional ceasefire agreement in April 2004 and deployed 60 ceasefire monitors to supervise it, with 300 Nigerian and Rwandan troops to protect them.[18]

Obasanjo inherited this situation when he was elected chairman of the African Union in July 2004. Visiting Khartoum in August, he played down military intervention. 'From what I hear,' he said, 'three battalions would be a drop in the ocean' in Darfur. Rather, 'We have to mix disarmament with a political solution.'[19] For this purpose, he hosted peace talks in Abuja later in August, the first in a sequence of negotiations, chaired largely by the former OAU Secretary-General, Salim Ahmed Salim, which continued with agonising slowness for nearly two years.[20] On 5 May 2006, Obasanjo chaired the final meeting, designed to force a decision by presenting a draft settlement, prepared largely by Salim's negotiating team, to the Sudanese government representative and the leaders of the three main rebel groups. These were the sophisticated Islamist, Khalil Ibrahim, of the Justice and Equality Movement (JEM), and the two rival leaders of the Sudan Liberation Army, the ruthless Minni Minawi, who probably had the largest following and was considered the key figure, and the more populist Abdel Wahid.

An eye-witness account of this meeting gives a vivid picture of Obasanjo as negotiator at this late stage of his career.[21] He first summoned Minni Minawi to face the international mediators. 'This is the moment of decision', Obasanjo warned him. 'What decision we make here tonight – or fail to make – will have monumental implications for Darfur and for Sudan. This opportunity will not come again.... A grave responsibility falls on you.'[22] Minni accepted part of the settlement but demanded changes to the power relationships. The American representative said there could be no changes. Obasanjo told Minni to reconsider and return. Abdel Wahid, called next, expressed similar reservations:

> Obasanjo concluded: 'We stand for the victimized. You go and decide.' Abdel Wahid asked to return to the hotel to consult his team. Obasanjo blazed: 'Who the hell do you think you are?' Then Abdel Wahid's chief negotiator ... intervened ... Obasanjo gave leave to Abdel Wahid and his team to hold a meeting of their negotiating council in Aguda House.[23]

It was 2.15 a.m. when Khalil Ibrahim entered the room and rejected the settlement out of hand:

> Obasanjo was abrupt. 'You must take responsibility for what happens in Darfur. Go. Leave.' Khalil interrupted him: 'The AU will be responsible too.' Obasanjo became angry and sarcastic. 'The AU started this war? Are you saying the AU started this war? What nonsense. You are utterly irresponsible. What the hell are you saying?' He thumped the table. 'An African of good family who is well brought up does not treat his elders like that. I can see that you are not from a good family or well brought up.' [Khalil was from a ruling family.] He paused. 'See what will happen.' Obasanjo gestured dismissively. 'The floor is open.'
>
> International representatives lined up to condemn Khalil.... Obasanjo concluded: 'You insulted us.' Khalil replied: 'I didn't mean any offence that might have been taken. We need knowledge and patience. I represent the people, the will of the people.' He turned

to address the mediation, 'Reconsider how to manage our cause and don't blame us.' Obasanjo said curtly: 'JEM you can go.'[24]

The meeting adjourned at 4.55 a.m. and resumed four hours later. Minni Minawi appeared first and accepted the settlement with reservations. 'There was a long pause before Obasanjo asked for applause.' Minni asked to discuss with the other two leaders. Obasanjo refused: 'No. What we have we keep, then we try to get more.' He called in the government delegation: 'As a government the initiative is essentially yours…you have more to keep than to receive. We called you for your reactions to minor modifications. Anything acceptable to the Sudanese parties is acceptable to us.' The delegation's leader stated reservations but accepted the settlement. Obasanjo, always a man of the state, thanked him for the government's 'responsible and proper reaction'.

While they waited for the final text to be printed, Abdel Wahid returned:

> Obasanjo confronted Abdel Wahid, springing into the posture of a boxer. 'You let me down!' he said, his fist in Abdel Wahid's face. Abdel Wahid began to explain, 'You are our Baba, not just the Baba of Nigeria but the Baba of Darfur, but I am demanding the rights for our people …' Before he could continue, Obasanjo seized him by the collar and pulled him into a side room, 'I need to talk to you, boy.' For more than two hours, a shuttle followed … pressing Abdel Wahid to sign.

It was no good. Although most of his delegation favoured agreement, 'I, Abdel Wahid Mohamed al Nur, will never sign!' At 5.55 p.m. the government representative and Minni Minawi, alone, signed the Abuja Agreement.[25]

It was a disaster. The agreement had been imposed by the mediators rather than negotiated by the contestants. The military leaders in the field had not been involved. Minni Minawi's acceptance of the settlement lost him much of his following. Instead, he allied with the government forces. The violence in Darfur continued, but most of it was now fighting among the rebel groups or the Arab militias, while the government in Khartoum sat out the conflict and obstructed the deployment of a more effective force by the United Nations, which took over the formal control (and expense) of the peacekeeping force in January 2008, although routine management remained with the African Union.[26]

By the time of the final negotiations at Abuja, Obasanjo was no longer the chairman of the African Union. He had hoped that his term would be extended again beyond January 2006, but Mbeki and other leaders at the meeting refused and Obasanjo appears to have left the meeting early in disgust.[27] Apart from Darfur his tenure had largely been peaceful, but it had been a thankless task, with Gaddafi, on one side, pressing for rapid expansion into a United States of Africa and the bulk of members, on the other, reluctant to meet the costs even of the existing structure. By 2007, contributions were $44 million in arrears, eleven member states were consequently prohibited from speaking at meetings, and the parliament remained an expensive formality.[28]

Instead, Obasanjo's chief diplomatic problem during the last year of his presidency lay within Nigeria. When the International Court had allotted Bakassi Peninsula to Cameroun in 2002, Obasanjo had temporised, knowing that cession would be deeply unpopular within Nigeria and that he would soon face re-election. Once his second term was safely won, the government declared in 2003 that it would

284

withdraw troops from the peninsula once the border demarcation was completed and the future of the affected population was settled. While the National Assembly insisted that the cession could be made only with Senate approval, the government obtained a High Court ruling that the judgment of the International Court could not be questioned.[29] On 12 June 2006, ignoring the advice of a security committee that the peninsula was vital to Nigeria's defence, Obasanjo signed an agreement at Green Tree, in New York, embodying the border demarcation and implementing the International Court's decision.[30] Next day, he sent the agreement to the Senate President and asked for 'expeditious ratification'. On 14 June the President read the letter to the Senate, which promptly forgot about it. An area on the Nigerian side of the border was renamed Bakassi so that no change in the constitution was needed. The Nigerian army withdrew from the peninsula in August 2006, leaving a civil administration in place for another two years.[31] At the parade to mark the withdrawal, Obasanjo told his troops, 'We have set a lesson for Africa and the world. We have shown that it is possible to resolve a difficult border problem without war and unnecessary loss of lives and property.'[32] The wisdom of that decision and the *fait accompli* skill of its execution formed an apt conclusion to his conduct of foreign affairs.

NOTES

1. Peter Kagwanja, 'Zimbabwe's March 2005 elections: dangers and opportunities', *African Security Review*, 14, 3, 2005 (electronic resource); Adebajo in Adebajo et al., *South Africa in Africa*, p. 230.
2. Kaye Whiteman, 'The switchback and the fallback: Nigeria-British relations', in Adebajo and Mustapha, *Gulliver's troubles*, p. 271.
3. Soares de Oliveira, *Oil and politics*, p. 334.
4. Gillies, 'Obasanjo', pp. 571–2; Paden, *Faith and politics*, pp. 18–23.
5. Sharath Srinivasan, 'A "rising Great Power" embraces Africa: Nigeria-China relations', in Adebajo and Mustapha, *Gulliver's troubles*, pp. 341, 344; above, p. 275.
6. *Guardian*, 25 and 28 July 2003; Soares de Oliveira, *Oil and politics*, pp. 238–42; *Petroleum Economist*, October 2008, p. 34.
7. *Africa Research Bulletin (Political)*, September 2003, pp. 15439–42, and October 2003, p. 15481.
8. *Africa Confidential*, 4 February 2005, p. 8; *Guardian*, 11 May, 8 August, and 14 December 2007.
9. Paul Simon Handy, 'The dynastic succession in Togo: continental and regional implications', *African Security Review*, 14, 3, 2005 (electronic resource).
10. Paul D. Williams, 'From non-intervention to non-indifference: the origins and development of the African Union's security culture', *African Affairs*, 106 (2007), 274.
11. *Times*, 19 January 2006; Médard in Adebajo and Mustapha, *Gulliver's troubles*, p. 321; Adebajo in Adebajo et al., *South Africa in Africa*, p. 234; D.O. Zounmenou, 'Côte d'Ivoire's 2008 elections: is there hope?' *African Security Review*, 17, 2 (2008), 66–71.
12. Kagwanja, 'Zimbabwe's elections'; *Sunday Times* (London), 10 July 2005; *Africa Research Bulletin (Political)*, August 2005, p. 16335.
13. Adekeye Adebajo and Helen Scanlon (ed.), *A dialogue of the deaf: essays on Africa and the United Nations* (Auckland Park, 2006), pp. 19–26; Bola A. Akinterinwa (ed.), *Nigeria and the United Nations Security Council* (Ibadan, 2005), passim; Adebajo in Adebajo et al., *South Africa in Africa*, pp. 233–4.

14. Landsberg in Adebajo and Mustapha, *Gulliver's troubles*, p. 214.
15. Adebajo in Adebajo et al., *South Africa in Africa*, p. 234.
16. This account relies heavily on Alex de Waal (ed.), *War in Darfur and the search for peace* (Cambridge MA, 2007).
17. Julie Flint and Alex de Waal, *Darfur: a new history of a long war* (revised edition, London, 2008), p. 128.
18. Samuel M. Makinda and F. Wafula Okumu, *The African Union: challenges of globalization, security, and governance* (London, 2008), pp. 83, 91; Murithi, *African Union*, pp. 91–2.
19. *Africa Confidential*, 6 August 2004, p. 3.
20. Akinjide Osuntokun, 'Foreign policy challenges: Olusegun Obasanjo as President of Nigeria and Chairman of the African Union', in Bola A. Akinterinwa (ed.), *Nigeria and the development of the African Union* (Ibadan, 2005), p. 225.
21. Alex de Waal, 'Darfur's deadline: the final days of the Abuja peace process', in his *War in Darfur*, Ch.11.
22. Ibid., p. 273.
23. Ibid., p. 274.
24. Ibid., p. 275.
25. Ibid., pp. 277–9.
26. Flint and de Waal, *Darfur*, pp. ix–xii, 187, 230–3, 269–76; *Africa Confidential*, 20 March 2009, pp. 1–3.
27. Adebajo in Adebajo et al., *South Africa in Africa*, p. 234.
28. Makinda and Okumu, *African Union*, pp. 37, 91.
29. *Daily Trust*, 7 August 2003; *Guardian*, 24 March and 13 August 2008.
30. Text in *This Day*, 14 August 2008.
31. *Nigerian Tribune*, 2 December 2007; *Guardian*, 18 December 2007.
32. Obasanjo, *Standing tall*, p. 258.

23
Managing the Succession

For many Nigerians, whatever services Obasanjo had previously rendered their country were negated by his political behaviour during his second presidential term. They believed that, being a natural autocrat further corrupted by power, he had attempted to defy the constitution by seeking a third term of office or perhaps even attempting to make himself president for life.[1] To achieve this, he had been willing to bribe and coerce legislators and to abuse his power by illegally excluding Vice-President Atiku from seeking election as president. When Obasanjo's bid for a third term failed, so it was said, he had tried with greater success to secure the election of a weak and compliant successor by making the presidential election of 2007 the most corrupt and undemocratic that Nigeria had seen.

This is a formidable charge and Nigerians were surely right to feel that to understand Obasanjo's behaviour on this issue is crucial to understanding the man. Part of the charge is certainly true, especially the treatment of Atiku and the character of the election. Yet there are two objections to the predominant opinion: it does not recognise the complexity of the political situation facing Obasanjo during his second term, and it does not appreciate the depth of his lifetime dedication to Nigerian unity and stability. To meet these objections requires a more subtle interpretation, although much must remain speculative until the relevant documents are publicly available.

Obasanjo's behaviour as civilian president was shaped chiefly by his experience twenty years earlier as military head of state, especially the failure of the political transition that he had supervised. This had resulted in the weakness and corruption of Shagari's regime, the military coup that had overthrown it, and the subsequent sixteen years of military rule that had brought Nigeria to its knees. 'Obasanjo's really palpable fault in government', journalists had perceived in 1986, 'is the vicarious sense of failure he continues to suffer in the death of the Second Republic: the reasoning being that no responsible regime can distance itself from the quality and performance of its successor.'[2] As he entered his second term of office as president in 2003, Obasanjo was determined to avoid the mistakes of 1979. One of those had been to believe that it was enough to organise a free election, which would automatically produce a satisfactory successor. Nine days before he finally left office in May 2007, Obasanjo claimed that the new succession he had managed 'had corrected the mistakes observed in 1979 when he, as military head of state, handed over power to Alhaji Shehu Shagari. "One thing that was not properly done in 1979 was that we were not really interested in the personality of who succeeded us."'[3]

The Second Presidential Term (2003–7)

Obasanjo's first priority – and, as he saw it, his first duty – during his second presidential term was therefore to ensure that whoever became president in 2007 would make a good president. This had three implications. One was that Obasanjo himself must retain control of the political process until the moment of electoral victory in 2007. That would be difficult, for, as Americans knew, a president entering his last term was a lame duck from whom power rapidly slipped away. Obasanjo had experienced being a lame duck in 1979[4] and can scarcely have wished to repeat it. By November 2003, only six months into his second term, politicians were already saying, 'In two years' time, Obasanjo will no longer be relevant in Nigeria's politics.'[5] He had to find ways of remaining relevant and powerful if he was to control the outcome of the 2007 election.

The second implication of that duty, in Obasanjo's eyes, was that he had to exclude Atiku, whom he pursued as obsessively as he had once sought to unseat Babangida. The reasons for this will be considered in more detail later in this chapter, but they probably combined a belief that Atiku was no more than a corrupt politician who would make a bad president, a violent resentment of the humiliation to which Obasanjo believed Atiku had exposed him during the PDP convention of January 2003, and the poisoning of the President's mind by close advisers anxious to prevent Atiku succeeding.

To exclude Atiku, however, created the third difficulty in controlling the succession: there was no other obvious candidate with any claim to the loyalty of most Nigerians. There would certainly be many aspirants, but to throw the competition wide open would be to invite a level of inter-regional rivalry that might tear the country apart and ensure that whoever gained the victory would have a large majority of enemies. For Obasanjo to select and promote a candidate from an early stage, on the other hand, would assuredly range all the potential rivals against him. The best way to handle the problem was to delay the competition for as long as possible and then intervene decisively at the last moment on behalf of the contender most likely to make a good president.

Obasanjo later insisted, correctly, that he had never expressed a wish to remain in office after 2007,[6] but he could certainly have stopped his supporters campaigning for constitutional change to allow him a third term. His failure to do so needs to be seen in the context of controlling the succession. The campaign ensured that rather than becoming a lame duck, he continued to dominate politics for at least the first three years of his second term.[7] No other aspirant could campaign effectively until the third term issue was settled in May 2006, nor did Obasanjo need to choose among the aspirants until late in 2006, except to work against Atiku's aspirations. Once the third term project failed, he had to find other methods of retaining political control, but the shortened period of less than a year before the election made it much easier.

Yet Obasanjo's motives were probably more complicated than this. He had never coveted power, but he certainly enjoyed it, perhaps all the more as he grew older. He had grounds to think that he was still the best president available to Nigerians. His economic reform programme and oil-for-infrastructure deals were still at early stages, his National Integrated Power Project required another presidential term to deliver results, and the African Union needed leaders of his weight and experience. He cannot have enjoyed knowing that, like any Nigerian leader, he could expect denigration once he left power. At the same time, however, he knew that tenure extension had ruined the reputations of Gowon, Babangida, and Abacha.

288

He also knew that a bid for a third term would be widely unpopular, especially among northerners, who expected the presidency to return to their region in 2007. To threaten that regional compact was to endanger everything that Obasanjo had worked for throughout his life, which is the most powerful reason to think that he would not have done so purely from motives of personal ambition. It is possible that, as a man of ruthless political guile, he realised from the start that the third term campaign would fail and allowed it to proceed chiefly because it occupied time and dampened competition. It is more likely that he realised, once others began the campaign, that it could be to his advantage whether successful or not, and this is perhaps the most convincing interpretation of his behaviour. He may also have recalled the criticism that in 1979 he had left power too early, deciding on this occasion to leave the choice to Nigerians. A stronger motive may have lain in his providential beliefs. As he had said in 2002, 'My gut feeling and my faith tell me that until God shuts a door, no human can shut it. And when He opens a door, it remains open until He chooses to close it.'[8] By allowing others to put him forward, without himself campaigning, Obasanjo put the issue in the hands of the people and of providence. As will be seen, he accepted their verdict instantly. These possible motives were not mutually exclusive. All may have been in the mind of an exceedingly complicated man.

Even before the President began his second term in May 2003, he assured Nigerians that he would not support any constitutional amendment to extend his tenure beyond 2007.[9] He was already under pressure from Atiku's supporters to endorse him as successor. By July 2003 an 'Atiku for 2007' campaign had been launched in his home state, Adamawa.[10] This can only have angered Obasanjo, who resented his deputy's 'disloyalty' at the recent PDP convention, was hearing rumours that Atiku had encouraged Na'Abba's impeachment campaign, and was convinced of the Vice-President's corruption.[11] Late in 2003, Obasanjo asserted the power to appoint and dismiss Atiku's aides, claiming they were presidency staff. Early in 2004 the President was reported to have warned Atiku to abstain from campaigning for at least the next eighteen months. In March, at Obasanjo's request, the National Assembly revoked the Vice-President's automatic chairmanship of the National Council on Privatisation, which Atiku was alleged to have abused.[12] His political base in Adamawa was also weakening because his candidate, a Christian, had only narrowly won the governorship in 2003, losing Atiku's own ward, and a new rival was threatening his control of the state in the person of Senator Jubril Aminu, the formidable former Ambassador in Washington.[13] When Obasanjo replaced Atiku's supporter Audu Ogbeh as PDP chairman in January 2005, the Vice-President's colleagues in the PDM faction considered leaving the party.[14] By then it was common gossip that Obasanjo was determined to prevent his deputy from succeeding him because he could not be trusted to maintain the President's cherished economic reforms.[15]

In the meantime, the possibility of extending Obasanjo's tenure had again surfaced. During 2003, he had denied any such ambition. 'Do you think he wants to soil his name?' one associate asked.[16] During 2004, however, the presidents of neighbouring Togo and Chad both extended their tenure through constitutional changes.[17] Early in 2004, associates began to press Obasanjo in the same direction. In July, Anenih declared publicly that the President ought to continue, 'because he is doing well, but the problem is that he is statutes barred.' By September, a committee had been established, apparently including governors, politicians, and businessmen, to lobby for an extended tenure for both the President and state governors, 26 of whom were due to retire in 2007. 'Unsolicited advocates,' as Yoruba described them, were taking control. Obasanjo, however, continued to deny any desire for extension.[18]

Executive tenure became an issue of national debate in February 2005 when Obasanjo opened a National Political Reform Conference. Throughout his presidency he had resisted demands for a sovereign national conference, insisting that Nigeria already possessed in the National Assembly an institution empowered to initiate constitutional changes. The Assembly agreed and established a constitutional review committee in May 2000. Among its many proposals, it favoured a single five-year presidential term rotating among the six geo-political zones. Obasanjo submitted a bill to enact this, but in January 2003 the Assembly abandoned the proposal as too contentious.[19] In October, he revived the suggestion and activated a new committee. When nothing resulted and critics began to plan their own national conference, Obasanjo induced the Council of State to convoke a National Political Reform Conference of 400 members, 50 appointed by himself and the others mostly by state governors. Asked whether its mandate included extending the president's tenure, the chairman of the planning committee denied it.[20]

Opening the conference on 21 February 2005, Obasanjo insisted that he had no hidden agenda and attempted to restrict debate by listing principles that he claimed were beyond dispute.[21] The conference ignored him and revealed the range of Nigeria's political conflicts. Igbo complained that the conference organisation marginalised them. Muslims denounced their underrepresentation and feared an attack on Sharia law.[22] The most contentious issues were resource control and revenue allocation, with delegates from the oil-producing states demanding that 50% of revenue should accrue to the state of derivation. This won sympathy from Middle Belt delegates in a novel alliance of minorities, but it was resisted by northerners, whose insistence on a maximum of 17% by derivation led South-South delegates to walk out and the conference to collapse.[23] In the meantime it had also deadlocked over the presidential term. Obasanjo had mentioned that one paper to be considered was a revised version of a draft constitution produced during his first term. This was apparently made available only to certain delegates and at a late stage.[24] It proposed a single six-year term for president and governors, specifying that those who had already served two terms would not be eligible for election. This, too, was rejected chiefly by northerners who expected a northern president to serve for eight years from 2007.[25]

In the mood of suspicion prevailing, the conference was widely seen as a defeat for Obasanjo and especially for his unsolicited advocates, who, as he put it in March 2005, 'keep worrying me, maybe you should stay a little longer.'[26] One informant declared a month later that the President's backers 'are aware that President Obasanjo is reluctant in contesting for a third term in office, but said "once we are sure that the six year term is inscribed in the constitution, then we begin our campaign for him to stay till 2009. This is to ensure that his reforms are at least over eighty per cent concluded".'[27] In November 2005, a sub-committee of the National Assembly went further to propose that president and governors should be eligible for three four-year terms.[28] In a later interview in January 2007, at the height of his dispute with Obasanjo, Vice-President Atiku claimed that shortly after the national conference he had seen a draft in Obasanjo's handwriting recommending that the president should enjoy such a third term.[29]

For Atiku, the third-term campaign created a no-win situation. If he opposed it, he would alienate Obasanjo irreparably. If he supported it, not only might he destroy his hopes of securing the presidency in 2007, but he would anger his northern supporters. In August 2005, shortly after the conference ended, he declared that it would be politically and constitutionally impossible to extend Obasanjo's tenure and that the President had sworn to him that he had no plan to do so. Obasanjo replied angrily that he had made no vows to Atiku and had sworn only to observe the constitution.[30] Atiku's enemies seized the opportunity to swing the PDP machinery against him, using the distribution of new membership cards as a means of excluding his supporters, especially in Adamawa, where Atiku himself was unable to obtain a card and his local rivals worked to destroy his influence.[31] Publicity was given to allegations of his corrupt dealings in the United States, which he denied and were later shown to be untrue. His supporters replied with allegations against the President.[32]

By August 2005, Obasanjo had denied publicly at least six times that he wished to stay in office after 2007, although many refused to believe him, much as he had disbelieved Babangida in 1993.[33] Popular opinion was strongly against extending his tenure. An Afrobarometer survey late in 2005 found that 84% of respondents opposed a third presidential term.[34] Longstanding critics of Obasanjo like Afenifere – which warned of civil war – the Nigerian Labour Congress, Roman Catholic bishops, alienated PDP Aborigines, human rights activists, and most of the press were vocal in their hostility.[35] Also opposed, at the elite level, were the young modernisers of Obasanjo's economic team and a large proportion of northern legislators and other notables. The Arewa Consultative Forum announced that it would not recognise an Obasanjo presidency after May 2007.[36] In the United States, the Director of National Intelligence warned Congress that if Obasanjo stayed beyond his second term, it might 'unleash major turmoil and conflict' leading to 'disruption of oil supply, secessionist moves by regional governments, major refugee flow, and instability elsewhere in West Africa'.[37]

Support, by contrast, came especially from the presidential circle – perhaps led by younger men like Andy Uba rather than the more experienced Anenih, who reportedly warned that it could not be done[38] – from Corporate Nigeria, from amenable legislators, and from state governors who hoped to share in the extension of tenure and had much to fear from prosecution once they lost office, although many governors were ambivalent in backing what they often knew to be an unpopular project, so that press estimates of those in favour varied from as many as 31 to as few as 14.[39] The governors were crucial, for they were expected to sway both the state assemblies and their representatives in the National Assembly, the latter through control of reselection. In addition, in mid April the PDP's National Executive Committee formally endorsed the third term without discussion, Ahmadu Ali warning that any party member opposing it would be sanctioned. Some 25 members of the committee walked out in protest.[40] Enormous sums were, as usual, said to have been amassed to bribe legislators, although the EFCC found no hard evidence of bribery.[41] 'The all-consuming question,' wrote a far from impartial editor, 'was … which will prevail, the wishes of the people or the desires of a cabal?'[42]

By late April 2006, when the Constitution of the Federal Republic of Nigeria 1999 (Amendment) Bill 2006 was tabled in the National Assembly, the chance of securing the necessary two-thirds majorities was clearly fading, despite police action to disrupt opposition gatherings.[43] Early in May the House of Representatives passed the first reading by only 171 votes to 109 and Danjuma, the President's alienated former colleague, had a conversation (by his own later account) in which he asked Obasanjo whether he was behind the campaign: 'He said, "Well, not exactly." That at first, he didn't think so, "but in the circumstances of the present situation, in view of Atiku's disloyalty", he could not just walk away. He thought that this campaign was also good, that he would need to continue.'[44]

The Senate debate, broadcast live on independent television despite a security raid on the television station, began on 3 May, with a majority of speakers opposing the proposal.[45] Eight days later, Obasanjo summoned the Senate President and the Speaker, complained bitterly of 'unprintable words' spoken about him during the debates, and sought to insist that voting must comply with party policy. The legislators pointed out that their rules prevented such manipulation.[46] On 16 May, the strong-minded Senate President, Ken Nnamani, put the question of reading the bill for a second time to a voice vote. Only half a dozen senators said Aye. Astonished, Nnamani asked them again and even fewer responded. Then he asked for the Nays and 'The Senate chamber exploded with "Nay" answer.' He repeated the procedure, received a more resounding reply, and declared the bill lost.[47]

Obasanjo's critics predicted that this would not end the matter, that he 'will try some tricks', perhaps 'something dishonourable to democracy'.[48] He did nothing of the kind but described the vote as a victory for democracy, insisting, 'Throughout the debate, I maintained a studied silence. I was maligned, insulted and wrongly accused but I remained where I am and what I am.' Ahmadu Ali even claimed the result as a party decision because the party controlled both houses of the National Assembly.[49] Unconvincing as this was, it indicated that Obasanjo and his colleagues had switched to a new strategy to control the political process. The first step was to tighten party discipline. In June 2006, an attempt by dissident party founders to launch a 'reconstituted' PDP was squashed when police sealed off its Abuja office.[50] In September, a meeting of the party's National Executive Committee declared Obasanjo 'life leader of the party, father of the nation, and founder of modern Nigeria,' agreed to restrict eligibility for the chairmanship of its Board of Trustees to former national presidents or creditable party chairmen, and empowered the Board's chairman 'to call to order any officer of the party whose conduct falls below the norms'. The party also required all candidates for office to sign a bond making them liable to punishment for breaches of discipline. Obasanjo announced that he would not endorse a presidential candidate until the PDP convention in December, thereby retaining his hold on the political system.[51] Instead, he let it be known that he expected to be succeeded by one of the state governors and encouraged them to enter the race for nomination, thereby ensuring that neither Atiku nor any one governor could recruit a widespread following.[52]

All was now ready for the first step towards the elections of 2007: the primary contests to choose party candidates for state and federal offices other than the presidency. The PDP primaries of late 2006 were probably the most grossly manipulated that Nigeria had seen. In seven states they had to be postponed owing to violence or the disqualification of candidates.[53] Even when they produced clear winners, party headquarters might override the result. The extreme case was in Imo State, where no candidate secured the necessary 50% of votes in the primary. Citing numerous allegations against the frontrunner, headquarters replaced him by a former President of the Manufacturers' Association of Nigeria, who had come fourteenth in the primary poll but had strongly supported the third term campaign and was backed by Obasanjo and the state governor. The Supreme Court ordered the frontrunner's restoration, at which the PDP expelled him and instructed its supporters to vote for a candidate from another party who undertook to switch to the PDP if elected. He was, and fulfilled his pledge two years later.[54]

The election of state governors and legislators was scheduled for 14 April 2007, to be followed a week later by the federal and presidential voting. Interest in the presidential poll focused chiefly on the selection of the PDP candidate. The front-runner, Atiku, launched his campaign a week after the Senate rejected the third term, insisting that he would fight on the PDP ticket. Yet the popularity he had gained by leading the opposition to extending Obasanjo's tenure had only strengthened the President's determination to exclude him. Obasanjo had long ceased to allocate him vice-presidential duties. In June 2006 his aides were reduced to two, from the 22 who had once surrounded him.[55] On 6 September, Obasanjo launched his main attack, asking Atiku to leave a meeting of the Federal Executive Council so that it could discuss allegations of financial malpractice against him based on the EFCC's enquiries. Following the meeting, Obasanjo reported the Council's acceptance of the EFCC's indictment to the Senate, seeking thereby to establish grounds for barring Atiku from standing for election.[56] On 28 September, the PDP's National Executive Committee suspended Atiku from party membership for three months, thereby excluding him from its presidential primary contest on 16 December. A month later, Atiku declared his candidacy without mentioning his party, perhaps because open departure from the PDP, on whose ticket he had been elected, might give grounds for his removal from the vice-presidency.[57] It was widely assumed, however, that he would be the candidate of a coalition of small parties led by the Action Congress (AC), a recent amalgamation of former members of the Alliance for Democracy with dissident PDP notables. When Atiku finally committed himself to the Action Congress in December 2006, the PDP expelled him and Obasanjo declared the vice-presidency vacant, an action that the Court of Appeal was to declare *ultra vires*.[58]

During the last months of 2006, Nigeria teemed with presidential aspirants. Babangida still exercised his fascination over political minds, collected a party nomination form with great fanfare, and was reportedly vetoed brutally by Obasanjo.[59] Rumour had it that elements within the PDP favoured Buhari, the austere general with much popular northern support, but in December he was reconciled with the northern governors who controlled the ANPP and again became its candidate.[60] Many northern members of the PDP believed that their region had a right to the presidency in 2007, but they lacked an agreed candidate: several governors were mentioned, together with General Aliyu Gusau, Obasanjo's former National Security Adviser.[61] The Middle Belt Forum staked a claim to the nomination as a quasi-northern zone that had not hitherto provided an elected president, but was reticent about naming a candidate.[62] There was no such reticence in the South-South zone. The wealthy and ambitious Governor Odili of Rivers State toured the country assiduously and generously.[63] His rivals included the young Governor Duke of Cross River, whose campaign was described unkindly as 'designed for Plato's Republic instead of the largest Banana Republic on earth'.[64] The South-East, too, restated its demand for full equality within the federation while demonstrating its inability to agree on a candidate, eventually fielding two idiosyncratic party leaders: the 76-year-old Ojukwu of the APGA and the maverick Governor Orji Uzor Kalu of Abia with his Progressive People's Alliance. By November 2006 the PDP alone had at least 29 presidential aspirants.[65]

Obasanjo had told a delegation in July 2006 that 'even if his mouth was forced open with a knife, nobody would have an inkling of who he wants as his successor in 2007.'[66] There was indeed no obvious successor and the President was determined to retain political control for as long as possible, to make his choice only when there was no time to challenge it, and until then to keep all the aspirants in play. That he could do so at a time when his own reputation had been so severely damaged was an indication of his political skill. Although insiders claimed that there had been a clear understanding in 2003 that Obasanjo's successor should be a northerner, the President denied it, insisting at a party convention in December 2005 that as party leader he should be left 'to interpret our policy and principles of power shift to suit the occasion which will definitely consider the seeming agitation from the North of the country'.[67] To the very eve of the nominating convention in December 2006 he managed to leave the candidates and the country uncertain whether or not the office had been zoned to any particular region.[68] At his meeting with PDP governors and senators immediately after the third term project collapsed, he pledged his own neutrality, told them that they were the natural pool of candidates – thereby suggesting at least that he favoured a civilian successor – and urged the governors to produce an agreed candidate, excluding only contenders from his own south-western zone.[69] During the next six months the governors held several meetings and, predictably, failed to agree. At a meeting early in December, they apparently produced a short list of six governors from three regions, but accounts of the names on it varied. The PDP Working Committee insisted on conducting a parallel screening process. Obasanjo also asked northern traditional rulers to identify their best candidate, apparently without response.[70]

Meanwhile the EFCC and, it appears, the National Security Organisation were compiling dossiers on potential candidates for the President's use. In September 2006 Ribadu of the EFCC told the Senate that 31 of 36 governors were under suspicion of corruption, which was probably in part a warning that nothing should be taken for granted. Only one thing was certain: after his experience in 1979, Obasanjo intended to choose his successor, not simply to let him emerge.

As the convention date of 16 December approached, several candidates were still rumoured to have the President's blessing, but during November, it appears, he urged candidacy on one of the few reticent governors, Umaru Yar'Adua, Governor of Katsina and younger brother of Obasanjo 's former Chief of Staff and fellow prisoner. Early in December he was added to the governors' short list, apparently at Obasanjo's suggestion, and by 10 December, one well-informed newspaper thought that he might win the nomination on the first ballot if the President finally signified his support.[71] Yar'Adua's background was impeccable. Aged 55 and the son of a First Republic minister and senior emirate official, he had been influenced by the Marxist historian Bala Usman at ABU, worked as a chemistry lecturer, and joined the radical PRP during the Second Republic. He later belonged to the PDM, which partly neutralised Atiku's appeal, and in 1998 he was an early member of the group that encouraged Obasanjo to seek the presidency, himself winning the Katsina governorship for the PDP as a strong Obasanjo supporter. Unlike many northern governors, he backed the third term project strongly.[72]

An austere, earnest, and retiring man in the northern manner, Yar'Adua had gained a reputation for honesty (as the only northern governor not suspected of corruption), economy (he had cleared Katsina's debts and built up large reserves), moderation (especially in administering Sharia law), and political toughness (mobilising youth groups and imposing his nominees on his divided state).[73] 'I have

294

demonstrated in Katsina that things can work,' he claimed.[74] These were qualities that Obasanjo valued. Yet in other respects, Yar'Adua was the President's antithesis: modest, reluctant to involve himself in national affairs, without international experience, and with an apparent lack of energy that had caused his initial administration in Katsina to be described as 'transparency without development'.[75] Warned that Yar'Adua's health was uncertain, Obasanjo's response, as he later described it, suggested misunderstanding of the medical issues involved:

> I knew that Yar'Adua has kidney problem and was under dialysis and that he went abroad for the treatment when he was the governor of Katsina State. Before I picked him, I asked him questions and he gave me the medical report that states that he is no longer under dialysis. I asked medical experts to interpret the report and they told me that once you had completed your dialysis, you have had a successful kidney transplant and can live as long as God wants you to live. If medical experts had said that, who am I to begin to think that the dialysis will fail?[76]

Critics alleged that Obasanjo favoured Yar'Adua because he expected to dominate him after leaving office: 'another third term agenda'.[77] Certainly the President insisted on 'a reliable successor, who would continue his reform programme' and could be trusted not to destroy macroeconomic stability by wild spending.[78] After his retirement, Obasanjo claimed that the many people he had consulted had agreed that only Yar'Adua possessed the five qualities necessary: a northerner, a former governor, well educated, with a record of fiscal discipline, and sharing in the policies and programmes of the administration for the sake of continuity.[79] Moreover, the President's close relationship with the Yar'Adua family offered him some hope of protection once power had passed from him.[80]

When some 5,000 delegates assembled at the PDP convention at Abuja on 16 December 2006, many were probably unaware that the decision had already been taken. During the previous few days Obasanjo had apparently told the northern governors that the party's nominee must come from the North, not least because northern delegates might otherwise support a northern military aspirant such as Aliyu Gusau or even switch to Buhari or Atiku. The decision throws an interesting light on the seriousness of his own third term project. Among the northern governors he favoured Yar'Adua, as did wealthy southern governors like James Ibori of Delta State, who would eventually provide much of Yar'Adua's campaign finance.[81] Other strong candidates among the northern governors were persuaded to withdraw.[82] Then, on 14 December, Obasanjo met the southern aspirants, including Odili, who had been encouraged to campaign so lavishly and was still presented as the frontrunner by dedicated southern newspapers, and told them that the party had zoned the presidency to the North.[83] This meant that the vice-presidential candidate must be a southerner. According to Nasir El-Rufai, a minister who claimed to have been closely involved, Obasanjo wanted this post for Odili, but Yar'Adua – who had experience of a strong-willed deputy in Katsina State – was firmly opposed. It took a reference to Odili's EFCC report to change the President's mind.[84] Instead the governors chose the relatively young Governor Goodluck Jonathan of Bayelsa, who not only had an exemplary record of loyalty to his predecessor and Obasanjo but, as an Ijaw, might help to pacify Niger Delta dissidents.[85]

When the convention finally met, the outcome was so clear that many delegates had apparently left and about a thousand did not vote.[86] Yar'Adua received 3,024 votes. Another 372 delegates cast protest votes for a south-eastern candidate, Rochus Okorocha, while the military aspirant, Aliyu Gusau, secured only 271 ballots and the seven remaining candidates polled 323 between them. By the standards of earlier PDP conventions it was a lacklustre occasion, punctuated by three power cuts. There was a widespread feeling that it had produced a lacklustre ticket.[87]

The opposition, however, was in even worse condition. Removal of many obstacles to party registration had led to a proliferation of parties – 49 eventually contested one or other election – and further entrenched PDP domination. Of its two main opponents, the ANPP was short of money and was divided between its governors and the popular but unbending Buhari, while the newly-formed AC, although supported by Atiku's personal wealth, was a loose alliance of dissidents and was to be severely obstructed by rigging. The PDP, by contrast, was lavishly financed. A new Electoral Act limiting presidential expenditure to N500 million (about $4 million) and individual contributions to any candidate to Nl million (about $8,000) discouraged the grandiose donations of earlier years, but Governor Ibori was reputed, doubtless with exaggeration, to have contributed N5 billion to Yar'Adua's campaign, which was said to have allocated N35 million to each of the 36 state organisations. None of the three major parties had submitted the legally required accounts eight months after the specified deadline.[88]

Although the official media gave disproportionate coverage to the PDP, Nigeria's roughly 100 newspapers and magazines, 100 television stations, and over 200 radio stations ensured an extensive and lively election coverage.[89] Yet campaign tours and public meetings were still central features of electioneering, and Obasanjo, who took full control of the little known Yar'Adua's campaign, was by now a master of the genre. At the age of seventy, usually clothed in an opulent version of local dress,

> He toured every nook and cranny of Nigeria, climbed high podiums with ease, gave long speeches in his characteristic guttural voice and in most cases, he would force other co-campaigners into frenzy dancing while on the podium. He was occurring each time like a good comic relief at the PDP campaign grounds.[90]

When Yar'Adua was taken ill and flown to Germany during the campaign, Obasanjo called him on a mobile phone from the election platform to prove that he was still alive. In Taraba, the President was stoned following a dispute over a governorship candidacy. In Ekiti shots rang out while he was speaking and three PDP activists were killed.[91] As a journalist mused, 'Watching him on the campaign trails, jarrating [sic] to music and song, throughout the breath [sic] and length of the vast land whilst the opposition slumbered, one wonders the necessity of the blatant rigging.'[92] Obasanjo supplied the answer: this was a 'do or die affair'.[93] He was not going to make a mistake this time.

The chief victim of his determination was Atiku. Once the Vice-President had accepted the AC's presidential nomination in December 2006 and the PDP had expelled him, Obasanjo sought some means to prevent him contesting the election. The courts refused to endorse his removal from the vice-presidency. Attempts to impeach him faltered when it became clear that PDP legislators were just as likely to impeach Obasanjo.[94] Instead, the President turned to article 137 of the constitution, which stated that a presidential candidate was disqualified if he had been indicted (not convicted) by a judicial commission of enquiry or a properly constituted tribunal and the indictment had been accepted by the federal or a state government. Early in January 2007, the Independent National Electoral Commission (INEC), appointed by the President, announced that anyone so indicted would be barred from contesting election.[95] On 5 February, the EFCC produced a list of 135 electoral candidates from six parties (including 51 from the PDP) whom it declared unfit for public office. It was headed by Atiku, eight incumbent governors, and 23 gubernatorial candidates. Report had it that Obasanjo removed several names from the list before publication, which he denied.[96] Two days later the government constituted a panel of enquiry, which indicted Atiku and others. INEC declared them to be automatically disqualified from contesting election. Atiku and others appealed to the courts, claiming that their appeal stayed INEC's action. INEC insisted that the constitution, not INEC, had disqualified them.[97] During March, while the law took its desultory course, damaging accusations of corruption against President and Vice-President were traded before the Senate. There was talk of suspending the elections and appointing an impartial interim government to conduct them.[98]

On 7 April 2007, INEC published a final list of candidates, excluding Atiku, and printed corresponding ballot papers. Atiku's case was still before the Supreme Court. On 11 April, Obasanjo declared the next two days public holidays, ostensibly to enable workers to travel to vote in the state elections but with the effect of delaying the court hearing.[99] It finally took place on 16 April. The Supreme Court, maintaining the reputation for independence it had gained during Obasanjo's presidency, declared that INEC could not disqualify a candidate without a court order, thereby clearing the way for Atiku to contest and simultaneously throwing into doubt many of the state elections already held.[100] INEC now had less than five days in which to print 65 million new ballot papers (in South Africa) and distribute them to over 100,000 polling stations. Obasanjo made available the necessary money, transport, and personnel.[101]

The elections of 14 and 21 April 2007 would in any case have been turbulent. The uncertain status of candidates and the need for last-minute rearrangements made them, by general consent, the worst that Nigeria had ever held. Because INEC organised both state and federal voting, it faced the world's largest electoral undertaking, requiring 400 million ballot papers and employing some 500,000 staff on election days.[102] Major problems had arisen in attempting to register voters with supposedly rigging-proof digital technology, but there was much anxiety to register – the Catholic Church in Nsukka made it a requirement before receiving communion[103] – and INEC ultimately claimed to have registered 61,567,036 people, or about 44% of the population, some of them perhaps more than once.[104] As usual, the worst rigging took place at the primaries long before election day, as did most of the violence. Reports suggested that 200 or 300 people were killed during the entire electoral process, including 37 policemen, and on this occasion many of the deaths were in the North where the contest was most intense, including at least 50 in one incident of inter-party warfare in Nassarawa State.[105] By February, two months before the poll, 12% of those interviewed said that had been offered an inducement and 4% had been threatened; the evidence was that inducements were ineffective and threats deterred people from voting.[106]

Large numbers turned out to vote at the state elections on 14 April and were widely disappointed by the late arrival of officials and voting materials. Only one-fifth of polling stations observed by European Union monitors opened on time and many never opened at all. Where voting did take place, it was seldom secret and was confused by uncertainty about the identity and legitimacy of candidates.[107] In

Atiku's Adamawa State, for example, his party's governorship candidate was disqualified on orders from Abuja ten hours before polling began, although his name was on the ballot paper. In the Ondo South election to the Senate, a week later, the PDP won by 318,153 votes to 13,333 without even specifying a candidate.[108] In the delta region, as usual, over 90% turnouts and PDP victories were reported in states where little if any voting took place.[109]

The ballot papers for the presidential poll on 21 April reached Nigeria at 10 p.m. the previous evening.[110] Where they reached polling stations, the long delays and blatant rigging of the state elections had already reduced the turnout, which observers generally estimated at about 20%.[111] INEC later claimed that the election was properly conducted in 27 of the 36 states, but 78% of polling stations observed by European Union monitors lacked essential materials when the polls opened.[112] Where voting took place, it was often better conducted than a week earlier, but the falsification of results was similar. Buhari's lawyers later claimed that only some 30,000 voters' names were ticked on the registers in Rivers State, where the PDP alone claimed some 2.7 million votes, the highest number in the country. In Anambra, where there was little voting, Andy Uba was awarded 1.9 million votes by a registered electorate of 1.8 million.[113] INEC later ordered fresh elections of some kind in 27 of the 36 states. There were no prosecutions for electoral irregularities.[114]

Obasanjo had not gained a third term or excluded Atiku from the contest, but the election at least gave him what he wanted. Whereas pre-election opinion polls were said to have suggested roughly equal votes for and against the PDP, Yar'Adua won 70% of the reported presidential vote – a larger proportion than Obasanjo's victories – with 19% for Buhari and only 8% for Atiku, but with far higher reported turnout in states that Yar'Adua won than in those he lost. The PDP won an even more sweeping victory in the National Assembly elections, winning some 90% of the seats.[115] The results showed two outstanding features. One was regional fragmentation. Only the Middle Belt gave solid support to the PDP; all the other five zones were split between the parties, the ANPP losing its clear dominance in the North and the PDP in the South-East. The other feature, however, was the consolidation of the PDP as the dominant party in the country as a whole.

The President was elated. 'I don't deny that there were imperfections in the elections,' he assured the BBC, 'but the magnitude does not make the results null and void. We should not be measured by European standards. Nigeria has come a long way from when I first voted. We are better than 20 years ago.'[116] Other Nigerians, with higher expectations of democracy, were humiliated and embittered. Soyinka described the elections as 'an insult on the intelligence of the Nigerian people'. He warned Yar'Adua, 'A gentleman does not accept stolen goods.'[117] 'In the last one year or so,' Atiku later reflected, 'Mali and Senegal have conducted peaceful and credible elections. Even the war ravaged Liberia and Sierra Leone with all their difficulties conducted peaceful and credible elections to the admiration of Africa and the rest of the world. But Nigeria, with her claim to leadership in Africa, has been unable to do so. What a tragedy!'[118] Reuben Abati described the election as 'a coup ... against the Nigerian people'.[119]

Election monitors generally echoed the criticisms. Nigeria's Transition Monitoring Group, with 50,000 observers, denounced the exercise as 'a charade' and called for the presidential poll to be reconducted.[120] European Union monitors, among the most critical, judged that the elections 'fell far short of basic international standards', leading the European Parliament to recommend that financial aid should be withheld from Nigeria until fresh elections were held.[121] A Commonwealth Commission thought the polls 'fell short of the standards Nigeria had achieved in 2003' and focused its criticisms especially on INEC and its apparent dependence on the presidency, described by a group of American academics as 'brazen and systematic collusion'.[122] INEC replied by blaming 'the political class' and especially Obasanjo's quarrel with Atiku. In December 2008, an Electoral Reform Commission identified INEC's lack of independence as the key weakness and proposed its replacement by new electoral bodies.[123]

Defeated candidates had meanwhile turned to the courts, which, guided perhaps by the Supreme Court's decisions in Atiku's favour, showed themselves more willing than in the past to overturn INEC's declarations, denouncing it in one case as a 'spineless body' acting at the PDP's bidding.[124] At least fifteen governorship results were contested, but where the courts annulled elections, those initially elected generally won the rescheduled contests with wider margins than before. The most striking reversal was in Edo State, where the courts replaced the initial victor by the trade unionist Oshiomhole of the Action Congress.[125] Attention naturally focused chiefly on the challenge by Buhari and Atiku to the presidential result, a challenge the Supreme Court rejected in December 2008 by only four votes to three, declaring that 'despite all the non-compliance with the Electoral Act, the result of the election was not substantially affected.'[126]

Whereas the peaceful transition in 1979 had made Obasanjo's reputation, the electoral fiasco of 2007 ruined it. In Washington, President Bush found himself too busy to receive a farewell visit.[127] Obasanjo's final broadcast, by contrast, was characteristically triumphal as he celebrated Nigeria's first peaceful transition from one elected government to another, its elimination of military coups, improved international image, developing economy, freedom from external debt, and unprecedented level of unity.[128]

Next day, after the inauguration ceremony at which Yar'Adua had called him 'one of our nation's greatest patriots', ex-President Obasanjo returned once more to Abeokuta.[129] The crowds were there again to greet him at the stadium. The Alake was there again to list his achievements and express their pride. Three days later, however, at a thanksgiving service at St Peter's Cathedral, Archbishop Peter Akinola struck a note different from those of the past, urging Obasanjo to dedicate the rest of his life to the service of his poor neighbours and reconciliation with those he had antagonised. 'What is left for you', the Archbishop counselled, 'is to be humble and shed off every [part?] of that excess luggage – those side attractions – every political expediency; all those military adventurisms; all those unholy financial pursuits. They must go.'[130]

NOTES

1. Nwabueze, *How Obasanjo subverted law*, p. 165.
2. Ted Iwere and others in *African Guardian*, 5 June 1986, p. 21.
3. *Punch,* 21 May 2007.
4. Above, p. 94.
5. *Tell,* 24 November 2003, p. 23.
6. *Tell,* 30 May 2006.

7. This interpretation was suggested in *Africa Confidential*, 9 September 2005, p. 2.
8. Obe, *New dawn*, vol. 3, p. 366.
9. *This Day*, 10 May 2003.
10. *West Africa*, 9 June 2003, p. 13; *Daily Trust*, 1 August 2003.
11. *Insider Weekly*, 14 July 2003, pp. 21–2; *Tell*, 30 June 2003, p. 22; Danjuma in Guardian, 17 February 2008.
12. *This Day*, 28 December 2003, *Tell*, 2 February 2004, pp. 17–18; *Insider Weekly*, 5 April 2004, pp. 21–2.
13. *Tell*, 28 April 2003, pp. 14, 18, Adinoyi Ojo Onukaba, *Atiku*, p. 244; *Newswatch*, 18 April 2005, p. 50.
14. *Newswatch*, 24 January 2005, p. 10; *This Day*, 11 February 2005.
15. *Newswatch*, 25 April 2005, pp. 13–15; *This Day*, 5 February 2005.
16. Bode George in *This Day*, 28 December 2003.
17. Handy, 'Dynastic succession'; Soares de Oliveira, *Oil and politics*, p. 283.
18. *This Day*, 7 March, 4 July, 18 and 27 September 2004; *Newswatch*, 24 January 2005, pp. 20–1; Wole Soyinka, *Ibadan: the penkelemes years: a memoir: 1946–1965* (London, 1994), p. 82.
19. *This Day*, 24 May 2000, 7 October 2002, 28 January 2003; *West Africa*, 9 September 2002, p. 19.
20. *Newswatch*, 17 November 2003, p. 26; *This Day*, 13 January 2005; *Guardian*, 8 December 2004.
21. *This Day*, 22 February 2005.
22. *This Day*, 1 April 2005; *Newswatch*, 14 March 2005.
23. *Newswatch*, 2 May 2005, p. 13, 27 June 2005, p. 10, and 25 July 2005, pp. 19–20; *This Day*, 6 May 2005.
24. *This Day*, 24–8 April 2005.
25. *Newswatch*, 2 May 2005, p. 40, and 9 May 2005, pp. 17–21; *This Day*, 14 and 27 June 2005.
26. *This Day*, 28 March and 27 June 2005; *Newswatch*, 25 July 2005, p. 26.
27. *This Day*, 23 April 2005. See also Olusegun Adeniyi in *This Day*, 5 May 2005.
28. *This Day*, 16 November 2005.
29. *Vanguard*, 30 January 2007.
30. *This Day*, 20, 29, and 31 August 2005; *Africa Confidential*, 9 September 2005, p. 1.
31. *This Day*, 20–1 September and 4 and 18 October 2005; *Newswatch*, 10 October 2005, p. 12; *Source*, 17 October 2005, pp. 16–23.
32. *Newswatch*, 12 September 2005, pp. 14–24, and 19 September 2005, p. 21; *This Day*, 15 September 2005.
33. Sola Odunfa, 'General decline', *BBC Focus on Africa*, 17, 3 (July 2006), 13.
34. Afrobarometer Briefing Paper no. 35, 'Term limits, the presidency, and the electoral system: what do Nigerians want?' (April 2006), p. 2: http://www.afrobarometer.org/papers/AfrobriefNo35.pdf (accessed 26 August 2007).
35. Paden, *Faith and politics*, p. 82; *This Day*, 3 August 2005, 24 February and 11–12 March 2006; *Guardian*, 1 June 2006.
36. *Guardian*, 18 May 2006; *This Day*, 21 January 2005 and 25 January 2006; Paden, *Faith and politics*, p.81.
37. Paden, *Faith and politics*, p. 81.
38. *Guardian*, 14 May 2006; *This Day*, 24 September 2006; *Newswatch*, 16 October 2006, p. 32.
39. *Newswatch*, 27 February 2006, p. 14; *Africa Confidential*, 14 April 2006, p. 7.
40. *Guardian*, 8 May 2006; *This Day*, 14 April 2006.
41. *Guardian*, 16 May 2006; *This Day*, 27 June 2006.
42. *This Day*, 17 May 2006.

43. *This Day*, 29 April 2006; *Insider Weekly*, 3 April 2006, pp. 19, 21, and 10 April 2006, p. 18.
44. *Guardian*, 24 February 2008.
45. *Guardian*, 4 and 16 May 2006.
46. *Guardian*, 13–16 May 2006.
47. *Nigerian Tribune*, 17 May 2006.; *Guardian*, 17 May 2006.
48. Balarabe Musa in *Guardian*, 17 May 2006.
49. *Newswatch*, 29 May 2006, p. 28; *Nigerian Tribune*, 19 May 2006.
50. *Guardian*, 10–11 June 2006.
51. *Newswatch*, 16 October 2006, pp. 30–2; *Vanguard*, 19 June 2007; *This Day*, 9 July 2006; *Nigerian Tribune*, 29 October 2006.
52. Nasir El-Rufai, 'Umaru Yar'dua: great expectation, disappointing outcome', 31 May 2009, http://www. saharareporters.com (accessed 25 December 2009).
53. *Guardian*, 19 and 27 November 2006; *This Day*, 10 December 2006.
54. *Vanguard*, 27 March 2007; *Nigerian Tribune*, 26 July 2009.
55. *Guardian*, 23 June 2006.
56. *Newswatch*, 18 September 2006, pp. 16–23; *This Day*. 8 and 10 September 2006; *Guardian*, 14 September 2006.
57. *This Day*, 1 October 2006; *Guardian*, 26 November 2006; *Nigerian Tribune*, 24 November 2006.
58. *Nigerian Tribune*, 3 October and 20 November 2006, 24 April 2007; *Guardian*, 21–4 December 2006, 13 January 2007.
59. *Newswatch*, 13 April 2006, p. 21; *Guardian*, 9 and 26 November 2006.
60. *Nigerian Tribune*, 7 and 12 November and 19 December 2006; *This Day*, 4 December 2006.
61. *This Day*, 28 May and 27 July 2006.
62. *This Day*, 18 May 2006; *Nigerian Tribune*, 26 May 2006.
63. *Daily Champion*, 11 October 2006; *This Day*, 28 October 2006; *Nigerian Tribune*, 29 October 2006.
64. *Vanguard*, 7 January 2007.
65. *Daily Champion*, 4 March 2007; *Nigerian Tribune*, 30 December 2006; Moses Tedheke and Idris Tanu Ejenavwo (ed.), *The Obasanjo administration 1999–2007: chronicle of events and issues* (Kaduna, 2007), p. 233.
66. *Daily Champion*, 22 July 2006.
67. *This Day*, 20 March, 30 May, and 30 November 2003; *Guardian*, 5 and 7 December 2004; Obasanjo, *Standing tall*, p. 140.
68. *Vanguard*, 29 October 2006; *Nigerian Tribune*, 11 November 2006.
69. *This Day*, 27 May 2006.
70. *Nigerian Tribune*, 5 December 2006; *This Day*, 27 July and 5 December 2006; *Guardian*, 29 August and 12 December 2006; *Newswatch*, 29 May 2006, p. 22.
71. El-Rufai, 'Umaru Yar'dua'; *This Day*, 12 November and 5 and 10 December 2006; *Daily Champion*, 21 November 2006.
72. *This Day*, 26 and 29 January and 28 February 1999, 12 March 2004, 1 December 2006; El-Rufai, 'Umaru Yar'dua'.
73. *Guardian*, 16 December 2006 and 12 June 2007; *Newswatch*, 2 June 2002, p. 50, and 25 December 2006, p. 21.
74. *Vanguard*, 8 March 2007.
75. *Guardian*, 18 December 2006; *Weekly Trust*, 19 June 2000.
76. *Guardian*, 22 January 2010.
77. *Vanguard*, 14 December 2006.
78. *Nigerian Tribune*, 8 April 2007; *Guardian*, 8 April 2007.
79. *Nigerian Tribune*, 27 June 2009.
80. Paden, *Faith and politics*, p. 90.

81. *This Day*, 26 November and 21 December 2006, 25 January 2007; *Guardian*, 7 and 13 December 2006, 7 August 2007; *Nigerian Tribune*, 15 December 2006.
82. *Vanguard*, 14 December 2006.
83. *Daily Champion*, 15 December 2006; *Guardian*, 16 December 2006.
84. El-Rufai, 'Umaru Yar'dua'; *Daily Independent*, 13 March 2007, quoted in Albert, 'Review', p. 62.
85. *This Day*, 24 February, 15 August, 18 and 21 December 2006; *Guardian*, 15 December 2006.
86. *Nigerian Tribune*, 17 December 2006; *Daily Champion*, 18 December 2006.
87. *Guardian*, 17–18 December 2006; *Vanguard*, 20 December 2006.
88. E. Remi Aiyede, 'Electoral laws and the 2007 general election in Nigeria', *Journal of African Elections*, 6, 2 (2007), 43, 49; *Daily Champion*, 5 February 2007; *Guardian*, 7 August 2007; *Nigerian Tribune*, 25 March 2007; *Punch*, 6 December 2007.
89. Commonwealth Secretariat, 'Report of the Commonwealth Observer Group: Nigeria state and federal elections: 14 and 21 April 2007' (2007), p. 32, Commonwealth Secretariat library, London.
90. *Nigerian Tribune*, 27 February 2008.
91. Commonwealth Secretariat, 'Report', p. 30; *Nigerian Tribune*, 7 February 2007.
92. *Punch*, 20 May 2007; Commonwealth Secretariat, 'Report', p. 30.
93. *Guardian*, 13 January 2007; *Nigerian Tribune*, 27 January 2007.
94. *This Day*, 5 March 2007; *Nigerian Tribune*, 6 January 2007. On the legal issues, see Nwabueze, *How Obasanjo subverted law*, Chs 14–17.
95. Commonwealth Secretariat, 'Report', p. 23; *This Day*, 7 February 2007; *Guardian*, 2 March 2007. Different sources give slightly different figures.
96. *Vanguard*, 25 February and 6 March 2007.
97. *Guardian*, 14 and 16 February 2007; *Vanguard*, 25 March 2007.
98. *Guardian*, 28 February and 19 April 2007.
99. *Guardian*, 8 and 12 April 2007.
100. *This Day*, 17 April 2007.
101. *Guardian*, 11 March and 25 April 2007; *Punch*, 31 January 2008.
102. *Guardian*, 29 November 2006 and 14 March 2007.
103. *This Day*, 16 January 2007.
104. *Nigerian Tribune*, 16 February 2007.
105. *Punch*, 1 June 2008; Human Rights Watch, 'Criminal politics', p. 19; *This Day*, 1 May 2007; *Daily Champion*, 3 April 2007.
106. Michael Bratton, 'Vote buying and violence in Nigerian election campaigns', Afrobarometer Working Paper no. 99 (2008), pp. 4–5, 9–11: http://www. afrobarometer. org/papers/AfropaperNo99.pdf (accessed 22 October 2008).
107. *Guardian*, 26 April 2007; Ben Rawlence and Chris Albin-Lackey, 'Nigeria's 2007 general elections: democracy in retreat', *African Affairs*, 106 (2007), 497–8.
108. *Guardian*, 14, 15, and 26 April 2008.
109. *Nigerian Tribune*, 16 April 2007.
110. Emmanuel O. Ojo, 'Nigeria's 2007 general elections and the succession crisis: implications for the nascent democracy', *Journal of African Elections*, 6, 2 (2007), 23.
111. *Guardian*, 23 April 2007; *Daily Champion*, 25 April 2007.
112. *Guardian*, 26 April and 14 August 2007.
113. *Guardian*, 28 October 2007; Uno Ijim-Agbor, 'The Independent National Electoral Commission as an (im)partial umpire in the conduct of the 2007 elections', *Journal of African Elections*, 6, 2 (2007), 83.
114. *Nigerian Tribune*, 27 April 2007; Human Rights Watch, 'Criminal politics', p. 45.
115. Rotimi Suberu, 'Nigeria's muddled elections', *Journal of Democracy*, 18, 4 (2007), 102; Richard Joseph and Darren Kew, 'Nigeria confronts Obasanjo's legacy', *Current History*,

107 (2008), 170; *Guardian*, 24 April, 2007; Rawlence and Albin-Lackey, 'Nigeria's elections', p. 501; *Vanguard*, 30 May 2007.

116. *Guardian*, 25 April 2007.
117. *Nigerian Tribune*, 28 April 2007; *Punch*, 30 June 2007.
118. *Guardian*, 4 April 2008.
119. *Guardian*, 27 April 2007.
120. *Nigerian Tribune*, 24 April 2007.
121. European Union: Election Observation Mission, 'Nigeria: final report, April 2007', http://www. eueom-ng.org; *Guardian*, 25 May 2007.
122. Commonwealth Secretariat, 'Report', pp. 24–5, 49; Ademola Oshodi, 'Return to civilian rule in Nigeria: problems of electoral culture and transparency over the past three Nigerian elections (1999–2007)', *The Round Table*, 96 (2007), 628.
123. *Guardian*, 15 October 2007 and 12 December 2008; *Newswatch*, 18 January 2009.
124. *Guardian*, 12 April 2008.
125. *Guardian*, 28 October 2007; *Nigerian Tribune*, 26 July 2008; *Punch*, 11 November 2008.
126. *Guardian*, 13 and 17 December 2008.
127. *Guardian*, 27 May 2007.
128. *Guardian*, 29 May 2007.
129. *Guardian*, 30 May 2007.
130. *Punch*, 4 June 2007.

24
Retirement

In the Reverend Samuel Johnson's great *History of the Yorubas*, the most dramatic incident concerned the Basorun Gaha, the senior chief of the Oyo kingdom in the mid eighteenth century, who 'was noted for having raised five Kings to the throne, of whom he murdered four, and was himself murdered by the fifth.' 'He was credited', Johnson wrote, 'with the power of being able to convert himself into a leopard or an elephant, and on this account was much feared. He lived to a good old age, and wielded his power mercilessly.' At the last, however, the King of Oyo raised the country against him. As his enemies closed in, 'Gaha in vain tried to transform himself into an elephant as of yore.' But he was too old and feeble, so they took him and killed him.[1]

When Obasanjo left office in May 2007, he too needed to turn himself into an elephant, to thicken his skin and prepare to defend himself. He well knew that Nigerians who had shouted 'hosanna' to the saviour of the moment would cry 'crucify' when he fell. He had cried it himself at General Gowon thirty years before. 'The best attitude to the pull him down syndrome', he had counselled in 1990, 'is caution with consistency in performance and believing in the dictum "the hatred of the high is the involuntary homage of the low".'[2] Now he needed his own lofty advice. An occasional ally rallied to him. The astute Jubril Aminu called to congratulate him on his 'very smooth transfer of power' to Yar'Adua.[3] But they were outnumbered by enemies. 'He is an embarrassment to Nigeria', an Afenifere leader declared. 'He is an embarrassment to Abeokuta. He is an embarrassment to Egba people and he is an embarrassment to [the] Yoruba race.'[4] Danjuma made a point of not inviting him to his seventieth birthday party, commenting, 'I don't know what I would have done if he came uninvited. I would probably have called the police to throw him out.'[5] Reuben Abati wrote in January 2008, 'Obasanjo is at his lowest depths. He is being kicked by anyone with a foot.'[6] Publicly, the former president played the elephant. 'Regardless of biased campaign against him,' he assured an audience at his old school at Abeokuta, 'history would vindicate his administration.'[7] Privately, it was said, he told his friends that 'he has been worried for the future of the country for failure by Nigerians to show even a modicum of appreciation to all he had done only for critics, more especially the media, to declare his eight years of leadership in democracy an utter failure.'[8]

To provide the defence that he knew he would need, Obasanjo had induced the PDP in September 2006 to make him the only candidate qualified to chair its

304

Board of Trustees, with the power to 'call to order' the party's officers.[9] A month after leaving office, he ousted the previous chairman, Anenih, and let it be known that he would also head a committee 'to set the legislative agenda for all PDP legislators for the next four years'.[10] This provoked the party's 'Aborigines' to seek revenge for their marginalisation at his hands. Led by Ekwueme, they succeeded in restoring the Board of Trustees to its former advisory role by a vote of 3,916 to 15 at a party convention in April 2009 that Obasanjo was careful not to attend.[11]

If he had hoped to control his successor – which, given the character of Nigerian politics, is unlikely – Obasanjo was disappointed. Yar'Adua, with his own northern team of economic advisers, defended macroeconomic stability and rejected demands to 'probe' the whole of Obasanjo's administration, but he immediately scrutinised the last-minute contracts it had awarded, cancelled the sale of refineries and steel mills, revoked Transcorp's ownership of NITEL, and scrapped the oil-for-infrastructure deals from which Obasanjo had hoped so much.[12] Initially, also, Yar'Adua halted the National Integrated Power Project, asserting unwisely that Obasanjo had spent $10 billion on the power sector with nothing to show for it. This encouraged a committee of the House of Representatives to launch a widely televised enquiry into the power sector, concluding that the true sum wasted had been $16 billion. Amidst much public obloquy, Obasanjo refuted the charge in detail and the House eventually disowned its committee, reducing the estimate of expenditure to $3 billion.[13]

As his political influence in Nigeria waned during 2008–9, Obasanjo may have found relief in his continuing international travels and his appointment late in 2008 as the UN Secretary-General's representative in the Eastern Congo, returning after 47 years to the region where he had served as a young subaltern. The situation was depressingly similar. Hutu forces involved in the Rwandan genocide had taken refuge there, provoking local Tutsi to arm themselves under the leadership of Laurent Nkunda, whose defiance of the Congolese army had turned hundreds of thousands of civilians into refugees.[14] Obasanjo met Nkunda at his village in the foothills of the Virunga mountains and persuaded him to take part in peace talks. These failed, but the formerly hostile leaders of the Congo and Rwanda agreed to take joint action against the armed Hutu who were the main cause of violence. The action had little success, but for Obasanjo this joint assertion of state power was an important achievement.[15]

Back in Nigeria, Obasanjo was drawn increasingly away from national affairs into the local issues of Yorubaland, Ogun State, and his own Egba and Owu communities in which he acted as a senior chief. In defending his chairmanship of the PDP's Board of Trustees, he even sought support lest his opponents 'deny the Yoruba race the opportunity of holding a highly placed position in the PDP', an argument that led a journalist to remark that the former president had 'descended into fighting a narrow Yoruba cause'.[16] His family, too, drew him into parochial disputes. In backing his daughter Iyabo's ambition to become the next Governor of Ogun State, he found himself at odds with the incumbent Governor Daniel, who wanted his successor to come from another section of the state.[17] The publication in 2008 of Oluremi's account of their marriage was deeply embarrassing.[18] Worse was his alienated son Gbenga's divorce suit with his wife, in which he claimed, *inter alia*, that she had slept with his father in order to secure business contracts, an accusation she denied.[19] Nigerians rushed to assume that the allegations were true. 'Obasanjo … has now been stripped naked in the market place,' a journalist commented.[20] The elderly Solomon Lar, whom Obasanjo had eased out of the PDP chairmanship, urged him to resign from the party.[21] Obasanjo remained silent, but he was deeply affected. When the Alake of Abeokuta arranged a reconciliation meeting, it was reported, Obasanjo put three questions to his son. 'Thereafter the ageing farmer was said to have asked leave of the gathering so that he could tend to his plants and chickens as he had no more to say.'[22]

The Ota farm was one consolation. At its thirtieth anniversary in October 2009, Obasanjo claimed that his various agricultural holdings employed over 6,000 workers.[23] Nearby were two other enterprises, the Bells Secondary School and the Bells University of Technology, which he had founded and patronised. At Christmas 2007, moreover, Obasanjo moved into a newly-built Hilltop View Mansion in Abeokuta. There, two years later, he welcomed a new wife, a woman who had borne a child for him some years before. Only a kilometre away from the mansion, the Presidential Library was taking shape with the support of UNESCO and the relentless opposition of Wole Soyinka, who had christened it the Presidential Laundromat.[24] In January 2009, the Open University awarded the 71-year-old General a Post-Graduate Diploma in Christian Theology, undertaken 'to hone his skills as a Sunday Schoolteacher as well as to gain more insight into his faith'.[25]

Such consolations were needed, for Obasanjo's political reputation seemed to reach its nadir in November 2009, when President Yar'Adua suffered acute pericarditis and was flown to Saudi Arabia for treatment, returning in February 2010 but remaining hospitalised, screened from public view, and incapable of conducting business. He had not formally transferred responsibility to Vice-President Jonathan, thereby creating a leadership vacuum that, according to the constitution, could be filled only if the Executive Council declared Yar'Adua incapacitated or the National Assembly impeached him, which neither was willing to do. Obasanjo's attempt to avoid a repetition of the failed transition of 1979 by imposing his own candidate in 2007 had thus ended in yet worse failure. Critics not only blamed him for it but accused him of deliberately planning it in the hope of regaining power in the resulting vacuum,[26] an accusation he fiercely denied. 'Nobody picked Umaru Yar'Adua so that he will not perform', he protested. 'If I did, God will punish me because I love this country so much so that there is no reason for me to do that.'[27] Yet when he suggested in January 2010 that the 'path of honour and the path of morality' was for Yar'Adua to give way to Jonathan, the PDP denounced his statement as 'an insincere attempt at self exoneration'.[28] Obasanjo declared that he would not speak on the subject again.[29]

In the event, however, the crisis was resolved as Obasanjo recommended. First the National Assembly declared Jonathan to be Acting President. Then, when Yar'Adua died in May 2010, Jonathan succeeded to the substantive office until a fresh election in 2011. Obasanjo gave President Jonathan full support, perhaps recalling the moment 34 years earlier when he too, modest and inexperienced, had been thrust into a position of great responsibility. In such ways could an elderly patriot still serve Nigeria, before his fifth and final homecoming.

NOTES

1. Johnson, *History*, pp. 178, 184–5.
2. Obasanjo, *Not my will*, p. 235.
3. *Punch*, 11 June 2007.
4. *This Day*, 11 May 2008.
5. *Guardian*, 17 February 2008.
6. *Guardian*, 26 January 2008.
7. *Nigerian Tribune*, 5 August 2007.
8. *Nigerian Tribune*, 13 April 2008.
9. *Newswatch*, 16 October 2006, pp. 30–2.
10. *Guardian*, 28 June 2007; *This Day*, 30 June 2007.
11. *Newswatch*, 26 April 2009.
12. *Guardian*, 18 June and 27 July 2007, 3 January 2008, 21 July 2009; *Nigerian Tribune*, 21 February 2008; *This Day*, 9 February 2009; Vines et al., 'Thirst for African oil', pp. vii, 2–3, 21–4.
13. *Newswatch*, 3 and 31 March 2008 and 1 March 2009; *This Day*, 12 May 2008 and 12 May 2009.
14. For the background, see Monika Thakur, 'Demilitarising militias in the Kivus (eastern Democratic Republic of Congo)', *African Security Review*, 17, 1 (2008), 52–67.
15. *Guardian*, 18 November 2008; Koen Vlassenroot and Timothy Raeymaekers, 'Kivu's intractable security conundrum', *African Affairs*, 108 (2009), 482–4; *This Day*, 20 March 2009; *Africa Confidential*, 24 July 2009, pp. 9–10.
16. *Nigerian Tribune*, 2 and 7 February 2008.
17. *Nigerian Tribune*, 21 June, 17 September, and 16 November 2008; *Tell*, 11 July 2009, p. 32.
18. Obasanjo, *Bitter-sweet*.
19. Gbenga's submission was published in http://www.nigerianmuse.com/spotlight/Son_Gbenga_Accuses_Obasanjo. Mojisola's denial was in http://www.nigerianmuse.com/spotlight/Alleged_sexscandal_Moji_Obasanjo_speaks_Denies_All (both accessed 15 September 2008).
20. *This Day*, 20 January 2008.
21. *Nigerian Tribune*, 23 January 2008.
22. *Nigerian Tribune*, 22 March 2008.
23. *This Day*, 10 October 2009.
24. *Daily Champion*, 25 December 2007; *Guardian*, 5 March 2009.
25. *Nigerian Tribune*, 8 January 2009; *Punch*, 8 June 2007.
26. *Guardian*, 24 January 2010.
27. *Guardian*, 22 January 2010.
28. *This Day*, 22 and 25 January 2010; *Guardian*, 24 January 2010.
29. *Nigerian Tribune*, 7 February 2010.

Appendix: exchange rates

The naira (N) replaced the Nigerian pound in January 1973 and was valued at U.S. $1.52. It was pegged first to the U.S. dollar and then to a basket of major currencies until 1983. By then a substantial differential existed between the naira's official value and that on the parallel (free) market. From 1983–4 both official and parallel exchange rates fell sharply until the naira had lost over 99 per cent of its value. The official rate became increasingly artificial during the 1990s but was in effect realigned with the parallel rate thereafter.

In order to make sums expressed in naira meaningful and comparable over time, I have generally inserted an *approximate* current dollar equivalent, using the official exchange rate until 1982 and the parallel rate thereafter, where evidence can be found. Different sources give somewhat different values for both rates. The rates used are shown in the Table opposite:

Sources

1973–1981   Olivier Vallée, '"Système naira" et crise financière,' in Daniel C. Bach, Johny Egg, and Jean Philippe (eds.), *Le Nigeria: un pouvoir en puissance* (Paris, 1988), p. 46.

1982–1990   David Bevan, Paul Collier, and Jan Willem Gunning, *Nigeria and Indonesia* (Oxford, 1999), p. 75.

1991–1994   Peter Lewis and Howard Stein, 'Shifting fortunes: the political economy of financial liberalization in Nigeria,' *World Development*, 25 (1997), 11.

1995   Jane I. Guyer, LaRay Denzer, and Adigun Agbaje, *Money struggles and city life: devaluation in Ibadan and other centers in southern Nigeria, 1986–1996* (Portsmouth NH, 2002), p. xxxii.

1996–2000   Economist Intelligence Unit, 'Country profile: Nigeria,' 2002 (electronic resource)

2001   Olayiwola Abegunrin, *Nigerian foreign policy under military rule, 1966–1999* (Westport, 2003), p. 177.

2003–2007   Economist Intelligence Unit, 'Country profile: Nigeria,' 2005–8 (electronic resource)

Naira to U.S.$1

Year	Official rate	Parallel rate
1973	0.66	
1974	0.63	
1975	0.62	
1976	0.63	
1977	0.65	
1978	0.64	
1979	0.60	
1980	0.55	
1981	0.61	
1982	0.69	1.14
1983	0.72	1.82
1984	0.76	3.23
1985		3.7
1986		3.8
1987		4.8
1988		6.3
1989		10.8
1990		9.6
1991		12.8
1992		22.2
1993		c.43
1994		c.90
1995		80
1996		83
1997		85
1998		88
1999		99
2000		111
2001		112
2002		
2003		129
2004		133
2005		131
2006		128
2007		119

Bibliography

Newspapers and Journals

Africa (London)
Africa Confidential (London)
Africa Forum (London)
Africa Research Bulletin (Exeter)
Africa Today (London)
African Concord (London)
African Guardian (Lagos)
BBC Focus on Africa (London)
Daily Champion (Lagos)
Daily Independent (Lagos)
Daily Sketch (Ibadan)
Daily Telegraph (London)
Daily Times (Lagos)
Daily Trust (Kaduna)
Economist (London)
Financial Times (London)
Guardian (Lagos)
Hotline (Kaduna)
Insider Weekly (Lagos)
Jeune Afrique (Paris)
Mail and Guardian (Johannesburg)
National Concord (Ikeja)
New African (London)
New Nationalist (Ibadan)
New Nigerian (Kaduna)
New York Review of Books (New York)
New York Times (New York)
Newbreed (Lagos)
News (Lagos)
Newswatch (Ikeja)
Nigerian Tribune (Ibadan)
Obanta Newsday (Ijebu-Ode)
Observer (London)
Petroleum Economist (London)
Post Express (Lagos)
Punch (Ikeja)
Source (Lagos)

Bibliography

Sunday Concord (Ikeja)
Sunday Telegraph (London)
Sunday Times (Lagos)
Sunday Times (London)
Tell (Ikeja)
This Day (Lagos)
Times (London)
Vanguard (Lagos)
Weekly Trust (Kaduna)
West Africa (London)
West African Pilot (Yaba)

Works cited more than once

Abegunrin, Olayiwola. *Nigeria and the struggle for the liberation of Zimbabwe: a study of foreign policy of an emerging nation.* Stockholm, 1992.
Abegunrin, Olayiwola. *Nigerian foreign policy under military rule, 1966–1999.* Westport, 2003.
Adamolekun, Ladipo. *Politics and administration in Nigeria.* Ibadan, 1986.
Adamu, Haroun, and Alaba Ogunsanwo. *Nigeria: the making of the presidential system: 1979 general elections.* Kano [c.1983].
Adebajo, Adekeye. *Building peace in West Africa: Liberia, Sierra Leone, and Guinea-Bissau.* Boulder, 2002.
Adebajo, Adekeye. *Liberia's civil war: Nigeria, ECOMOG, and regional security in West Africa.* Boulder, 2002.
Adebajo, Adekeye, and Abdul Raufu Mustapha (eds) *Gulliver's troubles: Nigeria's foreign policy after the Cold War.* Scottsville, 2008.
Adebajo, Adekeye, Adebayo Adedeji, and Chris Landsberg (eds) *South Africa in Africa: the post-apartheid era.* Scottsville, 2007.
Adebanwi, Wale. 'The carpenter's revolt: youth, violence and the reinvention of culture in Nigeria', *Journal of Modern African Studies*, 43 (2005), 339–65.
Adekanye, J. 'Bayo. *The retired military as emergent power factor in Nigeria.* Ibadan, 1999.
Adekunle, Abiodun A. (ed.) *The Nigeria Biafra war letters: a soldier's story.* Volume 1. Atlanta, 2004.
Ademiluyi, 'Femi. *From prisoner to president: the metamorphosis of Olusegun Obasanjo.* Osogbo, 2006.
Aderinwale, Ayodele. 'For leadership's sake: the story of the Africa Leadership Forum', *Africa Forum*, 1, 1 (1991), 45–7.
Adeshina, R.A. *The reversed victory (the story of Nigerian military intervention in Sierra Leone).* Ibadan, 2002.
Adeyi, Olusoji, Phyllis J. Kanki, Oluwole Odutolu, and John A. Idoko (eds) *AIDS in Nigeria: a nation on the threshold.* Cambridge MA, 2006.
Adinoyi Ojo Onukaba. *Atiku: the story of Atiku Abubakar.* Abuja, 2006.
Adinoyi Ojo Onukaba. *In the eyes of time: a biography of Olusegun Obasanjo.* New York, 1997.
Albert, Isaac Olawole. 'A review of the campaign strategies', *Journal of African Elections*, 6, 2 (October 2007), 55–78.

Alli, M. Chris. *The Federal Republic of Nigerian army: the siege of a nation*. Ikeja, 2001.

Aluko, Olajibe. *Essays on Nigerian foreign policy*. London, 1981.

Amadi, Tony. *Power and politics in the Nigerian Senate*. Garki Abuja, 2005.

Andrae, Gunilla, and Björn Beckman. *The wheat trap: bread and underdevelopment in Nigeria*. London, 1985.

Anifowose, Remi, and Tunde Babawale (eds) *2003 general election and democratic consolidation in Nigeria*. Lagos, 2003.

Anthony, Douglas A. *Poison and medicine: ethnicity, power, and violence in a Nigerian city, 1966 to 1986*. Portsmouth NH, 2002.

Anwunah, Patrick A. *The Nigeria-Biafra war (1967–1970): my memoirs*. Ibadan, 2007.

Anyanwu, Chris. *The days of horror - a journalist's eye-witness account of Nigeria in the hands of its worst tyrant*. Ibadan, 2002.

Anyaoku, Emeka. *The inside story of the modern Commonwealth*. London, 2004.

Avwenagbiku, Patrick. *Olusegun Obasanjo and his footprints*. Abuja, 2000.

Awolowo, Obafemi. *Awo on the Nigerian Civil War*. Ikeja, 1981.

Babatope, Ebenezer. *Not his will: the Awolowo Obasanjo wager*. Benin City, 1990.

Babawale, Tunde (ed.) *Urban violence, ethnic militias and the challenge of democratic consolidation in Nigeria*. Lagos, 2003.

Bach, Daniel C. 'The politics of West African economic co-operation: C.E.A.O. and E.C.O.W.A.S.', *Journal of Modern African Studies*, 21 (1983), 605–23.

Bach, Daniel C., Johny Egg, and Jean Philippe (ed.) *Le Nigeria: un pouvoir en puissance*. Paris, 1988.

Barnes, Sandra T. *Patrons and power: creating a political community in metropolitan Lagos*. Manchester, 1986.

Barrett, Lindsay. *Danjuma: the making of a general*. Enugu, 1979.

Bevan, David, Paul Collier, and Jan Willem Gunning. *Nigeria and Indonesia*. Oxford, 1999.

Biobaku, Saburi O. *The Egba and their neighbours 1842–1872*. Oxford, 1957.

Birmingham, David, and Phyllis M. Martin (eds) *History of Central Africa*. 3 vols, London, 1983–98.

Central Bank of Nigeria. *The changing structure of the Nigerian economy and implications for development*. Lagos, 2000.

Červenka, Zdenek. *The Nigerian War 1967–1970: history of the war, selected bibliography and documents*. Frankfurt A.M., 1971.

Clapham, Christopher. *Africa and the international system: the politics of state survival*. Cambridge, 1996.

Coleman, James S. *Nigeria: background to nationalism*. Berkeley, 1960.

Collier, Paul, Chukwuma C. Soludo, and Catherine Pattillo (eds) *Economic policy options for a prosperous Nigeria*. Basingstoke, 2008.

Commonwealth Group of Eminent Persons. *Mission to South Africa: the Commonwealth Report*. Harmondsworth, 1986.

Commonwealth Observer Group. *The National Assembly and presidential elections in Nigeria, 12 and 19 April 2003*. London, 2006.

Commonwealth Secretariat. *Report of the Commonwealth Observer Group: Nigeria state and federal elections: 14 and 21 April 2007*. London, 2007.

Diamond, Larry, Anthony Kirk-Greene, and Oyeleye Oyediran (eds) *Transition without end: Nigerian politics and civil society under Babangida*. Boulder, 1997.

Dike, Victor E. *Nigeria and the politics of unreason: a study of the Obasanjo regime.* London, 2003.

d'Orville, Hans (ed.) *Beyond freedom: letters to Olusegun Obasanjo.* New York, 1996.

d'Orville, Hans (ed.) *Leadership for Africa: in honor of Olusegun Obasanjo on the occasion of his 60th birthday.* New York, 1995.

Dudley, B.J. *Instability and political order: politics and crisis in Nigeria.* Ibadan, 1973.

Dudley, Billy J. *An introduction to Nigerian government and politics.* London, 1982.

Easum, Donald B. 'Interview with Donald B. Easum, 17 January 1990', http://memory.loc.gov/cgi-bin/query/r?ammem/mfdip:@field(DocID+mfdip 2004es0l) (accessed 15 February 2009).

Economist Intelligence Unit. 'Country profile: Nigeria', annual, 1996–2008 (electronic resource: Business Source Complete).

Ehonwa, Osaze Lanre. *Behind the wall: a report on prison conditions in Nigeria and the Nigerian prison system.* 2nd edn, Lagos, 1996.

Ejindu, Dennis D. 'Major Nzeogwu speaks', *Africa and the World,* 3, 31 (May 1967), 14–16.

Eke, Kenoye Kelvin. *Nigeria's foreign policy under two military governments, 1966–1979: an analysis of the Gowan [sic] and Muhammed/Obasanjo regimes.* Lewiston, 1990.

Ekeh, Peter P., Patrick Dele Cole, and Gabriel O. Olusanya (eds) *Nigeria since independence: the first twenty-five years: volume V: politics and constitution.* Ibadan, 1989.

Elaigwu, J. Isawa. *Gowon: the biography of a soldier-statesman.* Ibadan, 1986.

El-Rufai, Nasir. 'Umaru Yar'dua: great expectation, disappointing outcome', 31 May 2009, http://www.saharareporters.com (accessed 25 December 2009).

Environmental Rights Action. *A blanket of silence: images of the Odi genocide.* N.p., 2002.

Falae, Olu. *The way forward for Nigeria: the economy and polity.* Akure, 2004.

Falola, Toyin. *Violence in Nigeria: the crisis of religious politics and secular ideologies.* Rochester NY, 1998.

Farris, Jacqueline W., and Mohammed Bomoi (eds) *Shehu Musa Yar'Adua: a life of service.* Abuja, 2004.

Fasehun, Frederick Isiotan. *Frederick Fasehun: the son of Oodua.* Lagos, 2002.

Fayemi, John Olukayode. 'Threats, military expenditure and national security: analysis of trends in Nigeria's defence planning, 1970–1990', Ph.D. thesis, King's College, London, 1994.

Forrest, Tom. *The advance of African capital: the growth of Nigerian private enterprise.* London, 1994.

Forrest, Tom. *Politics and economic development in Nigeria.* 2nd edn, Boulder, 1995.

Fourchard, Laurent. 'A new name for an old practice: vigilantes in south-western Nigeria', *Africa,* 78 (2008), 16–40.

Garba, Joe. *Diplomatic soldiering: Nigerian foreign policy, 1975–1979.* Ibadan, 1987.

Garba, Joseph Nanven. *'Revolution' in Nigeria: another view.* London, 1982.

Gbulie, Ben. *The fall of Biafra.* Enugu, 1989.

Gbulie, Ben. *Nigeria's five majors: coup d'état of 15th January 1966: first inside account.* Onitsha, 1981.

Gevisser, Mark. *Thabo Mbeki: the dream deferred.* Johannesburg, 2007.

Gillies, Alexandra. 'Obasanjo, the donor community and reform implementation in Nigeria', *Round Table,* 96 (2007), 569–86.

Gleijeses, Piero. *Conflicting missions: Havana, Washington, and Africa, 1959–1976*. Chapel Hill, 2002.

Handy, Paul Simon. 'The dynastic succession in Togo: continental and regional implications', *African Security Review*, 14, 3 (2005) (electronic resource).

Harneit-Sievers, Axel, Jones O. Ahazuem, and Sydney Emezue. *A social history of the Nigerian Civil War: perspectives from below*. Enugu, 1997.

Harnischfeger, Johannes. *Democratization and Islamic law: the Sharia conflict in Nigeria*. Frankfort, 2008.

Human Rights Watch. 'Chop fine: the human rights impact of local government corruption and mismanagement in Rivers State, Nigeria', January 2007, http://hrw.org/reports/2007/nigeria2007/nigeria0107web.pdf (accessed 29 August 2007).

Human Rights Watch. 'Criminal politics: violence, "godfathers" and corruption in Nigeria', October 2007, http://www.hrw.org/en/reports/2007/10/08/criminal-politics (accessed 10 October 2010).

Human Rights Watch. 'Revenge in the name of religion: the cycle of violence in Plateau and Kano States', May 2005, http://hrw.org/reports/2005/nigeria0505/nigeria0505text.pdf (accessed 30 September 2007).

Human Rights Watch. 'Rivers of blood: guns, oil and power in Nigeria's Rivers State', February 2005, http://hrw.org/backgrounder/africa/nigeria0205/nigeria0205.pdf (accessed 23 September 2007).

Iloegbunam, Chuks. *Ironside: the biography of General Aguiyi-Ironsi, Nigeria's first military head of state*. London, 1999.

International Labour Office. *First things first: meeting the basic needs of the people of Nigeria*. Addis Ababa, 1981.

International Monetary Fund. 'Nigeria: staff report for the 2004 Article IV Consultation', 22 June 2004, http://www.imf.org/external/pubs/ft/scr/2004/cr04239.pdf (accessed 21 December 2008).

Irele, George Taiwo. 'Land and agricultural policy in Nigeria under military governments, 1966–1985', Ph.D. thesis, University of Cambridge, 1990.

Jega, Attahiru (ed.) *Identity transformation and identity politics under structural adjustment in Nigeria*. Stockholm, 2000.

Johnson, Samuel. *The history of the Yorubas*. London, 1921.

Jolaoso, Olujimi. *In the shadows: recollections of a pioneer diplomat*. Lagos, 1991.

Joseph, Richard, and Alexandra Gillies (eds) *Smart aid for African development*. Boulder, 2009.

Katjavivi, Peter H. *A history of resistance in Namibia*. London, 1988.

Kayode, Femi, and Date Otobo (eds) *Allison Akene Ayida: Nigeria's quintessential public servant*. Lagos, 2004.

Kayode, M.O., and Y.B. Usman (eds) *Nigeria since independence: the first twenty-five years: volume II: the economy*. Ibadan, 1989.

Kew, Darren. '"Democrazy – Dem Go Craze, O": monitoring the 1999 Nigerian elections', *Issue*, 27, 1 (1999), 29–33.

Khan, Sarah Ahmad. *Nigeria: the political economy of oil*. Oxford, 1994.

Kirk-Greene, A.H.M. (ed.) *Crisis and conflict in Nigeria: a documentary sourcebook 1966–1969*. 2 vols, London, 1971.

Kissinger, Henry. *Years of renewal*. London, 1999.

Last, Murray. 'The search for security in Muslim Northern Nigeria', *Africa*, 78 (2008), 41–63.

LeVan, A. Carl, Titi Pitso, and Bodunrin Adebo, 'Elections in Nigeria: is the third time a charm?' *Journal of African Elections*, 2, 2 (October 2003), 30–47.

Lewis, Peter M. *Growing apart: oil, politics, and economic change in Indonesia and Nigeria*. Ann Arbor MI, 2007.

Lewis, Peter, and Etannibi Alemika. 'Seeking the democratic dividend: public attitudes and attempted reform in Nigeria', Afrobarometer working paper no. 52, October 2005, http://www.afrobarometer.org/papers/Afropaper No52–17nov06. pdf (accessed 19 August 2007).

Lewis, Peter, and Michael Bratton. 'Attitudes to democracy and markets in Nigeria', Afrobarometer paper no. 3, April 2000, http://www.afrobarometer.org/papers/ AfropaperNo3.pdf (accessed 29 July 2007).

Lewis, Peter, Etannibi Alemika, and Michael Bratton, 'Down to earth: changes in attitudes towards democracy and markets in Nigeria', Afrobarometer paper no. 20, August 2002, http://www.afrobarometer.org/papers/AfropaperNo20.pdf (accessed 12 August 2007).

Luckham, Robin. *The Nigerian military: a sociological analysis of authority and revolt 1960–67*. Cambridge, 1971.

Mabogunje, Akin, and J.D. Omer-Cooper. *Owu in Yoruba history*. Ibadan, 1971.

Madiebo, Alexander A. *The Nigerian revolution and the Biafran war*. Enugu, 1980.

Maier, Karl. *This house has fallen: Nigeria in crisis*. London, 2000.

Makinda, Samuel M., and F. Wafula Okumu. *The African Union: challenges of globalization, security, and governance*. London, 2008.

Malan, Magnus. *My life with the SA Defence Force*. Pretoria, 2006.

Mandela, Nelson. *Long walk to freedom*. London, 1994.

Meagher, Kate. 'Hijacking civil society: the inside story of the Bakassi Boys vigilante group of southeastern Nigeria', *Journal of Modern African Studies*, 45 (2007), 89–115.

Miners, N.J. *The Nigerian army 1956–1966*. London, 1971.

Mitchell, Nancy. 'Tropes of the Cold War: Jimmy Carter and Rhodesia', *Cold War History*, 7 (2007), 263–83.

Momoh, H.B. (ed.) *The Nigerian Civil War, 1967–1970: history and reminiscences*. Ibadan, 2000.

Moser, Gary, Scott Rogers, and Reinold Van Til, with Robin Kibuku and Inuta Lukonga, 'Nigeria: experience with structural adjustment', IMF occasional paper 148 (Washington, March 1997).

Moss, Todd, Scott Standley, and Nancy Birdsall. 'Double-standards, debt treatment, and World Bank country classification: the case of Nigeria', Center for Global Development working paper no. 45, November 2004, http://www.cgdev.org/ content/publications/detail/2741.pdf (accessed 4 March 2009).

Murithi, Timothy. *The African Union: pan-Africanism, peacebuilding and development*. Aldershot, 2005.

Nigeria. *Obasanjo's economic direction 1999–2003*. Abuja, 2000.

Nigeria. *Report of the Constitution Drafting Committee*. 2 vols, Lagos, 1976.

Nigeria. Federal Office of Statistics. *The Nigerian household 1995*. Lagos, 1996.

Nigeria: Federal Office of Statistics. *Poverty profile for Nigeria 2004*. [Abuja] 2005.

Nigeria: Human Rights Violations Investigation Commission. 'Report', 7 vols, May 2002, http://www.nigerianmuse.com/nigeriawatch/oputa.pdf (accessed 27 August 2007).

Nigeria: National Population Commission. *1991 population census of the Federal Republic of Nigeria: analytical report at the national level.* Abuja, 1998.

Nigerian Economic Society. *Poverty in Nigeria: proceedings of the 1975 annual conference.* Ibadan, 1976.

Nigerian National Planning Commission. *Meeting everyone's needs: national economic empowerment and development strategy.* 2 vols, Abuja, 2004.

Njoku, H.M. *A tragedy without heroes: the Nigeria-Biafra war.* Enugu, 1987.

Nnebe, Hobson E. (ed.) *Policies of the Federal Republic of Nigeria; the Obasanjo years (1999–2007).* 3 vols, Kaduna, 2006.

Nolte, Insa. 'Ethnic vigilantes and the state: the Oodua People's Congress in south-western Nigeria', *International Relations*, 21 (2007), 217–35.

Nolte, Insa. *Obafemi Awolowo and the making of Remo: the local politics of a Nigerian nationalist.* Edinburgh, 2009.

Nwabueze, Ben. *How President Obasanjo subverted Nigeria's federal system.* Ibadan, 2007.

Nwabueze, Ben. *How President Obasanjo subverted the rule of law and democracy.* Ibadan, 2007.

Nwokeforo, Ukeje Jonah. *Obasanjo's presidency and King David's rule (overwhelming similarities).* Ibadan, 2006.

Nwosu, H.N. *Laying the foundation for Nigeria's democracy: my account of June 12, 1993 presidential election and its annulment.* Lagos, 2008.

Obasanjo, Oluremi. *Bitter-sweet: my life with Obasanjo.* Lagos, 2008.

Obasanjo, Olusegun. *Africa embattled: selected essays on contemporary African development.* Ibadan, 1988.

Obasanjo, Olusegun. *Africa in perspective: myths and realities.* New York, 1987.

[Obasanjo, Olusegun]. *Call to duty: a collection of speeches.* [Lagos] n.d.

Obasanjo, Olusegun. *Constitution for national integration and development.* Lagos, 1989.

Obasanjo, Olusegun. 'The country of anything goes', *New York Review of Books*, 24 September 1998, pp. 55–7.

Obasanjo, Olusegun. *Guides to effective prayer.* Abeokuta [c.1998].

[Obasanjo, Olusegun]. *Hope for Africa: selected speeches of Olusegun Obasanjo.* Abeokuta, 1993.

[Obasanjo, Olusegun]. *A march of progress: collected speeches of His Excellency General Olusegun Obasanjo.* Lagos, n.d.

Obasanjo, Olusegun. *My command: an account of the Nigerian Civil War, 1967–1970.* Reprinted, London, 1981.

Obasanjo, Olusegun. *Not my will.* Ibadan, 1990.

Obasanjo, Olusegun. *Nzeogwu: an intimate portrait of Major Chukwuma Kaduna Nzeogwu.* Ibadan, 1987.

[Obasanjo, Olusegun]. *Selected speeches of President Olusegun Obasanjo: volume 2.* Abuja, n.d.

Obasanjo, Olusegun. *Sermons from prison.* Ota, 2000.

Obasanjo, Olusegun. *Standing tall.* Lagos, 2005.

Obasanjo, Olusegun. *This animal called man.* Abeokuta [c.1998].

Obasanjo, Olusegun. *Women of virtue: stories of outstanding women in the Bible.* Abeokuta, n.d.

Obasanjo, Olusegun, and Hans d'Orville (ed.) *Challenges of leadership in African development.* New York, 1990.

Obasanjo, Olusegun, and Akin Mabogunje (ed.) *Elements of democracy*. Abeokuta, 1991.

Obasanjo, Olusegun, and Felix G.N. Mosha (ed.) *Africa: rise to challenge*. Abeokuta, 1993.

Obe, Ad'Obe (ed.) *A new dawn: a collection of speeches of President Olusegun Obasanjo: volumes 2 and 3*. Ibadan, 2001–4.

O'Brien, Donal B. Cruise, John Dunn, and Richard Rathbone (eds) *Contemporary West African states*. Cambridge, 1989.

Ogunkola, E. Olawale, and Abiodun S. Bankole (eds) *Nigeria's imperatives in the new world trade order*. Nairobi, 2005.

Okafor, Obiora Chinedu. 'Remarkable reforms: the influence of a labour-led socio-economic movement on legislative reasoning, process and action in Nigeria, 1999–2007', *Journal of Modern African Studies*, 47 (2009), 241–66.

Okoi-Uyouyo, Mathias. *M.D. Yusufu: beyond the cop*. Calabar, 2005.

Okonjo-Iweala, Ngozi, and Philip Osafo-Kwaako. *Nigeria's economic reforms: progress and challenges*. Washington DC, 2007.

Okonjo-Iweala, Ngozi, Charles C. Soludo, and Mansur Muktar (eds) *The debt trap in Nigeria: towards a sustainable debt strategy*. Trenton NJ, 2003.

Olagbaju, Folabi K. 'Seasons of cooperation: a study of peasant politics in south-western Nigeria (1960–1989)', Ph.D. thesis, George Washington University, 1999.

Olonisakin, 'Funmi. *Peacekeeping in Sierra Leone: the story of UNAMSIL*. Boulder CO, 2008.

Olukoju, Ayodeji. '"Never expect power always": electricity consumers' response to monopoly, corruption and inefficient services in Nigeria', *African Affairs*, 103 (2004), 51–71.

Oluleye, James J. *Architecturing a destiny: an autobiography*. Ibadan, 2001.

Oluleye, James J. *Military leadership in Nigeria 1966–1979*. Ibadan, 1985.

Omeje, Kenneth (ed.) *State-society relations in Nigeria: democratic consolidation, conflicts and reforms*. London, 2007.

Omoruyi, Omo. *The tale of June 12; the betrayal of the democratic rights of Nigerians*. London, 1999.

Onslow, Sue. 'South Africa and the Owen/Vance Plan of 1977', *South African Historical Journal*, 51 (2004), 130–58.

Osaghae, Eghosa E. *Crippled giant: Nigeria since independence*. London, 1998.

Osaghae, Eghosa E., Ebere Onwudiwe, and Rotimi T. Suberu (eds) *The Nigerian Civil War and its aftermath*. Ibadan, 2002.

Oshun, Olawale. *Clapping with one hand: June 12 and the crisis of a state nation*. London, 1999.

Ould-Abdallah, Ahmedou. *Burundi on the brink 1993–95: a UN envoy reflects on preventive diplomacy*. Washington DC, 2000.

Owen, David. *Time to declare*. Revised edition, Harmondsworth, 1992.

Oyediran, Oyeleye (ed.) *Nigerian government and politics under military rule, 1966–79*. London, 1979.

Oyediran, Oyeleye (ed.) *The Nigerian 1979 elections*. Lagos, 1981.

Paden, John N. *Faith and politics in Nigeria: Nigeria as a pivotal state in the Muslim world*. Washington DC, 2008.

Panter-Brick, Keith (ed.) *Soldiers and oil: the political transformation of Nigeria*. London, 1978.

Peil, Margaret. *Lagos: the city is the people*. London, 1991.

Practical Sampling International. 'Summary of results: round 3 Afrobarometer survey in Nigeria, 2005', January 2007, http://www.afrobarometer.org/Summary%20 of%20Results/Round%203/nig-R3S0R-24jan07-final.pdf (accessed 26 August 2007).

Rawlence, Ben, and Chris Albin-Lackey. 'Nigeria's 2007 general elections: democracy in retreat', *African Affairs*, 106 (2007), 497–506.

Read, James S. 'The new constitution of Nigeria, 1979: "the Washington model"?', *Journal of African Law*, 23 (1979), 131–69.

Rotberg, Robert I. (ed.) *Crafting the new Nigeria: confronting the challenges*. Boulder CO, 2004.

Sala-i-Martin, Xavier, and Arovind Subramanian. 'Addressing the natural resource curse: an illustration from Nigeria', IMF working paper WP/03/139, 2003, http://www.imf.org/external/pubs/ft/wp/2003/wp03139.pdf (accessed 5 October 2008).

Saliu, Hassan, Ebele Amali, and Raphael Olawepo (eds) *Nigeria's reform programme: issues and challenges*. Ibadan, 2007.

Sampson, Anthony. *Mandela: the authorised biography*. London, 1999.

Saro-Wiwa, Ken. *On a darkling plain: an account of the Nigerian Civil War*. Port Harcourt, 1989.

Schlesinger, Arthur M., Jr. *The imperial presidency*. New edition, Boston, 1989.

Shagari, Shehu. *Beckoned to serve: an autobiography*. Ibadan, 2001.

Sklar, Richard L. *Nigerian political parties: power in an emergent African nation*. Princeton, 1963.

Smith, Daniel Jordan. *A culture of corruption: everyday deception and popular discontent in Nigeria*. Princeton, 2007.

Soares, Benjamin F. (ed.) *Muslim-Christian encounters in Africa*. Leiden, 2006.

Soares de Oliveira, Ricardo. *Oil and politics in the Gulf of Guinea*. London, 2007.

Sotunmbi, Abiodun Olufemi. 'Nigeria's policy towards southern Africa – 1966–1979', Ph.D. thesis, University of Keele, 1989.

South Africa: Truth and Reconciliation Commission. 'Proceedings' (typescript, Cambridge University Library).

Soyinka, Wole. *You must set forth at dawn: a memoir*. London, 2007.

Stewart, Elizabeth Kirk. 'Banks, governments, and risk: medium-term, syndicated international capital market loans to Nigeria, 1977–1983', Ph.D. thesis, London School of Economics, 1985.

St Jorre, John de. *The Nigerian Civil War*. London, 1972.

Stremlau, John J. *The international politics of the Nigerian Civil War 1967–1970*. Princeton, 1977.

Suberu, Rotimi T. *Federalism and ethnic conflict in Nigeria*. Washington DC, 2001.

Suberu, Rotimi T. 'The Supreme Court and federalism in Nigeria', *Journal of Modern African Studies*, 46 (2008), 451–85.

Tamuno, Tekena N., and J.A. Atanda (eds) *Nigeria since independence: the first twenty-five years: volume IV: government and public policy*. Ibadan, 1989.

Tedheke, Moses, and Idris Tanu Ejenavwo (eds) *The Obasanjo administration 1999–2007: chronicle of events and issues*. Kaduna, 2007.

Tieku, Thomas Kwasi. 'Explaining the clash and accommodation of interests of major actors in the creation of the African Union', *African Affairs*, 103 (2004), 249–67.

Turner, Terisa E., and Leigh S. Brownhill. 'Why women are at war with Chevron: Nigerian subsistence struggles against the international oil industry', *Journal of Asian and African Studies*, 39 (2004), 63–93.

Udoma, Sir Udo. *History and the law of the constitution of Nigeria*. Lagos, 1994.

UNAIDS. *Report on the global AIDS epidemic 2008*. Geneva, 2008.

United States: National Archives. 'Declassified documents reference system' (electronic resource).

Usman, Yusufu Bala. *For the liberation of Nigeria: essays and lectures 1969–1978*. London, 1979.

Usman, Yusufu Bala (ed.) *Nigeria since independence: the first twenty-five years: volume I: the society*. Ibadan, 1989.

Usman, Yusufu Bala, and George Awale Kwanashie (eds) *Inside Nigerian history 1950–1970: events, issues and sources*. Ibadan, 1995.

Utomi, Pat. *To serve is to live: autobiographical reflections on the Nigerian condition*. Revised edition, Ibadan, 2002.

Vance, Cyrus. *Hard choices: critical years in America's foreign policy*. New York, 1983.

Vines, Alex, Lillian Wong, Markus Weimer, and Indira Camros. 'Thirst for African oil: Asian national oil companies in Nigeria and Angola: a Chatham House report', August 2009, http://www.chathamhouse.org.uk/files/14524_r0809_africanoil.pdf (accessed 24 August 2009).

West, Deborah L. 'Governing Nigeria: continuing issues after the elections', World Peace Foundation, Cambridge MA, 2003, http://www.ciaonet.org/wps/ wed04/wed04.pdf (accessed 30 September 2007).

World Organisation Against Torture. 'Hope betrayed? A report on impunity and state-sponsored violence in Nigeria', Geneva, 2002, http://www.omct.org/pdf/ Nigeriareport0802.pdf (accessed 12 October 2008).

World Bank. *World development report*. New York/ Washington DC, annual.

Yakubu, A.M., R.T. Adegboye, C.N. Ubah, and B. Dogo (eds) *Crisis and conflict management in Nigeria since 1980*. 2 vols, Kaduna, 2005.

Index

Index

Index

New Partnership for African Development 221, 281
Ngige, C. 262–3
Niger Delta 40, 59, 146–7, 185–8, 194, 228, 258, 260–1, 272
Nigerian Institute of Policy and Strategic Studies 127
Nigerian Labour Congress *see* trade unions
Nigerian People's Party 91–2, 103
Nigerian Telecommunications Corporation *see* telecommunications
Nkomo, J. 75, 77, 79
Nkunda, L. 305
Nnamani, C. 242
Nnamani, K. 292
Northern People's Congress 9–10, 17
Not My Will (1990) 112–17, 126
Nujoma, S. 80–1
Nwabueze, B. 1, 3, 258–9
Nwobodo, J. 170, 173
Nwobosi, Capt. 20
Nyerere, J.K. 77, 80, 94, 101, 128
Nzeogwu, C.K. 13, 15, 20–1, 111–12
Nzeogwu (1987) 111–12
Nzeribe, F. 140–1

Obafemi Awolowo University, Ife 170
Obasanjo, Gbenga 1, 156, 256, 305–6
Obasanjo, Iyabo 101–2, 305
Obasanjo, Oluremi 9, 12, 16–17, 22, 31–2, 39–40, 45, 101–2, 131, 156, 305
Obasanjo, Stella 40, 102, 156, 173, 184, 256
Obe, Ad'Obe 127–8
Odi 187, 193–4, 234
Odili, P. 170, 231, 242, 244–5, 293, 295
Offor, E. 165, 222, 242, 244
Ogaden dispute 82
Ogbeh, Audu 231, 241, 263, 289
Ogomudia, A. 260
Ogoni 146–7, 187
Ohanaeze Ndigbo 148, 174, 185, 189, 233
oil industry 40, 59–60, 67, 76, 103–4, 137, 147, 201, 203–5, 209, 222, 256–7, 259, 261–2, 268–71, 275, 281, 305
oil refining 61, 175–7, 205–6, 208, 257, 271, 305
Ojukwu, E. 15, 20, 22–9, 109, 244–6, 293
Okadigbo, C. 228–30, 238–9, 244
Okija shrine 202–3
Okonjo-Iweala, N. 209, 259, 268–70, 277
Okorocha, R. 296
Onagoruwa, O. 145

Oodua People's Congress 170, 188, 233, 239–40
Operation Feed the Nation 58, 99
Ore 26, 28, 109
Organisation of African Unity 46–7, 75, 77–9, 81–3, 130, 220–1
Organisation of Petroleum Exporting Countries 40, 59, 103–4, 184, 209, 271
Orji Uzor Kalu 189, 293
Oruh, G. 40, 102
Oshiomhole, A. 206, 228, 233, 239, 276–7, 299
Ota Farm 7, 99–104, 127–8, 139–40, 148, 152–3, 156, 160, 167, 256, 306
Otedola, F. 244, 273, 275
Owen, D. 76–9, 81, 120
Owu 7–8, 12, 99, 184, 305

Palme Commission 120–1, 130
Patriotic Front of Nigeria 137
People's Democratic Movement 165–7, 169, 174, 241, 289, 294
People's Democratic Party 165–75, 184, 225–7, 229–35, 239–47, 256, 258–9, 261–4, 291–9, 304–6
People's Redemption Party 92, 294
Plateau State 192–4, 261–2
police 64, 103, 185, 193, 195, 255
polygyny *see* gender relations
population 3, 9, 42, 64, 128–9, 185, 200
poverty 64, 201, 273, 276–7
Presidential Library 257–8, 306
press freedom 195, 258
prison 153–60, 195, 230
privatisation 115, 129, 204, 207–8, 257, 275, 289
providentialism 158–9, 168, 176, 254, 289
public opinion polls 186, 193, 204, 208, 210, 231, 238–9, 246–7, 255, 276, 291

Ransome-Kuti family 8–9
Rawlings, J. 83, 104, 140
Reagan, R. 84, 121, 124
resource control 185, 187, 190, 241, 290
Rhodesia *see* Zimbabwe
Ribadu, N. 255, 257, 294
Rilwan, A. 155
Rimi, A. 1, 140, 173–4, 227–8, 235, 242
Rivers State 31, 170, 175, 188, 244–5, 260, 275, 298

Salim Ahmed Salim 283
São Tomé e Príncipè 222, 281–2